DISCIPLINE AND DEVELOPMENT

Perhaps the most commonly held assumption in the field of development is that middle classes are the bounty of economic modernization and growth. As countries gradually transcend their agrarian past and become urbanized and industrialized, so the logic goes, middle classes emerge and gain in number, complexity, cultural influence, social prominence, and political authority. Yet this is only half the story. Middle classes shape industrial and economic development rather than being merely its product; and the particular ways in which rural and urban middle classes shape themselves – and the ways historical conditions shape them – influence development trajectories in multiple ways. This book tells the story of South Korea's and Taiwan's economic successes and Argentina's and Mexico's relative "failures" through a historical examination of each country's middle classes and how they facilitated or limited the state's capacities to discipline capitalists during key phases of twentieth-century industrialization. It also raises questions about the likelihood that such disciplining can continue in a world context where globalization squeezes middle classes and frees capitalists from state and social contracts in which they historically have been embedded.

Diane E. Davis is Associate Professor of Political Sociology at MIT. She is the author or editor of several books that explore the intersections among cities, politics, and national development, including *Urban Leviathan: Mexico City in the Twentieth Century* (1994) and *Irregular Armed Forces and Their Role in Politics and State Formation* (Cambridge University Press, 2003).

DISCIPLINE AND DEVELOPMENT

*Middle Classes and Prosperity in East Asia
and Latin America*

DIANE E. DAVIS

Massachusetts Institute of Technology

CAMBRIDGE
UNIVERSITY PRESS

PUBLISHED BY THE PRESS SYNDICATE OF THE UNIVERSITY OF CAMBRIDGE
The Pitt Building, Trumpington Street, Cambridge, United Kingdom

CAMBRIDGE UNIVERSITY PRESS
The Edinburgh Building, Cambridge CB2 2RU, UK
40 West 20th Street, New York, NY 10011-4211, USA
477 Williamstown Road, Port Melbourne, VIC 3207, Australia
Ruiz de Alarcón 13, 28014 Madrid, Spain
Dock House, The Waterfront, Cape Town 8001, South Africa

http://www.cambridge.org

First published 2004

Printed in the United States of America

Typeface Garamond #3 11/12 pt.   *System* LaTeX 2ε [TB]

A catalog record for this book is available from the British Library.

Library of Congress Cataloging in Publication Data

Davis, Diane E., 1953–
Discipline and development : middle classes and prosperity in East Asia and
Latin America / Diane E. Davis.
    p.   cm.
Includes bibliographical references and index.
ISBN 0-521-80748-4 – ISBN 0-521-00208-7 (pb.)
1. Middle class – East Asia.   2. Middle class – Latin America.   3. Industrialization – East Asia.
4. Industrialization – Latin America.   I. Title.
HT690.E18D38   2003
338.95 – dc21

/179

2003051487

ISBN 0 521 80748 4 hardback
ISBN 0 521 00208 7 paperback

CONTENTS

PREFACE

For most development scholars the East Asian "tigers" have long been a source of wonder and curiosity. Among them, South Korea and Taiwan garnered special attention during the 1980s and 1990s for their increasing per capita incomes, declining rates of inequality, and the fact that they had transcended a predominantly agrarian past to become formidable industrial giants in a remarkably short period of time. Many have pondered why these particular countries achieved considerable economic stability and prosperity while in the same decades so many other late industrializers lurched from one debt, financial, employment, or inflation crisis to the next. What made it possible for South Korea and Taiwan to escape from the trap of problem-ridden import-substituting industrialization and pursue the more profitable export-led industrialization so early on, thereby setting themselves on such a promising path vis-à-vis so many other late developers?

When I began to seek answers to these questions several years ago, after having completed a detailed case study of political and economic development in twentieth-century Mexico, I turned to the case of South Korea first. I was totally unprepared for what I discovered. The regime uniformly identified as responsible for establishing the South Korean development miracle, that of General Park Chung Hee, counted on South Korea's farmers and rural-based small producers as a key political base and cultural reference point. During his first decade in office, when South Korea's development path initially was set, Park did not rely upon *chaebols* or other large industrialists, foreign investors, or U.S. military advisors, all of whom spent the first several years repudiating Park's administration and criticizing the nature and direction of his development policies. Rather, Park initially developed his industrial policies with small rural producers in mind. With modest farmers backing his regime at almost every turn, Park became a heavy-handed disciplinarian of bankers and large industrial capitalists, who were soon goaded (if not forced) to generate sufficient industrial export earnings so the South Korean state might foster the growth of a dynamic agricultural sector and a strong rural middle class of farmers.

As a Latin Americanist I knew this story demanded further attention. I had not read an account of successful late development in which small rural proprietors seemed so important to a government's larger developmental vision and to the content of its industrial policies. Nor had I seen a focus on small-scale rural producers to explain the uniqueness of the East Asian model, even among those scholars who had already identified the state's disciplining of capital as key to South Korea's successes. To be sure, scholars such as Alice Amsden and Robert Bates had highlighted the state's disciplinary measures, but little had been said about the social origins or political foundations of this extensive disciplinary capacity. Tantalized by these findings and the revisionist theoretical possibilities of focusing on small rural farmers, I immediately turned to the history of Park's ascent to power. The evidence shows that he was a charismatic leader, a provincial middle-class son of schoolteachers born in the countryside who valued rural life more generally. Park viewed South Korea's urban populations as overly acquisitive and insufficiently austere; he particularly despised bankers; and he viewed most large-scale industrial capitalists and their financier counterparts as pampered and unworthy social groups whose speculative impulses and accumulation instincts should be harnessed in the service of national development. Far from envisioning South Korea as a leading industrial nation preparing itself to compete and consume more in a world of major industrial manufacturers, Park's own preferred model for South Korean development was not a big industrial power like the United States, Germany, or even Japan, but the bucolic, rural middle-class country of Denmark. Denmark? What Latin American country would have tried to build its economy using this small and relatively modest country as a guide? How much of this owed to Park's own idiosyncrasies as opposed to a realistic reading of the country's developmental possibilities and constraints?

Park's constant invocation of Denmark as a model further reinforced my resolve to consider the possibility that the South Korean state's desire and capacity to discipline capital, and thus achieve such great developmental gains, rested on rural middle-class foundations. But then again, if these modest goals of rural development really were Park's aim, and he relied so strongly on a rural middle-class ethos of discipline to sustain this vision, why did South Korea end up looking so heavily urbanized and industrialized, with a relatively weak rural sector and a dominant class of industrialists, and not at all like the northern European agricultural welfare state that served as his inspiration? This was a story that had to be told, not only for its own sake, but in comparison to other late industrializers.

Once I had made the decision to use material drawn from the South Korean case as a springboard for understanding East Asian "successes" – especially vis-à-vis the Latin American economies that have suffered so many economic troubles during the last several decades – I reformulated this project into a more general study of "middle classes" and late industrialization in which discipline was a key conceptual notion. I chose for study South Korea, Taiwan, Argentina, and Mexico, because when they were grouped as "matched pairs," conventional class-centered, state-centered, and world-system explanations could not account for their developmental differences and commonalities (see Appendix A for more on case study selection and methodological logic). My originating point of departure became smaller producer-owners, both rural and urban, and their role in establishing the disciplinary foundations of state development policy during key decades of industrial expansion. In conceptual and theoretical terms, the book's focus on these forces, and the decision to view them in middle-class terms, stemmed from a desire to liberate development theory from the shackles of its myopic preoccupation with the power of capital, labor, and the state.

Enter History

As the research for the project unfolded, it became clear that I harbored an equally fundamental aim: to reintroduce history into contemporary development studies. I had long been uneasy with the contemporary development literature's overly presentist orientation. I found far too many efforts to theorize successful development with a focus on the policies enabling those successes, rather than with a view to what made those policies possible in the first place. An emphasis on the period of success rather than on its antecedents further reinforced the search for simple policy paradigms whose ingredients could be altered or modified to produce greater government efficiency, expedient global management techniques, "right" or "wrong" prices, new public-private partnerships, post-Fordist production techniques, and/or reconstituted global commodity chains, to name but a few. Granted, many of these prescriptions hold the potential to bear fruit, and there is nothing wrong with embracing such normative aims in the social sciences. But an overriding concern with market failures and the policies necessary to "correct" them has dislodged the long-standing scholarly commitment to historically grounded, complex explanation of the variety that led to a focus on South Korea's unique disciplinary development trajectory in the first place. By first turning to the post–World War II rural middle-class origins of Park's disciplinary development model, and then contrasting South Korea with countries at an equivalent historical moment where such class foundations and developmental visions were absent, this book raises the possibility that economic prosperity in late developers is as much the outcome of social structures and political processes rooted in historically grounded geographical, cultural, and social class arrangements that favored some countries over others as it is a matter of knowing what general policies will magically correct market deficiencies and thus lead to sound economic growth.

In addition to recognizing the constraints of history, this book also seeks to transcend them in some fashion. Much of the development literature is built on the assumption that the history of the world's "early" industrializing nations, namely, Britain, France, and much of western and northern Europe, stands altogether apart, and that economic progress in twentieth-century industrializers, or "late developers," differs fundamentally from the early developmental experience. To be sure, the extent and dynamics of global capital and commodity flows in the twentieth-century world are entirely different from those in the eighteenth and nineteenth centuries when countries like Great Britain first initiated industrialization. So too are the size, character, and role of the state, factors which affect whether, where, and how the governments in "late" industrializers will intervene in markets and productive activities. But in the effort to specify what makes late development unique, scholars may have thrown out the baby with the bath water, ignoring the class actors and social conditions that were most relevant among early industrializers, namely, middle classes and their disciplinary orientations. With its analytic focus on middle classes and discipline, this book shows some elective affinity with arguments offered by scholars of early development, particularly those advanced by Max Weber in *The Protestant Ethic and the Spirit of Capitalism*. Far from conceiving of the distant past as an obsolete legacy to be shed in contemporary model building and analysis, I suggest that the history of "early" developers can serve as a central theoretical and analytical reference point for a more contemporary period.

For further guidance in historicizing and theorizing late development, and any similarities or differences between late and early industrializers, I turned not only to the literature on states and bureaucratic decision making and to that which explores the relations between business investors and their factor inputs (labor and technology), but also and most especially to the classics in comparative-historical sociology and economic history written by Max Weber, Henri Pirenne, Karl Polanyi, Barrington Moore, Perry Anderson, Robert Brenner, Eric Hobsbawm, David Landes, Michael Mann, and Charles Tilly. The model that emerged is a hybrid, a contemporary mix of the "new" and "old" dynamics examined in both bodies of literature. Think of it as Robert Brenner's and Barrington Moore's yeoman farmers meeting Alexander Gerschenkron's and Peter Evans's developmental states.

History enters these pages in yet another way: in the analyses of individual country trajectories. Not only did each of the four countries studied here (South Korea, Argentina, Taiwan, and Mexico) face distinct social, political, and economic histories, these unique national histories affected rural and urban middle-class formation, the institutional and cultural foundations of the disciplinary ethos, and thus how and why each country pursued the twentieth-century industrial development path that it did. For precisely this reason, much of the narrative of this book is devoted to presenting what I would call "foundational" histories of late industrialization, or the historical conditions associated with middle-class formation in each of the four countries that led their national states to foster rapid industrialization at a particular time and in a particular form.

Acknowledgments

Speaking of histories, I have one myself. I would like to thank those who inspired and mentored me over the years, especially those who taught me the importance of thinking historically. I start with my mother, Dorothy F. Davis, whose eight-year personal project of mapping the genealogies, wars, monarchical lineages, and imperial dynasties of early modern Europe belied her seemingly narrow role as a 1950s suburban housewife. My love for historical scholarship began with her and with the reams of paper she transformed into charts and diagrams, rolling and clandestinely stuffing them into an upstairs hall closet before her four kids returned home from school. This initial interest in historical research was reawakened in graduate school under the watchful eye of Maurice Zeitlin, who mentored me in the academic pursuit of historical sociology. Other luminaries in the fields of history and historical sociology furthered my commitment to the marriage of history and social science through their personal encouragement during my first several teaching appointments. They include Charles Tilly, Janet Abu-Lughod, Ira Katznelson, and Eric Hobsbawm, with whom I had the fortune of working in one way or another while at the New School for Social Research; David Landes, who graciously approved my very first academic job as a Lecturer in Social Studies at Harvard University; Theda Skocpol, who permitted me to join her CROPSO workshops during my year at Harvard; John Coatsworth, also at Harvard, who many years later gave me an opportunity to join a dynamic group of Latin Americanists at the David Rockefeller Center, and who still inspires as a master economic historian of Mexico; and most recently, Robert Fogelson, a colleague at the Massachusetts Institute of Technology and brilliant urban historian to whom I owe a great personal and professional debt.

For help and guidance with the aspects of this book that mainly concern economic development, another interest tracing to Maurice Zeitlin, I relied on yet another circle of scholars, and they too deserve thanks. First, I am most grateful to Alice Amsden, whose seminal work on the South Korean state's policy measures to discipline capital inspired much of the thinking and preparation for this book. Amsden's work interfaced nicely with my own long-standing research on middle classes in Mexico and helped inspire the basic argument of the book, the idea for which emerged during an enjoyably raucous and stimulating political economy class we taught together at the New School for Social Research in the mid-1990s. I also thank Judith Tendler, whose guidance, writings, and advice drawn from her years studying and implementing rural development policy were and continue to serve as a source of inspiration and knowledge. Many others have read or made insightful comments on the history and theory of development in this project at different stages of its formulation, starting with an initial paper on middle classes and development in comparative perspective prepared for an international conference in Taiwan organized by Hsin-huang Michael Hsiao. They include an especially welcoming group of scholars from the Sociology Department of the University of Hawaii at Manoa, namely, Hagen Koo, Alvin So, and Peter Manicus; long-standing friends and colleagues Susan Eckstein, Leslie Sklair, Deborah Poole, and Tony Pereira; and newfound professional colleagues Mauro Guillén and Vivek Chibber.

As usual, my husband, Bish Sanyal, served as my fiercest critic, but his comments were invaluable. I also thank Susan Browne for typographical and first-rate editorial assistance, Yu-wen Fan and Sun Hee Yoon for library assistance and translations of key works on South Korea and Taiwan, and both Mary Child and Alia Winters at Cambridge University Press for their patience. Initial institutional support for preliminary study of middle classes in Latin America came from the Social Science Research Council and the United States Institute of Peace. More recent research on the relationships between military and middle-class identities was partially funded by the Andrew W. Mellon Foundation, through its sponsorship of a Sawyer Seminar on the Military, Politics, and Society in Comparative and Historical Perspective.

This book is dedicated to my daughter, Alexandra Indira Sanyal.

Diane E. Davis
Cambridge, Massachusetts
September 2003

DISCIPLINE AND DEVELOPMENT

Middle Classes and Prosperity in East Asia and Latin America

1

AN INTRODUCTION TO MIDDLE CLASSES, DISCIPLINE, AND DEVELOPMENT

The Middle Classes and Economic Growth

One of the most commonly held assumptions in the field of development is that middle classes are the bounty of economic modernization and growth. As countries gradually transcend their agrarian past and become urbanized and industrialized, so the logic goes, middle classes emerge and gain in number, complexity, cultural influence, social prominence, and political authority. Yet this is only half the story. Middle classes *shape* industrial and economic development, rather than being merely its product; and the particular ways in which middle classes shape themselves – and the ways historical conditions shape them – influence development trajectories in multiple ways. This is especially true in late industrializers. Whether they choose rapid and successful export-oriented industrialization (EOI) grounded in an integrated and robust sectoral development based on strong forward and backward linkages, or whether they remain overly wedded to industrial policies that protect import-substitution activities (ISI) and reinforce sectoral imbalances and a disarticulated domestic economy careening from one economic crisis to the next, will depend on the alliances, character, composition, and political sway of their middle classes, both rural and urban, and the extent to which these forces and conditions engender strong state disciplining of capitalists and laborers in the service of national development.

This claim rests on several interrelated premises, themselves built on a definitional understanding of middle classes as comprised of three basic occupational categories: 1) *salaried employees* in commerce, services, industry, and the professions, as well as those employed by the state;[1] 2) *self-employed* artisans,

---

[1] In Marxist terminology, salaried employees would include both semiautonomous wage earners and managers, two different categories of middle classes defined by their contradictory class location between capital and labor. See Wright, *Class, Crisis, and the State.* For more on this, see Appendix B.

craftsmen, and other independent rural and urban-based producers, who in developing countries are frequently called petty commodity producers (or yeomen farmers in the rural sector); and 3) owners and operators of *small enterprises*, including family firms, in service, industry, and agriculture.[2] Granted, nothing raises the academic red flag faster than the concept of the middle class. Perhaps the best statement on this comes from Loic Wacquant, who charges that the "epistemic ambition of defining, once and for all, the 'real' boundaries of the middle class is doomed to failure because it rests on a fundamentally mistaken conception on the ontological status of classes: the middle class does not exist ready-made in reality."[3] And I agree. Still, if one is interested in understanding this particular occupational range of difficult-to-categorize social forces that are pervasive in most late industrializers, it is necessary to begin analysis from some vantage point. I chose the notion of middle classes and use the above definition because it is the most consensual and inclusive in accommodating this occupational range while also spanning the classificatory lexicon of multiple theoretical perspectives. (For more on this logic, and further discussion of "middle classes," see Appendix B: Defining the Middle Class.)

The first leading premise of this book is that under certain historical, cultural, political, and discursive conditions, key actors in one or all three of the above classified occupational groupings will see themselves, their social and political dynamics, and their economic policy priorities as sufficiently distinct from large industrialists and wage laborers to suggest some form of "middling" class identity. When they do, they will enable the state's use of a variety of measures to politically and economically *discipline* capitalists and laborers for the purpose of generating national prosperity and balanced growth. With capitalists and laborers strictly disciplined in this manner, the economy is less prone to distortion and waste, industrial policy decisions are more likely to be made with long-term frameworks in mind, national industrial growth objectives are more apt to be achieved, and sustained macroeconomic development is more likely to materialize. We call administrations that pursue these policies *disciplinary regimes*. In contrast, where middle classes are absent or politically weak, states are less likely to impose discipline and more likely to accommodate the demands of capital or labor in ways that allow rent-seeking, short-term profit maximization, higher wage rates, and/or protectionist measures that in

---

[2] For a general theoretical understanding of the middle classes, both new and old, I draw upon the important work of the following authors, among others: Abercrombie and Urry, *Capital, Labor, and the Middle Classes*; Wright, *Class, Crisis, and the State*; Carchedi, "On the Economic Identification of the New Middle Class"; Goldthorpe, "On the Service Class"; Ross, "Marxism and the New Middle Classes"; Burris, "The Discovery of the New Middle Classes"; Hindess, *Politics and Class Analysis*; and Wacquant, "Making Class."

[3] "Making Class," p. 57.

the long run limit firms' capacities to compete domestically and abroad. We call these *accommodating regimes*.

A second main premise of this book is that among the fractious groupings that comprise the middle class(es), it is those in rural as opposed to urban locations who endow the state with its greatest disciplinary capacity vis-à-vis capital and labor, thus making rural middle classes especially critical to a nation's developmental prospects. Rural middle classes are defined as those self-employed, salaried, or small-scale producers whose economic livelihood is structured primarily around agricultural activities. Whether directly involved in agricultural production on small or family farms, or in town-based activities linked to trade, exchange, or even processing of agricultural goods produced on farms, folk are considered rural if they see themselves and their economic priorities as spatially and socially linked to agriculture and the development of the countryside more than to industry and the development of cities.

It may seem counterintuitive to suggest that successful patterns of industrial development rest in the cultural orientations, social networks, and political relations between rural populations and the state. After all, in the social sciences these forces are more likely to be identified as critical in studies of revolution, not macroeconomic development;[4] and if they are seen as central in the latter body of literature, they are more often than not conceived as "fetters" on development, an idea that can be traced to Marx but has reappeared in a variety of forms since his time, especially in modernization theory. The failure to examine rural folk generally and rural middle classes in particular is also due to the fact that most contemporary development scholars who study late industrialization focus primarily on the state alone or its relations to urban classes, since cities are where one encounters what are generally thought to be the principal protagonists of industrial development and thus modern economic growth – ranging from owners of large manufacturing firms and their industrial workers to more affluent folk who consume these processed industrial goods. Yet by focusing on cities to the exclusion of villages and the countryside, development theorists gloss over the rural context of industrialization and economic growth and the possibility that small-scale rural producers may influence or affect states in ways that can guide the overall contours of national development policy, be it ISI, EOI, or a hybrid combination of the two.

Several decades ago this urban bias in development studies was not so well entrenched. During the 1960s and 1970s, Alain de Janvry and others made great advances in linking the state of rural agriculture to national development trajectories by examining the negative impact of sectoral disarticulation (i.e., insufficient articulation of agricultural and industrial production) on both rural progress and national economic growth. One of the most popular claims

---

[4] The best statement on this can still be found in Skocpol's *States and Social Revolutions*. The seminal equivalent in the developing country context would be Paige's *Agrarian Revolution*.

associated with this school of thought was that truncated or distorted industrial development owed to the inordinate political power of large landlords whose capacities to set the basic terms of macroeconomic policy in their favor through exchange rates, pricing policies, investment in infrastructure, subsidies, etc., disadvantaged industrial manufactures. Yet with a very few exceptions, including recent work by Cristóbal Kay,[5] the concern with agricultural growth and rural class structure has slipped off the research and policy-making agenda since the 1980s, perhaps because cities have continued to grow and industries continue to locate there, provoking many contemporary scholars to assume that these developments are the key to national progress.[6] This book attempts to bring the rural perspective back into studies of industrial policy making by highlighting its enormous significance for late industrialization in Latin America and East Asia.

In light of these aims, more recent work by Jeffrey Sachs is distinctive primarily because he is one of the few who focus on rural conditions as a key determinant of the ISI-EOI divide in late industrializers. Like Kay, who argues that without state policy measures that produce agricultural growth with equity, successful industrialization will not materialize, Sachs focuses on the economic problems posed by depressed agricultural conditions and how to counteract them. And, like Kay, Sach argues that sustained "rural influence" will tip the balance against inflationary import-substituting regimes by spurring the state to set "realistic" food prices and favorable exchange rate policies, thereby strengthening a country's balance of payments situation and reducing the likelihood of external debt.[7] Sachs, however, links rural "influence" to population distribution and the ways that demographic patterns uphold political power in the countryside, in a way that suggests that all one needs to know is whether more of a nation's populations live in rural as opposed to urban areas. This book offers a related but theoretically distinctive approach. It suggests that the key to understanding development lies not in a focus on rural-urban demographic balances more generally, or even the power of rural landlords, as suggests Kay,[8] but on the middle-class character and composition of the countryside, and especially the extent to which small-scale rural producers and suppliers wield political influence within the state.

---

[5] See *Asia's and Latin America's Development*.

[6] Some of this may owe to the fact that de Janvry's 1981 book, *The Agrarian Question and Reformism in Latin America*, was rather pessimistic about the prospects for sustained rural development in capitalist economies. De Janvry's normative emphasis on the contradictions of commercial agriculture, even in the context of land reform, may in fact have pushed policy-oriented scholars to bypass the agrarian question altogether and, therefore, to turn their full attention to industrial policy instead.

[7] "External Debt and Macroeconomic Performance in Latin America and East Asia," p. 550.

[8] *Asia's and Latin America's Development*, pp. 27–28.

Of course, a countryside dominated by large landlords might be equally likely to push national policy makers to set realistic food prices and favorable exchange rates. But it also would be prone to rural poverty or rural class polarization, conditions that further limit self-sustaining rural development. Large landlords also would be less willing to push the state to invest in widespread rural credit, education, and other factor inputs that lay the foundations for longer-term productivity and growth. If it is smaller farmers and other small-scale agricultural producers, processors, or distributors politically calling the shots, however, not only do we generally see more government support for these types of policies, we also are more likely to see national policy limitations on luxury imports and other goods associated with higher income consumption and/or modernization. This is because rural middle classes are more likely to fashion themselves, their political allegiances, and their economic policy demands as distinct from urban-based capitalists than are affluent landlords — who in the late-developing world frequently are interlocked with the banking and industrial elite. In short, rural middle-class political influence translates into a different combination of industrial and agricultural policies than does rural elite or rural poor influence; and it is the particular combination of development policies grounded in rural middle-class political sway that is most generative of successful development trajectories.

State Discipline and Development

Equally central to the argument presented here are both the notion of state-imposed discipline and the ways that middle-class political sway sustains the late-industrializing state's disciplinary capacity. Some of the most ground-breaking work on East Asian development traces macroeconomic successes to the state's regulatory actions vis-à-vis industrial firms. In the terminology and thinking of scholars such as Alice Amsden and Robert Bates, it is the imposition of performance standards, and the use of these standards as a benchmark for determining future financial support or privilege, that most engender successful industrial development. When the state applies performance standards, there is no free ride for big industrial firms; rather, they are required to show evidence of productivity and economic success in return for continued state support or accommodation.[9] To be sure, it could be argued that all capitalist

---

[9] One way to assess the developmental outcomes associated with these disciplinary measures is to understand what happens at the microeconomic level when performance standards and strict control over banking capital are in fact absent. In such conditions, capitalists and laborers receive financial support, preferential treatment, or accommodation of demands (be they related to wages, prices, protection, financing, or lowered taxes) whether or not they meet sales, manufacturing, or productivity targets. Rather than discipline based upon performance standards, the state plays the role of benefactor no matter how successfully industrialists and

states impose regulations and, by so doing, discipline in some fashion. But most scholars who recognize this as a positive externality associated with state power do so only when these disciplinary measures are applied to labor. State efforts to regulate or interfere with private-sector activities, in contrast, are usually seen as obstacles to market growth and economic prosperity. And for many, it is market discipline that is considered most central to development success, with state action seen as getting in the way of this.[10] I take issue with this bias and argue that state actors can indeed be central protagonists in economic discipline, especially when they are middle-class-embedded.

To suggest that the relationship between the state and middle classes can shape development trajectories is to depart from the common view of the state and its relationship to classes in the late-industrializing world. Most scholars assume that "developmental" states are autonomous, not class embedded,[11] and that autonomy – be it derived from internal bureaucratic dynamics,[12]

---

    laborers meet national economic development priorities such as achieving market compet-itiveness or increasing national wealth without producing inordinate deficits, inflation, or foreign exchange balances. Trust that capital and labor will work conscientiously to achieve national development goals, rather than actual performance indicators grounded in an envi-ronment of discipline, governs the state's expectations in granting developmental assistance in these accommodating regimes.

[10] It is of course true that market dynamics, or discipline, can be used to prod performance gains or inspire capitalists' self-regulatory measures. After all, state controls on banking and the setting of performance standards, among other possible disciplinary actions, are frequently fueled by the state's desire to have key economic actors "work" the market to its greatest potential (and, by so doing, achieve performance goals). It is for precisely this reason that so many scholars assume that the East Asian tigers are developing their economies around free-market dynamics. But in many of those countries, as we shall see shortly, it is the state that is disciplining capitalists' and laborers' relationship to the market, not merely the market itself laying disciplinary foundations.

[11] The argument was that *autonomous* states – or those not beholden to capitalists – were a key force behind successful development. Much of the work on this topic was inspired by *Bringing the State Back In*, coauthored by Rueschemeyer, Evans, and Skocpol, which contained several articles on the state and development in newly industrializing countries. Yet one of the best statements on the class context of state autonomy in late industrializers is still one of the first: Hamilton's *The Limits to State Autonomy*. A more recent and equally compelling work that situates East Asian state autonomy in class, cultural, and historical conditions is offered by Castells in "Four Asian Tigers with a Dragon Head," who argues that the destruction of the oligarchy and an attendant debilitation of the capitalist class – along with strong sentiments of nationalism and a disorganized and repressed working class – explain state autonomy and developmental successes in East Asia.

[12] Among the best works that focus on the workings of the state as an automous bureaucratic institution are Amsden's *Asia's Next Giant*, Alam's *Government and Markets in Economic Devel-opment Strategies*, Haggard's *Pathways From the Periphery*, and Wade's *Irrigation and Agricultural Politics in South Korea* and *Governing the Market*.

world-systemic and geopolitical conditions,[13] domestic or international fiscal constraints,[14] and/or accelerated class conflict between capital and labor[15] – gives certain states the developmental capacity to introduce sound macroeconomic policies even as it prevents them from becoming predatory in terms of rent seeking or other economically disastrous policies. Among the few scholars who do choose to examine state-class articulations, the preferred partner for the state is almost always capitalists,[16] at least if the state is considered to be developmental. This focus on the positive developmental gains of state and capitalist-class embeddedness was first proposed by Peter Evans in his seminal book *Dependent Development*,[17] and later articulated even more expertly in a theory of state-capitalist class embeddedness in his equally groundbreaking study *Embedded Autonomy: States and Industrial Transformation*. Our model shares this appreciation for the notion of state-class embeddedness, but focuses on the state's embeddedness with middle classes as laying the foundations for economic progress or, in our terminology, for *disciplinary development*.

By examining the middle-class contours of late developmental states, like Peter Evans we proceed under the premise that some form of class embeddedness is necessary in order to prevent rent seeking and other forms of predatory behavior that often arise when the state is so institutionally autonomous that it acts with impunity and disregard. But our model presupposes a slightly different understanding of who gets disciplined, by whom, and why. To be sure, I acknowledge that the notion of state autonomy used by so many other

---

[13] See Stallings, "International Lending and the Relative Autonomy of the State"; and Glasberg, "International Finance Capital and the Relative Autonomy of the State." One of the most provocative and compelling case studies available that links domestic state autonomy to global conditions, both geopolitical and economic, is Woo's *Race to the Swift*.

[14] See Fitzgerald, "The Financial Constraint on Relative Autonomy."

[15] See Anglade and Fortin (eds.), *The State and Capital Accumulation in Latin America*; and Gulalp, "Capital Accumulation, Classes, and the Relative Autonomy of the State."

[16] Exemplary in this regard were Eckstein's *The Poverty of Revolution,* and Waisman's *The Reversal of Development in Argentina*, both of which examined the relationship between capitalists and the state. The writings of Gary Gereffi, John Walton, and Alejandro Portes also took a similar view, although they more purposefully integrated a domestic focus on capitalists and the state with an analysis of global conditions. See Gereffi, *The Pharmaceutical Industry and Dependency in the Third World*; and Portes and Walton, *Labor, Class, and the International System*.

[17] In this book, rather than pitting global explanations against domestic ones, Evans integrated a focus on global capital with an understanding of domestic capitalists and their relations to each other and the state. The book was very important at the time because it challenged some of the central tenets of dependency theory. Indeed, its main argument was that the global context of accumulation did not impede development because industrialization and some degree of economic progress were indeed occurring; rather it structured and limited the capacity of domestic industrialists to initiate development without the aid of multinational capital.

development scholars may appear to closely approximate what I mean by the middle-class-embedded state, at least to the extent that such a state will not be acting in the interests of capitalists. Generally speaking, however, the notion of state autonomy – at least as it has come to be defined – presupposes a state that acts independently of all class forces. Our disciplinary states, on the other hand, have identifiable class foundations – primarily rural middle class – that sustain a government's will and capacity to discipline capital and labor.[18]

How this dynamic works is well seen in one of the most effective forms of state discipline imposed on private-sector actors, which is government control of banking and investment capital. With such measures, the state holds the power to limit capitalists' capacities to spend themselves into or out of a market collapse or production dilemma. This constraint places considerable limits on individual firm strategies for weathering a difficult supply or demand situation, but it also limits inflation and the unproductive use of scarce financial resources in ways that may be good for the economy as a whole. This example is particularly relevant to the middle-class-based argument presented here because it reveals the way that state disciplinary measures (performance standards, government control of banks, etc.) frequently force big industrial firms to *behave like small producers*. That is, these measures generally insure that large firms work in the context of strict financial constraints and market unpredictability, turning only to their existent resources (and not a financial bailout) as they struggle to meet performance targets.

State discipline also can come in the form of macroeconomic regulation and not merely microeconomic restrictions on industrial firm behavior. Generally understood, macroeconomic policies are those that affect or establish aggregate demand conditions (while microeconomic policies affect supply conditions). States of the Keynesian variety traditionally have used macroeconomic policy to stimulate demand for productive investment with the expectation of drawing the private sector away from unproductive (or perhaps even speculative) activities, to great developmental success. A disciplinary state takes this logic even further by regulating and controlling conditions of demand across almost all fronts simultaneously, not just domestic and international but also

---

[18] Granted, most scholars have operated under the premise that autonomy is defined in terms of the state's institutional or policy-making independence from capital or labor, and thus what we see as a middle-class-embedded state they would see as an autonomous state precisely because neither capital nor labor is in the equation. It is important not to confuse cause and effect. One should not fall into the tautological trap of assuming that states which discipline capital and labor are autonomous. States may be able to cultivate policy-making independence from capital and labor, or discipline them, precisely because they count on middle classes as their principal source of legitimacy or political support.

rural and urban.[19] Measures intended to control demand conditions include agricultural and industrial pricing policy, the setting of exchange rates, and the establishment of interest rates to channel savings for national investment. The state's aim is not just to intervene in both domestic and international markets to bolster demand in some general sense but, rather, to link aggregate demand to the microeconomic management of supply conditions (and vice versa), and to relate both sets of measures to domestic production and consumption. Such robust state control of both supply and demand conditions is rarely understood to be a feature of capitalist states, since this practice is more commonly identified in communist states with centrally planned economies. What differentiates our disciplinary regimes from communist regimes, however, is not just the fact that both domestic and international markets serve as principal reference points around which microeconomic and macroeconomic policy measures for supply and demand management are crafted, but also the fact that profit making and capital accumulation are still principal aims. It is just that both are to be achieved within a framework that subordinates them to a hierarchy of class and social needs in which the rural middle class – rather than the usual suspects, "mass" society in communist states or big industrialists and perhaps even organized labor in their capitalist counterparts – leads the pack.

Once we recognize that it is primarily the state's rural middle-class foundations that help politically establish this particular hierarchy of class needs and social aims, we further understand why these states are prone to apply their micro- and macroeconomic regulations on the basis of a sectoral logic as well, mainly for the purpose of nurturing the productive gains of rural producers. This can be done directly, through rural pricing and other policy prods and infrastructural investments, or indirectly by channeling the activities of urban-based capitalists and laborers to contribute to overall rural aims. Among the many policy measures that frequently are used to achieve such gains are those which guarantee the existence of small and medium-sized plots for self-cultivation (i.e., land reform), those which keep the internal terms of trade relatively favorable to agriculture, those which help generate forward and backward linkages in rural areas and between them and cities, and those which increase domestic and international demand for goods produced in and

---

[19] The distinction between the concept of disciplinary regime and those strongly interventionist states frequently called "developmental states" is also worth noting. Practically all late-industrializing states, whether democratic or authoritarian, autonomous or class embedded, protectionist or market oriented, are highly interventionist; and most have the capacity to impose some form of regulation or restriction on micro- and macroeconomic activity. But not all states with the capacity to intervene in the market will discipline both capitalists and laborers in ways that aid the development process, and sometimes their interventions make it easier for capitalists to sidestep market constraints.

by rural sectors. In the context of late development, achievement of these sectoral aims often requires considerable foreign exchange earnings and/or high savings rates, with both deposited in state banks or a state-regulated financial sector, as well as monetary policies and other measures to keep overall inflation rates low. Yet just as telling, the achievement of these goals generally presupposes aggressive state support for export-led industrialization rather than import-substitution industrialization, not only because the former would be expected to generate export earnings but also because it would not overly disadvantage rural over urban sectors of the economy even as it kept overall domestic consumption down and thus savings high, owing to the paucity of industrial goods for purchase.

Development scholars might be quick to note that many of the disciplinary measures and policy components I identify as comprising this *disciplinary regime of development* already have been promoted or implemented in the developing world, albeit perhaps under a different rubric; and some already have been identified as producing great successes. For example, the importance of recasting industrial policies to nurture exports rather than imports of processed industrial goods is one of the most popular ideas these days, seen as a magic bullet for many late-industrializing countries. The emphasis on rural development and the value of balancing rural and urban development have also had their day in the sun, two aims that are equally reflected in this model. As noted earlier, it was not that long ago that scholars such as Alain de Janvry argued that governments which supported agriculture along with industry were more likely to generate balanced economic growth and eliminate income extremes, with more recent work by Michael Lipton and his colleagues underscoring the positive economic impact of farm-nonfarm linkages on reducing rural poverty in ways that parallel the disciplinary regime's efforts to coordinate cross-sectoral gains.[20] So too Cristóbal Kay's emphasis on agriculture-industry connections as central to East Asia's economic success vis-à-vis Latin America seems consistent with my claim, although he identifies the timing of agrarian reform and the state's autonomy – not middle-class embeddedness – as key to this outcome.[21] Where my approach – and this model of disciplinary development – differs from these authors' is in its recognition of the fact that it is the

---

[20] The way this works is well specified in Hazell and Haggblade's "Farm-Nonfarm Growth Linkages and the Welfare of the Poor," pp. 190–204 in Lipton and van der Gaag's *Including the Poor*. They argue that "non-farm linkages generated by technical change in agriculture can enhance both growth and its poverty-reducing effects" because a "growing agricultural sector demands non-farm production inputs, and supplies raw materials to transport, processing, and marketing firms. Likewise, increases in farm income lead to greater demand for consumer goods and services" (p. 190).

[21] In fact, in Kay's conception of rural class structure, middle classes are practically absent, as evidenced by the subtitle to his most recent monograph on Latin American versus East Asian

combination of each of these particular industrial and agricultural development priorities that brings great gains, and in its recognition of the fact that it is an aggressively interventionist state embedded with rural middle classes that husbands this outcome through use of microeconomic, macroeconomic, and sectoral discipline.[22]

Middle Classes and the Cultures and Practices of Self-Discipline

So why is it that rural middle-class embeddedness produces a state committed to the imperatives of capital accumulation and eager to prod market gains by microeconomic regulation of individual producers, willing to connect agriculture and industrial exporting, yet also keen to manage and regulate the macroeconomy, its sectoral contours, and its key protagonists with harsh disciplinary measures? This is where an understanding of the notion of discipline as a cultural construct enters the picture. Earlier we defined discipline in terms of state-sanctioned microeconomic and macroeconomic regulations and sectoral priorities whose purpose is to coerce firm output or aggregate productivity while fostering rural development and overall economic growth. Here we focus attention on a disciplinary ethos which assumes a certain degree of austerity, self-regulation, and self-imposed personal restraint marshaled in the service of an individual producer's output or productivity. When this type of disciplinary ethos infuses both society and the state, and vice versa, the developmental gains are enormous.[23] For precisely this reason, we use the notion of

development, in which he targets "Landlords, Peasants, and Industrialization." See *Asia's and Latin America's Development*, pp. 13–14, 27–28, 44–45.

[22] Understanding the rural middle-class, disciplinary, and statist dimensions of this model not only allows us to differentiate what I am calling a disciplinary regime of development from other development models built around a rural *versus* urban orientation or a prioritization of EOI *over* ISI, it also allows us to understand how this development model differs even from that promoted by rural oligarchies sharing power with urban industrialists, a very prototypical model for many late-industrializing countries. In these instances, the government also had fostered a macroeconomic connection between rural and urban sectors of the economy and microeconomic support for both large landlords and urban industrialists. But without a rural middle-class disciplinary orientation built into the model, there was practically no disciplining (only accommodating) of rural landlords or urban capitalists and laborers. The result was often the worst of both worlds: a highly protected, uncompetitive version of ISI coexisting with the development of large-scale agribusiness, two sets of activities which often work at cross-purposes in terms of foreign exchange policy and which ultimately lead to the development of an unstable economy unable to develop one or the other sector completely, let alone establish a synergy that leads to greater gains for both.

[23] Our desire to link the emergence of disciplinary regimes both to state institutions and the political or cultural practices of middle classes also draws inspiration from Philip Gorski's

disciplinary *regime* of development to emphasize that the foundations of economic success are most entrenched when discipline comes from both "above" and "below," existing as an ethos that permeates both state and society.[24]

To be sure, middle classes do not hold a monopoly on the disciplinary ethos, be it directed toward self or others. Such behaviors are often variably displayed, owing to personal idiosyncrasies, family upbringing, or general cultural and moral practices emergent in subgroups or societies at large. Capitalists often ruthlessly discipline their workers. Certain religions also advocate discipline. But there also is something about middle-class work aims and practices that is central to the development of a disciplinary ethos, especially as applied to self. Derek Sayer, for his part, defines the middle-class mentality constitutive of a disciplinary ethos. It is one in which "both the idle poor and the idle rich are equally deserving of condemnation,"[25] and where middle classes hold certain expectations of themselves in terms of ability, shrewdness, industry, providence, and thrift, to paraphrase Chamberlain's classic phrase.[26] A deeper logic underlying such self-consciously aggrandizing claims would be that those who are self-employed depend considerably on their own expenditures of energy and the deployment of their own labor in activities that self-reproduce their

efforts to distinguish between and rearticulate disciplinary "carriers" and "strategies" (sometimes referred to as "disciplinary ethics" and "disciplinary techniques") in his study of early modern state formation. In "The Protestant Ethic Revisited" (p. 270) Gorski argues that "a social group acts as a *carrier* of discipline to the extent that it bases its status claims and strategies of domination on discipline. An institution [read state] forms part of a disciplinary *strategy* to the extent that its operation and legitimacy are premised on certain disciplinary techniques and ethics. New disciplinary carriers and new disciplinary strategies generally emerge together. The ideal and material interests of a carrier group affect how disciplinary strategies are institutionally deployed. Conversely, the character of available disciplinary techniques conditions the formation of carrier classes."

[24] To advance my thinking about the origins, meaning, and dynamics of discipline in this more ubiquitous sense, I also find Foucault's *Discipline and Punish* to be quite helpful, precisely because it examines the pervasiveness, centrality, and significance of social norms and constraints and how they manifest themselves in disciplinary and regulatory practices both imposed by the state and embodied in individuals. In that sense, Foucault's understanding of the combined effect of coercive discipline (imposed by powerful institutions like states or organized religion) and self-discipline (as embodied in the social norms and practices of individuals and society) is similar to mine. Where I differ is by locating the origin of the disciplinary ethos in certain class foundations, and not merely in society or institutional structures of power more generally.

[25] *Capitalism and Modernity*, p. 131.

[26] Lewis and Maude, in their study of the English middle classes, cite Joseph Chamberlain's claim as archetypal: "I belong to the middle class, and I am proud of the ability, the shrewdness, the industry, the providence, and the thrift by which they are distinguished, and which have in so considerable a degree contributed to the stability and prosperity of the Empire." See *The English Middle Classes*, p. 37.

own livelihood.[27] Thus the values of thriftiness and industriousness often hold meaning to middle classes themselves, even if their monopoly on such virtues is questionable. And for rural middle classes, especially small farmers, the commitment to discipline will be even greater.

Some of the elective affinity between rural middle-class location and discipline owes to the fact that small-scale agrarian production, by its very nature, generally entails a much greater degree of self-regulation, austerity, and savings than urban-based artisan production. This probably holds true whether rural production is for use or exchange value. This is not to say that surviving in rural areas is merely a matter of will and disciplined effort; nor is it to suggest that urban residents do not gain from a similar self-disciplinary ethic. But in the countryside, the conditions of self-reproduction are directly in an individual's (or family's) hands. To be sure, any differences in degrees of disciplinary orientations across city and countryside will be historically specific, with these dynamics playing out differently in different locales and in different historical moments. Yet no matter the time period, small-scale farming and other forms of agrarian production are extraordinarily difficult activities requiring considerable self-discipline, savings, and austerity. Even Lenin affirmed this idea in his analysis of nineteenth-century society where he argued that small agricultural producers, or what we might term the rural middle class, may be among the most self-disciplinary and hardworking social forces, having "reduce[d] their needs to a level inferior to that of wage laborers and exert[ing] themselves in the work incomparably more than the latter do."[28] This is still true in much of the developing world.

The general idea that something about agriculturally based self-employment or the demands of small-scale rural production will generate or sustain a self-disciplinary ethos is frequently acknowledged in the work of historians of class and consumption. Robert Redfield, for example, analyzed early economic progress in European locales (where Protestantism was absent, in an effort to test Weber's thesis) and found that rural-based, self-employed, small-scale

---

[27] This claim is relatively compatible with that advanced by Bendix in his seminal *Nation-Building and Citizenship*, in which he sees class and occupational factors as being as relevant as religious affinity in his discussion of the origins of the work ethic. Although Bendix focuses on yet a different historical context than Gorski (see fns. 22 and 29), he also posits an explanation for his subjects' disciplinary orientation that owes as much to work conditions and the requisites of self-reproduction or economic success as to religion and culture. The "ethic of work performance," Bendix claims, "developed among the masses of English workers out of the combined legacies of *craftsmanship* [emphasis mine], the Puritan ethic, and the rising ideology of the individual striving and success – *prior to the growth of modern large-scale industry* [emphasis his]." See *Nation-Building and Citizenship*, p. 183.

[28] *The Development of Capitalism in Russia*, p. 7.

producers – or those forces that we might term the rural middle classes – held strongly to values of "hard work, frugality . . . and productive industry as a prime and central duty" that others had identified with the Calvinist middle classes.[29] Scholars who studied the emergence of market cultures and class differentiation in later periods also have long documented lifestyle patterns that differentiate rural and urban populations on a continuum of disciplinary behavior. One of the earliest and best-known accounts is that of Frederick LePlay, whose nineteenth-century study found high levels of consumption and spending among Parisian workers when compared to rural populations. He also found that the high wages and high spending of city-based workers led to what Judith Coffin has characterized as "lack of discipline and feckless spending."[30] This stood in stark contrast to the habits and practices of rural folk who, according to LePlay, evinced "less market involvement (less earning and spending)" and "drew on and preserved the resources of land and family" in ways that sustained a much more austere – and morally superior in LePlay's eyes – set of norms and values.[31]

Granted, much of the austerity and discipline of rural folk in the historical context LePlay examined owed to lack of infrastructure such as good roads, networks of communication, and the transportation necessary to bring goods to the far reaches of the countryside. Thus rural people had little to buy and rural savings often outstripped expenditures. Yet such insights can readily travel to the late-industrializing context, where patterns of rural austerity also owed to key lifestyle differences due to limited developmental gains in the countryside (especially when contrasted to the city), including the fact that rural folk were more likely to be self-sufficient in food and had little rent to pay.[32] Indeed, although LePlay was concerned with urban versus rural location and not class position per se, his findings could be applied to the daily lives and

[29] See *Peasant Society and Culture*, p. 65. Recent work by Philip Gorski (see fn. 23), who has studied what he calls disciplinary movements in early modern Europe, also hints that an important part of the disciplinary ethos may have owed to the middle-classness of the movement participants, and not merely their religious orientation. Indeed, in highlighting "the predominance of Calvinists within Dutch political institutions" that sustained a disciplinary ethos in society at large, Gorski identifies his key protagonists as "*merchants*, many with Protestant sympathies [emphasis mine]," thereby identifying these individuals in terms of an occupational and class status first, and only secondarily in terms of their religious affinities, which he subsequently acknowledges as less than absolute ("The Protestant Ethic Revisited," p. 280).

[30] "A 'Standard' of Living?" p. 9.

[31] Ibid.

[32] It is noteworthy that rural-urban differences have existed in most countries throughout most of the twentieth century, even in communist nations where reducing inequalities was an explicit political aim. For more on the latter context, see Merkel, "Working People and Consumption Under Really-Existing Socialism," pp. 92–111.

activities of rural middle classes, especially small farmers, with even greater certitude.

Whether in early or late industrializers, farmers tend to exhibit great caution in expenditure and relative austerity in outlook, and this is especially so for smaller-scale agricultural producers whose operations are not large enough to be well capitalized and employ wage labor. The very nature and cycle of agricultural production is usually so unpredictable that most farmers are driven to save more and consume little, particularly when it comes to the purchase of luxuries or other goods not necessary to agricultural production. The impossibility of predicting weather, disease, or other potential obstacles to income generation also mitigates against any regularities or guarantees for self-reproduction, so that adopting a self-disciplinary and austere outlook buttressed by savings is almost a necessity. The seasonal requisites of farming, in short, further reinforce the ethos of fiscal self-discipline and savings, especially if the farmer is producing for exchange rather than use value, since harvests come irregularly and the profits generated from them must last long enough to survive the year (if not another one, failing good weather).

Among the multitude of goods that can be produced on one's own account, in fact, probably the hardest and most unlikely to be shifted in midstream are agricultural goods, since the planting, cultivation, and harvesting cycle unfolds over a set and (more often than not) extended period of time, no matter how much labor is invested and no matter the demand.[33] In the exit, voice, loyalty lexicon of Albert Hirschman, one would say that farmers are most likely to remain "loyal" to their activities, at least from the beginning to the end of the cultivation cycle; and this in itself imposes a discipline on their actions.

Bridging Historical Divides

But how exactly will work conditions and/or the requisites of self-reproduction among rural middle classes sustain a disciplinary ethos in both the state and society sufficient to lead directly to developmental gains, especially in late industrializers? I return to the literature on early modern Europe to help

---

[33] In short, it is not so difficult to imagine why urban middle classes – i.e., those producing on their own account, such as self-employed artisans in cities – might be somewhat less disciplinary than their rural counterparts, at least to the extent that they would not face the same acutely unpredictable circumstances. The very diversity of urban economic activities, and the somewhat greater ease and rapidity with which production orientations could potentially change among urban artisans, make all the difference in the world. And this, in turn, might explain why we often see urban middle classes allying with capitalists: They are more connected in terms of production and consumption dynamics than are rural middle classes, a point to which we return in the upcoming chapters.

answer these questions and, by so doing, to unearth the foundations for a modeling of a disciplinary regime of development that can apply even in the contemporary period. The most powerful reason for revisiting historical literature is the fact that scholars of European capitalist development also have identified middle classes as central protagonists and discipline as a key notion.[34] To be sure, most scholars of early modern Europe fail to examine rural versus urban differences in middle-class formation, a key element in our analysis, mainly because middle classes are assumed to be an urban phenomenon – a conceptual bias I take to task in the next chapter.[35] Likewise, few who study the early modern experience examine the state's role in development, despite the fact that it is an absolutely central actor in almost all late industrializers and one of the principal agents of discipline examined here. Instead, when the notion of discipline is employed in the literature on "early" industrializers, it is frequently attributed to Protestantism or other normative developments (including the rise of rationality) manifest in European religious history and culture.[36] But if we return to this classical literature and examine it anew, there is considerable evidence to suggest

[34] Generally speaking, the argument is that small-scale producers sustained the emergence of economies based on the accumulation and reinvestment of capital, leading to the growth of markets and overall economic dynamism in early modern Europe. To be sure, among those who took this position there were differences in the weight attributed to class and material versus cultural explanations for how and why these so-called middle classes mattered. Materialists argued that it was in the economic interests of smaller-scale urban producers to get behind the larger project of capitalist industrialization, either on their own (in the effort to become bourgeois), or in political alliance with a nascent class of capitalists who allied with them in the fight against the economic stranglehold imposed by feudal landlords. In contrast, those more sympathetic to cultural explanations saw values, especially as conceptualized in terms of disciplinary work attributes and orientations, as more central than class, although even Engels produced a provocative argument about the role of religion and the rise of science and mechanics in spurring urban middle classes' defeat of feudalism. Engels, "Socialism," pp. ii, 102–103 (quoted from Abrams, *Historical Sociology*, p. 45).

[35] To be sure, scholars disagreed about whether it was urbanization per se or middle-class formation that was of determinate analytic significance in understanding capitalist development. For example, following Weber's work on the history of cities and capitalist development, Pirenne argued that the development of long-distance trade and commerce in cities was an external factor that accounted for the rise of middle classes and led to the demise of feudalism and the ascendance of capitalism. Dobb, in contrast, focused more on the endogenous character of feudalism and argued that it was because feudal social relations were inherently unstable that the transition to capitalism occurred, a situation that sustained the emergence of cities and urban artisans along with other nascent urban middle classes. For more, see Pirenne, *The Economic and Social History of Medieval Europe*, and Dobb, *Studies in the Development of Capitalism*.

[36] According to Weber, the Protestant ascetic would "always demand of the world an ethically rational order and discipline, corresponding to his own methodical self-discipline," which

that small-scale rural production, and not merely urban artisanal production and/or Protestantism,[37] sustained both discipline and development in "early" developers in ways that show striking parallels to some contemporary late industrializers.

Some of the most powerful evidence for this possibility comes from scholars who still stand as leading interpreters of the early capitalist experience: Max Weber, Robert Brenner, and Barrington Moore. Weber's discussion of the economic differences between northern and southern Germany in the nineteenth century, Brenner's work on agrarian class structures, and Moore's seminal discussion of the different paths to capitalist development all demonstrate an elective affinity between the predominance of rural middle classes and successful capitalist development trajectories. And although none of these works focuses explicitly on the disciplinary orientations of farmers or other small-scale rural producers,[38] they all locate the origins of self-sustaining economic development and prosperity in the flowering of these particular class forces, who are more accurately identified as yeoman farmers despite the anthropological propensity to label them as peasants. We see this most clearly with a view to Barrington Moore's treatment of Great Britain's economic successes, in which a significant cadre of "middling" yeoman farmers contributed to the commercialization of the countryside. Countries with a polarized class structure, he argues in contrast, where the lord dominated the serf and where few commercially oriented small-scale rural producers materialized, missed out on these early developmental gains. For Moore, then, it was the presence or

---

can entail "a revolutionary transformation of the world." See *The Protestant Ethic and the Spirit of Capitalism*; cf. Sayer, *Capitalism and Modernity*, p. 173.

[37] Other historians who also have focused on the material conditions underlying middle-class identity include Thompson and Hill, and they too raise questions about the primacy of cultural or religious explanations for the disciplinary ethos. According to Sayer, they and others "stressed that this capability of Protestantism to confer respect – and respectability – on the everyday activities of the 'middling sort' . . . was one reason for its widespread appeal in a society already moving in the direction of capitalism" (*Capitalism and Modernity*, p. 131). Christopher Hill takes this argument one step further by noting that world economic fluctuations made these early modern middle classes economically vulnerable, thereby pushing them to Calvinist conversion in the first place, in order to weather the difficult times. See "Protestantism and the Rise of Capitalism," pp. 45–47.

[38] This is also true for Weber, author of *The Protestant Ethic and the Spirit of Capitalism*. Although he was clearly interested in cultural and religious differences (especially Protestantism versus Catholicism), in a separate discussion of small farmers and their role in producing regional disparities within Germany he took a much more materialist view and examined distinctions in property ownership and size, particularly how and why the small-farmer economy of certain regions of Germany sustained regional prosperity and self-generative development (while large landlord-dominated areas did not).

absence of a rural middle class of yeoman farmers that was key to early and successful capitalist development (and democracy).[39]

But what about the state? While, unlike late development analysts, scholars of early modern Europe do not place great emphasis on state actors, they do identify the importance of political structures and institutions in sustaining both middle-class formation and discipline, and in this sense their applicability to the contemporary context is partially assured. It is worth remembering that Calvin's great social experiment in Geneva, which has served as a reference point for countless studies of vibrant capitalist development, embodied an unparalleled combination of both top-down (i.e., coercive or state-imposed) and bottom-up (self-imposed) discipline, reinforced by middle classes and others through religious institutions and their leadership. Citizens' compliance with the Reformation's principal tenets of discipline was mandated twice weekly in the pulpit as well as through the rule of law.[40] Equally important, many of these citizens were former farmers who had migrated to Geneva in order to partake in the new socioreligious order, and who took up residence in a city that, while increasingly Protestant, still remained strongly connected via social networks and economic activities to its own rural "hinterland."

All this suggests that the great economic gains in Geneva that so many scholars attributed to Protestantism may have owed not just to religious orientation, or even just to the fact that a considerable number of its citizens were subject to a top-down form of discipline institutionalized in the local structures and practices of political and religious power. Geneva's stunning economic successes also may have owed to the fact its residents carried with them a farmer's self-disciplinary attitude and a persistent rural orientation, despite their urban location.[41] Thus it was not merely urban middle-class formation, or even rural

---

[39] In creating a framework for understanding the countryside built on the "pre-class" notions of lord and serf, Moore may have developed an accurate understanding of the earliest developers, but the language did not translate as well to some of his late-industrializing cases, including Germany. Moreover, he also missed an opportunity to identify, analyze, and/or theorize yeoman farmers in rural middle-class terms, and thus was in no position to ascertain whether it was also a disciplinary orientation, grounded in the material conditions of production of these yeoman farmers, that along with material conditions helped make their agricultural activities so successful in the first place, leading in turn to their generative relations with larger landlords and bourgeois producers rather than vice versa.

[40] For more on this, see McNeill, *The History and Character of Calvinism*; and Hillerbrand (ed.), *The Protestant Reformation*.

[41] A between-the-lines reading of Gorski's empirical study of variations in Prussian and Dutch state formation (see fns. 23 and 29) in yet an earlier historical period further suggests some form of connection between rural life, discipline, and development – although he is more interested in political than economic development. Indeed, Gorski's account suggests that the differences in "disciplinary" orientations in these two nations, which he links to patterns of Pietest versus Calvinist influence in society, could be interpreted as reflecting the

middle-class discipline that generated capitalist development in Geneva, but the "transference" of a rural-based disciplinary orientation into an urban setting where strong state institutions reinforced both the disciplinary ethos and the interchange of rural and urban activities. And this in turn suggests, more generally, that a rural middle-class ethos may engender its greatest developmental gains in conditions where town and countryside remain economically and socially connected.[42]

The Forward and Backward Linkages of Disciplinary Development

The population movement from countryside to city that sparked Geneva's developmental successes has been a common occurrence in the late-industrializing world; yet in the latter situation, rural-urban migration usually is identified as sustaining some of the most problematic features of late industrialization, ranging from rural neglect to overurbanization and regional imbalance. The common view of rural-urban migration in the late-industrializing context is that it serves as a fetter on balanced national development even as it sustains distorted patterns of urban and industrial development. Yet in Geneva and in early modern Europe more generally, the movement of rural people to cities is seen as one of the key building blocks of economic progress.[43] How do we reconcile this discrepancy? Does this mean that early and late development

political salience of different factions of the middle classes (civil servants and entrepreneurs, respectively) and even more to the point, differences in the involvement of rural versus urban populations in the state. See "The Protestant Ethic Revisited," pp. 298–299. It is also noteworthy that he identifies differences in Prussia (vis-à-vis the Dutch case) as owing to the use of the Prussian army as the "main vehicle of popular disciplinization," and that the army was comprised mainly of rural recruits, since "urban burghers and craftsmen had been exempted from military service beginning in 1714" (p. 301, fn. 36). As we shall see in the next chapter, it was precisely the mixture of military *and* rural middle-class mentalities that sustained such a strong disciplinary state in South Korea.

[42] There are good reasons for this: Urban economies allow a greater scope for the productive application of self-disciplinary efforts, and thus they may be an even more fecund host for the intensely disciplinary ethos so pervasive among small farmers. This would be especially true when urban activities are linked to rural cultivation in ways that allow an urban "hedging of bets" against farm disasters, and vice versa, resulting in a synergy of production and consumption that can buoy the entire economy.

[43] Most works on the origins of capitalism, in fact, identified the successful transition from feudalism to capitalism – or the emergence of industrialism, as Abrams calls it in his masterwork, *Historical Sociology* – as intricately linked to a shift from agriculture to industry and from the countryside to the city of people, investments, and economic growth, transformations that many sociologists have identified in social or cultural terms (i.e., a change from traditional to modern values or a change in social relations based on *gemeinschaft* to

are fundamentally different and that we err in trying to use models drawn from the former to explain the latter? Much of the answer to this question lies in a closer understanding of the articulations (or disarticulations) between city and countryside in both these contexts.

In many late developers, the lack of forward and backward linkages between rural and urban activities sustains rural poverty (and hence serves as an obstacle to rural middle-class formation in the first place), urban privilege, and overinflated prices for urban goods. Each of these conditions chips away at the prospects for disciplinary development. In early industrializers, in contrast, one generally is more likely to see macroeconomic gains associated with strong forward and backward linkages between city and countryside, a situation which also helps eliminate the likelihood of stark regional or urban/rural inequalities. Balances of political power are more equally distributed, as are prices, wage rates, and supply and demand for goods and services, thereby eliminating urban economic and political dominance while increasing the likelihood of rural middle-class political sway. Accordingly, it is not merely the formation of rural middle classes or their contact with cities that sustains disciplinary development, then or now, but also the extent to which larger political, social, economic, and even geographical conditions generate strong articulations between rural and urban economies.[44]

A version of this may have been what was occurring in the commercialization of the English countryside, where the connections between town and country were so "organic" that industrialization must be considered a rural phenomenon as much as an urban one, uniting town and country in production and consumption cycles on the backs of folk whose primary and economic commitments were to the English countryside more than anything else. In David Landes's classic work *The Unbound Prometheus*, the notion of "self-sustaining" growth is used to refer to similar dynamics. Landes locates England's early industrial successes in sustained production and consumption, which he attributes to greater purchasing power, a higher standard of living, and reduced expenditure on foodstuffs, a set of rural-urban interactions that

---

gesellschaft). Among other things, the movement in space, especially from countryside to city, was hypothesized as fueling economic progress, by both material and cultural means.

[44] In substance these claims resonate with a more contemporary body of literature and debate in the field of agricultural economics, in which linkages between farm and nonfarm growth are seen as the key to ending rural poverty. See Hazell and Haggblade, "Farm-Nonfarm Growth Linkages and the Welfare of the World Poor"; Ranis and Stewart, "Rural Linkages in the Philippines and Taiwan"; and Mellor and Johnston, "The World Food Equation." They also are relatively consistent with claims advanced by proponents of the "secondary city thesis" during the 1970s and 1980s, such as Rondinelli, who identified the economically generative possibilities associated with the emergence of strong linkages between city and countryside in a defined and well-integrated territorial context.

produced and were produced by a "thickening" of the countryside around cities.[45] A similar dynamic seems to have been what fueled the early and unparalleled successes of city-states in Europe, not only Geneva but also Amsterdam, Brussels, and those smaller countries whose economies flourished in a relatively limited environment circumscribed enough in spatial terms to politically, economically, and socially link urban and rural populations and activities to each other. But perhaps the best example of this and of the positive gains produced when rural middle-class discipline thrives in a town-linked setting is seen in the case of the early United States. In the United States, many of the small-scale rural producers who settled on farms in and around the towns and villages of New England during the eighteenth and early nineteenth centuries saw themselves and the new society they forged in the postcolonial era as rural middle-class in spirit and disciplinary in ethos.

Some of this may have owed to the Protestant roots of settler migration, or so it has been argued. Yet it also is true that many early settlers considered themselves yeoman farmers – and often even gentlemen farmers – but certainly not peasants or landlords.[46] Granted, the insistence on these as collective American identities may have involved a certain degree of denial;[47] but such attitudes and linguistic categories were part of the popular lexicon and the stubbornly middle-class self-identity that prevailed across some of the most economically prosperous regions of New England. And owing to the fruits of their labors as yeoman farmers, by the early-nineteenth century most of these regions had achieved relative prosperity, associated with a farm-based economy and accelerating agricultural productivity that interfaced with rural and then urban industrialization to lead to tremendous regional and national economic gains.[48] What gave the early American rural producers a head start, then, may have been not only their disciplinary orientation as Protestant farmers, but also the fact that their conditions of livelihood paralleled those seen in the most successful city-states of early modern Europe, by virtue of the strong

---

[45] *The Unbound Prometheus*, p. 52.

[46] These yeoman farmers, as they were sometimes called, were also idealized in Jeffersonian thought as "better citizens as well as healthier, nobler, and more affluent men," a view that fit well with their sense of themselves as upstanding middle-class citizens. See Rourke, "Urbanism and American Democracy," pp. 344–345.

[47] Clearly, during this period indentured servitude existed, farm labor was employed, and the entire south of the country was built on slavery and a plantation economy reminiscent of feudal social and economic conditions.

[48] To be sure, small-scale farmers were soon matched in economic prowess by southern plantation owners – closer to feudal lords in Moore's terminology – who prospered through slaveholding. But the path, prospects, and successes of U.S. industrialization lay in the Northeast, where small farming predominated.

economic bonds established between the urban and rural economies – or town and country – as it is generally called in the U.S. literature.

Observations of eminent American historian Gordon Wood seem to further support this interpretation, although his point of departure in the study of American economic development was consumption more than production. Wood argued that rural productivity in the postcolonial United States increased because of a burgeoning consumer revolution, which itself was fueled by the growing possibilities of buying and selling ever more luxury goods which were produced in or imported to towns and cities along the eastern seaboard. These new consumption practices, however, should not be understood merely in cultural terms; they also developed in a certain spatial context where the propinquity of rural and urban activities and orientations fueled the possibilities of a well-connected and generative production-consumption cycle. As Wood puts it,

> Ordinary farmers began working harder and increasing their productivity when they found that there were genteel goods available for them to purchase. They did not just grow crops but scrambled every which way to produce goods for exchange in local markets – putting their wives and children to work spinning cloth or weaving hats, making hoops and barrels, distilling rum or cider, fabricating whatever might sell – all in order that there might be an increasing variety of consumer goods.... New England farmers worked harder and produced surpluses during the war [for Independence], not, as traditional thinking would have it, out of poverty and necessity, but in order to increase their purchase of luxury goods and to raise their standard of living.[49]

For our purposes, what is significant about Wood's observation is not only that hard work and self-discipline fueled the cycle of production and consumption, but also that spatial conditions were central to positive economic outcomes. For Wood the spatial connections between city and countryside – brought together in the economic, social, and political dynamics of the New England town – insured that American farmers were more than just that: They farmed *and* they produced nonagricultural goods for sale in an integrated town-farm context, with these two sets of activities sustaining and reinforcing each other and the overall gains associated with the American settlers' clearly self-disciplinary mentality. As such, not only were New Englanders solidly middle class in terms of ownership and labor process; their middle-classness rested in a hybrid of rural and urban sensibilities and activities that together fueled one of the world's most enduring and prosperous experiences of postcolonial economic development.

[49] "Inventing American Capitalism," p. 49.

Modeling "Disciplinary Development": Then and Now

In focusing on the rural middle class and disciplinary dynamics that produced developmental gains in the early European and American context, we have journeyed far from the late-developmental experience of East Asia that led us down this path in the first place. Our focus on cases where the state's role in development is hardly mentioned at all seems to further the sense of distance, not just because the state is so significant in late industrializers but also because it is central to our notion of disciplinary development. But even though the absence of such a strong and economically interventionist state is one of the main differences between early and late developers, it still is possible to conclude that there are a variety of ways in which the early modern experience could serve as analytic inspiration if not as a model. To get the ball rolling, let us return once again to Calvin's Geneva and contrast it to what we already know about the case of South Korea.

Geneva's great gains and that city's special place in the history of self-sustaining capitalist development owed in no small part to the coercive discipline imposed by church leaders in tandem with local authorities as it did from the self-discipline of citizens themselves. Without the elite's coercion "from above," working in tandem with the "bottom-up" disciplinary mentality of migrated farmers, it is unclear whether the same heights of productivity would have been reached. This experience bears striking parallels with South Korea under Park Chung Hee. And conversely, one might say that a "functional equivalent" to South Korea's late-developmental state may have existed in the religious/cultural, spatial, and governing institutions that dominated social, political, and economic life in Geneva. We could further extend the search for functional equivalents among early and late developers by posing other questions about middle-class dynamics in these two contexts. To the extent that many of the economic gains in both Geneva and South Korea seem to have owed to the demographic and social importance of small farmers and other self-employed rural producers, whose self-disciplining combined with "top-down" measures produced an overall disciplinary ethos in state and society, similar dynamics seem to have been at play.

So how might we integrate these various experiences into a predictive model that would help explain why some late-industrializing countries achieve out-of-the-ordinary developmental success? By specifying: 1) some sort of institution (state, church, army, depending on historical time period) with the authority and legitimacy to discipline key economic actors; 2) some social class or group that supplements, legitimizes, or sustains these institution(s) and their disciplinary orientation; 3) an economic, political, social, and/or cultural environment in which citizens themselves are committed to self-discipline and market productivity; 4) middle classes – if they do constitute these disciplinary forces – that are independent enough of other class forces to politically sustain a coercive and self-disciplinary ethos in both the state and society; 5) material conditions that make it feasible for these smaller-scale producers to pursue productive and profitable commercial activities in the countryside; and 6) a combination of spatial, political, and social conditions and institutions that connect rural activities and residents to urban ones, and in which middle-class producers socially and economically straddle both territorial domains.

My aim in the upcoming chapters is to examine the explanatory utility of this model as a predictor of successful and failed late development, and to determine the conditions under which they have been most likely to materialize. What historical peculiarities – both domestic and international – have sustained these six conditions sufficiently to produce a disciplinary regime of development in the late-industrializing context; and conversely, what has prevented them from materializing? To answer these questions I employ a comparative-historical method, analyzing matched pairs of countries (again, see Appendix A: Cases, Comparisons, and a Note on Methodology and Sources). Starting with an examination of South Korea, and then moving on to Taiwan, Argentina, and Mexico during the first half of the twentieth century up through the post–World War II decades, I assess cultural practices, state and class formations, patterns of political power, social and spatial relations between city and countryside, and industrialization policies to determine the relationship among these forces and conditions, discipline, and development trajectories. This is a complex and interrelated task which rests on our capacity to ascertain the extent to which rural middle classes, alone or in combination with other classes, become key political bases of the state; the extent to which rural middle-class political influence, understood as a form of state embeddedness, translates into the government's willingness and capacity to discipline key economic actors; and the extent to which, through these disciplinary measures, rural middle-class-embedded states reduce domestic overall consumption, increase savings, enhance productivity, generate export earnings, and establish sufficient forward and backward linkages among rural and urban sectors to generate nationally self-sustaining economic growth in both agricultural and industrial sectors.

The book is structured as follows. Chapter 2 provides the analytical and empirical justification for our efforts to bring middle classes back into the study of development, by first demonstrating how and why they fell out of view. In this chapter I also examine the construction of middle "classness" from a scholarly perspective, underscoring the ways in which preconceived notions and blinders about who constitutes the middle classes prevented most development scholars from examining – let alone theorizing – these actors' role in either successful or failed development trajectories. Chapters 3 through 5 present the case studies, which contain detailed empirical analyses of middle classes, their relationships to other classes and the state, the historical, political, cultural, and discursive conditions which made (or prevented) rural middle classes from becoming a key political force, and how these patterns affected each country's likelihood of pursuing a disciplinary regime of development.

Each of the case study chapters, which focus on South Korea, Taiwan and Argentina, and Mexico respectively, are presented as historical narratives in which particular development decisions and industrial trajectories are discussed in light of patterns of middle-class formation and identity as well as the middle-class political foundations of the state and how they led to the emergence of disciplinary or accommodating regimes of development. Each chapter also addresses a particular analytic problematic in the construction of a disciplinary (or accommodating) regime of development. For example, the South Korean chapter focuses on the state's active efforts to reinforce and construct a rural middle-class disciplinary ethos, how this initially brought great developmental gains, and why the country later suffered a temporary reversal of fortune. The Taiwan and Argentina chapter, which also entails comparative reflection on the South Korean case, analyzes the problematic of rural middle-class formation and the impact of working-class political discourses on rural middle-class unity in Taiwan and disunity in Argentina. It further highlights the role of culture, language, and space in creating predominant class identities among self-employed rural and urban workers. The concluding case study chapter, on Mexico, highlights the role played by regional conflict, racial identities, and revolutionary trade-offs in the political defeat of rural middle classes, developments which undermined the initial promise of disciplinary development and led to a macroeconomic strategy that accommodated the aims of industrialists and their workers.

Chapter 6 presents final remarks about middle classes and development. In addition to discussing the theoretical implications of similarities and differences between early and late developers, and what this says for key current debates like the asserted relationship between democracy and development, this concluding chapter considers the diminished prospects for rural middle-class formation and disciplinary development in an increasingly globalized world in which internationally networked capitalists, among others, appear to be increasingly undisciplined by their societies and home nation-states.

2

MIDDLE CLASSES AND
DEVELOPMENT THEORY

Stalking the Path Not Taken

Forty years ago, long before the East Asian tigers roared loudly enough for the world to notice, it was unusual to find scholars who did not focus on middle classes in the study of development in the late-industrializing world. Today middle classes have practically vanished from the literature. In fact, most contemporary scholars of late industrialization focus on practically every social or class force *but* the middle class, while capitalists, laborers, and/or the state are invoked without pause. While rounding up the usual suspects year after year may not be inherently objectionable as an analytic strategy, it does raise epistemological questions about why middle classes disappeared from the development literature in the first place. Some no doubt would account for this state of affairs by linking the fate of middle classes to the rise and fall of modernization theory, a paradigm built around claims of a morally superior and generative role to be played by the middle classes. When modernization theory held sway in the field of development, middle classes danced on center stage; when modernization theory fell out of favor, replaced initially by dependency or world-system theory and then a variety of state-centered paradigms, middle classes swiftly exited the theoretical limelight.

The problem with emphasizing shifting theoretical paradigms, however, is that it tells little about why a concern with middle classes was not reformulated in terms more compatible with the theories that replaced modernization theory. This need not have been. When dependency theory first nudged modernization theory off center stage, it came in a variety of forms and packaging, some of which were much more consistent with a focus on middle classes than others. In fact, Fernando Henrique Cardoso and Enzo Faletto's *Dependency and Development in Latin America*, considered one of the most nuanced and masterful statements on the class dynamics of dependency, conceptualized middle classes as key protagonists in the drama of development.[1] Yet Cardoso and Faletto's approach to dependency turned out to be the path least taken in the field of development studies, not only with respect to its discussion of middle classes but also with respect to its presumption that domestic class conditions – as opposed to global structures – should serve as a starting point for understanding late industrialization.

Likewise, the subsequent rise of the state-centered paradigm could, in theory, have provided room for some discussion of middle classes, especially as a conceptual tool to resolve the tensions between class- and state-centered theorists. Some of the most contentious issues in development theorizing revolved around conflicts over whether the state's capacity to engender successful macroeconomic development derives from its autonomy or its class embeddedness. In these debates, class embeddedness was almost always defined in terms of the state's relationship to capitalists, just as a state was considered autonomous if it was understood to be acting somewhat independently from capitalists. But if development scholars had taken middle classes more seriously in their theorizing about state structures and actions, and if they had chosen to assess the state in terms of its middle-class embeddedness, such conflicts might not have materialized. Not only would we have understood why a (middle) class-embedded state could act independently of capitalists, perhaps even disciplining them, we also would have been forced to consider that a state might be both autonomous and class embedded at the same time, albeit middle-class embedded, thereby moving forward the divisive debate that all but stalled development theorizing for a decade or two. What must be explained, then, are what Robert Merton calls the "pockets of theoretical neglect" into which middle classes disappeared.

My aim in this preliminary chapter is to resurrect the "disappeared" middle class and to offer an analytical, empirical, and theoretical justification for so doing. Later chapters sustain this logic with historical evidence and greater empirical precision based on material drawn from the case studies. Here I begin by demonstrating that the prevailing languages of class and assumptions about middle classes have long prevented contemporary development scholars of almost all theoretical persuasions from seeing middle classes as key forces in late industrialization. Through closer examination of who routinely has been assumed to constitute the middle class and why, I argue that the current failure

---

[1] In their attempts to make sense of the interaction between domestic class structures and global dynamics, Cardoso and Faletto paid considerable attention to the political orientations and activities of the middle classes, particularly the extent to which they participated in the so-called game of power, as well as the ways these orientations and activities helped determine developmental differences among Latin American countries. Enclave economy or not, Cardoso and Faletto declared, "in all cases, the domestic economy developed through pressure from *middle groups* allied with the existing bourgeois capital sector, or with the worker-peasant sector, or with both [emphasis mine]." See *Dependency and Development*, p. 125.

to seriously consider the role played by middle classes in molding national development trajectories owes less to the "facts" and more to the ambiguities in conception and definition of middle classes. Some of these ambiguities come from the peculiar nature of middle "classness," if you will, and some from the complexity of the developing-country context. But most of them derive from deeply ingrained scholarly assumptions about who or what constitutes a class and how to draw boundaries around it, as well as from the analytic blinders that directed attention to capitalists and laborers while bypassing the middle class. The gaps in research produced by these biases have not been benign. They have molded ways of thinking about key protagonists and processes of late development, and they have sustained the sway of certain theories and the importance of certain actors while precluding others. Only after examining the conceptual frames that kept these central protagonists out of the picture, then, and shedding them accordingly, can we consider bringing middle classes back into development history and theory. That is my aim here and more generally.

Searching for Silences in Development Theory

How simple it would be to claim that the fate of middle classes in the development literature owed to the empirical failures of modernization theory to account for developmental patterns.[2] Or even to argue that the political and/or ideological repudiation of modernization theory by scholars of the developing world, many of whom shunned the self-righteous (or at least self-referential) claims of North American scholars about the elective affinities between middle-class ideals and sustained economic development, explains middle classes' analytical demise.[3] Many development scholars did truly revile

---

[2] Much of this can be attributed to the demonstrated inadequacies of modernization theory. Its claims that urbanization tends to create a middle class willing to promote achievement over ascription and capable of pushing forward modern ideals, including the importance of democratic states, did not hold true in practice, and its claims that with urbanization society as a whole would become increasingly middle-class and the extremes of the class and status structure would disappear have failed to materialize. For a concise elaboration of these ideas see Ratinoff, "The New Urban Groups," pp. 62–65.

[3] Modernization theorists' emphasis on middle-class values and the importance of keeping middle classes in political power in order to insure the conditions for economic development fitted neatly with the conservative political culture of the cold war era, fueling many foreign policies of the time, some of which came to be associated with U.S. foreign intervention. Thus with the turn to the "left" in development studies over the 1960s and 1970s, these ideas were patently unpopular and few development scholars even tried to take them seriously. Even today, most of those scholars who argue that entrepreneurial values or middle-class culture plays a key role in development tend to openly identify themselves as politically conservative. Among the more recent cohort of scholars who still seek to link social and cultural values to development we would find Berger as well as a new crop of "communitarians," like Etzioni,

modernization theory because its principal tenets were based upon assumptions about the professed moral superiority and asserted democratic proclivities of middle classes, and because modernization scholars categorized most developing countries as backward precisely because they lacked middle classes with these sentiments.[4] As such, the disenchantment with this paradigm and its basic claims did affect the theoretical fate of middle classes in development studies. But advocates of modernization theory were not alone in highlighting the centrality of the middle classes in development, and thus the fate of middle classes as a subject of study cannot be reduced to the mere ideological rejection or embrace of the modernization paradigm. Middle classes reigned supreme in a wide variety of development theories, materialist, class-conflict, and culturalist alike, especially those crafted to account for the timing and character of industrialization in early modern Europe and America, as noted in the last chapter.[5]

So if modernization theorists were not the only ones appropriating the middle-class subject in their accounts of development, what explains their relegation to the theoretical sidelines in the post-1960s period? An equally compelling explanation might be the growing preoccupation with global dynamics among scholars of development, including those who practiced class analysis. This theoretical advance was perhaps best seen in the initial popularity of dependency theory and the tidal wave of studies examining late industrializers in a world-systemic context over the 1970s and 1980s. *Dependistas*, as the Latin American founders of this school of thought were subsequently called, proceeded under the assumption that it was impossible for late-industrializing countries to repeat European or North American patterns of development, in part because of the negative structural impact of past patterns of development in the "core," or advanced capitalist countries. That is, it was not the cultural or social traits associated with a country – especially the presence or absence of its middle classes – that kept nations from fulfilling their developmental potential, but the global context, and the fact that countries in the so-called

---

Wolfe, and, more recently, Fukuyama, all of whom are reintroducing these ideas into the study of American society.

[4] Middle classes were assumed to embody strong achievement-orientation, an unbridled work ethic, a commitment to savings, a flair for entrepreneurialism, and faith in the practical value of education, all of which were seen as critical determinants of steady economic progress (not to mention high national savings rates).

[5] In *The Class Struggles in France* and *The Eighteenth Brumaire of Louis Bonaparte*, Marx underscored the critical role played by urban middle classes – especially small shopkeepers, traders, and artisans who served as the foundation for the growing, nascent bourgeoisie or who allied with them behind the project of capitalist industrialization; and it was these same urban middle classes who figured so prominently as Calvinists in Weber's writings, especially *The Protestant Ethic and the Spirit of Capitalism*, as well as in Tawney's *Religion and the Rise of Capitalism*.

developing world were structurally linked in a dependent way to advanced capitalist "core" countries.[6]

Still, it was not just because dependency and world-system theory became so unquestionably popular and theoretically hegemonic that the modernization paradigm and its propositions about middle classes found ever fewer supporters. Or even the fact that dependency's successor, world-system theory, posed a frontal challenge to the long-standing focus on domestic political and social conditions and, as such, directed attention more toward external market factors.[7] Rather, to know why middle classes disappeared from development theory we must understand the larger interpretive frameworks and conceptual assumptions that most theorists carried with them as they studied development. And, by and large, most development scholars were burdened by ideas and assumptions about class categories and class dynamics that have prevented many of them from "seeing" middle classes as conceptually distinct, numerically significant, and/or politically salient class actors. As they disappeared from sight, they also disappeared from theory.

Four interrelated assumptions common among development scholars relegated middle classes to the blind spot in theories of late industrialization. The first was an assumption of a causal relationship between economic development and the appearance of the middle class. The second concerned definitions of capitalists and laborers and how to draw boundaries around them. The third had to do with locale or, better said, assumptions about where middle classes are – or are not – expected to reside. A fourth had to do with assumptions about the analytic distinction between state and class actors. Often, these four sets of assumptions conspired together within a body of literature to slight the middle class entirely; but even when they did not, they circumscribed the definition of these so-called intermediate forces so narrowly that the conceptual category of middle class began to disappear altogether as an analytically significant entry point for the study of development. While it may be possible to find the rare scholar who does not work under one or more of these assumptions, the combined weight of the four sets of assumptions so marked the field of development over the last several decades that discussions of the middle class still fail to seriously engage the scholarly community.

[6] Economists such as Prebisch, Singer, Furtado, Sunkel, and Dos Santos joined with Latin American sociologists such as Cardoso, Faletto, and Stavenhagen to chart the historical origins and nature of dependency.

[7] After all, it is not entirely inconceivable that in the effort to determine whether and how domestic classes interact with the global economy in some way, a key aim of world-system theory, middle classes could have been identified as central. Much of the current work on global commodity chains by scholars such as Gereffi builds on an examination of the important role of small-scale family firms involved in flexible industrial production, which clearly fall into the middle-class category.

Cause or Consequence of Development?

The first frontal challenge to efforts to consider middle classes as protagonists in processes of late industrialization can be traced to the assumption that middle classes are primarily the *result* of capitalist modernization and economic development. To the extent that for years scholars interested in the developing world have accepted this premise to a great degree, they never made serious efforts to examine the history or composition of middle classes in any meaningful way except to chronicle their demographic appearance on the scene as countries increase their per capita income and/or rise to the top of the ladder of global economic prosperity. The related assumption that middle classes should be seen as indicators of development, an idea that still prevails in many circles, pushed scholars to consider only certain "modern" occupations as middle class, moreover, and to ignore other significant occupations that also fall into a broadly defined intermediate stratum but that remain slighted because they are associated with "premodern" activities or "underdeveloped" economies. Consequently, a good portion of a developing country's population dropped off the conceptual map entirely.

Further adding to the problem, among the few who have analyzed the character and composition of middle classes in developing countries, it is usually the so-called new middle classes who capture attention – mainly white-collar professionals, managers, and technicians with higher levels of education who are employed in the modern industrial and service sectors. These are the occupations whose emergence is most frequently traced to a more complex division of labor and the increasing economic prosperity generally encountered in the move from traditional, agricultural economies to highly urbanized and industrialized societies. Traditional or so-called old middle classes, including artisans, merchants, small shopkeepers, and traders, even when they exist in highly industrialized and modernized cities of the developing world, have been surprisingly under-examined in the contemporary literature on development, primarily because the common notion is that they disappear as the economy modernizes and industrializes.

The assumption that only new middle classes deserve the middling nomenclature held true especially among advocates of modernization theory, perhaps because the teleology of their reasoning has been to work backwards from the modern condition: Take a snapshot of an advanced capitalist country (usually the United States or a European country), identify the class structure of its societies (i.e., the overwhelming presence of new middle classes as juxtaposed with declining numbers of old middle classes), and argue that in "underdeveloped" societies these particular middle classes are absent. This logic is then used to support the claim that it is precisely the absence of these middle classes that both characterizes underdevelopment and impedes development. Yet, as we shall see shortly, the assumption that the only analytically relevant middle classes are the so-called new ones is not exclusively the domain of modernization theorists or even those who study late industrialization. Many scholars of both the developed and the developing world, whatever their theoretical affinities, tend to assume that once the notion of middle class is invoked, it is the new middle classes who are the subject of study.[8]

This is especially evident with a closer look at scholars working in the Weberian tradition, where concerns with the relationship between modernization and bureaucratization suggest that a growing number of technical and salaried employees – both in and outside the state – would become increasingly visible as capitalist development proceeds. But it also holds for scholars of other theoretical perspectives, including those with Marxist sensibilities, who tend to see the old middle classes as disappearing with capitalist development, especially as the pressure for greater productivity and accumulation drives a concentration of capital and the attendant demise of smaller-scale individual producers.[9] For them, as soon as capitalism finds its foothold the most significant intermediate strata are not "old" petit bourgeois forces, but the new middle classes, or "salaried managers, overseers, and other capitalist functionaries," who according to Marx, "maintain[ed] themselves to an ever increasing extent directly out of revenue" and who thus burdened the working class while increasing the social security and power of the upper classes.[10] And even when the so-called old middle classes are actually the subject of study – which itself is quite rare in most theoretical traditions – they are referred to mainly by their occupational category (artisans, small businessmen, etc.) not their class status, whereas with new middle classes it is the other way around: Their class identity is invoked more than their occupational categories (i.e., typists, word processors, managers). Clearly, even the lexicon itself underscores the assumptions about who is or is not middle-class, and much of this bias is due to the use of the advanced capitalist experience as the yardstick for comparison.

It may be precisely because so many scholars assume that it is new middle classes that one has in mind when this term is invoked that we are now faced with an incomplete if not injudicious accounting of the diverse activities, orientations, and larger impact of middle classes in their entirety in the developing-country context. If significant groups of the population are

---

[8] See for example, the introduction to Vidich's edited volume, *The New Middle Classes*, p. 1.

[9] As Marx put it, "The previously existing small intermediate strata – the small industrials, merchants and rentiers, the artisans and peasants – all these classes sink down into the proletariat, partly because their small capital does not suffice for the carrying on of large-scale industry and succumbs in competition with the larger capitalists, partly because their skill is rendered worthless by new methods of production." Quoted in Draper, *Karl Marx's Theory of Revolution*, Vol. 2: *The Politics of Social Classes*, p. 616.

[10] Burris, "The Discovery of the New Middle Classes," pp. 19–20.

excluded from analysis, it is hard to know what exactly their impact is on development. And if assumptions about economic modernization and class formation insure that it is primarily managers and white-collar employees who are considered to be middle classes, these same groups will not be identified as central in the developing world because their number is still relatively small and they are often much less well organized. Alternatively, if middle classes are defined in such a way as to include some state workers or small commercial and industrial producers, then it would be much harder to ignore their role in late development.

If middle classes are defined primarily as highly educated managers and salaried employees, moreover, a further assumption is that they also have certain social characteristics and political priorities. More often than not, they are assumed to share little in common with the working classes and to identify much more with capitalists, an assumption that further fuels the analytic neglect of the middle classes and a scholarly preoccupation with capitalists, the working class, and their relationship to each other. But again, if middle classes were conceptualized or identified in all their complexity, as comprised of both new and old middle-class occupations with a variety of possible allegiances, such assumptions would be difficult to sustain. Instead, it would be necessary to actually examine these so-called middle classes – their homogeneity or heterogeneity as well as the extent to which they do or do not identify with capitalists and/or labor.

Granted, it is not only because scholars assume that middle classes result from economic development that they fall into the trap of ignoring a wide variety of middle classes and/or treating this category as an analytic extension of the bourgeoisie. This problem also owes to the popularity of the so-called "thesis of extinction" argument, as it is frequently called among Marxists, which posits that "with growing industrialization and in the course of increasing class struggles, . . . [the] 'class in between' was to be destroyed between the two antagonistic classes."[11] In many ways, this thesis is the opposite of modernization theory because it holds that middle classes disappear – rather than materialize – with industrialization and economic development. But the analytic implications are surprisingly similar: Patterns of capitalist development determine the fate of the middle classes, and to the extent that they are assumed to disappear in this process, attention is focused on other class actors.

Drawing Boundaries Between Capital and Labor

A second reason middle classes have been ignored in recent years is that there is little consensus about where to draw boundary lines between them and capitalists, as well as between middle classes and the working class. One result

---

[11] See Pappi, "The Petite Bourgeoisie and the New Middle Class," p. 106.

is that many scholars of the developing world, dependent on their theoretical proclivities, have collapsed middle classes into one or the other of these two main class categories. This may have been most explicitly acknowledged by Richard Adams, who not that long ago declared that

> the usefulness of the middle-class concept for the study of contemporary Latin American society has been greatly exaggerated and this has in turn obscured other processes which are of considerable importance. While it is possible to distinguish a growing middle-income sector, the older and basic dual structure of prestige and value system has not changed as much as has been supposed. Rather, the apparently new middle group is only an extension of the traditional upper class, both in terms of its economic position and basic values.[12]

To be sure, it is neither implausible nor unlikely that for certain sectors of the middle class or in certain countries – of Latin America or elsewhere in the late-industrializing world – these claims might be true. But rather than raising questions about the conditions under which this is the case, the tendency is simply to assume as a truism the analytic irrelevance of the category of middle class. Such assumptions have stifled intellectual curiosity and the conceptual wherewithal to theorize the role played by middle classes in large-scale processes of development.

This tendency to analytically define away the middle class is probably most evident in Marxist-inspired theories of development, which have dominated the development literature over the last several decades and thus have had greater influence on the fate of the middle classes than any other single paradigm. For many scholars schooled in this tradition, the principal motor of change is the antagonistic relationship between two polar classes, capital and labor; middle classes have only been significant to the extent that they ally with a nascent bourgeoisie against an oligarchy, or are themselves considered to be the nascent bourgeoisie.[13] In fact, the evolutionist assumptions of Marxist theorizing made it possible to conceptualize a force that was not yet a bourgeoisie in bourgeois terms nonetheless, owing to the presupposition that once the dynamics of capitalist development were put in place there was a natural tendency for accumulation and increases in size that would transform a petit bourgeois class of shopkeepers and small producers into large ones. This, in turn, meant that among most Marxist scholars, the petit bourgeois factions of the middle classes, such as small producers in commerce, services,

---

[12] Adams, "Political Power and Social Structures," p. 16.
[13] Even in *The Eighteenth Brumaire*, where Marx presents a much more nuanced and empirically grounded treatment of class structure, he refers to writers, lawyers, officers, and officials – clearly members of the middle class – as "republican-minded bourgeois." See *The Eighteenth Brumaire of Louis Bonaparte*, in Tucker (ed.), *The Marx-Engels Reader*, p. 445.

and industry, were frequently treated in bourgeois terms or, at minimum, as a predictable and crucial ally of the bourgeoisie.

To be sure, in studies of the advanced capitalist context, Marxist scholars occasionally qualified their treatment of small producers by classifying them as petit bourgeois, a terminology that allowed them to sometimes also consider these forces as middle class. Yet it is striking that in the developing-country context this terminology has been almost completely absent, even among Marxists.[14] Rather, the tendency among those trained in this tradition who study developing countries has been to discursively treat the class structure of late industrializers as divided between capitalists and laborers, or (bourgeois) owners and workers. If distinctions are made within the bourgeoisie, it is generally between domestic versus foreign firms, manufacturing versus financial enterprises, or exporting versus import-substituting capitalists, not between firms of different sizes, at least in such a way as to recognize the existence of a middle class.[15] Rarely are industrial producers or commercial and service enterprises of any variety, including small ones, discursively treated as anything *but* the bourgeoisie.

This was true even in the work of Cardoso and Faletto. In their *Dependency and Development*, they refer continually to industrialists as "the bourgeoisie," regardless of size; and in their wide-ranging and heterogeneous definition of the middle class, the one occupational group that is absent – or, better said, insufficiently specified – is small producers.[16] In fact, Cardoso and Faletto quite candidly claim that their use of the concept bourgeoisie is intended "to stress the character of 'capitalist producers,' or 'capitalist entrepreneurs,'" an acknowledgment that provides further evidence of an unwillingness to differentiate between small and large capitalist producers and entrepreneurs, and thus between middle classes and other capitalists.[17]

The failure to analytically distinguish between petit bourgeois forces as well as other small-scale producers and larger "bourgeois" capitalists is also apparent in José Nun's groundbreaking study of middle-class military coups. In this study, though, the problem is just the opposite of Cardoso and Faletto's: a tendency to treat all property owners, whether large or small, as

---

[14] For a fascinating discussion of the use of this term in socialist societies, and studies of them, see Misztal, "The Petite Bourgeoisie in Socialist Society." Much as we do, he defines them primarily as "small manufacturers, shopkeepers, craftsmen, and farmers [who] own their own means of production but also work themselves, only sometimes hiring labour in addition to their own" (p. 91).

[15] See, e.g., Chilcote and Edelstein's *Latin America*.

[16] *Dependency and Development*, p. 83. An acknowledgment that "those linked to the industries and services oriented toward the domestic market" are part of the middle class is the closest Cardoso and Faletto come to recognizing small producers as distinct from the bourgeoisie.

[17] Ibid., p. 77 fn. 1.

unqualified members of the middle class. To be sure, Nun's deliberate "use [of] the expression 'middle class' rather than 'bourgeoisie'" was inspired by a desire to recognize that processes of class formation in Latin America have unfolded differently than in Europe, where the urban middle class served as a nascent bourgeoisie whose struggles against agrarian oligarchies ushered in capitalist development.[18] Yet no matter the importance of Nun's efforts to underscore that Argentina never developed this historic bourgeois force, his decision to throw out the concept of the bourgeoisie altogether, and invoke just that of the middle class despite his concern with a wider range of class forces, leads to considerable etiological and theoretical confusion. To the extent that there is little consensus about when professionals, petit bourgeois forces, and/or big industrialists are middle class and when they are bourgeois capitalists, it may not be so surprising that they are shunted aside in those terms.

Of course, those concerned with the class dynamics of development, such as Cardoso and Faletto as well as Nun, are not the only ones to have worn blinders or meshed categories when analyzing the middle classes in late developers. Modernization theorists like Robert Scott also have grouped the middle class with the bourgeoisie, seeing it as "only an extension of the traditional upper class, both in terms of economic position and of basic values," very much in the same way as Nun, albeit for different reasons.[19] Yet more common in the modernization tradition is the tendency to reverse the order of this determination. That is, while scholars trained in the Marxist tradition tended to treat all producers – regardless of size – as the bourgeoisie, and by so doing to effectively ignore the middle classes, most modernization theorists see all capitalists as "entrepreneurs," regardless of size, and thus as members of the middle class. This is perhaps best evidenced in John Johnson's book on the middle classes in Latin America, in which he claims all "owners of commercial and industrial establishments" to be the most "stalwart members of the middle class."[20] The point here is that among development scholars of various theoretical stripes, with the recent and notable exception of Dietrich Rueschemeyer, John Stephens, and Evelyn Huber Stephens, middle classes as a category – analytically separate from capitalists – seems to have disappeared from analysis.[21] Groups like small producers in industry, commerce,

---

[18] "The Middle-Class Military Coup," p. 77.

[19] Adams, "Political Power and Social Structures," p. 16.

[20] *Political Change*, p. 3.

[21] One of the few exceptions is Rueschemeyer, Stephens, and Stephens's *Capitalist Development and Democracy*, although in this book the authors' focus on middle classes comes in the context of an argument about development and democracy, in which the emergence of these classes – as a result of capitalist development – leads to class alliances that make democracy more likely. In addition to recognizing the difference between a bourgeoisie and smaller, middle-class entrepreneurs, they consider forces as varied as small and medium-sized

and services are either ignored or discursively and empirically lumped into the category of bourgeoisie rather than middle class.

Despite the silences in the halls of academe, however, perhaps the most striking feature of the class structure of late developers is that in reality the extremes tend to be dwarfed by a relatively large and heterogeneous occupational middle, many of whom are self-employed in some fashion. As Chris Gerry and Chris Birkbeck put it, in most developing countries

> not only is the sectoral distribution of the working population much more heavily weighted towards agriculture, but there is also an apparent shortage of capital, and a marked structural inequality in the distribution of that capital and great unevenness in its accumulation. Foreign capital, as well as the capitalist class, is largely dedicated to relatively capital-intensive production. As a result, the creation of well-remunerated employment opportunities in the "western-style" enterprises is limited in comparison to the growth in the size of the working population. . . . The results are well known: a relatively small working class, and, whether we accept the dictates of labour surplus theory or not, a sizable portion of the labour force who appear to be "forced" into creating their own jobs with very scarce capital resources, "primitive technology," and little enterprise.[22]

It is of course doubtful that all these different sectors of the middle class would exhibit the same political praxis, even if they were to see themselves as holding a common middle-class identity – a state of affairs that itself is highly unlikely and cannot be assumed a priori for any country, let alone for the developing-country context as a whole. As with all other classes, middle-class identity and action are constructed in relation to other classes and under certain historical conditions; they are not objectively given. Yet it is only with a closer view of specific cases or certain conditions that we will know whether this is the case and whether it is appropriate to use the concept of middle class to refer to what other scholars have identified as laborers, capitalists, or merely the state.

Small-scale, self-employed producers – which would fall into the category of middle class by both size and self-employment criteria – are sometimes referred to as petty commodity producers, a nomenclature that has not helped them break into the ranks of development theories whose main point of reference

---

farmers, state workers, urban professionals, private-sector employees, and artisans and craftsmen as potential members of the middle class. And rather than analytically treating all those who work for a living as so-called "laborers," or as the "working class," as do most of their development colleagues, they recognize the fact that many of these folk should also be considered middle-class. We return to the importance of their ideas and the theoretical implications of their work in the book's conclusion.

[22] "The Petty Commodity Producer," p. 122.

is capital, labor, the state, and the global economy. Two elements define them as such: 1) direct ownership of the means of production, and 2) small-scale activities (in volume of output, size of workforce, amount of capital, and level of technology).[23] To the extent that these activities often lie substantially "outside the principal spheres of capitalist production," relying primarily on family members rather than wage labor, they further push these small producers into the middle class.[24] Of course, because these petty commodity producers often provide inputs which the capitalist firms are unable to produce profitably, they also are connected to the capitalist dynamic. Likewise, most scholars identify them as providing "cheap food and consumer goods for employees of capitalist firms (and the state which services them)...[which often leads to] opportunities for additional earnings, and the possibility... of establishing themselves as independent men."[25] All said, then, petty commodity producers exist between – and provide for – both capitalists and labor, mainly urban but also rural based. This state of affairs not only holds the potential to reinforce their numeric presence and middling status in the class structure of developing countries; it also means that the employment fate of these "middling sectors" is frequently connected to that of capital and labor.

To recognize that owners of small industrial firms and artisan-workers could constitute or hold elective affinity with middle classes leads us to a final category of folk whose existence is tied to the developmental peculiarities of late industrializers, but who are rarely understood in class terms: those in the informal sector. In developing countries, especially but not only in the beginning decades of industrialization before extensive economic growth, nonwage work is generally much more prevalent than wage work. This can be true in both rural and urban areas, owing to the general incapacity of industry to keep up with the rapid population growth that characterizes most developing countries. Self-employment, moreover, defined broadly enough to include small farmers and urban informal-sector workers, is still a dominant mode of employment in most developing countries, even after significant industrialization.[26] Yet because scholars tend to use frameworks of class categories drawn from study of the developed world, most of these informal-sector workers also tend to have fallen off the conceptual map. This is a serious problem if only because in most late-industrializing countries, the proportion of the population that works as wage labor will not come even close to the number of self-employed or nonwage workers, who are most easily recognized as artisans,

[23] Ibid., p. 128. Gerry and Birkbeck draw substantially on the work of Allison Scott.
[24] Ibid., p. 129.
[25] Williams and Mutebile, "Petty Commodity Production in Nigeria," quoted in Gerry and Birkbeck, p. 134.
[26] See Portes, Castells, and Benton (eds.), *The Informal Economy*.

craftsmen, traders, informal-sector workers, and workers in family firms but are also present as small producers in rural areas.[27]

Languages of Class

The tendency to envision the class structure of developing countries as polarized between two conceptual extremes and the failure to see complexity in the middle are as evident in the language used to discuss late developers as in the self-conscious theoretical frameworks employed over the last several decades. In much of the writing on developing countries, especially during the period of so-called economic takeoff, scholars still spoke mostly of the rich and poor or of traditional masses and modernizing elites. In the Latin American context particularly, the literature also was replete with discussions of the oligarchy or bourgeoisie as pitted against the "popular classes," a term that many used – and still use – interchangeably with the working class. The notion of the popular classes itself is worth examining further, since it embodies in many ways the biases we are discussing here. Although rarely defined, the term "popular class" has been imprecisely if not uncritically used to refer to the poor, and the urban poor in particular. Its counterpart in rural areas is generally called the peasantry, with these agricultural folk conceived as standing in equally stark contrast to landlords and sometimes even referred to as "nonproletarian popular sectors."[28] Yet this language reinforces the image of a polarized society where self-employed urban artisans are analytically indistinguishable from industrial laborers or where poor small farmers are indistinguishable from rural wage laborers. Even Cardoso and Faletto continually refer to "the urban popular strata" as standing in opposition to "regional agro-exporting and urban-industrial groups," who throughout their work are treated as the two key factions of the bourgeoisie.[29] The problem, in short, is that this terminology – like much Marxist theorizing – sustains a conceptualization of class structure in developing countries that divides primarily between the elite and the exploited poor. In language if not in practice, it presupposes very little class diversity and only limited internal differentiation within the two extremes, thereby blinding scholars to the appearance or existence of "popular" groups who might act on or pursue middle-class concerns.

To make this criticism is not to suggest that developing countries themselves have completely avoided polarization on the basis of income, status,

---

[27] This was true even in the European context. The classic text on this is Sjoberg's *The Pre-Industrial City*. For a wonderful discussion of the self-employed, informally employed, seasonally employed, and even nonwage workers in London during the initial stages of industrialization, see Jones's *Outcast London*.

[28] Bartra, *Agrarian Structure*, p. 16.

[29] *Dependency and Development*, p. 87.

39

customs, or other significant factors. In recent years economic polarization, in particular, has increased in many developing countries, owing partly to liberalization and globalization. But it is to underscore the theoretical and empirical dangers of using concepts and categories that presuppose a polarized clustering of class forces that itself implies a certain preordained theoretical logic or basis for action and that fails to recognize differences among developing countries. Indeed, to consider that by definition urban artisans or street vendors are members of the working or even "popular" classes, in the same way as poor industrial laborers or seasonally employed construction workers, who are more commonly recognized as members of this class, is to assume that their interests and actions all will be similar. To recognize that urban artisanal work and street vending entail entirely different kinds of activities than does working in a factory, however, and that the former folk may have autonomy, more access to property, and a different set of economic and political priorities than factory workers or other wage laborers, is to be aware that their interests and actions may be quite different – and perhaps more similar to those characteristically called the middle class. Accordingly, perhaps more than the failure to distinguish between middle classes and capitalists, it has been the failure to distinguish between middle classes and the working class that has most characterized and distorted the literature on the class politics of development, and as such has contributed to the silences about the middle class.

To be sure, the lines separating middle classes and working classes in the developing-country context are extraordinarily ambiguous, hence the emergence of the term "popular classes" in the first place. Yet it is precisely this ambiguity that establishes the possibility that some of the professions routinely considered to be working class in the literature on developing countries may in fact share much more in common with the middle class. This was particularly clear in the economic history of "early" developing countries, in which most artisans, craftsmen, and traders made their living as independent producers, even during the initial stages of industrialization, before their professions were edged out by factory work. But there is a contemporary parallel in late developers today. In the cities of these countries are numerous artisans, craftsmen, and self-employed laborers as well as a wide variety of small enterprises, most frequently seen in the form of small retail shops and small-producer workshops.[30] Despite their poverty, those folks often have become politically powerful enough to question the state's systems of regulations and its biases toward the formal-sector activities.[31] And such small enterprises

---

[30] See Gilbert and Gugler, *Cities, Poverty, and Development*, and Gugler (ed.), *The Urbanization of the Third World*.

[31] Hernando de Soto built a reputation in Peru and Washington around the demands and concerns of small-scale, informal-sector producers who decried the state's regulations and constraints on their activities.

are dominant not only in commerce and service; they also tend to prevail in industrial production and processing, at least until they become squeezed out by large firms, which does not occur in any massive sense until considerably after extensive industrialization.[32] Indeed, even in those twentieth-century industrializers with a head start on industrialization, a considerable number of small factories or family enterprises continue to be found.[33]

All this means not only that the line separating artisans and proletarians has and continues to be unclear, especially to the producer himself, but also that the distinction between artisan and middle class may be just as problematic owing to the fact that factory production so often takes place in small-scale enterprises, sometimes known as industrial shops, where craftsmen and skilled artisans work in much the same manner as when they are self-employed.[34] This ambiguity in class status or identity is further reinforced by the fact that as the economy moves from artisan to factory production it is frequently the same individuals who make the transition.[35] Self-employed artisans and craftsmen are often the first to fill jobs in large-scale factories. Thus even though labor-process conditions may have changed dramatically for them, social and occupational practices – and thus identities – may be much more enduring.[36] This partly explains why in late-developing countries, where industrialization has been relatively rapid, deepening extensively even in the course of one generation, many folk consider themselves to be "artisan-workers" who are neither fully proletarianized nor without their original craft

[32] One of the best overviews of cities in the Third World is Roberts's *Cities of Peasants*. See also McGee, *The Urbanization Process in the Third World*, and Gwynne, *Industrialization and Urbanization in Latin America*.

[33] As noted by Bryan Roberts in his study of cities in the industrializing third world, "the urban economy was based on the proliferation of small-scale enterprises . . . [in which] the household, not the individual, became the basic wage-earning unit." See Roberts, "Transitional Cities," p. 55.

[34] In Spanish the word is *taller*, and industrial workers employed in *talleres* operated under very different labor process conditions than did those in large-scale factories.

[35] For a fascinating discussion of the durability of artisanal identity, even in the context of proletarianization (and after a revolutionary break), see Sewell, Jr., *Work and Revolution in France*.

[36] It is striking that the literature on artisan-workers in the developing world differs from the writing on these groups during early stages of industrialization in Europe and the rest of the advanced capitalist context. The latter displays much more nuance. Dobb, for example, argues that because "production was scattered and decentralized," the "artisan-craftsmen who both labored as individual (or family) units . . . retained a considerable measure of independence." He also argues that the "capitalist was still predominantly a merchant," thereby raising the possibility of a distinction between capitalists and middle classes. See Dobb, *Capitalism Yesterday and Today*, p. 21. For a more recent yet provocative study of the problematic of class identity among artisan-workers, see Calhoun, *The Question of Class Struggle*.

identity.[37] Another reason for this is that in these small-scale operations the division of labor is not well developed, and those involved in selling and accounting for products often are also the owners or producers. This further insures that salaried employees in industry tend to be few in number in early stages of industrialization, although they do multiply more rapidly when industrial firms and their accessory enterprises begin to proliferate. As such, even when we see significant increases in the capitalist class of developing countries, what we generally consider white-collar salaried employees are a relatively small and insignificant group within the larger class structure of late developers. And when salaried employees are few in number, the ranks of the middle class are dominated by those involved in more traditional occupations.

The failure to analytically distinguish working from middle classes also has become a problem among the large number of scholars who take organized labor or the labor movement as their analytic point of departure, and who are equally likely to collapse artisan-workers into a category with the working classes.[38] One would think that scholars of the developing world who focus on organized labor would be quite clear about its class composition, not only because use of the term "labor" itself conjures images of workers defined in specifically class terms (i.e., those workers who sell their labor power to others), but also because the emphasis on organization and movement dynamics resonates with Marxist theorizing. But again, the class definitional silences are notable. Take state workers, for example, who tend to be grouped in some of the largest and most influential organized federations in the developing world. Despite the fact that state workers consist primarily of salaried employees with considerable education and job autonomy, including teachers and doctors, in the literature they are almost always treated as working rather than middle class, at least in Latin America. Granted, maybe many state workers see themselves in working-class terms, and their organizational affiliations – often in national confederations that also include manufacturing workers – may reinforce this working-class identity. But there may also be conditions under which state workers do not identify themselves as working-class or as members of any class for that matter. It depends on a country's particular history and class organizational experience. To analytically collapse them into a theoretical category along with industrial workers who comprise part of the organized labor movement, as so many scholars do, may be to ignore important aspects of state

[37] The 1908 census for Peru is telling in this regard. In listing sectors of the economy (agriculture, commerce, transport, etc.), industry and "manual arts" (*artes manuales*) are grouped together. Note, moreover, that the ambiguous group of artisan-workers frequently served as the mainstay of anarcho-syndicalism. See Tejada, *La cuestion del pan*, pp. 31–33.

[38] For some of the best treatments of organized labor in the developing country context, see Bergquist, *Labor in Latin America*; Deyo, *Beneath the Miracle*; and Collier and Collier, *Shaping the Political Arena*.

worker self-identity, just as failing to recognize state workers as members of the middle class is to distort their complex nature and bypass their potential impact on development.

From City to Countryside

Another set of preconceptions that propels many development scholars to disregard the middle classes – and slight the rural middle classes in particular – stems from the assumption that middle classes primarily reside in cities. As John Johnson put it in his provocative study of the middle sectors in Latin America, "Whether they are salaried persons, self-employed professionals, or property owners and *rentiers*; whether they belong to the middle sectors because of their learning or their wealth, the members of the intermediate groups are almost solidly urban. It has been thus historically."[39] This assumption, shared by almost all contemporary scholars of development, effectively obliterates from view large numbers of rural peoples, primarily though not exclusively small-scale agricultural producers and cultivators. And even among development scholars who study rural areas, few offer accounts in which the notion of middle class is employed. Small-scale rural producers, especially farmers, are rarely ever conceived of as members of the middle class, especially among those scholars who take class struggle or class analysis seriously. Rather they are almost always referred to as peasants and, somewhat less so, as farmers.

There were theoretical reasons for this, of course. Most development scholars used the concept of the peasantry to track larger economic and political processes associated with capitalist development and to identify their historically specific features, both with respect to urban areas and with respect to the advanced capitalist world. The peasantry or, better said, the peasant economy embodied a set of productive and social relations that either eluded capitalist penetration or, at best, contained both traditional and capitalist elements and therefore failed to evince full-scale economic "modernization." Class categories were thus avoided with respect to almost all rural inhabitants except landlords, who themselves were more likely to be discussed as oligarchs or even large landowners rather than rural capitalists. Smaller producers, for their part, were discussed primarily as "peasants." Yet the analytic implications of their discursive treatment were not inconsequential. For one thing, the peasant category itself hid a multitude of diverse work experiences.[40] For another, pervasive

---

[39] *Political Change*, p. 5.

[40] Leeds, "Mythos and Pathos, p. 110; and Roseberry, "Beyond the Agrarian Question in Latin America," pp. 328–331. It is worth noting that Roseberry decries the inverse of the problem I am highlighting here: the fact that in a focus on urban middle classes, the "rural villager disappears from the analysis altogether," merely by virtue of his migration from country to

use of the term "peasant" concealed the class character of small producers or, perhaps better said, the contradictory class character of many rural folk, a state of affairs that should have motivated scholars to consider some small rural producers in middle-class terms, but did not.[41] Even Marx saw peasants as both owners and workers, a conceptualization that shares elective affinity with Erik Olin Wright's discussion of middle classes' contradictory class locations. So too did Lenin, who was even more explicit in his description. He found that the middle peasantry

> is a class that vacillates. The middle peasant is partly a property-owner and partly a toiler. He does not exploit other toilers. For decades the middle peasant defended his position with the greatest difficulty, he suffered the exploitation of the landlords and capitalists, he bore everything. Yet he is a property owner.... We must most of all refrain from being too hasty, from being clumsily theoretical.... Considerable practical ability and knowledge of local conditions is required here.[42]

Yet few development scholars actually pursued these lines of reasoning in their studies of rural folk.

Surprisingly, a degree of "Eurocentrism" helps explain this state of affairs. Marx and Engels's views of middle peasants not withstanding, most European-based social theory was built on the assumption of clear social distinctions between rural and urban worlds, a state of affairs generally conceptualized in the polar extremes of city versus countryside, *gesellschaft* (society) and *gemeinschaft* (community), or modern and folk society, all evident in writings by Marx, Weber, Durkheim, Tönnies, and Simmel. These sociological thinkers focused on the differences between rural and urban lifestyles in order to create ideal types that would help them theorize similarities and differences between preindustrial and modern industrial societies. Despite rancorous differences among them, one thing classical sociologists shared, besides the tendency to ascribe pathologies of modernity to urban life, was a conceptualization of social relations in rural areas as embodying a primordial state of being (*gemeinschaft,*

city (p. 331). As shall be clear from the case studies, however, in our framework the fact that urban middle classes trace their origins and experience to rural areas affects the process of middle-class formation, in such a way as to link these urban middle classes more to rural forces than to urban capital and labor. This, in turn, has implications for the emergence of a disciplinary state.

[41] Even Marx acknowledges the contradictory class position of rural producers when he notes that "the independent peasant or handicraftsman is cut into two persons. As owner of the means of production, he is a capitalist; as a worker, he is his own wage laborer" (*Marx's Economic Manuscripts of 1861–1863, Part Three,* p. 20).

[42] See Lenin, *Collected Works,* Vol. 1, cited from Pouchepadass, "Peasant Classes in Twentieth Century Agrarian Movements in India," p. 144.

or community), where people were untouched by the throes of modernization and the iron cage of rationality. By virtue of its isolation from the urban-based structures and practices of capitalist development, rural life was considered to be relatively untouched by modernity and capitalism, equated with precapitalist social relations, and as such classless by definition. For this reason, the concept of the peasantry was used to evoke the classless rural world bounded by kinship ties and other close personal networks.[43]

Scholars of the developing world carried forward a strikingly similar vision. For Marxist and modernization-inspired scholars alike during the 1960s, the concept of peasant was meaningful precisely because it captured more than purely economic activities of rural producers. It also suggested a certain set of social relations and cultural activities that by nature were assumed to mediate – if not prevent – rural producers from responding to markets as purely class actors or with purely accumulation objectives.[44] Nowhere is this clearer than in Eric Wolf's seminal article on the peasantry, in which he distinguishes the peasant from the small farmer because the former is devoted to subsistence and the latter to reinvestment.[45] Many subsequent studies of the peasantry frequently referred to "the peasant economy" and juxtaposed it against the capitalist economy, working under the assumption that a whole different set of social and productive relations by definition governed peasant life and as if class were totally irrelevant.[46]

---

[43] This is especially clear in the work of anthropologist Redfield. "I shall call peasants [those] who have, at the least, this in common: their agriculture is a livelihood and a way of life, not a business for profit"; they do not "carry on agriculture for reinvestment and business, [or look] on the land as capital and commodity" (*Peasant Society and Culture*, p. 18). Following Wolfe he further claims, "One sees a peasant as a man who is in effective control of a piece of land to which he has long been attached by ties of traditional and sentiment. The land and he are parts of one thing, one old-established body of relationships. This way of thinking does not require of the peasant that he own the land or that he have any particular form of tenure or any particular form of institutional relationship to the gentry or the townsman" (p. 19).

[44] Weber made the argument that peasants and peasant life were divorced from the market economy sufficiently enough to limit the development of class activities and identities. He also noted that "the past two thousand years did not train the peasant to produce in order to gain a profit," a state of affairs owing to the fact that "as far as possible, the city prohibited rural trade and the exploration of cereals" ("Capitalism and Rural Society in Germany," p. 365).

[45] "Types of Latin American Peasantry," p. 454.

[46] Moreover, for many scholars of both the late-developing and the European worlds, the notion of peasant was grounded on recognition of the family as the key unit of production, a condition that helps explain why kinship group was so frequently identified as the basis of social relations in rural areas (Shanin, "The Peasantry As a Political Factor," quoted in Franklin, *The European Peasantry*, p. 15).

For some, of course, the term "peasants" conjured up images of savages and barbarians, something which, unfortunately, may further explain its persistent use in the study of the developing world. Even the educated academic elite of developing countries themselves, not to mention foreign scholars, have easily fallen prey to this dichotomized understanding of themselves as "civilized" and peasants as "other," that is, barbarians.[47] Much of the national political culture of Argentina, for example, was built on just such a dichotomized conceptualization which distinguished the "modern" *porteños* of Buenos Aires from the "uncivilized brutes" in the hinterlands. But not all scholars who used the concept of peasant shared these disdainful and patronizing ideas. Those who professed great affection and sympathy for rural peoples, including a whole generation of anthropologists, historians, and development scholars influenced by Marxist theory, also found the concept of the peasantry a valuable one for their studies because it shed light on social relations in situations where the extent and nature of capitalist penetration was partial, incomplete, or under question.[48] But this view of rural folk as exploited by the class dynamics of capitalism precluded most reference to small farmers as small-scale capitalist producers understandable in rural middle-class terms, and sustained languages of the peasantry. As such, the concept of the peasant was used to understand the poor, exploited, and overworked rural producer whose life and livelihood ebbed and flowed in relationship to the capitalist activities of large landlords.

---

[47] In his *Peasants Into Frenchmen* (p. 6), Eugen Weber notes that "city dwellers, who often (as in the colonial cities of Brittany) did not understand the rural language, despised the peasants, exaggerated their savagery, insisted on the more picturesque – hence backward – aspects of their activities, and sometimes compared them unfavorably with other colonized peoples in North Africa and the New World. In nineteenth-century Brest it was not unusual to hear the surrounding countryside described as 'the bush': *brousse* or *cambrousse*." Of course, peasants all over have been routinely labeled and understood in pejorative terms, as this classic study of the French peasantry demonstrates with such masterful detail. In this and other studies of Europe, it is telling that the language used to talk about peasants sometimes even takes the developing world as its point of reference. Yet in studies of Europe and the developing world, the common frame of reference upon which these conceptualizations rest is that the countryside in its entirety sustains barbarism, which is juxtaposed against the modern city and the urban attributes of modernity. As Weber says, and for France no less: "Civilization is urban (civic, civil, civilian, civilized), and so of course is urbanity; just as polity, politeness, poetics, and police spring from the *polis* – the city again. Civilization is what the peasants lacked" (*Peasants Into Frenchmen*, p. 5).

[48] Mallon's seminal study of Peru, which chronicles the ways peasants' lives changed with the introduction of capitalism, is a case in point, as is Chatterjee's provocative theoretical discussion of peasants and the communal, feudal, and capitalist mode of production in India. See Mallon, *The Defense of Community in Peru's Central Highlands*; and Chatterjee, "More on Modes of Power and the Peasantry."

From Classless to Over-"Class"ified

Granted, as scholars began to view peasants as exploited by capitalist dynamics rather than sitting outside of them, class languages did start to emerge. But again, when they did, most scholars of rural areas conceived of the class structure in polarized income terms with class conceptions relevant for understanding the extremes but not the middle, and especially not for discussing peasants or small farmers.[49] This was especially so in studies of Latin America, the region of the late-industrializing world that captured most attention among development scholars in the early decades of theory building. The emphasis on rural class extremes is evident in the writings of Ricardo Pozas and Isabel H. de Pozas,[50] who analyze the Mexican countryside in terms of an agrarian bourgeoisie and an agricultural proletariat, as well as in the oft-cited work of Roger Bartra who categorizes small farmers as super-exploited workers or would-be proletarians who stand "on one side" of the class structure with "the bourgeoisie on the other."[51] This occurs, Bartra argues, mainly because "the structural relation of the small peasant economy with the large capitalist enterprise inevitably involves the disintegration, pauperization, and proletarianization of the former."[52] Moreover, when Bartra speaks of exploited rural producers, much of whose exploitation he argues comes from the low-wage or nonremunerated employment of family members, he almost always uses the notion of the peasantry, even avoiding the terms "small farmer" or "family farmer."

Some scholars have been more catholic in their understanding of these rural middle sectors than Bartra or the Pozas, seeing them in both middle-class and peasant terms. Alberto Escala's 1982 study of Argentina offers a six-tiered rural social structure ranging from "rural workers, or agricultural proletarians" to "semiproletarians" to "smallscale peasant producers (*pequeños campesinos*)," the latter of which he acknowledges will "constitute a large part of the rural petite bourgeoisie." Still, by sandwiching these small-scale, petit bourgeois producers between "semiproletarians" and "middle peasants (*campesinos medios*)," who are succeeded in turn by a fifth category for "rich peasants, who constitute the agrarian bourgeoisie" and a final category of "large landlords (*terratenientes latifundistas, la oligarquía agropecuaria*)," he offers a somewhat ambiguous grouping that suggests middle-classness for only some nonwaged peasant producers, that simultaneously refers to the same group in both peasant and bourgeois class

---

[49] This may owe in large part to Marx and the popularity of his writings among scholars of development. Marx, most developing country scholars would remind you, did not consider peasants to be a class, primarily because their isolation and disorganization made them incapable of representing themselves as such.

[50] *Los indios en las clases sociales de México*, p. 139.

[51] *Agrarian Structure*, p. 13.

[52] Ibid., p. 22.

terms and that is based on income more than mode of production definitions.[53] And more to the point, work like this remains the exception that proves the rule.

Many of course will argue that the "real world experiences" of the people studied in these works will account for the languages used as much as does the telos of the categorization.[54] They would be right to a great extent, if only because it is primarily (though not exclusively) Latin Americanists who have tended to dominate the field of peasant studies, and income and class polarization in the countryside is a common state of affairs in this region of the world. In Mexico, for example, where Bartra and the Pozas examined rural life, there is no denying the stark income and lifestyle polarization, a point to which we return shortly. Nor would many deny the importance of recognizing the incredible labor and toil involved in small-scale production, especially in contrast to other similarly categorized middle-class activities such as small shopkeeping. Yet hard work does not a class make, nor does income inequality for that matter. Equally important, the degree and nature of polarization in rural areas is not fixed across time and place, despite the fact that the polarized languages and peasant orientation used to study rural life often seem to suggest otherwise. In conceptual terms, then, polarized language and continual references to exploited peasants only reinforce silences about the composition and character of small-scale rural producers, at least in certain regions or at certain historical moments. It is not necessary to fit rural populations into conceptual boxes that presuppose polarized conflict between capital and labor in order to recognize that class or classes can exist or matter, either subjectively or objectively, in rural life.[55]

---

[53] See *Argentina*, p. 87.

[54] Although even in studies of East Asia, including many writings on South Korea and Taiwan analyzed for this study, use of the concept of the peasantry and similar sets of assumptions about polarization prevail.

[55] To see rural farmers as members of the middle class is not as foolhardy a leap as some might be wont to believe. The existence of a rural middle class in Latin America has been implicitly acknowledged, in fact, by several eminent agrarian scholars, including de Janvry, who created a classification for studying rural land and labor regimes which included "precapitalist estates," "subsistence farms internal to the precapitalist estates," "commercial farms," "family farms," "external subfamily farms," "subsistence farms in corporate communities," "capitalists estates," and "landless workers." With the exception of the last two, which acknowledge the presence of rural capitalists and a rural working class, the remaining categories closely match our definition of the middle class, that is to say, they refer to those who work on their own account or in family settings. And while commercial farms could in fact be capitalist enterprises in some general sense, if they were small in size – as is implied by de Janvry's categorization of them as distinct from capitalist estates – their proprietors would also be considered middle class.

All this is not to say that scholars who identified rural class polarization absolutely failed to recognize the importance of intermediate distinctions in the countryside, something evident even in Bartra's own use of a fourfold categorization of different types of rural producers, using size or (Weberian) income differentials, and in the highly regarded writings of Rodolfo Stavenhagen, whose late-1960s studies of agrarian class structure influenced many analysts of the developing world, especially of Latin America. For Stavenhagen, at least as elaborated in his early and most influential works, there are four main class categories in the countryside: the rural bourgeoisie, minifundista peasants, property owners, and the agricultural proletariat. However, of these four the two "middling" categories are presented as either peasantry or as property owners without any middle-class qualification,[56] despite the fact that in later work Stavenhagen suggests even more differentiation and less polarization.[57] And Bartra, who like Stavenhagen comes very close to using middle-class languages for discussing the peasantry,[58] still insists on referring to rural folk primarily in class-polarized languages. The willful effort to gloss the potential middle-class status of rural producers is evident in his claims that the "specificity [of peasants] lies in the fact that they are exploited as proletarians owing to their petty bourgeois condition."[59] Translation: Because they are middle class they are proletarian.

The empirical evidence, however, is much more complex, especially if we consider all late industrializers and not just Latin America. Rural producers come in many different sizes and operate under a variety of ownership dynamics, even in the same country, and even in the highly land-polarized context

---

[56] *Neolatifundismo y explotación*, pp. 43–55.

[57] In later writings, Stavenhagen changes the contours of his categories, identifying five groupings, one of which is called mid-level property owners, a group that comes even closer, both conceptually and linguistically, to our understanding of the rural middle class. But he still carries forward the assumption that more differentiated class structure and more commercially oriented production characterize cities and remain in the hands of large producers. For example, in his *Las clases sociales en las sociedades agrarias*, Stavenhagen (p. 95) uses the phrase "peasant bourgeoisie," together with the term "rural bourgeoisie" to refer to a contemporary stratum of commercial landowning farmers who combine commerce with agricultural activities. In a later work he dropped the term peasant bourgeoisie and retained that of rural bourgeoisie to define a new class of commercial middlemen, residing in medium-sized cities, who have displaced the *hacendados* as a dominant class in rural Mexico.

[58] In 1960, for example, family and medium-sized multifamily farms generated 47 percent of the country's total agricultural production (*Agrarian Structure*, p. 59). At various times Bartra calls peasants "simple commodity producers"; he acknowledges that many own their land, work on their own account, and, at certain historical moments at least, have been important aggregate contributors to national agricultural production totals.

[59] Ibid., p. 109.

49

of Latin America.[60] As anthropologist Anthony Leeds notes, the countrysides of the developing world are filled with small, self-employed farmers who are as likely to produce and consume in a commercialized setting as in an isolated, noncapitalist environment.[61] Moreover, if we want to ascertain the class character of rural producers, middle class or otherwise, it is important not to look for generalizations based solely on an understanding of the farm simply as a unit of production. We need to be "materialists," in Henry Bernstein's words, and examine "different units and forms of production and social classes as they are constituted through the social relations of production in specific concrete conditions."[62] We also need to know each country's unique history. All late developers (or "early" ones, for that matter) are not alike, both within and among themselves. This is exactly what Max Weber acknowledged in his study of Germany, an exercise which allowed him to chart differential patterns of economic success in the eastern and western parts of the same country, dependent on the extent of landowners' direct involvement (versus subcontracting) in agricultural production and cultivation.[63]

[60] This not only speaks to the question of which form of production (i.e., wage labor or tenant farming) produces the principal part of one's livelihood. Another equally important criterion for understanding class position among rural property holders, middle-class or otherwise, is the terms of their contracts. To the extent that sharecroppers are required to give landlords a fixed percentage of their product, the incentives for production (and discipline) are limited. Moreover, the contractual relationships of production and the social relation between landlord and sharecropper may readily produce antagonistic relations paralleling those between capital and labor, especially since in this situation landlords tend to oversee production more directly. Tenant farmers, in contrast, generally pay a fixed rent no matter what their cultivation output. As such, although this situation may produce more economic vulnerability (i.e., if crops are down one year, their margin of profit can squeeze the producer to the point of near extinction), it also reinforces a sense of autonomy and offers the possibility for greater profit (Alavi, *Peasants and Revolution*, p. 295). Tenant farmers usually do so in order to maximize crop yields, from which their revenues as landlords derive. For a fascinating discussion of the differences between sharecropping and tenant farming, and the differences in landlord supervision in each, see Emigh's "The Spread of Sharecropping in Tuscany," especially pp. 424–425.

[61] *Mythos and Pathos*, passim. Farmers correspond more closely than any other form of agrarian labor to the notion of a firm or enterprise making allocational decisions for profit. According to Leeds, this enterprise, located in the farmer role and role set, has jural rights to its own product and to the profits from its alienation. As such, the firm in question is basically a family-household unit, sometimes with secondary additions, which serves as the central unit of production but may, as an allocating firm exchanging in a money market, also buy labor as a commodity or buy capital goods to replace labor.

[62] "Concepts for the Analysis of Contemporary Peasantries," p. 4.

[63] In Weber's analysis, however, his emphasis was on the differences between lords in the east and landlords in the west, with the former involving themselves in actual cultivation of the land and the latter deriving their income from land rent, interest, and peasant taxes. It is obvious that this analysis greatly influenced Moore's *Social Origins of Dictatorship and*

Deconstructing the State in Class Terms

One last set of assumptions in the development literature that has routinely limited scholarly capacity to see middle classes as potentially central protagonists has to do with prevailing understandings of the state. Again, the spectre of European-based social theory hangs heavy. In studies of European economic development, most scholars start with the premise that an extensive state bureaucracy grew hand in hand with the capitalist economy. There may be considerable disagreement about the central driving force in this process (e.g., whether in the transition from feudalism to capitalism it was class struggle, the absolutist state, demographic shifts, trade, or even war making that fueled and/or mediated the process of the state). But it is well accepted that the main impetus and dynamic of development rested less in the hands of the state and more in the conflicts and actions of classes and/or other social forces, including the monarchy and feudal lords, whose subsequent triumph fueled processes of state making. This is clear in classic works such as Barrington Moore's *The Social Origins of Dictatorship and Democracy*, noted earlier, in which the relations between lord and "peasant" serve as the main starting point while the state is hardly mentioned at all as a critical actor. Even in Charles Tilly's seminal book, *Coercion, Capital, and European States, 990–1990*, which shows that various forms of states have existed for centuries, national policy-making bureaucracies – which form the underpinnings for what we have come to know as the modern state – are discussed more in terms of their functions than their constituent class and social actors.

Scholars of late development, starting with Gerschenkron, have challenged the European-derived assumption that capitalist development preceded modern state formation, highlighting the late-developing state's central role in fostering economic growth. But despite joining ranks behind Gerschenkron, such that there has been remarkable agreement among scholars of the developing world that the state is a key actor, most have failed to recast their definitional understanding of the state in ways that capture its social or class composition as understood by the occupations that comprise it. Rather, even among scholars of late development, languages used to discuss the state suggest a Eurocentric understanding more relevant for ancient than modern times, with the state treated as an organizational structure in which only the highest-level political leaders and a few key decision makers, such as heads of states and cabinet ministers, are conceived as conceptually relevant state actors. It may be for this reason, in fact, that we see continual references to "the State" as if it were a relatively homogeneous and well-contained institutional actor, and few efforts to discuss states as heterogeneous collections of actors, including

Democracy and his attendant focus on the relations between lord and peasant in the making of the modern world.

those employed in its ranks. The result is that development scholars pay attention primarily to high-level decision makers and not those many personnel whose salaries come from the state, who themselves constitute a large portion of the population of most developing countries, and many of whom could be understood in middle-class terms.

To be sure, in the developing world the hierarchy and organizational structure of the state does grant unparalleled power to its principal political leaders and high-ranking officials in a pattern similar to that of the premodern state. It also is true, however, that the late-developing state is extraordinarily complex and diverse in both its organizational form and occupational structure, despite the convergence of political power in the executive branch (with the legislative and judicial arms much more emasculated). Often, the state is the single largest employer in late-industrializing countries, responsible for the livelihood of a considerable percentage of the national labor force. All this, moreover, owes not just to the bureaucratic residues of colonial empires, but also to the broad range of activities that late-developing states generally undertake to both jump-start their economies and establish social legitimacy and political power. In addition to its characteristic role in controlling the means of violence, as a highly interventionist apparatus it generally offers widespread health and educational services, regulates commerce, and coordinates parastatals, to name but a few of its wide variety of activities. This in turn means that it holds within its institutional ranks not only clerks and bureaucrats, but also military personnel, the police, and a wide range of educated professionals. Among the occupations that predominate among the general category of "state worker" in the developing-country context are low-level paper pushers, drivers, office helpers, and bodyguards; semiprofessionals such as tax collectors, accountants, and teachers; more educated and technically skilled professionals such as doctors, lawyers, and engineers; and myriad government employees involved in propping up state power, ranging from the police to the military.[64]

---

[64] Of course, skill levels and degrees of autonomy on the job vary considerably among different types of state workers, and the ways in which each articulates with or views other sectors of the economy and society also differ markedly, especially in the case of military personnel. Yet, all are also salaried employees, which further means that all stand in a rather ambiguous, if not middling, position vis-à-vis capital and labor. For those employed in this broad range of occupations, the conditions of work rarely replicate those of factory workers and other heavy laborers; yet neither do they have the resources and property of capitalists. And by virtue of the fact that many of these folk owe their employment directly to the state, and not to capitalists, despite the fact that many nonetheless work in difficult or exploitative conditions, an antagonism toward capital is rarely a defining feature of their work or work identities. In all these senses, then, we must at least consider that state workers, including the military, could see themselves in middle-class terms. Note that in *Dependency and Development* (p. 83), Cardoso and Faletto define government employees, both civil and military, as falling into

That few scholars of development acknowledge this broad variety of occupations among the ranks of state workers underscores not only the narrow conception of the state that prevails in the literature but also the silences about the potential middle-classness of many of those who comprise the state apparatus. Being employed by the state does complicate the matter of class identity, of course, both objectively and subjectively, since state workers often face juridical restrictions that elude other workers or employees, and since state employment puts these workers in a rather ambiguous relationship to capitalists (if not also laborers, against whom they have the power to police, manage, and control). Yet precisely because of this, many state workers see themselves as middle-class, a posture that is surprisingly consistent with Marx's view, insofar as he directly included in his category of middle classes "the horde of flunkies, the *soldiers, sailors, police, lower officials* and so on, mistresses, grooms, clowns and jugglers, . . . ill-paid artists, musicians, lawyers, physicians, scholars, (and) schoolmasters, inventors, etc. [emphasis mine]."[65]

It is noteworthy, perhaps, that rural-based occupations are noticeably absent from this list. But that does not mean that rural folk fail to take on these occupations, or even that rural middle classes are unconnected to the state, which after all extends its institutions and personnel (especially police and lower officials) into the rural realm. In these regards, Antonio Gramsci picked up where Marx left off by claiming that, in the early-twentieth-century Italian case at least, state administrators often traced their origins to the rural middle strata. And although Gramsci, like Marx, also saw intellectuals as middle classes, he went even further to identify the *rural* middle-class intellectual as a key political force with great developmental significance: "democratic in its peasant face, reactionary when its face is turned toward the big property owner and government."[66] Gramsci's analysis, in short, built on three critical assumptions that are quite central to the argument presented here: 1) Rural middle classes are quite likely to exist in late-industrializing societies; 2) it is not uncommon in these conditions to find rural middle classes dominant within intellectual circles and the state;[67] and 3) their intermediate status is as likely to be seen

---

the middle class. See also Johnson, *Political Change*, pp. 1–2; and Rueschemeyer, Stephens, and Stephens, *Capitalist Development and Democracy*, p. 185.

[65] *Theories of Surplus Value*, Part I, p. 218, quoted in Burris, "The Discovery of the New Middle Classes," p. 20.

[66] "The Southern Question," p. 43. Gramsci makes this claim in the context of an argument about old and new intellectuals, the old being organically linked to small and medium-sized farmers (rural bourgeois) and the new "the technical organiser, the specialist of applied science" produced by industry (p. 43). He further links the presence of these two types to differences between more agricultural and more modern (read industrial) societies.

[67] Ibid., p. 42. Gramsci claimed that "three-fifths of the State bureaucracy is composed of southerners," primarily drawn from these small and medium-sized property owners.

in a contradictory political ideology as in a contradictory class location, both of which can shift rapidly depending on the larger context.

As Gramsci's work makes clear and as I suggested earlier, to claim the existence of a significant middle strata – either rural or urban – is neither to ignore income inequality nor the sheer misery of daily life for large sectors of the population, including the middle classes themselves. Nor is it to make any assumptions about overall wages, living standards, or income polarization. In most late industrializers, intermediate class occupations such as artisanal and craft work, for example, are not paid better than industrial wage work, nor have small farmers and independent cultivators prospered substantially more than agricultural wage workers. In many developing countries, in fact, salaried workers actually earn less than skilled manual workers, and small-scale farmers are consistently poorer than wage laborers.[68] It is precisely such facts – and the narrow use of income criterion as a guide – that frequently prevent development scholars from making use of the notion of middle classes in the first place. But again, we also must recognize that income is not the only basis for identifying class position; labor process and ownership conditions also matter. Moreover, in the economy and society of late developers, capitalists and wage workers – especially in industry – generally have been but a fraction of the population, and thus are not necessarily the most salient class forces in either politics or society, especially in the beginning stages of industrialization when developmental paths are truly set; while middle classes, albeit very broadly defined, are quite pervasive. And states, for their part, in addition to being key actors in the late-industrializing context, generally are composed of middle-class personnel who may share elective affinities with a wider range of nonstate middle-class forces.

Creating a Model by Speaking to the Silences

Even if it is clear that the middle classes consistently have fallen into the discursive cracks of prevailing development paradigms and scholarship, the real challenge is to determine the theoretical implications of these silences, and to ascertain whether and how contemporary theorizing about late industrialization might have been different if middle classes – as such – were brought in. To a great degree, that is the objective of this book in its entirety, and the upcoming chapters sustain this aim with empirical evidence. But before doing so it is worth considering what the disappearance of middle classes from the scholarly lexicon has meant for the evolution and content of development theory on its own terms. As noted earlier, the silences in the research have not been benign. They have pushed support of certain theories over others, with one

---

[68] This was documented in a fascinating dissertation on the Peruvian middle class. See Parker, *The Idea of the Middle Class*.

of the biggest casualties being those theories whose focus is on internal class structures and on the politics of state-class alliance building. This becomes especially clear if we return to the 1970s and reexamine the fate of dependency theory.

As noted earlier, Fernando Henrique Cardoso and Enzo Faletto built their ideas about dependent development partly around the claim that it was middle classes' decisions to ally with either the "existing bourgeois capitalist sector, or with the worker-peasant sector, or with both" that determined developmental paths in late industrializers.[69] Dependency theory, however, had a very short shelf life. As such, the question arises as to whether the fate of dependency theory – mainly its relegation to the sidelines and the ascendance of world-systems, state-centric, and class-conflict models of development – had anything to do with Cardoso and Faletto's analytic embrace of the middle classes. At first glance, this line of questioning may appear strangely illogical. After all, dependency theory could have disappeared from the scene not because it embraced middle classes, but because its explanatory power as a whole did not prevail in the competitive market of development theorizing. The focus on global forces and conditions from scholars such as Immanuel Wallerstein, Giovanni Arrighi, and Gary Gereffi, for example, did bear remarkable fruit; while the power of states and their relations to capitalists, as exemplified in work by Peter Evans, Stephen Chiu, and Stephan Haggard, among others, became just as popular as a theoretical frame. Both these elements were present in dependency theory. Still, it is possible that the dependency paradigm and, more specifically, the focus on internal class conditions in which middle classes were key, lost its competitive edge because Cardoso and Faletto also got middle classes "wrong" so to speak and, by so doing, failed to provide material that could fully sustain their theoretical claims about middle-class politics and development.

This possibility is lent some credence with a closer focus on the argument itself. Although Cardoso and Faletto do identify middle-class alliances as determining whether a country developed an enclave versus domestically controlled economy, in none of these situations did they see the middle classes as toeing their own developmental line or the state acting on their behalf in such a way as to impose restrictions on big capital. That is, they failed to truly "see" middle classes on their own terms, despite their conceptual and analytical recognition of their political importance, always subordinating middle-class actions and interests to those of other class forces. Specifically, middle-class actions and orientations were uniformly assumed to be determined by a structurally given allegiance to capital or labor, rather than on the basis of middle classes' own unique productive situation as relatively autonomous

---

[69] *Dependency and Development*, p. 125.

producers.[70] Moreover, the interests of capital always dominated, no matter the middle classes' allegiances.

These assumptions prevailed even in the study of countries whose political systems were built upon populist politics, such as Argentina, Mexico, and Brazil. In these populist countries, where historiographers and sociologists have shown that middle classes allied with labor during the period of industrial expansion, dependency theory operated under the assumption that some faction of capital predominated in the political and economic "system of domination," as Cardoso and Faletto called it. Stated simply, regardless of which class force the middle classes were assumed to throw their political allegiances to, be it capital, labor, or both, the assumption was that capitalists were always calling the shots, at least when it came to industrial development policies. And this, in turn, meant that their theory left very little empirical scope for understanding the possibility that middle classes, rural or otherwise, disciplinary or not, had some analytically autonomous effect on development, independent of other classes. That in itself may have been a good reason for other scholars to empirically or theoretically ignore them, and possibly even to shed the dependency theory that upheld their centrality. One result was that even among *dependistas*, the analytic focus shifted to capitalists; and once this occurred, even the domestic class and political orientation of dependency theory was nudged out by the preoccupation with the global conditions that sustained capitalist class power.

The conclusion that capitalists were calling the developmental shots is not that surprising, of course, especially within the body of theory that prevailed after modernization theory was displaced by class analysis and world-system theory. Many scholars of the developing world viewed industrial capitalists as dominating the political system, and usually for good reason. If they did not, it was often because they alternatively saw landlords — or agrarian rather than industrial capitalists — as playing this role.[71] Moreover, a variety of political conditions common in the developing-country context further validated these

[70] To be sure Cardoso and Faletto wore their own particular blinders about the middle classes which prevented them from seeing certain of its configurations, especially small-scale and self-employed industrial producers. They also were primarily interested in explaining the establishment of enclave versus nationally controlled export economies, two different forms of primary product dependency, and in explaining whether and why a certain faction of capital predominated both in the economy and in politics — conditions that they claimed could push a country toward or away from nationally generated versus dependent development. As such, they were not necessarily concerned with the conditions that pushed some countries down the road of ISI while others took the EOI path. These caveats notwithstanding, Cardoso and Faletto did in fact see developmental outcomes in the various Latin American countries they studied as contingent on middle classes.

[71] It is in light of this argument that we can understand the power of Zeitlin's pathbreaking historical study *The Civil Wars in Chile*. This book was one of the few that suggested caution

ideas about capitalist class power and middle class inconsequentiality. One was the fact that absence of democracy in many developing countries made it difficult for middle classes to toe their own political or economic line vis-à-vis capitalists, let alone within the state.[72] Another was that the global context itself reinforced the overwhelming power of capitalists, either on their own or in alliance with multinational capital and the state (as argued Peter Evans), in ways that would prevent middle classes from voicing alternative development models, especially in contexts where states themselves become beholden to capitalists, given the requisites of global investment priorities and dynamics. It is also worth noting that few at this time conceived of the state as an autonomous actor, and as such all power relations were established in the context of class relations. Given their contradictory class location, the above-noted reasons, and the weight of class-conflict models in which the extremes were theorized as most relevant, middle classes were not considered relevant.

Yet I want to suggest a third possibility that has less to do with the structuralist proclivities of most dependency theorists, or even the empirical realities of capitalist-class power in a globalizing world, and more to do with the prevailing conceptual and definitional biases noted earlier as well as the geographic focus of study for theory building. Stated simply: The failure to consider that under certain conditions middle classes may either challenge capitalists or toe their own line may derive from the fact that Cardoso and Faletto, like most of their contemporaries who studied Latin America, were theoretically preoccupied with a very narrow conception of middle classes, mainly salaried urban middle classes, who were indeed most likely to politically support the urbanization-led industrialization projects advanced by capitalists. Had Cardoso and Faletto been liberated from these assumptions about the locality and definitional contours of "middle-classness," or had they taken the early modern literature more seriously and understood that development trajectories

about losing the focus on domestic classes in the shift to global (world-system or dependency) dynamics, and in that sense it carried forward the path not taken by most subsequent interpreters of Cardoso and Faletto. Yet Zeitlin's study also sought to expose the Eurocentrism inherent in classical propositions about middle-class/bourgeois revolutions associated with Weberian and orthodox Marxist theorizing, which lay buried within Cardoso and Faletto's focus on middle classses. By arguing that Chilean development – both political and economic – proceeded the way it did precisely because dominant class configurations *prevented* the flowering of an independent urban industrial bourgeoisie, in this book and in other writings with Ratcliffe, Zeitlin questioned this Eurocentric preoccupation with urban middle-class/bourgeois alliances even as he helped direct scholarly attention toward agrarian oligarchies and the conditions that turned landlords into capitalists.

[72] Authoritarian and even populist states have been quick to use military force and other forms of repression to punish any class that challenges the power of capital or the project of capitalist development in a national context, a response taken to extremes in the cases of Chile, Argentina, and Guatemala, to name but a few.

rested in a wide variety of these middling social forces, including rural middle classes as much as their urban counterparts (as did Robert Brenner and Barrington Moore), they also might have found more scope to conceptualize middle classes – and perhaps even the late-developmental state if it relied on rural middle classes as a political base – as capable of acting independently of capitalists.[73] This would be so not just because rural middle classes are much less likely than urban middle classes to be big consumers of processed industrial goods produced by capitalists either abroad or domestically, an attribute which itself has a direct impact on the state's industrial development priorities and its support for ISI versus EOI. It also owes to the fact that rural middle classes are much less likely to forge political alliances with urban capitalists, at least in contrast to those urban middle classes connected to urban capitalists in terms of employment, consumption patterns, and possibly even economic linkages (i.e., producing for or consuming from big industrial firms, etc.), as noted earlier.

But if this argument about the analytic importance of rural middle classes is so logical, one might ask why it eluded Cardoso and Faletto, who were among the few to conceptually identify middle classes at all? This is where comparative method and geographic scope factor in. In addition to their preoccupation with *urban* middle classes, their failure to fully consider the state as a relatively autonomous actor, and their theoretical assumptions about the power of capital, Cardoso and Faletto focused only on Latin America. As such, although their claims about the power of capital over the state and their failure to focus on rural middle classes may have reflected the real political, class, and developmental peculiarities of this region, they were in fact completely limited to this experience. This was not a liability for Cardoso and Faletto, of course, as their aim was precisely this. The problem, however, was that most scholars chose to read Cardoso and Faletto's *Dependency and Development* in universal terms, as a theoretical treatise about dependency in general, not merely as an account of historical conditions unique to Latin America. And while there is sufficient empirical evidence to suggest that in the "real world" of Latin America, the continent that Cardoso and Faletto examined almost exclusively, middle

---

[73] This argument is not that different from one offered by Gramsci, whose writings on Italy support the notion that a state linked to rural middle classes is perfectly conceivable even in the context of late industrialization. Italy is neither South Korea nor Argentina, but Italy can be classified as one of Europe's later developers. Gramsci identified rural middle-class intellectuals as customarily linked to the state; and he further suggested that when combined, these forces routinely struck a harsh stance vis-à-vis big property and the privileges of bankers and urban-based industrial capitalists. As such, his claims lend some credence to the proposition that rural location, and the rural middle-class experience in particular, can endow the state with a strong disciplinary orientation toward certain key capitalists and perhaps even industrial laborers. See "The Southern Question," pp. 42–44.

classes – especially rural middle classes – neither pursued an independent political or class project nor dominated politics or the state, such an assumption did not necessarily apply to all late-developmental contexts. Even so, this theory was transported to other late-industrializing contexts (especially the countries of East Asia, the next new kids on the late-developmental block); and when it was found wanting, dependency theory and its middle-class focus both were shunted aside.

The point here is Cardoso and Faletto's claim that capitalists always prevailed had as much to do with the peculiar processes of rural and urban middle-class formation and the historically specific political alliances these processes engendered in Latin America as with any structurally inherent or universal power of capital and weakness of middle classes in late developers more generally. Had rural or urban middle classes seen or organized themselves as an independent force distinct from both capital and labor, or had they achieved greater power in the state than capital or labor, states might have possessed a greater disciplinary capacity to set their economies on a prosperous path, more akin to East Asia perhaps, where EOI replaced ISI early on and where, we shall see shortly, rural middle classes were powerful and embedded in the state. Furthermore, a development theory that focused on middle classes might have remained a key paradigm for understanding their process.

So far the discussion of theoretical paths not taken has focused on the watershed moment in the history of development theory when dependency analysis was outpaced by world-system and state-centered theory. But the exercise could be applied to more contemporary ideas about development. Let us consider how theories of industrial development successes and failures offered by Nicole Woolsey Biggert and Mauro Guillén in their late 1990s study of Taiwan, Argentina, Spain, and South Korea might be different if middle classes were recognized as potentially critical actors. Among these four countries, Biggert and Guillén classified Taiwan and Spain as more successful because their private sectors were able to meet world quality standards in automobile production, while South Korea's and Argentina's producers were judged to have failed in doing so. In both of the successful cases the key economic actors were small-scale direct producers (defined by Biggert and Guillén as small family businesses in Taiwan and local families and worker co-ops in Spain), whereas in the failed cases they argued that it was large business groups who predominated, either alone (as with the chaebols in South Korea) or in alliance with local elite families (in Argentina).[74] In the latter case, moreover, even when the "government provided incentives to encourage auto components production and exports,... they tended to benefit the [large] vertically integrated assemblers rather than the small and medium-sized firms."[75] Accordingly, we

---

[74] Biggert and Guillén, "Developing Difference," p. 741 (Table 3).
[75] Ibid., p. 739.

might suggest that one of the key features that distinguishes the two "success-ful" cases from the "failures" is the salience of what we term middle classes and their production priorities. And although the term "middle class" is absent in their theorizing, with little in the article that details how and why these smaller middle-class producers carried the day in Taiwan and Spain but not in South Korea and Argentina, when read in light of this book's revisionist claims about the importance of these key forces, Biggert and Guillén's overall findings are quite consistent with what I am suggesting about middle classes and development strategies.[76]

Disciplinary Development in Comparative Historical Perspective

But in order to transform these two examples in to a more robust claim about middle classes and development success, we still need to know why smaller producers carried the day in some countries (like Taiwan) but not in others, especially in Latin America. Is there some general proposition that could ac-count for this; or is it merely historical contingency? Let us try to answer this question by returning to the Latin America and East Asia comparison once again and considering the possibility that the salience of rural middle classes and their role in engendering disciplinary regimes of development derives not just from contingent peculiarities but from systematic historical and regional differences in patterns of class formation that are regionally and/or country specific. Indeed, while most Latin American countries have shared with East Asia a highly polarized class structure, factory production in Latin Amer-ica was much more advanced by the first decades of the twentieth century. Thus most Latin American countries hosted a relatively sizeable urban work-ing and middle class alongside a growing industrial bourgeoisie, frequently based in cities. This in fact is one of the key findings upon which Cardoso and Faletto built their theory of dependency. These conditions suggest a para-dox of sorts, or the fact that the "early" late-industrializers of Latin America were much less likely to develop a rural middle-class-embedded state than were the "late" late-industrializers of East Asia.[77] This in turn meant that

---

[76] At this juncture, it is also worth noting the parallel between our claims, Biggert and Guillén's findings, and the corpus of literature known as flexible specialization. Works by scholars like Piore and Sabel or Locke, for example, on the flexibility of small-scale production in countries like Italy and elsewhere, further sustain the idea about successful economic development presented here, despite applying their application to regional or sectoral (rather than national) economic prosperity.

[77] To be sure, when I distinguish between "early" and "late" late industrializers I am not re-ferring to these solely as chronological distinctions, despite the fact that this categorization makes considerable sense in the comparison of East Asia and Latin America. What I really

the "early" late-industrializers of Latin America, who seemed to have a head start on economic modernity by virtue of their industrial advances, actually suffered in the long term. And why? Because the class structures that emerged in the late-nineteenth and early-twentieth centuries in the course of Latin America's foray into self-sustaining industrialization privileged urban populations in general, and urban workers, industrial capitalists, and (somewhat less so) urban middle classes in particular. Thus, urban-based classes had both a size and political visibility that made it difficult for Latin American states to respond to rural middle classes, given the stark differences in their lives and livelihoods.

Most Latin American countries' large size and immense distance from colonial rulers further contributed to this state of affairs, because these factors helped reinforce the development of one or two main cities that served as the key nodes in mercantile trade, and whose populations became politically and economically salient. Of course, the fact that industrialization also had time to trickle "out" to the countryside somewhat, particularly because most of it was centered on the processing of agriculturally based or derived consumer durables and nondurables, insured that a strong agrarian bourgeoisie emerged nonetheless, despite accelerated urban development and domination. Combined with embryonic struggles over state formation and class power that fostered urban growth and urban centralization, and with Latin America early on evidencing some of the world's highest rates of urban primacy, that part of the world came to the twentieth century with a much more complex class structure and a more problematic tussle between rural and urban populations and aims than did most of the countries in East Asia.

What I am suggesting here is that the so-called "early" late industrializers of Latin America seem to have been much less likely to host rural middle-class-embedded states and more likely to develop states beholden to urban political coalitions dominated by capitalists and laborers or urban populations in alliance with an agrarian bourgeoisie, owing partly to the timing of industrialization. East Asian countries, in contrast, benefited from the paradox of being "late" even among late developers, at least to the extent that these countries tended to remain more agricultural than industrial for a much

---

want to underscore here is the extent of industrial manufacturing and production already under way, as opposed to the weight of or influence of agriculture in the national economy at the moment of industrial takeoff, and the extent to which either of these profiles would generate the greater likelihood of a rural middle-class-embedded state with sufficient disciplinary capacity to further industrialize in an effective fashion. Accordingly, it is more fruitful to think of differences between these two categories of late industrializers in terms of class structures and sectoral balances, instead of their sequencing in chronological time, and the ways that these characteristics facilitate or impede subsequent development trajectories.

longer period of time.[78] These countries' primarily agricultural profiles, accompanied by only limited advances in industrialization, insured that urban classes in general, and urban middle classes in particular, would not have had the same opportunity to develop in size or political influence, especially relative to the agrarian populations.[79] In theoretical terms, the proposition would be the following: The social, spatial, and political conditions associated with minimally industrialized and agriculturally oriented economies are more likely to sustain the formation of rural middle classes with the political wherewithal to produce a disciplinary regime of development.[80]

In methodological terms, these findings also seem to suggest a new form of comparison, which itself has theoretical implications, because in class and disciplinary developmental terms, there may be many more parallels between the "early" early industrializers (such as the United States) and the "late" late industrializers (e.g., East Asia) than among "early" and "late" late industrializers (e.g., East Asia and Latin America). Whatever one thinks of this typological categorization, it underscores the importance of taking national history seriously in a substantive as much as a chronological sense, and the importance of highlighting the search for a theoretical model that can explain developmental differences and similarities both between and among early and

[78] Such a claim builds directly on the work of Gerschenkron, who was one of the first to identify the advantages of late development and to highlight the state's role in this process. But rather than highlighting the potential for technological learning inherent in starting the game later in time, for example, as Gerschenkron does in his study of Germany as a prototypical late industrializer, I highlight the ways in which class and sectoral legacies of a nation advantage the state by endowing it with a class structure that sustains the state's disciplinary capacity to impose sustainable macroeconomic development policies. It may be in these regards, then, that Germany and East Asia share a common heritage. While the "late" late industrialization of East Asia came decades after Germany's much earlier late industrialization, which in chronological time occurred closer to Mexican and Argentine industrialization, at least in terms of rural class structures and the political and economic salience of rural middle classes, Germany and East Asia may have been much more similar because of the common salience and political influence of farmers and the rural middle classes.

[79] This situation also helped generate stronger government support for land reform alongside the state's serious efforts to industrialize, in no small part to keep the majority of the population from rebelling or challenging industrialization projects. To be sure, not all East Asian countries introduced successful land reforms. But there were more in East Asia than in Latin America; and without them, East Asia would have remained (and did in some cases) dominated by an agrarian bourgeoisie, as in Latin America, such that rural middle-class formation would not have materialized to the same extent.

[80] There is some elective affinity between this argument and Kay's claim that the timing of land reform explains differences between Latin America and East Asia. But while Kay focuses on the *economic* effects of this timing differential, I focus on the political and class effects and how they affect states and their policies.

late industrializers. And to do this we also need a new way of "seeing," so we can recognize the role played by middle classes, both urban and rural.

The search begins with a focus on South Korea, primarily because it is one of those wildly successful East Asian tigers whose remarkable economic progress has captured the attention of scores of development scholars armed with very different theories than ours, from state-centered to market-centered to world-systemic. For decades academics painted a picture of South Korea as a poor, exploited country, peopled by backward peasants with few skills. Within a few short decades, it became a country with high economic standing, whose successes were attributed to the efforts undertaken by huge conglomerates of urban-based capitalists, organized as chaebols, and/or a strong and authoritarian state ruthlessly directing the nation to prosperity through integration in a global marketplace. Moreover, this is a country that scholars routinely point to as a model of middle-class development, having produced a large and educated middle class out of the ashes of "peasant" society in a relatively short period of time. Middle-class formation, in fact, is routinely trumpeted as one of the shimmering *by-products* of successful industrial development in South Korea.[81] So in between the focus on capitalists and the state or successful patterns of insertion into the global marketplace, and in the context of assumptions that middle classes are a new and primarily urban phenomenon in a long-standing peasant society, is there room for a new argument about the rural middle-class foundations of South Korea's development miracle? It all depends on where and during what time period you start to look.

---

[81] There is a whole new body of literature emerging in East Asian countries to document the rise of these new middle classes. For some of the best, see Hsiao (ed.), *Discovery of the New Middle Classes in East Asia*.

3

DISCIPLINE AND REWARD

Rural Middle Classes and the South Korean Development Miracle

The Present in Hindsight

Throughout the 1980s and much of the 1990s, South Korea earned its reputation as one of the darlings of the development jet set, a fabulously successful late developer committed to export-led industrialization and touted by policy makers and international aid agencies as a model for other developing countries. As the South Korean economic miracle captured scholarly attention, most analysts took as their analytic starting point that exact same era of unparalleled bounty in the 1980s, or at best the final years of the 1970s when significant gains first were apparent. Rather than looking to the pre-1970 period for clues as to which state or class forces were responsible for South Korea's buoyant economy in those later decades, the tendency was to cultivate a presentist understanding of the structure and nature of the South Korean economy during the period it reached its heights. This meant that certain actors and conditions – namely, those most visible and powerful by the late 1970s and into 1980s, such as the *chaebols* – were routinely identified as key sources of South Korea's success. Others, most notably for our purposes the middle classes, were routinely ignored.[1]

---

[1] Because the *chaebols* were clearly the leading economic forces in domestic industrial production and global trading during the economic boom of the late 1970s and throughout the 1980s, and still are today to a great degree, many scholars attribute South Korea's developmental successes wholly or partly to the efficiency and strategic capacities of these well-organized, highly networked, and strategically diversified conglomerates of capitalists. Even leading scholars such as Haggard, Moon, and Evans, who took great pains to acknowledge that the state also was a key actor in this development miracle, still linked the government bureaucracy's involvement and actions to its relationships with the chaebol-dominated private sector. Hence the popular use of the phrase "sword-won alliance," coined by Haggard and Moon. The "won" is the South Korean currency. For more on state-capital relationships, see Haggard and Moon, "The State," p. 52; and Evans, *Embedded Autonomy*, passim.

But the economic and banking crisis that hit that country several decades later, in the 1990s, changed all that. Owing to the role that large firms (i.e., chaebols) and banks played in the crisis, some scholars began to consider that large capitalists may have contributed to South Korea's late-1990s economic problems, at least to the extent that their unparalleled size brought unchecked economic and political influence of industrialists and their banking clients, a state of affairs which in turn allowed both to sustain ever more inefficient, fiscally questionable, and seemingly corrupt business practices. The possibility that South Korea's economic crisis may be somehow related to its earlier chaebol-driven successes suggests that we more carefully examine the country's large corporate actors and their role in the country's post–World War II macroeconomic development. What brought the unparalleled power of the chaebols in the first place; how exactly did they contribute to economic gains in the period from 1970 to 1990; and why after two decades of accolades for their positive role were they associated with economically questionable behavior and the nation's macroeconomic crisis more than its developmental gains? In this chapter I pursue these questions through a closer examination of the middle classes, especially the rural middle classes.

I will argue that in order to understand why South Korea achieved such unparalleled economic successes in a relatively short period of time, as well as why this country found itself unexpectedly mired in serious financial crisis, we need to examine the country's small-scale agrarian-based producers who, as rural middle classes, laid the political foundations for the Park Chung Hee administration in the 1960s. I will suggest that these rural middle classes originally endowed Park's administration with the will and capacity to discipline industrial capitalists (i.e., chaebols) during the 1960s and early 1970s, and that these disciplinary actions set South Korea on its post-1970s path to a shining industrial future. I will further argue that it was the rural middle classes' declining political and economic significance over time that ultimately limited the state's capacity to regulate large industrialists as well as keep the economy on a sound economic course over the 1990s. This set of propositions constitutes a twofold critique of conventional views of the South Korean economic miracle: that scholars have focused attention on the wrong set of class actors and on the wrong time period. By so doing, they have fallen into the worst sort of methodological trap. Not only have they mistaken correlation for causation, they also have been overly – and perhaps erroneously – preoccupied with an autonomous state, industrial capitalists, labor, and even the global marketplace. In order to correct these biases, a deep understanding of mid-twentieth-century Korean history must be incorporated into any study of the South Korean miracle.

The chapter proceeds as follows. I begin with a discussion of the South Korean development literature and what has been lost, theoretically, by focusing on the present rather than the near past and by examining only the usual

suspects of capital, labor, the state, and even the global economy. I then seek
to "correct" the biases in this literature by drawing attention to small farmers
and other rural middle-class small producers. I focus on the political and social relationships they forged with the Park administration and how and why
these forces pushed South Korea to support export-led industrialization (EOI)
beginning very early on. Subsequent sections link the selection and success of
the EOI route to Park's disciplinary policies vis-à-vis industrialists and to his
rural middle-class foundations and agrarian-oriented macroeconomic policies
more generally. The chapter concludes with a double paradox: first, that Park's
rural middle-class-embedded administration did achieve enormous gains, but
that this ultimately led to rural impoverishment and extensive urban and industrial growth; and second, that the latter state of affairs economically and
politically empowered the chaebols sufficiently to change the class structure
and balance of power, thereby eliminating the state's capacity to discipline
capitalists and thus temporarily reversing South Korea's fortunes during the
late-1990s economic crisis.

The (A)Historical Origins of South Korean Development Theorizing

If one looked back in time to the foundational decades before the period
of boom, to the late 1950s and early 1960s when the country initiated its
comprehensive industrialization program, it would be apparent that chaebols
would not be considered significant players in either the economy or politics.
In fact, far from being leading economic – or even political – actors in the
scene, most of the businesses that eventually grew to be large chaebols would
have to be envisioned as small, fledgling industrial operations. They possessed
unproved track records, evidenced little economic potency domestically or
globally, and carried few of the skills, insights, experiences, and so-called bold
entrepreneurial ethic that would later turn them into central players in the
economy and in national economic policy making.[2] A more accurate view
would be that for the first and most critical decade of the economic miracle,

[2] Lie, "Review: Rethinking the 'Miracle,'" p. 70. Of the four main exports as of 1970 (textiles,
plywood, wigs, and minerals), sociologist John Lie claims, chaebols were significantly involved
only in textiles. Lie has suggested the possibility that we are focusing on the wrong class forces
to explain South Korea's economic successes, and he has argued that chaebols should not
command so much attention in development theorizing because "the products and produce
that led Korea's early exports did not significantly involve chaebols" but, rather, were processed
primarily by small-scale entrepreneurs. Similarly, economic historian Eckert has suggested
that the South Korean bourgeoisie did not really become much of a political or economic
force until the late 1970s and, as of the late 1980s, still remained surprisingly "unhegemonic"
in social, even if not political, terms. He attributes this not only to the effects of Japanese

private sector forces – including the industrial firms that we now identify as chaebols – were highly disciplined, regulated, controlled, and clearly on the receiving end of orders from the state, rather than vice versa.[3] They were quite restricted in their capacities to conduct industrial activities, and hardly in a position to profit from business decisions. Rather, these big firms were forcefully goaded by the state – dragged kicking and screaming in many cases – into the particular economic projects that later would transform their owners into millionaires and their firms into formidable chaebols. In Robert Wade's words, the Korean state "aggressively orchestrated" the chaebols' growth and the activities that sustained them, sometimes even assigning individual firms specific projects to carry out.[4]

Of course, knowing that the Korean government had to "twist arms to compel businesses to export" during the initial stages of rapid industrialization, as Clive Hamilton puts it, would not fully undermine the prevailing view that the activities of the chaebols mattered in some way, especially with respect to economic growth.[5] Still, I am suggesting that the large industrial groupings known as chaebols might be as well understood as the product of the South Korean economic miracle as its source. In Clive Hamilton's words, which echo Carter Eckert's view of the absence of bourgeois hegemony in early- and mid-twentieth-century Korea, "Industrial capital . . . [was], in a sense, the creature of the [South Korean] state," born in the aftermath of strategic economic policies introduced in the postwar period after the Japanese left the country without a significant indigenous bourgeoisie.[6] This outcome could be considered quite similar to what happened in Mexico (and various other Latin American countries, for that matter), where state intervention produced a cadre of "revolutionary capitalists," as Nora Hamilton called them, who with state support and protection founded large industrial conglomerates that ultimately played a leading role in the national economy.[7]

The ahistorical preoccupation with the decades of the miracle itself, and the failure to look back in time to the originating policies that laid the foundation for later economic successes, also have reinforced certain misleading assumptions about labor repression and labor's leading role in South Korean

colonialism and Korean culture, but also to the powerful role of the state ("The South Korean Bourgeoisie," p. 100).

[3] See Amsden, *The Rise of the Rest*, and Amsden's earlier *Asia's Next Giant* for more on how this worked on the firm level. For general discussion of business restrictions, see Hamilton, *Capitalist Industrialization*; and Wade, *Governing the Market*.

[4] *Governing the Market*, p. 320, quoted in Evans, *Embedded Autonomy*, p. 53. See also Eckert, "The South Korean Bourgeoisie," pp. 100–103; and Amsden, *Asia's Next Giant*, passim.

[5] *Capitalist Industrialization*, p. 44.

[6] Ibid., p. 118.

[7] See *The Limits of State Autonomy*.

economic development.[8] While it is undeniable that a highly regulated and re-pressed industrial labor force helped insure low wages and thereby contributed considerably to economic growth, and while there has been considerable government control and repression of labor, it also is true that during certain periods, especially in the initial decade of the economic miracle from 1961 to 1971, organized labor in South Korea fared relatively well, not only with respect to other class and social forces but also in comparison to labor in other developing countries pursuing rapid industrialization. Labor, while not formally incorporated into the governing pact,[9] could hardly be considered more politically repressed in South Korea than in most Latin American countries, owing to relatively benevolent domestic labor legislation that guaranteed the rights to association, collective bargaining, and collective action. According to Jang Jip Choi, in fact, during the first decade of Park's rule the chief priority of organized labor was a wage increase, and for the most part unions were successful in achieving this aim, as evidenced by the fact that "in real terms, wages rose, albeit sluggishly, throughout the decade."[10] Choi further argues that "unions enjoyed a great degree of associational autonomy" during this period, and that although they were clearly not able to place any significant constraints on state elites, they did participate in a considerable number of labor disputes and strike actions.[11]

Closer examination of the first decade of the Park Chung Hee administration – starting in the post-1961 period during which rapid industrial takeoff first became a reality – also shows that labor's rights were actually expanded somewhat, especially compared to the situation under the ISI-oriented administration of Syngman Rhee.[12] Indeed, although broadly similar labor laws were

---

[8] This argument is made by many, although some scholars see repressed labor as only one among several factors contributing to the South Korean economic miracle. See, for example, Appelbaum and Henderson (eds.), *States and Development in the Asian Pacific Rim*; and Deyo, *Beneath the Miracle*.

[9] Under Park Chung Hee, efforts were made to separate unions from the ruling party, a semicorporatist state of affairs that had characterized the Syngman Rhee administration and more closely paralleled the situation in countries like Mexico, Brazil, and Argentina.

[10] *Labor and the Authoritarian State*, p. 89.

[11] Ibid., pp. 89, 90. In *South Korea*, Ogle (p. 17) recounts that there were 97 labor disputes registered with the Office of Labor Affairs in 1965 and 112 in 1969, with 205,000 workers taking part in the latter year. As in Mexico and many other countries where labor was linked to the government, however, most of these disputes never made it to the strike stage.

[12] All this is not to say that the Park administration, even in those early years, was patently or unproblematically pro–industrial labor. There clearly was a bias against industrial working classes that manifested itself in restrictions on the locus and nature of labor organization and association at the factory-level, both of which set important constraints on the national power of labor. In point of fact, in the first decade of the Park administration there existed three types of bargaining arrangements for labor, depending on type of industry. Eight unions bargained

formally on the books during these two administrations, Rhee did not apply them while Park did, thereby seeking a more judicious and constitutionally rigorous treatment of labor, at least until 1971 when strike actions started to threaten industrial production and Park introduced a new constitution.[13] If anything, it was not until after 1972 that labor really suffered under the repressive hand of the state, according to Choi and most other analysts of the South Korean labor movement.[14]

Of course, scholars also have turned to the state – and not just chaebols or labor regression – to explain South Korea's success. Among the most accepted theories about South Korea's economic successes is the "state autonomy argument," based on the claim that a strong and relatively autonomous state produced the country's extraordinary economic successes. Those who accept the autonomy argument often seek evidence in the period of military rule that Park Chung Hee initiated in 1961, in which a strong and interventionist state with a clear developmentalist vision initiated industrial takeoff and thereby ushered in subsequent decades of prosperity. They tend to argue that

at the national level, three bargained regionally, and the rest locally. Still, labor repression was hardly a distinguishing feature of the initial decade of Park's rule, or even of South Korea's history in general, especially when juxtaposed with the larger universe of late developers. Of course, this historical evidence about labor also raises several questions about how best to understand and explain what I suggest is the relatively benign treatment accorded labor by the country's most developmentally oriented administration, that of General Park Chung Hee. The Park administration, after all, was known to be rabidly anticommunist and is still considered to have been quite socially and politically conservative, despite the initial view taken by the U.S. State Department repudiating Park's rise to power and suggesting he was some sort of communist. Moreover, Park Chung Hee was no apologist for his authoritarian and militarized regime. Why did the single administration considered most responsible for setting and then sustaining South Korea on its developmental path also safeguard the rights and respond to the claims of industrial workers, at least initially; and how did this stance factor into South Korea's industrial successes, especially as compared to its Latin American counterparts? For more on this see "Enter Discipline" below.

[13] While there were changes in the law in 1963, they in fact helped protect the rights of labor more than previous clauses.

[14] See Choi, *Labor and the Authoritarian State*, pp. 82–91; Ogle, *South Korea*, pp. 11–16; and Cumings, "The Abortive Abertura," p. 7. Note however that there is some disagreement about when things really changed dramatically, and why. Choi identifies a 1969 revision to the labor law as setting changes in motion, particularly because they made strikes more possible. This became particularly bothersome to the government because in 1971 it was actively courting foreign investors and labor stability was one of the prime incentives for Direct Foreign Investment (DFI). Others, including Ogle and Cumings, identify 1972 as a key year, because policy changes associated with the Saemaul movement further restricted labor's capacity. Most agree, however, that Park became a "dictator" with respect to labor and South Korean society starting in the early to mid-1970s, sustaining what Cumings calls a "bureaucratic-authoritarian industrializing regime."

the military underpinnings of the South Korean state as well as the existence of a well-trained and meritocratic civil service, the weakness of organized labor, and/or the absence of a landed oligarchy, coupled with massive foreign support (both political and economic), combined to provide Park and subsequent administrations with the bureaucratic capacity to implement successful macroeconomic development policies. Yet despite their temporal forays into the Park period, most of the scholars who take this line of reasoning fail to offer a genuinely historical account of why Park Chung Hee, in particular, was able to implement such highly successful economic policies with his purported autonomy.[15] This is because most still prefer to identify general conditions of state autonomy rather than temporally specific forces and conditions as the main source of Park's successful policy making. Stated differently, most development scholars have tended to treat both Park's administration and the post-Park military administrations as if they were all of a piece – the same "autonomous" piece. This has prevented them from analyzing the differences between Park's regime and subsequent military administrations on labor issues or anything else for that matter, as well as from seeking alternative explanations for why Park's own policies varied over time despite his reliance on connections to the military throughout his years in power.[16] To buttress this view, scholars are as likely to cite general cultural traditions (what Peter Berger and Byung-nak Sung call the "Confucian ethic," Steward Clegg calls "post-Confucianism," Richard P. Appelbaum and Jeffrey Henderson call "neo-Confucian cultural forms," and Gustav Papanek calls the "New Asian Capitalism"), conceptualized in terms of work-oriented values free-floating in time, as opposed to specific historical events or conditions.[17]

---

[15] It also is possible to offer a historically specific account of state autonomy, with a focus on the Park period or any other period. The work of Woo, noted earlier, is exemplary in this regard. She argues that cold war geopolitical dynamics in the aftermath of the Korean War afforded the South Korean state a remarkable capacity to do what it wanted within its borders, which included strong state intervention into financial and industrial activities, despite efforts by the United States and other forces to push the economy in a more market-oriented direction. See *Race to the Swift*.

[16] The upshot is that most scholars using the state autonomy perspective tend to invoke the Park regime mainly as symbolic or representative of the South Korean state's characteristic profile in these regards, not as a particular historical instance in which a certain type of autonomy may have been achieved, and only vis-à-vis specific actors at a specific moment in postwar administration. Rather, they see the period of Park's rule as a prototypically "developmental" regime that in its very nature is uniquely South Korean, if not East Asian.

[17] All these conceptual formulations rest on an understanding of the principal tenets of Confucianism, which according to Clegg, Higgins, and Spybey entail "a concern for the courteous and correct conduct of one's duties, particularly towards the family, based on a profound respect for social conventions." They further link this to state power and state capacity, by arguing that "Confucianism, in its concern with ritual, order, imperial patrimonialism,

To be sure, not all scholars who invoke culture or who accept the South Korean state's relative autonomy shun historical grounding for their explanation. Nor do they agree on basic questions of theory, method, or explanation.[18] Appelbaum and Henderson, for example, identify neo-Confucian cultural forms as working along with free markets, foreign capital, a repressive labor system, and historically unique geopolitical conditions as giving the South Korean state its developmental capacities.[19] Thus it may be scholars who incorporate the world-system perspective into their analysis of state autonomy, such as Appelbaum and Henderson as well as Woo, who hold the most potential to achieve a historical grounding for their claims. This is so because they argue that the historically specific character of the world economy in the 1960s, 1970s, and 1980s, especially the rapid increase in global trade between 1960 and 1973, combined with Park's hold on power to facilitate South Korea's successful efforts at EOI.[20] Still, this type of world-system argument tends to be historical only in a partial sense, in that the focus is mostly on external factors with little said about the domestic historical conditions – especially political ones – that pushed the South Korean government to accommodate changing global conditions and new geopolitical pressures.[21]

service and the meritocratic achievement of these virtues, was profoundly anti-individualist: it legitimated a corporate, bureaucratic elite unified around the highly developed monopoly of complex literacy enjoyed by the mandarinate." See " 'Post-Confucianism,' Social Democracy, and Economic Culture," p. 38.

[18] It is telling that many scholars who cite these cultural traditions seem to read history – and culture – rather selectively. For example, Berger insists that Confucian traditions fuel the hard work ethic among South Koreans, an ethic identified as partly responsible for their developmental successes in much the same way the Protestant ethic reinforced the spirit of capitalism in early modern Europe. See "An East Asian Development Model," p. 5. In contrast, however, other scholars of South Korean Confucian culture find almost the opposite. Kim, for example, in *Man and Society*, argues: "Not unlike many other preindustrial societies, work in traditional Korea was not looked upon with respect and envy. It was primarily conceived in terms of manual labor which was not certainly the responsibility of the landed gentry class" (p. 31). In particular, those groups who were most central to capitalist development in the West, merchants and craftsmen, were actually considered inferior in Confucian culture, because "craftsmen . . . dirtied their hands; and merchants . . . were considered close to the menials because they played dirty tricks" (p. 31).

[19] "Situating the State in the East Asian Development Process," in *States and Development in the Asian Pacific Rim*, p. 5.

[20] See also writings by Gereffi, especially "Industrial Restructuring and National Development Strategies," p. 59, in which he traces shifts in ISI to EOI, and a modification in the latter, to patterns of world trade between 1960 and 1973.

[21] Even this understanding is predicated on an unspoken presupposition: that an autonomous state would automatically be in a position to respond to the new market niches presented by a changing global economy, and would do so merely because the global opportunities were there. Such an argument itself seems doubtful, or at least it would be argued so by

So the question arises as to what – or whose – history matters most for explaining autonomy or any other characteristic feature of the South Korean state, and why. Among the scholars who have been particularly conscientious in their efforts to trace the South Korean state's autonomy and policy-making actions to long-standing preconditions and/or historical developments, most shun class analysis and focus instead on the institutional character of the state and its historical origins. The dimensions of state formation that have captured most attention include the long tradition of meritocratic civil service examinations, which some scholars trace to as early as 788 A.D., as well as the impact of the Japanese colonial occupation – which is seen as laying the regulatory and infrastructural foundations for competent bureaucratic organization, especially in the financial sector.[22] Yet the problem with these arguments, like the general claims about neo-Confucian culture, is that they may be too historical, in the sense that they conceive of history mainly as a distant past which hangs over the present in a temporally unfettered fashion. Of course, the effects of late-nineteenth- and early-twentieth-century Japanese colonialism are not nearly as distant as civil service traditions tracing all the way back to the eighth century. But the question is whether they have occurred far enough in the past to require some understanding of historical mediations. At minimum, we would have to take the post–World War II period and South Korea's formal political independence as a significant point of departure. But even then, would the state under Park really work in exactly the same way, organizationally and administratively, as it did decades or even centuries earlier?

If one were to understand history as more than just institutional and cultural antecedents, however, but also as significant events of the past that imprint themselves on the present, then it would be as important to identify the critical junctures and specific events that reinforce, transform, or even destroy past practices as it would be to cite these earlier legacies. This, in turn, requires a better understanding of history as it is made in time, not just as a general and unproblematic backdrop in which past structures or patterns are written on the present. In the case of South Korea specifically, this would entail a better understanding of the immediate post–World War II period and the

---

scholars such as Hamilton who have challenged the South Korean case by asserting that "the 'export-oriented' strategy was stumbled on quite accidentally." Even if it were true, such a claim gives little insight into the domestic historical conditions that made it possible for the South Korean government to pursue the EOI strategy, autonomously or not. To know this, we would have to turn inward and examine domestic historical conditions with greater care, especially those leading to the administration of Park Chung Hee and his policies. See Hamilton, *Capitalist Industrialization*, p. 44.

[22] Kook, quoted in Evans, *Embedded Autonomy*, p. 51. For more on the effects of Japanese colonial administration, see Myers and Peattie, *The Japanese Colonial Empire*, as well as recent work by Kohli.

differences between the Syngman Rhee and Park Chung Hee administrations. And a closer look at both administrations, along with John Chang Myong's, briefly sandwiched between them, shows that macroeconomic policies and even the state's character varied considerably in this relatively short period of time from the mid-1950s to the mid-1970s, despite sharing the same colonial Japanese institutional heritage, a similar nationalist sentiment, and a reliance on the same civil service exam system.

President Syngman Rhee governed Korea with U.S. backing from the end of the Korean War until 1960 and was considered to preside over an increasingly corrupt state apparatus (or what Peter Evans might call a "predatory state"). He was directly implicated in scandals and questionable financing agreements with a new cadre of businessmen and industrialists, which began to openly materialize after the Korean War. ISI was the policy of choice then, and government bureaucrats were so well known for lining their pockets that one scholar has claimed that "in its services to the public, the bureaucracy was perhaps less effective during the 1956–1960 period than at any other time in modern Korean history."[23] Park's administration, in contrast, was considered highly moralistic and uncorruptable;[24] and it may be for precisely this reason that decades later, during the banking crisis and corruption scandals of the late 1990s, South Koreans polled in a national survey identified Park Chung Hee as the one leader they would most like to clone. Most important for our purposes, however, was the fact that the Rhee administration emphasized ISI while the Park administration developed EOI. The question of course is why.

The Rural Underpinnings of Park's Ascent to Power

Some scholars would direct us to the global economy for answers, and they would not be entirely mistaken to do so. One key difference between the 1953–1960 period of Rhee's rule and the 1961–1979 period of Park's rule was the changed world economy. Most analysts of globalization target 1960 as a year when global trade began to accelerate rapidly, in part due to the accumulated effects of international financial agreements signed at Bretton

---

[23] Kim, *The Fall of Syngman Rhee*, p. 19.

[24] Arguments about the militarized foundations of the Park regime do not appear to fully explain the differences between the Rhee and Park administrations either, at least to the extent that Rhee was known to rely heavily on a well-trained and violent cadre of police which was the largest single source of state manpower personnel and received the greatest budgetary expenditure of all the ministries. According to Kim, "As the strong arm of the Rhee regime, the police force was more or less openly used to secure electoral victories for the ruling party and the incumbent administration. It suppressed political opposition, discouraged individuals connected with the opposition party, and created fear on the part of the common people in the countryside" (quoted in Janelli, *Making Capitalism*, p. 21).

Woods, and partly due to the subsequent revitalization of Western (and Eastern) economies in the aftermath of the Marshall Plan. In these conditions, EOI was both possible and likely. However, it is equally true that in the South Korean case, the years 1960 and 1961 also served as a key *political* watershed in the country's modern history. In 1960 Syngman Rhee failed in his efforts to capture the presidency, only to be succeeded by an ineffectual and short-lived politican, John Chang, who was subsequently deposed in a military coup and replaced later that year by Park Chung Hee. Starting in 1961, the South Korean economy and politics fell under Park's forceful guidance, and he set out to change the political and economic course of the nation.

Not only was Park's administration responsible for laying the foundations of the South Korean economic miracle, Park also sought to politically distance himself from the past, especially from the political priorities that sustained Rhee's grip on the post–Korean War political economy. Thus Park's hold on power was sustained by an entirely different political coalition than Rhee's, which had been tied to a highly corrupt, urban-based bureaucracy strongly linked to ISI industrialists. As such, there were important social, class, and political changes occurring within South Korea in the early 1960s that both motivated and sustained Park's new approach to macroeconomic policy making, particularly the unique combination of ISI and EOI that brought South Korea dazzling rates of industrial growth and economic prosperity. And among the class and social forces that factored most into Park's personal and political vision, and that allowed him most leeway to openly distance himself from Rhee and his primarily urban-based political allies, were rural classes, especially family farmers and other small-scale agricultural producers who could be considered a mainstay of the rural middle class.

In South Korea at the end of World War II, the far majority of rural populations were not landless peasants or rural wage laborers, but small-scale producers and other self-employed or family farmers, whose ownership of land, employment of family members and occasional wage laborers, and small farm size made them a key component of the rural middle class. As of the early 1960s, in fact, both large landholdings and tenant farming had almost disappeared. There was some tenancy, but the rate had remained remarkably low since the successful introduction of land reform starting in 1958, at which time less than 6 percent of the population were landless tenants.[25] Upon coming

---

[25] At this time only 6 percent were part-tenants who owned less cultivatable land than they rented but were still considered small-scale producers because they did own and cultivate their own property too, and 9 percent were part-tenants who owned the majority of the land they cultivated. These are 1958 figures from a study by Lee cited in Janelli, *Making Capitalism*, p. 36. See also Brandt, *A Korean Village Between Farm and Sea*, p. 55, who notes that there was little tenancy because "with the furor over land reform and intensive indoctrination under the Communists it . . . [was] vaguely felt to be illegal"; Kim also notes that after land

to power in 1961, Park programatically and ideologically bathed his regime in small-farmer sentiments, including an overwhelming concern with rural development. And it was the Park administration's deep respect for and allegiance to small farmers, and theirs toward him, that accounts for much of the content of the general's macroeconomic policy making, why it differed from Rhee's, and why it shifted over time even during his own time in office.

Granted, General Park also began as an earnest promoter of industrialization, a developmental objective that most scholars choose to identify as the defining essence of his administration. But scholars err in assuming that Park's unwavering support for industrialization automatically emerged from – let alone correlated with – his political regard for industrialists and a desire to accommodate their interests. Rather, Park's concern with industrialization was always tied to his preoccupation with rural middle classes and rural development, with the latter set of concerns conditioning the former, and not vice versa. Park's key aim was not just to regenerate the historically given stature of Korea's farmer classes and further ensconce them in the country's social and cultural fabric. He also sought to nurture and sustain their economic position in the national economy. As such, he imposed a great deal of discipline on industrial capitalists and laborers, promoting considerable industrial development but harnessing most of it in the service of rural development.

In pondering why the rural middle classes were so important to the Park administration, it is tempting to revert to a long-standing cultural explanation, namely, the fact that small-scale rural producers – whether called farmers or peasants – have historically been perceived as one of the most valued and respected strata in Korean society. In contrast to many other late-industrializing nations (Argentina, for example, where political culture has characteristically relegated rural folk to the status of barbarians and savages), in Korea rural populations devoted to farming, even at such a small scale as to be considered peasants, have historically been perceived with high social and cultural status. According to Confucian culture, in fact, these folk are considered the "Great Foundation of Life under Heaven,"[26] and among rural peoples, farmers have always held higher prestige than others who also work on their own account in the village setting, including fishermen.[27] In contrast, urban populations and persons employed in business and commerce historically have been considered of relatively low status, and rarely have they merited the same general respect as farmers, at least culturally speaking. In fact, the traditional value system of South Korean Confucianism places commerce and industry at the absolute bottom of the status hierarchy, a fact which should give pause to

---

reform "low rents and guaranteed tenure . . . [made] tenancy an unattractive proposition for a landowner" (*The Fall of Syngman Rhee*, p. 21).

[26] Kim, *Man and Society*, p. 31.

[27] Brandt, *A Korean Village Between Farm and Sea*, p. 3.

scholars like Peter Berger who argue for a direct cultural parallel between a Protestant-ethic-driven commercial route in the West and in East Asia.[28]

Despite their broad appeal, such cultural explanations that focus on the high value ascribed to rural farmers can only go so far, especially if they are not also historically contextualized and grounded in an understanding of general political and economic conditions in post–World War II South Korea. After all, the Syngman Rhee administration was also nationalist and just as eminently "South Korean" – in what might be considered a purely cultural sense – as most of the postindependence administrations. Like Park's it also touted its nationalist and anticommunist character. Yet unlike Park, Rhee pretty much ignored small farmers and their concerns, leaving rural populations to fend for themselves as massive government resources fed ISI. Thus, we must move beyond general cultural explanations and identify additional factors if we want to explain Park's uniquely rural sensitivities. They include first, and foremost, the comprehensive rural land reform implemented in the post–Korean War period. But equally important were historical factors such as the primarily agricultural nature of the South Korean economy under Japanese colonialism and at the point of independence, as well as the demographic, class, and political impact of the Korean War, including the division of the more industrialized north from the more agricultural south.[29]

When Park Chung Hee muscled his way into power in a 1961 military coup, South Korea was still primarily agricultural. As late as 1955, farmers constituted 70 percent of the population; 7.5 percent were nonfarm self-employed and 4.8 percent were nonmanual workers; while only 12.5 and 0.3 percent of the population were involved in manual work or were business owners and top executives, respectively.[30] Of course, Korea had long been much more agricultural than industrial, even before partition, owing to the domestic political and economic constraints associated with Japanese colonial rule. Under Japanese administration there had been some industrial development, mainly

---

[28] The rank-order is 1) scholar-official, 2) farmer, 3) artisan, 4) merchant. Noted in Mason et al., *The Economic and Social Modernization*, p. 281.

[29] These priorities in turn diverted Rhee's attention from rural considerations even to the point of his backtracking on U.S.-backed land reform. The actions of the Rhee administration, then, further moved Park to resuscitate the country's rural development project, thereby even more firmly establishing the rural middle-class foundations of his unique developmental vision. Last, the rural middle-class foundations of the South Korean military, foundations which Park himself shared, further connected him and his administration to rural folk. Of course, several of these historical factors might have pushed Rhee in a similar direction, but they were counterbalanced by his strong political and social connections to urban and industrial forces, as well as to foreign investors who buttressed Rhee's ISI priorities. Land reform differentiates Park's administration from Rhee's even more firmly, establishing the rural middle-class foundations of his unique developmental vision.

[30] Koo, "Middle Classes, Democratization, and Class Formation," Table 1, p. 489.

directed at the processing of agricultural goods (including textile production), as is frequently the case with colonial economies. Still, it was the Korean War and the resultant division of the country into north and south that most dramatically transformed the demographic character of South Korea and further reinforced its primarily agricultural character. It was not just that most of the industrial infrastructure was concentrated in the cities of what became North Korea. A far greater proportion of the economic infrastructure in the south than in the north was destroyed during the war. As such, greater economic opportunities, combined with an ideological allegiance to the communists on the part of many, motivated a good number of industrial workers and landless peasants to migrate north upon partition.[31] Those who remained in the south were more likely to be rural property owners, both small and large.

City Versus Countryside in Newly Partitioned South Korea

It was precisely because of this unique demographic and political situation that the initial independence government of Syngman Rhee committed itself to land reform, a program that intensified the agrarian orientation of South Korean citizens after 1952 and helped produce expectations that the country would be populated by a burgeoning class of small farmers. Given that the majority of the new nation's population was impoverished and consisted mostly of farmers with few other skills and long ties to the land, it made political sense for the new South Korean government to offer land to its people. Clive Hamilton reminds us that "between 1945 and 1965 the proportion of farm households wholly owning their land rose from 14 to 70 percent [while] the proportion of pure tenants fell from 49 percent to 7 percent."[32] One reason the South Korean government had been able to implement such a large-scale land reform owed to the fact that many of the large holdings in the country belonged to the Japanese, who fled their ex-colony in defeat after 1945. Much more important, however, was the enormous volition on the part of South Korean authorities and their U.S. allies – fueled by cold war fears on the part of Americans and South Koreans alike about the rural inroads to be made by communists in the larger propaganda battle over rural landlordism and agrarian exploitation.[33] As in Taiwan, land reform was seen as a politically expedient means to preempt rural rebellion.

---

[31] Keon, *Korean Phoenix*, p. 73, claims that most of the two million persons displaced from North into South Korea by politics and war came from farm families.

[32] *Capitalist Industrialization*, p. 30.

[33] One other issue that factored into these deliberations was the fact that a radically comprehensive land reform was implemented in North Korea in 1946, thereby putting pressure on South Korean authorities to follow suit even as it subsequently split the populace over the desirability of South Korea's more moderate reform. For more on this, see Pak and Gamble, *The Changing Korean Village*.

Still, the positive effects of the land reform, especially its capacity to remedy the conditions and bolster the livelihood of rural populations, were long in coming, a state of affairs that Park eventually parlayed into his own political advantage. According to Stephan Haggard and Chung-in Moon, "Limited [land] reforms had begun [during the Korean War] under the military government with the sale of Japanese properties to tenants, but the American reforms had not touched Korean holdings,"[34] and in the postwar period few actions were taken to remedy this situation. Syngman Rhee, for example, who governed South Korea in the post–Korean War period, dragged his feet so that very few actual transfers of property took place.[35] With only a superficial commitment to land reform during most of the 1950s, and most of it formally kicking in only around 1958, very little was accomplished in terms of reviving small-farmer production in South Korea until the year immediately preceding Park's grasp for power. As one scholar observed, over the 1950s the South Korean government did nothing in particular for farmers except to "make great efforts to manipulate them for political objectives."[36]

In addition to the slowness of land transfers under Rhee, much of the obvious neglect of the small farmer owed to the fact that the land "reforms were not followed by a political commitment to rural development; Rhee gave greater emphasis to industry and the urban areas."[37] More than anything else, the Rhee administration prioritized urban-based industrial development, using U.S. military and other foreign aid to support processing and manufacturing activities.[38] It also hosted the growth of a "new commercial class, which grew rapidly from the supply shortages of the war economy and increased foreign trade."[39] As a result, the gross domestic product grew at an average rate of 3.9 percent in 1953–1955 and again in 1960–1962, while manufacturing grew at 11.2 percent a year.[40] In more or less the same period, during the Rhee administration, the annual growth rate of domestic grain production was 1.72 percent, while the rate of foreign grain imports increased 23.1 percent annually for the same period.[41] In contrast, from 1953 to 1961, mining and manufacturing grew at an average annual rate of 12.2 percent.[42] Significantly,

---

[34] See Haggard and Moon, "The State." For more on the failure to implement reforms on the books until after the Rhee administration, see Mitchell, "Land Reform in South Korea."

[35] Haggard and Moon, "The State," p. 60.

[36] Lee, "Rural People and Their Modernization," p. 76.

[37] Haggard and Moon, "The State," p. 61.

[38] The United States was a strong supporter of ISI in South Korea, especially during the Rhee administration. For more on the role of the United States in pushing Rhee to neglect agriculture and promote industry, see Hsiao, *Government Agricultural Strategies*, pp. 82–83.

[39] Haggard and Moon, "The State," pp. 61–63.

[40] Ibid., p. 61.

[41] Hsiao, *Government Agricultural Strategies*, p. 84.

[42] Hamilton, *Capitalist Industrialization*, p. 34.

because most of the manufacturing and commercial activities were urban based, the nation experienced a political alignment under Rhee in which urban classes and their demands for the restoration of urban and industrial infrastructure took center stage, especially in Seoul, the capital city. In stark contrast to the following two administrations of Chang and Park, for example, who drew their cabinet membership much more from the provinces, under Rhee almost one-third of the national cabinet came from Seoul.[43]

Further tipping the developmental balance toward cities in general and Seoul in particular was the rapid growth of the South Korean bureaucracy under Rhee. Some of this was the natural organizational by-product of massive monies lent to the new government for the purpose of rebuilding after the war. In 1955 Rhee established the Ministry of Reconstruction (MOR), which employed technicians and trained administrators in the service of rebuilding the South Korean infrastructure. Some bureaucratic growth also owed to the government's strong commitment to jump-start urban-based industrialization, which entailed the establishment of numerous government agencies to finance, license, and coordinate new manufacturing activities. However, a large portion of the growing size and political visibility of the state bureaucracy headquartered in Seoul owed directly to the patronage policies of Syngman Rhee. Faced with declining political support and intense political competition after 1956, Rhee found it increasingly necessary to bolster his hold on power by expanding patronage networks, a strategy which rapidly deteriorated into a downward spiral of corruption and favoritism.[44] At the same time, he strengthened his relations with a new cadre of urban-based ISI industrialists who owed their origins and livelihood to his administration's policies. Many of these businessmen secured their influence by making direct contributions to President Rhee's campaign coffers, with the expectation that he would respond with favorable lending or licensing, something which occurred frequently. The result was a bloated government bureaucracy, expanded in volume and influence, riddled with corruption, and well linked to a growing class of ISI industrialists in Seoul.

The clear favoritism toward ISI industrialists and the corrupt economic practices of the bureaucracy came to haunt Rhee, setting the basis for his political

---

[43] Paik, "The Formation of the Governing Elites in Korean Society," p. 49. Paik notes that during Chang's administration, the Cholla Province was overrepresented, while in the Park administration most cabinet members came from Kyongsang Province.

[44] In fact, most scholars identify corrupt practices as occurring early on in the Rhee administration, starting when he "sold off formerly Japanese factories and equipment for small amounts to the industrialists and later granted special foreign-exchange and import licenses, allowing these men to make profits through privileged access to resources rather than through risk taking, competition, and other entrepreneurial activities" (Janelli, *Making Capitalism*, p. 83).

defeat, even in Seoul, where many patronage and infrastructural perks had been distributed to the local population. As early as 1956, urban populations, those most likely to see the visible effects of the conspicuous consumption and corruption of both the bureaucracy and the industrialists, began withdrawing political support from Rhee. While in 1952, 82.3 percent of Seoul's voters supported Rhee's candidacy, a scant four years later this figure had dropped precipitously to 33.7 percent, in part because he also lost the support of the urban middle class.[45] Nationally, Rhee's political popularity continued its free fall as misguided economic policies and clear industrial biases produced an overvalued exchange rate and a fiscal crisis that steadily wreaked havoc in the domestic economy for both rural and urban populations. Most troublesome for his administration, however, was what Michael Hsiao called "the ever-widening gap between the average earning of farmers and that of urban dwellers."[46] When a student revolution in April 1960 focused its attention on the illicit wealth, growing inequality, and corruption associated with the Rhee administration, it became a catalyst for his political defeat and electoral replacement by John Chang Myong. But the new Chang government was equally hard-pressed to revive citizens' confidence. Perhaps most damaging to his fragile new administration were the declining conditions in rural areas, primarily the result of Rhee's blatant neglect of rural development in the rush to support ISI industrialists and expand the government bureaucracy. Given that the majority of South Koreans still lived in rural areas, and that tensions over the division between north and south persisted and remained highly charged in the countryside, political instability loomed large. That Chang was considered too weak and indecisive to inspire much enthusiasm further limited his political future.

The already precarious political situation worsened dramatically when the Chang government devalued the exchange rate in February 1961. Forced to devalue and also implement rate hikes for government services, Chang's administration incurred the wrath of various sectors of society, including urban residents who directly or indirectly lived off the bureaucracy as well as those who relied on primary or secondary imports for production and/or consumption needs, namely, ISI industrialists and a small but emergent urban middle class. As such, even the small but visible pressure groups who originally supported Rhee were ready for some sort of significant change in 1961. Yet again, perhaps the most aggrieved citizens in the wake of Chang's devaluation were rural populations, primarily because the devaluation generated severe food shortages by accelerating the costs of agricultural imports. Already, rural populations had become ever more dependent on food imports, owing to the dismal state of

[45] Kim, *The Fall of Syngman Rhee*, p. 15; for more on the urban middle class, see Park, *Economic Development and Social Change in Korea*, p. 282.

[46] Hsiao, *Government Agricultural Strategies*, p. 55.

rural infrastructure and the paucity of rural credit for agricultural production. When devaluation raised the prices of food to new heights, rural populations were doubly hit: neither were they producing food nor could they afford to consume it. In these conditions any political leader who could rally the support of rural populations and establish the potential for sustained agricultural production was likely to go far, given that they still constituted close to 70 percent of the national population. Park Chung Hee did just that: He came to power openly "sympathetic to the plight of the farmer"[47] and brandishing what Haggard and Moon labeled a strongly "antiurban tone."[48]

Restoring the "Great Foundation of Life Under Heaven"

The May 1961 coup led by Park Chung Hee ushered in a dramatic new shift in development priorities in which rural populations took center stage. Some scholars, among them Michael Hsiao, go so far as to say that it was only with Park's military government, which counted on military personnel drawn mainly from the rural areas, that "agricultural economic problems for the first time received close official attention."[49] Like Rhee, Park of course concerned himself greatly with national unity and an effort to triumph politically and economically, especially in comparison with North Korea. Yet his means differed significantly, as did some of his key objectives. Among other things, Park and his allies were concerned about both Rhee's and Chang's obsessive preoccupation with politics and conditions in the main urban center of the country, that is, in Seoul, and their neglect of the countryside. Park's concern in these regards owed not only to his astute recollection that many of the communists' successes in the prewar period were due to their capacity to organize thousands of peoples' committees in rural areas and the hinterlands.[50] It also stemmed from his personal disdain for cities: "'Rotten' and 'filthy' . . . [were] two words he frequently . . . [used] to describe urban life."[51] From the beginning, rural citizens were a key audience of the Park administration.

In his first five-year plan, Park prioritized rural development and displayed an unambiguous commitment to carrying out any stalled land transfers in the hopes of firmly establishing the land tenancy and property rights upon which a rural middle class of farmers could grow and prosper. Among the government measures introduced within the first months of the coup were: promulgation of a farm price maintenance law on June 27; the purchase of summer grains to stabilize prices of summer yields; raising the purchase prices

[47] Hamilton, *Capitalist Industrialization*, p. 39.
[48] "The State," p. 65.
[49] *Government Agricultural Strategies*, p. 86.
[50] For a discussion of this see Cumings, *The Origins of the Korean War*, especially Chap. 8.
[51] Kim, *The Politics of Military Revolution*, p. 90.

of export farm products, including peppermint, hemp, and silk cocoons; setting grain prices at pre-revolutionary levels; releasing government reserve grain horded by military personnel; maintaining price stability through the release of five million bushels of rice; and government purchases of grain crops to avoid a seasonal slump during the fall harvest. Writing at the time, Kyung Cho Chung claimed that "these measures aim at freeing farmers from heavy losses resulting from low farm prices. The government is well aware that an increase in farm incomes is a 'must' for the development of the national economy."[52]

Just as notably, while Park did seek to encourage some form of industrialization, he initially targeted his support to firms concentrated in those manufacturing activities that were geared to generating greater rural production, mainly fertilizers and energy, and to construction and infrastructure activities that would facilitate rural-urban transportation and communication.[53] As Cristóbal Kay notes, in South Korea (and Taiwan) the government "encouraged the creation of industries which would allow improvement in agriculture such as the chemical fertilizer, and farm machinery and equipment industries. Furthermore, agriculture-supporting industries received an even higher allocation of foreign aid funds than other types of industries."[54] And as General Park himself stated so simply and more than once, albeit in slightly different incarnations, "Farming is and will be the basis on which industry is built. Self-sufficient food production and supply is the prerequisite to building an industrial state."[55] As such, the industrial development that Park pursued, especially during his first five years in office, was informed as much by his rural development objectives as by an overwhelming obsession with industrialization per se. As another scholar put it, "Overall economic development was both a prerequisite for and corollary to agricultural development. Korean agriculture could not begin to modernize until the country was capable of building such essentials as fertilizer plants and road networks."[56] Thus even when urban-based industrialization was advocated, it was expected to take some of the pressure off rural farmers by offering urban employment for surplus labor, opportunities which in turn were expected to help ease the pressure on farm life. Initially this was as much intended to absorb migrants fleeing from North Korea, who would have been forced to seek employment on already overcrowded farms or would have ended up even more destitute in cities, desperately trying to eke out a living. Yet even then, Park rarely ceded that employment in cities was a key objective, at least early on, which may

---

[52] *New Korea*, p. 163.

[53] See Vogel, *The Four Little Dragons*, pp. 55–56.

[54] See *Asia's and Latin America's Development in Comparative Perspective*, p. 39.

[55] Shik (ed.), *Major Speeches*, p. 156.

[56] Salem, "Korean Rural Development, p. 39.

help explain why a 1966 Ministry of Public Education document profiling Park's first five years heralded his successes in reversing the trend toward urbanization.[57]

This closer examination of Park's rural orientation, both in terms of population priorities and development strategies, suggests that Park initially conceived of industrialization as a means to an end, not an end in itself, and not necessarily as his principal developmental goal. "Whatever else we may consider at this moment," Park claimed in 1962, "the most urgent and fundamental need is that the rural communities should have precedence over everything else. It is the top priority."[58] In contrast to Rhee, also an unreconstructed nationalist but one who ignored rural populations and conceived of rapid industrialization as his main goal and a strategy for one-upping the Japanese,[59] Park's first priority was rural South Korea and its small-scale agricultural producers. For Park, no less a nationalist than Rhee, it was rural populations and small farmers, not urban Koreans, and certainly not industrialists or chaebols, who served as the great foundation of the society he hoped to build. He pledged his devotion to the plight of the farmers and fervently identified them as the "economic backbone of our, as yet, underdeveloped country."[60] Some scholars will suggest that Park's concern with farmers and his plans for rural development were merely window dressing: propaganda efforts planted into five-year plans and public discourse in order to sustain a harsh and controlling military regime's legitimacy as it poured resources into industrialization at all costs. And it surely is true that in his first five-year plan Park was careful not to overcommit scarce resources to the rural sector, placing as much fiscal and policy emphasis on the development of the energy sector (mainly coal production and electric power) and heavy industry as on rural development per se. However, as Ban, Moon, and Perkins have also noted, "It was agriculture that benefited from the industrial and export boom rather than the reverse." South Korea, these

---

[57] While propaganda and fact are hard to separate in these reports, what is unmistakable are the priorities and images the government wished to highlight. Owing to Park's policies and objectives, the document boasts, "the farmers who had desperately migrated into the cities, where they often remained unemployed, thus now turn back to their villages, and are 'resettled'" (Ministry of Public Education, *Profile of President Park Chung Hee*, p. 52).

[58] *The Country, the Revolution, and I*, p. 36.

[59] According to Carl Strom, a counselor of the embassy in Korea until July 1956, Rhee's obsession with repudiating the Japanese was such that he occasionally jeopardized relations with the United States, which in the postwar period was as eager to influence the rebuilding of the Japanese economy and society as it was to aid South Korea (Source: Department of State, Central Files, 033.100-ST/3-855, quoted in Lim, "The Developmental State"). See also Woo, *Race to the Swift*, p. 53.

[60] Radio transcript of Park Chung Hee speech, broadcast by WGBH Boston, May 16, 1962, during "South Korea: A Year Under Military Rule." Archived at Yenchang Library, Harvard University.

authors of the often-cited Harvard study of rural development claimed, was "a model of how an industrial revolution can precede and help bring about an agricultural revolution."[61] Industrialization, in short, was a means, not an end.

It may be worth noting that skepticism about Park's rural commitments and a tendency to see Park as clearly favoring industrialization are most likely to surface among scholars writing about the later years of the Park administration, at least after 1972 and primarily after 1975, a situation which may underscore my earlier admonition about the theoretical importance of taking history seriously and not reading the past through the lens of the present. It also is a view that tends to predominate among "foreign" (i.e., non-Korean) scholars. Conversely, scholars taking a more historical perspective on Park's ascent to power, especially those writing during or about the first decade of his administration, and those domestic scholars generally cognizant of South Korean rural life and thus not overly influenced by later successes with industrialization, have a very different view of this early period. Writing in 1971, for example, Se-Jin Kim defined Park as "a strongly anti-urban reformer," whose main interest was the countryside and who was most concerned about "the long neglect of rural interests by civilian politicians, except for occasional bribes (or harassment) to induce votes, [which] resulted in a greater privation in agriculture than in any other major sector."[62] Kim further suggested that the "massive grants and loans to agriculture during the initial period and the emphasis placed on constructing fertilizer plants by the junta government reflect Park's rural interest. . . . He does not, or cannot, seem to separate himself from rural life and values."[63]

Park, of course, had many aims besides a commitment to restoring rural development to the national agenda. His 1961 coup, or military revolution, as Park and his loyalists insisted on calling it, was inspired by a concern about the threat of communism; and once in office he worked hard to limit pro-communist agitation among students and labor organizations and to fight massive layoffs in the military.[64] Still, the evidence is considerable that Park's

---

[61] *Rural Development*, pp. 5, 12.

[62] *The Politics of Military Revolution*, p. 90. Likewise, Salem's arguments that industrialization was a prerequisite for agricultural development, noted in fn. 56 above, also may owe to her conscientious effort to take a historical perspective, as is stated in the subtitle of her article, "Korean Rural Development: A Historical Perspective."

[63] *The Politics of Military Revolution*, p. 90. As further evidence of Park's rural bias, Kim also noted that within several months of the coup the Supreme Council invalidated the rights of creditors who charged more than 20 percent on their land, but applied "these provisions . . . to farmers and fishermen only; commercial, industrial, or other types of loans more urban in occurrence, were not covered" (p. 106).

[64] South Korean military expert John P. Lovell noted that in the final stages of the Chang Myon campaign, "a statement was issued pledging a reduction of 100,000 in the armed forces if

original commitments to uplift the lives and livelihoods of the rural populations in general – and the rural middle class in particular – were among the reasons for his coup d'état in the first place, not merely cynical afterthoughts used to legitimize a hold on power. As one scholar put it,

> No one needed to sell Park on the farmer as the basic provider for the nation, and a social being with his own needs. . . . Looking ahead to a day of electoral test, Park knew that the majority of votes, and what real support he could expect, lay outside the towns. He had long brooded on rural-urban imbalance and, as noted, had worked out for himself the belief that, in a modern economy, any sustained betterment of rural work and living would not come from programs conceived and imposed as development exercise but from farmers' natural reaction to a waxing and diversifying national growth.[65]

Linking Rural Populations to the Military Government

So how deep was Park's commitment to the rural middle class of small producers? As of late it has been popular to cite the role of bureaucratic and political "entrepreneurs" in leading and successfully carrying out development schemes. Scholars who take this position generally fasten their sights on highly charismatic individuals like General Park as evidence of these dynamics. And clearly, Park Chung Hee played a major role in voicing concern for and personally identifying with the aims of rural development. Yet it is important to recognize that restoring prosperity to the countryside and dignity to small farmers were not merely the projects of one idiosyncratic individual. These developmental goals were also a high priority for the majority of South Koreans, who were still primarily rural; and as such, they can be seen as reflecting the national will in some limited fashion. Moreover, it was not merely a free-floating national support for rural development that reinforced Park's commitment to rural development and that sustained his institutional capacity to act on these goals. Equally important was the fact that rural development was considered to be both a viable and noble goal by many members of the military, and their support for Park's administration was absolutely central in explaining his hold on power and thus his willingness and capacity to sustain this particular developmental vision.

the Democrats were made the ruling party. This pledge was reiterated by the new Minister of Defense shortly after the Chang government came to power." See "The Military and Politics in Postwar Korea" (p. 172). With Rhee having promoted his political allies, especially those sympathetic to his ISI development goals, Park undoubtedly had good reason to believe that he and other rural-oriented military personnel might lose out big in these restructurings.
[65] Keon, *Korean Phoenix*, p. 69.

Scholars often trace the military's involvement in developmental regimes to their nationalist sentiments, which they frequently claim will translate into support for industrialization at all costs. Despite the popularity of this spectacular analytic leap from nationalism to industrialism, it is not always possible to know in the abstract which development policies the military is likely to support, since in theory, nationalism could be as easily directed toward industrial as agricultural development or ISI as opposed to EOI (think Turkey or Argentina). In South Korea, in fact, the military was a strong supporter of and motivation for Park's rural development priorities. Much of this owed to the fact that most military men associated with the Park regime had direct family connections to the rural areas, coming primarily from the rural middle class. As Larry Burmeister puts it, "As a social group, the military coup leaders did not have strong ties to the traditional rural aristocracy or the urban elites based in Seoul," and as such they were "social[ly] isolated . . . from other elite groups (particularly landlords-turned-entrepreneurs and the intelligentsia)."[66] That is, most of the officers who participated in the 1961 military coup came from modest farm families, counted on farmer friends and relatives in rural areas, and had little sympathy for the urban industrialists associated with the prior Rhee administration.[67] This means that the Park administration's concern with rural development and rural populations both derived from and reinforced a link between the military and rural populations, social and cultural linkages which gave further urgency to Park's plans for the countryside, and further embedded his administration in the lives and livelihoods of rural peoples.

The 1961 coup brought to power a new group of rural-based military personnel who, for the first time in Korean history, came not from the upper or upper-middle levels of Korean society but primarily from the middle or lower-middle classes, especially from rural areas.[68] According to Hahn and Kim, who studied the social background of cabinet members and the Supreme Council for National Reconstruction (SCNR) in 1962, the first year of the Park administration, the majority of members of the SCNR and the military government were sons of small landholders and laborers, while there was not a single representative from the business sector.[69] Park himself was the son of a

---

[66] *Research, Realpolitik, and Development in Korea*, pp. 41–42.

[67] Keon, *Korean Phoenix*, p. 69.

[68] For more on the junta's rural orgins, see Kim, *The Politics of Military Revolution*, p. 106; for more on the middle-class origins of the military junta, see Chang, *Economic Control*, p. 78.

[69] "Korean Political Leaders (1952–1962)," p. 305. Of course, as shall be clear shortly, much of this owes to the overrepresentation of military personnel in the junta. Paik claims that 68 percent of the cabinet members comprising the Commission of Military Revolution and Government came from the military; see "The Formation of the Governing Elites in Korean Society," p. 53.

small farmer. In 1977, a decade and a half after the coup, he was still described as "a farm boy himself by birth, upbringing, and continuing interest."[70] After initially working as a rural schoolteacher, Park found military service a lucrative source of middle-class employment, like many other farm youths, although restrictions imposed by the Japanese on military academy slots in Korea meant he went to Manchuria for training. At that time, military service was one of the few avenues available to the sons of small farmers that also allowed considerable educational betterment, long a concern of the middle class and of a schoolteacher like Park Chung Hee. To a limited degree, employment in the military as a viable occupational choice for rural populations initially began during Japanese colonialism; yet its role as a means of educational betterment and class uplift owes its origins to the Korean War. Before then, the role of the military had been highly circumscribed, with military men relegated to relatively low status in society. A career in the military was never intended as a source of upward mobility.[71] But after Japanese defeat and exile from Korea, efforts were made to bolster the military and to use it as a means for educating as well as mobilizing the rural masses in the fight against communism and forces from the north. The Republic of Korea's (ROK) army initiated special literacy, elementary, and junior high school education programs, such that between 1951 and 1970 a total of six hundred thousand soldiers became literate.[72] The result was that during the 1950s and 1960s, many rural boys joined the military, finding educational enrichment, employment, and a more privileged life in the process.

It was precisely the military's rural origins, then, and perhaps even the advantages they now enjoyed as recipients of government training and largesse, that helped sustain Park's efforts to use his newfound political power to do something for their families, friends, and neighbors in rural areas. Because these sons of the rural middle class now predominated in the national military and state bureaucracy, where policy decisions were made, they were in a position to prioritize rural development and challenge the unqualified urban and industrial biases of the Rhee administration.[73] It was not merely through

---

[70] Keon, *Korean Phoenix*, p. 3. Keon notes that Park encouraged his "image makers" to play with these sentiments by "photographing him in cornfields and piggeries, embracing elderly farm women, and lecturing to their husbands all over the country" (p. 3).

[71] Chang, *Economic Control*, p. 78.

[72] For more on the training of military personnel during this period, see Chang, *Economic Control*; and Lee, "Political Change."

[73] In Kim's study of "task elites" recruited to work in the government bureaucracy, 18.8 percent came from the military during the Park administration, while in the Chang and Rhee administrations the figure was 0 percent and 1.3 percent, respectively. See p. 35 (Table 25) in *Administrative Changes and Elite Dynamics*.

macroeconomic policy, or a common rural heritage, that Park and his political allies were linked to rural peoples, especially farmers. Park also used existent institutions, like the military, and created new ones, like the National Reconstruction Movement (NRM) and his own political party, to solidify his bases in rural areas. Park's political loyalists established the NRM several months after the coup, in June 1961, manning it with military personnel and representatives from country, township, village, and block organizations. Through legislative actions, the Supreme Council placed NRM headquarters under direct control and funded many of its activities. By offering specialized services on a very local level, the NRM created a network of social and political linkages between rural residents and the Park regime; and it was through these networks, institutions, and activities that the Park administration both responded to rural concerns and established political loyalty among these key populations. The founder of the NRM, former professor of agriculture Yu Tal-young, worked hard to direct most of the movement's energies toward the village, especially the youth and women's wings, arguing that it was "wiser to emphasize the rural communities in the formative stage [of the movement] and to slow down the pace in the urban communities."[74] This decision seems to have had both a demographic and a political logic. Not only did villages still host the majority of the nation's residents, they also were the home for "many able young veterans who . . . [had] served in the military forces," who in addition to offering a natural political base for Park were also "expected to provide leadership in local projects" after being given proper training and financial support.[75] Among the institutions and programs created through the NRM were reconstruction and youth training centers, an adult education and literacy program, a rural library movement, and a farm youth school. By 1963, the NRM registered nearly four million members, at which time it was transformed into a voluntary organization that eventually expanded into some thirty thousand branches throughout the nation.[76]

Along with the NRM, the military continued to serve as an essential point of contact to insure the embeddedness of the Park administration and rural populations. As John P. Lovell has explained so well in his discussion of the first years of Park's rule,

> At the level of official military policy, a substantial commitment exist[ed] to major participation by military units in developmental activities through Korean society. This commitment is most clearly revealed in military policy statements and actions supporting "civic action" programs. "Civic action" denotes a program for the utilization of military

---

[74] *The National Reconstruction Movement in Restrospect and Prospect*, p. 293.
[75] Ibid.
[76] Huer, *Marching Orders*, p. 93.

units in activities such as agriculture, construction, public education, public health and the like. . . . ROK military men have assisted farmers in rice planting and harvesting. They have built dams, roads, and schools; they have distributed food, medical supplies, machinery, and equipment to needy civilians; they have brought transistor radios to villages previously without them; they have entertained and educated villagers and provided them with medical treatment; military units have established fraternal relationships with civilian communities and schools; and have organized civilian youth groups.[77]

The Park administration also used the bureaucracy and various new government programs to engage the rural masses. Park's efficiency in this regard was "prodigious," according to John Huer, especially with respect to "national mobilization, creating organizations and public works projects."[78] A 1961 Agricultural Cooperation Law, for example, organized a Land Reclamation Movement for which, in 1965 alone, over forty-five million worker-days of employment were provided by the government, while the National Agrarian Cooperative Federation provided subsidies to marginal farmers and the various youth programs run by the Park administration. The government also mobilized and dispatched medical professionals to doctorless villages, underscoring Park's antiurban biases by assigning doctors born in Seoul "to especially remote areas for two years of public service."[79] In addition to the NRM, the Park administration used organizations as diverse as the Cooperative Association, the government's Offices of Rural Development, the Irrigation Association, the Livestock Association, 4H Clubs, Offices of Regional Construction, the Veterans Association, and the Forest Cooperative to expand and strengthen its network with farmers and other rural-based populations. John Huer cites one study indicating that 64 percent of villagers surveyed belonged to at least one organization.[80]

Through these various institutional networks and activities, the Park administration further established connections with rural peoples, embedding the practices and personnel of his administration with rural populations, especially its small-scale producers. Park subsequently used these networks to entrench support for his Democratic Republican Party (DRP), which by late in the decade counted more than any other party on rural constituents for

[77] "The Military As an Instrument for Political Development," pp. 21–22. See also Huer, *Marching Orders*, pp. 96–97.

[78] *Marching Orders*, p. 93.

[79] Ibid., pp. 93–94. For more on these and other rural-based programs, see Jacobs, *The Korean Road to Modernization*, pp. 103–108.

[80] *Marching Orders*, p. 94.

political sympathy and electoral loyalty.[81] And while the DPR under Park – and the party system more generally – never developed the institutional autonomy to countervail the power of the South Korean state, the programs, networks, and linkages that the DPR used to connect citizens to the state did thrive. It was these networks and programs that allowed Park to rely heavily on rural villages and rural peoples for political support even as they relied on him to speak to their developmental concerns. Rural middle classes became institutionally embedded in the governing apparatus (or tentacles) of the Park administration even as he and his military allies became dependent on them for political support. And once he established these political and institutional bases in the first years of rule, Park both drew inspiration from and sought to transform the wretched lives of "demoralized farmers," as he often called them, who had long suffered "through thoughtless former governments turn[ing] their face from agriculture and . . . [indulging] in corruption and political strife."[82] It was these demoralized and neglected farmers who, almost inadvertently, ultimately yielded Park the secret to his stunning economic successes.

Imagining Denmark

As Stephan Haggard and Chung-in Moon have noted elsewhere, before the developmental state paradigm redirected attention to the institutional foundations of state autonomy, a considerable number of Korean scholars tried to link South Korea's economic gains to the conservatism of the Park regime, which purportedly was matched by a conservatism in "the rural sector and portions of the emerging middle class."[83] In many ways, what we have been suggesting so far underscores the importance of returning to a similar type of analysis, albeit with several important distinctions. First, because we also conceptualize Park's political bases as mainly rural, to the extent that small farmers and a rural-based military counted in development policy making, it was mainly the *rural middle class* that mattered in Park's developmental policy making, and only secondarily the urban middle class.

Second, while most early scholars conceptualized rural social and political bases of the Park administration as somehow distinguishable from the regime itself, which was seen as empowered and institutionally isolated from society

---

[81] In *Marching Orders*, Huer notes that in 1971, "in contrast to 57 percent of the opposition, 75 percent of the DRP Assemblymembers were born either in small towns or in rural areas" (p. 125). Huer also notes that much of the recruitment into the party owed to the top-down strategies employed by the Park administration to engage rural peoples; whereas the opposition party relied more on bottom-up, voluntary membership.

[82] *The Country, the Revolution, and I*, pp. 35–36.

[83] "The State," p. 57.

through military rule, we see them as institutionally, socially, and culturally embedded in each other. This embeddedness rested not only on the organizational networks and linkages to government programs, discussed earlier, which cemented the Park administration to rural folk. It also rested in no small part on the key mediating role played by South Korean military personnel and regime leadership, who also traced their roots to rural society. Stated differently, to the extent that we see the military's hold on the state as institutionally relevant, it is primarily in terms of the military's rural origins, and its historically bounded and institutionally reinforced elective affinity with the rural middle class of farmers and other small-scale producers, not merely the fact of military rule itself.

Third and most important, while earlier claims rested on the assumption that it was merely the political conservatism of the rural sector and its traditional middle classes that was meaningful for Park's development ideology, primarily because scholars thought that this was what inspired his later efforts to tough it out with the labor movement and to accommodate the big industrial capitalists who developed export activities, we depart from this view slightly by suggesting that it was not political conservatism per se, which could have been equally shared by rural peoples and various urban classes, but specific cultural and social expectations borne primarily by rural middle classes that seemed to matter most. Rather than guaranteeing accommodation of the demands of industrial capital, as is generally assumed when the notion of political conservatism is bandied about, I argue that these cultural and social expectations brought the Park administration to impose harsh disciplinary measures on industrial and financial capitalists, and eventually on laborers too, actions that helped engender much of the Korean miracle.[84] Disciplining capitalists – not accommodating them – was the modus operandi of the culturally and socially conservative Park regime, and this disciplining ethos originated in Park's rural middle-class bases.

The distinction between political conservatism, on the one hand, and the cultural/social fabric of economic expectations transmitted by the rural middle class and supportive of a culture of discipline, on the other, is critical not just because it suggests that Park's macroeconomic policy program and its successes owed to more than just your generic brand of red-baiting political conservatism. It also gives some explanation as to why the Park administration was as restrictive with capitalists as it was with labor, at least in the first several decades of policy making, as well as why it was able to pull off these disciplinary stances. What good anticommunist red-baiter also punishes big industrialists as much (and perhaps even more in the first decade at least) as the workers? One who sees his allegiance as lying with rural small producers rather than large urban-based industrial ones, and one who contrasts the moral decay

---

[84] See, for example, Amsden, *Asia's Next Giant*; and Wade, *Governing the Market*.

of urban industrial life with privileged moral high ground of hardworking, self-disciplined, and family-centered village life. This, in many ways, was the attitude shared by Park Chung Hee, his military associates, and significant portions of the South Korean populace. As such, most of the harsh and punitive stances that the South Korean state took with capitalists and laborers during the period of industrial takeoff owed to the rural middle-class embeddedness of the Park administration, an embeddedness that produced its distinctively disciplinary character and antiurban tone.

So in what concrete ways did this peculiarly rural middle-class ethos of discipline manifest itself in macroeconomic development policy making? In addition to the general support for generating rural prosperity and increasing rural production, combined with the early efforts to marshal industrialization in the service of agricultural development, we see it – in very broad strokes at least – in the overall vision of development that Park frequently advanced. In some of his very first public speeches and documents, Park proposed a macroeconomic development model for South Korea's future that imagined a treasured world of small-scale producers. Those countries he saw as exemplary were anything but highly industrialized and urbanized. In fact, rather than the large, advanced industrial economies that many late developers typically try to emulate, what seemed to inspire Park most were small, agriculturally based economies built on the the hard labor of small, self-employed farmers such as those in Denmark. "We must put an end to the chronic poverty of our peasant population," he proclaimed in February 1962, "and devote whole natural resources to the creation of prosperous farming communities after the pattern of Denmark."[85] Denmark – which was routinely invoked in speeches and public documents of the era – appealed to Park not just because it was a modern and advanced agriculturally based economy, but also because it had achieved its success without sacrificing its reliance on small-farmer classes and their privileged position in the economy and society.

Park desperately wished to do the same in South Korea. At the time of the 1961 military coup, South Korea was close to 70 percent rural and filled with numerous small farmers who owned and cultivated land of relatively small sized plots. As Clive Hamilton noted, "The revolution in agrarian relations did not . . . have any large impact on plot size or farming technique (apart from some initial decline in investments with the withdrawal of landlord capital), and the serious problem of land fragmentation persisted."[86] In 1962, within a year of the coup, nearly half of all farmer-owned parcels still were only 1.25 acres, and 75 percent of all farms were under 2.5 acres.[87] In

[85] *Our Nation's Path*, p. 1.

[86] *Capitalist Industrialization*, p. 30.

[87] Kyung, *New Korea*, p. 145.

addition, most landholdings had been and would remain relatively small, if not centered around the family, owing to size restrictions mandated by the 1950 Land Reform Law. This situation stood in stark contrast to that in other countries that introduced land reform, including Taiwan, where landholdings were allowed to grow much larger after the initial phases of land reform. Accordingly, Park's vision was not just one of agricultural development per se, which could have occurred by allowing larger landholdings and fostering large-scale agribusiness concerns. Rather, Park envisioned an economy built around an enormous class of relatively small farmers, marginally differentiated among themselves, who could maintain traditional agricultural activities but were able to produce enough to maintain economic and social viability in a modernized economy. All this was to occur, moreover, in the context of an advanced national economy liberated from economic backwardness and graced with social and technological modernity yet neither profaned nor constrained by the weight of overindustrialization.

That Park conceived of a particular means of agricultural development as a central goal (i.e., small-farmer production), an aim which he considered to be as vital as increasing output (i.e., agricultural growth at any cost), further explains why he made such great efforts in his first years in office to introduce financing, set grain prices, and control taxation and credit policies, all with the intent of helping small-scale producers make a secure living. With these measures Park expected little in terms of export earnings, despite his public and private recognition of the importance of securing foreign exchange. What he did expect was a social and political payoff, as well as an economic one. Indeed, Park implemented these measures in order to encourage efficiency and increases in small-farmer production, basing his policies on the assumption that even small-scale farmers could, if provided the right aid and inputs, be self-sufficient and produce a respectable livelihood and lifestyle. For Park, thrifty and disciplined small-scale farmers were not merely a political constituency; nor did he regard small farmers as a predatory constituency whose principal role was to divert resources away from other activities like industrialization that could have helped the nation progress. Rather, for Park small-scale producers were the backbone of the country's overall transformation, the social, economic, political, and moral foundation on which he was to build his "miracle on the Han."[88]

Park's desire to modernize his nation while keeping small rural holdings predominant in the national economy further explains why Park worked so hard at disciplining capitalists so that they would increase their industrial exports. Export earnings were not merely a way to achieve national economic

---

[88] Park's reference to a miracle on the Han was also intended to draw a parallel between the experiences of South Korea and Germany, which achieved impressive economic development after a war shattered its economy and broke its nation in two.

independence in some aggregate sense, they also helped guarantee funds to support Park's rural development programs in general and his financing, credit, and grain price policies for small farmers in particular. Without industrial exports, there were almost no domestic sources of capital for financing rural development, especially with agricultural production in shambles after the Rhee administration's neglect. Moreover, ISI industrialists, operating financially unsound factories, saddled the economy with current account deficits and tremendous public and private debt. With industrial exports, however, Park would be able to spend a considerable amount of money on infrastructure, fertilizer production, technical inputs, and technical training, as well as to directly support farmers in the first several years of transition as technical and infrastructural inputs were implemented. And these exports had to be generated in the industrial sector, since Park's desire to keep rural landholdings relatively small, so that all agricultural families could receive the benefit of land reform in some fashion, meant that he expected few export earnings to be gained through agricultural exports. This stands in stark contrast to the situation of countries where large rural landowners provide export earnings. In the absence of agricultural exports from large or even smaller landowners, it was particularly incumbent on Park to put even greater pressure on industrial firms to export if he wanted to generate foreign exchange for rural development.

To be sure, some scholars will claim that Park's orientation to exports emerged out of his desire to generate foreign exchange to facilitate domestic industrialization, especially production of capital goods, and by so doing to decrease national dependence on manufactured imports.[89] This is a strategy that is quite common in developing countries, that makes considerable sense in the long run, and that at first glance seems quite consistent with Park's nationalist fervor. Yet those who favor this interpretation are working under the assumption that Park's development plans gave priority to industrialization in and of itself, and were built around an understanding of the forward and backward linkages generated by a carefully balanced support for production of primary and secondary goods and based on explicit openness to the political and economic priorities of domestic capitalists and their industrial laborers. This assumption seems to better fit the country's macroeconomic plans during the Rhee rather than of the Park period, however; and careful scrutiny of the timing of Park's policy decisions casts considerable doubt on this interpretation. In his first five-year plan, when Park's orientation toward exports was already evident, and even in the second plan, which built upon these priorities by committing to the development of new activities, Park was only just beginning to think about capital goods production and the other

---

[89] Hamilton, *Capitalist Industrialization*, p. 119.

traditional elements of ISI.[90] His main priority was still rural development, and in the industrial sector he was most concerned about producing goods and services, including energy and infrastructure, that would increase agricultural productivity. Both in word and deed, EOI was as much intended to support rural development as vice versa, as is generally assumed for Korea; and this commitment was clear from Park's first year at the helm.[91]

But what about the requisites of the global economy, or the economic and political dynamic associated with an emergent world system linking developed and developing countries in unequal trade and exchange? This is an argument that has frequently been advanced to explain South Korean development. Scholars such as Hagen Koo and Bruce Cumings have long suggested that Park's macroeconomic policies, especially his EOI policies, were formulated under foreign pressure, either in 1964, or later, in 1971, when labor union activity and balance of payments deficits hit a peak.[92] The argument generally given is that during this watershed period the United States wanted to reduce its direct foreign aid and subsidies to South Korea, and U.S. advisors, especially those from USAID, felt that the Korean economy needed to become more macroeconomically sound, either with respect to exports and/or competitiveness, especially when labor unrest emerged with force in the late 1960s and early 1970s.[93] Yet despite real concern about balance of payments deficits and U.S. pressure to get South Korea off the dole, it may be misleading to assume that Park's EOI policy choices owed primarily to foreign intervention or influence, or even the new opportunities presented by an increasingly globalizing economy in which cheaply produced industrial exports were in high demand in the United States and Europe.

---

[90] It is noteworthy that while most scholars will agree that export-led industrialization ultimately became the macroeconomic strategy of choice, there is little consensus on what preceded this shift, let alone why and when. Indeed, some scholars prefer to refer to the first years of the Park regime as focused "inward, [on] agriculture, and rehabilitation" (Song, *The Rise of the Korean Economy*, p. 169); while others see it as the typical first stage of ISI (see e.g., Haggard, *Pathways From the Periphery*; or Kim and Roemer [eds.], *Growth and Structural Transformation*).

[91] Vogel, *The Four Little Dragons*, pp. 51, 56.

[92] See Koo, "The Interplay of State, Social Class, and World System"; Cumings, "The Origins and Development of the Northeast Asian Political Economy"; and McCormack, "The South Korean Economy." One of those who dates the EOI shift somewhat later is Hamilton, in *Capitalist Industrialization in Korea*. See also Ogle, *South Korea*, p. 34.

[93] Some scholars (Mason et al., *The Economic and Social Modernization*, p. 47; and Koo, "The Interplay of State, Social Class, and World System," p. 169) openly argue that powerful international institutions, most specifically the Agency for International Development and the World Bank, are said to have played leading roles in prompting the shift to an export-oriented economy (see also Janelli, *Making Capitalism*, p. 72).

For one thing, the timing is slightly off. Park, after all, publicly stated his commitment to exports many times in speeches and public documents published between 1961 and 1963, before the 1964 domestic economic crisis and long before the United States renewed efforts to pressure the government to harness labor in the late 1960s.[94] For another, as Michael Keon has noted elsewhere, the United States was far from the architect of Park's macroeconomic policy, at least in its first years of formulation. If anything, "domestic, U.S., and other foreign critics were quick to point out that Park's plans were 'almost impossible – unprecedented not only in Korea but in other developing countries.' "[95] The United States, in fact, had not supported the Park administration in its early years and long opposed his agricultural orientation, especially Park's desire to marshal industrial exports in the service of small farmers' prosperity.

Even more important, while it undoubtedly is true that the global economy in the 1960s offered new scope for late industrializers like South Korea to find a market niche for their low-wage exports, the mere possibility of doing so does not necessarily insure that this will be the strategy of choice. One need only look at the Philippines in the same period of time or myriad other late industrializers in the 1960s and 1970s, including Turkey and the whole of Latin America, to see that it is not merely a changing global opportunity structure that explains why a country selects a certain development strategy. Domestic political and economic conditions will also factor into government decision making. And in these regards, what made the South Korean case exceptional, again, was Park's rural middle-class orientation. Indeed, to the extent that his development vision prioritized rural over urban populations, with agricultural activities and lifestyles serving as the heart of the country's economy and culture, there were internal limits to ISI that militated against developing it as a national strategy. These limits had to do primarily with the truncated domestic market for industrial goods produced domestically, a constraint which in turn motivated Park to shift his preferences from ISI to EOI in the mid-1960s.

After pursuing a modified form of ISI during the first five years of his administration, it became evident to Park that low-wage industrial workers were hardly in a position to jack up domestic consumption of these ISI goods that they were producing, or at least sufficiently to fuel further production and gains

---

[94] See Supreme Council for National Reconstruction, *Military Revolution in Korea*, p. 39; Park, *The Country, the Revolution, and I*, p. 40; and Park, *Rebuilding a Nation*, p. 13. In *Man and Society*, Kim also identifies the government's macroeconomic commitment to exporting consumer goods as being evident as early as 1962 (p. 73); and as noted earlier, in *The Four Little Dragons*, Vogel argues that "Park in 1961 immediately began to promote industrial production for export" (p. 51).

[95] *Korean Phoenix*, p. 69.

in economics of scale. This was especially so given that the lifestyles, consumption patterns, and income constraints of the still troubled rural sector made them an even less likely market for these goods, especially in the mid-1960s after only a few years of directed agricultural investment. The only way to increase domestic consumption under these conditions would have been to raise urban wages, a policy that would have undermined Park's initial rural orientation considerably, especially his desire to reduce the stark differences between rural and urban folk. Accordingly, both political and domestic economic prerogatives and constraints pushed Park to redirect industrial production toward exports. This way urban labor could stay employed, agricultural producers in turn would have a domestic market for their products, and the country would generate foreign exchange that could be funneled back into agriculture, keeping the whole cycle moving. The result, Park hoped, would be an articulation of agricultural and industrial development that would engender balanced economic growth and overall economic prosperity.

The favorable global environment made this whole integrated framework both possible and highly successful, at least to the extent that it was the match between these domestic and global circumstances that brought such great gains without pains. But if not for the commitment to rural areas and agricultural development in the first place, we probably would not have seen these policies. There would have been much less incentive to export industrial manufactures and much greater incentive to prioritize an integrated program of urban-based industrial production and consumption as the means for achieving national prosperity.

Enter Discipline

Park's decision to eschew the Fordist strategy of a self-sustaining, domestic-oriented cycle of industrial production and consumption and instead build agricultural prosperity through a system of industrial exports, built on and reinforced South Korea's low-wage policy for industrial workers. In that sense as well, the weight of a changed global economy was incorporated in the *success* of this strategy – even if in itself it cannot explain the choice of the strategy in the first place. But Park's support for a development policy geared toward the export – as opposed to domestic consumption – of industrial goods owed as much to his own elective affinities with modest rural farm folk and their generally negative view of industry, urban lifestyles, and conspicuous consumption of unnecessary luxury goods. From the vantage point of the small farmer (and Park too), many of the problems of rural underdevelopment in South Korea owed to the lavish, improvident, and uncontrolled consumption of greedy capitalists, not just the ISI industrialists of the Rhee period, but also big bankers and numerous rural-based moneylenders whose pockets grew fat while their countrymen starved and the country suffered. Controlling the practices of these two types of capitalists, eliminating those actions deemed particularly egregious, and bringing greater resources directly to the state for distribution to farmers or other so-called worthy small-scale entrepreneurs with the moral fortitude to rebuild the economy were principal objectives of the new military junta. And in achieving these microeconomic aims, Park relied directly on yet another aspect of rural farm life – a disciplinary ethos – to both justify and foster these measures.

Park's commitment to disciplining capitalists was clear almost from the beginning of his administration. One of the first and most controversial of his measures after the military coup was the arrest of Korea's leading businessmen and bankers and the announcement of plans to permanently confiscate their assets. While their assets were frozen under the Park government, a deal was struck whereby criminal charges would be dropped if the businessmen agreed to build new factories and donate them to the state.[96] Early on, Park also introduced rigid new constraints on banks and announced a greater centralization of government control over finance, including interest rates and investment decisions. This meant that the government made decisions about who received credit and the terms under which it would be allocated, a power that Park later used "to mobilize businessmen for major economic programs such as export promotion . . . [as well as to] maintain control over, and cooperation from, the business community."[97] Third, within months of taking office, Park established restrictions on who could participate in certain economic activities, stipulating that exports of goods over five thousand dollars would be the minimum requirement for registry as a foreign trader.[98]

Again, many scholars are prone to argue that these and other successful macroeconomic measures employed by the South Korean government owed to technical training, skill, sound economic policy advice, and/or developmental intuition on the part of Park and his allies. And in economic-theoretical terms, some of Park's policies were textbook examples of how to curtail rent seeking, generate savings, build an export sector, and stimulate overall macroeconomic development. What their accounts fail to note, however, is that Park's decision to implement these policies and, equally important, his government's willingness and political capacity to do so, owed to his political bases among rural small producers. After all, it was small farmers perhaps more than anyone who had first cultivated a vitriolic hatred for the "usurious class" of bankers and moneylenders, branded as earning their livelihood by speculating on agricultural prices, and for urban-based ISI manufacturers, seen as squandering scarce foreign exchange on their own conspicuous consumption or on the production and/or importation of luxury items. Park carried through on these sentiments

---

[96] Hamilton, *Capitalist Industrialization*, p. 35.
[97] Mason et al., *The Economic and Social Modernization*, p. 336.
[98] Hamilton, *Capitalist Industrialization*, p. 36.

by introducing policies that would fundamentally eliminate these activities, not only through "simple prohibition," as Clive Hamilton asserts, "but also by the series of big devaluations of the won which followed."[99]

Park, like many rural residents, had little confidence in the bankers and industrialists who had controlled big amounts of capital during the Rhee period. In his classic study of South Korea in the 1960s period, Edward Mason was among the many to recognize that Park shared with much of the rural populace the view that "rich businessmen and moneylenders were holding large cash balances that they would exchange for goods at the first sign of rising prices," and thus they needed to be restricted or controlled because, when left to their own devices, they only would repeat the mistakes of the past.[100] As the son of a desperately poor farmer himself, Park knew only too well that most farmers barely surpassed subsistence, because of debts they owed to rural moneylenders, and he was genuinely proud to commit himself to their elimination so as to destroy the middlemen who prevented small rural producers from accumulating capital and reinvesting in their own activities.[101] One of the aims of government, Park thought, was to create new institutions that provide financial resources to rural farmers without regard for profit, or even the market.[102] Combined with strict discipline of the usurious class of capitalists who squandered the nation's scarce resources, these measures were intended to set South Korea on a path of sound and socially just economic growth. As such, it is not surprising that among the factors that economists such as Alice Amsden cite as accounting for South Korea's economic success, and that differentiates this country from almost all Latin American late developers, is the remarkable degree of government control over the banking sector.

Park's antagonism toward speculators and those whom he considered to be overprivileged big capitalists, especially those who had lived lavishly during the Rhee administration, seemed to have been grounded in Park's appreciation of scale or, better said, a middle-class antagonism toward the excesses of size. From early on, for example, Park used banking policy and other carrot-and-stick measures to limit the proliferation of large industrial enterprises, encouraging small-scale development in industry to match that of agriculture. And in the first documents of the military government, as well as the

---

[99] Ibid.

[100] *The Economic and Social Modernization*, p. 329.

[101] Park noted this again and again in public documents, using numerous opportunities to express repulsion of rural moneylenders. See, for example, *Profile of President Park Chung Hee*, published by the Ministry of Public Education, January 1966, especially pp. 50–52.

[102] As Mason et al. have noted, Park "resisted repeated advice (mainly foreign) to let interest rates and competition among independent financial institutions determine the allocation of such credit," preferring instead to establish his own criteria for supporting small-scale production. See *The Economic and Social Modernization*, p. 336.

first five-year plan of his elected administration when he proposed new policies for industrial development and industrial export, Park always justified his policies by framing them in the context of what they would accomplish for medium and small-scale enterprises.[103] With respect to financing industrial development, moreover, he "created a new bank to serve small industry and commerce," concerning himself more with "help[ing] the lower income groups expand their production and income" than with directly facilitating economies of scale for big industrial ventures.[104] As such, in his developmental vision, Park preferred petit bourgeois industrial activities, consistent with a small-scale, middle-class outlook more generally, not big enterprises that would sustain big capitalists who might again reproduce the plundering and inequality of the Rhee regime.[105]

Park's sense that big capitalists could not be trusted with charting the course of the country's economic future also manifested itself in the introduction of multiple measures and policies intended to actively discipline industrialists and guide their economic behavior. As Alice Amsden has demonstrated, imposing discipline on capitalists was the modus operandi of the South Korean economic miracle:

> No matter how well-connected they are politically, all subsidy recipients in Korea have been subject to four blanket controls imposed by the government. First, all firms have had to export sooner or later, in larger or smaller quantities. Minimal export targets have been set even for unpromising industries. . . . Exports have provided the Korean government with a transparent measure of the progress of those in receipt of subsidy. . . . Second, all commercial banks were until recently owned by the government, and all financial institutions continue to operate under government control. This has discouraged speculation on the part of the recipients of cheap credit. Third, discipline has been imposed on "market-dominating enterprises," through annually negotiated price controls, in the name of curbing monopoly power. . . . Fourth, investors have been subject to controls on capital flight, or the remittance of liquid capital overseas.[106]

Although Amsden was writing from the vantage point of the late 1980s, the disciplining of capitalists, especially applied to those involved in generating exports, had been evident from almost the beginning of Park's ascent to office. In March 1962 Park introduced the Export Promotion Law, which "limited the eligibility for the use of Korean foreign exchange to those who exported at least

[103] Park, *The Road*, pp. 92–93.
[104] Mason et al., *The Economic and Social Modernization*, p. 329.
[105] Supreme Council for National Reconstruction, *Military Revolution in Korea*, p. 39.
[106] *Asia's Next Giant*, p. 22.

$10,000 worth of goods, and the existing External Trade Law was revised so as to strip any trader failing to sell the legal minimum of his qualification."[107] The trend continued throughout his administration, with new carrot-and-stick measures imposing discipline and allocating rewards in accordance with performance. By 1967, the government resorted to "the more frequent use of export monopoly rights offered to a restricted number of traders who had exported new products to new markets. Exporters of outstanding achievement were exempt from mortgages against special as well as general customs duties, free from extraordinary tax investigations, and given priority in the allocation of foreign exchanges for marketing activities."[108] Note that capitalists who yielded to the state's disciplinary measures were protected and privileged, a quid pro quo which underscores the fact that state discipline, not market discipline, was the operative concept. Under Park, industrial capitalists in South Korea were protected by import quotas, special low-interest financing, and a wide variety of other measures generally used to protect and encourage infant industries, just as occurred in most other developing countries, including the two Latin American nations we will discuss later. But the essential difference was that in South Korea these rewards were contingent on industrialists' acquiescence to the disciplinary hand of the state, and this hand was anything but invisible.

It is telling that Park's disciplinary ire, at least in the initial years, was primarily directed against big capitalists (including chaebols), bankers, and other big moneymakers, and not against the urban working class or industrial laborers. This could be partially explained by the fact that many of those who found themselves in this class during the early 1960s were primarily rural people who had migrated to the city looking for work because of increasing rural unemployment and destitution. Their modest wages already imposed a form of consumption discipline and, furthermore, Park worked under the assumption that most rural folk – like himself – were already highly self-disciplined. To make this point is not to say that Park was a true friend to the urban working class or that he did not eventually direct his repressive hand against them. Even in the 1960s, he spearheaded the purging of all communist membership in labor unions, and he showed little tolerance for any pro–North Korea sentiment among urban workers. But by and large, labor organizations were not repressed with the same disciplinary hand used with capitalists in the first decade of his administration; that came later, after 1971. Moreover, for someone who would soon cultivate the image of unwavering repression of labor, Park was surprisingly open in his public speeches to the plight of the urban poor and the working class. If he had any other targets for his disciplinary actions, it was usually the white-collar, upwardly mobile urban middle classes,

---

[107] Kim, "Recent Trends in the Government's Management of the Economy, p. 271.
[108] Ibid., p. 272.

especially professionals and those with discretionary income directly hit by his restrictions on the import of consumer goods.[109]

This view of the early Park administration's support for rural folk, the urban poor, and the independent working class shared much in common with the view of semipopulist Latin American countries during the initial stages of industrialization, a point that casts doubt on the mounting claims these days, from neoliberal economists and social scientists, that populist rhetorics and policies are always the enemy of sound economic development. The key distinction between South Korea and Latin America, however, a difference to which we will return again in our discussion of Argentina and Mexico in the next chapters, was that in South Korea this was a rural-based populism, built first and foremost around a privileged cultural, political, and economic place for small farmers in the national economy. While urban working-class populism generally builds on a strong dose of commitment to class struggle, or opposition to all capitalist accumulation, small-farmer populism is not necessarily anti-accumulation or anticapitalist per se, especially in a highly charged geopolitical context of anticommunism as was the case in South Korea. Small-farmer populism, at least in this case, was predicated on an understanding of the cultural and economic superiority of small-scale, petit bourgeois production where unnecessary speculation on others' productive activities or losses is eliminated and where manageable scale and size – not to mention family-based production – will produce the most efficient use of resources and generate the most equitable distribution of output. In South Korea small-scale rural producers were assumed by their very size and nature to be hardworking and disciplined enough to effect these outcomes, and to restrict their consumption as well, so that conspicuous living would be avoided, savings multiplied, and the economy propelled on a path toward growth rather than stagnation. As such, it was as small capitalists, or the "old" middle classes if you will, that rural populists were imagining as their country's economic future. And it was this vision writ large, with a heavy dose of industrial disciplining and direct control over bankers to generate export earnings to fuel this rural populist vision, that became the blueprint for South Korea's successful development.

The Languages of Development: Discipline, Austerity, Thrift

Small-farmer populists may have trusted few but themselves to exercise self-discipline, but in these regards Park was a perfect leader, democratically elected or not. Heavy-handed state-imposed discipline served as the watchword of the

[109] Hamilton, *Capitalist Industrialization* (p. 122), notes that "restrictions on imports of consumer goods mostly affected urban professionals and moneyed classes since it was they who could afford them."

Park administration. It was applied to big capitalists and bankers with a public volition and moral authority that marked the new South Korean government as entirely different from its immediate predecessors. As one observer put it, Park was "reputed to be a strict disciplinarian who would close down a business if it did not measure up, or if it tried to evade specifications set down by the government."[110] Yet as one might have expected given his rural middle-class and military roots, Park heralded a disciplinary ethos as the moral compass for guiding the entire nation's behavior, not just capitalists but all citizens, both inside and outside the government. As a primer for action, self-discipline was expected of everyone, even bureaucrats; those who failed in this regard could expect to be disciplined directly by the state. In addition to imposing performance standards on capitalists, then, the "raison d'être of most of the bureaucratic organizations of the state," according to Timothy Lim, was "based on explicit performance goals: failure to meet these goals meant, at least for the civil servants appointed to head each bureau, complete loss of power and prestige."[111] Park's disciplinary hand with the bureaucracy, many of whom were his own appointees, was further seen in the introduction of an enforced "rotation system" intended to help reduce lax behavior and corruption among public officials.[112] The disciplinary ethos of the Park administration also was seen in the numerous public speeches and government documents where the notion of discipline was repeated and reinforced. It was not uncommon, for example, to hear Park plead for the "self-discipline of an irresponsible press," or the "establishment of official discipline" in his calls to the nation and in his characterization of the goals of his administration.[113]

Undoubtedly, much of Park's obsession with self-discipline and his coercive crafting of a disciplinary ethos also was fueled by his own military experience and the preponderance of military personnel in the government and among his political allies. Like military leaders everywhere, the South Korean military leadership worked hard to install a cult of discipline in its ranks. Yet unlike many other countries, South Korea's history and its geopolitical location insured that the military had an inordinate and long-standing presence in the life and political culture of the nation: first, during the period of Japanese colonial rule and World War II, second, during the postwar period of U.S. military occupation, and third, during and following the Korean War. As Kyong-dong

---

[110] Ogle, *South Korea*, p. 31.

[111] "The Developmental State," p. 25. For further discussion of Park's actions vis-à-vis the bureaucracy, see Bark and Lee, "Bureaucratic Elite and Development Orientations."

[112] Although public documents justified the rotation system as "prevent[ing] boredom and stagnancy in office," these in turn were frequently seen as encouraging and/or facilitating rent seeking (i.e., corruption). See Supreme Council for National Reconstruction, *Military Revolution in Korea*, p. 30.

[113] Ibid., *Revolution's First Two Months' Achievements*, pp. 2–3.

Kim argues, the South Korean people had long experienced the weight of discipline, beginning in the colonial period when a

> militaristic discipline [was] inculcated from early in life starting in schools. This has continued through the days of war and afterwards. Ever since the truce was signed in 1953, Korea has been in a state of quasi-war without battle, at least officially. To meet the challenge of possible invasion from the North, youths have been subjected to military or quasi-military training in school, and every able young man has to serve in the military in one form or another. The reserve corps is well maintained, subject to regular roll call and drills, until the man reaches the age of 50. By law, the government conducts civil defense drills every month.[114]

Clearly Park's disciplinary ethos was consistent with the military foundations of his government and the overall militarization of South Korean society and its state, not just its rural middle-class origins and embeddedness. Still, it is also important to recognize that the disciplinary ethos Park cultivated, and from which he derived much of his policy orientation, was part and parcel of a larger code of "business morals and economic ethics" that he personally held, and which he characteristically associated with middle classes in general and small farmers in particular.[115] From Park's vantage point, two key goals for both the nation and its individual peoples were "independence and self-sustainment," ideals that have long been identified with self-employment and small-scale production.[116] Discipline, moreover, was of value insofar as it helped citizens attain these ideals, in no small measure by encouraging hard work, sustaining efficiency, and contributing to positive economic outcomes for individuals and the nation. Sound national ethics and the nation's economic future, Park liked to point out in speeches, had to be built on a code of conduct of "diligence, savings, and thrift" in which self-discipline was the foundation of action.[117]

In championing these values of discipline and independence, Park frequently cited the "natural" tendencies of small farmers, whose lifestyle he felt served as a model for behavior because it contrasted with the luxury, vanity, overconsumption, and waste of bureaucrats and businessmen.[118] And with the rural

---

[114] "The Distinctive Features of South Korean Development," p. 211.

[115] Shik (ed.), *Major Speeches*, p. 152.

[116] Choue, *The Way to Korea's Prosperity*, p. 76.

[117] Ministry of Public Education, *Profile of President Park Chung Hee*, p. 62.

[118] Keon, *Korean Phoenix*, p. 66. In one of his speeches, Park criticized the Rhee administration's dependence on foreign aid, which he saw as encouraging an emphasis on consumer goods. In lambasting that path, he cried that "it breaks our hearts to think that tens of millions

experience in mind, he further emphasized the value of a simple and austere life, or the "spirit of austerity" as he sometimes called it,[119] where saving was more important than luxury or conspicuous consumption. If the people carried through on the values of thrift and austerity, Park declared, the nation would gain; and hard work, savings, and discipline were the key. "In order to build an affluent society, devoid of corruption and poverty, where honest, diligent, and sincere citizens constitute its nucleus," he said in 1967, "I hope you each will work harder, be faithful to your assignment, improve your environment, beginning with even seemingly trifling matters, and respect the morals and order of our community life."[120]

Of course, Park did not leave the inculcation of a disciplinary ethos to chance, despite the fact that he generally assumed this orientation to be present among a large portion of the population already. To further insure the assimilation and institutionalization of the values of savings and thrift, Park initiated a national austerity campaign, but directed primarily at cities, because he assumed that the urban population most lacked these essential values.[121] Moreover, Park introduced several new macroeconomic measures, including a dramatic change in interest rates, to help motivate saving. By 1965 he had mandated markedly higher interest rates on time deposits, pushing them from 15 percent to 30 percent in 1965, so that within three months the level of time and savings deposits had increased by 50 percent, and over the next four years at a compound rate of more than 100 percent.[122] This unique combination of disciplinary "public policy and . . . self-imposed standards of austerity" paid off, producing increases in the size of Korea's financial system which were considered by most economists to be unparalleled in recent world experience.[123]

Some may be quick to remark that the notions of discipline, austerity, and thrift which Park invoked are almost identical to the concepts noted and analyzed by German historical sociologist Max Weber in his seminal study of

---

of dollars are spent . . . for luxury and consumption. . . . The problem goes far more deeply into politics, economics, culture, and overall social facets [*sic*]; encouraging and creating laziness, corruption, vanity, and luxury" (Park, *The Country, the Revolution, and I*, p. 37).

[119] Choue, *The Way to Korea's Prosperity*, p. 76.

[120] Shik (ed.), *Major Speeches*, p. 144.

[121] The urban-directed austerity campaign dedicated itself to increased savings – mainly of rice, electric power, and potable water – and to decreased consumption, which would entail "rejecting imported luxuries, restraining luxurious entertainment, wearing simple clothes, simplifying the formalities in wedding and other celebrations, etc. [for the purpose of] making both ends meet in daily life" (Supreme Council for National Reconstruction, *Military Revolution in Korea*, p. 94).

[122] Mason et al., *The Economic and Social Modernization*, p. 334.

[123] Ibid., p. 290.

the impact of religion on capitalist development, aptly titled *The Protestant Ethic and the Spirit of Capitalism*. And in what could be more than coincidence, in looking for other signposts early in his administration, Park actually identified postwar Germany as a premier example of a highly disciplined nation whose "unflinching fighting spirit inspired the people to renew their determination to establish economic self-support," and where diligence, perseverance, and austerity paid off.[124] But Park was no Calvinist, despite the fact that some scholars have called him "puritanical";[125] and while he often invoked a quasi-religious emphasis on spirit, it was generally the spirit of labor or the spirit of hard work or the spirit of independence, not capitalism per se, that he had in mind. As such, it is important to underscore that the disciplinary ethos so central to Park's developmental vision was not based on Protestant religion, or, as Weber suggested, on the open embrace of capitalism and its free market ethos, but on an appreciation of village-based, small-scale craft production and farming, and the set of values that sustained and made this type of work productive.

To be sure, it is possible to consider that this behavior also reflects the Confucian ethic of "personal cultivation, self-improvement, and spiritual and psychological discipline of the self."[126] South Korea, after all, was a Confucian nation, and this no doubt played a role in the population's accommodation to Park's disciplinary rhetoric and actions. But it is important to remember that despite his frequent references to his country's history and culture, Park himself never conceptualized his code of conduct as Confucian or neo-Confucian, although he had a deep grounding in Confucianism, having studied and taught it before military service. In fact, scholars have noted that Park publicly identified himself as opposed to "decadent confucian [sic] ideas and customs," especially those which encouraged hedonism and conspicuous consumption;[127] and he is on record as emphasizing what he called the "natural" origins of morals and conduct.[128] Moreover, while Park underscored what he considered an "Eastern" reverence for nature, he insisted that "in the final analysis . . . the question of how better to solve our problems and how effectively to accomplish the task of regenerating our nation depends to a large extent on whether or not we are capable of creating a new culture of an even superior quality" which uses daily life as its starting point.[129] For Park, farming and "the long hours of hard

---

[124] Ministry of Public Education, *Profile of President Park Chung Hee*, p. 60.

[125] Haggard and Moon, "The State," p. 65.

[126] Sung, *The Rise of the Korean Economy*, p. 51.

[127] Lovell, "The Military and Politics in Postwar Korea," p. 175.

[128] Supreme Council for National Reconstruction, *Revolution's First Two Months' Achievements*, p. 2.

[129] Park, *Korea Reborn*, pp. 31–32.

work before any results can be seen" served as both metaphor and inspiration for this new culture.[130] As Park put it:

> The traditional wisdom garnered throughout previous generations is best preserved by the farmers. . . . The spirit of diligence, self-help, and cooperation, for example, was neither imitated from other countries nor imported from the city. They are native virtues that the Korean people, agrarian in their tradition, have long cherished and practiced. Farming was not, and still is not, possible without hard work and diligence, self-help, and cooperation. Nature, being just and unerring, seldom rewards those who do not work patiently. The qualities of diligence, self-help, and cooperation have been part of the ethics of Korean farmers for a long time, and must continue to be so.[131]

Park's philosophy, in short, was a unique mix of materialism and pragmatism, and these ideals seemed as relevant as any religious ones in sustaining his great spiritualist commitment to discipline and austerity. If the South Korean people shared anything ideologically in common with Max Weber's early European Protestants, moreover, it was the small-farmer economy and the cultural and social experience of small-scale agricultural production, in which Nature (as opposed to God) sternly metes out rewards and punishments. Notably, this experience and ethos seems to closely replicate that which occurred in North America (a case that Weber also had in mind when he wrote *The Protestant Ethic*), where small farmers more than isolated urban merchants drove the nation's economic, social, and political developments. Accordingly, it may be worth revising Weber, and considering that the rural experience and the cultural discourse and practice of small farmers and other small-scale rural producers, not a Calvinistic commitment to the afterlife, is what gives rise to the disciplinary repertoire of values which we have identified as reflective of a rural middle-class ethos of self-discipline, thrift, and austerity.

Once we accept that small-scale rural production lays the infrastructural foundation for discipline and development, we actually can see similarities between several "early" developers in Europe and a handful of "late" developers of East Asia, especially South Korea, a point alluded to in our introduction and to which we return in Chapter 6. The most successful cases in both developmental contexts, I suggest, shared a similar collection of rural-based values that led to a transformation from an agrarian economy to a more industrialized one, and to similarly remarkable gains in the standard of living. Of course, in South Korea the transformation occurred in a fraction of the time that it took in Europe, a state of affairs which generally encourages scholars to overlook the commonalities between the two periods or contexts, and to identify

---

[130] Ibid., p. 74.
[131] Ibid., p. 76.

late development as a fundamentally distinct process. Moreover, in contrast to most "early" developers, in South Korea the state was an active instigator of the process. But this does not mean that the state's actions were based on a different logic. Park and many of the military elite who formed the core personnel of the state embodied the values of small-farmer populism, and Park himself used the power of the state and the military to nurture and promote this ethos. As such, while a strong role for the state differentiates the "late" and "early" developmental contexts, the cultural and class dynamics that underlay the actions of state personnel were not that different. Under Park's watchful eye and strong hand, South Korea was poised to follow a small-farmer, populist path to modernity. The result was an economy built around industrial exports produced by a highly disciplined class of capitalists morally regulated in the service of an economic modernization that privileged the values and activities of small farmers.

From Idealized Vision to Realist Practice

Park's developmental vision and disciplinary philosophy, despite its unorthodox and seemingly backward-looking romanticization of small farmers, brought considerable gains to South Korea. As early as 1966, after only five years in office, Park would announce that "the rate of domestic savings exceeded 10% of GNP for the first time in the history of the republic," an achievement attributed to "the increase in income, the successful application of the anti-inflationary policies of the government, the increase in the rate of interest, and public programs for increased savings."[132] Control of the banking sector and the capacity to direct financing into targeted activities also helped considerably. As a result, from 1962 to 1972 the average annual rate of GNP growth was 9 percent; per capita income rose from $75 to $255; the volume of exports saw a thirty-fold growth from $55 million to $1.624 billion; and the import/export ratio went from 8/1 to 3/2.[133]

All was not perfect, however. While industrial exports rose dramatically, and employment in industry began to rise enough to absorb substantial portions of surplus urban and rural labor, economic and social advances in the countryside remained relatively circumscribed, despite desperate efforts to promote them. There were some unmitigated successes, to be sure, as evidenced by the thirteen-fold increase in farm income between 1962 and 1965.[134] Yet despite these gains, rural conditions started to deteriorate after 1965 (see Table 1). Also, Park's political support in urban areas was understandably precarious, an

---

[132] Office of Planning and Coordination, *Evaluation of the First Year Program (1967), The Second Five-Year Economic Development Plan*, p. 26.
[133] Lee, "The Politics of Democratic Experiment," pp. 30–31.
[134] Ho and Hee, "The Economic Plight of Korean Farmers," p. 15.

Table 1. *Income of Farm Household and Salary and Wage Earner's Household, South Korea*

| | Income of Farm Household (per Household) | | | | Salary and Wage Earners (per Household) | | | | |
| | Nominal Income | | Real Income | | Nominal Income | | Real Income | | |
Years	Amount	Index	Amount A	Index	Amount	Index	Amount B	Index	A/B × 100
1961	67,885	27.3	206,337	80.7	96,600	25.3	203,617	77.0	70.3
1963	93,179	36.4	234,708	91.8	80,160	21.0	201,914	53.0	116.2
1964	125,692	49.1	244,537	95.6	97,300	25.5	166,610	43.7	129.3
1965	112,301	43.9	192,125	75.1	112,560	29.5	192,740	59.6	99.7
1966	130,176	50.9	199,046	77.8	161,520	42.4	246,972	64.8	80.6
1967	149,470	58.4	206,165	80.6	248,640	65.2	342,951	90.0	60.1
1968	178,959	70.0	222,033	86.8	285,960	75.0	354,789	93.1	62.6
1969	217,874	85.2	245,630	96.0	333,600	87.5	376,099	98.7	65.3
1970	255,804	100.0	255,804	100.0	381,240	100.0	381,240	100.0	67.1
1971	356,382	138.3	317,348	124.1	451,920	118.5	402,422	105.6	78.9
1972	429,394	167.9	341,874	133.6	571,400	135.7	411,975	108.1	83.0
1973	480,711	187.9	371,205	145.1	550,200	144.3	424,865	111.4	87.4
1974	674,500	163.7	421,299	164.7	644,520	169.1	402,573	105.6	104.7
1975	872,933	341.3	431,718	168.8	859,320	225.4	424,985	111.5	101.6
1976	1,156,254	452.0	499,246	195.2	1,151,800	302.1	497,306	130.4	100.4

Note: Amount: in won; index: 1970 = 100; deflated by index number of Seoul consumer prices.

Sources: Report on the Results of Farm Household Economy Survey, Annual Report on the Family Income and Expenditure Survey. Adapted from Kyong-dong Kim, *Man and Society in Korea's Economic Growth: Sociological Studies* (Seoul: National University Press, 1979), p. 155.

electoral crisis situation made worse when deteriorating economic conditions threatened to limit political support from rural populations too. In the 1963 presidential election, for example, only 30.2 percent of Seoul's residents voted for Park while 65.1 percent supported his opponent Yun, and in the country-side the latter polled 45.1 percent to Park's 46.7 percent.[135] Eventually, by the late 1960s, Park was able to recoup much of his political support from rural populations; but for the better part of the decade he faced relatively slow economic growth in the countryside, a condition that troubled him and his po-litical allies. Moreover, during this period the country's cities, especially Seoul, began to grow and prosper in relation to the countryside, mainly through slow but steady industrialization but also through continued rural-urban migration, such that by the end of the decade the agricultural terms of trade had moved sharply against the country and in favor of cities.

So why did a regime that so ardently heralded rural development have so many problems sustaining rapid rural growth and prosperity; and why after less than a decade in office did cities seem to be doing more to carry Park's econ-omy forward than his small farmers? This state of affairs is rather paradoxical given our claim that Park's administration was antiurban and that his main constituency lay in rural areas among small farmers, as these populations were perhaps most hurt by these deteriorating conditions. Why would a regime that relied for its support on rural populations allow that base to be threatened by questionable economic advances in the countryside and/or overshadowed by rapid industrialization and greater prosperity in the cities? Some would answer this question with unabashed cynicism, claiming that Park's discursive orien-tation to the rural masses in general, and small farmers in particular, was never anything but a sham. To many observers from a wide variety of theoretical and disciplinary perspectives – ranging from Clive Hamilton to Michael Hsiao – problems in the rural economy throughout the 1960s are merely further evi-dence of Park's industrial biases and his orientation toward big capitalists, if not an indicator of his wholesale abandonment of rural priorities. For them, the combination of rural deterioration and urban prosperity under Park was not a paradox at all. As Larry Burmeister, put it, Park was quick in "reneging on promises to implement an 'agriculture first' policy,"[136] mainly because his commitment was no more than skin deep. And as further evidence of Park's shallow – if not patently disingenuous – commitment to rural areas, Burmeister points to the deteriorating terms of trade between city and countryside, a sit-uation which owed in no small part to the fact that the government kept rural grain prices "artificially low."[137]

---

[135] Kim, *The Politics of Military Revolution*, p. 122 (Table 9).
[136] *Research, Realpolitik, and Development in Korea*, p. 42.
[137] Those who take this position include Hamilton, *Capitalist Industrialization*, pp. 41–43; and Cho and Kim, "Major Economic Policies of the Park Administration," p. 23.

It is true that the government-set grain prices offered Korean farmers for their products were capped during most of the 1960s, especially in comparison to urban wages and urban prices, thereby contributing to the unequal terms of trade. It also is true that these pricing policies benefited both urban workers and urban capitalists, since they kept down food costs for urban consumers. A limit on food prices not only lowered consumption costs of urban laborers, it also meant urban wages did not need to rise, and therefore businesses were more likely to generate profits. Still, a closer look at the broad range of Park's rural policies, as well as at his price-setting system, suggests that things were not so clear cut. At minimum, there could be several interpretations of the meaning and origins of low grain prices.

For one thing, despite the fact that Park kept grain prices low in comparison to urban prices, during his first decade in office he still devoted a substantial portion of his resources and energies to developing rural infrastructure; and he was fairly well regarded for these efforts. Brandt noted that during the Park administration, "any largess from above [i.e., Seoul] in such forms as cheap, subsidized chemical fertilizer, school construction, or agricultural credit . . . [was] of course welcomed."[138] During this time, the government spent considerable money in agricultural research and extension, developing and distributing improved seeds of various crops (rice, barley, soybean, and corn); disseminating improved fertilizer; teaching new farming techniques; and distributing water pumps, power sprayers, and dusters together with hand-driven equipment such as deep plows and hand pumps.[139] Although the agricultural inputs were never enough to fully turn conditions around in the countryside, farmers did not necessarily see Park as abandoning their cause. Moreover, in the context of Park's obvious political commitment to farmers – and their clear recognition of it – declining prices relative to urban wages were hardly a major problem for rural producers. Their principal concern, at least in the early years, remained credits, subsidies, and infrastructure, and Park's record on all these inputs remained relatively good.

Second, declining agricultural terms of trade do not necessarily translate into declining rural conditions; and this was true in South Korea, at least initially. For most of the 1960s, "farm income was made up not only of agricultural income, but also of side business income and non-business income."[140] The fact that most farmers were also involved in other forms of income generation, rural and sometimes even urban (including working in factories), meant that their livelihoods did not depend only on grain-pricing policy. This situation made Park's grain-pricing policy much less noxious than is generally assumed. The fact that small rural producers frequently were also involved in various

---

[138] Brandt, *A Korean Village Between Farm and Sea*, p. 13.
[139] Ban et al., *Rural Development*, p. 170.
[140] Ho and Hee, "The Economic Plight of Korean Farmers," p. 16.

other economic activities besides farming also sheds light on the rural class structure of South Korea at this time, and the ways this helped further sustain – rather than undermine – Park's rural middle-class embeddedness. Specifically, given the history of land reform, which drove many rural capitalists and their middlemen servicers out of the countryside, there was not always a clear differentiation between rural folk who were farm producers and those involved in farm-related trade or services. Remember that one of Park's key objectives was to actually eliminate speculative middlemen; and in many ways, his efforts to introduce the arm of the state into rural middleman types of activities (credit, marketing, transport) helped him achieve this objective. As such, without a well-developed class of merchant elite who would take a different position on grain-pricing policy than farmers, because their capacities to sell services were at stake, the Park government continued its grain-pricing policies with little controversy. This also meant that Park could count on relative unity within otherwise potentially competing factions of rural middle class, if not a great degree of consensus over agricultural policy in particular. Both situations reinforced the Park administration's rural middle-class embeddedness in these early years.

Third, and perhaps most important, declining agricultural terms of trade did not mean declining prices for agricultural goods *relative to the past*, which was what seemed to matter most to Park's rural constituency. As Clive Hamilton notes, before Park came to power "the government's purchase prices for rice were much lower than the estimated costs of production, but as the share of government in the harvest rose in the sixties it was necessary to raise the prices above production costs."[141] Stated differently, while Park's predecessor had set prices so low that they did not even meet production costs, Park actually raised the price offered farmers to a level that exceeded their production costs, something that most small farmers appreciated because they benefited directly by receiving more disposable income. This is even clearer if we look more closely at the agricultural terms of trade (in which a rise would result in increasing income in the agricultural sector), which catapulted from 71 and 70 in 1961 and 1962 respectively to 98 and 92 in 1963 and 1964. In short, conditions in rural areas were not as bad as is generally suggested, and on some counts there were improvements, especially in comparison to the immediate past under Rhee. In fact, even with the so-called squeezing of agriculture, during the 1960s the agricultural sector grew at an annual average rate of 4.5%.[142]

All this means that despite their imbalance with respect to urban prices, Park's agricultural pricing policies should not automatically be taken as evidence of rural neglect and urban bias, nor should they automatically be

[141] *Capitalist Industrialization*, p. 41.
[142] Ban et al., *Rural Development*, p. 178.

interpreted as a repudiation of his rural political bases. Many rural farmers felt relatively advantaged by Park's policies, and they indeed were, with respect to the past, with respect to agricultural production costs, and with respect to agricultural growth. It was just that the government-set price was still lower than the market price, a measure that if anything fueled Park's final commitment to disciplining small farmers and other key economic protagonists.

This is not to say that Park's agricultural pricing policy was without flaw. In the years after 1964 the agricultural terms of trade worsened dramatically, falling from an index of 83 in 1965 down to 78 in 1968 before moving back up to the 1964 level of 92 in 1971 and then to a new high of 101 in 1973.[143] The dramatic dip between 1965 and 1971, again, is generally presented as evidence of Park's neglect of the rural areas and his desire to sacrifice rural populations so that low food prices could be transferred to urban populations and thus "the hiring of industrial workers could be kept cheap."[144] Still, to conclude that Park abandoned his rural objectives because of a momentary dip in price and productivity conditions suggests a biased and highly selective reading of his administration, based on a focus on exceptional years in a longer-term trend that was clearly favorable to agriculture. Moreover, when analyzing agricultural development and productivity, one can never make assessments with short-term data since agriculture, unlike many other productive activities, is always vulnerable to weather conditions out of the control of government policy

---

[143] Data on agricultural terms of trade are drawn from Hamilton, *Capitalist Industrialization*, p. 40 (Table 2–2).

Agricultural terms of trade (1974 = 100):

1961	71
1962	70
1963	93
1964	92
1965	83
1966	78
1967	79
1968	78
1969	81
1970	90
1971	92
1972	98
1973	101
1974	100
1975	100
1976	99
1977	99
1978	99

[144] Ibid., p. 41.

makers and rural producers themselves. Conditions can deteriorate for reasons that have nothing to do with government policy; and this is precisely what happened in the mid-1960s in South Korea. In fact, much of the agricultural decline in this period is traceable to several extraordinarily bad harvests. Disastrous weather conditions in these years negatively impacted the agricultural terms of trade not only because they reduced agricultural productivity and output, but also because the ensuing crop failure inspired a massive wave of rural-urban migration, which put pressure on urban wages and urban prices. Still, for every decline, there were also rises. When weather conditions were good, as occurred in the 1965–1966 harvest, South Korea saw a 127.5 percent increase in the production of food crops overall, with potato production, rice, and wheat and barley up 253.4, 199.8, and 131.9 percent respectively.[145]

I suggest, then, that scholars who focus primarily on these several years of agricultural crisis and the attendant deteriorating agricultural terms of trade carry biases that prevent them from neutrally assessing the overall agricultural situation, biases that are further evident in the way they treat the years of agricultural crisis. Clive Hamilton, who is just one of many insisting that Park's agricultural and industrial development policies were intended primarily to aid industrial capitalists, notes that between 1964 and 1967 rice imports rose from none to 6 percent, and then again to 25 percent in 1970, all with foreign aid. But rather than seeing these imports as evidence of Park's desire to respond to several bad harvests and the food crisis they produced for rural as well as urban populations, he claims that they are evidence that "the government could afford to neglect agricultural development and to ignore the disincentive to production of its pricing policy."[146] The greatest irony of this interpretation, which is grounded in the urban biases of most development scholars, is that it glosses over the causality of the process, and may even partially invert it. If anything, Park was quite worried about bad rice harvests, which created havoc in 1964, and overall bad weather in 1966, which brought a 6.1 percent decline in agriculture, forestry, and fishing, because they challenged his efforts to keep rural development as the centerpiece of his strategy.[147] And because the latter decline could be accommodated in his larger developmental vision, precisely because manufacturing production was up by 21.4 percent that same year,[148] it is not fair to say that Park purposely neglected agricultural development, or even that his imports of rice (up 6 percent) were seen as a long-term alternative to agricultural development. After all, he only imported the amount necessary to cover the shortfall (down 6.1 percent), no more and no less. If anything, the increases in manufacturing, accelerated by a new round of disciplinary policies

---

[145] Ho and Hee, "The Economic Plight of Korean Farmers," p. 13.
[146] *Capitalist Industrialization*, p. 41.
[147] Office of Planning and Coordination, *Evaluation of the First Year Program*, p. 21.
[148] Ibid., p. 21.

introduced after the bad rice harvest in 1964,[149] made it possible to live with a momentary agricultural decline.

One could further subvert the prevailing view of the Park administration and suggest instead that the dramatic gains in manufacturing were actually seen by Park as a problem as much as a solution. This was evidenced by his lament that the bad rice harvest, "offset by a remarkable increase of production in the non-agricultural sector" had unfortunately produced "unbalanced growth" in the economy, as well as price instability, both of which he intended to remedy by imposing new constraints on the consumption of nonagricultural goods and services.[150] Park's aim, in short, was always to establish incentives for farmers, themselves, to be better, more efficient producers. And these incentives usually came in the form of disciplinary prods to production rather than a free lunch, be it in the form of inflated agricultural prices or other subsidies. This is well demonstrated in his decision in the autumn of 1964 to discontinue fertilizer subsidies to small farmers and to replace them with new policies to promote land development, technological improvement, and greater market efficiency aimed at accelerating the growth of the agricultural sector.[151]

To be fair, the view that Park actually had little concern for rural development also is based on the claim (by Hamilton and others) that Park and his policy advisors failed to recognize the "disincentive" to production of agricultural pricing, which set government prices lower than market prices. This is a claim that, despite Hamilton's neo-Marxist interpretation of the Park regime, puts him in much the same camp with neoclassical economists who analyze the same period of the South Korean development miracle. Indeed, both schools of thought treat Park's agricultural pricing policies as formulated with industrial capitalists and industrialization in mind, mainly because both base their claims on the assumption that in a "rational" economic world, agricultural pricing policies that keep the costs of urban food relatively low (especially with respect to market prices) economically favor industrial capitalists and workers while disadvantaging rural producers. Moreover, both schools of thought assume that in this rational economic world, had the state's agricultural prices been set higher or more in sync with the market price for food, small farmers would have produced more, thereby easing any evidence of rural decline and the steadily deteriorating agricultural terms of trade. If only Park had gotten the prices right, so to speak. Yet these arguments may be totally off the mark as well, especially for South Korea of the 1960s. Why? Because not only do they

---

[149] Indeed, in August 1964 the government lowered the interest rate on loans from banks to exporters to 6.5 percent from 8 percent; at the same time it offered exporters privileged exemptions from taxations by 50 percent of regular income tax and exemptions of customs duties on imported raw materials for production of export goods. See Park, *The Road*, p. 140.

[150] Ibid., p. 21.

[151] Hsiao, *Government Agricultural Strategies*, p. 87.

fail to recognize that for Park industrial production was part of rural development, insofar as that was seen as a key resource to develop the countryside; they also are based on the presupposition that small-scale rural producers were "economically rational" actors, to use Weberian terminology,[152] who would have vigorously responded to market (i.e., price) and other productive incentives if they had been offered.

A closer look at rural South Korea during this transition period, however, suggests that small-scale producers may have been quite alienated from this type of calculating logic and that they were still embedded in a cultural and social ethos that emphasized use-value, family sustenance, and community more than exchange-value, profits, and accumulation. Although this cultural embeddedness meant that many small-scale rural producers in South Korea also embodied the so-called middle-class cultural values of thrift, savings, and austerity that sustained Park's developmental vision, they did not necessarily behave as middle-class actors in the economic – or market – sense, at least to the extent that they were not socialized to react to production incentives even when they were provided, either in terms of market prices or in terms of financial credit, infrastructural inputs, and/or technology advances. Some of this owed to the fact that Korea's land reform failed to produce as large a class of owners as its proponents expected. In fact, "contrary to the intention of land reform legislation, tenancy . . . increased continually since the 1960s to the extent that by 1986, 30.5 percent of the country's total farmland was under tenancy."[153] And the fact that so many remained in a rental-type relationship surely affected their incentives – and most important, their capacities – to produce, reinvest, and grow. To put it another way, they still responded as "peasants" more than as members of a small-scale owner class committed to economic accumulation and reinvestment. So despite Park's many efforts to spur greater agricultural production, South Korean farmers consistently failed to respond to his rural development efforts.

That small-farm production remained relatively unresponsive to several key macroeconomic policy inputs and rural production incentives is a very important part of this story, mainly because this placed Park's administration in a terrible bind, severely limiting his capacity to realize many of his developmental goals. Remember that Park had committed himself to finding a way to promote economic growth and sustained national development based on a vision of small-scale rural production. But he soon found himself promoting

---

[152] I am of course referring here to Weber's theory of rationalization and how it links to modernization and economic development. Most scholars of modernization and economic development, however, including Marx, base their theories on these assumptions about rational actors who make decisions based on a calculation of costs and benefits rather than social ties or solidarity.

[153] See Kay, *Asia's and Latin America's Development*, p. 19.

this plan in an environment where small-scale rural producers appeared unprepared, if not patently unable, to carry the vision forward. And this meant that despite his efforts to prioritize rural development and to harness industry in the service of rural prosperity, rural areas kept falling behind. One of Park's greatest disappointments during his first five years in office, to which he often referred in public speeches and government documents, was the modest agricultural growth registered in national accounts, which in turn produced a growing gap between agriculture and industry. Park had thought that what he called the natural diligence and work ethos of small farmers, which he heralded with public vigor and confidence, would surely generate rural production, especially if government absorbed the infrastructural costs to help market and sell agricultural products. They did not. And it was this unanticipated state of affairs, which stemmed from rural producers' incapacities to cultivate and sell in accordance with government targets in Park's first years in office, that accounts for the unique macroeconomic policy package ultimately developed by the Park administration and its subtle shifts over time, ranging from an initially balanced mix of agricultural and industrial policy to one in which, by 1974, rural development goals were minimized and industrial exports maximized, thereby ushering in a decade of phenomenal and historically unprecedented economic and industrial growth.

Recalibrating the Model

Park first began to see the limits to his small-farmer-based populist developmental vision as early as 1968, although even at that point, he still remained relatively steadfast in giving priority to conditions in the countryside and in stemming the growing gap between rural and urban populations, as evidenced by his first two five-year development plans. Nonetheless, after starting out relatively well in achieving several moderate rural development goals between 1961 and 1964, two bad harvests later in the decade and surprisingly robust manufacturing development threatened to set the economy on a different, more urban-industrial, path. At first, despite the clear evidence that manufacturing production promised to bring considerable economic growth and a more diverse economy, Park did not fully abandon his policy commitment to the countryside, owing to the earnestness of his administration's devotion to rural development and rural farmers. Rather, after reassessing the first year of his second five-year plan, in 1968 he introduced several new macroeconomic policies that he hoped would rein in the growing urban-rural disparities while still providing economic resources for future growth in the countryside. Among them were a commitment to improve the system of agricultural loans to farmers, a plan to increase prices of agricultural products, a proposal to study possible agricultural exports and new land uses, and efforts "to develop industries germane to the rural areas."[154] There was also some discussion of establishing dual prices for rice, although this did not occur until 1969. Still, far from only establishing new "incentives" for rural populations in order to increase agricultural production, as is often the practice of policy makers attempting to balance rural and urban development, Park ardently devoted a good proportion of his efforts to limiting urban consumption. That is, rather than merely increasing production to counterbalance rural decline, he also introduced various policy measures to stem consumption; and in keeping with his rural middle-class ethos, in order to achieve many of these goals he relied on the state's disciplining of urban populations, especially the wealthy but also the more consumerist urban middle class.

Whether this dual strategy of providing incentives for rural production and placing restrictions on urban consumption can be seen as reflecting Park's growing recognition that rural producers were not readily going to carry the banner of national development without any further prompting and government support is unclear; for as we shall see shortly, it was not until yet a few years later that Park openly acknowledged the social, cultural, and material barriers to rural productivity and sought to transcend them, mainly through initiation of a program called Saemaul Undong in 1971. Overall, however, the macroeconomic reforms Park introduced starting in 1968 were still quite consistent with his long-standing rural middle-class ethos of development, not just because urban populations bore the brunt of restrictions but also because savings, thrift, and austerity were again the government's guiding themes. Among the ten policy objectives identified in the government's 1968 plan for macroeconomic reform, all but one ("mobilization of surplus labor for productive activities") were directed to increasing savings or decreasing consumption, especially of luxury goods. Measures to achieve these objectives ranged from "forcing savings" through higher taxes, diverting any increase in national income to investment, and reducing the government's own spending and consumption to restricting or suspending the production and import of luxury goods, increasing the commodity tax on luxury goods, restricting advertisements which stimulate consumption of these goods, and "holding down the supply of goods and services to restaurants and entertainment facilities." Among the direct recipients of moral admonition in the plan, moreover, were those in cities where such facilities and luxury goods were most available. "The tendency of the middle and high income groups to indulge in a luxurious mode of living has to be discouraged," Park's government spokesman proclaimed, especially because "this tendency is contagious even to the low-income groups through demonstration effect."[155]

---

[154] Park, *The Road*, p. 112.
[155] Ibid., p. 106.

Equally important, the increased emphasis on reducing urban consumption of luxury items – be they imported or produced by local industrialists involved in ISI manufacturing – sheds further light on why the government ratcheted up its commitment to EOI at about the same time. Of course, as noted earlier, Park had always expressed a commitment to generating industrial exports, seeing it as part and parcel of his plans to finance rural development and national modernization. But in the first years of his administration, he also devoted considerable government financing to ISI; and in fact, many scholars have argued that Park's macroeconomic policies during his first several years in office encouraged both goals equally. The shift to a much more conscientious reliance on industrial exports, to the near exclusion of ISI manufacturing, first becomes evident in 1968 and 1969, on the heels of the above-noted reforms introduced after a first-year evaluation of the second five-year plan. Given that the thrust of these reforms was to eliminate both the supply and consumption of manufactured goods, it made sense for Park to direct government resources and financing away from production for the domestic market and toward production for the external market. By so doing, he hoped to kill several birds with one stone. One would be to generate foreign exchange to help pay for food imports (especially given the vulnerability of agricultural production and the growing rural-urban migration); another would be to fund the government's infrastructure expenditures, many of them destined for rural areas, without dipping into domestic savings too deeply; and yet another would be to limit the source of much local consumption, thereby reducing inflationary pressures and encouraging domestic savings, two key goals in his larger developmental vision. By reducing the gap between rural and urban incomes, moreover, one of the key determinants of the unequal agricultural terms of trade, Park would further strengthen his commitment to rural populations and increase his popularity in the countryside.

As occurred between 1961 and 1964, Park's calculations and his commitment to both rural development and industrialization at first seemed to work, at least to a degree, as evidenced by the fact that the economy did relatively well in 1968 and the first half of 1969, closing out the decade of the 1960s with an aggregate 4.5 percent agricultural growth rate. But there were limits to the long-term viability of this plan, and again they appeared to rest in the capacities of rural populations and in rural conditions more generally. Basically, despite considerable government subsidies and massive infrastructural expenditures, including sustained policy efforts to induce farm mechanization starting in 1966, rural productivity rates and overall agricultural output were not climbing as rapidly as urban demand, thereby necessitating a steady increase in food imports. Part of the problem owed to the steady flow of rural-urban migration, which started with a vengeance in 1962 and 1963 and accelerated thereafter in the wake of two particularly bad harvests. It is important to acknowledge that much of the rural-urban migration came in response to the still relatively sluggish conditions in the countryside, since it took several years for many of the government's infrastructural investments and rural development programs to take hold. Yet with more people turning to the cities, even if only as a source of temporary employment before sustained rural development took hold, it became necessary to produce a greater volume of food staples for the expanding urban market; and when this did not happen the government had to turn to imported rice and grains, which produced further pressures to intensify industrial exports.

The relatively modest agricultural growth rates also owed to problems in the countryside itself, and not just to urban migration. As already noted, rural farmers had not been producing at the rates generally expected by government policy makers, even during years with favorable weather conditions. Some of this owed to the rugged agricultural terrain and the harsh nature of the Korean climate, which made farming difficult. Unlike Taiwan, which we will see in the next chapter relied on sugar that was easily sold abroad, the Korean agricultural economy had been based primarily on rice (in addition to barley and wheat) cultivation as well as fishing, activities that required considerable human labor and could not be readily parlayed into export products, at least without more investment in industrial processing. Moreover, efforts to introduce new, more productive crops tended to be slow in paying off, as with the introduction of livestock, sericulture, and the cultivation of various fruits and vegetables. Last and perhaps most significant, the small average size of plots set serious limits to overall productivity, since they frequently discouraged farmers from incurring greater expenditures on technological inputs and labor-saving devices known to increase productivity (see Table 2). As Vincent Brandt put it in his study of rural Korea in the mid-1960s, farming was considered "a respectable way of life but not a means of achieving prosperity" unless radical innovations like new cash crops combined with access to markets or a revolutionary change in agricultural technology were to be wholeheartedly implemented.[156]

In 1968, with newfound resolve to deal with these problems, the Park government initiated a new program to develop "specialized production areas," whose purpose was to more actively "boost agricultural production and to upgrade farm income."[157] Yet this program also failed to bring satisfactory results, in part "because marketing, processing, and storing facilities were totally inadequate to the task of absorbing the increased farm products," and in part because "severe fluctuation in the prices of fruits, vegetables, and other cash crops proved to be a major impediment to individual farmers considering

---

[156] *A Korean Village Between Farm and Sea*, p. 101. See especially pp. 75–87 for Brandt's extensive discussion of small plot size, terrain, and environmental obstacles to rural productivity in South Korea.

[157] Ban et al., *Rural Development*, p. 178.

Table 2. *Proportions of Farm Households by Size of Cultivated Land (%), South Korea*

Year	Total Farm Households (in 1000s)	Non-crop Farms	Below 0.3 ha	0.3–0.5 ha	0.5–1 ha	1–2 ha	2–3 ha	3 ha and over	Total
1965	2507	–	17.2	18.7	31.7	25.6	5.6	1.2	100.0
1966	2540	–	17.0	18.2	32.2	25.8	5.4	1.4	100.0
1967	2587	–	17.8	17.8	32.0	25.7	5.2	1.5	100.0
1968	2579	2.2	15.9	17.4	31.8	26.0	5.1	1.6	100.0
1969	2546	2.3	15.7	17.4	31.7	26.2	5.1	1.6	100.0
1970	2483	2.9	15.7	15.9	33.2	25.8	5.0	1.5	100.0
1971	2482	3.4	15.6	17.1	31.7	26.0	4.8	1.4	100.0
1972	2452	3.5	15.8	16.9	31.7	25.9	4.8	1.4	100.0
1973	2450	3.5	15.4	17.0	31.5	26.3	4.8	1.5	100.0
1974	2381	4.7	12.8	15.5	34.0	26.5	5.0	1.6	100.0
1975	2379	4.0	13.0	16.0	34.8	26.5	4.7	1.5	100.0
1976	2336	4.6	13.2	16.3	34.9	25.2	4.5	1.4	100.0

Sources: Ministry of Agriculture and Fisheries, *Yearbook of Agriculture and Forestry Statistics*, 1975, for data through 1974; and Economic Planning Board, *Korea Statistical Yearbook*, 1977, for otherwise. Adapted from Kyong-dong Kim, *Man and Society in Korea's Economic Growth: Sociological Studies* (Seoul: National University Press, 1979), p. 155.

specialization."[158] Furthermore, the small size of many South Korean farms again limited many cultivators' capacities to plan ahead, thereby limiting the potential impact of these policies.[159] To put it simply, there were serious material obstacles to generating greater rural productivity.

Limited by the costs and a longer-term timetable for remedying these material deficiencies, the Park government worked hard to change one input that it felt it had control over: farmers' motivations. In so doing the government turned its focus as much to the demand as the supply side of the equation. In 1969 Park's administration established a two-price system for barley and rice. This policy, which set a higher price for farmers and a lower price for urban consumers, represented one of the government's last-ditch attempts to keep its original rural-oriented developmental vision relatively intact, although it did renege somewhat on the expectation that only basic infrastructural investments and additional factor inputs on the supply side would be enough to spur the honorable and diligent, self-disciplinary small farmer to produce. Rather, the government now felt compelled to introduce market incentives (i.e., higher government purchase price for agricultural commodities) through which it hoped to further inspire farmers to produce more, a state of affairs that would help it achieve its twin goals of fueling rural development and reducing food imports, thereby reducing its balance of payments deficits.

This new policy temporarily stemmed the growing inequality between urban and rural per capita real income, with the latter jumping considerably from 1968 to 1970 (rural per capita real income rose from 92 to 106 in these two years respectively). Yet some of this owed to the fact that in order to sustain its long-standing objective of keeping inflation down, the government also found it necessary to counterbalance higher rural prices with lower urban prices for agricultural commodities. Moreover, all this meant that the government purchase price as compared to market price rose dramatically, to a level even higher than before the two-grain policy, shifting from a ratio of 81.7 in 1968 to 97.9 in 1970.[160] As such, the two-price policy, even though it first appeared to be helping Park achieve his rural development objectives, laid the foundation for several changes in the economy which ultimately forced him to drastically alter his developmental vision. One problem was increased government expenditures, as seen in the rising gap between market and government

---

[158] Ibid.

[159] As Brandt (*A Korean Village Between Farm and Sea*, p. 55) noted in his study of village life, the small-scale landholding of one-quarter or three-quarters of an acre, which was still common in many villages, provides only a marginal subsistence. For these farmers, where "good management, extra skills, and conscientious frugality exist," "poor" households could replicate the practices of "middle farmers" of the next higher category, but any shift in weather or personal tragedy could throw them into abject poverty.

[160] Hamilton, *Capitalist Industrialization*, p. 40.

purchase price. By continually raising the price paid for rural commodities, the government increased its spending enormously, and the budget suffered greatly by paying more for crops when there was less money available for the key infrastructural inputs also necessary to facilitate production and marketing. Another problem stemmed from the fact that once urban prices were set low enough (relative to rural purchase prices) to keep inflation in check, the specter of overconsumption that Park so ardently worried about reemerged on the horizon with a vengeance.

Both problems called for a new approach, or at least a recalibration of his original model, a shift which became most evident in 1970 and 1971. Park's new approach was built on two fundamental premises: 1) the increasing importance of shifting away from ISI to export-oriented production almost entirely, and not just partially, since this was one of the few reliable ways to both insure that domestic consumption would remain under control and guarantee foreign exchange for further rural investment; and 2) the increasing importance of motivating more vigorous, self-sustaining agricultural productivity. While the first merely reflects the intensification of Park's original concerns with generating foreign exchange through industrial exports, the second suggests a somewhat new policy direction, one that more clearly defines the 1970–1971 shift and was based on Park's realization that small farmers, as economic actors in the business of rural production, were not doing their jobs well enough. Underlying their original unwillingness and incapacity to respond to government incentives were material as well as cultural and social obstacles, each of which convinced Park that the key to South Korea's economic future lay not just in his government's capacity to increase exports, but also in its capacity to teach small farmers and other rural producers how to be economically calculating, strategically rational actors willing to take risks, to introduce innovation, to find new ways to identify market niches, and thus to increase their own productivity. In the context of Park's developmental vision as well as his small-farmer cultural biases and social bases, this meant imbuing small farmers with a small-scale capitalist mentality so that they would invest more of their own energies and resources in order to produce more. It meant, in short, teaching small farmers a petit bourgeois ethos that both encouraged and enabled them to behave as members of a rural middle class.

This was a rather strange, if not paradoxical, state of affairs. After all, it was this administration's highly disciplinary, rural middle-class ethos – which stemmed from Park's (and the military-linked bureaucracy's) political and personal embeddedness with South Korea's small farmers – that explains much of the desire to foster agricultural development and rein in industrial development in the first place, just as it helps explain many of the restrictive and heavy-handed disciplinary strategies Park chose for achieving these aims. Yet even as Park's own understanding of himself and the small-farmer experience led him to embrace and promote a middle-class ethos, many other small farmers without his distinctive profile or political access to wealth, power, class mobility, and the obvious payoffs to economic rationality, understood things quite differently. As Kyong-dong Kim underscored in his seminal study of socio-cultural transformation in rural Korea over the 1960s, a considerable number of rural Koreans still had little understanding of life outside the village. As such, they "tend[ed] to resemble the ideal-typical image of peasants [*sic*]: attachment to land, familism, or family-centrism outlook, traditionalism, and superstitious orientation . . . confounded by moralist obligation and collective particularism chiefly embodied in strong kinship ties and familism."[161] A calculating economic rationality and the urban and industrial experience that is so frequently identified as kick starting the middle-class frame of mind both seemed far from the rural farmers' grasp.

Vincent Brandt's late-1960s anthropological study of one rural village in South Korea came to many of the same conclusions.

> The typical villager cannot be seen simply as an individual competing with his neighbors in order to maximize material possessions, or any other egoistic satisfaction for that matter. The traditional ideological system imposes many limitations on what might be called rational economic motives. In Sokp'o people dwell constantly on the extent of their poverty, but in actuality they are far less preoccupied with acquiring material goods than their cousins in the city. The subordination of individual goals and satisfactions to those of the collectivity − family, lineage, neighborhood, or village − is nearly automatic, while excessive individualism stands out and is likely to be criticized.[162]

Owing to the clear distinctions between rural and urban life, then, and their own cultural experiences, for many small farmers family and collective betterment mattered more than individual economic success, and certainly accumulation for accumulation's sake was not a high priority. Indeed, for most small farmers use value rather than exchange value still motivated cultivation decisions, as evidenced by one study of the late 1950s demonstrating that Korean small farmers marketed less than 30 percent of their product while consuming the rest.[163] Productive activities, when they were pursued, were generally developed in keeping with traditional social and kinship practices as much as on the basis of current or future market potential.[164]

---

[161] Kim, *Man and Society*, p. 146.

[162] *A Korean Village Between Farm and Sea*, p. 76.

[163] Sorensen, *Over the Mountains Are Mountains*, p. 5

[164] As early as 1962, observers of South Korean agricultural development were arguing that much of the agricultural crisis in the first years of the Park regime owed to the fact that South Korean farmers were not "inclined towards radical changes in methods," as one scholar put it, adding that "if they would be willing to change from rice growing on the non-irrigated

Necessarily, these claims and the somewhat stereotypical views of small farmers upon which they are built must be taken with a note of caution. They certainly would not necessarily hold for all rural South Koreans during the Park period, and for how many they would hold and why is still a matter of debate among Korean social scientists. Whenever they are identified, these features are as likely to be traceable to long-standing material constraints – unfavorable natural conditions for farming, the lived experience of colonial exploitation, inaccessibility to markets, problems in obtaining credit, and so forth – as to some inherent cultural "backwardness" that characterizes peasants in general and South Koreans in particular. Yet regardless of origins or even of the veracity of these culturally essentialist claims, there is consistent evidence from a wide variety of studies of rural South Korea in the 1960s that small farmers – or peasants, as they are generally called in most of these writings – were reluctant and/or unable to change production and farming techniques on the spot, or at least to do so as rapidly, efficiently, and wholeheartedly as Park anticipated and his macroeconomic policy advisors projected would occur, even when material conditions did start to change through active government intervention.

This may not be surprising, of course, as we would expect some lag time – if not resistance to change – among almost any population faced with a threat to long-standing practices and traditions. Similar points have been made by sociologists as far back as Emile Durkheim, although Durkheim himself preferred to see this type of response as an anomic rather than cohesive route to a more "modern" division of labor.[165] Countless anthropological studies of social change all over the world also have observed the same behaviors. Regardless of the so-called normative understanding of this process, however, this body of scholarship reminds us that modernization, a more complex division of labor, economic development, or whatever theoretically informed phraseology one prefers to use must be seen as contested, and that the contestation is part and parcel of the process, no matter the outcome. South Korea's transformation was no exception; this was the challenge for Park, a challenge he ultimately recognized. The slowness with which rural populations changed their personal visions and daily practices posed a serious obstacle to Park's rural middle-class-based developmental vision, suggesting that his personal expectations about the disciplinary and productive capacities of small farmers rested as much on

paddy lands, they would not be so dependent upon weather conditions" (Pak, "The Outlook of Korean Agriculture in the Five-Year Plan," p. 20).

[165] As Abrams put it, one of Durkheim's main arguments was that "the speed and discontinuity of social change create situations in which in entering new occupations or embarking on new enterprises, people simply do not know where they are; the whole context of their activity is socially unregulated; there are no taken-for-granted ground rules for the conduct of the new social practices and relationships." See Abrams, *Historical Sociology*, p. 28.

nascent capacity and wishful thinking as anything else. It was the expectation that small farmers would indeed behave like the middle-class actors (that their property ownership made possible) that fueled Park's developmental programs, an expectation that seemed perfectly reasonable to him, or reasonable enough for him to structure development policy around it. Thus, when it became clear to Park that his expectation was not being matched by reality, and that small farmers' identities and practices were more tradition- and kinship-bound than "rational" and class oriented, he then used the strong arm of the state to try to make it happen. And this too explains some of the country's economic gains.

Creating a Rural Middle Class: Saemaul Undong

Perhaps most exemplary of Park's heavy-handed efforts to change the behavior and values of rural cultivators to "match" their material conditions was the Saemaul Undong program, a social and cultural crusade loosely translated as the "New Community Movement." In South Korean scholarship this movement generally is analyzed in political terms, with most scholars identifying it as evidence of Park's efforts to co-opt rural populations into his regime, to offer an institutional rationale for the state's penetration of civil society, and/or to buy off (through subsidies and government grants) rural populations for electoral purposes.[166] Moreover, most scholars' arguments about the timing of Saemaul Undong, conceived a year or so earlier but implemented starting in 1971, belie their views of its purely political purposes, since most scholars underscore that the program was initiated after a relative decline in political support for Park from rural populations and at a time when growing urban labor unrest gave the state greater motivation to strengthen its long-standing political bases in rural areas. Those who make the latter argument tend to see Saemaul Undong as providing political maneuvering room for Park's EOI strategy, meaning that they see it as the consequence of the government's long-standing commitment to industrial exports, by virtue of the fact that politically strengthening rural bases through Saemaul Undong would give Park even more centralized power. This was hypothesized to be especially necessary starting in 1971 when striking industrial workers threatened to sidetrack the government's efforts to accelerate EOI.

But the reality is far more complex. To be sure, these explanations are credible and many could serve as partial explanations for the timing, development, and policy content of Saemaul Undong. It is true, moreover, that in the 1971 elections President Park barely defeated opposition candidate Kim Dae Jung, an election in which for the first time Park's political strength was more pronounced in urban centers than in rural districts, suggesting that he may have been losing part of his long-standing rural base of support as population and

---

[166] See, for example, Ban et al., *Rural Development*, p. 163.

employment moved to cities. There also is no doubt that, in the long run, the establishment of Saemaul Undong, and the organizational infrastructure created to administer and evaluate local development projects implemented under its auspices, did provide the government with the personnel and tools to monitor, control, and selectively benefit local populations. And clearly, the program also fostered even stronger political relations between the Park administration and his rural middle-class base, as "farmers and bureaucrats learned to work together to achieve common objectives."[167] But still, claims that Park developed Saemaul Undong solely for the political purpose of strengthening his repressive and authoritarian hand do not square with local-level evaluations of how the program actually operated.

In his study of the government's direct involvement in the program, for example, Ronald Aqua found very little evidence of such machinations:

> While there can be no doubt about the positive spillover effect of SMM [Saemaul movement] for Park's government, and in particular for the post-1972 Yushin system, it is important to note that Park did not attempt to convert SMM into a personal instrument for maintaining his political power base. Whether because such an instrument already existed in the guise of the KCIA, or because of his well-known distaste for political parties and legislative affairs, Park did not form a new type of political party based on membership drawn from the ranks of SMM cadres nor did he promote SMM leaders to high policy-making positions within the central government. On the contrary, the recruitment possibilities seem to have been left largely unexploited.[168]

Equally telling, scholars who focus primarily on a political rationale for Saemaul Undong miss another central aspect of the program: its predominantly economic aims. Indeed, with the exception of government-trained or -funded scholars, most independent or critical analysts of Saemaul Undong have become so concerned with its political rationale and repercussions that they frequently fail to pay more than lip service to its developmental objectives. Even those who believe Saemaul Undong was intended to help South Korea increase general rural productivity usually see it primarily as a clearinghouse for Park's rural investment schemes; few see it as a serious rural development program. However, a closer look at the program's content and at Park's own characterization of Saemaul Undong, as well as a broader historical understanding of the failures of previous rural development policies, suggests that the program was intended to transform rural people as much as infrastructure, and that rural investments, subsidies, and incentives offered through the program were linked to expectations about purposively changing cultivators' behavior.

---

[167] Aqua, "The Role of Government in the Saemaul Movement," p. 420.
[168] Ibid., p. 418.

Moreover, the program was implemented nationwide and not focused – at least initially – only on certain villages. Far and away, then, the main objectives of the movement were to increase the income of an entire class of farmers by teaching them how to innovate, produce, and market, as well as to make their communities better places to live. Stated simply, Saemaul Undong was as much intended to turn small-holding peasants into rural middle classes by making them economically rational and efficient small producers, and by so doing increase their agricultural productivity and market responsiveness; it was not merely a ruse for political control of the peasant masses, although that may have been one by-product. And precisely because a new round of foreign exchange resources was required to mount this highly costly movement which entailed transforming en masse the material, social, and cultural conditions in the countryside, Saemaul Undong and the rural objectives it embodied must be seen as the cause as much as the consequence of Park's dramatic shift to EOI in the early 1970s.

Much of this is well evidenced through a closer examination of the movement, which has been termed an integrated rural development program by some technical observers,[169] as well as the ways in which material, social, and cultural incentives and investments articulated with each other. Sung Hwan Ban identifies the stated purpose of Saemaul Undong as "upgrad[ing] the quality of village life by promoting cooperation, self-help, and the transformation of conservative rural attitudes."[170] Still, unlike previous efforts at rural development which were directed, in Kyong-Dong Kim's words, "at some minor aspect(s) of rural change, such as technical assistance, improvement of rural environment, health, and educational conditions, reform of social organization, and the like,"[171] Saemaul Undong aimed at multiple levels of rural life simultaneously, working comprehensively to address material conditions, moral outlook, and standards of behavior. In one study conducted at the National Agricultural Economics Research Institute, the Saemaul Undong program was analyzed as comprised of several key elements intended to produce "attitudinal change," including inculcation of upright values, materialization of the spirit of self-reliance, and "rationalization," or development of a more scientific way of life; each of these value shifts was intended to correspond to a particular aspect of the country's economic modernization (rising income, innnovation in agriculture, and "re-adjustment of cultivating land and enlargement of the cultivating scale," respectively).[172] Moreover, rather than targeting certain activities or markets selectively, as had many previous

---

[169] For in-depth discussion of the component parts of Saemaul Undong, see Kim's *Man and Society*, esp. pp. 84–101.

[170] Ban et al., *Rural Development*, p. 163.

[171] Kim, *Man and Society*, p. 162.

[172] Cf. ibid., p. 84 (Chart 1).

rural development programs, the activities of Saemaul Undong were spread across the entire country. As one Korean scholar put it, "Every village in the country has, to a greater or lesser extent, felt the economic, political, and cultural pressures" of the movement, evidenced by the fact that Park mobilized all government personnel, ranging from police and the military to teachers, extension agents, and village leaders, into "putting in long extra hours working on self-help projects or in 'raising village consciousness.' "[173] The end product, in Ki Hyuk Park's words, was to be a widespread enough change in "farmers' 'consciousness structure' " so as to "transform the traditional family farm into the modern farming business."[174]

In its first years, the emphasis was on improving the villages' physical environments, a recognition of the fact that obstacles to small-farmer productivity lay as much in rural poverty and lagging infrastructural investment as in cultural conditions. Yet, over time, the program shifted its emphasis toward the promotion of greater agricultural productivity and increased rural incomes through self-help and reinvestment. In keeping with the traditional village orientation of most rural families, the village was generally the focus of the program, such that most were ultimately classified according to which of the three phases of Saemaul Undong they had achieved (basic, self-helping, and self-managing). But again, most aspects of the program emphasized incentives and behavior modification for individuals as much as entire communities. President Park himself noted in a public address in late 1970, "If we can create and cultivate the spirit of self-reliance and independence and hard work, I believe that all rural villages can be turned into beautiful and prosperous places to live.... We may call such a drive the Saemaul Undong."[175] And his words served as inspiration for the subsequent development of the program a year later, at least as it has been characterized in scholarship on its content and goals:

> The components of the "Saemaul spirit" were diligence, self-help, and cooperation. Through diligence, the people would develop a better work ethic, and as their incomes increased, they would be able to save more. By focusing upon self-help, the regime sought to foster among the farmers feelings of personal efficacy and confidence in their personal abilities. On the matter of cooperation, it will be recalled that mutual assistance and reciprocal activity were traditional features of the Korean villages. But this behavior was generally characteristic of small-scale endeavors, such as helping a neighbor build a new house, assisting in the fields at harvest time, or coming to the aid of a family during an emergency. As

---

[173] Ban et al., *Rural Development*, pp. 163–164.
[174] Park, "Contribution of the Saemaul Movement," pp. 170, 166.
[175] Turner et al., *Villages Astir*, pp. 75–76.

a rule, little cooperation was evident in the development of large-scale projects such as the building of roads and bridges, the construction of an irrigation system, erosion control, and the creation of community workshops – programs aimed at developing infrastructure that would improve the economy of the community and at the same time benefit individuals directly.[176]

In keeping with its dual focus on individuals and the community, the movement employed a stage-by-stage strategy built around "an initial phase – one of self-help – [which] was designed to improve the living conditions of individual households. . . . In making life more comfortable, the individual was to practice self-reliance rather than depend upon cooperative effort."[177] After encouraging changes in individual behavior in this first stage, however, a second emphasized the community by prioritizing the development of economic infrastructure (i.e., building feeder roads, bridges, and small-scale irrigation works and drainage systems; electrification; construction of public meeting halls). The third and last phase focused on generating increased income. This last phase not only brought together the program's dual emphasis on individuals and community infrastructure, it also emphasized collective behavior and organization by encouraging a higher degree of cooperation among individuals. The emphasis in this final stage was on "increased food production through new agricultural techniques, soil conservation, the specialization of crops, the reclamation of unused land, the introduction of high yielding varieties of rice and grain, and the assistance of agricultural extension agents. Farmers were encouraged to engage in group farming and marketing, to use common seedbeds, and to develop community forestation projects."[178]

What is most telling about the program's three-stage hierarchy is that it legitimized a status ethos in which the normative emphasis lay on villages exhibiting more "upwardly mobile" behavior, as it were, an aspiration commonly identified with the middle class. Villages were formally classified as falling into one of three ordinal categories – basic, self-helping, or self-managing – depending on the amount of energy and commitment invested by residents to produce common funds for self-sustaining development.[179] And the more valued "higher" stages of village classification were defined in terms that also reflected an eminently middle-class sense of attaining self-sufficiency and increased

---

[176] Ibid., p. 76.

[177] Ibid., p. 77. In this stage, for example, individuals completed such tasks as replacing thatched roofs with tile or tin, renovating kitchens, and improving sanitary facilities.

[178] Ibid.

[179] There is some disagreement as to the labeling of the highest stage of villages. Kim identifies the top tier as "self-reliant, self-suffcent (or developed) villages"; while Turner identifies them as "self-managing." See Kim, *Man and Society*, p. 92; and Turner et al., *Villages Astir*, p. 78.

production (from basic to self-helping), and then achieving a sufficient level of productivity to create a surplus to coordinate (self-managing) and perhaps even reinvest. Significantly, these distinctions replicate conventional wisdom held by Park and others about the differences between the old and new middle classes, with the first two stages illustrating the traditional sentiments associated with the self-employed and the third with a more modern and managerial outlook to be attained.

Additionally, the entire approach of the program both embodied and replicated long-standing middle-class ideologies about personal success, hard work, and competition and their impact on productivity, capital accumulation, and thus overall development. The first targets of "reconstruction" were individuals and their attitudes, a programmatic decision predicated on the assumption that the "correct" individual attitudes were a necessary – although not sufficient – foundation for transforming villages from being poor to being rich. In strict keeping with a middle-class ethos, moreover, rewards were meted out to villages in accordance with how successful they were in achieving their goals of moving up the hierarchy, not on the basis of greatest need, a policy shift that itself differentiated this program from most of Park's previous rural development attempts. That is, the poorer and least developed villages were not rewarded; only those who showed evidence of fostering individual incentives and improving community infrastructure received government monies, especially when they poured agricultural surpluses back into new activities (like processing plants or marketing services) that themselves helped achieve greater productivity and efficiency. As John Turner notes in his description of Saemaul Undong, "In the competition for funding, preference was given to communities in which the inhabitants had exhibited sincerity of purpose and capacity to use the resources efficiently"; while "community residents . . . were judged on the amount of their voluntary contributions to the projects, including a share of the investment costs, but primarily through donations of man-hours of labor."[180] Moreover, as just noted, the program structured its carrot-and-stick incentives in such a way as to generate a taste for competition among villages, if not among individuals, for the resources allocated by the government.

To the extent that the program was so obviously committed to producing and legitimizing prototypically middle-class sentiments about hard work, self-sacrifice, competition, efficiency, and reinvestment, it may seem strange that languages of class never entered the picture. But once we put the program

---

[180] *Villages Astir*, p. 78. Turner also notes that "the undeveloped villages, deficient in leadership and resources, received no financial support from the government"; whereas those whose residents had already started to supplement their cash incomes through greater cultivation and productivity received government support to establish light industrial plants and handicraft centers (p. 77).

in a larger social and political context, this is not entirely surprising. Historically, even those Koreans most likely to accept categorizations of class, that is, scholars trained in universities where imported theories of modernization and development privileged these notions, had long shunned languages of class – especially those predicated on the notion of class struggle – to understand Korean society. This was true even of factory workers, let alone self-employed rural and urban producers. Gi-wook Shin argues that as early as "the 1920s, Korean intellectuals, finding orthodox Marxist theory difficult to apply to colonial agrarian Korea, also used general and vague categories such as 'propertied' (*yusanja*) and 'propertyless' (*musanja*) instead of bourgeoisie and proletariat," a formula which "pitted 'the small minority of the rich, comprised of capitalists, landlords, and elements of an urban leisure class, against the overwhelming majority of poor Korean peasants and laborers.'"[181]

Conditions did not change much after World War II during the nation's encounter with independence, in part because the economy remained unstable and poverty was still rampant. When the nation was divided at the 49th parallel, with many communist sympathizers making the grand exodus north, the likelihood of embracing languages of class appeared further diminished. Even in the 1970s, when citizens' groups comprised of industrial laborers, among others, mobilized against the privileged elite in either the government or the private sector, they still tended to avoid class languages, resorting instead to a peculiarly South Korean version of populism, known as *minjung* ideology, that emphasized the people rather than class.[182] It was not until the 1980s, in fact, that class languages truly permeated the minjung movement or that significant groups of the South Korean people began to see themselves as working class or organize themselves around working-class identities or concerns.[183] Even so, this was mostly an urban phenomenon, fueled by the struggle and activities of workers allied with academics and dissident politicians. In rural South Korea, in contrast, class concepts and class languages remained relatively alien.

However, it may be precisely the absence of class languages and class logics in the countryside that explains the all-out efforts undertaken by the Park administration to create and disseminate the Saemaul Undong program as one which promoted a middle-class ideal and discourse without actually labeling

[181] "Marxism, Anti-Americanism, and Democracy in South Korea," p. 531 fn. 22.

[182] Despite being directed "against monopoly capital," as Koo has noted, the *minjung* movement avoided class-struggle issues and concentrated more on achieving political goals, especially democratization. See "The State, *Minjung*, and the Working Class in South Korea," p. 143.

[183] Koo (ibid., p. 145) shares the formulation of a well-known Marxist scholar writing in the mid-1980s, Pak Hyonch'ae, who claims that "minjung is composed of the working class as its core element and of small farmers, small independent producers, the urban poor, and a segment of progressive intellectuals."

it as such. If anything, in fact, the movement's commitment to cultural in-doctrination, its excessive deployment of symbolism (which included its own flag and anthem), and the almost fanatical commitment to changing attitudes and material conditions through heavy-handed moral persuasion reflected the enormity of the task at hand as well as the importance the Park administration placed on creating a rural middle class in deed if not in word. Park's efforts were almost obsessive in this regard, as seen in the lengths to which he went to inculcate values of hard work and his desire to link individual and village performance to government subsidies. Park often warned that the material or financial support must not be extended "to those unwilling to help themselves. Equal distribution of government funds among the diligent and idle alike," he proclaimed, "would be simply unfair."[184] Instead, just as with industrialists, bankers, and other major big capitalists, Park relied heavily on reward and punishment to enforce the self-discipline of small farmers as a new class, frequently noting in public speeches that "only for those farmers who struggle hard to improve farming methods, the government will provide positive assistance . . . [reiterating that] no matter how hard the government tries for the welfare of the farmers, it cannot accomplish a great deal if the farmers lack a spirit to help themselves."[185]

Moral and Material Incentives to Rural Middle-Class Formation

Given the energy and resources that both the government and rural citizens themselves invested in Saemaul Undong, it should be no surprise that it was considered relatively successful, at least in terms of its rural development objectives.[186] As Ban, Moon, and Perkins put it, the story of Korea's rural development was in many ways "a story of farmers making the best use of their resource endowment by putting greater emphasis on cash crops;"[187] and much of this owed to the projects and principles of the Saemaul Undong movement. After its implementation throughout the 1970s, farm income rose dramatically, especially as compared to its precipitous fall between 1965 and 1969. The index of farm household (real) income rose from a low of 75.1 in 1965 to 100.0 in 1970, almost doubling to 195.2 in 1976, just six years later (see Table 1). Equally important, these gains did not come at the expense of greater income inequality, as is often the case with rural development programs. In part due to the small size of landholding, but also due to the self-disciplinary, reinvestment orientation of the program, most families continued

---

[184] Keon, *Korean Phoenix*, p. 92.
[185] Shik (ed.), *Major Speeches*, p. 218.
[186] Turner et al., *Villages Astir*, p. 85.
[187] *Rural Development*, p. 9.

to emphasize production over consumption and to direct their agricultural gains to village and community development rather than personal aggrandizement. The result was "improved overall farm income, but without significantly increasing inequality in the distribution of income among farm households."[188]

Rural conditions also improved dramatically in relation to the city. As of 1973 the ratio of farm household income to urban-worker household income had narrowed almost to the point of parity, closing the rural-urban income gap that had so worried Park; in 1974, farm household income in real terms had even surpassed urban income. By 1977, moreover, South Korea finally achieved self-sufficiency in rice; and although there have been some declines since then, some scholars cite this as the principal source of the trebling of rural incomes between 1965 and 1977.[189] Additionally, according to the standards applied by the Korean authorities, the Saemaul Undong villages had all "progressed to higher forms" by the end of the decade.[190] As such, the perception in the countryside was fairly positive. Studies of rural residents in 1977 found that "89.7 percent of the respondents in rural villages reported that the economic conditions . . . [had] improved over the past five years; there was only one person who said they have worsened."[191]

Equally telling, Saemaul Undong seemed to have achieved at least minimal successes in transforming the daily activities and individual value orientations of rural residents. As one scholar put it, "The sort of change that has been encouraged, consciously or not, is going in the direction of further economic prosperity," owing to the enhanced "consumer orientation and economic achievement motivation" generated through the program.[192] Statistics seem to support these claims. Studies of changing morality and rural values in South Korea evidence a dramatic shift in priorities consistent with that which Park had hoped would occur when he first undertook the program. One such study, for example, showed that while in 1964 only 9.7 percent of rural residents were committed to "risk taking by investment rather than hoarding," this figure had jumped to 29.1 percent by 1977. Similarly, while in 1964, 15.6 percent and 50.0 percent of the population identified themselves as committed to

---

[188] Ban, "The New Community Movement," p. 234.

[189] Turner et al., *Villages Astir*, p. 85. In his account of rural improvements in this period, Turner cites numerous other studies, including those of Wickman (1982) and Hinton (1983), that reached the same conclusion about overall rural gains.

[190] Turner et al., *Villages Astir*, p. 85.

[191] Kim, *Man and Society*, p. 157. Brandt, in *A Korean Village Between Farm and Sea*, also reports that rural families noted a slight improvement in economic conditions starting with Park and accelerating in the late 1960s (p. 100).

[192] Kim, *Man and Society*, p. 168.

"personal mobility" and the goals of achieving "success by ability and determination," respectively, these rates had risen to 52.5 percent and 84.9 percent by 1977. As these more "economically rational" outlooks began to take hold, moreover, several long-standing traditional family and kinship obligations declined accordingly. While 62.6 percent emphasized "family obligation at [the] sacrifice of individual success" in 1964, only 29.3 percent did so in 1977.[193] The work of anthropologists also appears to sustain similar claims. Vincent Brandt notes that in rural areas by the 1970s, "younger men and fishermen increasingly tend[ed] to think in terms of money capital and alternative kinds of investment" rather than just holding oxen or land.[194] As such, many observers concluded that Saemaul Undong did make a difference. As Kyong-dong Kim put it, this movement must be considered "the backbone of rural development and change in this country. It has made great strides in the area of rural economic improvement together with the creation of environment, physical, economic, social, and cultural, conducive to economic betterment [*sic*]."[195]

In many ways, these findings offer considerable evidence to arrive at a new position on the age-old sociological debate about the role of structure versus agency, economy versus culture, state versus society, and even individuals versus classes in large-scale processes of economic transformation. Park's strategy straddled all these domains, precisely because he used the state to actively cultivate personal and shared social values, as well as individual and collective daily practices that would be reinforcing and consistent with rapid and sustained economic development. Moreover, it was his own personal and collective experiences and values that helped motivate him to use the state to recreate these experiences and values in others. As such, it was a dynamic interaction between state and society, structure and agency, individuals and classes, that helped fuel South Korea's stunning economic transformation from a "traditional" rural society to a "modern" industrial one.

Similarly, this scenario also suggests a very different picture than the one created in classical studies of economic transformation, especially as exemplified in the competing positions of Adam Smith and Karl Marx about the early origins of self-sustaining economic (i.e., capitalist) development. Both sought to explain what was called "primitive accumulation," or the appearance of sufficient economic surplus to fuel a process of capital accumulation and investment. Smith found the roots of so-called primitive accumulation in the hard work and personal strivings of individuals, an argument that foreshadowed Weber's later arguments about Protestantism and capitalism; while

---

[193] Ibid., p. 160.
[194] *A Korean Village Between Farm and Sea*, p. 52.
[195] *Man and Society*, p. 168.

Marx, labeling this argument as ideological, focused more clearly on the myriad political conditions (including state actions) that separated individuals from the land and thus forced them into a world of commodification, a theme picked up in later writings by Polanyi and others. For Smith it was individual character and cultural contingency, whereas for Marx it was larger political structures and conditions, most especially the state's concerted efforts to break the ties of tradition, that led to capitalist development. The South Korean experience, in contrast, suggests that it was neither one nor the other, but both processes that mattered. Purposeful state actions, including those that eliminated material obstacles to greater productivity, were necessary to change individuals and to try to make them behave as capitalists, albeit small-scale ones; yet without individual transformation, the state would not be successful in creating these small-scale capitalists and thus advancing the larger process of economic development.

Still, if the Saemaul Undong program achieved so many of its spiritual, cultural, and material objectives, and as such was so central to the developmental successes of the South Korean nation, the question arises as to why rural populations – and, more specifically, rural development as a principal government priority – steadily faded from the picture throughout the 1970s? Why did South Korea become known primarily as a major industrial power right after this period, with rural development aims slipping off the policy-making agenda with ever greater frequency? It was during this later period, after all, that South Korea reaped its greatest industrial successes, such that those big industrial conglomerates, known as chaebols, cemented their hold on the economy, and such that the balance of political, economic, and social power – not to mention the problems of poverty and income inequality – shifted to the cities, especially to Seoul. Does the focus on rural development and the historical framework I have employed to understand the timing and rural middle-class character of Saemaul Undong and its affiliated rural development programs help answer this question? The answer is a cautious yes, and in such a way as to underscore the importance of looking at the state's class embeddedness – in this case the state's rural middle-class embeddedness – and not merely the interaction of state and individual actors in charting developmental trajectories.

First, there were several short-term limitations which had less to do with the difficulties of inculcating individual small farmers with self-discipline and a rural middle-class ethos and more to do with the temporal and material obstacles that prevented them from turning themselves into a self-sustaining class of small-scale capitalist producers, at least immediately. The goal of transforming the psyches and investment decisions of individual citizens is a long-term project that even in the best of circumstances can take years to pay off. Thus, while over the decade of the 1970s Saemaul Undong did show evidence of achieving many of its objectives, these changes were not necessarily established in the early years of the program, nor were they always reflected in long-term and immutable patterns of investment and reinvestment among small farmers. Second, and perhaps more important, even if some values and behaviors did change in this short period of time, there were still other more tangible obstacles to generating sustained rural development. Perhaps the most important ones had to do with farm size and natural resource endowments, which set medium- and long-term limits to the viability of a sustained strategy of rural development based on small-scale land ownership and production, especially in resource-poor South Korea, even if and when farmers were adequately socialized to increase productivity and reinvest. That is, even if there were some initial changes in agricultural productivity as a result of the implantation of more "economically rational" values in various rural individuals, these changes could not necessarily restructure the entire South Korean economy enough to shift its emphasis away from industrialization and toward sustained agricultural development.

Remember that Park's original developmental aims revolved around a vision of small-farmer production (i.e., small plots, family-run farms) where overall community and rural development were still more important than accumulation for accumulation's sake. Yet these "dwarf farms," as many agronomists called them, were known to hamper agricultural output, especially in South Korea's rice-producing sector, which for many years had remained a mainstay of the economy.[196] Of course, small plot size was a principal social and political priority for Park, given his commitment to widespread land reform, and thus it was seen by the government as beneficial on other counts. Not only did it hold the promise of culturally sustaining the rural middle class toward whom Park was so inclined, small plot size also would help insure that farm income could rise without increasing income inequality. However, it also meant that few individual producers commited themselves to a sustained capitalization of agriculture, a commitment that generally entails increasing plot sizes and/or hiring wage labor or tenants. Most of the agricultural advances, in fact, came through cooperative endeavors. As Edward Reed put it in his study of Saemaul Undong in several rural locales,

> The villagers seem to have perceived a wide range of potential collective goods, most of them having to do with the agricultural production process. In fact, Korean farmers cannot be completely independent operators. Most of the critical farming decisions – timing of operations, labor supply, farm equipment acquisition, water use, even credit – must be made in coordination with fellow villagers. This is especially true in

---

[196] Oh, "Agrarian Reform and Economic Development," p. 92.

rice farming which seems to create a rationale for cooperation based on ecology and agronomics."[197]

These factors help explain why the structure of rural land ownership remained basically the same both before and after Saemaul Undong. Indeed, rather than seeing a notable increase in plot size, a transformation which most economists suggest would both result from and produce greater efficiency, accumulation, and reinvestment among individual farmers (owing to economies of scale, among other things), farm size stayed relatively stable and on the small side – miserably small in fact. Between 1965 and 1976, the proportion of farms between one and two hectares remained practically stable and still constituted the largest single category of farms (25.6 percent in 1965 and 25.2 percent in 1976), while those between two and three hectares dropped from 5.6 percent to 4.5 percent and those over three hectares rose only marginally (from 1.2 percent to 1.4 percent) (see Table 2).

The question arises as to why this was the case. One answer could be related to our earlier claims about the cultural and social obstacles to changing individual behavior in a short amount of time. That is, even with a greater appreciation for austerity, discipline, and reinvestment, rural farmers were neither socially prepared nor personally inclined to become capitalists as such, even small-scale, petit bourgeois capitalists, preferring instead to maintain a more traditional status as small, self-employed farmers involved in small-scale production primarily for use value.[198] Another may be the rugged terrain and climate of the nation, which limited crop selection and the incentive to use more capital intensive technology, although such material considerations may also help explain the more ideological and cultural accounting of farmers' personal proclivities just noted. Equally important, however, is the fact that with small plot sizes and small farmers leading the way, there were insufficient market and material incentives for greater capitalization, even when appropriate new technologies might have been available or even if there existed the personal wherewithal to achieve this goal, since economies of scale were severely limited by small plot size. The result: It was difficult to induce enough change in rural economic performance to turn agriculture into a centerpiece of the national economy, even though overall rural attitudes, conditions, and productivity rates for farm families did steadily improve.

---

[197] "Village Cooperation and the Saemaul Movement," p. 281.

[198] As evidence as to why small farmers were reluctant to enter into relations of capitalist exploitation by increasing plot size and hiring laborers, scholars have turned to family structure. Kim cites Lee as claiming, albeit awkwardly, that "the tenancy system does not have the significance of economic relationship of exploitation insofar as cultivating land is concerned. This, he explains, is mainly due to the fact that many of the landowners are either relatives or acquaintances of the tenant farmers." See Kim, *Man and Society*, p. 154.

Moving Beyond the Countryside

Still, the fact that resources and technology limited Park's rural development vision is only half the story of why urbanization-led industrialization for export ultimately triumphed and, more important, why it had the character it did. Several additional factors having to do with concurrent urban successes – not just rural failures – also counted. For one thing, from the beginning government policy makers had been well aware that sustained income generation from EOI was still an important element of Park's overall development strategy, especially his plans to "correct the inequities between the rural and urban sectors and to uplift the economic lot of the nation's farm economy."[199] As Ki Hyuk Park put it, "The task of transforming the traditional family farm into the modern farming business, which is capital intensive, required a provision of a large amount of capital investment."[200] And this meant that the government could not easily renege on its commitment to regulate, discipline, and prod capitalists in the service of sustained export-led industrial growth, since this still remained the key to rural transformation. As such, EOI developed around manufacturing activities based primarily in cities and the trend continued.

Yet it was not just that urban-based industrial activities continued to exist while the government emphasized rural development, since after all they had been around from almost the very beginning as part of Park's overall vision without fully challenging his insistence on the primacy of rural development. The difference in the 1970s, however, was that the government was extraordinarily successful in developing and sustaining this type of EOI. Put another way, it was not just that Park's administration continued to foster export-led industrialization, a commitment which itself helped tip the balance to cities and to a deeper and more diverse plan of industrialization. The important thing to recognize is that these EOI activities became even more productive and generated more profit than even Park had anticipated, a state of affairs which soon changed the demographic composition, political balance of class power, and overall economic structure of the nation. And again, some of this had to do with the onerous rural conditions that had predominated until Saemaul Undong kicked in, primarily because any employment gains in the city, even marginal ones, tended to draw migrants from the still problematic countryside.

Over time, especially as the goal of transforming the countryside seemed to be stymied by material, social, and cultural obstacles, more and more rural citizens moved to the cities. This demographic shift helped the nation's capitalists achieve their industrial and economic goals, partly because they could rely on an increasingly larger and relatively impoverished mass of urban

[199] Park, "Contribution of the Saemaul Movement," p. 163.
[200] Ibid., p. 166.

laborers for their factories. This, in turn, brought a notable change in the national class structure. Whereas during the first decade of Park's administration rural farmers constituted the large majority of the national population, by the 1970s a growing urban working class – and a not insignificant cadre of urban poor – began to statistically challenge their preeminence. By the end of that decade, more South Koreans were living in cities than in the countryside. And the more this occurred, the more the political and economic balance of power began to shift to the cities and in support of all-out industrial development. All this means that, despite Park's good intentions, Saemaul Undong may have been too little too late to stop the demographic flood of migrants that ultimately challenged his original rural development priorities and eventually transformed a vision of small-farmer populism into one of unrestrained commitment to EOI.

Of course, it would be foolhardy not to recognize that the intensified emphasis on urban-based EOI in the early 1970s can be partly explained by favorable conditions in the global economy and a new round of direct foreign investment during this period, both of which fueled the growth of export manufacturing, and not just rural-urban migration. But again, this argument can only go so far. After all, it was just about the same time that Park gave up on rural development alone and started pouring more energies into EOI that the global economy experienced a major downturn and crisis. This was evident by early 1973, owing to both the oil crisis and the collapse of the Bretton Woods agreement, both of which put a major damper on world trade and limited the extent to which the West would be able to import processed industrial goods, even cheap ones like those produced in South Korea at the time. Given these conditions, it is important to consider that the tremendous industrial successes of South Korea's export-led model that became apparent by the late 1970s owed not just to favorable global conditions and greater foreign investment, nor just to the demographic shifts noted above, but also to the government's intensified disciplinary measures. The content and character of these disciplinary measures, moreover, owed as much to past conditions, priorities, and practices as to conjunctural developments in the early 1970s, and to the rural-based Saemaul Undong program in particular.

Before 1971, as we have seen so far, the South Korean state evidenced a clear will and demonstrated capacity to discipline classes and social groups in the city, although most of the discipline was imposed on capitalists, both industrialists and bankers, owing to the small-farmer ideals on which this disciplinary ethos was based. Yet, after 1971, we start to see greater state disciplining with respect to industrial laborers and the urban working class too; and it was the application of the disciplinary ethos to these subordinate classes in the city that further nurtured the country's industrial miracle. All this means that Park's intensified commitment to disciplining industrial labor and capital in the early 1970s was historically grounded in a logic and disciplinary ethos, which itself grew out of Park's political and social embeddedness with the rural middle class in earlier periods, and that emphasized discipline and austerity in the service of greater productivity and efficiency. Not only did Park work hard to impose these small-farmer sentiments on the city and its populations; the application of these disciplinary measures to the factory level and to urban life in general played as critical a role as the global economy and demographic changes in producing the extraordinary industrial successes in the cities over the 1970s.

The overall effect of moving the program from the countryside to the city was not just to establish a new set of disciplinary practices and ideals that mitigated against the development of a strong urban working-class activism and consciousness. These new urban-based disciplinary programs and practices made South Korea's industrial manufacturing activities extraordinarily productive, not just in comparison to agriculture, but also with respect to the global marketplace. With factory-level production shooting through the roof, export gains were enormous and industry flourished, as did Seoul where most firms were located. Ultimately this combination of factors signaled doom for rural development objectives and irretrievably set South Korea on the path toward EOI.

In order to understand why this occurred in the early and mid-1970s and not earlier, we must return to the countryside and to Saemaul Undong. Why? Because despite the material limits to the program in rural areas deriving from small plot sizes and other impediments to greater productivity, it nonetheless was considered enough of a success to spur Park and government policy makers to implement a reconstituted version of the program in urban areas. This assessment helps explain the timing of urban-based Saemaul Undong, which began in 1973, at the time of Bretton Woods and almost two years after it was implemented in the countryside, and within a year of the time that the Park administration started to conscientiously concern itself with the problems of over-urbanization.[201] As was evidenced in the late-1960s austerity campaign and noted earlier, Park had long viewed urban residents as lacking the sound moral sentiments of rural dwellers, and by the early 1970s there were plenty of "moral" problems in South Korean cities that the government hoped Saemaul Undong could address, especially in Seoul. In addition to growing labor militancy, there were the distressing levels of poverty and the inadequate infrastructure, two additional sets of problems that may have stemmed from Park's original neglect of cities, itself a product of his obsessive emphasis on the problems of rural poverty and rural infrastructure, and his earlier failed

---

[201] See the position on urban problems, and discussion of a need to build a subway in Seoul, taken by Park's Democratic Republican Party in *DRP: Today and Tomorrow*, pp. 27–29.

agriculture programs which spurred rural-urban migration.[202] As in the countryside, however, Park chose to attack Seoul's social and economic problems by introducing a combination of moral and material incentives, with the emphasis on the former. "City residents," it was said, "had benefitted from the improvements in the economy but were lacking in spiritual development." Accordingly, "one of the key themes [of the urban-directed Saemaul Undong] was cooperation, including the fostering of better relations between employers and workers in the factories and friendship among neighbors."[203]

Given the extent and diversity of the problems in the cities, the Park administration developed five distinct branches of Saemaul Undong for urban areas, each targeted to a particular activity, social, or class grouping: the Factory Movement, the Movement of Office Workers, the School Movement, the Movement of Service Groups, and the Movement in Residential Areas. Of these five branches, most energy was directed toward the Factory Movement, which along with the School Movement was considered to be the most successful of the urban branches, although not nearly as successful or well received as the rural Saemaul Undong.[204] In applying the program to the cities, and primarily to Seoul, the government sought to impose the same strong standards of cooperation, self-discipline, and austerity as were applied in rural areas. Its three guiding principles were: 1) the establishment of Saemaul Undong citizenship to practice love for people and for the country; 2) the establishment of changes in the productive environment directing people away from the propensity to consume toward thrift and saving; and 3) the acceleration of national development by establishing solid unity between urban and rural Saemaul Undong.[205]

The urban movement prioritized rural and urban unity more than had its rural predecessor, a position that may have affirmed Park's view that both branches of the movement, working together, were necessary for sustaining national development. More important, the urban program differed from the rural in that it devoted its energies to slightly different productive and

---

[202] As Rho, *Public Administration and the Korean Transformation*, pp. 67–68, puts it: "The net result of this overwhelming concentration of population in the urban centers" over the late 1960s and early 1970s was "massive unemployment, overcrowded living conditions, proliferation of squatter settlements, and serious strains on urban services and facilities. . . . Moreover, problems such as overcrowding, the deterioration of the physical environment, rising crime and delinquency rates, overextension of service facilities (transportation, water, electricity), and rising environmental pollution place extreme demands on urban administrative systems and hinder the implementation of comprehensive development plans."

[203] Turner et. al., *Villages Astir*, p. 87 fn. 2.

[204] For more on the programs associated with the five branches of urban Saemaul Undong, see Park, "Contribution of the Saemaul Movement," pp. 175–180.

[205] Ibid., p. 175.

infrastructural activities, mainly those linked to manufacturing and urban development. But it worked just the same. As Ki Hyuk Park described it, "Because of the labor intensiveness of light industry [in cities], the [urban] Saemaul Movement has been geared for elimination of waste, diligent work, and mutual cooperation amongst workers," an organizational ethos that he claims not only aided in such projects as environmental beautification and road pavement, but also helped Korean industry to raise productivity and to "meet the foreign competition by reducing the production cost and by improving quality through stringent zero defect (ZD) movement and by co-operative and efficient employer-employee relationships."[206] In the factories in particular, where most resources were directed, the movement was directed at four areas of behavior modification: "1) job performance ability, 2) moral enlightenment to cultivate a lucid outlook on the nation, life and occupation, 3) problem-oriented group discussion, [and] 4) work ethics enhancing the consciousness of individual responsibility for the objectives of collective ventures and creating a congenial working climate."[207] Overall, then, the emphasis was not primarily on changing material and infrastructural conditions in and of themselves, as was the case in the first stage of rural Saemaul Undong, but on transforming attitudes and individual behavior so as to achieve greater factory-level productivity.

Whether the government's explicit aim was to undermine working-class consciousness is unclear, because much of the program seemed more directed toward the "positive" objective of creating a common, shared sense of identity as participants united behind the goal of achieving greater cooperation and productivity and less toward the "negative" objective of eliminating working-class identity as a salient basis for action. Nonetheless, the program's encouragement of individual innovation on the shop floor did indirectly challenge collective solidarity on the basis of a common working-class experience or position, even as it also sought to reify behavioral attributes more commonly associated with a traditional if not rural middle-class ethos, like the one that had materialized in and sustained rural-based Saemaul Undong, including an emphasis on self-discipline, austerity, and rewards for reinvestment and greater productivity.[208] Whatever the motivation, with the program emphasizing many so-called traditional middle-class values, as well as the unity of workers and owners, the

---

[206] Ibid., pp. 165, 183.

[207] Ibid., p. 184.

[208] In "the Saemaul Movement in factories . . . [the] corps which have demonstrated outstanding skill performances are rewarded, which [*sic*] give credits to the promotion of individual members concerned. The contributions by the corps are manifested in the saving of material resources and energy and the improvement of the production process" (ibid., p. 187). Ki Hyuk Park also notes that these productivity gains were not marginal. In the first quarter of 1979, for example, they were equivalent to 654 billion won.

Factory Movement "hinder[ed] the growth of class consciousness of the industrial workers and their labor movement, by inculcating the fantasy of familial relationships between labor and business managers."[209]

Of course, precisely because of the ways it sought to recast relations between capital and labor, it was generally understood that Saemaul Undong was not as popular in cities as in the countryside. In the countryside, this program and the middle-class ethos it embodied were considered to be much more in line with labor process and productive conditions associated with small farming; and direct gains to the farmers themselves and to the community in general were more readily recognized by the rural citizenry. In the city, in contrast, the movement and the values it presented were more often seen as an ideological and material threat to a significant portion of the population, primarily those involved in the organized labor movement. That this was the case, in fact, may explain why most scholars tend to see Saemaul Undong's main function to be one of repression. Yet even with many in the working class decrying the heavy hand of the program and its overall aims, urban Saemaul Undong did find some converts even in the city and, most important, it did make some gains.

In a 1977 survey of attitudes toward the Saemaul movement, 62.2 percent of urban residents saw it as successful and 32.1 percent were indifferent, while 86.3 percent of rural residents saw it as successful and 13.1 percent were indifferent. More telling, perhaps, of the factors identified as being most integral to the program's success (good leaders, cooperation, governmental support, right selection of the task, others), rural and urban residents were actually quite close in attitude, suggesting that the Saemaul program worked similarly in the city and in the countryside, at least from the point of view of citizens, despite the fact that it targeted different classes and different economic activities. Indeed, "cooperation" was chosen as the program's most important feature by an almost equal percentage of rural and urban residents (23.5 percent and 23.3 percent respectively); although there were some marginal differences on other factors: 19.1 percent of rural residents and 16.2 percent of urban residents selected "government support" and 16.6 percent of urban residents and 17.1 percent of rural residents identified "right selection of the task" as most important. Still, country residents were somewhat less likely to be critical of the program's accomplishments than were city dwellers, with urban residents marginally more likely to identify lack of interest, lack of governmental support, and wrong selection of task (28.5 percent, 26.2 percent, and 20.2 percent respectively) as impeding the program's developmental aims than were rural residents (20.1 percent, 14.15 percent, and 14.8 percent respectively), whose more tempered criticism seems to indicate a sense of overall satisfaction with the program.[210]

---

[209] Hahn, "The Political Philosophy of the Saemaul Movement," p. 120.

[210] Saemaul Study Group, *Saemaul Movement Research Collection* No. 1, A, 1978, p. 174, quoted in Park, "Contribution of the Saemaul Movement," p. 180.

The point here is that with regard to both hermeneutics and content, the moral and material incentives embodied in the Saemaul Undong program were applied in much the same fashion in city and countryside, they functioned similarly in both locales, and the overall reputation and successes of the program were evaluated by citizens in much the same way in both locales, despite the fact that this program was first developed as a means to help turn small agricultural producers from peasants into disciplined, efficient, productive, and "rational" rural middle-class actors. To say that the movement was intended to function in the same manner in both cities and the countryside, and that urban and rural citizens saw it in similarly favorable terms, however, is not to say that it produced the same outcomes. Indeed in contrast to the rural movement, the urban Saemaul Undong's impact on factory productivity in cities was absolutely extraordinary, in part because there were fewer material obstacles to greater productivity in the city than the countryside. If anything, in fact, introducing a program of discipline, hard work, and austerity in an industrial shop-floor environment was bound to be successful if the material infrastructure (equipment, inputs, marketing, financing) was already in place and readily available – which it was, given the government's control over and development of these inputs during its previous efforts to discipline capitalists. Thus it is important to underscore the paradox that although the program was initially developed to create a petit bourgeois or middle-class work ethos for rural small producers, it brought startling urban successes.

This occurred in a stepwise manner. First, once the values of self-discipline, cooperation, and austerity were initiated in the countryside with rural peoples in mind, and on the basis of a rural experience that then resonated nationally, they helped build the coherence and sustain the legitimacy of the project. Second, although these values might not have emerged as "naturally" in an urban-industrial environment of owners and workers without considerable innovation or prodding, once developed, implemented, strictly imposed, and practiced with an eye toward rural locales, they become easier to apply to the city and to the industrial shop floor. Indeed, the program had already achieved demonstrated successes as a national blueprint for the majority's increasing productivity in the countryside, in theory if not in practice. Moreover, South Korea was still a rural country in many regards, at least culturally, with many urban industrial workers themselves recent migrants from the countryside. Thus, when this program could only go so far in the countryside, owing to the intractable material limits to small-farmer production, when applied to manufacturing activities and an industrial labor force in the city these same programs and values took root and flourished. One result was a diminished working-class consciousness and reduced likelihood of class conflict, which combined with readily available factor inputs to considerably enhance productivity at the urban workplace and in the industrial sector as a whole.

The Industrial Exporting Miracle Arrives at Last

The economic gains engendered by Park's disciplinary ethos and by the South Korean people's own self-discipline, especially at the level of the industrial shop floor, were phenomenal. By 1974, scarcely a year and a half into urban Saemaul Undong, the number of manufacturing establishments had increased 40 percent (in comparison with 1962), while the average size tripled in terms of employment and rose ninefold in terms of value added.[211] It was during this same period that the smaller manufacturing firms started turning into big chaebols and the South Korean economy took off like gangbusters, absorbing a growing stream of foreign capital, breaking productivity targets, exporting beyond all projections, and starting the move from consumer to capital goods production. Much of this owed to the disciplinary ethos now applied so forcefully to the shop floor, the neighborhood, the schools, and to various other key institutions in South Korean cities. And the more these programs inculcated an environment of self-discipline among labor, the less important it was for the government to use macroeconomic policy prods to discipline capitalists in the service of economic growth, as it had originally sought to do. This further meant that the rural middle-class disciplinary ethos as imposed on the urban industrial workforce not only helped fuel unrestrained EOI; because it made industrial manufacturers so successful, it also fueled the growing power of urban industrialists. This turn of events signaled the beginning of the end of the Park administration's rural development orientation, even as it cemented the country's journey down the path of rapid, urban-led industrialization for export. In a stunning reversal, by the mid-1970s this industrialization model had become an end in itself and not merely a means to sustain rural development.

Some will rightly caution against overemphasizing Saemaul Undong's impact on the deepening of EOI and the attendant application of a rural middle-class ethos to the city, especially in the service of accounting for the greater quiescence of labor and/or for the remarkable productivity gains in manufacturing and industrial exporting during the 1970s. The standard line of argumentation about many of these developments usually focuses on what is referred to as the Yushin Constitution of 1972. Following principles begun in the declaration of a state of emergency in late 1971, the Yushin Constitution institutionalized legal restrictions on the capacity of labor to engage in collective bargaining and collective action, thereby diminishing the power of labor, forcing workers to push for their own wage and workplace demands. In that sense, the Yushin Constitution does factor into our understanding of the state's increasingly disciplinary hand with the organized working class over the 1970s. Still, the constitutional changes enshrined in the Yushin reforms of

[211] Mason et al., *The Economic and Social Modernization*, p. 278.

1972 do not fully explain why the urban economy and EOI ultimately crowded out Park's initial plans for rural development; and they may be the effect as much as the cause of these shifts.

For one thing, when the constitutional reforms were first introduced in late 1971, they were still explicitly coupled with a heavy rural development drive and thus were still intended to provide national resources many of which were intended for rural development. It was only in 1974, after urban Saemaul Undong had a chance to start working in the cities, that a marked shift toward industrialization in and of itself became evident, thereby suggesting that something else besides marshal law and the Yushin Constitution served as the key turning point. Accordingly, we would do well to remember that the legislative changes embodied in the Yushin constitutional reforms were introduced at about the same time as Saemaul Undong was being implemented in the countryside. That is, we might be better served by seeing the Yushin Constitution as part and parcel of a larger disciplinary package, newly imposed by the Park administration in the early 1970s, in which the urban working class also was explicitly targeted for the first time.

Additionally, the Yushin constitutional reforms of 1972 did not achieve all their aims in terms of restricting and marshaling labor in the service of rapid industrialization. If anything, these new restrictions on labor's right to strike and bargain collectively were probably more responsible for inspiring working-class consciousness and militancy than for snuffing it out. An alienated labor force is bound to be a very bad partner in development, since resentful workers would be highly unlikely to cooperate in a drive for increasing productivity while wages stay low and restrictions high. As such, with the implementation of the Yushin Constitution of 1972, the effort to recast the ethos and productive activities of the urban working class took on even greater urgency. With rural Saemaul Undong showing great gains on these fronts in the countryside at just about the same time, it served as a prototype and model for the cities, and one by-product was that the South Korean industrial unions' efforts at class struggle were sidelined. Yet, even with the state's heavier disciplinary hand now sanctioned in the Constitution, Park did not immediately loosen up on capitalists, or toe the hard line with labor, as is generally supposed. In his in-depth account of the South Korean labor movement, Jang Jip Choi suggests that Park's introduction of new, emergency measures on January 14, 1974, both "palliated the LSMSNS (constitutional restrictions on labor) and included a strengthening of penalties against employers' unfair labor practices and their violations of labor standards."[212] The result of this strong disciplinary action with capitalists was a renewed capacity for collective bargaining, albeit within constraints, and a dramatic "upsurge after 1974 in union membership

---

[212] *Labor and the Authoritarian State*, p. 92.

growth."[213] In fact, it may have been precisely because urban Saemaul Undong had been so successful in changing values and behaviors that the Park government even backtracked a bit on its constitutional restrictions vis-à-vis the industrial working class.

In short, the Yushin constitutional changes and post-1972 state policy shifts with respect to organized labor and industrial employers are significant not just because they suggest that urban Saemaul Undong was sufficiently triumphant in inculcating a shared sense of self-discipline and cooperation among urban workers so that it was not always necessary to uphold harsh constitutional restrictions to keep labor in line. They also suggest that it was not unbridled repression of organized labor that laid the groundwork for the mid-1970s economic miracle, but a transformation of behavior, attitudes, and disciplinary practices on the shop floor among laborers themselves, transformations which owed both their programmatic origin and contents to a Park-inculcated rural middle-class ethos which valued sacrifice, austerity, and commitment to productivity without personal aggrandizement.

By 1975, it was becoming clear that South Korea was starting to move in a slightly different direction, both with respect to macroeconomic policy making and in terms of the application of its disciplinary ethos. For one, although the state had not fully abandoned its initial commitment to disciplining capitalists, it had shifted its vision to one that reserved a central place for disciplining labor as well as capitalists. This new vision may have signaled a departure from Park's original small-farmer populism, in which big capitalists were the primary enemy, but in its initial form at least, it still was quite consistent with a rural middle-class ethos in that neither capital nor labor was overly privileged, either vis-à-vis each other or vis-à-vis other classes, including small farmers themselves. This is perhaps best evidenced in the fact that, even after the mid-1970s, the government still continued to use its full control over the banking sector, licensing, tariffs, and tax policy to discipline capitalists in such a way as to keep industrialists in line, reinvesting and producing for the national economy and not merely striving to accelerate their own profits. After 1974, in short, it was the continued, albeit revamped, disciplinary ethos, and even more so its widespread application not just to rural classes but also to the urban-based working class as well as industrial capitalists, that truly catapulted South Korea into the ranks of the world's fiercest developmental "tigers." If the Park administration or its successors had continued to be preoccupied with small-farmer development throughout the 1970s and 1980s, South Korea would never have prospered the way it did over this boom period, especially in terms of overall GNP, strong export earnings, and other financial gains which in turn were used on education, technology, and other key infrastructural components of sustained national

[213] Ibid. •

development. But once the Park administration had committed itself to the all-out goals of fostering urban based EOI and employing urban populations in these industries, and once it pursued these new goals with the same rural middle-class disciplinary ethos it had used in the countryside, then and only then did the South Korean economy cement its unparalleled and rapid ascent into the ranks of tremendous economic achievers, garnering world attention for its rapid industrial successes in this regard.

In retrospect, we should not be surprised that Park eventually started moving down this path, despite the fact that to do so entailed reversing his previous rural development commitments. After all, he was hardly in a position to look the industrial exporting gift horse in the mouth, especially after struggling so hard to foster rural prosperity. The long-term effects of this about-face opened a floodgate of economic growth. Still, despite the fact that this full-steamed shift to EOI was initially conceptualized as consistent with Park's original desires to discipline capitalists, and with his desire to generate external revenues for rural development, the rushing waters could not be contained, and in that sense the gift horse may have become a Trojan horse. Over the 1970s and throughout the 1980s, rural development goals and the agrarian populations who advanced them were irreversibly marginalized, dwarfed by urban-industrial gains. In their place, big industrialists organized in chaebols catapulted directly into the political and economic limelight. And with both the state and big industrialists on the receiving end of extraordinary gains over the next decade or two of nearly unstoppable economic growth, their fates became ever more linked with one another.

New policy measures soon reflected these changes, as capitalists increasingly were able to push the government to work more actively for them, the cash cow that could not be ignored. It may be quite telling that it was in 1974 – approximately two years after Saemaul Undong was implemented in factories and the city in general – the South Korean government first started to let up on previously ironclad domestic restrictions on imports and worked much harder to foster industrialization, including manufacture of previously imported goods. At this time, the government began to much more earnestly protect South Korean industrialists too. As Chung-hyun Rho notes,

> [From] 1973 to early 1979, import protection was strengthened and incentives expanded for the "strategic" industries. The import liberalization ratio, or the proportion of items that could be imported without prior government approval, decreased from 61.7 percent in 1968 to 50.5 percent by 1976, . . . [while] starting in 1974, import restrictions were reinforced with controls on the level of foreign ownership allowed in companies operating in South Korea.[214]

---

[214] *Public Administration and the Korean Transformation*, p. 26.

By the end of the 1970s, South Korea was husbanding a whole new approach to development, in which the balance of economic and political power shifted from the countryside to the city. Industrialization was pursued for itself, not merely as a means to generate resources for rural development and balanced sectoral growth, and the balance of disciplining shifted from industrial capitalists to laborers, with chaebols much more routinely accommodated as the years passed. It is only the latter part of this story, focusing on the industrial gains of the late 1970s and 1980s, as well as the growing economic power of the chaebols, that is well known in the development scholarship. What has been lacking, however, is an understanding of how and why South Korea got to this position in the first place, and how the disciplinary regime of development associated with a rural middle-class disciplinary orientation, embodied in Park's administration during its initial years, both materialized and reconfigured itself in such a way as to bring about this industrial giant.

Rethinking the Miracle, Rethinking the Chaebols, Rethinking the State

I have argued that it was the Park administration's embeddedness with rural middle classes that laid the foundations for the developmental path that eventually bore fruit and earned South Korea its unparalleled status as one of the world's most successful late industrializers. These rural middle-class political bases not only explain Park's strong disciplinary ethos, and his obsession with bringing this ethos to life through state actions in the service of his particular developmental vision, they also help account for the content and character of his macroeconomic policy making during these initial key decades of sustained growth and economic development, especially with respect to export-led industrialization as well as the shift away from rural development starting in the mid-1970s. Because the Park administration relied on the rural middle classes for developmental inspiration and political support during his first decade in office, the state chose to subordinate industrial development to rural development priorities, as well as to select an industrial strategy (EOI instead of ISI) that complemented this aim. Equally important, the state's rural middle-class political bases endowed the state with the capacity to impose relatively strict constraints on the micro- and macroeconomic behavior of capitalists – and later laborers – as well as to foster an environment of self-discipline, austerity, and efficiency in both industrial and agricultural sectors. By struggling to achieve these three goals simultaneously, Park helped turn a relatively "backward," primarily rural, nation into one of the world's most prosperous and successful late industrializers in a stunningly short amount of time.

The key to South Korea's remarkable economic success lay not just in overall support for industrialization, however, or industrialization at any cost, but in Park's decision to foster EOI rather than ISI early on, and his decision to use the former as a means to sustain rural development, not as an end in and of itself. These choices reflected the relative political weakness of urban based classes as well as the personal and developmental importance of rural populations for his administration. Moreover, South Korea's remarkable gains lay not merely in the selection of EOI policies, crafted in order to sustain rather than draw resources and attention away from rural development; they also owe to a developmental vision that prioritized production rather than consumption, that sought a healthy balance between rural and urban development, at least initially, and that counted on self-discipline and coercive discipline as the means to prod and guide economic behavior. All these goals also can be traced to the rural middle-class bases of Park's administration. Combined, these priorities not only turned South Korea away from the deepened, deficit-producing, consumption-oriented ISI model that proved so disastrous for Latin America and other late industrializers, they also made the selection of EOI a more logical outcome. In the global economic environment of the 1960s and 1970s, this policy choice was extraordinarily fortuitous, giving South Korea the opportunity to generate considerable external resources and foreign exchange even as it accommodated domestic political and social conditions and priorities.

The latter point is critical because it underscores the fact that in this accounting of South Korea's successes, the decision to wholeheartedly pursue EOI was not necessarily a technically expedient calculation made by autonomous state elites who knew a priori that this was the best way to achieve stunning growth rates or sustain national development. Rather, in many senses the South Korean government "backed into" this post-1974 industrialization strategy, as it encountered obstacle after obstacle throughout the 1960s and early 1970s while initially pursuing a different set of developmental goals derived from its specifically rural-class political bases. In short, serendipity rather than strategic calculation was at play here, for much of the time at least.

All this of course raises the question of why rural development and a rural middle-class ethos were pursued and promoted so wholeheartedly in the first place, an issue which speaks to the importance of looking for a more general theoretical logic and not just serendipity, and which also forces us to confront the limitations of thinking about development policy making only in terms of economic expediency, or the rationally chosen strategies of state actors. I have shown that Park's originating desire to build the national economy on a small-farmer populist vision of development was not capricious but purposeful, given his embeddedness in rural political bases and his own vision of the moral superiority, thrift, and efficiency of rural middle classes. Whether it was economically rational or technically expedient is yet another story. It clearly was strategical and perhaps even "rational" on a political basis, given the large farmer population in South Korea and the strong links Park's own military loyalists established with rural populations. It also was quite consistent with Park's personal experience and his own repertoire of values (themselves embedded in a material understanding of small-farmer lifestyles and priorities, plus the military training), something that could be considered in terms of a methodologically individualist, rational choice model.

Still, on purely market or macroeconomic terms, this developmental vision and the policies it brought to life would hardly be considered "rational" by most economists, despite the fact that Park actually sought to "write" rationality into the larger developmental equation through the implementation of purposeful and strong-armed government programs intended to introduce a culture of economic rationality into the countryside. It does not take a rocket scientist to determine that small farmers, especially in the historical, geographic, and geopolitical terrain of South Korea, would suffer incredible obstacles in generating the aggregate productivity levels necessary to sustain a national economy, even if they were inculcated with an ethos of economic rationality, especially given the small plot sizes that predominated. Moreover, what card-carrying economist would have calculated that the most strategically rational way to generate incredible industrial and macroeconomic advances would be to discipline capitalists as much as laborers? Yet it was precisely by following these policies, which together comprised a macroeconomically "irrational" vision of development, that South Korea ultimately ended up with an extraordinarily successful set of measures which brought great industrial and developmental gains and that analysts would later classify as strategically rational and expedient.

In addition to challenging rational-choice models, all this underscores something of a political and sociological paradox: Park Chung Hee spent considerable effort and more than a decade trying to sustain the rural middle-class vision in South Korean society, an objective which entailed introducing social, cultural, and material programs for nurturing and transmitting rural middle-class values to all corners of society, urban as well as rural, and for disciplining big capitalists. Yet, ironically, in the long run his administration has been considered successful because it laid the foundation for a highly industrialized, overurbanized economy with a powerful class of large industrial capitalists, thereby practically eliminating small farmers, the rural middle class, and South Korea's small-farmer-based agricultural economy. This occurred not because Park's active support of small farmers or the rural middle classes brought this outcome directly, but because this rural program had unintended consequences that mattered. Indeed, Park's "defensive" actions against big industrial capitalists, particularly by virtue of the strong-armed disciplinary and regulatory measures he imposed on them, spurred capitalists to organize among themselves, with economically beneficial effects. As Tun-jen Cheng sees it, the collective action of leading businesses was the most decisive factor in ultimately creating a strong and influential state-capital alliance over the late 1970s and thereafter. To the extent that Park's administration "forced businesses to organize themselves to protect their property rights by acting on behalf of the interests of the political elite," they were better prepared to take up the banner of development and point it in a new direction; and one result was that "organized business drafted its version of economic plans, designed industrial estates, and volunteered to secure international capital," all actions which increased their own political salience as they pushed South Korea down the road to rapid, urban-based industrialization.[215] Combined with the positive effects for industrial productivity engendered by the application of a self-disciplinary cultural ethos among the urban working class, these developments shifted the political and economic balance away from the countryside.

The longer-term gains from disciplining capitalists and laborers can be presented as evidence of what Albert Hirschman had in mind when he called for more attention to the role of "intended but unrealized effects of social decisions."[216] As noted up front in this chapter, most scholars of South Korean development start with a focus on the inordinate power and concentration of industrial capitalists, or chaebols, to explain the remarkable economic achievements of this country. Big chaebols were seen as inherently endowed with the power to discipline laborers and control the state sufficiently enough to insure successful operations and private economic gains, both of which were seen to fuel the South Korean development miracle. But what I am suggesting here, if anything, is that the extraordinary growth and development of chaebols and other large capitalists were the unintended consequence of initial efforts by Park to foster rural development and rural middle-class formation, efforts which paid off not just by fostering amenable macroeconomic conditions for sound export-led industrialization, but also by nurturing a self-disciplinary working class that contributed to capitalist's productivity gains (and did not throw EOI offtrack by demanding domestic goods for consumption).

But would Park himself have agreed with this assessment? Would he have acknowledged that his initial aspirations were so different, even after the economy fully shifted gears and transformed itself? This will remain forever unknown, since Park was assassinated in 1979, in a military coup planned by fellow generals known to wholeheartedly support urban-based industrialization.[217] While few scholars have tried to understand the reasons for Park's assassination by his own intelligence chief, preferring to cite unspecified "internal differences" in the military government as an explanation, it may very well be that Park's concerns about shifting the direction of macroeconomic development so rapidly, or his worry about the growing power of chaebols and

---

[215] "Political Regimes and Development Strategies," p. 159.

[216] *The Passions and the Interests*, p. 131.

[217] For more discussion of Park's successor, Chun Doo-Hwan, and his more supportive position on chaebols, see Choi, "Political Cleavages in South Korea," p. 36; and Bello and Rosenfeld, *Dragons in Distress*, pp. 71–75.

the dismal future for rural South Korea were at the source of at least some of these tensions. Whatever the reason, with Park eliminated from the picture the chaebols started influencing government policy in ways that he had long sought to avoid, growing and profiting in unparalleled fashion with a new, more friendly administration in power. Scholars who gloss over these administrative distinctions and see the military-backed post-1961 South Korean state as all of a piece lack the basic conceptual tools to understand why there were fundamental macroeconomic differences in that period or identify them as significant. They are relevant, however, especially with respect to development policy, because they highlight the sharp break in Park's initial economic aims, with respect to both his predecessors and his successors. After Park's death, South Korea became an entirely different place than it had been just a decade or two before, not just in terms of industrial development, but also in terms of class structure and rural-urban balance.

Since the 1980s, the South Korean government has pretty much abandoned rural development as a main priority and has embraced urban-based industrialization at all costs. The nation also has seen continuing decline in the countryside, steady rural-urban migration, a tremendous growth in the size of the urban working class, and greater income inequalities both between countryside and cities as well as within cities themselves.[218] While in 1960, 65.25 percent of the population were farmers, by 1985 the figure had plummeted to 23.9 percent, despite staying over 51 percent in 1970. The working class (defined as manual workers) has become the single largest class, comprising 34 percent of the population in 1985, a marked increase from 14.6 percent in 1960.[219] And as cities have grown to host the new, and now much larger, manufacturing firms, the urban class structure has become more diversified, ushering in an ever larger urban middle class of professionals and managers. In qualitative terms, the rural middle class in general and farmers in particular have found themselves increasingly without the inputs and policy support necessary to sustain sufficient levels of production, especially as they have lost their political influence. The urban working class, much larger in numbers now after two more decades of rapid industrialization, has only limited power to mold development policies, to be sure, in part because the state's disciplinary hand with labor remained even as it disappeared with capital. Chaebols are no longer the restricted and relatively insignificant political forces they were in the 1960s and early 1970s. As of the 1980s, they attained the heights of

---

[218] For a more thorough discussion of contemporary South Korea and political and economic transformations since 1975, see Bello and Rosenfeld, *Dragons in Distress*. They have a particularly good discussion of the crisis in the countryside and the ways in which failure to continue aiding small farmers, as well as the disastrous effects of market liberalization on the domestic and foreign demand for agricultural goods, have contributed to rural decline.

[219] Koo, "Middle Classes, Democratization, and Class Formation," p. 488 (Table 1).

power and influence, ever more capable of directing macroeconomic policy in their own interests and ever more linked to the state, which itself became increasingly corrupt as it answered to few but these big capitalists.

It should be no surprise, then, that one of the key mechanisms for directing and developing South Korea's economic potential during Park's administration – control over banking and the financial sectors – has now become a thing of the past. Chaebols themselves have been calling the shots in ways that have not boded well for South Korea's economy in the last decade, ranging from an overvalued currency to a highly speculative real estate market, financially insolvent credit and banking institutions, and an indebted public sector. In response to the unrestrained power of the chaebols and the corruption of the state, labor unions have increasingly struggled to push for recognition of labor's right to make wage demands. Urban residents, as well, have begun organizing around the growing service scarcities in the city, especially affordable housing, and struggling for more equitable distribution of the so-called miracle. One result has been the appearance of new class coalitions between the working and middle classes, mainly in cities. These social forces now stand together to challenge the strong-armed government both on economic policies and its unparalleled power, two complaints that in recent years have increasingly concerned the nation's destitute farmers. As a result of their mobilization and struggle, South Korea has now started down the path of democracy, after years of military rule. And with these transformations, South Korea has become an entirely different place than it was in the 1960s under Park, when rural development and rural populations still mattered and when public political opposition was confined to a relatively small group of intellectuals and working-class activists. Indeed, South Korea is a much more democratic place than it was even only fifteen years ago, when the working class was forced to buckle under the power of a chaebol-state alliance, and when democracy was still elusive.

Just as significantly for our purposes, however, contemporary South Korea is a different place economically speaking. And in these regards, the prospects are not quite so rosy, precisely because South Korea has taken on the profile and problems of so many other late developers, particularly those of Latin America. It is not just overurbanization, a growing and active urban working class, and urban-based coalitions of working and middle classes united against the government's economic policy that may make contemporary South Korea start to look a lot more like Mexico and Argentina. It also is the country's recurring economic problems, which themselves have been intricately related to the growing power and corruption of big business groups, which probably contributed to popular movements and the recent democratization of politics in the first place. Even in the early 1990s, before South Korea suffered through a serious banking crisis at the end of that decade, some renegade economists were warning of South Korea's growing foreign debt and its precarious balance of payments. Many argued that the South Korean national economy was nearing a full-blown crisis, plagued by a bailout-sized foreign debt, a weakened currency, a real estate crisis, growing evidence of business corruption, and an insolvent and overextended banking system. Not only did these problems echo those of numerous Latin American countries that so many observers used to chastise for not following the East Asian tigers' path over the late 1980s and 1990s, they actually seemed worse in South Korea than in some of Latin America's most renowned basket cases. Indeed, the November 1997 economic crisis that tarnished South Korea's international reputation as one of East Asia's loudest roaring tigers provoked the South Korean government to ask the IMF for a currency bailout that exceeded $65 billion dollars, easily surpassing the previous record of $48 billion given to Mexico,[220] a country that few would have compared to South Korea a mere decade ago.

Many of those economic problems can be traced to weaknesses in the South Korean economy, especially its banking sector, problems which themselves emerged only after the move to industrialization at all costs in the late 1970s and early 1980s, and after the unparalleled rise of the chaebols as a result. The shift in development policy and priorities over the 1980s not only reflected the government's diminished enthusiasm for fiscal austerity; it also took leave of the earlier government's opposition to conspicuous consumption and its over-all commitment to discipline industrial and banking capitalists so as to keep the economy sound. And this, in many ways, directly reflected the growing po-litical power of chaebols and their increasing capacity to loosen the constraints of state discipline and turn the financial system into a vehicle for market and currency speculation, rather than a motor for sustained national development, both industrial and agricultural. As Meredith Woo Cumings reminds us in her masterful study *Race to the Swift*, the latter state of affairs was probably best evidenced by the privatization of all banks in 1987, ending decades of government control over financing industrial development, and thus ending its capacity to guide and regulate industrial capital. And this suggests that many of South Korea's more recent economic problems can be traced to the new class structure of the nation, both the enlarged urban working class and middle class and the diminishing rural middle class, which no longer has the political salience within the state to push for the discipline of capitalists and bankers that brought much more sound economic development in earlier years.

This transformation in the class structure, and how this transformation has changed patterns of state-class embeddedness first fostered by Park, may in-deed be the greatest irony of all. South Korea's initial successes, particularly its rapid ascent into the club of industrializers by fostering EOI from the

---

[220] Kristof, "Seoul Plans to Ask the IMF for a Minimum of $20 Billion," *New York Times*, 22 November 1977, p. A1.

very beginning, owed to the salience of rural middle classes and their embeddedness in the developmental state of Park Chung Hee. Yet as EOI brought tremendous successes in generating foreign exchange and in bolstering the development of profitable manufacturing industries, the country fell victim to its own, almost unintended, industrial successes. These successes, combined with other endogenous limits to small-farmer production, killed the rural middle-class goose that laid the golden egg. Without a strong rural middle class embedded in the state, keeping capitalists in line as much as laborers, and without the benefit of a rural middle-class ethos that privileged production over consumption and rural development as much as urban, the economy set off on the same path that proved so rocky in highly urbanized and relatively industrialized Latin America. Given its current class structure, the salience of urban populations in the national economy and society, the disintegration of the rural sector, the elimination of the rural middle class as a key player and inspiration in national politics, and the ongoing tensions between capital, labor, and the state that now preoccupy politicians and industrialists alike, South Korea's prospects today do not look nearly as good as they did just a decade or two ago, although in the recent banking crisis, citizens returned to old habits of self-discipline and reduced consumption sufficiently to bolster savings and comply with IMF-imposed austerity measures enough to set the economy back on track. It may not be that farfetched to suggest that history has had its day, that this East Asian tiger cannot roar as loudly as it used to, and it is now humbly finding its place in the late developmental cage with the other big cats.

4

DISCIPLINARY DEVELOPMENT AS RURAL MIDDLE-CLASS FORMATION

Proletarianized Peasants and Farmer-Workers in Argentina and Taiwan

Rural Middle Classes in Comparative Perspective

The disciplinary development model pursued by General Park in South Korea over the 1960s and 1970s based its promise on gains to be generated by a vibrant class of small-scale rural producers. For a while, this unfulfilled promise was sufficient to sustain the government's commitment to disciplining industrialists, who were then expected to generate foreign exchange earnings through manufacturing exports so that revenues could be recycled into self-sustaining and nationally generative rural development. But a thriving rural economy and a vibrant middle class of farmers with the productive capacity to generate robust forward and backward linkages between city and countryside never truly materialized in South Korea, at least not to the degree and in the form that Park imagined. Without a strong rural middle class of small agricultural producers stoking the fires of South Korea's economy, much of the glittering appeal of disciplinary development steadily lost its shimmer. The South Korean state still prioritized the export of manufactured goods after 1979, to be sure; and this brought foreign exchange gains and a contented class of industrial capitalists who continued to lead the country down the road of relatively successful export-led industrialization. But without rural economic gains, the countryside languished terribly. Farmers increasingly migrated to cities to work in factories, tipping the rural-urban balance and further limiting the national government's political capacity to discipline manufacturing industrialists and their urban-based laborers in a macroeconomically efficient fashion. Exports continued, but firms became bloated, inefficient, and self-serving, as did many of the government bureaucrats of the post-Park administrations, who placed themselves on the receiving end of the *chaebols'* unparalleled economic gains. Bureaucratic corruption further limited the state's will and capacity to discipline. The upshot was that even as economic gains accrued from a steady rise of manufacturing exports, blemishes tarnished the miracle and the country suffered through some rocky times with the debt crisis of the 1980s and the banking crisis of the 1990s.

To the extent that South Korea's economic trajectories were so intricately connected to the political and economic decline of the rural middle class, or what one might term the obstacles to rural middle-class formation, it is prudent to turn to these actors and that process more conscientiously. What conditions explain whether small-scale agricultural producers will form a social force with sufficient economic clout and political sway to sustain a government's disciplinary stance vis-à-vis urban industrialists and laborers? What obstacles might prevent them from doing so? Is the fate of rural middle classes contingent on certain country-specific factor endowments which lie beyond the practical reach of governing authorities or small producers themselves? Or, can state decisions, deeds, and dynamics work to effectively produce and/or sustain a vibrant rural middle class and its support for a disciplinary development model, even when unanticipated industrial gains seem to challenge such outcomes? These are the questions that guide this chapter.

In the service of answering them, I bring two new cases into the picture: Taiwan and Argentina. These countries lie at the extreme ends of a developmental spectrum in which South Korea stands in the middle, both in terms of rural middle-class formation and in terms of successful versus "failed" macroeconomic development trajectories. Taiwan, like South Korea, has earned kudos as one of the loudest roaring tigers of the East, and it is considered by most observers to be even more economically successful than South Korea, mainly because it too achieved early industrial exporting gains even as it avoided the debt and financial crises that plagued South Korea in the 1980s and the late 1990s. Of course, there are some important similarities between these two East Asian tigers that explain why they are generally lumped together as "success" cases, especially when contrasted to most of Latin America. Like South Korea, Taiwan pursued export-led industrialization early on, thereby shedding the import-substitution preoccupation that saddled the economies of Latin America over the decades of the 1960s, 1970s, and 1980s. And like South Korea, Taiwan hosted a relatively successful rural land reform during the 1950s and over the 1960s, a move which established important ownership conditions necessary for building a relatively significant rural middle class. Yet in contrast to South Korea, Taiwan's rural middle class blossomed and grew as a key economic force, giving life to the dream that slipped from General Park's hands.

As most of South Korea's rural farmers struggled through decades of disappointing harvests, poverty, and eventual abandonment of the countryside to work in big urban factories, large numbers of Taiwan's agricultural producers stayed put, invested, reinvested, and expanded their farm activities. In contrast to South Korea, where 30 percent of small farmers remained as tenants despite the introduction of land reform, all but 5 percent of Taiwan's small farmers achieved ownership after land reform.[1] Partly for this reason, Taiwanese farmers increased their productivity rates, average farm size, profitability, and overall economic gains, so that by the late 1970s and early 1980s, farmers themselves served as major sources of investment and social capital in the development of urban industrial activities in Taiwan, and not vice versa. Urban activities remained connected to rural ones and agriculture and industry continued to fuel each other. Urban industrial activities, in fact, were generally undertaken by small family firms – i.e., urban middle classes – with strong family investment connections to the farm economy.

The early buoyancy and sustained centrality of Taiwan's rural middle class, then, may lend insight into why Taiwan pursued a disciplined development strategy even earlier than South Korea, why it continued to do so even after years of great industrial exporting successes brought sufficient gains to empower urban industrialists, and why Taiwan's disciplinary path toward prosperity has been more deeply entrenched and economically generative than South Korea's. Despite a shared experience of Japanese colonialism, similar cold war geopolitical dynamics, early commitment to EOI, and extensive global integration, Taiwan has avoided many of the economic problems currently plaguing South Korea. Not only does Taiwan continually place in the top rankings of world exporters, but, as early as 1992, when South Korea was desperate for the resources to pay off external debt, Taiwan ranked first in the world, above Japan, in foreign exchange accumulation.[2] In 1990, moreover, as South Korea suffered through the tail end of a debt crisis that hit its citizens hard, the "poorest 40 percent of Taiwan's populace apparently had a larger share of national income than their counterparts in any noncommunist country in the world."[3]

The experience of Argentina could not be more different. This is a country that has fostered almost no rural middle class to speak of, and in contrast to both Taiwan and South Korea, Argentina has been in a perpetual state of deep economic crisis, or in some version of it, since its own very early "reversal of development" in the 1930s, so well chronicled by Carlos Waisman.[4] Unlike its East Asian counterparts, Argentina has suffered a chronic imbalance of payments and steadily growing external indebtedness over the past several decades, owing partly to an enduring commitment to ISI. And these problems continued even when the country formally embraced neoliberalism. When Argentina joined the regional free trade pact known as the Mercosur in the 1990s, for example, government policies continued to prioritize industrial imports over export-led industrialization and to protect highly inefficient and

[1] See Kay, *Asia's and Latin America's Development*, p. 19.
[2] Bullard, *The Soldier and the Citizen*, p. 2.
[3] Tien, *The Great Transition*, p. 27.
[4] *Reversal of Development in Argentina*.

noncompetitive manufacturing industrialists.[5] For this reason, as well as the fact that the market for its agrarian exports has been declining, Argentina recently suffered a major economic crisis – further related to its failure to sustain sufficient exports to justify recent policy efforts to "dollarize" its currency – which has all but thrown the country into political, social, and economic chaos. With the future still unknown as this book goes to press, it is not too farfetched to consider Argentina as perhaps the *least* successful of a promising group of twentieth-century industrializers, especially given its relatively high level of industrial and economic development nearly a hundred years ago.

What may be most significant for our purposes is the fact that of the major industrialized nations of Latin America, and in contrast to Taiwan especially, Argentina stands out in terms of the political and economic dominance of its large landlords within the country's rural class structure. For this reason, Argentina's rural middle class is considered extraordinarily weak if not effectively nonexistent in political and economic terms. This state of affairs further suggests that Argentina's macroeconomic problems may owe to the absence of a rural middle class economically or politically capable of sustaining government imposition of a disciplinary development model that prioritizes industrial exports and/or generatively connects urban and rural economies in terms of production, consumption, and forward-backward linkages. To be sure, the inclusion of Argentina in this analysis may at first smack of an over-reliance on materialist explanations for developmental trajectories. Or so this might be the conclusion given the fact that most scholars uniformly consider that Argentina's geography and Spanish land-grant history prevented its rural middle class from forming into a significant force. As an ex-Spanish colony whose unequal patterns of large landholdings were established early on, long-standing conditions favored the development of large agricultural landlords while subsequent failures to implement a serious land reform reinforced land-lord power.[6] All these factors make the absence of a significant rural middle class neither a surprise nor an issue of current sociological or historical inquiry.

---

[5] For a masterful accounting of this as seen from the level of the firm, as well as its impact on Argentina's integration into the global economy, see Guillén's *The Limits of Convergence.*

[6] What matters most is not the presence or absence of reform per se, as we shall see in the next chapter when we discuss Mexico, but rather, the rural class and power structures that materialize with or without land reform and the extent to which they are marshaled in the disciplining of industrial capital and labor. Even with a similarly timed land reform that eliminated the agrarian oligarchy, South Korea did not achieve the same enduring developmental successes as Taiwan. And even in countries where large landownership flourished in the absence of land reform, as in the case of Argentina, the state's unwillingness to discipline industrial capital and/or labor cannot be assumed. In theory, an agrarian oligarchy could just as easily use its power and influence to promote strong state regulation of industry, as occurred in the case of South Korea (although not under the hand of the oligarchy); and in fact, such a policy would make great sense to an agricultural elite if industry were seen as competing with

However, closer scrutiny of twentieth-century Argentine history paints a very different picture, suggesting that its truncated economic progress and its politically emasculated rural middle class were neither preordained nor unproblematic by-products of the country's postcolonial factor endowments. Indeed, if we reexamine Argentina's early historical successes in fostering sustained and unparalleled levels of economic growth in the late-nineteenth and early-twentieth centuries, we see that for a short period of time the country did host a considerable rural middle class and that their political sway in the late-nineteenth and early-twentieth centuries may be part of the country's economic story. During these early periods of economic and industrial expansion, it was the provincially strong, middle-class-based Unión Cívica Radical, or Radical party, that led the nation to these unsurpassed heights. It was in the heyday of the party's administrative hegemony (under Hipólito Yrigoyen and Marcelo T. Alvear) during the first decades of the twentieth century, in fact, that "protection for domestic manufactures was conspicuous by its absence."[7] Thus we might consider that some of Argentina's great industrial and economic gains, in early periods at least, owed to the political salience of a relatively broad spectrum of rural and urban middle classes in the governing coalition.[8] This was especially so during the administration of Hipólito Yrigoyen, a charismatic political leader of the Radical Party whose occupational origins as a schoolteacher and "moonlighting" experience as a farmer raising livestock on rented agricultural lands echo Park Chung Hee's own rural middle-class identity and personal background.[9]

But when Juan Perón came to power in the 1930s, and his Partido Justicialista defeated the Radical Party, middle classes of both urban and rural origins, especially the latter, were much more likely to be excluded from the national political picture and the governing coalition in particular. Perón's government relied on urban classes for political support, mainly labor and industrialists, and it fostered rapid ISI while protecting the urban-based industrial capitalists and a good portion of the industrial working class. Accommodation of capital, not discipline, was the modus operandi of the Argentine state; and despite the

agriculture for state influence or favor. Likewise, there is no guarantee that the absence of a strong agrarian oligarchy, something that frequently results from land reform, automatically translates into the developmental successes that South Korea and Taiwan experienced.

[7] Whittaker, *Argentina*, p. 78. He also claims that in general, the Radicals neglected domestic manufacturing (p. 88), something which suggests that even in the absence of strict disciplining, there was little favoritism either. Cornblit further argues that the Radical party has long opposed protectionism ("European Immigrants," p. 246).

[8] According to Johnson, the Civic Union (established in 1892), which was the precursor to the Unión Cívica Radical, "drew support from wide segments of society and had a broad geographic base, [although] it was from the start the party of the middle sectors, particularly those in Buenos Aires" (*Political Change in Latin America*, p. 98).

[9] For more on Yrigoyen's background, see Whittaker, *Argentina*, p. 67.

fact that Perón had his enemies among the economic elite, he pretty much failed to keep their activities regulated. One result was that industrialists called the shots, and thus the Argentine economy began lurching and jolting downhill from one crisis to another.[10]

Still, even this rather depressing outcome should not be considered "given" by Argentina's industrial or landowning past so much as conceptualized as the product of class conflict and political struggle in which rural middle classes might have been successful but were not. After all, rural middle classes were not always absent from the landscape. As late as 1937, when Argentina was poised on the edge of a major governmental push toward urban-based industrialization under Perón, the number of persons both living and working on Argentine farms was over 2.5 million, outpacing rural laborers (both permanent and transient) five to one.[11] Carl Taylor has gone so far as to suggest that as late as 1948 approximately "84% of all farms in Argentina ... [were] family operated,"[12] while the esteemed sociologist Gino Germani argues similarly that as of 1940 "small property owners, middle-sized leaseholders (*arrendatarios medieros*), and others who cultivated less than 200 hectares carried out production with family labor or alone, controlled 10% of the land," yet constituted 80 percent of all cultivation units.[13] Many among this relatively sizable cadre of rural middle-class farmers had struggled politically and economically against large landlords for control of the government and its macroeconomic policy making throughout the first four decades of the century when subsequent industrialization patterns were firmly set.

Ultimately, however, rural middle classes lost out and one of our aims in this chapter is to understand why. What combination of social, political, and economic conditions prevented Argentina's rural middle class from empowering themselves and the government to sustain a disciplinary development strategy, and why did Taiwan "succeed" (and, somewhat less so, South Korea) on these grounds instead? Part of the answer undoubtedly rests in the unique geopolitical, military, and cold war conditions in East Asia during the 1950s

---

[10] As Rock puts it, most of "Argentina's [economic] misfortunes originated in Perón's heyday during the 1940s and early 1950s." See Rock, *Argentina*, p. xxiii.

[11] Taylor, *Rural Life in Argentina*, p. 107 (Table 17). While there were 286,468 permanent laborers and 260,309 transient laborers working on Argentine farms, the total number of farm "entrepreneurs," as Taylor calls them, plus their spouses, children, and "other members of these same producers' families" working on the farms, was 2,535,999. (A caveat: Taylor does not clearly distinguish among farm sizes in these aggregate statistics, but focuses instead on what he calls family production units.)

[12] Ibid., p. 241.

[13] *Estructura social de la Argentina*, p. 13. (Translation note: Germani claims these small producers "*representan el 80% de las explotaciones*"; hence I use the term "cultivations" in order to differentiate between raw numbers of people working and the overall magnitude of small-scale production.)

and the extent to which they produced carte blanche U.S. support for Taiwan and South Korea, which in the 1950s and 1960s stood at the front line of the international anticommunist movement. South Korean and Taiwanese loyalty in the United States' struggle against China and North Korea is part of the reason why American armed forces did not intervene to overthrow their governments even when they sought to discipline capitalists within their borders. Such intervention commonly occurred in Latin American countries when leftist governments introduced land reform and/or challenged the hegemony of capitalists.[14] Still, Argentina did not suffer a U.S. invasion to topple its government, perhaps because Peronist anticommunist rhetoric was not altogether that different from that heard in South Korea under Park. Indeed, during much of the time Peronists were in power, government and party leaders not only developed anticommunist sentiments (and actually repressed and jailed many communist leaders), they also relied on populist languages to accommodate certain disenfranchised forces in society and chart an independent (or "third") route between communism and free market capitalism, just as occurred in South Korea and to a great extent in Taiwan.[15] One key difference that did exist, however, was in the extent to which in East Asia these ideological mantras were marshaled in the service of supporting rural middle classes and behind a disciplining of capitalists that also became part of this "third" way. Neither occurred in Argentina.

It is also worth noting the ways that differences in the spatial and territorial distribution of political power affected political discourses and disciplinary actions in such a way as to privilege rural middle classes in Taiwan (and South Korea) but not in Argentina. Owing to the sheer size and dominance of Buenos Aires, most of the Peronist Party's class-based political support lay in the capital city and its surrounding province, even as a large number of pro-communist or anarchist elements settled in the countryside (a result of historically specific patterns of European working-class migration to rural Argentina). Both factors limited Peron's use of anticommunist rhetoric to appeal to rural folk. The privileging of populations in Argentina's capital city in periods both before and after the 1940s industrialization boom stands in stark contrast to patterns evident in the more economically successful Taiwanese and South Korean cases,

---

[14] Guatemala and Chile are two cases in point.

[15] In the South Korean and Taiwanese cases, the emphasis was toward a state-guided economic development, albeit capitalist. In Argentina, the aims were similar, although Perón used anticapitalist rhetoric much more than did Park Chung Hee and Chiang Kai-shek and was less willing to champion the unrestricted hand of the state. According to Gillespie, *Soldiers of Perón*, p. 18, Perón's so-called third position "counterposed itself equally to capitalism and communism," or the two imperialisms, presupposing "neither the exploitation of man in the name of capital nor in the name of the State." (Quoted in an interview with Perón by Pavón Pereyra, *Perón tal como es.*)

especially the former. One of the most remarked upon features of Taiwan's history and its post-1950s developmental gains has been that they equally span city and countryside. Most of Latin America's late industrializers built their successes through the development of a modern urban industrial infrastructure that draws rural migrants from the countryside to one or two principal cities, often the capital. This usually produces economic decline in the countryside, mainly because states continually ignore the "sending" rural areas, or because they deliberately choose to foster the growth of the "receiving" cities where population and resources are more concentrated, some combination of both. For this reason, some scholars have even gone so far as to use a focus on the overdevelopment of a nation's cities, or the extent of rural-urban imbalance, as limiting a country's developmental gains.

Notably, on these same measures Taiwan also is exceptional. Not only does it stand on the opposite side of the urbanization spectrum from Argentina, it also differs from its East Asian cousin, South Korea, in these regards. In the words of one observer, "The squalor of Taipei, compared with the more impressive face of Seoul, is itself a reflection of social equality," such that in Taipei there is no "elite wealthy enough to support the elegant shops and finance the imposing office buildings that give Seoul its appearance of affluence."[16] As we seek to understand Argentina's tango with economic disaster, then, as well as similarities and differences between Taiwan and South Korea, we examine urbanization patterns and how these affect rural middle-class formation and rural middle-class political sway. In pursuing a focus on the conditions that sustained a vibrant rural middle class in Taiwan but not in Argentina, we proceed under the assumption that a combination of historical factors and active political struggles, and how they unfolded spatially, produced divergent economic outcomes. In this sense, the fate of each country's rural middle classes, and in turn each country's development trajectories, was determined through active conflict or alliance building in which rural middle classes sought to promote their own formation as a class as well as a larger developmental agenda that would sustain their aims. This explains why we choose to conceptualize disciplinary development as intricately connected to the process of rural middle-class formation, and vice versa, a process that combines both agency and structure.

The chapter proceeds as follows. I begin with an analysis of the agricultural and colonial histories of Argentina and Taiwan and how these experiences laid the seeds for more sustained and self-generating rural middle-class formation in Taiwan than in Argentina or even South Korea. In the next several sections I focus on the social, spatial, economic, and political conditions that prevented Argentina's rural middle classes from strengthening their position in politics and society even as Taiwanese rural middle classes were able to do so. I then

---

[16] The quote is from Domes, cited in Moody, Jr., *Political Change on Taiwan*, p. 4.

discuss the role that party politics, geopolitical conditions, ethnicity, and prevailing discourses of class played in processes of rural middle-class formation in both countries. I conclude with an account of how these processes led to economic prosperity in Taiwan and economic troubles in Argentina.

The Colonial Foundations of Rural Middle-Class Formation in Argentina and Taiwan

Patterns of rural middle-class formation in both Argentina and Taiwan trace their roots to the colonial period, although this is not to say that both countries carry exactly the same legacies of colonialism. Long before the introduction of land reform in Taiwan in the 1950s, colonialism in Taiwan produced a relatively consequential class of small rural producers who existed side by side with large landowners of Taiwanese and colonial Japanese origin. Argentina, in contrast, weathered colonial and postcolonial rule with a heavy concentration of large landowners, who over time employed an increasingly larger class of agricultural laborers, many of whom abandoned their own farming activities and turned to wage labor as the rural economy declined. As of 1914, long after colonial independence, "78.3 percent of all land in Argentina was held in farms of 2,500 acres or more; [while] there were some 4,400 properties of 12,000 to 60,000 acres, and 485 with more than 60,000."[17]

The proliferation and persistence of large landowning elites in the Argentine countryside owes partly to geography, horticulture, and animal husbandry, as well as their combined impact on patterns of land cultivation and production.[18] Much of the Argentine economy (both domestic and export-oriented) developed around cattle, for food consumption and processing (as in hides), as well as around crops that could feed cattle. These activities required large tracts of land where cattle could graze relatively freely. Additionally, many of the country's agricultural crops, such as corn and wheat, could not be cultivated annually without significant damage to the land's ecological potential, thereby pressuring agricultural producers to pursue a pattern of crop/livestock alternation. This not only linked the political and economic fate of grain farmers to large *estancieros* involved in cattle breeding, it also reinforced large landholding across the board, not just in cattle, since to alternate grains with livestock entailed having the land capacity to produce livestock, even if only

---

[17] Whittaker, *Argentina*, p. 53.

[18] "The pampas region, heartland of Argentina's agricultural wealth, accounted for some 60 percent of the nation's agriculture and 80 percent of cattle production, but only 38 per cent of the land there was cultivated. . . . Indeed, it remained a standard practice of the agrarian magnates to withdraw land from production so as to control supply levels and thereby manipulate prices." See Gillespie, *Soldiers of Perón*, p. 27.

occasionally.[19] The result, according to Edwin Williamson was as follows:

> The system of land grants following the conquest of the pampas from the nomadic Indian tribes in the 1870s had failed to produce the class of independent small farmers envisaged by liberal reformers. Instead, the pampas had been carved up into *estancias*, vast estates owned by cattle ranchers and wheat-growers, who perpetuated the seigneurial values of the Hispanic nobility.[20]

For much of its history, then, Argentina was reported to be highly divided between a strong landed class with roots in the agrarian oligarchy on one hand, and exploited rural wage laborers on the other.

At first glance, the Taiwanese case seems to share many of Argentina's historical antecedents, at least insofar as it too was a colonial economy whose agriculture was geared toward export production. Taiwan also lived under the oppressive hand of colonial rule (albeit Japanese not Spanish) after decades of incorporation into the sphere of Chinese mercantilism. It thus found its economy similarly directed outward. In Taiwan, foreigners were key players in the economy, as in Argentina; and in the early stages of colonization Taiwanese "business and banks were controlled by the Japanese and 70 percent of the agricultural land was owned by them. . . . By the end of the war, 80 percent of the cultivated land and 95 percent of the forest land was under the control of the Japanese Government."[21] Moreover, as in Argentina during its initial preindependence period, Taiwan's foreign occupiers were more concerned with their own mercantilist gains. This too distorted the rural

---

[19] Of course, many additional factors help account for the concentration of large landowning, some more convincing than others. Calvert and Calvert, for example, offer a purely cultural explanation, arguing that "the emphasis on urban living is . . . thought to have worked against the development of lower-class enthusiasm for small-holdings." However, there is considerable disagreement as to whether the problem is really a culturally grounded absence of will. A more widely accepted claim locates landowning patterns in the system of Spanish land grants and the economic distortions toward large-scale agricultural exports produced by this political system. To the extent that native peoples frequently were forced to labor on *estancias*, they generally directed their own production activities toward rural production of subsistence needs, thereby reinforcing the pattern of large landowning and the economic marginality of small capitalist farmers. Calvert and Calvert, *Argentina*, pp. 193–194.

[20] *The Penguin History of Latin America*, p. 459. As Rock concludes similarly but with more qualification, "not even the embryo of [a rural middle class] appeared until the middle of the nineteenth century"; and even then, this fledgling class of small-scale rural producers tended to be overshadowed by large landlords and urban classes, both politically and economically. For a detailed discussion of the political economy of Argentine agricultural development, see Rock's *Argentina*. For more on the absence of small producers, especially before the 1860 wave of European immigration, see p. xxvi.

[21] Bullard, *The Soldier and Citizen*, p. 31.

economy, especially in the early decades of the twentieth century. In Tom Gold's words, the

> Japanese did not intend ... to industrialize Taiwan as they had their motherland, but rather to develop its agriculture to supply foodstuffs and raw materials to the industrializing home islands. There was thus to be a functional and geographical division of labor within the integrated economy of the expanding empire. ... [And] as in most European colonies, the economic structure [of Taiwan] was disarticulated as production was geared to external demand and the daily necessities of life other than foodstuffs could not be produced domestically.[22]

Yet despite these similarities, in Taiwan colonialism and the initial foreign domination of the economy did not produce quite the same highly polarized rural class structure as in Argentina, which is to say that it did not preclude the development of a vibrant rural middle class of small farmers. This state of affairs laid a critical foundation for later developmental differences in the two countries.

Taiwan's "gains" in terms of rural middle-class formation owed largely to the fact that Japanese economic might was imposed on a semifeudal, semi-imperial environment which for various reasons was characterized by an already considerable number of independent small-scale producers and small landowners who persisted despite the colonial penetration of the rural economy. Throughout the nineteenth century, the island's agricultural economy was based on small peasant owners and tenant cultivators engaged in small-scale commodity production whose experience and activities laid the foundation for subsequent patterns of rural middle-class formation.[23] Alice Amsden notes, for example, that under the Japanese, Taiwan hosted an

> elaborate network of agricultural associations, under the aegis of the government and rich landlords, [which] provided peasants with extension education, the cooperative purchase of fertilizers, warehousing, and other services. When persuasion failed, the police were employed to force modern techniques onto rural communities that resisted change. The experience that small tenants gained in experimenting with new seed strains and their familiarization with scientific farming ... prove[d] to be of immense value.[24]

That is, rather than destroying small-scale cultivators, as colonial rulers frequently do through large land grants allocated to occupying forces and/or

---

[22] *State and Society in the Taiwan Miracle*, pp. 36, 45.

[23] Ibid., p. 29.

[24] Amsden, "The State and Taiwan's Economic Development," p. 81.

through taxation and trade policies, Taiwan's Japanese colonial rulers tended to politically, socially, and economically reinforce the country's small-scale rural producers.

Taiwan's main agricultural products were rice and sugar, which by the late nineteenth century were in great demand in Japan for both consumption and processing, and which were imported in exchange for the export of manufactured goods back to Taiwan. Unlike cattle, then, which served as a centerpiece of the Argentine economy, sugar could be productively cultivated on small plots. The result was to further buttress small agricultural producers, a situation that the Japanese reinforced through the introduction of policies that gave incentive to small-plot cultivation in cane and which strengthened the economic position of native sugar producers. The impact of government policy on rural middle-class formation was evident as early as 1902, when Japanese authorities introduced a law to encourage small-scale sugar cultivation and established a Sugar Bureau on Taiwan to coordinate these efforts. Soon thereafter the Japanese introduced a new species of cane from Hawaii, the Rose Bamboo, which was heralded as sustaining small-scale production among cane farmers' because it "could withstand rougher treatment and an unsatisfactory water supply, and yet yield an output gratifying in all respects."[25] Almost immediately, the colonial authorities further sustained cane farmers' activities by promoting the widespread construction of sugar factories with government subsidies – and in some cases by directly providing and leasing the machinery to local producers. Last and perhaps most important, colonial authorities made it possible for cane planters to "get land on very moderate terms, and even manure was gratuitously provided by the Government, on condition that the planters pledged themselves not to leave off sugar cultivation for the following five years."[26]

Needless to say, these measures reflected neither benevolence nor a calculated concern with fostering rural middle-class formation on the part of the Japanese. Rather, they were intended to guarantee the steady supply of locally produced sugar to modernized, capital-intensive cane-processing plants, which thereafter were built, owned, and/or controlled by the Japanese and which supplied the Japanese domestic markets.[27] Small cultivators were often

[25] Geerligs, *The World's Cane Sugar Industry*, p. 83. Geerligs also notes that in 1900, with a subsidy of 60,000 yen per year, it was the Japanese government which helped establish the Taiwan Seito Kaisha (Taiwan Sugar Company), whose aim was to purchase cane and export sugar.

[26] Ibid.

[27] In *State and Society in the Taiwan Miracle*, p. 38, Gold notes that colonial authorities "divided the island into fifty sugar districts, each with a Japanese-owned mill at its core that purchased cane from Taiwanese peasants at a previously announced price." He also suggests that "farmers' associations functioned as instruments of control as well as a channel for

forced to produce against their will.[28] One unanticipated consequence was the strengthening of a class of small-scale rural producers throughout the colonial period. Colonial authorities also abolished the old land tenure system (*ta-tsu-hsu*) while introducing a land tenure reform (in 1905), measures that created and reinforced free and absolute ownership.[29] With mandated sales and a guaranteed market, small-scale cane producers responded and began to flourish. The results were tremendous, at least with respect to cane production. Within five years Taiwan saw a major increase in native sugar production and, most important for our purposes, the strengthening of small-scale cultivation and processing of sugar on a district by district basis.[30]

new technology and capital. In . . . [these] way[s], the peasants' activities became increasingly integrated into the cycle of capitalist reproduction with its origin and endpoint in Japan."

[28] Frequently "farmers refused to sell their cane to the manufacturers, and chose to grind it in their own buffalo mills in the old primitive way," while "natives, too, refused to plant the new kind of cane, although the tops for planting could be had gratis, and although they were provided with manure and irrigation facilities and enjoyed a subsidy if they would only plant a better kind of cane" (Geerligs, *The World's Cane Sugar Industry*, p. 84). But when the first round of subsidies and policies did not generate enough small-scale cultivation to locally supply and sustain the Japanese-controlled sugar processing factories, colonial authorities redoubled their efforts with stronger regulation. In 1905 the Japanese issued an ironclad set of ordinances obliging farmers to sell cane to district-level local factories (rather than processing it themselves via older methods), although the government also guaranteed that district factories would be responsible for buying up all the cane planted in a district, even if this entailed exceeding their processing targets. According to Geerligs (ibid.), these government measures dictated that "anyone wishing to erect a modern sugar factory must first obtain permission from the Director of the Sugar Bureau, who will mark out the district within which the applicant is to be allowed to buy cane sugar, and where no other sugar works may be started. Anyone planting sugar cane in that district is under obligation to sell it to the factory, and is not free to export it outside the district, nor to use it for any other purpose, so that the factory enjoys the monopoly of buying all the sugar cane planted there. On the other hand, the factory is bound to take all the cane planted in the district, and is not free to refuse a part of the planting should the supply exceed their wants. Cane planters are not allowed to grind their cane in their own buffalo mills, unless permitted to do so, and as the Sugar Bureau means to promote modern methods of sugar cultivation, these licenses are not easily granted. In some districts which have no cane cultivation of their own, large extensions of soil may be ceded free of cost to sugar undertakings."

[29] See Ka, *Japanese Colonialism*, p. 26. Of course, they also levied a heavy land tax, so these measures were by no means benign.

[30] By 1910 gains were such "it was announced that no more charters would be granted for the time being for the formation of sugar manufacturing companies, nor for the extension of existing mills, the object being to check the expected over-production of sugar in the island in excess of the demands of Japan for direct consumption and for refining, pending the opening of foreign markets" (Geerligs, *The World's Cane Sugar Industry*, p. 85).

On the down side, colonial dictates brought the gradual erosion of native production techniques and the replacement of native traditional mills with modern Japanese-owned sugar factories. The latter became a principal mechanism for the penetration of capitalist market and social relations on the island, a situation which in most environments sustains a greater likelihood for income polarization. And again, it is worth reiterating that the Japanese saw the development of locally owned small-scale production activities as a means to their exporting and mercantilist ends, not as a valued goal in and of itself. But even so, Japanese colonial practices tended to reinforce rather than undermine a nascent rural middle class of native agricultural producers, primarily because Japan acquired most of its sugarcane for processing and export largely via contractual arrangements with small family farms. Also, by erecting sugar-processing factories in every district, and thereby lowering transport costs for all cane producers, colonial authorities further eliminated undue pressures for greater economies of scale in farming, thus further nurturing a prosperous class of family and small-scale producers. The feedback effects of these dynamics were further sustained by a buoyant property market.[31]

Still, it is important not to overstate the causal extent to which Taiwan's relative success (especially as compared to both Argentina and South Korea) in sustaining a small- and medium-sized farmer class owed purely to the dynamics of sugarcane production. The entire structure and nature of the agricultural sector was an equally important determining factor, especially owing to concurrent developments in the rice sector, which by the end of the nineteenth century comprised 50 percent of farm output value and accounted for 70 percent of land use.[32] Indeed, Taiwan's agricultural economy had historically been structured around *both* sugar and rice, in a pattern that few other Japanese colonial economies shared. As such, the dynamics in one sector influenced the other. Rice was always an option if sugar became unprofitable for small-scale producers, or if the pressures for capitalization and concentration in cane production threatened to drive cane farmers to lower their prices or sell their lands to larger enterprises. In fact, farmers in Taiwan were known to return their lands to rice cultivation if sugar capitalists did not provide cane growers with the same income standard and possibility for profits as rice growers.[33]

These agricultural dynamics furthered colonial authorities' interventionist resolve, a situation which worked to the benefit of Taiwan's rural middle class as

---

[31] The persistence of smaller-scale farms under Japanese rule owed partly to the high cost of land – which itself was a product of the booming successes of the Japanese export trade – and the fact that in order to motivate small producers to supply sugar processing factories, the Japanese had been compelled to install a legal framework to protect private property in land. Ka, *Japanese Colonialism*, pp. 97–98.

[32] Myers and Peattie (eds.), *The Colonial Empire*, p. 421.

[33] Ka, *Japanese Colonialism*, p. 136.

much as to the benefit of the Japanese themselves. Precisely because the balance between rice and sugar cultivation was so hard to maintain through market (i.e., land and pricing) mechanisms, the colonial government frequently intervened directly by monopolizing rice exports and/or reducing the purchase price of rice so as to prevent the luring of small-scale cane producers into rice. And it was precisely these actions that reinforced smaller-scale units of production in the rice sector – to parallel that of sugar, since they undercut the economic strength of the native landlord class that earlier had dominated the upper reaches of the rice sector.[34] The results were striking. According to Chih-ming Ka, "As a result of the replacement of (rice) landlords' economic functions by the government and their declining strength, the amount of owner-cultivated lands increased drastically while tenant-cultivated lands dropped."[35] And with processing mills in the rice sector also relatively small, on average employing fewer than three workers (primarily family members), small-scale factory owners flourished alongside small-scale cultivators,[36] thereby reinforcing the strength and visibility of the rural middle class. One significant by-product was an expansion in the "number of households with property rights."[37]

But again, it was the nature and composition of the agricultural economy that mattered most, and not merely Japanese colonial practices, a point that becomes obvious if we contrast the South Korean case with that of Taiwan. In both these East Asian countries colonial authorities promoted rice cultivation; both experienced land reform and land tax levies under the Japanese; and in both countries, the colonial authorities established and nurtured farmers' associations and agricultural experiment stations to facilitate rural production for export. Yet Taiwan's more favorable temperature and rainfall gave it two seasons of rice cropping rather than just one, as in South Korea. Moreover, as just noted, the concurrent development of sugar gave Taiwan a more buoyant economy, brought more overall agricultural investment in an early stage, and most important for our purposes, established a diversity and type of competition within the agricultural sector between rice and sugar that reduced tenancy and increased owner cultivation of small and medium-sized plots. South Korea, in contrast, suffered through the same colonial occupation with

---

[34] In this and other regards, Japanese colonial administrators struggled to curtail the traditional power of the Taiwanese landlord class, which posed a potential obstacle to their plans to monopolize the export sector, all to the advantage of smaller producers. One particularly effective way they sought to limit the potential competition from the native Taiwanese landlord class was to reshape tenancy relations in the rice sector, policy measures crafted with the explicit aim of increasing the solvency of small-scale rice producers so as to undermine their large landlord competitors.

[35] *Japanese Colonialism*, p. 176.

[36] Ibid., p. 155.

[37] Myers and Peattie (eds.), *The Colonial Empire*, p. 449.

a much less dynamic rural economy, something that itself put limits on the growth of a rural middle class of farmers, as did the country's reliance mainly on rice alone, cultivated only once a year.[38] In South Korea, moreover, the rice sector was almost fully dominated by the Japanese, who owned 54 percent of rice-processing mills, compared to a rate of only 7 percent in Taiwan.[39] As a result, in South Korea tenancy increased, while owner-occupied cultivation failed to take root, and impoverishment and stagnation prevailed in the rural sector throughout the colonial period.

Unlike South Korea, Taiwan survived the colonial experience with the seeds planted for the development of a potentially vibrant rural middle class of small and medium-sized agricultural producers, even if it did not fully materialize until after the Japanese defeat and departure. By 1950, when the newly formed Taiwanese government led by the Kuomintang (KMT) sought to pursue an independent course of rapid economic development, the country's existent ranks of small farmers were already organized and experienced enough to pursue cultivation on their own, and the immediate introduction of land reform made this potential a reality. This stands in stark contrast to the situation in South Korea at independence, where the sheer rural impoverishment, inequality, and relative absence of a small-producer class with the experience and know-how to produce for the market were fundamental obstacles to rural growth. Their failures in these regards explains why Park struggled so hard over the decades of the 1960s and early 1970s, even after a serious land reform, to turn South Korea's so-called peasants into small-scale capitalist producers who would become a vibrant rural middle class of efficient producers. And it is this difference that explains why, when the KMT-led government's "efforts to rebuild its industrial base were, at first, given second priority to agricultural development,"[40] in much the same manner as Park, this strategy worked relatively well in Taiwan but not South Korea. As Tom Gold put it, in Taiwan,

> in retrospect it can be argued that [national planners'] concentration on agriculture helped prepare the way [for industrialization]. An ample supply of agricultural products helped keep down inflation, and valuable foreign currency did not have to be spent for food imports. Production increased rapidly enough that some refined sugar and other food products could even be exported to earn additional foreign currency.[41]

In Argentina, the colonial experience laid only a minimal groundwork for the development of a vibrant rural middle class, more in keeping with the

---

[38] For a wonderful comparison of overall similarities and differences in the agricultural economies of Taiwan, South Korea, and Japan, see ibid., esp. pp. 428–449.

[39] Ka, *Japanese Colonialism*, p. 153.

[40] Bullard, *The Soldier and the Citizen*, p. 32.

[41] *State and Society in the Taiwan Miracle*, p. 19.

South Korean experience. Equally important, there also were fewer clear or successful government efforts to try to nurture small-scale rural producers through general development policy or land reform, as seen in Taiwan and even in South Korea under Park, despite his long-term failures in this regard. When rural-based industrialization materialized in Argentina in the meatpacking and -processing industries, it developed in large factories with a labor force of wage workers, not in the smaller-scale rural-based enterprises that were so pervasive in the sugar-refining industry in Taiwan, and certainly not through conscious government efforts to create a substantial cadre of small-farmer capitalists. By the time Perón came to office, in the 1940s and 1950s, rural middle classes and their economic policy preferences hardly factored into the government's manufacturing or agricultural development plans at all. This meant that the developmental path that Argentina took in the post–World War II period was more similar to that pursued by South Korea *after* 1975, at which time the Park government started to renege on its commitment to the rural middle class. As such, Argentina's path was built on an obsession with urban-based industrial development and a reluctance to alienate a nascent and growing class of large industrial manufacturing capitalists producing for the domestic market and urban consumers. In Argentina it was ISI and not EOI that preoccupied the government and industrialists, an orientation that further shifted the political and economic balance away from rural populations in general and the rural middle classes in particular. And in Argentina, economic problems were much worse than even in South Korea, putting it on the opposite end of the developmental spectrum from Taiwan and the East Asian cases more generally.

Failed Land Reform Versus Urban Dominance: Cause or Effect of a Debilitated Rural Middle Class

But why did Argentina's rural middle class not develop the political salience or economic wherewithal to impose a development model similar to that which ultimately materialized in South Korea after Park abandoned his rural development aims, even if the Taiwanese model remained out of reach? As just noted, Argentina and South Korea faced similar postcolonial agrarian conditions and constraints, yet the Korean government still disciplined urban industrialists and turned its attention to nurturing agrarian development and a vibrant class of rural middle-class producers. Why were the same state-led measures not undertaken in Argentina? Some might turn to the absence of land reform in Argentina for answers, since such a focus could be used to suggest that too few small-scale rural producers existed in the first place. This argument, however, can only take us so far, because the absence of land reform does not mean that rural middle classes actually failed to appear in Argentina. Rather, the existence of a sizable cadre of small medium-scale farmers and agriculturists is one of the best kept secrets of Argentine economic history.

Some of this owed to the topography and the nature of the countryside itself.[42] During the late nineteenth century, farming was as popular an activity as ranching. In the northwest provinces, for example, sugar (the same product that was so central in transforming Taiwan's rural class structure) was parlayed into a strong local industry for both internal trade and export throughout the nineteenth century.[43] Wool (i.e., sheep) production and processing, activities that Barrington Moore identified as absolutely central to the great developmental gains made by the British (owing to their role in leading the commercialization of agricultural areas), also persisted and produced remarkable economic successes in several key Argentine locales, producing significant exports and the growth of a small-scale farmer class involved in animal husbandry that later expanded into cereals, at least temporarily. From the 1820s onward, in fact, sheep competed with cattle as the principal source of livestock wealth, especially in the most economically and politically central areas of the country, such that "by the 1870s sheep had effectively displaced cattle from much of the improved pasturage near Buenos Aires."[44]

Many of these small-farmer gains owed to the immigrant diaspora. A steady inflow of mainly European immigrants provided the country with unique opportunities to strengthen small-scale farming activities, since many of the immigrants were rural folk with farming and agricultural skills, who moved directly to Argentina's agricultural areas.[45] The result, according to David

---

[42] Detailed evidence shows that Argentina's rural economy was quite diverse for much of the nineteenth century, built around raw cotton, cereals, sheep, horses, mules, and a variety of animal derivatives, such as wool and hides, all used as key tradable goods. In short, Argentine producers raised and harvested more than just cattle, corn, and wheat.

[43] Rock, *Argentina*, p. 151.

[44] Owing to the changing rural economy and the immigration of foreigners who bolstered the farmer class, in fact, by the latter half of the nineteenth century "a vast semicircular farming belt had appeared around the city of Buenos Aires," ranging from Entre Rios in the north, across central and southern Santa Fe as well as eastern Córdoba through the province of Buenos Aires to the port of Bahia Blanca in the south, and expanding from almost nothing in 1852 to 600,000 hectares of cultivated areas in 1872 to 2.5 million by 1888. Ibid., pp. 135–136; Slatta, *Gauchos*, p. 141.

[45] According to Rock, "In 1853 the government of Corrientes contracted to locate one thousand French families on land in the province. From this beginning several hundred farm colonies and roughly the same number of new towns and villages were founded in Corrientes, Entre Rios, Córdoba, Santa Fe, and Buenos Aires. Many of these farms were sponsored by provincial governments, which drew up contracts with European entrepreneurs. The former selected and prepared land for colonization, subdividing it into lots of usually between thirty and forty hectares, and provided the farmers with animals and seed, while the contractors assumed responsibility for recruiting and transporting colonists from Europe. Once settled on the

Rock, was a stable, well-rooted rural middle-class society, similar in many ways to that of the Midwest of the United States. But equally important was the active financial support of government programs and policies, which nurtured several growing communities of successful farmers. Land reform and subsidies to small farmers were principal goals of several mid- and late-nineteenth-century administrations, despite the presence and looming threat of oligarchic opposition. Beginning with "Bernadino W. Rivadavia's efforts to create a nation of sturdy yeomen of small farmers during the 1820s,"[46] and continuing into the 1830s when Rosas submitted a tariff law whose declared "object was to help agriculture and the middle classes,"[47] the Argentine government's commitment to creating a rural middle class seemed unmistakable. But even with these measures and commitments, the "agrarian dream never materialized on the Argentine plains."[48]

So what happened to this country's nascent rural middle class of farmers and to the considerable rural enthusiasm for so-called yeoman farming so frequently cited by Argentine historian Tulio Halperin-Donghi? In theory it should have been possible for the Argentine government to insure that its economic and social programs or policies – including land reform – would continue to effectively nurture and sustain the activities of rural middle classes, making them central to twentieth-century industrial development plans in much the same manner as occurred in South Korea around the 1950s and 1960s. But the reality was otherwise, and to know why we need to examine the larger political priorities and social bases of power in Argentine politics more generally, so as to determine what specific social and political conditions prevented Argentina's nascent rural middle classes from achieving enough political sway to institutionalize their desired programs of agrarian reform, rural development, and small-scale rural production. It is tempting to look for explanations for this outcome in the larger political culture. In South Korea, remember, rural farmers were considered the great foundation of life under heaven. The situation in Argentina could not have been more different. In

---

land, the colonists received additional subsidies until they were able to discharge their debts. There were many highly successful ventures of this kind. By 1870 the colonies were the source of around 20,000 tons of wheat, about half the total domestic output. By 1880 there were 365 colonies and 18,000 farms in Córdoba, and 184 colonies and 15,000 farms in Entre Rios." See *Argentina*, pp. 136–137.

[46] Slatta, *Gauchos*, p. 151.

[47] Rock, *Argentina*, p. 108. With this reform, Rosas had in mind both farmers in the province of Buenos Aires and artisans in the city. As such, his interest was in the middle class more generally, not just the rural middle class, which further explains why Rosas was considered to have "undone" earlier attempts at land reform. See Whittaker, *Argentina*, p. 52.

[48] Slatta, *Gauchos*, p. 151.

Argentina it was the urban and not the rural populations who were generally considered the moral compass of the nation. In fact, rural folk were most likely to be considered "barbarians," while urban populations were seen as more "civilized," to appropriate the discourse of the Argentine literature and popular culture. In Argentina, in fact, perceived demographic, political, and even social asymmetries between rural and urban populations pushed divergent coalitions of political actors into a zero-sum game, such that political priorities – and thus development policies, generally – were ultimately portrayed or understood as being *either* rural- *or* urban-oriented, even though much of the time they spanned the two domains in practice.[49]

More important, much of this sentiment owed to the national preoccupation with Buenos Aires – both the province and the city – and its domination over the rest of the nation. Even now, Buenos Aires is more than ten times the size of Argentina's second largest city, Rosario, and more than twelve times its third, Córdoba. As such, the political history of the last century and a half has been driven by the unresolved territorial and then political conflicts between *porteños* (Buenos Aires residents) and the rest of the nation, although the enemies and alliances have changed as conditions have changed. From political revolt to interstate rivalries (with both Uruguay and Spain) to civil war and back again, these conflicts have fueled the "invention of Argentina," to borrow Nicholas Shumway's conceit.[50] And more than anything else, perhaps, the ongoing conflict between Buenos Aires and the rest of the nation helps explain why rural middle classes had a difficult time strengthening their economic position

---

[49] In some late industrializers, the political balance of power may span both city and countryside within the same province, or revolve around certain regions in which rural populations are as significant as urban ones, such that rural middle classes may be as likely as other classes to have a stake in the national state and development policy, even if they do not reside in the capital city. Hence it is not merely the presence or absence of large cities that sets the stage for the rural-urban balance of political power, and thus the salience of rural middle classes in the state and society, but the entire patterning and history of urban-rural relations as understood both on the levels of the region and the national state. And on these counts, Argentina is practically off the map, so to speak, both with respect to Taiwan and South Korea, not to mention most of the rest of Latin America.

[50] As early as 1610, the Portuguese who were based in Buenos Aires and preoccupied with the silver trade and commerce coexisted uneasily with the Spanish-speaking inhabitants of the inland provinces involved in trading cattle hides and other consumer goods. By the early nineteenth century, these conflicts had intensified rather than dissipated; and according to Rock, the tumultuous political struggles for independence and over state formation during the 1820s and again in the 1850s were reenactments of this long-brewing conflict (Rock, *Argentina*, p. 113). For more on the give and take between the provinces and Buenos Aires, see Rock's extraordinarily comprehensive account in *Argentina*. For a fascinating discussion of the ways in which these littoral-interior conflicts unfolded in the political and literary discourse of the times, see also Shumway, *The Invention of Argentina*.

or prevailing in national politics, up to and including their failure to guarantee a serious land reform.

The obstacles to rural middle-class formation and political power stemmed not just from the political centrality of Buenos Aires the city, but also from the fact that the entire province of Buenos Aires was fundamentally different in composition and character. Unlike the rest of the provinces in the nation, Buenos Aires province had always had a very small Indian population, something which had direct influence on patterns of urbanization and rural class formation.[51] The province of Buenos Aires grew mainly around the commercial activities undertaken in the city, and it was these commercial activities that determined prosperity in the province as a whole, thereby reversing the conventional pattern in which rural activities sustained urban growth. Equally important, these patterns reinforced class and economic differences that had an ethnic and racial underpinning. In Buenos Aires province, those few who initially became involved in direct agricultural production were blacks and Indians primarily, while *mestizos* became cattle peons or settled primarily in the city, becoming militiamen or employed artisans.[52] Because the activities were so differentially distributed in space – commercial, military, and artisanal employment in the city versus raising cattle and some farming in the hinterlands under conditions of relative population scarcity and a high land-labor ratio – a stark dualism characterized both the province and the nation as a whole. This dualism ultimately reflected in "the emergence of separate urban and rural societies: at the perimeter of the city's 'civilized' population lived the 'barbarian' society of the *gente perdida*," and those called *vagos* and *gauchos* in later periods.[53] Together these patterns diminished the social and cultural status of rural peoples nationwide. This in turn limited their political capacities to make material claims on the state too.

Historically, country and city embodied different meanings and experiences, such that most Argentines felt that the countryside was "in constant danger from ambush by wild Indian tribes, far from the city and from any protection by the government."[54] For many years, in fact, the countryside and its rural inhabitants were physically, culturally, economically, and even

---

[51] According to David Rock, the "absence of a large local pool of Indians inhibited widespread use of *encomienda* or *mita*, and this lesser dependence on forced labor created distinctive population trends in Buenos Aires. While the population of the interior cities waxed and waned with equal speed, in Buenos Aires slow, uninterrupted growth proceeded from a minute base. The shortage of Indians also inhibited the growth of agriculture in Buenos Aires; during its first forty years on several occasions the city was obliged to import grain from Córdoba" (*Argentina*, p. 24).

[52] Ibid., pp. 24, 38.

[53] Ibid., p. 38.

[54] Romero, *A History of Argentine Political Thought*, p. 26.

juridically marginalized from the urban populations in Argentina. "Spanish legislation looked on the colony as a group of cities, only urban life was efficiently regulated"; and it was from cities that all power emanated, insofar as "in the cities there were Spaniards who . . . depended on the exploitation of lands that were almost unknown to them."[55] The limited interaction between city and countryside and the pejorative attitudes about rural peoples carried over into the decades of independence and were reinforced in literature (as in Sarmiento's *Facundo*), among leading intellectuals, and in the public sphere throughout the nineteenth century, especially as struggles between Buenos Aires and the provinces persisted.

The consequences were twofold: for one, early on both the city and the province of Buenos Aires developed distinct economic, racial, ethnic, political, and sociocultural profiles, not only with respect to each other but also in comparison to the interior, especially those regions where large landholdings and exploited Indians initially fueled agricultural development and provincial prosperity. I will return to this point and its significance for rural class formation in a moment. For now, suffice it to say that when rural activities did develop in Buenos Aires province they were different in composition and in the nature of the connections established with the port city. In Buenos Aires province, farming of all varieties remained much more marginal – at least until the wave of foreign immigration late in the nineteenth century, when cattle ranching triumphed – while the interior provinces hosted a greater mix of these and other activities and farming generally brought greater gains. By the end of the eighteenth century, "most communities of the interior were self-sufficient in wheat and corn, often in rice, olives, mules, wool, and cattle hides."[56]

The second consequence was that the various cities in Argentina differed greatly among themselves. "Specialization was more highly developed among interior cities, commerce embraced a larger volume of goods, and artisan manufacturing, too, was advancing,"[57] whereas in agricultural terms, inhabitants of Buenos Aires and its immediate surrounds still preoccupied themselves mainly with cattle and a more narrowly defined external commerce. This, in the words Richard Slatta, owed to the fact that "farming faced much more serious obstacles than did sheep-raising in the surrounding pampa. The small internal market and conflicts between ranchers and farmers hindered crop production. European demands arose for wheat, corn, oats, and linseed, but until ranchers required alfalfa pastures for purebred stock during the latter decades of the century, farming held little importance."[58] Accordingly, most

---

[55] Ibid., p. 27.
[56] Rock, *Argentina*, p. 57.
[57] Ibid., p. 78.
[58] *Gauchos*, p. 150.

of the rural elite of the Buenos Aires province linked their fate to exporting cattle through the capital city, and as they soon developed into large cattle barons, they had little commitment to fostering the growth of a nascent rural middle class, especially farmers, either in Buenos Aires or anywhere else in the rest of the nation.[59] When farming did emerge late in the nineteenth century, moreover, fueled by European immigration, there was considerable social and political conflict not just between these foreign-born new farmers and large ranchers, but also occasionally between farmers and roaming cattle hands (gauchos), a complex situation which limited the unity and economic power of rural small producers.[60]

These conflicts spilled over into the political sphere. During the struggles in the late-nineteenth century between the Federalists and Unitarists over whether Buenos Aires would become the national capital, questions about whether its concerns would be integrated into, subordinated to, or determinant of the concerns of the provinces involved a broad variety of social forces with competing visions, juridical projects, class structures, and economic activities. What was at stake, moreover, was the balance of power not just between Federalists and Unitarists, but also between supporters and opponents of economic liberalism (i.e., free trade of commercial goods and currency), as well as supporters and opponents of protectionism, foreign investment, and even land reform. These struggles over the agricultural versus the industrial development of the nation persisted throughout the nineteenth century not only because the stark differences between the commercially oriented port of Buenos Aires and the more class- and agriculturally diverse provinces prevented an easy solution. When a political settlement was finally reached at the end of the nineteenth century, it was the porteño-based Unitarists who ultimately triumphed. Their political ascendance sealed the fate of rural middle classes as a declining national political force.

The diminishing influence of rural middle classes in the first decades of the twentieth century did not occur without a struggle, of course. In the first decades of the twentieth century small and medium-sized agricultural producers (*chacareros*), many of them family farmers, organized in their own independent national association, the Federación Agraria Argentina (FAA).[61]

---

[59] Indeed, Slatta notes that in Argentina as a whole, "farming held little importance except in partidos close to Buenos Aires," where it arose in the late-nineteenth century in the form of alfalfa production for cattle ranching. Ibid.

[60] Ibid., pp. 152–153.

[61] In *Estado*, Girbal de Blacha identifies *chacareros* as the *"pequeña y mediana burguesía"* rural," i.e., small and medium-sized rural bourgeoisie (p. 9), although in another section (p. 14) she defines chacareros as *"pequeños o medianos propietarios,"* i.e., small and medium-sized property owners. Eventually, she offers the term "rural subalterns" to describe both the small and medium-sized property owners and small and medium-sized tenant farmers (p. 15). Note,

The FAA existed separately from the main organization representing large landlords (*terratenientes*) and oligarchic interests, called the Sociedad Rural Argentina (SRA).[62] Among the founding concerns of the FAA, which was formally established in 1912 in order to protect small-farmer interests against those of large landlords, were scarcities of credit, problems with land access, and the rapid commercialization of cereal production, all issues that spoke to the problematic yet distinct "middling" rural economic position and concerns of smaller-scale producers.[63] Through the FAA, rural middle classes reasserted

moreover, that the classification of chacareros as middle class is seen in Taylor's *Rural Life in Argentina* (p. 111) in which a *chacra* is considered a diversified family farm which differs from a *granja*, the term used to identify a diversified family farm in which some processing occurs. It also is consistent with the definition offered by de Paoli in *La reforma agraria* (p. 26), as well as by Argentine scholars Forni and Tort in "Las transformaciones" (p. 143), who are even more precise in defining chacareros as comprising the middle strata between landed capitalists and peasant laborers. They argue that chacareros "appear clearly in the agricultural stratification system as middle class," and they further suggest that "although in certain moments and in certain ways they can be confused with the dependent peasant (*campesino dependiente*), their economic interests, their position as employers or potential employers, and their greater rootedness (*arraigo*) differentiate them from the agricultural proletariat." (Translation note: I use the term "rootedness" for *arraigo* in the text of the quote precisely because I suspect the authors are differentiating these producers from seasonal or transitional laborers who are waged workers and have been quite common in rural Argentina. The *Pequeño Larousse* also offers both "property" and "influence" as alternative translations of arraigo, which I could have used as well, since both would also imply the more middle-class status of chacareros clearly suggested by the authors.) It may also be worth noting that Forni and Tort argue for a new terminology in which English terms are used or embedded in Spanish. Specifically, they suggest that over time chacareros are becoming farmers or "farmer-contratistas" (i.e., "*allí es donde se concreta la transformación de chacareros en* farmers *y donde aparece con más claridad el predominio de la 'producción por terceros' o la figura del 'contratista'*"). I would like to suggest that this innovation comes partly in response to the particular stereotypes associated with the term "chacarero," especially the common understanding that chacareros are peasants and not farmers, a notion that may trace to Peronist discourses, as we shall soon see.

[62] This juxtaposition of *chacarero* (which is translated as farmer or peasant in the *Pequeño Larousse* Spanish dictionary) against *terrateniente* (translated as landowner or landlord) comes from Girbal de Blacha's fascinating account of agricultural policy during the ascendancy of the Radical Party. See Girbal de Blacha, *Estado* (esp. p. 36 as well as pp. 58–61), for a discussion of the tensions and conflicts between these two groups.

[63] For more on the membership of the FAA, which was strongest in La Pampa, Chaco, Tucumán, Mendoza, Río Negro, Santiago del Estero, Buenos Aires, Córdoba, Santa Fe, and Entre Ríos, see Forni and Tort, "Las transformaciones." The FAA's self-consciousness as a separate social sector representing rural middle classes had to do with its members' middling yet relational status between large landowners on one hand and *arrendatarios*, or renters, on the other. For this and other reasons, then, it is both possible and logical to consider these smaller farmers in the FAA in middle-class terms, or as small-scale middle-class producers (i.e., chacareros) and not peasants.

their political presence in the decades immediately preceding the urban-based industrialization boom of the 1930s and 1940s. And this occurred precisely as a rural middle-class defense against larger estancieros and cattle barons in the powerful and hegemonic SRA – who themselves were monopolizing production and the commercialization of the countryside by supporting the development of large industrial processing plants for cattle products. In some senses, in fact, one might say that the FAA served as the organizational arm of the rural middle class, or the closest thing to it. This possibility is evidenced by the fact that as early as 1919 the Radical governor of Buenos Aires province, José Camilo Crotto, had worked with the FAA to push for agricultural reforms that would facilitate "the rapid formation, by ingenious and simple means, of a stable and prosperous rural property-owning class" to counterbalance any social disequilibrium.[64]

But even with a membership of 24,703 in 1926 and 31,881 in 1930, the FAA was no match for the cattle-ranch oligarchy.[65] Why? Because despite their visibility and numeric strength, and despite their growing links to the Radical Party,[66] Argentina's rural middle classes had a hard time securing other class and political allies both within and outside the Radical Party to support their rural development aims. In a certain sense, then, the relatively limited visibility, agrarian influence, and political alliance building of Argentine rural middle classes during the mid-twentieth century foray into industrialization was the paradoxical consequence of their initial economic successes. When Buenos Aires province hosted a burst of small-scale farming and agricultural production in sheep and cereals, these activities grew in tandem with the burgeoning caudillo-dominated cattle economy as well as in response to the demands of urban populations (mainly in Buenos Aires city) for dairy products, affordable grains, and other foodstuffs, although these activities were frequently subsidized by the porteño government. With the rising economic tide lifting all boats, there was little incentive for small farmers to struggle against potential competition in either city or countryside. There was also little incentive to struggle to strengthen their position as a class, because they were doing relatively well in the province that mattered most nationally, that is, Buenos Aires.

[64] Girbal de Blacha, *Estado*, p. 29.

[65] Ibid., pp. 39, 36.

[66] Ibid., pp. 11, 36, 39, 45. See also de Paoli, *La reforma agraria*, pp. 27–30, for a discussion of the founding of the FAA and its strong relationship to the Radical Party, especially in Santa Fe province. One of the key bases of the Radical Party in the early-twentieth century, in addition to urban workers, sons of immigrants, and a number of landowners and commercial enterprises who had been "displaced from oligarchic circles," were "small and medium *estancieros* [and] some groups of tenant farmers."

Clearly, some of the failures to protect themselves as a (middle) class owed to "natural" divisions among small scale rural producers themselves, and their spatial distribution.[67] Among those whose numbers and employment were most bolstered by the overall economic vibrancy of Buenos Aires city and province, there existed two main groups. One was the gauchos, who became involved in trading hides and rustling cattle; a second was the small sheep and grain farmers.[68] Both groups coexisted throughout the nineteenth century, before the economic crisis and transformation of the twentieth century limited gaucho activities and reduced many to the status of wage workers.[69] As Richard Slatta suggests in his seminal study of them, "*gauchos* do not fit into a schema of slaves, serfs, proletarians, or peasants, however, and thus they represent something of an aberration in classical Marxist theory," because they "controlled some of their own labor power and some of the means of production." Indeed, because gauchos were often "paid partly with 'keep' (room and board, such as it was) and sometimes used [their] own equipment (mounts, lasso, knife, boots), the gaucho does not qualify as a proletarian," at least for most of Argentine history.[70] As such, gauchos and small farmers, had they united, would have constituted a formidable middle-class force in Argentine politics within Buenos Aires province and, by virtue of its economic centrality to the nation, in Argentina as a whole. This did not occur, however, because the gauchos' seasonal employment and their wandering lifestyle meant that they were less attached to a particular place or even to other rural

---

[67] In Peter Smith's compelling account of intraclass tensions in rural areas, their impact on the Radical Party, and their overall contribution to Argentine political development, he also differentiates within the rural sector, by employing the fattener-packer distinction, with the former including ranchers, breeders, and even *gauchos* and the latter involved in industrial processing of cattle products and related animal husbandry. But he does not analyze this distinction in class terms (as the middle class, or in terms of a distinction between middle-class and capitalist producers). From the vantage point of this book, I try to examine differences among rural groups on the basis of size, independence, use of family labor, and use of wage labor. By so doing, I concur with many of his findings, but work under the assumption that some categories (like breeders) do not necessarily imply a certain class position without further knowledge of the actual conditions of ownership and production. See *Politics and Beef*, esp. pp. 131–134.

[68] While it has been more customary to conceptualize Argentina's gauchos as "a class of the unclassified," to use Martínez Estrada's words (*Muerte y transfiguración de Martín Fierro*, Vol. 1, p. 251), mainly because they tended to shift from one socioeconomic and legal category to another, in many respects gauchos could be understood in rural middle-class terms, owing to their status as self-employed and to the general labor process conditions under which they worked, including their considerable independence on the job.

[69] Slatta, *Gauchos*, p. 46.

[70] Ibid,. p. 15.

middle-class producers in political and even spatial (or territorial) terms, and thus they did not always see eye to eye with farmers, especially in terms of support for land reform.[71]

The second group were the farmers. In contrast to gauchos, farmers and many other small-scale agricultural producers set down roots and established social and working relationships that reinforced their attachments to place and production. Farming in general and sheep farming in particular was "more suitable to family labor than cattle ranching,"[72] a state of affairs which together helped produce a demographic shift that further strengthened farmers' demands for government support of the rural sector in its entirety. But many of their demands were geared toward specific farming concerns, and this failed to bring gauchos to their side. In the absence of significant rural middle-class unity, national political power remained elusive.

All this is not to say that rural middle-class forces were politically insignificant at all times. Precisely because of small farmers' growing demographic and economic strength in several key provinces, the government often responded to their demands. One result was that by the early 1900s, smaller-scale rural producers were considered a key coalition ally for whichever class or social force sought to gain political control, especially of the city of Buenos Aires and the province, and even the nation as a whole. It would have been hard, after all, to govern the entire nation from Buenos Aires if populations surrounding the city were unsympathetic. As a result, the Radical Party frequently catered to rural middle-class demands for farm land and agrarian progress. Under one of the Radical Party's greatest leaders, Yrigoyen, the government sought money from the National Congress for "new colonization schemes on state lands, for subsidies to farmers caught by a recent drought, [and] for a new state bank to improve farmers' credit."[73] These moves were intended to sustain the Radical Party's popularity among what David Rock calls "the pampas' rural middle class," and were made in response to organized demands by associations like the FAA and its small-farmer constituents. In fact, the colonization schemes were intended "to assist Argentine-born farmers to gain farm-home ownership."[74] In 1921, the Radicals actually offered a land reform law (initially introduced by a Socialist government in 1900 in which Juan B. Justo participated as a deputy) that mandated greater property rights and freedom for tenant farmers of more than three hundred hectares in cereal-producing areas, which primarily meant Buenos Aires province and its immediate surrounds.

---

[71] According to Slatta, "the mobility necessary for ranch work, along with government harassment, prevented many gauchos from enjoying a stable family life" (ibid., p. 5).

[72] Rock, *Argentina*, p. 134.

[73] Ibid., p. 199.

[74] Taylor, *Rural Life in Argentina*, p. 388.

But as noted earlier, agrarian reform and the rural middle classes' political days in the sun were short-lived. Support for the small-farmer class in Buenos Aires province had always been highly circumscribed,[75] and the rural middle class itself was not united,[76] with the little independent farming that did prosper lying mostly in the periphery outside the pampas.[77] Additionally, the small farmers' newfound importance in making national political alliances as well as their growing ties to the Radicals ultimately undermined their capacity to push a purely middle-class agenda. Some of this again owed to the national economic and political centrality of the capital city. When Buenos Aires prospered so did the economy in the entire province, and thus so did the political power and influence of large estancieros and other oligarchic families who were involved in large-scale production and processing activities. These large *latifundistas*, in turn, used their power to limit the political and economic influence of rural small farmers both in the interior and in Buenos Aires province itself, such that even the supportive agricultural policies of the early- and mid-nineteenth century began to be replaced by less accommodating and more repressive measures with respect to rural tenants and other small-scale rural producers.[78] Indeed, even with the more rural middle-class-oriented Radical Party at the helm of the state, large *latifundistas* and the agrarian

---

[75] In contrast to the province of Santa Fe, for example, where the growth of a relatively prosperous small-farmer class was quite successful, in Buenos Aires province oligarch forces granted only meager support for farming, facilitating the development of small farms only to the extent that they aided their own larger-scale agricultural processing and exporting objectives. For more on this, see Slatta, *Gauchos*, pp. 153–156.

[76] Further damaging to rural middle-class unity and rural middle-class capacities to act as a powerful political force, many farmers tended to prosper more quickly as tenants than as independent smallholders. Why? Because in the context of cattle ranching and an associated rise in land prices, tenant farming was much more profitable, especially in the cattle-dominated Buenos Aires province. Also limiting the profitability of independent smallholdings was the fact that farmers still lacked adequate credit facilities and many were chronically indebted to landowners, rural shopkeepers, or the great cereal export houses in Buenos Aires that emerged in the late 1880s. For more on this, see Rock, *Argentina*, pp. 177–178.

[77] Ibid., p. 197.

[78] The Radical Party, for its part, was increasingly under pressure to include both urban and rural middle classes within its party structures and platforms, in response to the increasing prosperity of Buenos Aires and its commercially and industrially oriented residents. Further restricting its capacity to support rural middle-class formation through calls for land reform, the Radical Party had long been a strong supporter of private property. Combined with concern about establishing a broadly cast national presence, this position explains the Radical Party's "refusal to make an issue of the status of large rural holdings," a policy stance that ultimately restricted the claims of its rural middle-class base much more than its urban middle-class constituency. Johnson, *Political Change in Latin America*, p. 103.

oligarchy still held sway in politics and society, while urban middle classes themselves started to taste the fruits of political power.

One result was that the cattle industry prospered greatly under the Radicals, as did meat processing and other cattle-related industrial manufactures, many of them in the capital or in the towns and small cities of Buenos Aires province. These developments, in turn, fueled the development of urban-based manufacturing activities geared toward the growing consumption demands of the increasingly high-wage urban workers, mainly in Buenos Aires. "Between 1895 and 1914 manufacturing establishments doubled in number, and capital investment in manufacturing quintupled. For example, the dairy industry – insignificant in 1890 – appeared by 1914 to have a great future; while between 1895 and 1914 flour milling expanded fourfold, sugar refining threefold, and brewing beer eightfold."[79] And with the lure of urban prosperity just over the horizon in the first decades of the twentieth century, the demographic balance in the country also began shifting. Many rural residents abandoned farming activities and migrated to the city. These out-migrations not only helped deplete the rural middle class demographically and politically, they also signaled the re-subordination of sheep and agriculture to the renascent cattle economy, or so argues David Rock, and a further social and political division between farmers and gauchos. By the 1920s, it was clear that urban middle classes were increasing in number and visibility in the national class structure, even as rural middle classes declined.[80]

In terms of national politics and coalition building, the consequences were enormous. The internal division and declining significance of the Radical Party, and thus an unwillingness and incapacity to support the demands of the rural middle classes, were one set of by-products; another was the conspicuous economic neglect of the interior. The latter state of affairs further contributed to the declining national political salience of rural middle classes nationwide, and not just in Buenos Aires province.[81] After 1930, Argentina's overall farming population began its most dramatic free fall, after reaching a peak earlier that same year,[82] and by the mid-1930s, Pedro de Paoli argues, neither the Conservative Party nor the Radical Party was eager to pick up the banner

---

[79] Rock, *Argentina*, p. 169.

[80] With cattle ranching and related cereal agriculture as the main rural activities, Rock further argues, labor was free and highly mobile, and the wage form almost universal, such that along with large estates the province saw an uneven distribution of wealth and a large transient population. After 1914, in fact, the rural population was composed primarily of cattle peons or shepherds, seasonal laborers, and farm tenants, who by the 1930s comprised almost 44 percent of all farm families. Taylor, *Rural Life in Argentina*, p. 204.

[81] See Sawers, *The Other Argentina*.

[82] Taylor, *Rural Life in Argentina*, p. 108.

of Argentina's rural farmers.[83] Moreover, these demographic and economic shifts led to a more polarized rural class structure and to institutionalized underconsumption in the countryside, which further contributed to Argentina's "uneven, underdeveloped, and soon largely inflexible economic structure."[84] This, in turn, meant that not only was there insufficient demand in rural areas themselves for their own goods, but the basic source of consumption lay in the cities among urban populations whose appetites for imported goods permanently weakened Argentina's balance-of-payments situation. The countryside languished further except as a source of large-scale agrarian exports.

It is no surprise, then, that during his political ascendance in the 1930s and 1940s, General Juan Perón sided with urban populations almost to the exclusion of rural ones, especially those small-scale farmers who proved problematic to his larger political coalition. Nor is it a surprise that Perón's great twentieth-century push for industrialization took place largely without rural middle classes – let alone their disciplinary influence.

Territorial Dynamics and Taiwan's Rural Middle Classes

Despite its common colonial heritage and agricultural-exporting economy, Taiwan experienced an entirely different state of affairs, sharing the "best" of the rural middle-class formative experience, if you will, at least when compared to both the South Korean and Argentine cases, even as it dispensed with their most debilitating constraints. Like South Korea, Taiwan was still mainly agricultural and thus rural populations – and specifically, a rural middle class of small agricultural producers – figured strongly into national politics. Hence the widespread support for land reform. Yet, as in Argentina, certain class and social sectors in the city (mainly Taipei) also mattered to a great extent, mainly large-scale industrialists producing for a domestic market. This situation insured that the country's rural orientation would also be laced with a commitment to urban and industrial development. Most important, perhaps, Taiwan was blessed with a demographic and historical legacy that strongly linked rural and urban populations and priorities *together*, rather than pitting them against each other, as occurred in Argentina and somewhat less so in South Korea. This state of affairs further explains why the Taiwanese government ultimately supported small-scale rural industrialization and small-farmer agricultural production combined with strategically targeted large-scale industrial development. Together, this combination of policies both derived

---

[83] *La reforma agraria*, p. 34. The result, he suggests, was that despite their "liberal bourgeois tradition," neither of the parties succeeded in "rationalizing or ordering" Argentine agriculture.

[84] Rock, *Argentina*, p. xxvi.

from and reinforced patterns of rural middle-class formation, even as it fostered strong connections between the state and rural middle classes on one hand, and between the state and a small number of large-scale urban-based ISI industrialists on the other. This unique mix of state-class alliances set Taiwan on a much more durable and sound developmental path than that pursued by Argentina under both Perón and his successors during the post–World War II period.

Taiwan's success in these regards owes largely to the fact that the fate of rural middle classes was much less contested and problematic than in Argentina or even South Korea. Rural middle-class prosperity and influence accelerated steadily during the first stages of mid-twentieth-century industrialization rather than vacillating back and forth and ultimately declining, as occurred in Argentina. There are multiple reasons for this, but in keeping with our interest in the impact of urbanization patterns, one critical place to begin is a comparative examination of territorial patterns of population distribution, especially relations within and between regions and Taiwan's capital city, Taipei. Taiwan never experienced serious rural-urban conflicts, at least to the extreme degree that Argentina did. Nor was there significant uneven regional development during the initial process of postwar state formation, at least not enough to produce what would be considered paralyzing political or economic tensions. If one were to survey Taiwanese political and economic history throughout the nineteenth and most of the twentieth centuries, and compare it to that of Argentina, one would be surprised to find hardly a mention of Taipei at all. In fact, most development scholars tend to discuss the island as a whole, paying attention to different economic activities – i.e., rice versus sugar – but not to the regional underpinnings of these variations. There is hardly a mention of developmental differences among various parts of the country, let alone urban-rural or capital city–provincial tensions. Yet Taiwan's more even patterns of regional development, and the absence of an overwhelming core city, have been absolutely critical in its macroeconomic successes.

Size may explain many of the country's advantages in these regards. Taiwan is a very small island, petite in comparison with many of the world's late developers and absolutely minuscule in comparison with most of its counterparts in Latin America, Argentina in particular. In addition to being small, nearly two-thirds of the island is mountainous, a geological situation which limits the amount of arable land (about one-fourth is cultivable) and helps explain why much of the population is concentrated on the west coast. As such, the expanse, geopolitical character, and territorial magnitude of Argentina dwarf Taiwan and set these two countries apart from each other on many counts. However, the differences are not just geographic in some abstract sense; they also owe to the political and state-building dynamics associated with these territorial and geopolitical patterns. For one thing, as noted earlier, struggles over state formation and national power in Argentina were highly contentious precisely because of the nation's territorial expanse, the diversity of its economy, the variety of peoples, and geographic scope for state rule. In Taiwan, a much smaller size insured that national powers, colonial rulers, and externally imposed authorities, ranging from precolonial dynastic governments in sync with Chinese imperial powers (pre-1895), to the Japanese (1895–1944), to the KMT (post-1947), all were able to establish hegemony without the same divisive, regionally based civil wars that wracked Argentina. For another, given Taiwan's size and geography, there also was much less scope for extraordinarily large landholdings, since unlike Argentina, in Taiwan there was so little productive land. Last, and most important for our understanding of urban-rural tensions, most of the population in Taiwan was concentrated in one small part of the island, a state of affairs which limited the potential for conflict-ridden regional rivalries and overly profound urban-rural differences.

Yet it was not merely the size of the country that limited its internal differentiation into distinct rural and urban areas and that prevented the emergence of contentious provincial or center-periphery politics that would overprivilege cities. From early on, the lives and economic activities of most Taiwanese people straddled rural and urban areas, by virtue of their involvement in agricultural production for export, in the context of both Chinese imperial and Japanese imperial rule. According to Tom Gold, in fact, by the end of the nineteenth century most Taiwanese residents were what he calls "peasant owners" or tenants who "through the cultivation and marketing of cash crops . . . became increasingly linked into commercial networks that extended beyond the island to the rest of the world."[85] This meant that despite their rural location and involvement in small-scale agricultural production, most people in Taiwan were neither economically nor socially (or politically, for that matter) isolated from towns and cities, but somehow implicated in their orbit. The result was that there were fewer antagonisms between so-called rural and urban localities. This in turn meant that rural middle classes were more likely to be included than excluded from governing coalitions and larger projects of state building, no matter who was in power.

Whereas in Argentina colonialism helped generate territorial and class antagonisms within and between rural and urban populations, by virtue of its impact on patterns of landholding, agricultural exporting, and mercantile trading relations, in Taiwan Japanese colonial practices militated against the development of these patterns even as they helped reinforce the country's more evenly spread demographic and relatively balanced urban character. In Gold's words, "The infrastructure and factories built by the Japanese were dispersed throughout the island, thus avoiding the common phenomenon of a tiny modern channel in a sea of traditional society."[86] In fact, despite foreign ownership

---

[85] *State and Society in the Taiwan Miracle*, p. 29.
[86] Ibid., p. 45.

and control of great stretches of land, under Japanese colonial rule relatively few Taiwanese people were driven off their land either onto plantations or into a few key cities, as was generally the rule in many other colonies and had been especially the case in Latin America. Additionally, under Japanese economic and administrative policy, most of the already existing cities were expanded to make centers of industry, a practice that further contrasts with the Latin American experience where one or two internal cities and/or a single critical port city were developed to mediate trade and mercantile relations, leaving the rest to die on the vine.

Significantly, this apparently was as true in colonial South Korea as in Taiwan. Under colonial rule Korean "cities grew as administrative centers for colonial exploitation, assembly points of agricultural products to be exported to Japan, and production sites of raw materials and cheap manufactured goods destined to the Japanese factories and consumers."[87] By 1920, in fact, there were eight areas defined as urban (with a population of twenty thousand or greater); and by 1940 the number of towns and cities in Korea falling into this category had increased from eight to ninety.[88] Still, in terms of urbanization patterns as well as urban-rural balances, there were some differences between South Korea and Taiwan that shed light on their divergent fates, especially in terms of rural middle-class formation and the rural and urban embeddedness of their states. The predominance of sugar processing under Japanese colonial rule in Taiwan, built on the relatively decentralized and even distribution of rural-based sugar processing plants, helped sustain if not fuel small-farmer production of sugar, which in turn helped to economically justify Japanese investment in local processing plants in the first place. And these produced more integrated and balanced rural-urban patterns, providing a vibrant rural middle class with a market for its products and sufficient rural backward linkages to generate self-sustaining economic growth.

In South Korea, despite its shared status as a Japanese colony, the emphasis on rice rather than sugar meant that its economy developed differently from Taiwan's, and so too did urban-rural articulations and the urban system as a whole. Rice was not nearly as productive or lucrative a trade item in South Korea, with rice cultivation intended mainly for Japanese consumption, as noted earlier. Accordingly, the Japanese tended to foster the development of other activities – like industrial processing of textiles – to a much greater degree in South Korea than in Taiwan. This in turn brought more regional differentiation and rural-urban imbalance in South Korea, with a few central and northern cities growing as industrial centers and a "population shift away from densely settled agricultural southern provinces,"[89] in a manner that

---

[87] Kwon et al., *The Population of Korea*, p. 62. See also Lee, *Life in Urban Korea*, p. 18.
[88] Kwon, *The Population of Korea*, pp. 62–63.
[89] Ibid., p. 64.

seems to echo urban and industrial dynamics in Argentina. The geopolitics of partition made this initial imbalance even worse. When Korea split at the 49th parallel, the most urbanized and industrialized provinces fell under North Korean control, while the more agricultural – and poorer – provinces became what is now South Korea. In addition to changing the overall rural versus urban balance of the population within the country as a whole, a situation which may have had some advantages because it ultimately sustained Park's commitment to rural over urban development, and his efforts to sustain rural middle-class formation, partition also changed the intra-urban patterns in the south.

All this suggests that the developmental consequences of partition in South Korea, in short, may not have been as wholeheartedly beneficial to the economy's development – at least in comparison to similarly anticommunist Taiwan – as many scholars tend to assume, precisely because the relatively more balanced urban-rural spatial dynamics initially produced by Japanese colonial administrative practices actually were undermined in South Korea. One result was that in urban terms, South Korea began to look more like Argentina, with one or two large cities juxtaposed against a series of relatively under-urbanized rural provinces, and much less like its colonial cousin Taiwan. Of course, the partition of Korea did fuel much of the antiurban sentiment that General Park Chung Hee marshaled to sustain his rural middle-class ethos. In that sense, it did have some positive impact on South Korean developmental trajectories. But the partition of the urbanized and industrialized north from the more agricultural and impoverished south also contributed to demographic problems down the road, especially when rural agriculture and rural populations failed to prosper rapidly enough with Park's rural development programs. In these conditions, the lure of Seoul as the one industrial beacon on the horizon continually fueled rural-urban migration, a process which ultimately upset the demographic and political balance in South Korea. Once the balance of class power shifted away from rural to urban areas, these populations became ever more isolated from each other, as was also the case in Argentina, leading toward a highly concentrated and powerful cadre of urban industrialists who led South Korea down a more Latin American–style path to crisis.

Of course, the imbalances between Seoul and the remaining agricultural provinces in South Korea were not nearly as stark as were the differences between the port and the interior in Argentina, with Buenos Aires vying and ultimately achieving demographic and political dominance over a marginalized if not isolated interior. But neither were they as evenly balanced or integrated as in Taiwan, where early division of the country into fifty sugar districts produced much more extensive and evenly distributed rural-based industrialization and thus much more extensive urban-rural articulation, as in the United States, the U.K., and other early modern European cases described in Chapter 1. And these urban-rural differences between South Korea and

Taiwan on one hand and Taiwan and Argentina on the other produced major differences in rural middle-class formation and rural middle-class political power.

Geopolitics, the Military, Rural Middle Classes, and Discipline in Taiwan

It may be true that the history of sugar production and the attendant imbalance in urban and rural relations helped sustain the development of a vibrant rural middle class in Taiwan. We would be remiss, however, if we did not factor into the story the geopolitical dynamics and how in the case of Taiwan this spurred the postcolonial government to nurture both a rural middle class and a more widespread disciplinary ethos within the state. This unique history differentiated Taiwan from Argentina and produced parallels with South Korea in developmentally significant ways.

The conflict between the communists and the nationalists on China's mainland set the stage for these developments. Once finding themselves in retreat from China, the Kuomintang (KMT), or nationalists, set up shop in Taiwan. As they sought to establish a political hold on the state, they needed local allies. The country's nascent cadre of rural middle classes was a likely target. This owed in no small part to the fact that a large proportion of the KMT exiles who came to the island were themselves small farmers or holders of variously sized rural properties from agricultural provinces in the mainland.[90] True, some of those in the higher ranks of the KMT leadership were drawn from families of urban industrialists, particularly from Shanghai. But in general, most of the nationalists in Taiwan were from more modest small-scale commercial or farm families (i.e., urban and rural middle classes), with the most prosperous Chinese industrialists having fled to Hong Kong rather than Taiwan after Mao's victory.[91] They also were staunchly anticommunist. These features combined to remake the post-1949 Taiwanese state quite ideologically sympathetic to the resident small-farmer class of small private property owners who struggled to produce and prosper on their own account.

That the KMT-dominated state identified and sympathized with small-scale rural producers was in many ways reflected in the ideological contours of the nationalist movement, especially in the political and philosophical writings of its founder and figurehead, Sun Yat-sen. Along with Chiang Kai-shek, Sun

---

[90] That the KMT military rank and file, even if not the party leadership, saw themselves in small-farmer terms is partly evidenced by the fact that after they left the service, government provisions were made for most KMT veterans to retire to small farms (in Taiwan) run both cooperatively and individually.

[91] Gold, *State and Society in the Taiwan Miracle*, p. 70.

served as a dominant figure in the KMT's history. And in a fashion similar to that of Park Chung Hee, much of Sun's original writings highlighted rural middle-class virtues and sang the praises of a disciplinary ethos, as was perhaps most evident in his calls for "regulating capital [*chieh-chih tsu-pen*]," an idea that later became a key element of the KMT's ideology.[92] Additionally, Sun's more general concept of *min sheng* was, at least as one scholar has described it, "a vague concept akin to that of socialism in its advocacy of regulation of capital and equalization of land tenure, but minus class struggle and with a major role for free enterprise."[93] Of course, Sun's writings have been characterized as Leninist-style democratic centralism by Thomas Gold and others, but they also touched on many elements that suggest both nationalism and social justice in a fashion not very different from that which Park Chung Hee promoted. Monte Bullard, among others, suggests that although "Sun Yat-sen actually called his economic program 'communism,' it was in reality a form of capitalism which provided for strong government action at the beginning of the development and would gradually lead to an increasingly laissez-faire economy." Bullard further argues that "the degree of government participation or controls in the economy could allow it to be described as a socialist economy although [Sun] explictly rejected many of Marx's theories – such as class struggle, the theory of surplus value, or the inevitable collapse of capitalism – after studying them in detail."[94] Where KMT policy mirrored Park's, then, was in its so-called "'petty bourgeois' outlook" and in the high priority Sun gave to agriculture as a means for developing industry.[95] As with Park in South Korea, KMT leaders argued for a combination of "land reform and capitalism,"[96] which entailed support for

---

[92] Hsiao, "The Changing State-Society Relation in the ROC," p. 129.

[93] Gold, *State and Society in the Taiwan Miracle*, p. 48. For more on the KMT, its origins on mainland China, and its development in Taiwan, see Jiang and Wu, "The Changing Role of the KMT in Taiwan's Political System"; and Cheng and Haggard, "Regime Transformation in Taiwan."

[94] *The Citizen and the Soldier*, p. 53. Bullard suggests that Sun's principle of "People's Livelihood" had three meanings prioritized as follows: 1) develop material strength to support a strong nation-state in a world of exploitative nations, 2) enrich the nation to erase abject poverty, and 3) insure economic distributive justice.

[95] Metzger, "The Chinese Reconciliation of Moral-Sacred Values With Modern Pluralism," p. 10.

[96] Bullard, *The Citizen and the Soldier*, p. 54. "Land or the agricultural sector, in Sun's scheme, was to be a major producer of capital for investment in the industrial sector or overall modernization. . . . State capitalism was to be a policy for industries, like utilities, which were too large for private investment or corporations, which tended toward monopoly. This was tempered, however, by Sun's instruction that 'all matters that can be and are better carried out by private enterprise should be left to private hands, which should be encouraged and fully protected by liberal laws.'"

"restraining private capital in some form"[97] and an overwhelming sympathy for smaller-scale agricultural producers, namely, rural middle classes.

But it was not merely the personal affinities or even the ideological romanticization of small farmers or rural middle-class life among KMT leaders and sympathizers that reinforced the embeddedness of Taiwan's rural middle classes in the state. Just as important, the KMT-led military forces saw their occupation of Taiwan and their hold on the state in primarily strategic terms, seeing this small island as the location from which they could strengthen their own efforts to reclaim mainland China. For this reason, in fact, mainlanders dominated the public and state sectors, at least during the first decades of KMT rule. When Chiang Kai-shek and his forces retreated to Taiwan in 1949 during their ongoing struggle to wrest control of the Chinese mainland, they were confronted with an economy that was primarily agricultural, comprised of a considerable number of small-scale rural producers, and a relatively modest if not underwhelming urban metropolis. The single largest demographic constituency available to sustain the KMT's legitimate claim to the state were rural producers, mainly small independent farmers and tenant farmers. The KMT leadership had learned a bitter lesson through its experiences on the mainland, having lost its claim to China through a successful peasant revolution in which Mao Tse-dong's forces had managed to appeal to the rural masses. For this reason too, the KMT identified rural populations as the political cornerstone of their stay on Taiwan, with the recognition that "to strive for the final victory (on China) as well as to complete the revolutionary task, we should start our work all over again," especially with respect to village residents. In Chiang Kai-shek's words, "their likes and dislikes should be the yardstick to measure merits and effects of the local administration. We should help to relieve them from evils in time so that they can rejoice over the good in peace."[98]

Accordingly, in the KMT's party congresses in Taiwan, farmers were identified as "first and foremost among laboring masses."[99] As in South Korea, the government in Taiwan was very careful to cultivate the organization and unity of rural middle classes and to link them to the state and party. In so doing, they relied directly on institutional arrangements that the Japanese had originally established in order to coordinate small-farmer production in the colonial economy. In Monte Bullard's words, "These arrangements included farmers' associations, irrigation cooperatives and other agricultural institutions which promoted organizational rules and cooperative behavior patterns which 'in turn increased their power to manipulate their physical and biological environment

---

[97] Cheng, "Political Regimes and Development Strategies," p. 155.
[98] Chang, *The Kuomintang*, p. 11.
[99] Moody, Jr., *Political Change on Taiwan*, p. 20.

more in line with their needs and aspirations.'"[100] Party documents give further testament to the KMT's aims in these regards:

> We will spare no effort to strengthen leadership on the district level. . . . To magnify propaganda effects, electrical apparatuses have to be amply utilized to dissemilate [*sic*] information in rural districts. To promote mass movements, the farmers' associations will be improved to help push the program of the land-to-the-tiller policy, and labour unions will be activiated [*sic*] to coordinate with the four-year plan of economic reconstruction. In addition, scientific technology has to be applied to increase production and to better the livelihood of the people. We will arouse public zeal to serve the people, and urge the people to contribute free manual labour.[101]

The bottom line for the KMT was that it both needed and sought to establish its legitimacy with local populations, mainly rural. The KMT could not afford rebellion on its host island.

After a particularly serious uprising in 1947 known as the February 28th Incident, in which local Taiwanese demanded political autonomy, the KMT was very careful to accommodate or at least keep most of the Taiwanese people loyal. In its seventh national party congress in 1952, when the larger political and economic objectives of the KMT-led state were laid out, the social foundation of the party was identified broadly as encompassing "youth, the intelligentsia, and the laboring masses including the farmers, the laborers, and the producers in general."[102] Still, given the largely small-farmer, agricultural activities of most native Taiwanese, as well as the KMT's concerns that rural populations would be most susceptible to communist organizers at home and from abroad, the party made a concerted effort to lend economic and social support to small-scale agricultural producers, which the above-cited passage identifies as the first and ostensibly most critical representative of Taiwan's laboring masses. Farmers, in short, were seen as the backbone of the economy and the most critical political force to bring to the governing KMT's side, such that the KMT publicly summed up its mission and overall party objectives as the effort to "reconstruct the nation through rural reconstruction."[103] In these efforts, the officially labeled Farmers Associations (FA) played a key role.[104]

The KMT's commitment to rural reconstruction is seen in the early and accelerating implementation of land reform, starting as soon as the KMT

---

[100] *The Citizen and the Soldier*, p. 31.

[101] Chang, *The Kuomintang*, p. 9.

[102] See Chang, *The Rebirth of the Kuomintang*, p. 83.

[103] Chang, *The Kuomintang*, p. 13.

[104] For more on their origins in 1900, their development by the Japanese, and their subsequent role under the KMT, see Tien, *The Great Transition*, pp. 46–50.

arrived on Taiwan and continuing throughout the early 1950s, especially in its 1953 "land to the tiller" program. Studies of Taiwanese land reform are many and I will not take the time here to detail them, except to say that in contrast to South Korea before Park and even during that country's early years of land reform, in Taiwan the KMT was dead serious about making land reform work from the very beginning. Indeed, as ultimately occurred in South Korea after Park's coup d'etat in 1961, considerable monies were spent to supply the newly independent farmers with fertilizers, pesticides, improved seeds, technical advice, and credit.[105] The results were evident in both middle-class formative and productivity terms. According to Tom Gold, "Land cultivated by owner-cultivators increased from 50.5 percent of the total in 1949 to 75.4 percent in 1953. Tenant-cultivated land fell from 41.8 percent to 16.3 percent over the same period," and "small landowning families became the dominant force in Taiwan's countryside."[106]

In both South Korea and Taiwan, U.S. support and encouragement for land reform played a role in producing a rural middle class. But even with similar foreign aid packages, only in Taiwan did the program work well enough to bring major developmental gains, both in terms of foreign exchange and in terms of forward and backward linkages between agriculture and industry, owing again to the strong base of rural middle-class producers that already existed when the program first kicked in. In 1952, 22 percent of Taiwan's exports were agricultural products and 70 percent were processed agricultural products; by 1959, as per capita income grew steadily, nearly 90 percent of Taiwan's exports still consisted of agricultural goods and processed agricultural goods.[107] These figures clearly reflect the legacy of small-scale rural production buttressed under Japanese colonialism plus the KMT's strong initial commitment to agriculture. Yet they also help explain the extent to which Taiwanese farmers (in contrast to those in South Korea) both prospered through state-supported agriculture and remained committed to it in such a way as to fuel subsequent industrial development by growing rural demand for domestic industrial manufactures.[108] One especially striking by-product of the growing dynamism in the rural sector was an increase in average farm size, as smaller farms combined into somewhat larger production units that could adapt to

---

[105] For one of the fullest accounts of Taiwan's land reform, see Yager, *Transforming Agriculture in Taiwan*.

[106] *State and Society in the Taiwan Miracle*, p. 66.

[107] Vogel, *The Four Little Dragons*, pp. 19–20.

[108] Vogel, in ibid., p. 21, also notes that with growing agricultural exports the rural sector increased its savings rate, as we might expect given the rural middle-class ethos of Taiwan's relatively developed cadre of small farmers, which in turn the state later used for industrial development.

mechanization.[109] This also distinguished Taiwan from South Korea. While, in the former case, land reform enhanced small-farm production and agricultural productivity, activities which further buttressed nascent patterns of rural middle-class formation, in the latter, the effects were much less beneficial in terms of productivity, plot size, and thus rural-class formation.

On an institutional level, the state's rural development policies strengthened farmers' capacities to press their own macroeconomic and political demands, thereby cementing rural middle-class embeddedness in the Taiwanese state. With credit, fertilizer, and other state supports for agricultural development channeled through the long-standing FAs, rural middle-class producers became directly connected to the state apparatus, further cementing their influence. Accordingly, although membership in these state-linked associations was voluntary, by the mid-1980s about 85 percent of Taiwanese farming households identified themselves as regular members. Moreover, over the decades these Farmers Associations continued to grow, widening their scope as the organizational representative not only of rural middle-class farmers but also of small businessmen and small entrepreneurs who ultimately were incorporated as associate members.[110] In this sense, the KMT used land reform to reinforce the party-led state's middle-class embeddedness, first rural and then urban.

Many scholars choose to look at the darker side of these programs, identifying land reform in Taiwan as "an effective way for the Nationalist regime to remove the only potentially strong alternative locus of authority on the island"[111] and as a way of "coopting potential allies."[112] Such assessments echo many of the common scholarly interpretations of Park's Saemaul Undong program, in which it was seen only as a means for the top-down manipulation of rural masses. Still, Taiwan's land reform programs and the KMT's conscientious efforts to imbue farmers associations with the power of "direct democracy" – especially in terms of local leadership and organization – also brought significant gains, both political and economic, so much that the party felt particularly proud of its successes in agriculture and liked to think of itself "as the farmer's friend." Overall, then, KMT support for rural development and several decades of land reform paid off by cementing its political bases in the countryside and the provinces much more so than in the city. This in turn fueled "the continuing political influence of the peasantry both in the province as a whole and within the rank and file of the opposition and the KMT."[113]

[109] Lee, "Taiwan's New Land Reform," p. 13.

[110] Tien, *The Great Transition*, p. 47.

[111] Simon, "External Incorporation and Internal Reform," p. 147.

[112] Gold, *State and Society in the Taiwan Miracle*, p. 65.

[113] Moody, Jr., *Political Change on Taiwan*, p. 47. Haggard and Pang agree with this assessment, but phrase it slightly differently: The land reform "created a new class of smallholders that

Not surprisingly, the positive effects of land reform policies also were seen in electoral results, in which the KMT has consistently polled better in rural elections than urban ones, with cities on the whole being much less supportive of the KMT than the countryside.[114]

The nature of KMT organization and the ways in which the state actively linked itself to farmers and other rural populations are in fact important parts of the story of the Taiwanese state's rural middle-class embeddedness. In much the same way that Park used programs and government propaganda and rhetoric to underscore the elective affinity between rural farm populations and his government, the KMT worked conscientiously to do the same with native Taiwanese people. In fact, the KMT may have been under even greater pressure than Park Chung Hee to establish strong connections not just with rural populations but also between the military and the Taiwanese people, precisely because of the KMT's status as interloper and occupying force. Whereas in South Korea the cultural and social connections among the military, rural farmers, and the state were grounded in a shared past and thus already in place to some degree, only needing reinforcement by Park when times got bad, in Taiwan there existed a strong basis for antagonism between the KMT and the local population, who were ethnically distinct from their exiled Chinese leaders. This ethnic antagonism also had a spatial underpinning that threatened to make Taiwan more similar to Argentina than to South Korea, and which was manifest in the fact that the capital city of Taipei tended to be dominated by mainlanders while the native Taiwanese predominated in the countryside.[115] For these reasons, the KMT recognized the importance of developing multiple strategies to overcome the possible antagonism between rurally based native Taiwanese populations and Taipei-based mainlander populations, including the growing cadre of mainlander-drawn urban industrialists who also settled on the island.

The first strategy the KMT used, as noted earlier, was to actively support a multitude of provincial FAs. As in South Korea, the infrastructure of farmers associations was a remnant of Japanese colonialism, having been used in earlier times to control rural small-scale producers for integration into the Japanese-dominated colonial economy; but in Taiwan, in contrast to South Korea, farmers associations were still relatively vibrant at the initial point of KMT-led state formation, owing to the continued vitality of the small-farmer, rural-based economy during the final years of Japanese colonization. As such, farmers associations were not merely the tools of the state, as was suggested

---

provided the KMT with at least a tacit support base." See "The Transition to Export-Led Growth in Taiwan," p. 57.

[114] Moody, Jr., *Political Change on Taiwan*, p. 132. He also notes that while mainlanders tend to support the KMT, they are concentrated in the cities (especially in Taipei).

[115] Ibid., p. 122.

in South Korea. They functioned as relatively independent organizations reinforcing a strong two-way relationship between the KMT and rural peoples
even as they buttressed the numbers and influence of rural middle classes along
the way. A second developmentally more significant strategy revolved around
the government's plans for the military. In contrast to South Korea, the KMT
leadership took great pains to institutionally separate the military from the
state and link it to the citizenry, at least to as great a degree as is possible given
the intrinsic and obvious connections between the KMT state and its military.

This was accomplished in two ways. One was through the KMT's decision
to make the military part of the party and not the state per se, as is generally more customary under conditions of authoritarian rule and as occurred in
South Korea and Argentina. Placing the military into the party allowed the
KMT to argue that it had developed an inclusive institutional structure for
accommodating a variety of social and class forces, of which the military was
merely one, and in which all members were to share equal aims. From Chiang
Kai-shek's point of view, in fact, this was one of the key domestic and foreign
(i.e., China-directed) aims of his administration. In a 1953 party document
KMT leaders argued that "the most urgent of all is to build up the Party as a
fighting body, which is to function in such a way as to integrate Party activities,
political affairs, and military campaigns into the same fighting machinery."[116]
One additional way that the KMT linked the military to the citizenry was
through development of a variety of military activities which themselves targeted civilian populations. These included 1) the expansion of the military to
include native Taiwanese within its ranks, 2) the development of various programs of citizen assistance, aid, and propaganda for the purpose of increasing
the military's visibility, prestige, and appreciation among rural populations in
particular, and 3) efforts to reinforce the cult of discipline and austerity, both
of which were tied to military service and KMT principles of self-sacrifice and
capitalist development. These programs not only cemented the rural middle
classes to the state, both directly and via the ranks of the military as an institution, they also laid the foundations for the inculcation of a nationally
identifiable disciplinary ethos shared by the rural middle classes, the military,
and the state. And as we have seen in earlier chapters, it is the combined effect
of top-down and bottom-up discipline, embodied in institutions and practices
that operated in both the state and civil society – as well as among rural middle
classes themselves   that brings the greatest developmental gains.

The commitment to a disciplinary ethos was evident as soon as the KMT
arrived on the island. Because of their concern that years of Japanese occupation would automatically limit native Taiwanese support for the nationalist cause,[117] starting in 1949 the KMT began a period of active "political

---

[116] Chang, *The Kuomintang*, p. 13.
[117] Bullard, *The Citizen and the Soldier*, p. 12.

tutelage," inspired by Sun Yat-sen's 1946 program on the mainland of the same name, in which "emphasis shall be laid on developing the habits of physical labor, the way of making a living, the cultivation of the virtues of patriotism, loyalty, personal sacrifice and social service" and in "which military training [was to be] introduced in senior middle schools, colleges, and universities."[118] From the beginning, the KMT worked hard to produce what it called "formal and direct political education" both within the military and society at large, plans which included support for the principles of "hard work and study," even for military personnel, and example by demonstration.[119] Rural populations, as noted above, were a key target for these activities, much as had been the case with Saemaul Undong in South Korea.

The parallels between the KMT's militarized educational mission and Park's Saemaul Undong are indeed striking and go a long way in explaining both the strength of the disciplinary ethos and the rural middle-class-embedded state policies that led both countries down a similarly successful EOI-oriented developmental path, at least initially. Starting in June 1950, for example, the KMT initiated a program designed to improve civil-military relations in which the military both established new rural associations and helped spur rural productivity gains.

> Community leaders serve[d] as chairmen of the associations and they invite[d] all local dignitaries to join. . . . The main purpose of the associations was to 'serve' the people and win support from them by providing such assistance as: 1) working with farmers in cultivation and harvest work; 2) helping in local environmental cleanup activities; 3) assisting in the construction and repair of local infrastructure (bridges, roads, dikes, etc.); 4) showing respect for local seniors, leaders, and dignitaries to increase their prestige; 5) helping the poor with relief supplies and free medical service; 6) establishing small libraries for the local people to provide them with an information base; 7) providing a public letter-writer so that illiterates could write letters and fill out official forms; and 8) setting up special classes for illiterates to help them become literate.[120]

The KMT state, in short, just like the Park government, was well prepared to inculcate into the population as a whole a range of disciplinary values associated with both military service and rural life, not just for the purposes of sustaining the party's larger political and developmental goals and keeping citizens from sympathizing with communists, but also in order to experientially connect citizens to soldiers. One key difference in Taiwan, however, was that youth were identified as a special target, mainly because they were considered more

[118] Ibid., p. 67.
[119] Ibid., pp. 117–118.
[120] Ibid., p. 158.

prone to support communists. Party documents claimed that one could never "over-emphasize the historic mission of youth cadres," who "should fully grasp the significance of how to use hands and brains as well [as] how to 'incorporate military skills with literary arts.'"[121] Thus, among other programs, the KMT established youth corps whose purpose was to help harvest rice, distribute food, and perform other social services. These youth not only received military-style disciplinary training,

> they also participated in teams which would render public service activities in military units and in civilian rural communities. In military units the students would teach basic literacy courses to the soldiers, help them write letters, comfort the troops in hospitals, and provide entertainment. In the countryside they would help the farmers clear the area and actually work on the farm. This was partially to provide urban youths with a feel for farming and develop their character through labor.[122]

Overall, other citizens who came in contact with the military through local associations and other military-led services were continually exposed to the ideology and the practice of farm life and to the ethos of self-discipline and austerity, both of which were inculcated among recruits and the population at large by KMT loyalists. The KMT "Soldier's Chant" included phrases like "we will not be greedy for money and property and we will not lie to others. . . . We will strive to be self-reliant."[123] Similarly, the Anti-Communist Youth Corps promoted eight defining principles of organization and action which echoed the soldiers' self-sacrificing ethos and disciplinary concerns while contributing other principles which themselves reinforced a quasi-middle-class sense of being responsible for oneself and one's own actions: "1) Believing in the Three Principles of the People; 2) Upholding our leader; 3) Obeying commands; 4) Adhering to disciplining; 5) Independence and self-improvement; 6) Energetically practicing our principles; 7) Mutual assistance and cooperation; and 8) Service and sacrifice."[124] With these propaganda efforts, not to mention the elective affinities and organized activities that linked the KMT rulers, military personnel, and Taiwanese citizens behind a semi-militarized disciplinary ethos consistent with the promotion of small-farmer production and self-sacrifice, Taiwan pursued a version of deep disciplinary development that paralleled that initially introduced by Park in South Korea. Yet it one-upped South Korea by establishing a much more widely entrenched disciplinary ethos that pervaded urban as well as rural society and brought a wider range of class forces into the collectively shared ethos than occurred in South Korea.

---

[121] Chang, *The Kuomintang*, p. 12.
[122] Bullard, *The Citizen and the Soldier*, p. 141.
[123] Ibid., pp. 193–194 (Appendix 4–2).
[124] Ibid., p. 196 (Appendix 5–1).

The Military, Nationalism, and the Rural Middle Class in Argentina

But if the military's role in party politics and society in Taiwan – and somewhat less so South Korea – was so central in strengthening the rural middle-class embeddedness of the state and in establishing a disciplinary ethos, why did the same not occur in Argentina? After all, this was a country where the military-state connections were equally strong, especially during the postwar period when Perón came to power, and where nationalist sentiments also flowered. One explanation is that there were relatively few other cultural and institutional connections directly linking the military and rural middle classes, even during the critical administration of Juan Perón, who himself came from rural middle-class origins. If anything, the military leadership traced its self-identity and social connections to the landed oligarchy and urban middle classes, two sets of affinities which helped ensure that sympathy toward the rural middle class or their developmental aims was rarely forthcoming. In Argentina, moreover, the military's historical and cultural connections to both the oligarchy and urban middle classes meant that when military government did materialize, the state was much less likely to embody the rural-based disciplinary values or austere consumption orientation that came to characterize South Korean and even Taiwanese industrialization to a great extent. Complicating matters, the absence of pressing geopolitical threats after the initial period of state formation, in combination with its uniquely urban and oligarchic class origins, made the Argentine military more prone to division than the military in either of our two East Asian countries. This situation translated into internal political instability and a continual shifting of class coalitions within the Argentine military state, such that urban working classes eventually became a key class coalitional ally for military leaders, a condition that further limited rural middle classes' capacities to embed themselves in the military and thus have much long-term impact on development policy.

The strong connections between the military and working classes – matched by the exclusion of rural middle classes from the military-led Argentine state in the postwar period – owed partly to the fact that the military as an institution had long fostered connections to Buenos Aires. It was in Buenos Aires that the large majority of the nation's military personnel resided, having suffered repeated military conquest, including a successful military invasion by the British navy in 1806. Moreover, Buenos Aires made its reputation as the administrative headquarters of the Viceregal area, such that subsequent revolutionaries continually aspired to dominate this city.[125] Even after the British invasions shattered Spanish administration of the River Plate

[125] For a more detailed account of these conflicts and the rise of various militias and military forces in Buenos Aires and the rest of the nation, see Halperin-Donghi, *Politics*, esp. Chap. 4.

Viceroyalty, the eight thousand militiamen who had been employed by the Spanish remained in the city, ready for conflicts over the city and the nation, which in turn fueled a new round of battle with the native-dominated militia.[126] The result, in David Rock's words, was a complete "militarization" of Buenos Aires, with around 30 percent of the adult male population mobilized by military or militia activities in the decades after 1806.[127] The social origins of the military and patterns of conscription in the late-eighteenth and early-nineteenth centuries further reinforced the military's profile as dominated by porteños and helps explain why most leading military personnel held either urban middle-class or oligarchic affinities.[128] Part of this owed to the fact that militia and military service was a principal source of prestige for the sons of the provincial elite,[129] even as it was a common and relatively respectable route for the sons of the *porteño* urban middle and lower classes, given its status as paying better and holding more prestige than many other jobs.

In many countries, the military rank and file is drawn primarily from some of the most disenfranchised sectors of society, which often means poorer rural populations and even the rural middle class of small farmers whose opportunities for advancement are generally much more limited than those of their urban counterparts. This, in fact, was the situation in South Korea, owing in part to conscription patterns under Japanese rule, and it was a factor that reinforced the elective affinity between General Park, his military-based administration, and the rural middle classes. In Argentina this did not occur to the same extent, and both rural poor and rural middle classes were still a minority in proportion to their urban counterparts.[130] These general patterns of conscription

---

[126] Rock, *Argentina*, pp. 71–73.

[127] Ibid., pp. 75–76.

[128] The urban lower class fed the lower ranks, as did some of the rural poor (often via forced conscription under the tutelage of large landowning, oligarchic strongmen), while the urban middle class entered the middle ranks of the military, and the officer corps tended to be drawn from the sons of the oligarchy – although it was also common for these young men and their families to reside in Buenos Aires as well. The officer class from Buenos Aires was quite tight and highly interconnected through families and over time, something which Halperin-Donghi (*Politics*, p. 199) identifies as a "pattern of behavior characteristic of a group which attributes to itself a social position higher than others were prepared to accord it." Yet overall, as Whittaker notes, it was not the elite but "the middle class [that] supplanted the oligarchy as the main source of the officer corps" (*Argentina*, p. 85).

[129] Halperin-Donghi, *Politics*, p. 194. According to Canton, the support for conservative views and pro-oligarchic sentiments in the military was reinforced by the fact that "military officials from the interior of the country tended to marry into higher social positions than their own," meaning mostly into the oligarchy and other notable families. See *La política de los militares argentinos*, p. 121.

[130] Many of Argentina's poorest rural residents were confined laborers on the large estancias and thus did not join the military to the same extent as urban populations, instead offering their

not only meant that rank and file personnel and the officer corps both were much less likely to come to military service with sympathy for the experience, priorities, and sentiments of small farmers and other elements of the more traditional rural middle class. Moreover, precisely because the military straddled the urban middle class and rural oligarchic divide that had long characterized Argentine politics,[131] it suffered from potentially divisive internal conflicts, a state of affairs which limited its unity on many issues.[132] And in these regards, Argentina contrasts sharply with South Korea, where the predominantly rural social origins of the leadership and rank and file, the shared experience of Japanese colonialism, and a common struggle against North Korea united the military as an institution. It also contrasts with Taiwan, where internal military unity was reinforced by the shared experience of fighting communists in mainland China and a shared commitment to building a strong Taiwan in order to achieve these geopolitical goals.

Owing to these differences, in Argentina a nationalism drawn inward rather than outward was one of the few issues that gave the military a larger objective and helped to unite its urban middle class and oligarchic bases. So who were the internal forces against which the "nationalist" Argentine military was united? When not directing their ire toward Paraguay or other bordering neighbors, it was immigrants, and to some extent the rural middle classes, who along with immigrants (who because of their foreign status were exempt from military service) were least likely to be members of the military rank and file. This in turn meant that questions of citizenship and individual nationality were linked to questions of military loyalty or allegiance. In large part, debates about citizenship and nationality revolved around conscription and who should or could be eligible for military service, and in Argentina many immigrants declined to become citizens in order to avoid the burden of military service. From the

---

"military service" to local strongmen. Also, the rural middle class tended to hold a disproportionately large population of foreign immigrants – especially later in the nineteenth and in the early-twentieth century, many of whom failed to take Argentine nationality precisely in order to avoid military service. For more on this, see Whittaker, *Argentina*, p. 59.

[131] Military historian Johnson notes that in the nineteenth and early-twentieth centuries the military remained "closely aligned with the aristocracy and beef barons," who after all cemented their provincial influence within and through their control of Buenos Aires, and with the long-standing urban middle class of Buenos Aires. See Johnson, *Political Change in Latin America*, p. 107.

[132] It may have been precisely because of the potential for division within the military that its leadership undertook efforts at professionalization starting early in the nineteenth century, in order to build an esprit de corps within the military. But these efforts did not fully eliminate internal tensions, which kept cropping up throughout the nineteenth century, becoming especially critical in the first decades of the twentieth as struggles between center and region raged and as political parties themselves were unable to accommodate these conflicts.

point of view of most military personnel, then, immigrants were social outcasts or cultural aliens unwilling to fight for their adopted country.[133] One result was that nationalist discourses within the military, and eventually in society at large, became linked with conservative, anti-immigrant sentiments that estranged the military from a sizable sector of Argentine society.

Nationalism was a double-edged sword, then, not just for Argentine democracy as so many others have argued, but also for military-linked discourses of discipline and for the eventual fate of rural middle classes in politics and the national state. For one thing, anti-immigrant and antiforeign (especially anti-British) sentiment produced considerable tensions within the middle-class-based Radical Party,[134] especially among its military loyalists,[135] creating a situation that eventually undermined the party's concerted efforts to straddle the concerns of working and middle classes in Buenos Aires and its surrounding provincial countryside (especially given the high proportion of immigrants in these locales).[136] For another, with the Radical Party divided and thus politically weakened, rural middle classes lost the one political party that appeared prepared to take up their cause. This was disastrous for Argentine democracy because it left this particular class force with few options for formal political representation and participation, a situation which helped spur the rise of illiberal social movements that shunned democratically based competitive party politics and that subsequently supplanted military rule. It also meant that discourses of nationalism and discipline were linked more to these illiberal social movements than to the military per se, let alone to the state or wider swaths

---

[133] To be sure, these themes were often merely a cover for vicious anti-immigrant sentiment and racist feelings projected against a steady stream of newcomers whose alien language, ethnic heritage, and cultural practices often set them apart in terms of behavior and national origins. They also mixed in unique ways with the anticommunist sentiment present among many in the military and were reinforced by the pervasiveness of class-struggle ideologies among the immigrants, who David Rock identified as comprising three-quarters of the Buenos Aires working class in 1914 (*Argentina*, p. 175). This may further explain the frequent and often virulent intervention of the military against striking workers and other radical members of the working class in Buenos Aires, especially under Yrigoyen.

[134] Cornblit, "European Immigrants," p. 244, notes that Radicals of the littoral showed antagonism to the foreigner, in part because "there were bonds between Radicalism and the middle and lower classes – traditionalist, xenophobic, and nationalist – who joined the radicals because of the *autonomismo* of Alsina and Alem or through the provincial caudillos of Santa Fe and Entre Rios."

[135] For more on military loyalists to the Radical Party during this period, see Ciria, *Partidos políticos*, pp. 128–129.

[136] It was disunity, after all, that most scholars identify as the key to the Radical Party's failure to remain in power in 1930 and thus the failure of Argentine liberalism – or democracy. See Whittaker, *Argentina*, p. 97; Williamson, *The Penguin History of Latin America*, p. 463; and Johnson, *Political Change in Latin America*, p. 106.

of society as a whole. One result was that while a military–rural middle-class disciplinary nexus did flower, it did so in the context of a circumscribed, semifascist movement that failed to embed itself more broadly in either the state or the society.

Much of this is clear with a closer examination of the nationalist movements that blossomed in the countryside during the 1920s and 1930s. Among some of the most visceral nationalists were provincially based political leaders, like Carlos Ibarguren and Leopoldo Lugones, who sought to revive the "cult of the rural life," to champion the small farmer, and to identify Buenos Aires as "synonymous with 'bureaucracy, prostitution, and corruption'" as well as with "immigrants [who] were 'parasites and undesirables.'"[137] Some of these leaders may have traced their personal roots to oligarchic or elite rural families, but they tended to be downwardly mobile oligarchs in the business of smaller-scale farming or ranching, or what the prominent nationalist intellectual Arturo Jaureche calls "the déclassé of the ruling class, the poor cousins of the oligarchy,"[138] and as such could be considered part of the rural middle class. At minimum, many of these key sympathizers of the nationalist movement were known for cultivating an appreciation for the life and sufferings of the rural middle class. They also saw other small-scale rural producers as a key social base and political constituency for their movement, given the fact that most had been routinely excluded from the party platforms of both the Radicals and the Conservative Party, with the latter taking up the rural question but mainly from the vantage point of the oligarchic elite rather than the more humble farmer.

With a concern for their own newfound "middling" class situation and with eyes open to the strategic gains afforded by bringing a larger rural middle-class constituency to their political side, leaders of the nationalist movements played on the antiurban sentiments and small-farmer romanticism of traditional provincial culture in Argentina. The result was a mixing of rural middle classes alongside the descendants of more privileged oligarchic families into a nationalist movement that would exclude the increasingly vocal urban working class and other urban populations, especially those of immigrant origin.[139] For Lugones, or so he would argue publicly, "there was 'no better citizen than he who works the land,'" a claim echoed in the nationalist publication *Crisol*, in which the "man of the country" was declared to be "superior to the man of the city. The former is a producer . . . the latter is worthless."[140] The ruralist

[137] Rock, *Authoritarian Argentina*, p. 102.

[138] Cited from ibid., p. 96.

[139] As Rock reports, "the ruralist strain of the early Nationalist movement then resurfaced as Lugones complained at the 'excessive privileges of urban labor, most of it anti-foreign.'" See ibid., p. 74.

[140] Ibid., p. 102.

strain in the nationalist movement and the ways urban populations were seen as inferior to rural folk pose a much-needed academic challenge to the larger historiographical emphasis on "civilized" elites over rural barbarians, which has too often been interpreted as a universal Argentine discourse despite evidence to the contrary. In practice it also reinforced the anticommunist, antiimmigrant, and even anti-Semitic ethos that permeated nationalist discourse, since most of the nation's communists were found among the industrial working class employed in urban areas, especially Buenos Aires, which itself held many immigrants within its ranks.[141] This array of racist, anticommunist, and conservative pro-Catholic religious sentiments combined with the cult of the small farmer and a romanticization of rural life to explain why so many scholars describe Argentine nationalism as fascist.

That most scholars of Argentine nationalism and fascism tend to ground their analysis in a closer examination of the military and not the rural middle class may be explained by the fact that many of the nationalist discourses employed by these near-fascist movements frequently emphasized the importance of the military or a military ethos alongside that of rural middle-classness. Lugones, in particular, was a keen supporter of military rule who thought citizens and soldiers should be "synonymous," who felt support for urban reform and especially urban workers would disadvantage rural areas, and who argued that "the expansion of the military would strengthen 'discipline in general' and banish 'social immorality.'"[142] In fact, some of the most active nationalist movements organized themselves into paramilitary and militia groups, using military drill and other military-inspired routines and tactics. Among the key edicts routinely supported by nationalists was the importance of fostering "Authority, Discipline, and Hierarchy," an ethos that is routinely cultivated within the military.[143]

What may be most telling about this for our purposes is that it shows that Argentina's nationalist movement burst on the scene with much the same discourses of discipline as permeated South Korean politics under General Park Chung Hee and Taiwanese politics under Chiang Kai-shek, relying as it did on similarly strong connections between a rural middle class and a military ethos, targeting financial speculators and middlemen as enemies, and professing the superiority of farmers and rural life. Likewise, nationalists in Argentina were among those most responsible for the break from democratic politics and the advent of military rule, just as occurred in South Korea in 1961. With his successful coup on September 6, 1930, General José F. Uriburu brought the

---

[141] Jews were seen as residing primarily in urban areas and occupying middleman positions as merchants, creditors, and speculators.

[142] Rock, *Authoritarian Argentina*, p. 74.

[143] Ibid., p. 102. Rock (p. 94) also mentions the *milicias cívicas* and the *guardia Argentina*, among others.

rhetoric of rural middle-classness, a quasi-military emphasis on discipline and social order, and an antiurban sentiment to the government. Uriburu proudly proclaimed Argentina as "a country of farmers and ranchers," and he urged "co-operative action to join together rural workers in great and disciplined forces" to counter the previous domination of (primarily urban-based) lawyers, physicians, and workmen in the country's chamber of deputies.[144] But unlike South Korea and Taiwan where the military was relatively united, where in alliance with rural middle-class forces it controlled the state for at least a decade or more with relatively few internal conflicts and external challenge, and where it was able to stay in power by orchestrating elections and not just under the threat of military might, in Argentina Uriburu and his "disciplinary" nationalists seized the state only temporarily, maintaining their influence mainly through armed force rather than the ballot box, and with very circumscribed popular support.

All these conditions signaled disaster for the long-term capacities of rural middle classes to wield influence in the Argentine state and its larger macro-economic policy making. In order to keep the reins of power – especially given the illegitimacy of the military takeover – the nationalist movement as headed by Uriburu would have had to win over much more than the rural middle class. Urban populations would also have to count in some fashion, if not right away then down the road, given the long history of the hegemony of Buenos Aires in the nation and on the larger political scene. Moreover, while the nationalist movement in Argentina may have counted on the rural middle classes, their disciplinary rhetoric, and their cultural ethos to provide some sort of larger moral (some might say immoral) purpose to their claims about authority, discipline, and the perils of unregulated capitalists and labor, both the military and its oligarchic and urban middle-class constituents were equally implicated in the politics of illiberalism. And therein lay the problem. As in the military itself, strains that pitted class against class and rural against urban populations riddled the nationalist movement and society at large. Thus a broadly cast alliance of rural and urban forces with different interests, united primarily by conservative values of anticommunism and anti-immigrant sentiment, found it almost impossible to stay in power democratically, as did their opposing forces. Each set of parties or movements was forced to build a coalition, and eventually, when these failed again, to turn to military, rule.

Urban Biases in the Governing Coalition of Industrializing Argentina

In Argentina, historically determined class and regional tensions limited rural middle-class capacities to politically embed themselves in the state without

---

[144] Quoted in ibid., p. 92.

forging cross-class or rural-urban coalitions. This pattern first became evident in Uriburu's short-lived tenure and his replacement in 1932, less than a year after the military coup that had brought him to power, by another military general, Agustín P. Justo.[145] Justo was not nearly the ardent nationalist that Uriburu had been, supporting policies that many Argentines saw as selling the nation (*vendepatria*) in exchange for the favored treatment of cattle barons and the oligarchic elite, as was the case in his signing of the Roca-Runciman Pact and with his support for British tramways at the expense of local *transportistas* in Buenos Aires. But for Justo the most visible nationalist policies had to do with immigration and not foreign ownership, and this meant that most of the nationalist anti-immigrant sentiment that Justo and his rural middle-class "fascist" supporters carried forward from Uriburu was directed against urban working-class populations in Buenos Aires. As a result, once Justo came to power the urban situation deteriorated accordingly, a state of affairs only worsened by the 1930s economic crisis that hit Argentina hard. With accelerating anti-immigrant and anticommunist sentiment in the ever deteriorating urban economy, over the 1930s Buenos Aires saw a rise in industrial working-class activism, particularly linked to the syndicalism of the Communist and Socialist parties, as well as attendant responses of military repression. It also hosted the rising discontent of the urban middle class, a relatively new state of affairs in Argentine politics and something that also was partly traceable to the nationalist military interlude starting in 1930.[146]

By 1943, it was relatively clear to nationalists, military officers, and the oligarchy alike that a free, democratic election would bring urban working- and middle-class dissatisfactions to the forefront, most probably in support of the Radical or Socialist parties. It might even spur some of the rural middle classes, whom Justo generally ignored, into the arms of the Radical Party again. Nationalists again united behind military rule in 1943, in a coup planned by a secret clique of twenty senior officers known as the Group of United Officers

---

[145] A liberal conservative, Justo won national elections fraudulently, but because he headed a coalition of parties known as the *Concordancia*, he was able to stay in power – in contrast to Uriburu – by restoring the influence of the oligarchic elite. The result was a declining economic situation for both rural and urban middle classes; and in fact, during this period the Radical Party gained considerable support from among these elements, as it had in the past, albeit at the local level. For more on Justo's rural orientation, see Johnson, *Political Change in Latin America*, pp. 108–109.

[146] In Johnson's account, rising dissatisfaction over the 1930s and early 1940s owed to the "loss in self-confidence and a decline in the economic status of the salaried middle sectors; [and] the collapse in 1930 of the political system they were nourishing to maturity," which he argues was a serious blow to the morale of these groups, especially given their ever weaker economic position vis-à-vis the reempowered landed elite. See ibid., p. 111.

(GOU).[147] Among the leading officers in the new regime was Juan Perón, who was named head of the national labor department and who had long argued for a program of national industrialization to be led by the military.[148] Perón seemed a likely candidate in no small part because when he founded the Partido Laborista in 1945, in an effort to prepare for his rise to power during the 1946 elections, he included in his platform several of the key demands of rural middle classes and their advocacy organization, the FAA. Among the articulated goals of the Partido Laborista were

> the division of lands and elimination of the *latifundio*, the application of a progressive tax on inheritance and on land, the intention to carry out a policy *favorable to small agricultural producers so that they could transform themselves into a rural middle class*, the extension of social justice to the workers of the countryside, regulation of work conditions for rural wage workers, participation in the earnings of firms, obligatory minimum salary for all the country, extension of technical education to the interior, and establishment of sanitary living areas [*colonias*] in the countryside [emphasis mine]."[149]

Yet despite sharing many of the same pro–small producer sentiments as this earlier generation of nationalists, Perón differed from them in several ways. First, he sought to base governance on relatively broadly cast urban support rather than dictatorship (which is not to say democracy),[150] and, most importantly, he expressed strong sympathies for (noncommunist) urban workers and for a project of state-led, primarily urban-based industrialization. As such, from early on Perón worked to develop a strong urban popular base using his position in the department of labor to do so. Thus in a departure from the military rulers and nationalists who had preceded him, his key allies were more likely urban than rural folk, and working rather than middle classes.[151] Second, unlike previous nationalists and most high-level military officers,

---

[147] There is some ambiguity about the GOU, at least in nomenclature if not in function. While Rock identifies the GOU as standing for *Grupo Obra de Unificación*, Johnson and Norden both see this acronym as referring to the *Grupo de Oficiales Unidos*, the terminology we use here.

[148] Indeed, Perón saw industrialization as strengthening the military. For more on his views of national defense, the military, and industrialization, see Ciria, *Política y cultura popular*, pp. 13–24.

[149] Lattuada, *La política agraria peronista*, p. 46.

[150] Rock, *Authoritarian Argentina*, p. 126.

[151] Ciria argues that some of the strongest anti-Peronist forces in 1945 were "students, professionals, *comerciantes*, the [urban] middle class in general." For more on urban middle-class opposition to Perón, see Ciria, *Partidos políticos*, p. 112.

Perón demonstrated a clear openness to the country's burgeoning immigrant population, many of them recent migrants from the countryside who joined the industrial working class. Third, he rapidly abandoned his rural middle-class constituents after successfully coming to power.

Perón's calculated disregard for rural middle classes during his years in office was in many ways a paradoxical state of affairs, since rural middle classes' initial support for military rule helped Perón sustain enough influence within the GOU (and the country in general) to push for elections in 1946. Even after the 1943 coup in which Perón's actions were key, the military leadership in the GOU, with Perón's support, reformed an old agrarian law and signed a new one which would reduce rents for rural leaseholders, a move which brought public kudos from the rural middle-class-based FAA.[152] From 1943 to 1946, moreover, Perón used his position as secretary of labor to introduce several new policies and programs that appealed to rural middle classes, including the foundation of a Consejo Agrario Nacional (National Agrarian Council) and a plan for agrarian reform. Perón personally restructured the organizational setup of the Agrarian Council in 1945 so that its administrators would answer directly to him in the office of the secretary of labor (rather than to the Dirección de Tierras, or Land Secretariat); and at this time he also appointed Antonio Molinaria as presidente-interventor of the council. Molinaria was a man with rural middle-class roots, who had served as editor of *La Tierra* and who also had been a lawyer for the FAA. His appointment by Perón strengthened the general's relationships with and commitment to governing Argentina with the participation of rural middle classes.[153] So what happened?

The answer rests in the complex and divided class structure of Argentina, which limited the class alliance available to Perón, especially if urban workers specifically, and Buenos Aires residents more generally served as a key political base. Over the years Perón looked in many corners to find other stable allies to sustain his urban-based populist coalition, ranging from immigrant sectors of the urban middle class to leaders of the Radical Party, to different sectors of industry, and back to the military and the oligarchy, an exercise in futility that did not bode well for continuity in governance or economic policy making.[154] But at each turn, practically the only forces Perón was unwilling or unable to bring into his coalition were the traditional military-linked

---

[152] Lattuada, *La política agraria peronista*, Vol. 1, p. 30.

[153] Lattuada, *Política agraria del liberalismo-conservador*, pp. 54–57. La Tierra translates as "The Land."

[154] In *Política agraria y partidos políticos*, p. 25, Lattuada characterizes Perón's base as "a multi-class alliance whose principal classes and social sectors of reference were the owners of national industrial capital – a weak or local bourgeoisie – and the salaried sectors organized in unions, and to a lesser extent the military sectors" from which he himself had emerged to become leader of the Peronist movement.

rural middle classes, perhaps because of their xenophobic nationalist sentiments and relative unconcern for his project of industrialization.[155] Yet it was
precisely the *exclusion* of rural middle classes from his coalition which forced
Perón to rely even more on urban labor and a shifting mixture of agrarian and
industrial elites.[156] With these forces serving as the main political bases of his
governing coalition, the state's potential to sustain its disciplinary capacity
vis-à-vis industrial capital was greatly diminished if not eliminated almost
entirely, even during moments when Perón also could count on some portion
of the military to bolster his hold on the state.[157] And precisely because of

---

[155] Perón's actions in March 1946, just one month after the presidential elections, may illustrate
this point best. With his political position assured, Perón reversed his initial stance and
offered a new agrarian reform that increased the state's role in acquiring lands, mandated
certain prices for lands and terms of tenure, and put severe restrictions on the capacity of rural
producers to sell their lands. Among those groups most outraged by this reform were the rural
middle classes, who saw these reforms as transforming if not undermining rural property
rights and the value of rural lands. Clearly, these reforms constituted great advances for poor
tenant farmers, wage laborers, or other "would-be" rural middle classes seeking to obtain
their own property for the first time; and it was precisely these groups whom Perón sought
to aid. But these measures also threatened to limit the value of existent lands in ways that
could be catastrophic for the traditional rural middle class, especially the well-entrenched
smaller-scale farmers who often secured credit and other inputs mortgaged against the value
of their lands. According to Lattuada (*La política agraria peronista*, p. 61), in response to this
perceived threat the FAA "accused the government of wanting to transform the State into
the principal landlord." When Molinari upped the rural middle-classes oppositional ante by
resigning from the government, Perón hardly blinked. Instead, he immediately named Juan
Carlos Picazo Elordy, member of the SRA and unabashed spokesman for the large landlords
of the agrarian oligarchy, as minister of agriculture. With this appointment, Perón not
only helped insure that oligarchic concerns would weigh in the development of subsequent
rural policy, he also effectively eliminated rural middle classes from his governing coalition.
(ibid., pp. 60–62). For more on the new and stronger relations that Perón established with
the SRA after 1946, see Ciria, *Política y cultura popular*, p. 33.

[156] In *Soldiers of Perón*, Gillespie, p. 20, argues that "class membership of the Peronist 'alliance'
has altered considerably over the years. During the early years Peronism drew its support
from among local industrialists, part of the middle classes, and from the working class, but
by 1955 non-proletarian sponsorship had been far more seriously eroded than was the case
with labour backing; there were then eighteen years during which labour was the principal
bastion of the Movement, with entrepreneurs mainly conspicuous by their absence; and,
later, the final years of the 1966–73 military regime witnessed mounting support among
the university-based middle classes (students, intellectuals, professionals) and from local
businessmen associated with the General Economic Confederation (CGE)."

[157] As Gillespie notes, in ibid., p. 14, Peronism "was presented as an anti-oligarchic, anti-
imperialist movement based chiefly on the industrial classes, part of the middle classes, and
a nationalist wing of the military." Yet "only labour had stuck solidly with Peron to the
last" (p. 15).

the political influence of urban labor and agrarian and industrial elites in the governing coalition, the history of post-1940s Argentina is one in which ISI was the development policy of choice, and in which the state – especially under Perón – "bestowed unquestionable material favours upon the growing working class."[158] Industrial laborers, in turn, had the economic wherewithal to buy those domestically manufactured goods produced by the big firms in which they were employed.

Needless to say, the material benefits dispensed by Perón were good for workers and a clear improvement on their previous conditions, such that "between . . . [1943 and 1949], the real wages of industrial workers rose by 50–60 per cent, and between . . . [1946 and 1949], in sharp contrast to European fascist experiences, labour's share in national income rose from 40.1 to 49 per cent."[159] Yet these priorities also had their impact on the country's overall economic trajectory. For one thing, Perón's administration drove up the expectation and reality of consumption, a state of affairs which fueled a commitment to the production of consumer durables for domestic consumption and helped reduce domestic savings rates. According to Gillespie, in fact, "one of Peronism's legacies had been to boost expectations well beyond its development of the productive infrastructure of the country."[160] No individual austerity or self-discipline in production or consumption there. This in turn had an extremely negative impact on foreign exchange and the balance of payments. With demands for urban consumption high, it was difficult to calibrate foreign exchange rates in such a way as to sustain agricultural exports and vice versa. For another, the development of ISI that came along with Perón's clear commitment to industrial working-class employment, wage benefits, and sustained industrialization further privileged the political position of labor, sometimes even to the detriment of capitalists themselves and, to a great degree, to the agrarian oligarchy. Thus, when this model headed into dangerous economic waters, the administration was hard-pressed to shift gears, since the industrial working class held the key to Perón's power; but this too meant jeopardizing rural landlords' support, which in turn gave industrialists pause, since the former formed the productive backbone of the ISI economy, generating export earnings to pay for the import of industrial machinery used in ISI. In the words of one scholar, "When in the early 1950s and again in the mid-1970s Peronist governments attempted to introduce austerity measures

---

[158] Ibid., p. 9.

[159] Ibid., p. 10. "Apart from well-publicized wage rises, existing labour legislation was enforced for the first time, recognized unions were provided with a legal right to engage in political activity, and workers were able to enjoy cheap housing, a rent freeze, food and transport price ceilings, a shorter working week, greater job security, holidays with pay, annual bonuses, and pensions" (p. 9).

[160] Ibid., p. 27.

and boost productivity in response to economic crises, the latent strength of labour within the Movement [*sic*] moderated the impact of such efforts, leaving many industrialists ready to applaud military intervention."[161]

The question that remains, however, is whether the inclusion of urban labor in the governing coalition was as detrimental to macroeconomic progress as so many scholars of Argentina have suggested, or whether it was the *absence* of other factors – including a disciplinary ethos or the inclusion of rural middle classes – that should be identified as the analytical smoking gun here. After all, just as occurred in Argentina and in other Latin American countries that pursued ISI during the same period, from its inception Taiwan's KMT incorporated trade union concerns into party platforms and developed separate branches within the party for those working in railroads, highways, postal services, shipping, journalism, and industry, with many of these branches including representatives of both management and labor.[162] In addition to these efforts to bring management into the party, the Taiwanese state also fostered very strong linkages with industrial capitalists of mainlander origin, not just laborers, additional facts that at least should raise similar questions about the KMT's capacity to uphold a disciplinary stance vis-à-vis capitalists and labor. Given this evidence, can we really be sure that the political bases and disciplinary capacities of the Argentine and Taiwanese states during this key period of postwar industrial development were altogether that different, or as different as we have been suggesting so far?

Such questions about similarities and differences in the working- and capitalist-class underpinnings of the state's political bases and how they affect larger developmental strategies, even disciplinary ones, become even more pressing when we consider Taiwan in comparison with Argentina and even South Korea. In the latter case, we argued that it was an austere, disciplinary ethos identified primarily with the rural middle-class political and organizational bases of the Park administration that allowed the state to regulate both capital and labor for the larger common good. It was precisely when capitalists began to politically dominate the policy-making environment, our evidence suggests, that the larger disciplinary ethos started to vanish, as did the rural development orientation that allowed the state to regulate industrialization for export rather than domestic consumption in the first place. So why did this not happen in Taiwan, where preliminary evidence suggests the involvement of mainlander industrial capitalists in the governing coalition from the very beginning? And would differences in the presence or absence of industrial capitalists in the Taiwanese state affect the overall strategy of disciplinary development in any way, perhaps via its impact on the state's relationship to labor, who after all had a more prominent institutional role within the KMT

[161] Ibid., p. 22.
[162] Moody, Jr., *Political Change on Taiwan*, p. 21.

than South Korean labor had in Park's DRP (which itself was much more structured around farmers' organizations alone)?

Disciplinary Capitalists in Taiwan

We can begin to answer these questions by more closely examining Taiwan's industrial capitalists, their relationship to other classes, both rural and urban, as well as the state, and where all these forces fit into the disciplinary regime of Chiang Kai-shek. In Taiwan, the KMT established strong ties with large urban industrialists, embedding these class forces into the state and counting on them, as well, to sustain the disciplinary ethos. As noted earlier, some of Chiang Kai-shek's strongest military supporters on the mainland, and many of those who joined him in Taiwan, had been urban industrialists in China. For this reason, the KMT refugees included in number "wealthy Shanghai business-people who had managed to salvage their fortunes" and who subsequently parlayed them into prosperous industrial enterprises in Taiwan, often by taking over factories left by the fleeing Japanese.[163] During the initial period of state consolidation and industrial takeoff, the KMT made great efforts to create and sustain this new transplanted class of urban industrialists, mostly of mainlander origin.[164] Many KMT loyalists were catapulted to positions of prominence, named as overseers or managers of industrial enterprises that fell under state control. One result was that sympathizers of the KMT came to dominate most of the key industrial firms on the island, particularly the standard ISI manufacturing activities that are generally considered central to the development of local industry and infrastructure (including steel and iron), and to the development of consumer durables production for both home consumption and export, ranging from food processing and packaging activities to textile production. This budding class of industrialists supported the KMT's heavy-handed disciplinary rhetoric and developmental aims not just because they owed their livelihood to the state, so to speak, but also because most were mainlanders who shared a commitment to the nationalist cause and hoped to see Taiwan triumph economically vis-à-vis mainland China. As such, in Taiwan the state's embeddedness with large industrial capitalists alongside rural middle classes helped sustain (rather than undermine) the government's disciplinary ethos and those larger developmental aims in which self-sacrifice and small-scale agricultural production were as important for the country's future

---

[163] Ibid., p. 69. Moody also notes that "although the army was Chiang's main power base, it was not the only one. In his youth Chiang had been a stockbroker in Shanghai and he had connections . . . among the business community there" (p. 18).

[164] As Gold puts it, "It fell to the [KMT-led] state to foster the emergence of a bourgeoisie." See *State and Society in the Taiwan Miracle*, p. 70.

as industrialization. It also brought a concern with the interconnections between agriculture and industry into the rhetorical and developmental mix.

The inclusion of large-scale ISI urban industrialists in the KMT's governing coalition seems to parallel the Argentine and South Korean cases, or at least in the latter instance during the late 1970s, at which time large urban industrialists in South Korea came to wield enormous power over the state but rural middle classes fell out. In Taiwan, however, urban industrialists were part and parcel of the rural middle-class-based disciplinary regime established by the KMT from the very beginning, serving as a key political base for the new government and contributing to its agricultural as well as industrial development aims. The state's support for urban industrialists, and their loyalty to the state in turn, was predicated on a larger, shared nationalist commitment among KMT loyalists to a developmental model that reserved a place for agricultural production based on small farms, as much as industrial development.[165] As such, in contrast to South Korea, where most urban industrialists initially loathed Park's efforts to discipline capital and subordinate industrial development goals to those of agricultural growth and prosperity by focusing on the development of infrastructure and inputs for farm production, in Taiwan these aims grew together, hand in hand, with both state bureaucrats and parastatal managers (mainly KMT loyalists) critical to implementing these development plans. This more "balanced" program of development, built on strong support for ISI and agricultural development simultaneously, owed directly to the small-farmer and urban industrial base of the KMT. One result was that much of the initial industrialization undertaken in these large factories was devoted to the fertilizers and petrochemicals (for pesticides) necessary for agricultural production, something that Park also had insured through his early regulation of urban industrialists in South Korea.

The larger developmental benefits were enormous. As early as 1949, the goals of urban industrial and agricultural development were generally cast in complementary terms, and the Taiwanese state implemented economic policies that nurtured both sectors and the interrelationships between them.[166] Rural

---

[165] There is little doubt that many of the KMT-affiliated industrialists were able to nurture their ISI manufacturing activities so successfully precisely because the Taiwanese state protected them and their firms. In this way, Taiwan was no different than Argentina or even South Korea – and most other late developers for that matter – in the extent to which the state intervened to protect and advance "infant" industrial activities. In fact, as noted earlier, the Taiwanese state's support for and intervention in the development of domestically protected, large-scale industrial production was more intensive than in South Korea and almost any other late developer with similar economic successes. For more on the nature and extent of protection of ISI firms in Taiwan, see Li, *The Evolution of Policy*, pp. 40–44.

[166] The fact that the Taiwanese economy had floundered both in terms of agriculture and industrial goods exporting from 1945 to 1949 spurred the KMT's immediate efforts in these regards.

farmers were given support (credit, inputs, etc.) to help increase productivity and processing for both export and domestic consumption, activities which helped urban industrialists by keeping down the costs of consumption for the urban labor force, thereby keeping wages low as well. To the extent that agriculture contributed to foreign exchange earnings, urban industrialists had more leeway to import capital goods for production. Additionally, with strong government support for small- and medium-scale agricultural activities, the rural sector prospered and many citizens acquired the earning power to buy the consumer durables produced by the ISI manufacturers.

This strategy of integrating rural and urban development worked well for several reasons, not the least of which was the military state's embeddedness with both rural farmers and urban industrialists, which gave it the volition and vision for this combination of development policies. However, two other sets of historical conditions also mattered, one of which was the long-standing experience of small-scale farm production, noted earlier, that gave Taiwanese agriculturists a strong foundation for growth that was parlayed into prosperity when state support was forthcoming. Without a successful farm economy or agricultural sector, there would have been few export earnings and the state would have had to resort to deficit financing of agriculture, as in South Korea. Second was the fact that Taiwan already possessed the territorial or spatial "underpinnings" for a decentralized and integrated program of development. Indeed, the synergistic macroeconomic connection between agricultural and industrial sectors was kindled by the existence of an already relatively well-balanced and well-networked pattern of infrastructure, trade networks, and peoples evenly distributed across rural and urban domains. Much of this owed to Japanese colonial legacies, moreover. To the extent that rural and urban areas were not pitted against each other in geographical, cultural, social, or political terms, but rather were territorially and infrastructurally interconnected, the more integrated strategy of agricultural and industrial development introduced by the KMT over the 1950s and 1960s made sense and worked remarkably well. Moreover, under these conditions, a decentralized industrialization strategy ended up reinforcing both rural middle-class formation and overall industrial and economic development, thereby sustaining rather than undermining small farmers' livelihoods and lifestyles, as occurred in South Korea.[167]

Once we raise the spector of these urban-rural synergies and how they affect the broader class context of the state's rural middle-class embeddedness,

---

[167] It is telling that most scholars to date have identified these conditions in terms of their impact on working-class formation, all but ignoring rural classes. For example, in their important book *Political Change in Taiwan*, Cheng and Haggard argue that "the dispersion of industry and extensive linkages between rural and urban society served to reduce the possibility for autonomous working-class politics to emerge in cities" (p. 5).

we are forced to consider one more fundamental difference between Taiwan, Argentina, and South Korea, having to do with the centralized versus decentralized character of their political systems and the class inclusiveness of their party structures. The overwhelming centralization of the state and political structures in both Argentina and South Korea – as well as their hierarchically ordered concentration in Buenos Aires and Seoul – limited state capacities to recast political bases in order to transcend both space and class, as occurred in the Taiwanese case.[168] Smaller-scale rural producers were practically excluded from the picture in Argentina, despite the fact that there did exist associations of farmers representing them (FAA). In South Korea, in contrast, the situation was much more similar to that in Taiwan, at least to the extent that rural middle classes were a key element of both Park's political party and the South Korean state apparatus. In both Taiwan and South Korea it was the farmers' associations that played the critical role, linking rural middle classes to both the party and the state. However, in contrast to Taiwan where labor joined in as a key sector in the ruling KMT,[169] in South Korea neither the party nor the state effectively broadened its class base beyond the rural middle class and the farmers' associations that were so well prepared to advance the party's and the state's organizational interests.

Yes, labor unions did have some visibility and influence in South Korean party politics, and marginally so in the state by virtue of the bargaining capacities of labor unions, but never to the same degree as farmers associations, and in a rapidly declining fashion after the beginning of Yushin politics in the 1970s. Moreover, even when urban industrialists came to dominate the Korean state's economic policy decisions in the late 1970s and 1980s, it was primarily through informal and indirect connections to state bureaucrats, not through formal party structures. This may partly explain the capacities

---

[168] In Argentina, Perón relied primarily on a social movement of urban industrial workers to sustain his power, with Eva Perón helping to expand this base only somewhat by bringing women and some provincial workers to his side as well. Gillespie and others, moreover, have gone so far as to suggest that *Peronismo* is better understood as a movement than as a party, not just because it is based on a vertical integration of "classes and social forces, in contrast to the horizontal class base of many parties, but also to the fact that membership was more a question of identification than affiliation. To be a peronist did not necessarily imply regular political activity, and formal affiliation procedures, except in fulfillment of electoral registration requirements, were generally alien to the Movement. Membership in the Movement was a question of identification with Perón" (Gillespie, *Soldiers of Perón*, pp. 19–20). This further prevented Perón from fully extending or institutionalizing his party's territorial and class bases in ways that paralleled the experience of Taiwan. For more on *justicialismo* as a movement, see Ciria, *Política y cultura popular*, p. 54.

[169] Tien, *The Great Transition*, p. 60 notes that "among secondary associations the KMT has devoted the most energy to two mass organizations: trade unions and the farmers' associations."

for and explosion of corrupt relations between the chaebols and rent-seeking state bureaucrats in South Korea over the last two decades or so. In Taiwan, however, the political system was entirely different: The relatively decentralized political structures of the state combined with the broadly cast institutional contours of one-party rule to reinforce a much more territorially extensive base of support for the KMT, one in which rural middle classes and their concerns were absolutely central even though they also shared institutional influence with other classes. In Peter Moody's words, in both the party and the legislature the KMT had both functional and geographic representation.[170] Of course, this unique combination of "grassroots democracy" implanted into a strongly "democratic-centralist" party-led state was strategically calculated on the part of the KMT leadership in order to strengthen its legitimacy vis-à-vis village populations.[171] But even so, with direct suffrage, self-government, and the ruling party reaching down to the lowest levels, in Taiwan there was considerable scope for rural populations to forcefully bring their claims up to the national level, even though other important and economically powerful urban political bases, mainly urban industrialists and state workers – as well as the military – also formed part of the governing coalition and thus had direct access to the party and the state too.[172] Equally telling, with some of the most important sectoral associations organized within the KMT representing farmers, state employees (many of whom were ex-military personnel or KMT sympathizers from the mainland), the military, and as one scholar aptly notes, "broadly defined consumer and household savers,"[173] both a disciplinary ethos and a joint concern with rural and urban development readily permeated party and state politics, not just civil society.

---

[170] *Political Change on Taiwan*, p. 21. Tom Gold (*State and Society in the Taiwan Miracle*, p. 67) further argues that in Taiwan, national branches of government were directly linked to provincial bodies as well as to "elected county and municipal assemblies and governments, which have a great degree of say over local affairs," notwithstanding the strong party-led state.

[171] In Chiang Kai-shek's words, "In connection with the relationship existing between Party activities and the administrative arm, the village or county comprehensive political group has to be strengthened in order that the Party organ, the government administration, the economic interests, and the cultural institutions of the same locality can forge ahead as a four-pronged single striking force" (Chang, *The Kuomintang*, p. 12).

[172] In the first two decades of rule in Taiwan, a "full 60 percent of [KMT] members were politicians, civil servants, and military officers" (Jiang and Wu, "The Changing Role," p. 81).

[173] See Cheng, "Political Regimes and Development Strategies," p. 168. Remember that in its first two decades on the island, more than 60 percent of KMT members were mainlanders, and among them politicians, civil servants (especially bureaucrats, school teachers, university professors, and soldiers), and military officers predominated.

Further strengthening these commitments was the fact that most KMT leaders themselves were working under the assumption that one of the major sources of the nationalist defeat on the mainland had been rampant corruption in the state and among the economic elite. As such, there also was a considerable amount of *self-disciplining* going on among the KMT industrialists and among the KMT civil servants themselves, now of middle-class status primarily,[174] who manned the state, managed its regulatory capacities, and may even have run a considerable number of state-owned industrial enterprises.[175] In the party's Seventh National Congress in 1953, when the principles of governance for Taiwan were established, the KMT had identified three main objectives in meeting its two central aims of nationalism and democracy:[176] 1) recovery of the mainland and defeat of communism; 2) building a firm foundation for popular government; and 3) improving the way of life and reestablishing high standards, which meant that "our party members must be living examples for others by *disciplining their own personal lives*, cherishing the national culture, and *observing ethical standards* [emphases mine]."[177]

This third point speaks directly to the KMT's self-recognition of the paralyzing and destructive impact of corruption, on the part of both industrialists and state bureaucrats, which many party leaders had identified as the source of its defeat on the mainland. Ezra Vogel argues that

> Kuomintang leaders acknowledged that public support had eroded because of their failure to stop corruption and to provide for the common people's livelihood. Above all, they concluded, they should have done more to control inflation and implement land reform. They were determined to do better on Taiwan. They resolved to be strict with corruption, to expand the role of government enterprise in a way not susceptible to private influence, and to create a greater distance between the government and the private sector.[178]

---

[174] In *Taiwan's Politics*, Lerman argues the mainlanders "as a whole . . . did not become a rich ruling class," in part because they were "less movitivated or trained for commercial work," and instead valued education and government service (p. 12).

[175] According to Bullard, *The Citizen and the Soldier*, p. 32: "Most mainlanders who arrived in Taiwan were military or government workers and the government felt obligated to take care of them. They were given most of the key jobs in the government bureaucracy, in the education system, and in government enterprises."

[176] Again, it is important to remember that the KMT's view of democracy was highly centralized, built on Leninist principles that highlighted the role of the party in reinforcing and fueling democratic centralism.

[177] Chang, *The Rebirth of the Kuomintang*, p. 104.

[178] *The Four Little Dragons*, p. 18.

Some of this was accomplished with harsh and direct regulation of private sector activities, especially of exports and imports, as was the case in South Korea. Banks were strictly regulated in Taiwan, not just in number (the state allowed no more than sixteen) but also in terms of ownership and management (either state-owned or government-controlled) and in terms of lending practices (targeted to key industries with caps on interest rates).[179] But in contrast to South Korea, the Taiwanese state also directly took on the task of industrial production by putting numerous key firms under state control. As Gary Hamilton has noted elsewhere, in Taiwan the "state-owned sector has played a distinctive role in the overall economy . . . occupy[ing] a position furthermost upstream, supplying the basic raw materials (i.e. the steel and the petroleum) and the electrical power that runs most of the factories," with "all banks . . . government-owned or controlled, and their number limited to sixteen."[180]

Still, the KMT's aims in fostering efficient and solid forward-backward linkages were also accomplished with self-discipline, again, and not just state discipline. Economic policy makers and regulators, for example, were not allowed to engage in their own businesses.[181] The party also kept a strict eye on both public and private sector actors, and this stance endured through administrative generations. Chiang Kai-shek's son, for example, "aware of the corruption that existed on the mainland, insisted that government bureaucrats not only refrain from accepting presents and dinner invitations from those in business but avoid any social functions at which members of the business community were present . . . [even as he] detailed regulations [that] were considered annoyingly strict by many participants."[182]

Needless to say, the shared political objectives and nationalist sentiment among KMT loyalists probably did not eliminate all influence peddling, nor could it possibly have meant that personal connections between state and private sector actors played no role at all in the development of business enterprises. As discussed earlier, many of the large industrial firms inherited from the Japanese went directly to KMT loyalists with business experience on the mainland, itself a form of favoritism. However, "in general the [Taiwanese] bureaucrats were regarded by foreign observers as dedicated professionals who did not leak public goods into private hands or distort public policy to achieve

---

[179] Hartland-Thunberg, *China, Hong Kong, Taiwan, and the World Trading System*, p. 16. She also notes interest rates were subject to ceiling and floor limits and capital movements were strictly controlled. For more on banking and finance in Taiwan, see Silin, *Leadership and Values*, esp. p. 23.

[180] "Culture and Organization," p. 45.

[181] Vogel, *The Four Little Dragons*, p. 18.

[182] Ibid., pp. 33–34.

private aims."[183] They did not, in short, make a habit of cultivating so-called under the table – or even open – personal or rent-seeking relationships with the business sector per se, and as such they "manage[d] to avoid becoming captives of local business interests."[184] The explanation for this can be traced directly to the shared political experiences that linked KMT loyalists in the state and large industry to the party's organizational and unifying role as 1) the source of nationalist propaganda and sentiment, 2) the epitome of self-discipline, and 3) the proverbial hand of discipline with others. Moreover, as Ezra Vogel and others remind us, most government officials were mainlanders while the large majority of business people were "locals,"[185] that is, native Taiwanese. This ethnic and national division also made it easier for the party to distance itself from routine demands of much of the private sector and to maintain a strong regulatory hand.

This final point underscores yet another important difference between Taiwan and South Korea: the fact that the disciplinary measures imposed by bureaucrats whose aim was to spur the economy's growth and sustain integrated rural-urban development did not fall just on the shoulders of the large and economically successful mainlander-dominated industrialists. The state's most coercive disciplinary hand was applied mainly to small and medium-sized businesses, primarily small industrial workshops, many of them family-owned and -operated, and most of them run by native Taiwanese. Large industrialists used their mainlander and institutional connections with bureaucrats and networks in the KMT-run state to insure that it was the native Taiwanese-owned, smaller and thus more flexible firms – and not their own large industries – that were most harshly disciplined, so as to foster high productivity, low-wage, globally problematic industrialization for export. These small industrial exporters buoyed the economy in ways that cycled back to large, state-linked ISI industrialists, mainly by generating foreign exchange revenues that sustained their growth and expansion. And it was the small-scale industrial firms, who themselves comprised the backbone of the urban middle class, that most helped sustain the Taiwanese EOI miracle and that gave that country an industrial exporting profile similar to South Korea's, not the large mainlander industrialists.

To be sure, and as noted above, even large state-owned industrial firms were governed by harsh restrictions, some of which were intended to make it easier for smaller-scale, private firms to produce and export.[186] Additionally,

---

[183] Gold, *State and Society in the Taiwan Miracle*, p. 28.

[184] Vogel, *The Four Little Dragons*, p. 32.

[185] Ibid., p. 33.

[186] Hamilton, "Culture and Organization," p. 44, cites a study in the *Far Eastern Economic Review* which stated that "the charter for the 48.3 percent state-owned Taiwan Semiconductor Manufacturing Company states that the company is 'forbidden to make any products of its

most large mainlander industrial firms were limited in what they could do, although this often was the case because they were partners with the state in these raw material or intermediate goods-supplying enterprises.[187] In this sense, almost everyone in the country was directly affected by the government's efforts to forcefully impose economic self-discipline and a degree of austerity, something further evidenced by the government's regulation of interest rates on deposits, which were manipulated to insure high savings rates for individuals and firms rather than more expenditures on highly capital-intensive, labor-saving techniques of production (as often occurred in ISI economies) or consumer goods.[188] Yet all of these disciplinary measures were intended to sustain a vertically integrated economy with a clear division of labor that efficiently connected upstream and downstream producers or, better said, that linked firms of different sizes that were producing for a variety of domestic and global markets so that they coordinated rather than competed with each other. In this larger design, it was the coercive (i.e., top-down) regulation of small-scale firms and their self-imposed (i.e., bottom-up) capacities to succeed or fail in export markets as well as their forced reliance on cheap labor, rather than expensive technology to fuel the production and accumulation process, that kept the whole system running smoothly. In Gary Hamilton's words, "The small-firm tail of Taiwan's industrial structure wags the entire economy."[189]

Both ethnic division and the unparalleled power of mainlanders in the KMT government help explain why small industrial firms were on the receiving end of so much state discipline. To the extent that mainlanders were involved primarily in large-scale activities of domestic and capital goods production for the domestic market, they pursued rather traditional ISI activities and were highly protected by the state. Because they dominated this domestic niche, they also wanted to keep native Taiwanese out of many large-scale ISI activities, and thus it was necessary to find someone else to take up the

---

own.' Instead, 'partly to prevent it from becoming a rival to the small firms it was set up to serve,' the company was created to supply local firms with the semiconductors they needed to make their products."

[187] For more on the import restrictions on industrialists during this period, see Vogel, *The Four Little Dragons*, p. 30.

[188] Tsiang, in "Foreign Trade and Investment As Boosters for Take-off," p. 52. He also notes (p. 44) that "Taiwan was probably the first among developing countries to abandon, as early as 1950, the traditional policy of low interest rates," when it offered a "hitherto unheard of nominal rate of 4% a month," which when compounded "came to a remarkable 125% a year." This helped spur savings and reduce consumption, along the lines sought by Park Chung Hee in South Korea.

[189] "Culture and Organization," p. 47. For more on industrial structure in Taiwan, and the importance of small firms, see Kuo, Ranis, and Fei, *The Taiwan Success Story*; and Cheng and Gereffi, "The Informal Economy in East Asian Development."

slack with respect to exports. Small-scale native-Taiwanese-run firms were an obvious target, and for this reason they were held to very different standards and a much higher degree of state and market discipline. Yet this dynamic worked both ways: With large industrial firms dominated by KMT-linked mainlander loyalists, native Taiwanese themselves sought opportunities in the smaller industrial markets. The result was a clearly differentiated or "dual" economy, in which "the two sectors are quite distinct in technology, size, and market structure, such that the export-oriented sector tends to be more competitive (low degree of monopoly) and the domestic-oriented sector tends to be less competitive (high degree of monopoly)."[190] Gary Hamilton puts it slightly differently: "Taiwan has a dichotomous market structure in the private sector. The smallest firms are those that produce for export, and the largest are those that produce for local use."[191] Whatever the characterization, the payoff of this dual industrial structure for big industrialists has been enormous, not only because they remained a monopolized sector with almost no domestic competition from local Taiwanese businesses, but also because smaller firms' exporting activities generated considerable foreign exchange earnings, which were then used to sustain protection of mainlander-dominated ISI activities as well as the country's massive rural-development schemes.

In short, although the disciplinary hand the KMT bureaucrats applied to large industrialists surely helped strengthen the Taiwanese economy, at least to a minimal extent, by eliminating corruption and rent-seeking, the state's regulation of smaller-scale, native-Taiwanese industrial urban middle-class producers was just as critical to the success of the country's EOI strategy, its global integration, and thus much of the nation's developmental gains. Moreover, it was small industrial firms who, along with small farmers and other rural middle classes, were most expected to be self-disciplinary, austere, and market efficient. For small industrial firms this meant generating massive export earnings by developing products not already manufactured by the large ISI firms. Accordingly, small industrial firms were prodded into exporting so as not to compete with big ISI industries and to help the government generate foreign exchange. Yet from their own vantage points, this was a "niche" that seemed to make perfect sense to them as producers seeking markets for their goods. To the extent that most small industrial firms were quite successful in these regards, we have clues as to why Taiwan's recent trajectory has been much less problematic than South Korea's, where the small industrial sector failed to flourish under the shadow of the ever more powerful chaebols.[192]

---

[190] Chou, *Industrial Organization in the Process of Economic Development*, p. 84.

[191] "Culture and Organization," p. 46.

[192] Gold, *State and Society in the Taiwan Miracle*, p. 89. For a more complete discussion of the difference between Taiwan and South Korea in terms of firm size and character, see

With large industrial firms driving South Korea's exporting successes, and in the absence of an economically significant small-scale industrial sector, large industrialists ultimately monopolized economic and political power, a situation which made it harder for the South Korean state to discipline them further down the road. In Taiwan, in contrast, even though smaller firms were just as successful in selling their products and securing a powerful global niche as were the larger EOI firms of South Korea, their reduced size meant that they never came to fully dominate politics or the economy, even when they prospered. Small firms never became so politically influential that they called the macroeconomic policy-making shots as with South Korean chaebols; and thus they remained relatively subject to the state's disciplinary measures as time passed, especially as compared to South Korea's large exporting industrialists. Their enforced small size and flexibility, moreover, made them more efficient and better competitors. They were better able to respond to the "just-in-time" production ideas and market pressures that flexible specialization theorists now argue explains post-Fordist economic successes in the global economy. And this too helps explain why Taiwan was able to avoid much of the macroeconomic disaster that resulted in South Korea when large industrialists, freed from disciplinary market constraints as well as effective state oversight and heavy-handed regulation, borrowed themselves into a financial crisis.

From Structures to Languages of Labor: Understanding the Farm-Factory Nexus in Taiwan

But where does labor fit into this picture? Did this key social force impact the state's willingness and capacity to discipline capitalists, either small or large, in Taiwan or our other cases? Again, the comparison with Argentina is instructive. In Argentina, the relatively privileged political role of the industrial working class not only limited the government's capacity to discipline them, it also made it difficult to discipline capitalists too, since the government could not be seen as disciplining capital if it would not do so with labor. Two clear results of this constraint were the selection of ISI over EOI and the prioritization of urban over rural-oriented development. In Taiwan, the ruling party also paid considerable lip service to labor and sought to include leading sectors of the organized working class within the party, even if in a secondary fashion. This did not, however, limit the state's disciplinary hand. The KMT led state was pretty much able to keep labor marginal to its political and economic projects, unlike in Argentina. This and the fact that even large ISI firms were on the receiving end of some state and self-discipline made possible the strong

Dollar and Sokoloff, "Industrial Policy, Productivity, Growth, and Structural Change in the Manufacturing Industries."

control over industrial labor organizations, including a long-standing ban on strikes and painstaking efforts to keep wages low.

Of course, labor's weak position with respect to the KMT-run state owed to various factors. One was the rather polarized ideological climate in the region as a whole and within the party in particular. With the shadow of Mao and the Chinese revolution flickering across the Taiwan straits, the KMT was hardly open to ideologies of class struggle, and its doctrinal emphasis on class harmony limited traditional trade union strategies, among them strikes, which in most countries played an important role in producing solidarity and labor-movement power. Additionally, the disciplinary ethos that the KMT embodied with its primarily small-farmer, mainlander, and big-industrialist constituency held little room for an activist or independent trade union movement, either in terms of ideology or shop-floor practices. These ideological sentiments reinforced the organizational weakness of labor and buttressed the influence of other social forces, especially that of the rural middle class, whose interests lay not in workplace concerns such as wages, strikes, and job security but, rather, in government-provided inputs that fostered greater productivity and faster development of a booming market economy, ranging from credit and technology to agricultural pricing policies. Labor discipline, in short, was quite consistent with the internal structure of the KMT, the concerns of its key constituents, and the larger ideological contours of KMT rule in Taiwan. Accordingly, despite the fact that trade unions were mentioned as a key social constituency of the KMT in formal party documents, they never developed the visibility, numbers, and autonomous influence of farmers associations,[193] and as such they were generally relegated to a secondary position in party and macroeconomic policy deliberations.

Ideological factors, however, cannot tell us everything about labor's weak position in Taiwan, why it was more readily disciplined there than in Argentina, and how this state of affairs led to Taiwan's developmental successes. An equally important explanation was the fact that labor remained highly fragmented and thus was not easily able to unite as a strong political force, either within or outside the KMT. In Taiwan, after all, government employees were not allowed to unionize,[194] and as such they remained divided from industrial workers, a situation that stands in stark contrast to that seen in most Latin American countries, where government workers are among the most active federations and usually linked to industrial workers. In Argentina, in fact, industrial laborers of all varieties were grouped within the same labor federation (General Confederation of Labor, or CGT) as government workers. Because in Taiwan these

---

[193] Moody, Jr., among others, notes that labor has been relatively well co-opted within Taiwanese party structures and national politics. See *Political Change on Taiwan*, p. 21.

[194] Tien, *The Great Transition*, p. 49.

two key sectors of society were not allowed to organize together, the labor movement was much weaker than it was in most of Latin America, especially during periods of rapid growth when state involvement in the economy produced a spurt in government employment. This also meant that in Taiwan government employees rarely expressed support for labor activism or the rights of industrial workers, a state of affairs that was ideologically reinforced by the fact that most government employees – again, mainlanders – held little elective affinity with the primarily native industrial working class. And owing to labor's weak position, and the fact that middle-class identities were more likely to prevail than working-class identities in the state sector and in society as a whole, overall middle-class political influence began to flower.

One result was that overall rates of unionization remained relatively low in Taiwan (where about 30 percent of industrial workers in the private sector are unionized),[195] not just in comparison to Argentina but also in comparison to South Korea in similar stages of EOI development. Yet the single most important explanation for this traces to the dual nature of the industrial sector, and the fact that small industrial firms were leading the economy and its export boom. Small firms of fewer than ten workers comprise almost 70 percent of all businesses and employ almost 30 percent of Taiwan's industrial labor force, and those with fewer than thirty employees hold almost 50 percent, a proportion that continues to increase.[196] And in Taiwanese labor law, it takes at minimum thirty workers in an industrial enterprise to organize a union.[197] So with small enterprises outnumbering large ones, the labor force was much less organized. Still, the reduced power or salience of the labor movement owed to more than just these legal – or larger structural – barriers. Even when organization was possible, it tended to be highly problematic among smaller and medium-sized firms.

For one thing, many of Taiwan's small firms were and still are family-run, employing family members, friends, and neighbors. By their very nature, these relationships do not easily lend themselves to labor organization.[198] Workers in small and medium-sized firms also tend to enjoy less job security. Additionally, many of those employed in small industrial firms had long fostered great

---

[195] Ibid., p. 40. Tien further notes that "membership rates are much lower among young workers and employees of small enterprises."

[196] For data on firms, see Metraux, *Taiwan's Political and Economic Growth in the Late Twentieth Century*, p. 51. The proportion of industrial workers employed in establishments that held fewer than 30 workers increased from 46 percent to 51 percent between 1980 and 1990. Quoted from Sen and Koo, 1992; see also Burris, "Late Industrialization," pp. 265–270.

[197] Tien, *The Great Transition*, p. 49.

[198] For more on this and other obstacles to working-class consciousness, see Wu, "Class Identity Without Class Consciousness?" esp. p. 79.

expectations of becoming owners or employers themselves some day, a factor which further limited their allegiance to or support for industrial labor organization. This suggests that it was not merely the organizational co-optation, narrower occupational scope, or low membership in trade unions that explains why labor has been so easily disciplined in Taiwan. Equally important are the ways workers historically have been conceptualized in the larger political culture as well as the ways that they have come to see and talk about themselves. And this is where the self-discipline of labor enters the picture as well.

Specifically, class discourses in Taiwan differed from those in Argentina and even South Korea, especially with respect to the value and social significance accorded to working-class identity. This reduced the power of the organized labor movement, even as it reinforced the salience of middle-class identities and middle-class influence in national politics. Accordingly, it is not just that organizational factors made the industrial working class in Taiwan relatively docile compared to the more activist South Korean trade unions and the well-mobilized Argentine industrial workers. What is equally significant is that industrial laborers in Taiwan have been more apt to see themselves in rather broadly cast terms which frequently encompass middle-class as much as a working-class fealty, a state of affairs which itself can limit trade union membership and working-class activism. In these self-conceptualizations, moreover, rural and urban identities interfaced with working- and middle-class loyalties in complex ways, such that while in Taiwan rural middle-class allegiances colored the urban working-class experience, in Argentina we see precisely the opposite: urban working-class sentiments flowered in a so-called rural middle-class milieu. The point here is that the historical and spatial contexts of class discourse help explain who considered themselves middle- or working-class, why or why not, and why the disciplinary ethos started to seep beyond the rural middle class – and even the military and/or state – into wider class and industrial domains in Taiwanese but not Argentine society.

In Taiwan industrial laborers often are conceptualized (by the state and by themselves) in other than working-class terms, because their long-standing status as rural producers is seen as central to their industrial laboring identities. The notions of "farmer-worker" and "part-time farmer" are commonly used in Taiwan in reference to industrial workers. They also are applied equally in rural and urban settings, largely because many farmers engage in off-farm jobs as seasonal or temporary workers in factories or on other farms.[199] So too in both the popular and academic worlds, the notion of "worker-owner" is commonly used to describe prototypical elements of the Taiwanese working class, just as the term "peasant-capitalist" is often used to describe small-scale rural producers. All these hybrid notions, whether or not they include farmer

---

[199] See Gold, *State and Society in the Taiwan Miracle*, p. 89.

identity within them, are used primarily in reference to those employed in the small-scale industrial sector, which is as likely to be located in the countryside as the city. As Gary Hamilton observes, one "walks down dusty streets in central Taiwan and sees family after family working around tables in their storefront homes that are open to everyone's view or . . . one drives in the countryside and sees small concrete boxes located in the midst of rice fields that are factories employing only handfuls of people."[200] This suggests that industrialization for export is occurring in both rural and urban locales; and in both environments it is small-scale activity and self-employment that predominate.

Much of this has to do with the history and structure of the Taiwanese economy. Especially after the 1960s, when agriculture experienced a brief period of decline, many small farmers began to work in industrial activities in order to generate income for further investment in farming, an arrangement that itself became more possible because of government support for agriculture and the long-standing spatial and economic integration of rural and urban areas. Moreover, according to Cheng-kuang Hsu, much of the interplay between farm and industrial work owed to a shortage of farm labor during the immediate postcolonial experience when land reforms were first enacted. This situation spurred farmers to ask family members who had migrated to the city in search of higher-paying industrial work to return to farming on weekends.[201] Yet, even among those farmers who remained in rural areas during all these agricultural ups and downs, the distinction between workers and owners or between capitalists and laborers was generally a fuzzy one. In his study of farmers and their relationship to the state and to industrial sectors in Taiwan, for example, Chih-ming Ka argues that after implementing the land-to-the tiller program of the late 1950s, it was quite problematic even to employ the concept of tenant in the discussion of rural classes, a claim based on the fact that so many farmers who rented lands to till managed them in a business-like way, producing-high market-value products. It was far more common to call them "capitalist tenants," in fact, because of their propensity to rent huge land expanses and employ workers.[202]

On the industrial side, the ambiguities of class and overlapping rural-urban identities were just as apparent. The dream of many factory laborers in Taiwan has long been to start their own small businesses, either small farms or small industrial enterprises. As one scholar put it, "there is no real division between Taiwan's industries, small business people, and its industrial workers,

---

[200] "Culture and Organization," p. 49.

[201] "Ecological Change and Economic Activities in Yen Village," p. 28. Notably, this stands in stark contrast to the situation in South Korea, where there was little labor shortage in rural areas and where rural decline tended to push farmers into cities in a much more permanent fashion.

[202] "Farmers, the State."

for, by and large, the latter are the childen to the former, temporarily earning cash for family expenses."[203] As such, most analysts will argue that "although Taiwan became industrialized, it did not become 'proletarianized,'"[204] mainly because industrialization proceeded hand in hand with the development of an entrepreneurial middle class in both the countryside and the city, and because the discourse and practice of small entrepreneurship was central in both do-mains. Of course, the primacy of what some scholars call the "entrepreneurial spirit" was not merely an ideological or rhetorical construct, nor did it just miraculously materialize in the culture. The KMT actively promoted the prac-tice of self-employment and programs of assistance and self-improvement, as did Park Chung Hee with South Korea's rural farmers; and as in South Korea, the Taiwanese government initially directed these policies at both farmers and workers. The KMT's 1963 party platform, for example, called on the gov-ernment to "extend assistance to the organizations of farmers and workers in furthering their sound development, [to] protect the lawful rights and inter-ests of farmers and workers, [to] raise their technical and cultural standards, and [to] introduce the system of providing workers with the opportunities of becoming shareholders and receiving cash awards."[205]

In stark contrast to South Korea, however, the Taiwanese government was relatively successful in fostering the development of an entrepreneurial middle-class sentiment among rural producers in the countryside and among small producers in the city, something that paid off in self-disciplinary terms as well as macroeconomically. In the city this manifested itself in the flowering of small-scale urban entrepreneurs involved in labor-intensive factory production, not merely highly disciplined workers confined to large factory settings and employed in capital-intensive firms, as in South Korea. Gary Hamilton notes, in fact, that the "desire to be an independent businessperson and to earn one's living and possibly get rich . . . [had] a basis in reality."[206] Some of this is evidenced by the fact that the ratio of bosses or managers (*laoban*) to workers in post-1965 Taiwan has been extraordinary, having reached a rate of 1 for every 8 adults by the early 1980s. In this regard, Gary Hamilton quotes Tyler Biggs as "only slightly exaggerating when he said, 'If you stood in the middle of this city [Taipei] and tossed a stone in any direction, you'd probably hit a boss.'"[207]

To be sure, many of these so-called bosses are highly exploited themselves, with only minimal remuneration, while their firms are embedded in a verti-cally structured network in which they are the microenterprises that produce

---

[203] Moody, Jr., *Political Change on Taiwan*, p. 48.
[204] Ibid.
[205] Shieh, *The Kuomintang: Selected Historical Documents, 1894–1969*, p. 283.
[206] "Culture and Organization," p. 48.
[207] Ibid.

the materials that have been subcontracted out by others.[208] Still, the difference between them and industrial laborers – generally speaking, to be sure, but also in South Korea, where individual discipline and pride around production also were nurtured among waged-labor factory workers – was the fact that by and large these "bosses" were self-exploited, so to speak, and they owned their firms rather than selling their labor power. Thus most "bosses" in Taiwan's small industrial firms were in essence middle class, or at least they shared elective affinities with the middle class. These affinities, moreover, were most likely to extend to the rural middle class more than labor. The small size of industrial operations and scale of production made these "bosses" prototypically petit bourgeois, and discipline – or even self-discipline in their case – was of utmost importance to their firms' overall livelihoods, a trait that served them well in both city and countryside. Moreover, it was precisely the small-scale, vertically integrated production process prevailing in the urban sector that kept most native-owned industrial exporting firms from growing too large in size or economic scope. This in turn insured that both workers' and owners' outlooks resonated more with each other and with a petit bourgeois mentality than with the mind frame of large capitalists, thereby reinforcing rather than undermining the long-term conditions for (and middle-class underpinning of) a sustained disciplinary ethos. Equally important, the long-standing historical and migratory links between these small-scale urban industrialists and the farmer experience, noted above, further entrenched a powerful self-disciplinary ethos – most often seen among farmers – among both employers and workers in the urban industrial domain. As in South Korea, that was a formidable combination that more often than not produced great results in the factory setting.

The fungibility of class concepts, and especially the tendency to see both farmers and urban workers in middle-class terms, combined with the pervasiveness of a self-disciplinary ethos, have a lot to do with two characteristic features that are in many ways unique to Taiwan, at least among late developers. They include the predominance of small firms in the industrial economy and balanced patterns of urbanization or, better said, the strong social and economic relations between rural and urban areas. As Hung-mao Tien puts it,

> Taiwan's urbanization pattern differs from that of other countries, particularly the pattern in the Third World. The island is geographically compact, thus assuring that even rural residents had relatively easy access to a nearby urban center. Furthermore, many industries are located in smaller cities and towns, partly to absorb excess labor – part-time

---

[208] See Shieh's fascinating study, *"Boss" Island*.

farmers and agricultural workers. Hence Taiwan does not have a lop-sided concentration of population in a few metropolitan centers."[209]

These patterns not only helped create an environment in which urban and rural identities are not pitted against each other, they also sustain relatively facile flows of people back and forth from city to countryside, generally through seasonal or even daily migration. In these conditions, especially in an environment with relatively successful rural-based industrialization, rural versus urban class antagonisms subside. Workers are farmers and farmers are workers, even if only temporarily; and even those farmers who permanently move to the city often keep ownership of their lands or turn them over to relatives.[210] These practices stand in stark contrast to the situation in South Korea, where urbanization patterns, the relative absence of rural industrialization, and the predominance of Seoul mean not only that most rural-urban migration is relatively permanent, but also that farm life and the so-called rural experience still remain quite distinct from the urban and the industrial laboring experience.

The prevalence of small firms in the Taiwanese industrial economy also made family forms of ownership far more likely. And with "family ownership . . . the dominant form of enterprise" in Taiwan,[211] both the possibility of class conflict and the development of working-class identities were greatly diminished, at least among family members or family friends employed in these firms, even as the possibility of becoming an employer was enhanced. Equally important, precisely because "familism had strong roots in the Taiwanese farm family,"[212] the persistence of family forms of ownership has helped sustain rural outlooks even in urban firms, thereby contributing to the interchangeability of rural and urban identities and reinforcing a commonality of middle-class experience. To be sure, there may be a chicken-and-egg problem here, such that it is often difficult to ascertain whether it is rural orientation[213] or familism that

---

[209] *The Great Transition*, p. 30

[210] For a discussion of this and other ways in which farmers and workers may commingle, see Niehoff, "The Villager As Industrialist," and Ka, "Farmers, the State."

[211] The predominance of family firms may also explain why the Taiwanese government has been so austere and efficient, as well as why there have been such high savings rates. Indeed, because "individual families relied heavily on their own savings to start or expand enterprises, many borrowed from friends and relatives, or, in the rural areas, from local credit associations"; these practices made many Taiwanese see the value of having their own savings and reduced the burden on the government to finance industrial development. See Vogel, *The Four Little Dragons*, p. 37. In "Culture and Organization," p. 61, Hamilton further adds that "large businesses use bank loans much more frequently than small businesses," although even they use the private sector, including family members, as a source of financial resources.

[212] Vogel, *The Four Little Dragons*, p. 37.

[213] In *Political Change on Taiwan*, p. 47, Moody suggests that "Taiwanese folk self-identity . . . remains rural and agricultural (even as the island industrializes)."

permeates small firms' practices and sustains small size, or vice versa. Gary Hamilton, one of the most important scholars of the Taiwanese industrial economy and a keen observer of the anthropology of small firms, suggests that it is more the small size of the firm than family that matters, at least in terms of industrial successes;[214] whereas Ezra Vogel seems to suggest the opposite, claiming that "family" styles of management persist even in large firms.[215] Yet Hamilton takes this stalemate to more fertile gounds when he acknowledges that it is the interaction of these two dynamics that drives the small-firm nature of the Taiwanese economy. "One of the key aspects of management," Hamilton claims,

> is the maintenance of a double bond composed of firm and family . . . [which] often leads to the managers' exploitation of their employees. In Taiwan's highly competitive economy, the needs of business often overwhelm the decorum within families. In the end, the tension between family management and worker exploitation encourages those who are not close family members and those who do not share in the control of assets to escape from the direct control of management, to start their own firms and to exploit others in turn.[216]

In Taiwan, this interactive dynamic between family forms of ownership *and* small firm size, combined with the spatial integration that diminishes a rural-urban divide and brings farmers into the city, diminished the likelihood of strong working-class identities and sustained a vibrant entrepreneurial economy built on a disciplinary, quasi-rural middle-class ethos.

With working-class identities so thoroughly eclipsed by middle-class identities among those involved in both rural and urban-based activities, and with the remaining industrial laborers employed primarily in the small-scale industrial sector where family networks and personal ties envelop shop-floor practices, there has been only minimal commitment to securing the rights or protection of industrial labor, either from the state or from the labor movement itself, a state of affairs that reinforces labor's weakness vis-à-vis any disciplinary actions imposed by the state.[217] And because for many employment in industrial processing activities is still seen primarily as a way station on the road

---

[214] "The preponderance of family ownership does not, however, explain the success of Taiwanese firms. Quite the reverse is true. As Wong Siu-lun has so ably described, the Chinese family firm is inherently short-term and unstable" ("Culture and Organization," p. 50).

[215] *The Four Little Dragons*, p. 37.

[216] "Culture and Organization," p. 56.

[217] For more on the weaknesses of the labor movement, see Gold, *State and Society in the Taiwan Miracle*, p. 89. In addition to highlighting the fact that most laborers sought to become entrepreneurs, Gold also mentions the high proportion of female laborers and their rapid turnover rate, which also mitigated against working-class consciousness.

to self-employment, industrial laborers and small entrepreneurs alike engage in a considerable degree of self-discipline, or what one observer alternatively called "traditional thrifty habits."[218] The self-disciplinary stance of laborers and their pretensions and aspirations to become middle-class entrepreneurs, as well as the elective affinity with farmers and their experience in farm activities, further explains why labor's inclusion in formal party structures did not necessarily undermine the larger aims of the KMT with respect to disciplining large capitalists. And in tandem with the limited visibility and political power of the labor movement, these attitudes and experiences shed light on why the disciplinary ethos has been so much deeper, more durable, and more widespread among classes in Taiwan than in Argentina or even South Korea.

Turned on Their Head: Languages of Proletarianization and the Disappeared Middle Class in Rural Argentina

What is perhaps most striking about these conditions in Taiwan is that they stand in stark contrast to the circumstances in Argentina, especially during the country's concerted effort to rapidly industrialize under Perón, in which the class and political languages employed to appeal to rural peoples emphasized a proletarian or working-class (*obrero*) identity as much as popular or middle-class status, and where, because of the latter framing, industrial laborers tend to see both rural and urban entrepreneurs as enemies of the people (*pueblo*), that is, persons to be reviled more than models to be revered. Moreover, even those small-scale rural producers that in other countries might consider themselves farmers in Argentina saw themselves primarily as workers, or at least they have been referred to in these terms and have often responded politically to the languages that address them as such. With rural small producers finding elective affinity with working classes more than with the middle classes, polarized class conflict between large capitalists and laborers was much more likely to be on the agenda. This, in turn, helps explain why the Argentine state so ardently pursued discourses of class cooperation or accommodation more than coercion or self-discipline, and thus why it failed to discipline either of these two forces.

In Argentina, smaller-scale farmers might be considered the great losers in this discursive rhetoric, in part because they disappear from both the languages and practices of politics. Indeed, while in Taiwan the rural middle class is quite broadly defined, such that even industrial laborers are often seen or conceptualize themselves as farmers (hence the term "farmer-workers" noted earlier), in Argentina farmers are quite narrowly defined in both the culture and political discourse, such that they are more likely to be regarded and see themselves as workers (hence the commonly used term "rural proletarians"). As a result, in Argentina farmers and the rural middle class in general are much

---

[218] Tsiang, "Foreign Trade and Investment As Boosters for Take-Off," p. 47.

less visible, so to speak, and thus less capable of maintaining a presence as independent and valued social and political actors – especially when compared to their counterparts in Taiwan. Of course, some of the neglect or scorn accorded to farmers and other small-scale rural producers in the political culture and in discourses of Argentine politics owes to the history of relations between urban and rural populations, or between what Argentines termed "civilized" urban peoples and rural barbarians, as described earlier. Yet even within this particular cultural framing of the nation, there has been an obvious pecking order even among rural populations themselves, in which farmers and gauchos were on the bottom of a social hierarchy dominated by large ranchers or *estancieros*. Thus these classes looked for languages that reflected this unequivocably subordinate status.

In *A History of Argentine Political Thought*, Romero argues that from early on "ranching and commerce merited the highest social esteem," even though "agriculture in reality provided only a mere existence; its products lacked commercial value and, since it did not make men rich, labor in the fields seemed to be worthless compared with the ideal of wealth that was the polestar of the colonist."[219] He also cites an eighteenth-century chronicler, Azara, who wrote that "the Spaniards who live in the country are divided into farmers and ranchers, or *estancieros*. The latter say that the former are foolish, since if they were to become ranchers, they would live without labor and without needing to eat grass like horses."[220] Overall, then, the image of rural populations in general,[221] and small-scale self-employed farm producers in particular, has contributed to an environment in which many rural small producers have little cultural prestige and limited political or social influence in Argentine national politics, a state of affairs that was particularly striking under Perón. Of course nineteenth-century popular culture cannot fully explain the silences about small farmers in mid-twentieth-century Argentine political discourse, nor can it explain the tendency to conceptualize farmers and other rural folk as workers, two trends that contributed to the truncated development of an independent or politically salient rural middle-class discourse in Argentina and that contrasts so sharply with the Taiwanese case. As discussed earlier, the structural underpinnings of the Argentine rural economy also mattered, especially to the extent that there has been much more rural wage labor in

---

[219] *Argentine Political Thought*, p. 26.

[220] Ibid., p. 43.

[221] We might argue that the romanticization of the gaucho suggests some cultural sanction of small producers employed on their own account. But the gaucho is to be a particular variety of independent contractor, reified for his native (i.e., nonforeign) origins and appreciated for his loner lifestyle and rootlessness, not for staking a claim to farming or other more productive activities. For more on the gaucho as a cultural icon in Argentina, see Slatta, *Gauchos*, Chap. 11.

Argentina than in Taiwan, a situation that traced to the political and economic power of large landowners.

Most of the big estancias employed waged agricultural labor on their ranches, and there were a significant number of rural-based industrial workers employed in meatpacking and -processing plants (*frigoríficos*). By the early decades of the twentieth century, many farmers and other small-scale producers found themselves in extreme economic hardship, partly because of the nation's economic woes, yet also because many large landowners had been struggling for years to limit the growth of the rural middle classes. This state of affairs made it much more likely that working-class languages would resonate among these small rural producers and other similarly independent rural populations, like gauchos, since their capacity to be autonomous producers working on their own account eroded steadily over the nineteenth and early-twentieth centuries.[222]

Still, it was not just the steady proletarianization of rural Argentina and the dominance of the large landowner that explains why, especially during the critical period of industrial expansion under Perón, languages of rural middle-classness – along with rural middle classes themselves – effectively disappeared from the national political scene. Just as important was the larger political context in which these rhetorics developed and, in particular, the class coalitions that they were intended to sustain. Perón, in particular, was trying to politically craft a class coalition that would buttress his hold on power. For spatial and class-coalitional reasons discussed already, both of which were grounded in history, urban-based industrial labor was the main organizing base for Perón. For this reason his political discourse was highly circumscribed by a class-conflict mode of thought and discourse. Moreover, even among his working-class base, Perón was faced with the greatest opposition from the "white collar" or middle-class sectors of the organized labor force, such as government workers and commercial employees, who were more likely to support independent unions, even as the more "blue collar" – or traditionally working-class – unions of textile, metal, meatpacking, and rail workers tended to ally with Perón.[223] As such, Perón consistently referred to a class-divided society with workers pitted against owners; and this way of framing this problem left very little scope for ideologically or discursively accommodating middling sectors, be they small-scale producers or the self-employed who might practice a more petit bourgeois mode of production, either rural or urban. In a 1944 speech, for example, Perón proclaimed: "Our country is divided in two categories: one, made up of men who work, and the other, those who live from the men who

---

[222] In his study of perhaps the most renowned of all the rural self-employed, the gauchos, Slatta chronicles the Argentine ranching elite's "assiduous" efforts to reduce the gaucho's status from that of "self-sufficiency to patronage" (*Gauchos*, p. 5).

[223] Whittaker, *Argentina*, p. 12.

work. Against this situation, we openly place ourselves on the side of those who work."[224]

Granted, Perón was quite aware that working-class support was not enough to sustain his hold on the state, especially with an antagonistic class-conflict discourse that seemed to create as many enemies as friends. He also saw certain rural populations as central to widening his claim to power, especially in the critical province of Buenos Aires, even if he could not fully carry through on their claims or demands (as was the case when he dropped the idea of land reform in 1946, discussed earlier). For these reasons, Perón sought and crafted a language of rural classness that was broadly compatible with his industrial working-class bases even as it widened his political reach to include some heretofore neglected rural populations. The notion of rural proletarian fit the bill. The point, however, is that the discourse of rural proletarians in industrializing Argentina was as much socially constructed as objectively given, especially in the 1930s and 1940s when rural Argentina was undergoing such drastic social, political, and economic upheaval and was still relatively up for grabs. This becomes clear with a closer examination of the rural populations to which Perón was trying to appeal.

The folks Perón sought to fold into his political coalition were not merely rural wage laborers. Many owned their own farms, and even more rented land for cultivation on large properties. Yet even among the more "middling" category of tenant farmers, class identity was rather ambiguous, in a "realist" sense of the term. As one scholar writing in the 1940s put it, even in the face of evidence that most tenant farmers remained as such their whole life, most "do not think of themselves as a tenant class. They generally continue to aspire to ownership status and live in the expectation, or hope, that they will someday own farms."[225] He further suggests, arguably perhaps, that "farm operators and their families (both tenants and owners)" should be considered the "real middle class of Argentine agriculture."[226] In short, no matter the position one takes on classifying these rural social forces in middle-class terms, there is no denying that both class identity and rural social structure were quite fluid and diverse when Perón arrived on the political scene. Thus he responded with strategic political objectives as his guide. Among the groups he actively considered targeting for political support were tenant farmers (*arrendatorios*), small farmers (*pequeños propietarios*), rural wage workers (*trabajadores sin tierras*), and even some medium-sized farmers (*minifundistas*),[227] none of whom were natural allies for the Conservative Party (with its latifundista base) and only some of whom had strong connections to the Radicals. Why? Because given

---

[224] Cúneo, *Comportamiento*, p. 172.
[225] Taylor, *Rural Life in Argentina*, p. 191; see also pp. 394–395.
[226] Ibid., p. 419.
[227] Lattuada, *La política agraria peronista*, pp. 25, 42.

the unstable and quasi-dictatorial political situation in Argentina at the time, it was important for Perón to find a common political rhetoric with which he could appeal to as wide a variety of rural peoples as possible, still maintain his basic solidarity with industrial workers, and keep his hold on the state.

This was so especially after the economic crisis of 1941, when tensions between large landowners and tenant farmers became a political issue that even the Radical Party sought to address, and thus there was increased scope for acknowledging the declining economic and social position of all these rural producers. Owing to the earlier problems of rural neglect by previous governments, a good proportion of tenant farmers and small farmers were collectively organized in much the same way as were rural wage laborers, albeit in different organizations. In these post-1941 conditions of growing income polarization and economic decline for small farmers, use of the term "rural proletarians" insinuated a thematic and organizational unity that linked some (albeit not all) of the differing rural class segments under a common, broadly cast identity. The hope was that this particular political discourse could help bring certain rural populations politically closer to those organized urban workers already at Perón's side, who were themselves increasingly impoverished as well.

It may also be worth noting the spatial correlates of this strategy, primarily because they were so central in producing practically the opposite class discourses in Taiwan. By the late 1930s and early 1940s, the predominant pattern in Buenos Aires (BA) province was toward the increasing impoverishment of rural farmers. This was a key region for Perón since his capacity to hold the capital, and thus the nation, rested in his abilities to maintain political legitimacy in the larger province. Thus the vocabulary of "rural proletarians" had some grounding in the political realities of Peron's aspired ascent to power. It also owed to the power of the large estancieros in BA and other provinces, whom Perón soon recognized to be key to his capacity to stay in power and whom he thus failed to fully challenge (as evidenced by his stunning shift in support from the FAA to the SRA, as noted earlier). And it was concern about keeping loyalty from the large-landlord class bases, who generally pitted themselves against small, frequently immigrant, farmers, that further contributed to the circumscribed language and discursive machinations Perón used to appeal to rural peoples throughout the 1940s and into the 1950s and may, in fact, have defined the language he used much as did his linkages to urban working classes. These considerations were so great that in a 1952 public speech at the Teatro Colón, Perón went so far as to recast his definition of what a latifundista was in order to allow him to ignore the political demands of small farmers who decried the power of large landlords, saw themselves as small producers overwhelmed by the large capitalist ranchers, and/or were seeking a major land reform. "The *latifundista*" – he proclaimed in the Teatro Colón speech – "is not defined by the number of hectares or the extension of land that he makes productive; the latifundista is defined by the quantity of hectares, even though they may be few, that are unproductive." He added:

> God help us if we would be so limited in our understanding as to launch a struggle for the destruction of large properties to create small properties, having the immense extensions of land that we have [truncated] so that every agriculturalist (*agricultor*) could have all the fields (*campo*) he fancied! We don't want to make proletarianized peasants; we want happy and abundant agriculturalists.[228]

For a variety of political and economic reasons, then, Perón's discursive appeals to rural peoples and his identification of them either as rural workers or proletarianized peasants, on one hand, or classless agriculturalists on the other, differed substantially from the languages used in Taiwan, where farmer-worker languages prevailed and where an ethos of small entrepreneurial middle-classness permeated both city and countryside. Whereas in Argentina languages of working classes, themselves structured around a political platform based on urban industrial laborers, worked to help snuff out a rural middle-class identity, in Taiwan languages of middle-classness helped to snuff out a working-class identity. Stated simply, discursive processes and material patterns of middle-class formation, especially rural middle-class formation, were almost the mirror image of each other in these two countries, just as they represented two completely opposite ends of the spectrum in terms of the visibility and political importance of rural middle classes and in terms of accommodating versus disciplinary strategies of development.

So far, we have identified the importance of differences in rural land tenure, differences in class identities among the population, and the consciously crafted rhetorics and ideologies of governing authorities – themselves grounded in the prevailing class coalitional politics of the times – as accounting for some of the fundamental developmental differences between Argentina and Taiwan. But there is one other key variable in the construction of class discourses and identities that mattered considerably and which further distinguishes these two countries from each other and from South Korea: the role of ethnic division or conflict. Unlike South Korea, where the population remained relatively homogeneous in terms of race and ethnicity after the Japanese withdrawal,

---

[228] Cúneo, *Comportamiento*, p. 219. It may be worth noting that in response to this speech, the Sociedad Rural (SRA) – representing large landowners – published the following statement: "We are pleased to take this opportunity to underscore the magisterial dissertation pronounced by his excellency, señor Presidente de la Nación, General Juan Perón" (p. 219). Note also his invocation of the term "peasant" (and not even rural small producer) to refer to proletarianized rural populations in this particular context, as well as his use of the rather classless term *agricultor* rather than *pequeño propietario, minifundista*, or even *chacarero* to refer to agricultural producers.

both Argentina and Taiwan were heterogeneous societies plagued by ethnic division. Still, there was one key difference between them. In Taiwan ethnic division reinforced bonds within the rural middle class even as it facilitated a common identity across rural and urban populations that itself diminished the chances for the formation of a separate urban working-class identity. In Argentina, in contrast, ethnic tensions or conflicts divided rural and urban populations and split rural producers in such a way as to buttress languages of rural proletarianization, thereby diminishing the chances for the formation of a common middle-class identity under which rural and urban producers could unite.

The role of ethnicity and its impact on class politics and class identity in Argentina is better understood with a closer examination of the immigrant experience and the inflow of large numbers of Italians, Germans, and other Europeans to Argentina in the last half of the nineteenth century and the beginning of the twentieth. Most scholars who study the large-scale European immigration to Argentina chart its impact on the urban working class and the rise of Peronism as an urban popular movement. They identify cultural factors such as immigrants' exposure to anarcho-syndicalism or political factors such as their citizenship status (which meant that many immigrants did not vote) as contributing to the rise of Peronism. Yet far fewer scholars have examined the larger implications of the fact that many members of the immigrant working class that supported Perón initially were rural farmers who later journeyed to Buenos Aires city as economic conditions deteriorated in Buenos Aires province and its immediate surrounds. As Mario Lattuada notes, citing from Fayt, the so-called "new or recent industrial proletariate considered decisive for the triumph of the Peronist movement was comprised of a high percentage of migrants of rural origin, without any industrial experience, and understood as peons without lands, medium-sized farmers (*minifundistas*), small rural producers (*pequeños agricultures propietarios*), renters, tenant farmers (*medieros*), and other forms of non-owning tenancy."[229] Accordingly, Perón's use of languages of rural proletarianism not only allowed him to appeal to many of the occupational groups in the rural areas immediately surrounding the capital city, they simultaneously allowed him to generate sympathy with his existent urban working-class base *and* to strengthen social and political ties between these rural populations and urban workers, who frequently shared the same ethno-cultural origins and/or immigrant status. That is, it made sense in the immigrant, migratory, geographical, class, and political context of Perón's rise to power.

That a large proportion of these immigrants who ended up in the cities as members of the urban working class originally came to Argentina to start small farms is telling, not just because it helps us understand why Perón used urban

---

[229] *La política agraria peronista*, p. 43.

working-class languages to appeal to rural folk, and why so many rural small producers did in fact see themselves as proletarians. It also sheds light on why it was so difficult for rural middle classes to unite as a class or as a political force. Indeed, foreign immigrants who started farming in Argentine provinces often faced extraordinary ethnic discrimination and open social antagonism, which limited their capacity to own land and/or thrive as small-scale producers as well as their desire to take the rural middle-class route to prosperity.[230] To be sure, large landowners were often reluctant to sell their lands to small producers for fear of competition, while estancia domination of the rural economy hurt all small farmers no matter their ethnic origins. Yet most scholars do attribute the declining position of immigrant farmers to their foreign status, since there was considerable opposition among native populations to selling land to foreigners who spoke and looked differently, especially in Buenos Aires province,[231] and since a clear majority of the small farmers were indeed of foreign descent. Antiforeign sentiment, if you remember, was part of what fueled the fascist sentiment among native rural middle classes; and in this environment, those few small farmers that were able to buy enough lands to become large proprietors were generally of native origin.[232]

The point here is that in the everyday world of rural Argentina, or at least in the culture and perceptions of it, disentangling immigrant, small-farmer, and impoverished status was difficult. As Carl Taylor remarked, most immigrants and sons of immigrants "started farming as hired men and rose to the status of tenants but never advanced any further up the agricultural ladder."[233] Thus even if they were not fully proletarianized, they clearly were not advancing. And it was precisely these obstacles to immigrant small proprietorship and prosperity that help explain why so many of the foreign-born farmers would have been so open to Perón's political movement, receptive to a discourse that

---

[230] The result, according to Whittaker (*Argentina*, p. 55), was that most "immigrants found it easier to get ahead in the city than in the country, and easier in agriculture than stockraising. The acquisition of land was made difficult for them not only by the land system but also by the tenacity with which the native Argentines held onto their properties, whether because of the great social prestige of landowning or for one other reason. As a result, in rural areas relatively few of the foreign-born ever rose above the status of tenant or salaried manager. Even as common laborers they had only limited opportunities in stockraising, especially when the stock were horses and cattle."

[231] Most scholars agree that obstacles for foreign-born farmers were greatest in Buenos Aires province and its surrounds, with immigrant farmers in other locales finding greater success. See Taylor, *Rural Life in Argentina*, p. 114.

[232] Many observers of rural Argentina have argued that the main way that immigrant farmers have become successful and increased their scale of landowning is by way of owning petty trade activities in rural towns. Once they successfully accumulate capital in these towns, then they return to the countryside and buy large plots of land.

[233] *Rural Life in Argentina*, p. 175.

could unite them with their fellow foreigners in cities, and appreciative of his discursive acknowledgment of their exploitation and impoverishment, especially given their personal experiences and recognition of the real limits to their capacities to progress, reinvest, accumulate, and thus become successful petit bourgeois farmers, like the natives. Moreover, it was precisely this understanding among immigrants that they were bound to remain poor and economically marginal, while anti-immigrant natives would more easily prosper, that may further explain why a strong, unified, and thus politically salient rural middle class did not materialize in Argentina.

In Taiwan, ethnic differences between natives and foreigners also affected politics and society, yet rather than dividing the rural middle classes it united them, mainly because the large majority of rural producers were of native Taiwanese origin. Precisely because the foreigners in Taiwan were mainland Chinese refugees who controlled the state, and because they were a minority, they were quite cautious about exacerbating ethnic conflicts or tensions that would call into question KMT rule. Moreover, native Taiwanese identity helped unite rural middle classes and urban working classes (who themselves aspired to the urban middle class) in such a way as to overcome the conflicts seen between these groups in Argentina both before and after the rise of the immigrant-fueled Peronist movement. Remember, in Argentina bonds between rural and urban populations, when they did arise, often developed around a common immigrant identity that came to life in a working-class discourse. In Taiwan the pattern was different: Bonds between rural and urban folk developed around a common ethnic identity that came to life in a small-entrepreneurial discourse, which itself transcended "real" space and class in fundamental ways. As such, in Taiwan ethnicity united almost all classes, with the clear exception of the large mainlander industrialists, and even they shared the common developmental goal of fostering both rural development and EOI through the development of small-scale entrepreneurial classes. In Argentina, in contrast, ethnicity split rural classes in such a way as to undermine rural middle-class unity even as it tended to divide rural and urban classes, each of which had different attitudes about the priorities to be granted to rural versus urban development, ISI versus EOI, and the role of large-scale versus small-scale firms.

To be sure, in Taiwan all was not perfect with respect to the ethnic question. Many native Taiwanese felt economically exploited in the hard-driving economy piloted by the KMT, who identified with the Chinese mainland; and in the political sphere, tensions between the mainlander loyalists of the KMT and native Taiwanese persisted for decades. But in Taiwan it was the urban middle class, or small-scale family firms involved in industrial production for export – not farmers – who felt the economic exploitation most and who thus were more likely to promote ethnic resentment against mainlanders. As noted earlier, under the KMT's strict disciplinary hand, small industrial workshops were under tremendous economic and political pressure to produce quality goods for export through use of friend and family labor, especially since it was their EOI activities that sustained the economic miracle in Taiwan and thus kept the KMT a player in the region and in its longer-term struggle with China. These pressures came not only from the KMT government but also from larger industrial firms that contracted out their services. Both foreign-owned firms and mainlander industrialists promoted government policies and entered into regulation-bound contracts that pressured small producers to keep up with export targets and rely on each other, not on the state, for capital. It is not so surprising, in fact, given these pressures on small firms, that among the forces most active in the anti-KMT, pro-democracy movement were those small industrial producers tethered to EOI, considered by many to be the mainstay of the urban middle class, who joined with students and intellectuals to call for change.

Still, despite those tensions, in Taiwan ethnic differences did not divide the rural middle class nor did they divide the rural and urban populations, as occurred in Argentina. It is more likely, in fact, that ethnic tensions or identities *united* the middle class. This unity, especially in combination with the ethnically based tensions between small and large industrialists, prevented the urban middle class from joining a political coalition in which urban populations were pitted against rural populations, as occurred in Argentina. Most important, perhaps, the ethnic and discursive unity between urban and rural middle classes also prevented large industrialists from becoming so politically powerful that they could disregard rural development aims altogether and focus only on urban industrialization. Nor could large industrialists call their own shots with respect to government policy making and development financing. This was, in many ways, the key to sound macroeconomic development and to the successes of middle-class formation, both rural and urban (and the path from which South Korea ultimately swayed). In Argentina, however, it was the unique spatial, military, class, and ethnic conditions that pushed the country down a development path that was practically the opposite of Taiwan's – with the state ignoring rural development and pouring its energies into urban-based ISI – that the economy was so fragile.

In these conditions, the Argentine state could discipline neither capitalists nor laborers, a situation which brought rising wages plus sustained protectionism; nor could it privilege small-scale rural development. One result was more rural-urban migration from 1940 to 1960, which merely increased the urban working class and fueled the urban-based political pressure for ISI and for workers' rights. This in itself made it difficult for the government to shift away from ISI, even when global conditions called the utility of this strategy into question in the 1970s. Still another negative by-product of the wholesale neglect of rural areas in Argentina was the development of a dual economy in the countryside, which in many ways matched the dual class structure that resulted from the failure to implement a serious program of rural development. In this dual agricultural economy, the smaller, poorer farmers produced for domestic consumption, but they could hardly sustain the growing urban demand, which eventually pushed Argentina to import many foodstuffs. Large estancieros, in contrast, produced mainly for the export market, carrying out the foreign-exchange-earning function that small urban industrialists and large urban industrialists undertook in Taiwan and South Korea, respectively. This further limited the Argentine government's freedom to force the shift to EOI when ISI became "saturated" in the 1970s and thereafter – a move which would have threatened the large rural landlords' monopoly on the export trade. It also made Argentina quite vulnerable to fluctuating prices for export crops. Within a decade or two of Perón's rise to power, agricultural exporting had become so problematic that Argentina was forced to import staples like wheat. As a result, over the 1970s and 1980s its foreign exchange earnings began dropping precipitously even as the country's current account (balance of payments) was destabilizing under the weight of growing agricultural and industrial imports. The failure to develop EOI also meant there were few industrial exports upon which to rely if Argentina wanted to counterbalance the growing current account deficit. The situation was a disaster, and the long-term results have been clear in terms of economic instability, inflation, and a structurally weak economy. And as Argentina's standing in an increasingly globalized trading regime continued to deteriorate, Taiwan's position steadily strengthened to make it the roaring tiger it now is.

5

FROM VICTORS TO VICTIMS?

Rural Middle Classes, Revolutionary Legacies, and the
Unfulfilled Promise of Disciplinary Development in Mexico

Beyond Regime Type

If we were to choose just one other twentieth-century developer whose surface political profile most nearly parallels that of Taiwan, Mexico would be a principal contender. Both Mexico and Taiwan have been known over the past half century for their strong and enduring systems of one-party rule, fortified through forceful political, ideological, and institutional connections between a vanguard revolutionary party and the state. Both of these countries' party-state apparatuses, the KMT and Mexico's Partido Revolucionario Institucional (PRI), were highly centralized and carefully structured around corporatist principles that mandated the institutional inclusion of a wide variety of class forces drawn from both rural and urban locales.[1] Additionally, the long-term trajectories of political development in both countries are quite similar on many counts, including the timing of democratic opening in the late 1980s and the role played by grassroots democratic movements in bringing this political change. In Taiwan, it was the end of martial law in 1987 that marked the key point of democratic transition, while in Mexico this was the same year that opposition candidate Cuauhtémoc Cárdenas broke from the PRI, ran for the presidency on his own, and started Mexico down its current path toward democratic consolidation. Yet despite these political similarities, the economic development trajectories of these two countries over the last half century have diverged considerably. Clearly, political regime type

---

[1] The similarities between the PRI and the KMT are actually quite striking. According to Bullard, *The Soldier and the Citizen*, p. 34, the goals of the Central Reorganization Committee of the KMT, as early as 1950, included efforts to "1) make the KMT a revolutionary–democratic party; 2) broaden the social base of the Party by including peasants, workers, youth, intellectuals and producers; 3) adopt democratic–centralism as the organizing principle; 4) emphasize Party cells as the basic units of the Party; 5) have all decisions made by Party committees, and personnel and other policy matters handled by formal procedures; and 6) insist that Party members obey the Party, uphold its policies, and have a proper work style."

is not the best place for beginning to understand developmental differences or similarities between Taiwan and Mexico, or even between Argentina and South Korea for that matter, as both the latter countries have been similarly classified as bureaucratic-authoritarian regimes during their periods of rapid industrialization.

If we examine middle-class configurations in these varying countries, however, and the extent to which rural and/or urban middle classes formed a key political base for the state as it embarked on a program of rapid industrialization, we will be better able to account for many of the developmental differences between Taiwan and Mexico, on the one hand, and the similarities between Mexico and Argentina on the other. Generally speaking, during the periods of rapid industrial expansion in Latin America, rural middle classes were not considered key political forces; and even in Mexico, where they were formally represented within the PRI, they have held very little political sway. In both Mexico and Argentina, industrial capitalists and their laborers have wielded the greatest influence, and if middle classes mattered in the state and development policy making, it was generally urban middle classes who were employed in the bureaucratic sector or who consumed the ISI goods produced by domestic capitalists and their wage laborers. Thus it should be no surprise that their developmental paths also have coincided to a great extent. Since the late 1950s, both Mexico and Argentina have shown a preference for ISI and for protectionist policies, and both have paid little attention to accommodating concerns of the rural middle classes. To the extent that they also have shown very little willingness to discipline either capitalists or laborers, they have failed to generate widespread or self-sustaining rural development or a competitive industrial export sector. The result: an absence of strong forward and backward linkages between agriculture and industry (which brought economic prosperity to Taiwan), chronic high foreign indebtedness, and difficulties competing in international markets with industrial goods.

To be sure, over the years Mexico's party-led state has incorporated rural peasants and certain provincially based middle classes in ways that eluded Argentina and partially paralleled the KMT experience. This may help explain why now, as the new millennium unfolds, the Argentine economy is suffering through a serious economic crisis while Mexico is considered much more economically stable, a point to which I will return later in this chapter. In their openness to more modest rural populations, in fact, Mexico, South Korea, and Taiwan actually share some similarities. Yet even in Mexico, despite the PRI's avowed rural orientation, rural middle-class formation was not strongly encouraged by state policy. Only now, in fact, with the Partido Acción Nacional (PAN) defeating the PRI on the national level, do we see these biases beginning to change in Mexico. And if they continue to do so, we may see some of the longer-term economic stability that characterizes East Asian countries like South Korea and Taiwan. Indeed, one thing that differentiates the now-ruling

PAN from the PRI is its historically strong support from middle classes generally and rural middle classes in particular, especially those in the most productive northern agricultural provinces of the country. This party's rise to presidential power came in 2000 on the heels of changing agricultural and land policies that helped strengthen domestic and international markets for rural goods produced by many independent small farmers. Thus, it may be the contemporary Mexican state's new orientation toward rural production and the strengthening of rural middle classes, combined with the PAN's rise to state power, that could give Mexico a chance of nearing Taiwan on the development spectrum.

Still, the question that remains is why this has taken so long to happen. Why did rural middle classes fail to strongly embed themselves in party politics and the state in earlier periods, especially during the initial drive for industrialization at mid-century? This question is compelling not just because it may hold the key to understanding Mexico's past and future development prospects, but also because the limited political sway of rural middle classes in the post–World War II Mexican state seems both surprising and counterintuitive when considered in light of Mexico's much-celebrated revolutionary history and the agrarian reforms it generated. Mexico is one of the few Latin American countries to have committed to a serious land reform – a fact that should place it in a similar location on a rural middle-class formation continuum as Taiwan and South Korea. The imposition of land reform itself suggests that smaller-scale rural producers should have mattered much more in both national politics and the government's developmental vision than they did. Just as important, Mexico is a country whose Revolution, early in the period of modern state formation, was advanced in no small part by rural middle classes. It was rural middle classes who first dominated the state after the Revolution, not industrial workers or even big manufacturing capitalists, and with their ascendant political power and presence they were in a perfect situation to increase their institutional capacity to advance a disciplinary developmental model in which the concerns of smaller-scale agricultural producers were central. So why did Mexico's rural middle classes eventually fall out of the picture, and how did their fate in these regards establish limits to Mexico's macroeconomic development potential? These are the questions that guide this chapter.

Because by now I have shared evidence from three other cases that support my claim that rural middle-class embeddedness appears central to a country's disciplinary development potential, by virtue of the extent to which it will endow the government with a willingness and capacity to impose performance standards on capitalists and laborers while also tying industrial production to agricultural development through sustained forward and backward linkages, my principal aims in this chapter are somewhat different from those in the previous ones. First, I seek to account for the *disappearance* of rural middle classes from Mexican state institutions and from the government's overall development vision. Second, I seek to explain exactly how and why other classes – mainly urban-based capitalists and laborers – successfully embedded themselves in the revolutionary state instead. Both aims, together, give us a picture of twentieth-century Mexican state formation and how it differed from Argentina, Taiwan, and South Korea. Only after I have established how and why Mexican state formation took the form it did, without significant rural middle-class embeddedness (thus leading to the unfulfilled promise of disciplinary development), will I turn attention to the emergence of the alternative: the consolidation of an "accommodating" development strategy, defined in terms of the Mexican state's willingness to accommodate the short-term economic priorities of industrial capitalists and the employment concerns of their laborers.

In explaining the demise of the rural middle-class vision of small and medium-scale agriculture, and the emergence of an alternative developmental vision built on policies that accommodated the urban and economic requisites of industrial capitalists and their laborers, I draw on the analytic apparatus that has emerged as significant in the narratives of the previous chapters, primarily the spatial, social, political, and ethnic history of the nation. I demonstrate that struggles over regional, racial, and class identities and political power irreparably divided the rural middle class in Mexico, and then I suggest that it was the failure of rural middle classes to unite and forge stable political alliances among themselves and with the urban middle class, as occurred in Taiwan, for example, that accounts for the shift from disciplinary to accommodating development in Mexico. In short, it was Mexico's contested political history, with its peculiar middle-class and state-formative effects, that determined this nation's developmental trajectories. The chapter concludes with a discussion of the longer-term implications of the demise of the rural middle-class underpinnings of the PRI and the state, ranging from the dominance of the capital city and its populations to the relative neglect of the countryside and the failure to establish strong and generative forward and backward linkages between agriculture and industry. After chronicling the rural middle-class shift from being victors to victims of the Revolution, the chapter ends with a brief discussion of contemporary politics and the paradoxical ways that the accommodating development policies pursued by the PRI ultimately remotivated a rural middle-class and regional challenge to one-party rule, ushering in the possibility of a renewed commitment to disciplinary development in Mexico today.

Revolution and the Rural Middle Class

The most popular view of the Mexican Revolution is that poor, primarily landless peasants joined with industrial workers and semiskilled urban artisans to overthrow General Porfirio Díaz in 1910. Poor rural folk were most likely to have lost their lives in the violent struggle against the troops of the dictatorship, and their leaders Emiliano Zapata and Dorotco Arango (aka Pancho Villa) still stand as folk heroes of the Revolution.[2] Less celebrated but equally significant to the revolutionary process, however, were the military generals (Venustiano Carranza, Plutarco Elias Calles, and Alvaro Obregón) and liberal intellectuals (Franciso I. Madero) from northern provinces of the country who participated in battle and later commanded the Mexican state in the postrevolutionary period, a majority of whom were drawn from the rural middle class. Even when they came from large landowning families, these revolutionary forces nonetheless traced their social origins and political networks to regions where small and medium-scale agricultural production predominated.

That Mexico's Revolution is so frequently discussed in worker and peasant terms, with only minimal mention of its rural middle-class protagonists, except in terms of their political (not class) leadership, probably owes to the fact that most scholars of the topic have been directly influenced by class-conflict models of revolution. For this reason, Mexico's peasants, or *campesinos*, are usually treated as the rural equivalent of the working class: landless and exploited forces struggling against large landlords if not against the penetration of capitalism into the Mexican countryside.[3] But without small and medium-sized agricultural producers' and northern liberals' support for restoring *Tierra y*

---

[2] Both Villa and Zapata, who came from northern and southern Mexico respectively, were known for their courage in battling for the rights of an increasingly impoverished stratum of rural folk, who themselves struggled mightily to survive in a country increasingly dominated by large landowners (*hacendados*), and whose small-scale production activities and overall livelihoods were being threatened by the proletarianization, debt peonage, and increasing commercialization of agriculture during the last decades of the nineteenth century and the early years of the twentieth. Because many of these rural folk saw Porfirio Díaz's support for both foreign capitalists and hacendados as harbingers of their own economic and social decline, they joined Villa and Zapata in the revolutionary struggle against the Díaz dictatorship.

[3] The long-standing existence of the traditional village and communally owned land in Mexico partially explains why the concept of peasant is used more than rural middle class to describe small-scale producers. Generally speaking, it is the involvement in exchange rather than use value that serves as one of the main criteria used by anthropologists and other social scientists to distinguish the peasantry from other rural small producers; and generally speaking, studies of traditional societies have suggested that private property ownership is generally considered to facilitate production practices and the shift from use to exchange value. Yet in Mexico, owing to historical legacies of *ejidal* land ownership, production for market exchange is not uniquely tied to ownership status (or individual private property rights, to be more specific), or vice versa, as it is in many other contexts, given the historical patterns of communal and village land rights that fostered small-scale production by individual farmers even when land was collectively owned and operated. Moreover, many traditional Indian villages straddled both worlds, not just by virtue of the fact that small-scale cultivators and family farmers served as the mainstay of what is referred to as the village and communal economies, but also because these cultivators often produced for both exchange and use value.

Libertad (Land and Liberty), the rallying cry of the Revolution, Mexico might not have had its revolution at all.

Under the political leadership of Francisco I. Madero, a prominent provincial politician with a liberal agenda, Mexico began the slow process of revolutionary consolidation, in no small part built around the introduction of agrarian reform. Madero's support for the Revolution may have owed partly to his commitment to a liberalization of Mexican politics; but he also came from a rural property-owning family, and he relied for support upon a wide variety of like-minded rural-based independent producer protagonists who shared a great deal of his political vision.[4] One of Madero's first acts as president was to introduce new policies "favorable to the growth and protection of small-holdings (*pequeña propiedad*)," with "a division of landed wealth that would create a prosperous smallholding class, conducive to peace, stability, and constitutional government."[5] It was Madero who first acknowledged the postrevolutionary state's agrarian commitment and whose participation cemented the government's rural middle-class underpinnings.[6]

Like many Mexican revolutionaries, one reason Madero and his provincially based allies from both north and south supported agrarian reform was their worry that the government of Porfirio Díaz had begun to undermine smaller and medium-scale rural production on agricultural properties in the provinces, especially among those more modest producers less integrated into the increasingly globalized capitalist economy of Mexico. This concern, one

---

[4] Knight, among others, has argued that "the popular elements which contributed most to the overthrow not just of Díaz but of the entire Porfirian order came [first] from . . . the villagers, sharecroppers and small holders who had suffered from the rapacity of *hacendado, ranchero,* and *cacique,*" with *serrano* peoples (themselves small cultivators in large part) second, and urban artisans third. See his *The Mexican Revolution,* Vol. 1, p. 169. To be sure, Knight's text could be interpreted in two ways, with "agrarista peasantry, the villagers, sharecroppers and small holders" intended to refer to four distinct and mutually exclusive social forces. Yet given the larger argument in the book and Knight's own historically and empirically grounded attention to detail, I proceed under the assumption that he offers the phrase "agrarista peasantry" not to refer to a distinct class force but as a general rubric.

[5] Ibid., p. 418.

[6] Gilly, another leading interpreter of the Revolution, also identifies the middle-class roots of the movement, although in a much more pejorative way. He claims that Mexico's revolutionary forces differed "from [the leaders of] other peasant parties in history," in that they were composed primarily of "petty-bourgeois careerists, illusionists, adventurers, waverers, and spongers" (Gilly, *The Mexican Revolution,* p. 158). While in this characterization of the Revolution's petit bourgeois roots Gilly may fail to situate his protagonists in space, or employment dynamics, as specifically *rural* middle class, once we recognize like Knight that the forces to which he refers were involved in small and medium-scale agricultural production, or hailed from provinces where these activities predominated, we do see considerable analytic agreement between Gilly and Knight on the middle-class origins of key rural protagonists.

should note, was not that different than that which preoccupied Park Chung Hee in Korea, albeit a few decades later. Revolutionary opposition to Diaz and complicity in the project of agrarian reform also owed to concerns about the growing power and impunity of large landlords and an agrarian oligarchy that, through their connections to Mexico City and/or foreign investors abroad, were seen as dominating the regions and undermining the economic livelihood of smaller producers. Often this stance is identified as resting primarily in the southern forces of the Revolution, especially those allied with Emiliano Zapata. Yet, among the four revolutionary leaders responsible for crafting the Plan de Ayala, the so-called blueprint for Revolution, Madero was the only one to have actively advocated the formation of primarily small plots of land. Zapata did not specify plot size, preferring to struggle over the terms of expropriation; Villa argued for a much larger standard plot size (twenty-five hectares); and Carranza left size criteria unspecified, preferring to ambiguously call for an amount "sufficient to reconstruct."[7]

To underscore Madero's position on small plot sizes is by no means to place him on a staunchly "peasant" or "radical" end of the land reform spectrum, since he always balanced his support for small farms with an insistence that these plots should be sold to farmers (and only to original owners) on the basis of lands bought (not expropriated) from large landlords, who would be fully compensated for damages in return. Madero's policies on land reform were geared mainly toward the "reconstruction" of village-based *ejidal* lands that had been lost through previous constitutional reforms (which themselves had paved the way for the absorption of village lands by large property holders), and as such they did not grow out of any general commitment to revolutionizing the class structure of rural society, let alone any serious desire to use the state to catapult indigenous rural folk and impoverished village residents out of poverty in any wholesale fashion. As Madero himself stated in a newspaper interview in June 1912, "I have always advocated the formation of small holdings, but that does not mean that people should go and dispossess any landowner. . . . It is one thing to form small holdings through constant effort, and another to divide up the big properties."[8] This contrasted with the view advanced by Zapata and Villa, who called for massive expropriation and not compensation.

Essentially, Madero supported a market-based solution in which there were limits to expropriation, a view quite consistent with a more traditional rural middle-class vision of society. Moreover, just as in the South Korean experiment

---

[7] Sanderson, *Land Reform in Mexico*, p. 40. Madero's support for small plots was presented in his 1910 Plan de San Luis Potosi, while Zapata articulated his position in the 1911 Plan de Ayala. Villa and Carranza made their positions known somewhat later, in the Agrarian Law of 1915 and the Decree of 1915, respectively.

[8] Cf. Gilly, *The Mexican Revolution*, p. 90.

under Park, Madero's support for land reform was coupled with a concern for improvements in technology and productive inputs as much as a redivision of land, and they were built upon a basic philosophy "'that land should be made available to those who had the resources and the ambition to work it and make it pay; there were to be no gifts, nor was the government to sustain a financial loss from the program.'"[9] For these reasons, regulation of debt peonage and equalization of rural taxation were key elements in his new government's agrarian program, two elements that fitted well with the concerns of small and medium-sized producers who were disadvantaged by the stunning economic successes of large property owners under the Porfiriato.[10]

Still, it would be a mistake to trace the country's initial orientation toward agrarian reform to the personal whims or goals of one man. When Madero was assassinated in 1913 – in no small part because of his position on land reform[11] – the Revolution remained in the hands of those with a similarly petit bourgeois agrarian agenda, despite the fact that his death opened new space for more radical elements in the revolutionary coalition (including Villa and Zapata), to push for a more radical agenda. Some scholars have identified the next phase of revolutionary state building, beginning in 1914 after Madero's death, as signaling a "leftward" turn in the revolutionary struggle. But even then, the agrarian reform introduced by the revolutionary leadership

[9] Knight, *The Mexican Revolution*, p. 419.

[10] Taking a position on land reform was not easy for Madero, who also was concerned with cementing support from urban constituencies, especially the urban middle class that shared his liberal, antidictatorship vision. But especially as labor organizations began protesting the reformist character of many of his new policies, Madero found himself at greater political risk and in a highly unstable position, not just vis-à-vis the conservative forces still loyal to Díaz, but also vis-à-vis other revolutionary leaders who took a more radical view of the Revolution in its entirety. This was especially true with respect to those revolutionary leaders who were struggling on behalf of disenfranchised rural populations, namely, Zapata and Villa. Worried that he would not be able to count on fellow revolutionaries to support him as he struggled against conservative counterrevolutionaries, within a year Madero shifted gears slightly on the agrarian question, offering a new version of land reform that recognized the demands of peasant radicals while also keeping some commitment to property ownership. Working with the nation's leading agronomist, Luis Cabrera, Madero strongly argued for the renewed defense and reinvigoration of communal lands (ejidos) as a basis for employment and rural production, a policy stance that he and Cabrera articulated through the *Comisión Nacional Agraria* (National Agrarian Commission).

[11] Madero's position on land reform spurred the "creole" (mixed race) elite to withdraw support even as it alienated what Adolfo Gilly calls the right wing of the revolutionary coalition, identified most directly in the person of General Huerta. See Gilly, *The Mexican Revolution*, p. 98. According to Molina Enriquez, *La revolución agraria*, p. 119, moreover, both sets of forces rejected Madero's agrarian reform policies both as a sign of "a brutal, crude, and savage agrarian socialism for the popular classes" and as a fundamental challenge to their capacity to concentrate and own large parcels of land.

was not that far from the rural middle-class-inspired one originally offered by the more centrist Madero, especially in regard to the position on restoring lands to the original owners. These continuities in agrarian reform policy are clear with a closer view to the agrarian reform introduced by Madero's predecessor, General Venustiano Carranza, whose 1915 decree on agrarian reform was later enshrined in the 1917 Constitution. In the words of Andrés Molina Enríquez, Carranza "not only insisted on the principles already fixed by the Agrarian Government of Madero, and not only was it administered by the same body that [the Madero] government had created to resolve agrarian questions, it also established procedures to facilitate the positive execution of those [same] resolutions."[12] The 1917 Constitution thus gave the state the power to appropriate large holdings in order to support smaller plots, even as it "establish[ed] a guarantee for small property owners . . . insuring that in all cases of land grants [the state] would 'ALWAYS respect small agricultural properties' [emphasis in original]."[13]

All this is not to say that Madero's and Carranza's agrarian policies were identical. The Carranza regime actually ended up taking one step further than did Madero by making it constitutionally possible for the state to expropriate "necessary lands" immediately adjoining restored plots[14] and to encroach on large *hacendados* (in a modification that came much later, in December 1920), despite the fact that Carranza himself was a large hacendado and held greater elective affinity with this large landowning class than did Madero.[15] Yet it is also true that the appropriation clause was intended to serve as a last resort, to be realized primarily when other means for distributing land were judged to be insufficient. As such, Carranza's agrarian reforms also were conceived in the context of a genuinely rural middle-class view of the importance and aims of sustained agrarian production by independent farmers, with the state resorting to appropriation not just to insure "an equal distribution and conservation of the public wealth," but also to aid the "development of private property . . . and the development of agriculture."[16]

---

[12] Ibid., p. 161.

[13] Mendieta y Nuñez, *Política agraria*, p. 28.

[14] Sanderson, *Land Reform in Mexico*, p. 40.

[15] Some of this had to do with the fact that Carranza needed support from some of the more radical revolutionary forces to sustain his hold on power. Both Zapata and Villa found considerable elective affinity with small or independent producer ideals that were embodied in Carranza's agrarian reform proposals, perhaps because Carranza so skillfully left many of the land reform provisions unstated (compensation of large landowners, plot size, tenure type). Yet Villa himself came from a ranching family, while Zapata had long insisted on limiting the principal "aims of the peasantry . . . to land ownership," a fact that inspired Gilly to identify even Villa's ideology as "petty-bourgeois." See Gilly, *The Mexican Revolution*, p. 83.

[16] Molina Enriquez, *La revolución agraria*, p. 188.

With both Madero's and Carranza's legislations setting the initial course, a rural middle-class vision of land reform dominated government policies in the immediate postrevolutionary period.[17] Much of this owed to the fact that their political successors were probably even more authentically committed to the small-producer vision than even they were. Starting in 1918, Generals Plutarco Elias Calles and Alvaro Obregón came to power, two men whom Adolfo Gilly calls "the petty bourgeoisie from Sonora State" and who were assumed to have "finally prevailed over Carranza's bourgeois-landowner tendency."[18] Most of the officers who threw their loyalty and allegiance to these revolutionary generals of Sonora also "came from the provincial petty bourgeoisie (office-workers, schoolteachers, well-off farmers)."[19] Sonora itself was a northern state whose economy was built around ranching and whose people were heavily involved in yeoman farming and other forms of independent agricultural production.[20] The typical Sonoran *ranchero* was described as an agriculturalist who "lives on the land, works it himself, and depends for his living upon the crops which he cultivates."[21] The Sonoran economy and the orientations of its citizens and military leaders in many ways paralleled those which Park Chung Hee sought to

---

[17] Historical scholars might identify the source of continuities in agrarian policies after the defeat of Madero as owing to the long-standing tradition of Mexican struggles to establish the conditions for small proprietorship in the countryside, especially among Indian populations, as much as to any shared political vision between Madero and his revolutionary successors. The independence battles of the mid-nineteenth century had been fought in no small part over large landownership (although they revolved mostly around large plots of land owned and controlled by the Catholic Church and colonial rulers). Many of the same issues and themes that emerged in the independence struggles, moreover, were carried forward in the 1910 Revolution by moderate and radical forces alike. And in much the same way as their revolutionary descendants, the independence reforms also were intended to help establish a new cadre of "yeoman farmers" and thus a sizable rural middle class in the Mexican countryside. For more on yeoman farming, see Nugent, *Spent Cartridges*, p. 52. For more on rural claims during the colonial and independence periods, see Whetten, *Rural Mexico*, p. 153.

[18] *The Mexican Revolution*, p. 329.

[19] Ibid., p. 102.

[20] Calles and Obregón came from the northern state of Sonora, and both traced their origins to families with moderate or large landholdings. They also counted on loyalty and support from fellow *rancheros*, even those of more modest plot sizes, who predominated in this region. And within the revolutionary leadership, Calles and Obregón were not alone in bringing a rural middle-class vision into the policy embrace of the new government. Another of the Revolution's key northern generals, Francisco J. Múgica, also traced his roots to this northern property-owning region of the nation, although he took a more radical stance on land reform than did some of his geographic counterparts, closer in content to the position taken by Zapata and Villa, who represented the aims of smaller and medium-sized producers.

[21] McBride, *The Land Systems of Mexico*, p. 88. McBride further argues that the ranchero "is thus the agriculturalist of the country in a far truer sense than the *hacendado*, whose chief interest,

produce in rural South Korea during his first decade in office, further explaining both countries' common adherence to agrarian reform and to agrarian development policies built around considerable support for small and medium-scale agricultural production. And with these views and rural middle-class forces dominant within the newly minted revolutionary state, Mexico sat poised on a path that held the promise of delivering disciplinary development of the variety that benefited its East Asian counterparts.

Constructing a Rural Middle Class

So what happened? Clearly, the problem was not a lack of commitment, vision, or energy on the part of Mexico's new political leadership, which worked hard to inculcate the rural middle-class vision among the agrarian populace in ways that strongly paralleled the South Korean and Taiwanese experiences. Under the guiding hand of the Sonoran dynasty, the rural middle-class ethos of discipline and the commitment to small-farmer development were given life in the policy, rhetoric, and constitutional clauses that governed Mexican politics and society in the subsequent two decades. Starting in 1920 with the Obregón administration, the government accelerated land distribution to achieve its agrarian reform aims, with General Obregón's successor, General Calles, explicitly devoting much of his energies to developing a nation of rural middle classes. Calles was very deliberate in these regards, publicly identifying himself as "a firm believer in the institution of private property" who regarded "the *ejido* as a training school which should be encouraged for the purpose of developing a nation of peasant proprietors," an aim he advanced by enacting a "law to permit the crop *ejidos* to be divided into plots among the individual members."[22] Calles, in fact, was known for advancing "a prudent concern for public order [and] a profound Puritan sensibility," to use Alan Knight's words, sentiments further evidenced by his sacking of underlings for their "lack of 'discipline and morality' [and] for displaying 'deeply rooted, perverse habits.'"[23]

The pledge to establish and maintain a class of smaller-scale landowners was evident not just in statements or disciplinary moralizing endorsed by individual revolutionary leaders, it was also manifested in a variety of governmental programs and policies whose aim was to make peasants into economically productive rural middle classes. Some of the most visible of these policies were introduced by the Secretaria de Educación Pública (SEP), which was created in 1921 with a goal of inculcating the political culture of the Revolution in

as we have seen, is an assured revenue and the prestige which he may derive from possession of an estate and who, as a rule, lives upon his farm only a few weeks or days each year," p. 88.

[22] Whetten, *Rural Mexico*, p. 124.

[23] *The Mexican Revolution*, Vol. 1, p. 444.

the nation's youth. Early on, the commitment to a rural middle-class vision of agrarian transformation was identified as a key objective for the country's teachers, who were being trained to transform the country's rural folk into "scientifically informed commercial producers."[24] The SEP's dynamic founder and first minister, José Vasconcelos, felt that one of his ministry's key aims was to "take the *campesino* under [his] wing" and "teach him to increase his production through the use of better tools and methods."[25] Much of the Mexican state's rural education policy, in fact, was devoted to instructing rural populations on how to become more efficient farmers as well as more educated citizens. Subsequent national education policies built on a pedagogy of action education drawn from European and American theorists such as John Dewey, Adolfo Ferriere, and Maria Montessori, but directed this action to "creat[ing] the religion of duty" among rural folk.[26] This was a notion of education that, according to Mary Kay Vaughan, was shared by many middle-class pedagogues in Mexico at the time, whose aim was to "'liberate' Mexicans from their 'feudal' heritage prior to *disciplining them for development* [emphasis mine]."[27]

It is telling that rural teachers in Mexico played such a leading role in seeking to establish a cultural infrastructure for Mexico's future economic development, since this further echoes the experience of South Korea under Park Chung Hee, himself an ex–rural schoolteacher. In both cases, teachers channeled the hopes and aspirations of rural families toward an ostensibly modern and more prosperous future, often because many of these federally appointed educators "shared a common background in the modest middle class, predominantly rural but sometimes urban."[28] And as in South Korea under Park, and especially after the implementation of the Saemaul program, many of these activities were geared toward generating a disciplined, efficient, morally pure, and dutiful cadre of small rural producers. John Dewey's former student from Columbia Teacher's College, Moisés Sáenz, who was SEP undersecretary from 1925 to 1928, took the view that "the rural Mexican was an enslaved peon whom the school would convert into a farmer" capable of sustained production and reinvestment. Sáenz was not alone in conceptualizing peasants

---

[24] Vaughan, *Cultural Politics*, p. 4. This book provides a fascinating account of the role of the SEP in producing postrevolutionary political culture in Mexico.

[25] Ibid., p. 28.

[26] Much of this occurred under the administration of another revolutionary activist, Salvador Alvarado, a revolutionary activist who served as governor of the Yucatan in 1915 and who became secretary of education in 1923.

[27] *Cultural Politics*, p. 27. Secretary of Education Salvador Alvarado introduced various measures to achieve these aims. According to Vaughan, he "ended debt peonage on haciendas, closed cantinas to 'free' the poor from alcohol, excoriated the church as a repressor of human will and knowledge, and sought to free women from domestic cloistering through education, job opportunities and civic mobilization," p. 27.

[28] Ibid., p. 12.

as protopetit bourgeois, who only needed the proper discipline and training. Rafael Ramírez, architect of SEP's so-called Cultural Mission program, felt that "*campesinos* were ignorant, rude, inefficient, violent, and beset with vices. They did not properly disinfect or select seeds for planting. They misapplied water. By felling trees, they destroyed the soil." For Ramírez and countless others, one of the new government's main goals was to insure that "all customs, beliefs, and ideas that undermined the improvement of 'productive capacity' had to be swept aside."[29] Peasants, in short, had to be turned into small capitalists.

Sáenz's and Ramírez's remarks may have evidenced a cultural conceit and arrogant (if not racist) snobbishness about rural folk, bordering on repugnant moralizing. But these policies, whose main aim was to generate a productive class of small producers capable of leading national economic growth, were not entirely different from those advocated by some of the Revolution's more radical leaders, including those quite sympathetic to Mexico's peasant populations and indigenous peoples more generally. General Lázaro Cárdenas, who succeeded Calles as the head of the revolutionary family and governed Mexico from 1934 to 1940, was known for his strong commitment to both peasant and working-class causes; yet he also supported a version of this rural middle-class vision by promoting certain development projects. One of the most telling was his funding of the Bajo Rio Bravo agricultural project in the cotton-producing regions of the north, built on the assumption that "national progress depended on turning migrant and landless rural workers into property-owning, politically stable, middle class farmers; and that it was the state's responsibility to oversee this process."[30]

The postrevolutionary government's efforts to create a more efficient, morally pure, and well-disciplined cadre of rural producers, combined with the state's constitutionally sanctioned commitment to small-scale rural production and land reform as national goals, highlight several important similarities between the actions and orientations of political leaders in Mexico and post–World War II South Korea and Taiwan. Just as in the East Asian cases, Mexico's postrevolutionary government committed itself early on to land reform. And even though it did not make the same substantial headway as was made in East Asia, it did redistribute lands and support smaller-scale production starting in 1916 in ways that were entirely absent in Argentina. Equally startling is

---

[29] Ibid., pp. 28–29. The high-ranking official making comments about *campesino* productive capacity was Rafael Ramírez, architect of the SEP's *Misiones Culturales*.

[30] Walsh, "Eugenic Acculturation," p. 11. For more on the racial dimension of this, see Walsh's Ph.D. diss., Department of Anthropology, New School for Social Research, 2001. For more on state projects intended to turn agricultural workers and sharecroppers into property-owning small farmers, see Aboites, *La irrigación revolucionaria: Historica del sistema nacional de riego del Rio Conchas, Chihuahua, 1927–1938*, SEP, CIESAS, 1987.

the fact that both the individuals and political coalitions behind these policies shared a strikingly similar social profile. It was not just that the leadership of the postrevolutionary Mexican state traced its parentage and main political support to rural middle classes as much as any single other class base, as in South Korea and Taiwan, but also that those establishing the principal ideological contours of the revolutionary project found an elective affinity between rural middle-class and *military* identity, just as in East Asia, where the ethos of military discipline derived from and reinforced the ethos of rural middle-class discipline.[31] And this was true not just for Obregón, Calles, and Cárdenas, but also for some of the most fervently ideological rural protagonists of the Revolution, including Pancho Villa.

Villa, in particular, saw the mixing of small farmer and military identity and experience as laying the basic foundations for a new and more honorable society. In an interview with John Reed, who questioned Villa about his vision for the future, Villa once stated:

> We will put the army to work. In all parts of the Republic we will establish military colonies composed of the veterans of the Revolution. The State will give them grants of agricultural lands and establish big industrial enterprises to give them work. Three days a week they will work and work and work hard, because honest work is more important than fighting, and only honest work makes good citizens. And the other three days they will receive military instruction and go out and teach all the people how to fight. Then, when the Patria is invaded, we will just have to telephone from the palace at Mexico City, and in half a day all the Mexican people will rise from their fields and factories, fully armed, equipped, and organized to defend their children and their homes. My ambition is to live my life in one of those military colonies among my *compañeros* whom I love, who have suffered so long and so deeply with me. I believe that it would be desirable for the government to establish a factory to cut hides, where we could make nice chairs and horsebits, because I know how to do it; the rest of the time I would devote to working my small farm (*granja*), breeding cattle and planting corn. It would be magnificent, I believe, to help make Mexico a happy place.[32]

---

[31] Tannenbaum underscores the importance of the military underpinnings of the new state by noting that Mexico's Constitution "was written by the *soldiers* of the Revolution," while the main decisions about what key clauses were to form the constitutional foundations of the postrevolutionary state remained "in the hands of the soldiers – generals, colonels, majors – men who had marched and counter-marched across the Republic and had fought its battles." See Tannenbaum, *Peace by Revolution*, p. 166.

[32] Quoted in Córdova, *La ideología de la revolución mexicana*, pp. 158–159.

Villa's references to those working in both factory and field also suggest that his vision for Mexico's future was not that far from that which eventually materialized in Taiwan, where any stark dichotomization of city and countryside, farmer and worker, region and nation was effectively transcended. Moreover, in his conceptualization of veterans and ex-military personnel as central actors in the country's economic future and national defense, in his preoccupation with hard work, in his loyalty to small-scale production, and in his overall vision of a national economy built around work in both factory and farm, Villa's orientation keenly parallels the vision of disciplined soldier-farmers advocated in Taiwan if not also South Korea.

To be sure, Villa was ideologically sidelined in his efforts to triumph within the revolutionary leadership, a defeat which may account for some of Mexico's failure to pursue a more East Asian–like developmental path. But even so, the long-standing connection between military and rural middle-class identities was well entrenched in the history of the Mexican military, so that even if Villa's factory-farm nexus may have faded from the postrevolutionary state project, the small-farmer component did not. Generally speaking, there was a long tradition of connection between rural life and the military service, especially in northern regions of the country, home to much of the postrevolutionary leadership. According to Nathan Whetten, soldiers in Mexico formed the foundation for rural property-owning classes of all sizes, owing to the fact that some of the first land grants were "made to Spanish soldiers who had become farmers in Spain and who expressed a willingness to become colonists in the New World."[33] In the early 1800s an entirely new province (in the Isthmus of Tehuantepec) was created to give soldiers "opportunities to become farmers. Common soldiers were entitled to receive holdings of about 10 acres, and officers received larger grants according to their rank."[34] In subsequent years the government enacted further legislation for the purpose of promoting settlement in the sparsely populated northern areas of the Republic.

These northern parts of the country also were the site of long-standing wars between Apache Indians and Spanish (and later Mexican) colonizers, such that throughout the eighteenth and nineteenth centuries government troops who fought and triumphed in these wars were granted lands in this region as a form of payment.[35] Even when the overall purpose was to "colonize" these more problematic and remote regions, land was given to the military in order to insure their continued presence, not merely as a reward for past loyalty or service. One result was a constant shifting back and forth between cultivation and military activities, a pattern of employment later evidenced by the fact that

---

[33] *Rural Mexico*, p. 152.

[34] Ibid., p. 155.

[35] For more on this, see Nugent, *Spent Cartridges*, especially Chap. 2.

many of the northern troops loyal to Obregón and other northern revolutionary generals had traditionally "looked to army service as a means for subsistence for themselves and their families, in times when better-paid work was not available."[36] These historical legacies produced an elective affinity between the rural middle-class farming and military experiences, a factor which may further explain the strong support for the rural middle-class vision among the Revolution's northern leadership.

Whatever its origins, a military mentality was well entrenched among the rural middle classes in Mexico's northern provinces and vice versa, so much that it became a part of the revolutionary heritage. Daniel Nugent goes so far as to say that the political, economic, and military history of the country helped constitute "a new category of person" whom he refers to as "'soldier/farmers' or an 'armed peasantry.'"[37] And even if Nugent's appropriation of the term "soldier/farmer" as a common occupational category comes from a focused study of one particular village, Namiquipa, nestled in a highly militarized area of the country, the soldier/farmer identity was quite pervasive, especially in the north. Some of the Revolution's greatest leaders saw themselves in precisely these terms, that is, as embodying the combination of both military and independent producer mentalities in which self-discipline and self-sacrifice was a preeminent moral aim, while these views also were shared by scholars and laymen who ranged across the political and ideological spectrum.[38] One of the major agronomists of the postrevolutionary period and one whose political sentiments most probably lay with the liberal revolutionaries (if not the Porfirista sympathizers), Zeferino Domínguez, actually produced a 1913 book titled *El servicio militar agrario y la pequeña propiedad* in which he argued against big landholdings (*gran propiedad*), urged caution about industrializing agricultural production too rapidly, and philosophized about the elective affinity between sacrifice for country, family, and property (*tierra*).[39] Domínguez further argued that the government owed a great debt to those who actively participated in military service, an idea that inspired him to propose the creation of military colonies, or what he called either *haciendas militares* or *colonias agrario-militares*, to reward and economically sustain Mexico's military forces.[40]

---

[36] Gilly, *The Mexican Revolution*, p. 103.

[37] *Spent Cartridges*, p. 47.

[38] It is also worth noting that General (and then President) Calles, one of the most powerful and enduring leaders of the postrevolutionary period, served as a police chief in the northern state of Sonora before the Revolution. With his family identified as well-to-do farmers as well, he personally embodied the mixing of a quasi-military and rural middle-class mentality.

[39] See in particular the chapter (pp. 5–19) titled "El problema agrario y el problema agricola con relación a la paz y la prosperidad de la nación mexicana" in Domínguez, *El servicio military*.

[40] These ideas are advanced on pp. 23–27, in the chapter titled "El servicio militar-agrario y la pequeña propiedad" in *El servicio militar*.

But if Mexican ideas about the importance of creating a vibrant class of small producers and entrusting national development to soldier-farmers so clearly paralleled the ideas proposed in South Korea under Park, and even in Taiwan where the KMT was known for investing considerable government resources in the development of agricultural colonies for soldiers and veterans who fought against communist forces on the mainland, the question again arises as to why Mexico ultimately failed to pursue the East Asian model. Much of the answer lies in a closer examination of the contradictions and tensions within the rural middle-class coalition governing Mexico in the postrevolutionary period. In both the South Korean and Taiwanese cases it was a unity of military and rural middle-class identities that helped reinforce a disciplinary ethos between and among the state and its key social and political bases, a unity that further sustained the state's willingness and capacity to impose a disciplinary development model. This pattern was hard to replicate in Latin America. In Argentina, for example, both historically and especially under Perón, the military's urban origins provided more scope for alliance making with industrial laborers and capitalists in such a way as to dis-empower the rural middle classes both in the military and national politics at large, thereby foreclosing the option of disciplinary development. And in Mexico, the pattern was different still.

In contrast to Argentina and more like South Korea and Taiwan, Mexico's military historically was more rural than urban-oriented. Yet at the same time, Mexico's military was quite divided in class terms, especially after the Revolution. This owed not just to the historical development of the military as an institution, as in Argentina, but also to the fact that the Revolution itself enlarged the military to include peasants and a small cadre of large landowners alongside the rural middle classes. Thus, even though shared rural origins and a common concern for rural conditions helped bring the various revolutionary forces in Mexico together around the issue of agrarian reform, as occurred in East Asia, the social class and agrarian property-owning divisions that eventually permeated the revolutionary coalition – most of which were exposed if not reinforced in the constitutional and policy battles over land reform – ultimately divided the country's political leadership. And without unity, the shared commitment to a rural middle-class vision began to evaporate, as did the commitment to land reform and the promise of disciplinary development.

Whither Unity? The Contradictory Locations of Mexico's Rural Middle Classes

There were four main currents in Mexico's postrevolutionary leadership, at least as understood in terms of rural social class position, whose combined impact was to irreparably divide Mexico's rural middle class and its capacity to guarantee state discipline of industrial capitalists. These four currents corresponded largely to different positions on a property-owning spectrum, but they also divided along ideological lines, especially with respect to the question of state power versus community autonomy and the issue of compensation for expropriation. First were those who fell more on the "peasant side" of the rural middle-class continuum, many of whom organized around Emiliano Zapata. As noted earlier, Zapata unabashedly opposed large *haciendas* and prioritized smaller-scale production, although he advocated a communal form of land tenure, or at least one organized on the basis of villages.[41] Second were those who shared many of Zapata's ideals in terms of supporting the establishment of a class of individual small producers, but who differed somewhat in their support for private property ownership. Those falling into this category included Pancho Villa and his allies, who "were or wanted to be *agricultores de pequeña propiedad*" – that is to say, primarily small-scale agricultural private property owners.[42] Villa had been a small-farming sharecropper in Durango and knew the power and injustice of hacendados; and like Zapata, he felt that large landholdings – or what he once termed "grand territorial properties" – must be considered "incompatible with peace and prosperity in the Republic."[43] Both Villa and Zapata called for expropriation of all large properties and no compensation.

Standing at the opposite end of this continuum were those military leaders like Carranza and Calles who came from large landowning families. They supported agricultural development on landholdings of any size and were more interested in countering the political and economic marginalization of their region as a whole than in strongly advocating agrarian reform. Yet they did promote the importance of agricultural development and rural production. More important, these large landowners counted on smaller landowners who served with them within the military to sustain their position of leadership within the revolutionary coalition. General Alvaro Obregón and his forces, for their part, initially played this mediating role, but over time they embodied yet a fourth current in the revolutionary leadership, a "middling" position in terms of ownership and vision that straddled the claims of large and small producers.

---

[41] Zapata and his southern forces, for example, were comprised primarily of small family farmers of Indian heritage who were directly motivated in their struggle against Porfirio Díaz by the economic and political transformations that were creating new and accelerating threats to small-scale farm production. Their problems began with the collapse of small farms and whole villages, and because of their inability to compete economically with the large hacendados at the end of the nineteenth century. In the first decade of the twentieth century came the imposition of new restrictions on land titles and possession and local government edicts about whether land "could be farmed at all, on loan, rented, however possible." See Womack, Jr., *Zapata and the Mexican Revolution*, p. 53.

[42] Molina Enríquez, *La revolución agraria*, p. 156.

[43] Córdova, *La ideología de la revolución mexicana*, p. 161.

Adolfo Gilly consistently referred to Obregón as a "well-to-do small farmer" and traced much of his political ideology to this identity,[44] although Obregón's willingness and capacity to ally with both sets of forces also owed partly to the history of the region, Sonora, from whence he came. Most of the northern states of Mexico, like Sonora, were known for their more diverse rural class structure in which small, medium, and larger landholding coexisted. This state of affairs was reflected in the diversity of terminology used in these areas to refer to landholdings, ranging from *solares* and *granjas* to *medieros* (a name for small farmers with a slightly different legal relationship to their lands than ranchers) to *ranchos* to haciendas.[45] Support for some form of land reform thus emerged as a common project uniting many of the so-called northern forces into the dominant wing of the revolutionary coalition; and to the extent that in the early years of the Revolution they could count on the Zapatista-led southern forces to also rally around the call for land reform, the revolutionary coalition held. Still, given the property-owning differences within the coalition, underneath the surface conflict persisted over the exact character and extent of land reform, which ultimately blew wide open the uneasy political alliances within and between these four distinct currents.

In the beginning, emergent intra-coalition conflicts over land reform were shunted aside through a selective application of constitutional mandates and extralegal maneuvers. Carranza, who did not share Zapata's and Villa's views about expropriation, supported constitutional reforms to allow such actions; although he effectively ignored his own constitutional mandates and accomplished very little in the way of land reform or inputs for small-scale rural production, focusing his attention on military battle.[46] Even when constitutional reforms became firmly ensconced in 1917, with Carranza at the helm, large property owners still had recourse in the courts to prevent appropriation, a state of affairs that limited the sway and effectiveness of land reform policies. It took until 1932 for the Mexican Supreme Court to deny this right of *amparo* (injunction) and "remove the last serious obstacle to the

---

[44] *The Mexican Revolution*, p. 102.

[45] Whetten divides property holdings into the following categories: *solares*, or small lots less than one hectare; *granjas*, small privately owned lots from one to five hectares; *pequeña propiedad*, small holdings which were generally formed from subdivision of haciendas; *ranchos*, which range from five to a thousand hectares; and *haciendas*, or large holdings of more than a thousand hectares. For more on the different terms used to describe plots of different sizes, see *Rural Mexico*, pp. 173–177.

[46] One of the main purveyors of this view, in which Carranza is routinely lauded for efforts to address the agrarian question, is Molina Enríquez in *La revolución agraria* (Tomo 1). Molina Enríquez (pp. 163–164) sees Carranza as advancing a revolutionary position in many regards, including his implementation of monetary reforms that "scared capital and capitalists" but that ultimately "brought appreciable benefits of social renovation."

process of land redistribution."[47] Moreover, Mexico's land reform was limited in scope to certain types of village holdings and individuals, such that as early as 1921, the "law [had] automatically exclude[d] over 46,000 out of a possible 60,000 rural communities."[48] For those lucky ones who were eligible, it still took decades to redistribute land titles and institutionalize many of the ejidal and *pequeño propietario* land reform goals embodied in the Constitution, with different postrevolutionary administrations waffling on the extent of their commitment to land reform.

Originally, the enmity produced by these stances and the stalling or setbacks for land reform advocates was partially eased through the actions of Carranza's successor, Obregón, who worked hard to simplify the agrarian reform program, pursued it with somewhat more gusto, and reinforced the government's commitment to rural development, although he also turned some of his attention to industrialization.[49] Obregón's successor, Calles, went even further in acting on his agrarian concerns, albeit in a somewhat more staunchly rural middle-class direction. He was known for being a "firm believer in the institution of private property," and he sustained perhaps the most active promotion of small-scale rural development of all, enacting a law to "permit the crops of the ejidos to be divided into plots among the individual members."[50] Calles, in fact, distributed even more land than Obregón, a set of actions that explains why he initially was considered one of the strongest postrevolutionary supporters of the country's agrarian reform laws. Perhaps because his support and interpretation were so fully consistent with the rural middle-class ethos of small proprietorship, during his administration (1924–1928) Calles distributed much more land annually than did his predecessor Obregón, whose sentiments increasingly lay with the urban working class.[51] But even for Calles, there were limits to his support for agrarian reform, grounded as it was in expectations

---

[47] Tannenbaum, *Peace by Revolution*, p. 205.

[48] Ibid., p. 207.

[49] Whetten, *Rural Mexico*, p. 124.

[50] Ibid., pp. 124–125.

[51] All this is clear with closer examination of the deteriorating political relations between Calles and his immediate predecessor and main political rival, Alvaro Obregón, on the one hand, and Lázaro Cárdenas on the other. Obregón also came from Sonora, but unlike Calles, who came from a family of hacendados, Obregón traced his roots to medium-sized landowners. Because of these differences, during the 1920s Obregón became more concerned with the urban working class and labor peace rather than rural development, such that Calles and Obregón had already started to lock horns in the mid-1920s. Their conflicts were soon matched by an equally significant split in 1934 between Calles and his main political competitor for party leadership, Lázaro Cárdenas. President Cárdenas's efforts to reaffirm a national commitment to land reform, and to move the agrarian policy to the "left" of the revolutionary coalition's larger rural middle-class vision by reviving the importance of the ejido, expanding the state's powers of large landowner expropriation, and extending the scope of land reform to include

of producing a prosperous, small-farmer class of agricultural producers. He believed that market conditions and economic incentives would serve as the stimulus for greater productivity, not government programs or promotions to instill self-discipline and capitalist rationality. In the early 1930s, in fact, Calles used his influence to nearly abolish the agrarian reform program because it was not meeting his own expectations of fostering a thriving rural sector built on prosperous and self-sustaining small-scale producers. In a newspaper article published in June 1930, he is reported to have expressed such concerns frankly and with uncharacteristically minimal political camouflage:

> If we want to be sincere with ourselves we will have to confess as sons of the revolution that agrarianism, as we have understood it and practiced it up to the present time, is a failure. The happiness of the peasants cannot be assured by giving them a patch of land if they lack the preparation and the necessary elements to cultivate it. . . . On the contrary, this road will carry us to disaster, because we are creating pretensions and fomenting laziness. It is interesting to note the great number of ejidos in which the land is not cultivated; and, still, it is proposed to enlarge these ejidos. Why? If the ejido is a failure, it is useless to enlarge it. If, on the other hand, the ejido is a success, then it ought to have money to buy additional land needed and thus relieve the nation of further costs and promises to pay. . . . Up to the present we have been handing out land right and left, and the only result has been to load the nation down with a terrific financial burden. . . . What we must do is put an "up to here and no further" to our failures. . . . Each one of the state governments should fix a relatively short period within which the communities still having a right to petition for lands can do so; and, once this period has passed, *not another word on the subject*. We must then give guarantees to everybody, little and big agriculturalists [alike] so that initiative and private and public credit will be revived.[52] [Emphasis in original]

In short, Calles neither repudiated small and medium-scale agriculture nor fully embraced the type of large-scale cultivation that ultimately came to characterize many other Latin American countries – especially Argentina – in a similar period of time. He advocated a more intermediate path, itself quite consistent with a rural middle-class ethos. But he also began to place more emphasis on production and output, rather than on the importance of

agrarian workers (peons) on large haciendas, can be understood as a response to Calles's shift rightward, so to speak, and to his desire to also bring larger producers into the fold.

[52] Conversation of General Calles with "a group of friends," as reported in *El Universal*, June 23, 1930, quoted from Simpson's *The Ejido: Mexico's Way Out* and cited in Whetten, *Rural Mexico*, p. 126.

private property ownership per se, and to advocate a greater role for large as well as small producers in his vision of rural development. His position in this regard served as the glue that kept the revolutionary coalition precariously united. Yet precisely because over the long run this stance highlighted the contradictory character of the rural middle class, and exposed the differences in agrarian outlook that simmered within this rather broad political grouping, it pushed Mexico down a slippery slope of disunity.

To be sure, it was the slowly accelerating disunity that also brought new efforts to redefine the land reform program, thereby keeping this policy issue on the government's political agenda. But these measures, and the struggles over them, irreparably split the revolutionary coalition, polarizing the country enough to signal a fundamental break from the past. The irreversible nature of this growing divide became clear in the political leadership transition from Calles to Lázaro Cárdenas, who became president in 1935, and who continued the long line of military generals at the helm. Cárdenas sought to compensate for Calles's backtracking and neglect by renewing the government's commitment to land reform and pouring massive resources into rural development. Yet in reintroducing this commitment he needed political allies outside the rural sector, a requisite which brought him to match his rural development aims with an equal commitment to industrialization, which also received considerable energy and financial resources during Cárdenas's time in office. As a result, by the late 1930s a new cross-class political coalition with a distinct development vision began to materialize, one which prioritized urban concerns and urban classes over rural ones and wholeheartedly embraced urbanization-led industrialization.

But why did an issue that once united the revolutionary coalition ultimately divide it, and why did urban classes and urban concerns become so much more dominant than rural ones? One obvious explanation is that the large landlord class never disappeared, as in East Asia. Through all the ups and downs on land reform, Mexico never came close to eliminating the large landlord class or fully sustaining a substantial rural middle class. In fact, in some regions of the country – Chiapas being most infamous these days – Mexico's postrevolutionary governments tended to turn a blind eye to the persistence of large holdings and failed to foster small-scale development, even with legal and constitutional guarantees for doing so firmly in place. This situation developed in the context of informal political deals with local strongmen, or *caciques* in the local lexicon, who were treated in an extraconstitutional manner in return for their loyalty to the PRI. The persistence of an organized and politically influential (even if clandestinely operating) group of large landlords worked as a magnetic field polarizing the rural middle-class coalition from within, pushing its various currents to look outside the rural sector to strengthen their fragmented positions. Yet it was not merely the existence of property-owning divisions in the rural sector that sealed Mexico's fate. After all, it is possible to imagine conditions under which this type of contradictory class situation would offer considerable opportunities for compromise around a centrist position. This is exactly what occurred in the initial postrevolutionary period, in fact, as discussed earlier, when for the purposes of political victory political leaders proposed and supported a moderate land reform that appealed to a broad variety of farmers and independent cultivators of both small and medium sizes, that highlighted their intermediate status between peons and hacendados, and that allowed the revolutionary leadership to successfully walk a tactical line between the demands of small-scale cultivators originally allied with Zapata, medium-sized agricultural producers linked to Villa and Obregón, and larger producers who saw Carranza, himself a hacendado, as a probable ally. As such, there is nothing about a class-divided rural sector that inherently leads to unbridgeable division or self-destruction among its ranks. In order to understand why this occurred in Mexico, then, and why primarily in the latter (i.e., post-1930s) rather than the initial phase (i.e., 1915–1930) of postrevolutionary consolidation, we must look elsewhere to understand rural middle-class disunity and Mexico's abandonment of the East Asian path.

Three other factors unique to Mexico – which also distinguish it from both Taiwan and South Korea – further limited the capacity of the postrevolutionary political leadership to maintain sufficient rural middle-class unity to carry forward an independent small-farmer vision of agricultural development, or even to link rural development to industrialization in a way that sustained rather than undermined small and medium-sized agricultural production. First was the issue of regionalism, understood not just in terms of the salience of regionally specific cultural identities but also in terms of distinctive regional variations in agricultural production and economic development patterns, combined with a long history of struggle over regional autonomy. Second were questions of race and ethnicity, which divided rather than united middle classes. Third were territorial patterns of population distribution across space or, better said, the overall balance of urban and rural populations, plus the fact that national political decision making, both before and after the Revolution, emanated geographically and institutionally from Mexico City. With Mexico's rural middle classes also divided among themselves on the basis of these other identities and locations, the grounds for unity and compromise were considerably narrowed.

The persistence of different political, social, cultural, and economic traditions distributed across various regions of the country, or what I am calling regionalism, has long been a central issue in Mexico's political and economic development. Regional conflicts date at least to the period of colonialism and persisted throughout the nineteenth-century struggles for independence, emerging once again during the revolutionary period and continuing even today. Many of the stark regional differences in Mexico owe to the large territorial expanse of the nation (especially in comparison to its East Asian counterparts)

and its geophysical diversity, which embraces a topography and climate ranging from extremes of dry and barren desert plains to high mountains to trop-
ical rainforests. Colonization further exacerbated these differences, with the
Spanish settling in some of the most economically rich areas and leaving the less
resource-rich regions to native populations. A system of colonial land grants
known as the *encomienda* system, similar to that applied in Argentina, insured
that in those Mexican territories where the Spanish had most penetrated –
generally for the purposes of extracting mineral resources and primary products for mercantile trade – large property holdings predominated and these
regions were dominated by conservative political forces. Moreover, Mexico's
regions themselves varied in the extent of individually versus institutionally
owned land, the latter mostly under the hold of the Catholic Church. In regions less directly touched by Spanish colonizers and Catholic proselytizers,
property holdings tended to be smaller in size and more diverse in character, with more liberal political forces in power. In those areas dominated by
traditional Indian settlements, in contrast, communal properties were more
common, although they frequently existed side by side with large haciendas.
In traditional Indian settlements, in which land was communally held and
worked by the village (in a practice known as *calpulalli*, a preconquest system
that served as the foundation for later ejidal practices), Indians were also likely
to work full- or part-time on large plantations.[53]

Further complicating matters was the fact that in some parts of the country
each of the three forms of property ownership coexisted (individually owned,
institutionally owned, and communally owned). This had a direct impact on
the politics and culture of certain areas of the country, by making some regions
more diverse in terms of class structure, in the character of economic activities, and in the relative balance of colonial (white) to *mestizo* (mixed) to Indian
populations.[54] In central regions where farming and other agricultural activities directly fed into the Spanish-dominated mercantile trade, for example,
both urban and rural economic activities flowered, with an attendant variety
of urban and rural classes emerging.[55] In northern regions where mining or
ranching predominated, or where there was relatively little processing or exporting of agricultural goods, larger cities were absent, and so too the class
structure of that region was more rural than urban. Yet even among the latter

---

[53] For more on the historical origins and development of different landholding, see ibid.,
pp. 76–107.
[54] For a more comprehensive discussion of these regional variations, see Sanderson, *Land Reform
in Mexico*, pp. 10–37.
[55] The states of Jalisco, Veracruz, Nuevo Leon, and the central valley (in which the Mexico City
metropolitan area now rests) exemplified this pattern, hosting relatively bustling cities (i.e.,
Guadalajara, Veracruz, Monterrey, the Distrito Federal, respectively). These cities served as
intermediate points in processing and exporting the goods produced in the rural economy.

type of region, there were differences in the diversity of rural class structure, depending on the histories of land ownership and cultural traditions.[56] Southern regions, in contrast to both the above patterns, held a larger proportion of native peoples and tended to host a more polarized rural class structure, whereas in the north small, medium, and large landholdings existed side by side.

During the nineteenth century these initial differences played themselves out in independence struggles, with some regions having more or fewer colonial sympathizers, owing perhaps to their place in mercantile trading networks, and with some regions having more or less to lose with formal independence. Yet even after independence was achieved, these regional differences did not disappear, but rather accelerated, owing to further transformations in the structure of property ownership in some of the regions that had initially hosted primarily large church and other colonial property holdings. Many of the reforms introduced by the newly independent Mexican government in the mid-nineteenth century offered the incentive of individual proprietorship to Indians, which helped produce regional support for small farmers and their activities in later revolutionary battles, especially in center-south areas of the country. In fact, the regional question became one of the central dynamics in the 1910 Revolution, uniting a wide variety of classes in those provinces which felt they were missing out on the economic benefits produced under the dictatorship of Porfirio Díaz, who was seen as responsible for exacerbating regional inequalities and subordinating (both politically and economically) the country's many regions to its center.

In many ways, it was shared concerns about these issues that first made it possible for Mexico's revolutionary leadership to coalesce and pursue the small-farmer agricultural vision as a readily acceptable political project that would unite a number of distinct postrevolutionary factions. The fact that capitalist development and a political bias toward large hacendados were placing small and even medium-sized producers under threat in almost all regions of the country in the early part of the twentieth century, not to mention the

---

[56] The north of Mexico was much less populated to begin with, and thus the church had not developed its presence to the same degree. Moreover, it was also a region more "marginal to colonial development [because it] had no fixed indigenous population. In these huge, arid and mountainous stretches of land, above all in Sonora and Chihuahua, nomadic Indian tribes resisted the white and mestizo settlers until the middle of the 1880s. Captured land had to be continually protected from the Apaches," so that according to Gilly (*The Mexican Revolution*, p. 14), "apart from big *latifundia* like Luis Terraza's two million-hectare holdings in Chihuahua, a rural middle class sprang up on relatively small and medium-size ranches or mini-haciendas." As such, in Whetten's words (*Rural Mexico*, p. 154), "in spite of the tendency for small holdings to become absorbed into large ones, some progress was made in the development of small holdings," in this northern region and nationwide.

fact that under the Díaz dictatorship Mexico's regional political leaders were losing their autonomy and political capacity to democratically dispute such developments, as all major decisions emanated from the capital city, explains why so many different forces across the country united in a revolutionary coalition to bring down the Mexico City–based regime seen as responsible for this state of affairs. Yet paradoxically, it was these same regional differences that ultimately destroyed unity on the agrarian question, primarily by exacerbating tensions between the proponents of a more radical as opposed to a more conservative variant of this rural middle-class vision. Broadly speaking, support for the independent-farmer path unfolded in different ways in diverse regions of the country, because rural class structures varied significantly; and these differences hammered a wedge into the revolutionary coalition and thus shattered the common project that had originally united it. Further complicating matters, these differences in rural property ownership become irreparably divisive when they were cross-cut with other identities or were differentially distributed across distinct regions, with a large class of exploited small producers predominant in one part of the country and a more diverse rural class structure of farmers in another. In this instance, it was more difficult to find a common ground to unite a nationally diverse collection of rural middle classes in any long-term and viable fashion. Why? Because the same broadly cast support for family farming and small-scale rural production meant one thing in a region with a diverse rural class structure and quite another in a region dominated by large property owners.

In Mexico's northern regions where the rural class structure held farmers of all different sizes, support for a moderate agrarian reform was seen as an expedient and compromising position that did not necessarily entail a challenge to the idea of private property ownership but, rather, was more likely to be seen as a means to strengthen capitalist production generally – something generally viewed as beneficial to an already existent class of small and medium-sized producers. This stance also gained support from a much wider variety of rural class forces, small and medium to be sure, but perhaps even large. Hence the initial unity in the northern revolutionary leadership around land reform, despite the varying class or property-owning circumstances of Villa, Calles, and Carranza. Where the rural class structure was more highly polarized, however, as in Mexico's south, general discursive support for the idea of yeoman farming and smaller-scale production units was a much more politically difficult proposition. For one thing, it implied some sort of zero-sum game in which, in order to create these small and medium-scale farming units that did not yet exist, large property owners would have to give up either land or market hegemony. For another, even to push for moderate land reform in these conditions implied some sort of moral critique – if not an implied cap – on the activities of large property owners, whose market-oriented activities prevented the formation of middle-sized farms in the first place. To the extent that the meaning and viability of land reform as a universal political rallying cry – not to mention its larger impact – differed depending on the rural class structure of the regional or national context in which it was to be implemented, it is not so surprising that in a large and regionally diverse country such as Mexico it was difficult to maintain political unity on land reform. Accordingly, what initially emerged as a precarious unity among regionally distinct revolutionary forces around a common project soon devolved into ideological disunity and division, especially as political rhetorics intended to generate broad support turned into specific policies and programs. This explains why there was so much variation in the agrarian reform proposals advanced by different members of the revolutionary coalition, as well as enduring conflict over them.

Populations in southern parts of the country where Zapata and his revolutionary forces were most popular tended to advocate a more radical version of land redistribution, one which included strong support for ejidos and opposition to large landholdings in particular, while in Sonora and the other northern regions serving as home to Carranza, Obregón, and Calles, the emphasis was less on restoring ejidos and more on the legal and developmental infrastructure necessary to turn small cultivators into profitable farmers. In more central states landowning practices as well as agricultural and industrial employment patterns were sufficiently different (almost a mix of the two patterns we have referred to as northern and southern) that local political leaders supported yet other agrarian policies. In Tlaxcala, for example, a north-central state with a significant urban center (also called Tlaxcala) *and* a well-developed agricultural economy, key revolutionaries successfully campaigned for a different approach that included

> a fairly radical program that sought the return of stolen lands to communities, the abolition of the land tax for smallholder, the foundation of agricultural colonies for landless peasants on large haciendas, better labor conditions for workers, the transfer of the hated rural police, the *cuerpo rural*, to another state and, last but not least, the punishment of Porfirista officials guilty of repression and murder.[57]

This program, which strongly echoed the ideological program promoted by Park Chung Hee, grew out of the Tlaxcalan Anti-Reelectionist Party's (ART) active efforts to distinguish itself and its agrarian project from those offered by Carranza and Zapatista.

According to Buve, the ART's aims in these regards were successful precisely because the party united peasants and workers, even as it "obtained the support of the small Tlaxcala middle class for its essentially anti-elite program."[58] This

---

[57] Buve, "Neither Carranza nor Zapata!" p. 343.

[58] Ibid. Notably, by 1919 the elite in Tlaxcala had organized sufficiently to defeat the ART and its populist program.

was a cross-class alliance built on the unity of city and countryside that in many ways replicated the Taiwanese experience. But in contrast to the programs in both Taiwan and South Korea, this program was popular and this alliance successful only in one very small region of the vast country that comprised Mexico. It did not translate easily to the entire nation. Stated differently, the agrarian vision of Tlaxcalan revolutionaries may have fit the Tlaxcalan experience and its unique rural-urban class structure quite well, and it may even have fit Taiwan's and less so South Korea's, thereby laying the foundations for similar developmental gains. Had Mexico's revolutionaries taken this path nationally, the country might have crafted a development model very similar to that pursued by our two East Asian cases. But the Tlaxcalan path was hardly one that could be embraced in every other region of Mexico, let alone the national state, given the country's diverse regional and rural property-owning history. It was just one among many agrarian reform visions, each of which was advanced by different revolutionary forces from different parts of the nation, and none of which could prevail in the national governing apparatus without the support of revolutionaries in other regions. It was regional diversity, then, plus the fact that after Díaz's 1910 defeat different states used their newfound independence to introduce their own specifically tailored agrarian programs, that made the aim of finding one all-inclusive national position on rural land reform ever more difficult to achieve as time passed.

With multiple projects placed on the table in the postrevolutionary decade, the broadly cast revolutionary support for a general agrarian reform, even a moderate one, began to diminish starting as early as the first decade after the Revolution. And the failure to find unity on land reform affected several other key policy stances that the postrevolutionary leadership took, ranging from the extent of state centralization to support for urban-based industrialization.

Agrarian Conflict and the Centralizing State

The existence of regional conflicts and tensions did not of course fully prevent Mexico's new leaders from agreeing on all other changes to the Constitution relating to land, especially those that reflected some commitment to a petit bourgeois version of agrarian reform. Nor did it prevent the revolutionary coalition from finding common ground at every step toward revolutionary consolidation and future governance. Labor and the rights they would be accorded in the new political and economic order were important issues that, like land, held the potential to generate considerable division and conflict within the postrevolutionary political leadership concerned. Yet they somehow were "resolved." Indeed, in the debates between 1915 and 1917, and in the Constitutional Assembly where the various legislative clauses and regulations were hammered out, differences in opinion over labor legislation (Article 123) paled in comparison with the conflicts generated by the agrarian question

(Article 27). In Andrés Molina Enríquez's words, "The project of Article 123 did not present major difficulties for its approval; but Article 27 did "[59] And this not only meant that those agrarian reform clauses that actually made it into the Constitution were the result of deep political struggle and compromise fueled largely by competing expectations about what land reform was supposed to be and accomplish, differences which themselves were grounded in divergent rural class experiences and distinct disciplinary orientations.[60] This same regional diversity also meant that the agrarian reform legislation that did become law held the potential to produce different results in different regions, not merely in terms of its impact on rural middle-class formation and productivity, but also in terms of its impact on regional economies and power structures.

Given the political fragmentation that land reform threatened to produce, the revolutionary leadership was pushed to simultaneously introduce changes in the political structures of governance in order to accommodate different regional visions of land reform. But once the revolutionary leaders started playing with structures of state power, and allowing for regional differences in the implementation or application of land reform, they began to alienate previously loyal sectors of their rural constituencies, further splitting the revolutionary coalition rather than uniting it, and pushing certain factions of the revolutionary leadership to seek other class or political allies. Stated simply, political machinations (seen in the form of greater state centralization and

---

[59] *La revolución agraria*, p. 178.
[60] After uniting with his northern revolutionary counterparts during the initial struggle against the Porfirian dictatorship in 1910 and 1911, for example, and joining with them in opposition to Madero in 1912, Zapata soon realized that his ideas about the aims and larger meaning of land reform were coming under attack by most of his northern counterparts, despite their shared concern with independent cultivation and small-farmer production. This was first clear on the part of Carranza, who showed his ambiguous relationship to the idea of agrarian reform by failing to implement even his own initial constitutional mandates on the land question, formulated in the first stage of the revolutionary struggle. This happened in no small part because noncompliance of established codes allowed him to toe an ambiguous line of support for and opposition to land reform, a position which itself is somewhat understandable given the internal conflicts within the revolutionary leadership. But it also owed to the growing tensions between Zapata and Carranza, who began battling each other as early as 1913 in a struggle that ultimately led to Zapata's initial political defeat (followed several years later by his assassination). In this first round of struggle, another northerner, Villa, joined with Zapata, perhaps because his own background as a sharecropping small farmer in Durango made him more sympathetic to the agrarian aims of Zapata and his small-farmer forces than to those held by Carranza, who came from a large-landholding family in the northern state of Chihuahua. When Carranza politically and militarily routed Zapata and Villa, the way was cleared for more internal unity behind the petit bourgeois aims of agrarian reform, which then made their way into the 1917 Constitution.

more center-region domination) that were introduced in order to "deal" with the agrarian question themselves created new political and social problems and conflicts that ultimately led the Mexican state away from rural development and toward urbanization-led industrialization.

All this started to become clear as early as 1915, when Carranza decreed that state governors held the right to make provisional land grants to villages, with the national government later confirming these decisions. His intent was to give different regional elites some independent scope to deal with the agrarian question in a manner they saw fit, given their own distinct rural class structures and political or economic aims.[61] Yet this opened a Pandora's box of problems because these measures allowed political elites in regions less sympathetic to the revolutionary cause to publicly undermine the new government's articulated constitutional support for land reform, even moderate land reform. The measures also held the potential to empower conservative counterrevolutionary forces in their stance against any type of land reform, thereby provoking dissatisfaction among those rural masses who served as a principal basis of support for the revolutionary coalition. Complicating matters, these provisions also held the potential to empower regional supporters who were pushing for more radical land reform (the governor of the state of Veracruz was one). The upshot was growing political dissatisfaction on the part of those more moderate supporters of the revolutionary coalition who preferred the petit bourgeois path to land reform.

In response, within a year of the initial decree Carranza took this decentralized power away from local authorities, "practically bringing land reform to a standstill" until his hold on political power, not to mention a new agrarian program, could be worked out.[62] It was not until 1920, in fact, three years after enactment of the Constitution, that the original power of the governors to grant provisional landholdings was restored, since by this time the revolutionary coalition had much more firmly consolidated both its constitutional mandate and its hold on power, with Alvaro Obregón at the helm and many of his allies in place in the states. Yet even then, a new law of ejidos transferred authority back to the National Agrarian Commission, so that the "autonomy of state governors was again undercut."[63]

The steady disenfranchisement of regional elites and the strengthening of the centralized state in order to deal with conflicts over land reform, combined with the politically charged tinkering with the Constitution to achieve these aims, served as yet another wedge splitting the rural middle class. Part of the problem was that the Constitution was written in such a way as to allow for ambiguities in interpretation and enforcement of agrarian issues, with different

---

[61] Tannenbaum, *Peace by Revolution*, p. 202.
[62] Ibid.
[63] Sanderson, *Land Reform in Mexico*, p. 54.

regions offering their own views on what was allowed. Such ambiguity was evident in the fact that the Constitution sanctioned multiple forms of land ownership and left unsaid some of the most controversial yet key aspects of land reform, including specification of plot size and the conditions under which expropriation could occur. It also was reflected in the use of languages that were relatively ambiguous if not entirely contradictory when it came to land rights – a state of affairs that only begins to suggest why the Constitution, despite its centrality in Mexico's political historiography, is such a fragile and contested if not ineffective legal document. Indeed, the Constitution sanctioned both individual and collective property ownership, while conceptual overlaps in a variety of forms of property ownership were never completely resolved in its textual framing.[64] This was particularly evident in the language employed in Article 27, which "permit[ted] the juxtaposition of all types of ownership, from the nomadic group having nothing more than a vague sense of right to use, to that of a modern corporation with its complex titles, privileges, and prerogatives."[65] This language created problems down the road because it created discursive and rhetorical ambiguity about who comprised the middle class – a state of affairs that affected the state's capacity to foster citizen support for its rural middle-class vision. It also put the postrevolutionary political leadership in the difficult position of having to politically mediate among competing claimants to land whose property-owning status was sometimes in conflict. Given that mediation was in the hands of the state, the result tended to be biased toward the most powerful claimants, something clearly evidenced in the uneven application of expropriations across regions and over time. The result was that the constitutional provisions for land reform, even those formulated with relatively good intentions, ended up by exacerbating regional differences and citizen disunity, even as they reinforced an agrarian structure in which large landowners still remained a force to be reckoned with.[66]

Furthermore, the fact that many land and property ownership issues were never decided with any certitude in the original deliberations on the Constitution explains why Article 27 was crafted in such a way as to empower the national state to have last instance rights to determine the content and character of agrarian policy, both with respect to individual versus collective property

---

[64] For more on this, see Molina Enríquez, *La revolución agraria*, Tomo 5, esp. pp. 186–192.

[65] Tannenbaum, *Peace by Revolution*, p. 168.

[66] According to Tobler, many of the agrarian reform programs that were generated in accordance with these ambiguous constitutional dictates "created advantageous conditions for army chiefs to set themselves up in agriculture, because the army often exercised a decisive role of arbitrator in conflicts between *agraristas* and *latifundistas*. In this situation, the officers frequently acted as 'partners' or 'tenants,' of the landowners affected or endangered. In order to avoid expropriation of part of their lands, landowners were often prepared to offer favorable contracts to their protectors." See "Peasants and the Revolutionary State," p. 494.

rights, and with respect to the depth of land reform (i.e., appropriation). It may have been precisely because the 1917 Constitution mandated that the power to determine agrarian questions would rest in the hands of a centralized state apparatus rather than with the *pueblo*, or people, as had been dictated by the previous Constitution, that the revolutionary leadership's hold on power, not to mention its problems with respect to land reform, still persisted even after 1917, despite the appearance of disunity in the political coalition. Yet far from setting aside the most divisive issue within the revolutionary coalition, these aspects of constitution making further fueled regional and political conflicts. From 1917 onward Mexico suffered through round after round of struggles within and between the revolutionary leadership and competing regional forces – many of them initially sympathizers to the Revolution – to institutionally capture or control the postrevolutionary state.

Significantly, most of these battles were played out between varying gradations of rural property owners, from small to middling all the way up to large producers, who differed in their agrarian visions despite having shared a common support for the revolutionary defeat of Porfirio Díaz years before. In this period we first see rebellious large landowners, such as the Cedillo brothers in San Luis Potosi, militantly struggling to retake the national state by pitting themselves against the rural middle-class forces of Calles and Obregón,[67] who themselves later battled against fellow revolutionaries such as Cárdenas and others who were more sympathetic to the *campesino* poor. And as center-region struggles continued unabated, they were increasingly animated by both agrarian concerns and a preoccupation with the centralization of state power per se.

Race, Space, and "Middle-Classness"

By linking the agrarian question to state power and capacity, the stakes in postrevolutionary political consolidation were heightened even more, making consensus ever more elusive. The problem was not merely that the possibility of more centralized state power alienated rural constituencies, many of whom had fought against the Porfirian dictatorship on precisely these grounds. Nor was the problem merely the presence of so many regional variations in property ownership patterns and the difficulties of consolidating distinct rural forces into a single, long-term, broadly cast rural middle-class coalition that could see eye to eye on agrarian reform or general questions of governance. Complicating matters even further was the fact that race and ethnicity – or what Mexicans often refer to as "the Indian question" – also inserted themselves into these regional and agrarian conflicts in such a way as to reduce the common ground for sustaining the rural middle-class political unity.

---

[67] For more on the Cedillo opposition, see Falcón, "Charisma, Tradition, and *Caciquismo*."

Historically, Mexico can be considered among the most ethnically and linguistically diverse countries of Latin America, characterized by a large native population of Indians and the fortune of having avoided much of the large-scale Indian genocide that characterized many other Latin American countries, which explains why Mexico still hosts such a large indigenous population. Indian peoples have been well distributed across practically all parts of the nation, and they speak different languages, draw from different cultural repertoires, and represent a variety of native peoples, ranging from Mayan to Aztec to Yaqui, to name but a few. The colonial experience helped reinforce social differences among these groups and between them and Spanish-born settlers, although over the centuries it also contributed to ethnic and racial mixing. From the time of Spanish conquest and settlement, however, certain ethnic and racial groupings tended to be associated with certain class identities and to reside in certain regional locations. Generally, the pattern was for white-skinned Spaniards to employ dark-skinned Indians as peons on their haciendas. Yet because there were variations in the location of hacienda production, as noted above, the issue of regionalism also factored into the equation.

In northern areas, owing to military land grants as well as climatic and geological differences, populations were more likely to be relatively successful independent small farmers and of whiter skin; although, in the case of the relatively successful Yaqui farm settlements, this distinction was not hard and fast. Still, in these northern areas racial characteristics and ethnic traditions tended to differentiate rural middle-class producers from large hacendados, with the latter dominated by families landed through Spanish encomienda grants (identified as the Creole elite) and the former of Yaqui descent, of more mixed race, and of humble origins. In southern areas, in contrast, the clear majority of the population was both darker and of Maya or Aztec Indian descent, and by the early-twentieth century likely to be employed as wage laborers even if they also cultivated their own lands. These regionally distinct distributions of Indian populations are evidenced, albeit somewhat imprecisely, in census material on language acquisition. As late as 1940, the proportion of the population speaking an Indian language was 4.0 percent and 3.4 percent in the north Pacific and the northern regions of the country, respectively; 11 percent in the central region; 28 percent in the Gulf; and 38.2 percent in the south Pacific region.[68]

To the extent that race/ethnicity and class intersected systematically and distinctively in northern and southern regions, the debate on agrarian reform was further complicated. Darker and more "purely" Indian populations, who also tended to be poorer and more proletarianized, were more likely to support a radical version of agrarian reform; while whiter-skinned rural producers more readily sympathized with the rural middle-class vision of agrarian reform.

[68] Whetten, *Rural Mexico*, p. 582 (Table 7).

And it was this articulation of ethnic, regional, and class identities that further divided the revolutionary leadership and limited its capacity to unite disparate national political forces around a single, rural middle-class vision of land reform. Moreover, much of the divisiveness that emerged in postrevolutionary debates revolved around questions of how to incorporate the ejido tradition into agrarian reform legislation, an issue that itself had a racial if not ethnic subtext. Whether lands would be restored to all who needed them, or just to peoples organized in Indian villages, was a big issue of contention within the revolutionary leadership; and it in fact divided its two most like-minded protagonists, Villa and Zapata.

Remember that long-standing Indian traditions of communal land owner-ship had formed part of the agrarian programs of the nineteenth-century reform government, and there was considerable support for continuing the ejido tra-dition because it would help preserve traditional Indian communities and their lifestyles, not just because it protected small-scale production. This in turn meant that the issue of ejidal land was conflated with the issue of sustaining Indian populations almost from the beginning. This reality meant that some-times a position on land reform was advanced because it served as a means to support (or disempower) traditional Indian communities. Indeed, much of the counterrevolutionary opposition drew its political support from those groups concerned about the consequences of reempowering Indians, who were seen as barbarians incapable of modernizing themselves or the country. Like-wise, many Indians who sympathized with the Revolution, including Zapata, struggled because they were more concerned about restoring traditional Indian villages and customs than anything else.[69] Alan Knight notes that these con-cerns were long-standing within the Indian community, at least to the extent that the nineteenth century saw various Indian revolts representing "a protest against the community's incorporation into mestizo society and against the consequences which swiftly followed: taxes, forced recruitment into the army, vagrancy laws, and, often enough, agrarian dispossession."[70]

The complex interrelationship between race/ethnicity, scale of produc-tion, history of agrarian dispossesion, and divisive political positions taken on

[69] While Villa supported a similarly harsh position on expropriation as Zapata, his agrarian reform proposal was structured most definitely around creating a small-proprietor class of independent producers whose plot sizes would not exceed twenty-five hectares, and he wanted land to be available to all small producers without land, not just in a way that privileged restitution to Indian villages and communities. Zapata, in contrast, cared less about the size of plots and more about the communal character of land and the question of restitution, concerns that linked his agrarian reform proposals directly to the aim of reestablishing ejidal forms of property ownership associated with long-standing Indian communities and Indian traditions.

[70] *The Mexican Revolution*, Vol. 1, p. 116.

agrarian reform is clear in an account of the immediate postrevolutionary conflicts over land reform offered by Andrés Molina Enríquez, a leading postrevolutionary agrarian intellectual. For starters, Molina Enríquez identifies each of the protagonists as either *indio-mestizo* (mixed race of mainly Indian origin), *indio* (Indian), *criollo* (Spanish origin), or *criollo-mestizo* (mixed race of mainly Spanish origin). Stated simply, for Molina Enríquez there is no position on land reform that is not also understood in terms of the race/ethnicity of its proponents. Villa and Zapata, for example, would represent not just the *agricultores de pequeña propiedad*, or small-scale agrarian producers; they also are spokesmen for the country's disenfranchised Indian masses. In a chapter extitled "The Exclusion of the Villistas, Indio-Mestizos, Small Agriculturalists; The Abandonment of the Ejidos; The Haciendas Saved," Molina Enríquez further articulates the fusion of political, racial/ethnic, and landowning identities in ways that discursively place proponents and opponents on two extreme sides of the agrarian reform continuum. Yet, he also uses this racialized conceptual framing to understand why a more moderate position on land reform ultimately materialized.[71] To be sure, these are the opinions of just one man, even if a well-respected one. But they do reflect historical reality to a great extent, especially during the early decades of the twentieth century when Molina Enríquez was writing. Indeed, the divisions between criollos and Indians – as well as their overlaps with other identities and institutions – were not the figment of one man's imagination. They were an endemic and patterned feature of Mexican society, reflected in regional differences between north and south, in divisions between large and small rural property owners, and in access to the state and political power.[72]

[71] This is partially evidenced in Molina Enríquez's discussion of the personal characteristics of Luis Cabrera, the main protagonist of agrarian reform during the Madero administration, who, along with other criollos, controlled Madero's National Agrarian Commission. Cabrera, he suggests, "was a high talent and a true man of state; but he also was *"criollo de raza* or at minimum a *criollo-mestizo*," and because he "could not feel the inconveniences of the regimes of rural property owning linked to large haciendas with the same intensity as could those of Indian race," he failed to promote a more radical agrarian reform. See Molina Enríquez, *La revolución agraria*, p. 157.

[72] And this was true not just in society at large, which was politically and socially dominated by a small cadre of fair-skinned folk who prided themselves on their Spanish lineage and who saw the Indians and mixed-race peoples as physically and culturally inferior. It also held true even within the military, and this spilled over into the revolutionary leadership. Most Porfirian military leaders traced their origins to criollo ancestry, while the rank and file were comprised of poorer Indians and *mestizos*. Among those few soldiers of Indian or mixed-race heritage who did rise to the position of general, moreover, there was a much greater tendency to join the revolution, often in a military leadership position. That the Porfirian elite and armed forces were identified as sustaining a criollo dictatorship helped the revolutionary leadership because it inspired many Indians and mixed-race peoples to join the cause and

Still, the issue of race/ethnicity did not always work to the advantage of the revolutionaries. The disdain generally heaped upon Indians was so pervasive and ingrained in Mexican society, that ultimately this too appeared as a point of division and contention even within the revolutionary movement itself. It was hard to ignore the fact that criollos dominated among the revolution's own military generals and that Zapata stood practically alone as a glaring exception to this rule. One result was the emergence of divisions within the revolutionary movement over the question of race/ethnicity. Molina Enríquez goes so far as to suggest that "Indians and mixed-race Indians [were considered to have] formed a body apart that was considered offensive" even by many of the revolutionaries, who later "declared them enemies."[73] While this may be an overstatement, the division between criollo revolutionaries on the one hand, and Indian or mixed-raced revolutionaries on the other, was indeed evident in the tensions between Zapata, representing the latter grouping, and Carranza, Calles, and Obregón, representing the former. Their conflicts and particularly the divergent positions they took on agrarian reform cannot be fully understood without situating them in racial and ethnic context and without paying greater attention to the historical linkages between race and ethnic identity, property-owning status, and, as noted above, regionalism. It was the overlapping of all three sets of identities, then, that reinforced the fault lines of difference, leading to disunity in the revolutionary coalition and disrupting the common rural middle-class concerns about smaller-scale agrarian production that originally had united them.

The question still remains, however, as to how some factions of this irrevocably divided coalition of rural-based forces were able to triumph in their efforts to capture the postrevolutionary Mexican state, but not others. In some ways, the answer is disquietingly simple: Those factions which triumphed militarily, i.e., that were most successful using coercive means to undermine their opponents, secured the reins of state power. This surely was the case with Carranza and Obregón who, with help from Calles and other northern military allies, violently defeated the Zapatista and Villista forces. But this response only begs the question of how this was possible in the first place. Moreover, it does not tell us why, when certain rural factions triumphed, they rapidly abandoned their own rural middle-class and disciplinary priorities to instead embrace capitalists, their laborers, and a massive industrialization project, a stance that ultimately sealed the fate of "disciplinary development"

give their lives fighting the dictatorship. These tensions also divided the Porfirian army from within and in that sense further facilitated Díaz's defeat. Many on the front lines of the revolutionary battle were ex-Porfirian soldiers of Indian descent: what Molina Enríquez calls "Indio-mestizos and Indians who had common interests with the revolutionaries." See Molina Enríquez, *La revolución agraria*, p. 103.
[73] Ibid.

in Mexico. In both South Korea and Taiwan, after all, the military–rural middle-class nexus helped both countries pursue precisely that path. Given the fact that forging a centrist position on agrarian reform seemed to be a major aim of the Carranza-Obregón-Calles alliance, we might have expected the same: that once triumphant, the Sonoran generals would have pursued rather than rejected this agrarian path. Granted, they might have promoted a development policy more favorable to medium- and large-scale properties, but this would have evidenced a commitment to rural development nonetheless. Such a strategy clearly would have been more in keeping with the moderate agrarian reform program they initially proposed, albeit perhaps a bit more open to large-property ownership, and more in keeping with what occurred in East Asia.

The key to answering these questions is to situate the revolutionary struggle in a larger spatial and territorial context and not merely in a racialized and regionally diverse property-owning framework. This entails, first and foremost, a closer examination of the overwhelming importance of Mexico City and its urban populations in both national politics and in the country's economic and cultural history. Yes, the Revolution began in the regions; and, yes, the energy and military organization of a broad coalition of different-sized rural property-owning forces were enough to drive Porfirio Díaz from office in 1910. Still, the clear historical dominance of Mexico City in the national territory and in national politics, not to mention the extent of division among regions, made it unlikely that *any* purely rural-based coalition, no matter what position on agrarian reform it advanced, would be able to govern the entire country if it did not also have significant urban allies. In these regards, Mexico faced obstacles in politically institutionalizing rural middle-class embeddedness and the small-farmer vision that blessed its East Asian counterparts, which were not nearly so urbanized at the point of postwar state formation when agrarian reform hit the agenda. All this explains why Mexico's subsequent development trajectories differ substantially from those pursued in Taiwan and South Korea, and why they more clearly paralleled those in Argentina, whose urban dominance also colored agrarian politics.

Remember that Mexico City was not just the capital of the country but for years also had been the seat of the entire northern Spanish colonial empire. This meant that Mexico City and the central valley region which surrounded it were more privileged and class diverse than perhaps any other part of the nation, much like Buenos Aires and its surrounding province. By the early-twentieth century, the country's wealthiest and most powerful residents lived in Mexico City, as did most of the country's educated middle classes and a large majority of its organized laborers, most of whom were long-standing residents and not new migrants. More important perhaps, Mexico City was home or headquarters to all the major institutions of the state, not just the main legislative, executive, and judicial branches of governance, but also the army, the central bank, and myriad state regulatory bureaucracies involved in trade, taxation, foreign diplomacy, and so forth. Accordingly, it would have been difficult for a primarily rural coalition of forces to maintain power over the nation without some support from within the capital city, even if they had been unified. Given the racialized and property-owning splits among them, whichever faction of the rural middle-class coalition could count on support from the institutions and resident individuals of the capital city had the greatest likelihood of successfully capturing state power, and perhaps even legitimizing it. As in Argentina, then, the capital city was a central player in the nation's political – and thus economic – development trajectories; and as in Argentina, it was the inclusion and later domination of urban classes in the governing coalition that limited Mexico's capacity to pursue a rural-oriented disciplinary development model.

The importance of Mexico City to the revolutionary leadership and its agrarian projects was clear from the beginning, to such an extent that it even slowed the initial revolutionary break. Despite the multiple military victories of northern and southern revolutionary forces against the Porfirian army during 1910 and 1911, Porfirio Díaz was still able to maintain strict control of the national state and its institutions after official defeat, owing to his political monopoly on power in the capital city, not to mention the confidence he generated among populations there. For this reason, in fact, during the first months of active revolutionary struggle, most contentious military battles neither reached nor threatened seriously Mexico City citizens. As late as April 1911, after more than a year of bloody battle in the regions, Mexico City's local governing council (*ayuntamiento*) was still in place and operating under the publicly articulated assumption that the administration of Porfirio Díaz would continue indefinitely, with this ruling body proudly proclaiming itself to be unaffected by the skirmishes between the so-called marginal revolutionary forces and the army in the provinces.[74] Many in the capital were genuinely shocked, in fact, when Madero came to power in late 1911, despite the resounding military gains of the rebels in the countryside and their popular support nationwide, precisely because these struggles had been so effectively exorcized from most urban residents' everyday lives. And much of Mexico City was strongly behind Porfirio Díaz anyway, something which attests to the revolutionary forces' initial inability to enlist significant local enthusiasm or meaningful support for their cause.

---

[74] The *memorias*, or proceedings of the City Council, for the year 1911 note that the Council "began the year generally believing in the strength, power, and solidity of the government of Porfirio Díaz, and sustaining, officially at least, that the revolutionary movement initiated in Chihuahua by Francisco Madero was of little importance" (*Memoria del H. Ayuntamento de Mexico en 1911*, p. 3).

Moreover, even when Porfirio Díaz fled the country and was replaced by a shifting string of contending heads of the national state representing different factions of the movement, the revolutionary leadership's manifest incapacity to stabilize its grip on national power, no matter who was at the helm, rested on those leaders' capacities to control Mexico City militarily and/or generate support from the local populations. Madero's fate is a case in point. He lost control of the national state in part because he did nothing to challenge the Porfirian institutions of state power at their territorial bases. This was especially so with the army, which was left relatively intact in the capital city. This was a problem nationwide, of course, but it was felt most deeply in Mexico City, where the army was headquartered and where counterrevolution hung in the air like smoke from a blazing fire. Thus, it is not surprising that de la Huerta's successful counterrevolutionary coup against Madero in 1913 occurred in Mexico City, at a military barracks called La Ciudadela, home to members of the army most loyal to Porfirio Díaz and his brother, Mexico City's ex–police chief Felix Díaz. That de la Huerta was able to murder Madero, and for more than a year thereafter to thwart the efforts of Villa, Zapata, Carranza, and Obregón to take up the mantle of the postrevolutionary state, owed to the fact that Mexico's leading revolutionaries had few military allies in Mexico City itself, having come as they did from provincial regions to the far north and south of the city. De la Huerta, in contrast, counted quite heavily on local military and police-based support. It was not until the Mexico City–based ranks of the Porfirian army had been purged, then, and the revolutionaries had established strong alliances with the local police and other sympathetic military personnel, that northern revolutionary forces were able to ride freely and without peril into Mexico City several years later, in late 1916. Only then was Carranza truly able to wrench the reins of state away from the counterrevolutionary forces; and even that gain was hard-won.

Yet, as late as 1916, ten years after Díaz's defeat and despite the recognized establishment of a stable provisional government entrusted with the power to make national decrees, appoint governors, and start making national policy, Carranza's prospects of controlling Mexico City and physically moving into the offices of state were still so dismal looking that, in sheer desperation, he decreed the nation's capital was to be moved from Mexico City to Querétaro, a small town serving as the provincial capital of the contiguous and equally small state of Querétaro (in striking distance of Mexico City, of course). Ultimately, Carranza did generate sufficient support and military might to physically entrench himself at the institutional and territorial seat of national power; but this itself was a long, drawn-out process that brings us back to our originating questions about the conditions that made it possible. One decisive factor that facilitated Carranza's capacity to generate popular support from among populations in Mexico City was his decision to turn against Zapata and Villa.

Carranza desperately needed urban allies in order for his faction of the revolutionary coalition to triumph. He also needed supporters who would actually take up arms on his behalf, and he found them in the organized working class – most of whom embraced the Revolution's antiforeign and antimercantilist rhetoric and its repudiation of the political dictatorship of Porfirio Díaz – and in the Mexico City police. Yet these same forces also showed very little sympathy for the agrarian demands of Villa and Zapata. And when Carranza turned to these populations for political support and military assistance, he had both the justification and the motivation for breaking with the more peasant friendly forces in the revolutionary coalition or, more specifically, for defeating Zapata and Villa. Immediately after Carranza triumphed in his efforts to rout Villa and Zapata in 1914 and 1915, the question of agrarian reform was relegated downward on his list of priorities, leading to the tensions recounted earlier. Ultimately, then, the abandonment of the small-farmer vision of disciplinary development owed to the "real politics" of postrevolutionary times, themselves bounded by the country's larger geographic contours and territorial history.

To be sure, it may be difficult here to distinguish chicken from egg. Did Carranza betray Villa and Zapata – not only breaking up the balance (if not unity) of the revolutionary coalition, but also eliminating any necessity to respond to the more extreme demands about land reform – because he needed political support from Mexico City's populations? Or, conversely, did he seek support from urban residents for his more centrist revolutionary position on agrarian reform in order to defeat the more "radical" Villista and Zapatista agrarian currents in the revolutionary coalition? The former argument builds primarily on the assumption that Carranza was acting strategically, seeking the best way to gain hold of the state; while the latter suggests that his ideological position on the agrarian question was principled and based on his personal views as a large landowner, and that he cultivated political alliances in Mexico City in order to further strengthen or sustain an antagonism to a more radical, peasant-oriented and middle-class-challenging land reform. As frequently occurs in such matters, Carranza probably was motivated by both considerations. As noted earlier, we know that Carranza came from a large-landowning family and by nature had limited support for the extreme positions on land reform. This may help explain why even when he did push through agrarian reforms, he "did little to provide for either the decree or Article 27 of the Constitution."[75] But it is also true that as the counterrevolution progressed and as revolutionaries showed a surprisingly limited capacity to seize the institutions of the national state in Mexico City, Carranza steadily backed away from an initially stronger stance on land reform so that he could garner greater sympathy from among Mexico City's populations. He was living in a real world

[75] Whetten, *Rural Mexico*, p. 124.

of mighty antagonists, after all, and they were literally at his elbows in the capital city. And for most though clearly not all of Mexico City's residents, the idea of agrarian reform – not to mention its larger political significance – was practically a foreign concept, holding little significance in their everyday urban lives. This was especially the case among those urban residents who worked in small stores or struggled on the factory floors of central Mexico City. Thus support for Zapata and Villa was already highly circumscribed, and Carranza knew this.[76]

From 1913 onward, in fact, many Mexico City residents found themselves increasingly unsympathetic to the rural-based revolutionary movement, even to its more moderate northern forces like Carranza, since at that early stage the movement still rested precariously on the fragile unity among the forces led by Zapata, Villa, and Carranza. In the daily papers, especially those which were most sympathetic to the liberal vision of Madero, rebellious Zapatistas were generally portrayed as "savage hordes" against whom all the city's residents should be prepared to fight.[77] In these views, the spectre of race and ethnicity hovered, but linked to a pejorative view of the backwardness of regions. Evidence of this was best seen in the proliferation of ugly stereotypes about "uncivilized" Indians in the local press and popular culture, just as they had within the revolutionary coalition in the debate over ejidos and land reform. To the extent that race and ethnicity entered the picture in such a way as to distance many of Mexico City's residents from Zapatistas, the rural antagonism of urban residents also threatened to translate into opposition to the entire revolutionary movement. The instability and terror that the Zapatistas sowed among some urban residents further fueled this vicious cycle,

---

[76] As early as 1914, there was great concern that without the moderation of Madero, the radical demands of Villa and Zapata would ascend to the top of the revolutionary agenda. This realization fueled anti-Zapatista sentiments and inspired further opposition to the revolutionary movement, especially among Mexico City residents. As the urban-based counterrevolutionary forces picked up their speed, however, so too did Villistas and Zapatistas return the fire. This was particularly true with respect to the Zapatistas, who waged an increasingly violent campaign in the southern portions of Mexico City. The state of Morelos, home to Zapata and some of the most active Zapatista revolutionaries, bordered Mexico City on the south, so that from the beginning of the revolutionary struggle, Zapatistas were raiding sections of the capital within striking distance of their home bases and temporary camps. These attacks diminished as Madero assumed power, to be sure, despite Zapata's disagreements with Madero. But once the counterrevolutionary forces of de la Huerta took hold, Zapatistas found themselves concerned with the blatant repudiation of their revolutionary project, particularly as it affected the prospects for a deep agrarian reform. This state of affairs inspired a new round of Zapatista attacks on Mexico City, especially in its southern neighborhoods, which reached their peak in 1914 and 1915, further alienating urban populations as a consequence.

[77] "Los obreros de la capital," *Nuevo era*, 7 March, 1912, p. 7.

in turn legitimizing the actions of counterrevolutionary forces who justified their overthrow of Madero, their seizure of power in Mexico City, their efforts to control local police and military, and their subsequent efforts to defeat the revolutionary coalition by offering to defend Mexico City residents against Zapatista advances. Both these circumstances limited Carranza's capacity to wrest national power and generate support among the urban citizenry for the revolutionary movement as a whole, and they were key obstacles he was forced to overcome in order to thwart potential political defeat.

In this context, it is hardly surprising that Carranza responded to the urban public by distancing himself somewhat from the more radical agrarian priorities that had inspired much of the revolutionary ferment in the first place and by painting himself as the ideological successor to Madero. Madero, after all, was moderately popular in Mexico City despite his liberal critique of Díaz and his rural middle-class background, in part because he had embraced land reform not as a means of politically or socially empowering the peasant masses but as a means of bolstering private property and a petit bourgeois economy. Nor is it surprising that even after Zapata and Villa were considered to be militarily defeated, Carranza still evidenced considerable ambiguity in the extent to which he would commit to a deeper land reform and the extent to which he would conscientiously apply its provisions. In the aftermath of Madero's assassination and counterrevolutionary threats, Carranza's greatest and most pressing challenge was not to find the perfect compromise position on agrarian reform or to demonstrate a consistency in agrarian purpose so much as to establish a modicum of support for his revolutionary leadership among urban populations in the highly strategic capital city, something that itself presupposed a studied ambiguity on the agrarian question. Carranza's betrayal of Zapata and Villa and his embrace of Madero's original aims can thus be seen in light of these objectives. To the extent that there was only limited sympathy for the agrarian radicals in Mexico City, even among the organized working classes who may have expressed a proclivity to support the revolutionaries, but who also were quick to label Zapata's so-called dark-skinned barbarians as bandits and enemies,[78] any compromising dealings with Indian proponents of agrarian reform (mainly Zapata and less so Villa) could be seen as a great political liability.

---

[78] Mexican political historiographers have struggled with the fact that a good portion of the organized labor movement in Mexico City was antagonistic to peasant radicals of the Zapatista movement. The conventional explanation is a hypothesized failure of class consciousness, which prevented workers from seeing peasants as an immediate class ally in the struggle against elite political and economic domination. But racism and ethnic antagonism may be an equally compelling – if not more powerful – explanation, especially when coupled with a "cosmopolitan" snobbery among residents of the capital who preferred to see the modest rural cultivators as uncivilized and dirty peasants.

All this further explains why one of Carranza's most skillfull acts in the early years of revolutionary consolidation was not serious agrarian reform, but the signing of a pact in February 1915 with the Casa del Obrero Mundial, the Mexico City–based anarcho-syndicalist organization that served as the main source of organized labor organization and activism in the postrevolutionary period. The pact entailed a strong show of ideological support from both Carranza and Obregón for the organized labor movement (although the only real policy issue agreed upon was housing for workers), as well as a promise to work together to preserve order and reduce bloodshed in the city, in exchange for labor support of this revolutionary faction.[79] As such, this pact was significant not merely because it marked the beginning of a slow but steady end to the small-farmer vision, it also signaled the revolutionary leadership's recognition of the importance of maintaining a visible political foothold among organized working-class populations in the capital city, the foundation upon which the capital-labor-state pattern of "accommodation development" was later built. The result of this initial pact was not only the inclusion of urban workers in the revolutionary coalition, but a shift in developmental priorities so as to embrace industrialization. Both acts resulted in Zapata's defeat and the further isolation of Villa, even as they increased Carranza's chances of successfully boarding the ship of state in Mexico City.[80] When Carranza paraded into the capital a little more than a year later, it was these same workers' organizations that helped sustain his hold on the city, at least long enough for him to consolidate the strong position of the Sonoran dynasty and its main military and political leaders, Obregón and Calles.[81] Mexico, in short, even after sharing an initial state commitment to land reform similar to that of East Asia, was soon poised

---

[79] Araiza, *Historia del movimiento obrero*, Vol. 3, pp. 74–75.

[80] Within months, in fact, the majority membership of the Mexico City–based Casa del Obrero Mundial (which later transformed itself into an organized labor federation called the Confederación Regional de Obreros Mexicanos [CROM], and which showed distinct sympathies for Calles's and Obregón's governments) actively lent their services to the Carranza forces, with many joining the Red Battalions to fight against Zapata in Veracruz. It is also worth noting, however, that some of the affiliates of the Casa refused to support Carranza and joined Pancho Villa in his struggle.

[81] Shortly thereafter, Carranza showed his agrarian elite class origins and betrayed the labor movement as well by clamping down on the Casa del Obrero Mundial and other workers' organizations, a turn of events that lends further support to the contention that this initial alliance was forged without deep ideological commitment and for purely strategic reasons. But the connections that Carranza first forged with these organizations in 1915 were still nurtured if not strongly reinvigorated under Obregón and then Calles, two of the most powerful remaining members of the Revolution's original rural middle-class coalition. And according to Adolfo Gilly, with these alliances well established it was clear that "when Zapata was killed in 1919, the workers' movement had already begun to step onto the arena." See *The Mexican Revolution*, p. 316.

to embark on the Argentine path with a governing coalition built around a pact with the capital city–based labor movement and a clear urban-industrial bias, despite the agrarian origins of the revolutionary state.

From Rural to Urban Class Politics

Once Mexico's political leaders brought urban working classes into the governing coalition, they steadily lost sight of rural middle classes; and thus they appeared primed to pursue a developmental path much more similar to that followed in Argentina under Perón. But despite the state's common reliance on urban workers as key political bases in Mexico and Argentina, the political coalition buttressing the Mexican government in this key historical juncture – and immediately thereafter – differed considerably from its counterpart in the southern cone, Argentina, and as such, so did the macroeconomic policies the Mexican state implemented.

First and foremost, as early as 1916 it soon became obvious that the revolutionary coalition could not maintain its hold on Mexico City with support only from the urban working class. While the organized labor movement did make a "natural" ideological ally for the revolutionary leadership in some ways, given the important role played by a few key sectors of the labor movement in starting the revolutionary upheaval in the first place,[82] in Mexico City the labor movement did not have the numeric strength, economic salience, institutional power, or strategic significance to fully sustain Carranza's (and then Obregón and Calles's) grip on the state. In contrast to the situation in Argentina, where Perón could pretty much count on the military to back him up as he generated strong linkages with the urban working class, in Mexico the country was still in the midst of militarized conflict. Holdovers from the Porfirian army were still battling revolutionary forces, whose leadership itself was divided and engaged in internal battle. In these conditions, the leading faction of the revolutionary leadership still needed to solidify its hold on the state and, in order to achieve this, further control of the key institutions of local and national governance in Mexico City was necessary; military might was not enough. This was especially the case because it took more than military power to insure that the economy could function well enough to keep the overall population relatively loyal, especially in the face of the revolutionary state's strong alliance with the working class.[83]

---

[82] One high-profile strike among Cananea mining workers helped set the tone for the Revolution's antiforeign and anticapitalist tone. For more on the role of the organized labor movement in the Revolution and its immediate aftermath, see Hart's *Anarchism and the Mexican Working Class*, as well as his *Revolutionary Mexico*.

[83] For an elaboration of this argument about the larger strategic importance of facilitating the governance and urban service provision in Mexico City, see my *Urban Leviathan*.

Fully mastering the institutions of the state entailed expanding the organizational contours of the governing pact to include what were called state workers, or those employed by the state both directly (in the bureaucratic offices of governance) and indirectly – as in the case of urban service providers such as teachers, police, garbage pickers, streetcar drivers, and so forth. It also required an increase in the sheer numbers of those employed by the government, something that was accomplished in no small part by bringing veterans from revolutionary battles into public service. The latter feat actually killed two birds with one stone: Because many veterans were impoverished rural folk, this gave the government an opportunity to reward rural elements and integrate them into the revolutionary coalition even in the absence of a major land reform, while at the same time it increased the state's clientelistic hold on power. These acts shifted the balance of power in the political coalition to initiate the inclusion of a small portion of the urban middle classes as much as the urban working classes, since many of those employed by the state were considered – or saw themselves – as middle class, an issue to which I will return shortly. More important, bringing veterans and other revolutionary sympathizers into the state itself established a situation in which the dividing line between working- and middle-class identities was rather fuzzy. This was so not just because these more "middle-class" state employees (teachers, doctors, bureaucrats) were initially organized in the ranks of the labor federation – in no small part because this was where the revolutionary leadership had already established its strongest linkages. It also was true because the state ideologically embraced a working-class rhetoric and orientation (again, owing to the 1915 labor pact that it signed).[84] And once the state relied on this Mexico City–based cross-class alliance of urban working and middle classes, it became almost impossible to think of resuscitating support for agrarian reform, even a rural middle-class version of it, and even in the face of support for the idea from leading voices within the revolutionary movement.

Still, the urban path was not completely set. Ongoing internal conflict within the revolutionary leadership continued to transform the class and political coalitions of the postrevolutionary state, with struggle over its industrial versus agrarian contours fueled as much by the newly established discursive and legal ambiguities over who constituted a working versus middle class as by an abiding concern with agrarian questions. These tensions and their larger

[84] Initially, the state workers founded the Alianza de Organizaciones de Trabajadores al Servicio del Estado, which included street cleaners, teachers, and those employed in the water and sewage department, parks and gardens, graphic arts (i.e., newspapers), health care, communications and public works, and state-owned arms industries. Within a year, scores of other government agencies joined the organization, which was renamed the Federación Nacional de Trabajadores del Estado (FNTE) and which subsequently strengthened its connections with the CROM, the labor federation linked directly to Obregón and Calles over the 1920s.

developmental significance were especially clear in the ongoing personal and political conflicts between the more pro-labor Obregón, on the one hand, and Calles, on the other, who was oriented more toward the middle class (rural and urban) and who managed to wield the upper hand in the revolutionary family. Calles was regarded as the *Jefe Máximo de la Revolución* during the 1920s, and while he held the reins the country's commercial elites – especially in Mexico City – were relatively privileged. But infighting between Obregón and Calles, as well as among other potentially powerful labor leaders with national aspirations, such as Luis Morones, turned into a major political crisis when provincial rebellion accelerated over the late 1920s and early 1930s. As such, even with urban working classes, city-based government employees, and the urban commercial elite at their side, the revolutionary leadership faced a new round of political problems by the late 1920s.

Again, much of this stalemate owed to the legacy of Mexico's history of regionalism, racism, and continued center-region tensions. Spread across one corner of this vast national terrain stood the masses of impoverished rural folks, many of them of Indian descent, who were not covered by the highly circumscribed agrarian reform programs already enshrined in the 1917 Constitution and who felt betrayed by Villa and Zapata's defeat. In the other corner were regional elites, many of them large landowners, who were smarting from agrarian reform legislation and the growing centralization of power in the postrevolutionary state apparatus. Making matters worse, the shadow of an unhappy industrialist class of large entrepreneurs hovered ever more threateningly over this divisive conflict. With the economy at a near standstill after the disruption caused by the revolutionary upheaval, and with foreign capital already withdrawing from most local factories, Carranza, Obregón, and Calles now had to worry about growing dissatisfaction from industrial capitalists, especially those in the provincial cities of the nation where manufacturing production was well entrenched (e.g., Monterrey, Guadalajara, Veracruz). Elites in these cities may not have had a strong position on agrarian reform, but most were unenthusiastic about the new guarantees for the working class being forged vociferously in the alliance between Carranza and the labor movement. Provincial industrial capitalists also worried about privileging Mexico City, where the labor movement leadership resided, recognizing the fact that Carranza's specialized pact with labor might help industrialists in that particular locale and hurt them in the long run.[85]

Industrial elite opposition insured that the revolutionary leadership, for its part, was still divided on what strategy to pursue, especially with respect to widening its political coalition of support. Throughout the 1920s, during the administrations of Calles and Obregón, the government merely muddled

---

[85] For a more detailed treatment of tensions between industrialists in different cities of Mexico between the 1920s and 1940s, see Chap. 3 of my *Urban Leviathan*.

through these class-based and regional conflicts. It strengthened its relations with the urban working class and state employees and established working relations with a few key commercial and industrial capitalists in Mexico City, a tactic that also forced the postrevolutionary government to repress the most radical members of the labor movement and privilege its most corrupt elements. But with regional opposition heating up, and growing corruption and labor repression in Mexico City, the government's political situation remained precarious, especially considering its loss of support from rural folk who were still seething from the government's failure to make headway on the agrarian question.[86] It was thrown into further disarray in 1929 when Obregón was assassinated by a sympathizer of a Catholic opposition movement (*cristeros*) that had been gaining support in several key provinces of the country. With the world economic crisis further destabilizing the economy in both city and countryside, with urban unemployment and rural destitution rising, and with regional opposition simmering out of control, something had to be done to solidify political power among a constituency divided by class, race, and region. Only then could a set developmental path be taken, be it urbanization-led industrialization or not.

With these aims in mind, the revolutionary leadership turned to political reform and specifically to the development of a party apparatus that would embed several of these critical social and class constituencies directly into the state. The first efforts in these regards came in 1929, when Calles founded the Partido Nacional Revolucionario (PNR), Mexico's ruling party, primarily conceived as an extension of the existent pact with the urban-based labor movement and government employees. Shortly thereafter, under the leadership of Lázaro Cárdenas in 1934, the postrevolutionary state made yet another serious effort to recast and widen its political base of support to bring rural folk into the mix. Cárdenas, however, proceeded in a direction that created as many problems as it solved. Indeed, his preferred strategy for dealing with the problems of conservative opposition from large landowners and regional elites included efforts to further strengthen the institutional power of organized labor (which Calles and Obregón tried desperately to constrain) and plans to bring the agrarian question generally (and the plight of landless laborers) back into party politics and macroeconomic development policy making. Two years into office Cárdenas founded the Confederación de Trabajadores Mexicanos (CTM), a federation that united the key labor organizations in the country and that served as the institutional vehicle for linking the industrial working class

[86] Evidence for the diminishing commitment to agrarian reform is evidenced by statistics concerning the average plot size, its variation over time, and the differences between de facto and de jure provisioning. Nugent, for example, notes that "since 1920 the legal size of newly created [ejido] plots has varied between 4 and 20 hectares of *temporal*, but their actual size has always averaged less than 10 hectares per family." See *Spent Cartridges*, p. 131.

to the PNR.[87] Moreover, in contrast to Calles and other predecessors, Cárdenas made the ejido – or collective ownership – the centerpiece of agrarian reform rather than individual private property, that is, he targeted numerous large landowners for expropriation and granted land to agricultural wage workers.[88]

Combined with strong support for organized labor, Cárdenas's embrace of agrarian questions gave his administration a much more populist tone than that of previous postrevolutionary leaders. And in certain ways, the ideology of the Cárdenas administration faintly echoed the priorities that Park Chung Hee advanced in his several years of office, especially through Cárdenas's efforts to expropriate large estates and distribute them among the waged but land-less laborers working on rural haciendas that had been bypassed by previous agrarian reform legislation.[89] The structure of the party under Cárdenas, more-over, paralleled in many ways the KMT's inclusion of farmers, laborers, and nationalist industrialists; but Mexico still did not plant itself squarely on the East Asian path. Why? Because for historical and political reasons, Cárdenas built his developmental vision and political coalition around the concerns of organized labor first and agrarian populations second; while Park's and the KTM's aims were the opposite, with working-class interests and industrial goals generally subordinated to agrarian aspirations.[90]

Equally important, Cárdenas's vision of cross-class inclusion brought active military opposition, whereas in the East Asian cases the military supported both Park's and the KMT's strategies in these regards. One reason the military was not united behind Cárdenas was that his earlier efforts to integrate urban working-class and military institutions[91] had alienated many of the army's

---

[87] This organizational reform was followed almost immediately by conscientious efforts to respond to the country's most impoverished rural populations, best evidenced in the inten-sification of agrarian reform programs and the expansion of ejidal lands to accommodate a much larger portion of the national population. According to Whetten, "During the Cárdenas regime (1935–40) more land was distributed than in all previous administrations put to-gether. In not a single year of the six-year term did the area distributed fall below 1,700,000 hectares, while in 1937 it reached a total of over 5,000,000 hectares." See *Rural Mexico*, p. 127.

[88] Ibid., p. 128.

[89] Ibid., pp. 128, 132.

[90] That Cárdenas saw the urban working class as a primary rather than secondary base of support was evident not just in his efforts to jump-start industrialization in order to increase em-ployment, but also in the timing and manner in which he integrated laborers and small rural producers into the party: workers first and campesinos (literally, "those from the country-side") second. Indeed it was not until a year after the foundation of a federation for industrial laborers (CTM) in 1936 that Cárdenas established a similar pact with organizations of rural producers, who ultimately affiliated with the Confederación Nacional Campesina (CNC).

[91] For example, Cárdenas sought to extend state worker benefits – especially pensions – to military personnel, many of whom were employed in state-run factories and government

rural middle-class officers, as had Cárdenas's clear openness to the demands of impoverished peasants. To be sure, Cárdenas did count on considerable military support from a rank and file who traced their background to the peasant masses, many of whom had fought loyally with Zapata or Villa in the initial revolutionary battles. Still, most of the military leadership in Mexico traced their roots to more prosperous families of the rural middle class, and they felt Cárdenas to be too radical for their tastes.[92] The fact that the country's military elite were concerned about the agrarian and working-class biases of the Cárdenas administration also added to the tensions that were already brewing with regional industrialists. Large landowners, for their part, were also unhappy about the renewed efforts at land reform, while the industrial capitalists feared a more powerful organized working class. Both worried about the overall leftist tone of a government so clearly committed to advancing the claims of a united party of organized peasants and industrial workers.

But most telling for our purposes was the fact that Cardenas's overall developmental and party vision gave priority to industrial workers in alliance with the poorest of the poor rural producers, of primarily Indian heritage. This meant that relatively little scope was reserved for other self-identified middle classes – many of them mestizo in origin – to make their claims or establish their presence within the state. This not only was true with urban middle classes, especially those small commercial and industrial producers in Mexico City who saw Cárdenas introduce employment, housing, and other policy measures for the working class, and who themselves held little sympathy for either the country's industrial workers or its Indian populations. It also was true with respect to more prosperous rural producers, or those already established rural farmers with holdings larger than the twenty hectares being allotted to *ejidatarios*, who felt that Cárdenas's concerns with redistributing land politically privileged only a narrowly defined, highly radicalized spectrum of agricultural producers, albeit one that constituted the clear majority of rural folk.[93]

The fact that the Cárdenas regime seemed to alienate the rural middle class is particularly relevant for our understanding of why in subsequent decades

agencies, a move which alienated those military personnel who were loathe to see themselves in working-class terms. For more on this and the elective affinities between the military and the urban middle class in Mexico during this key historical juncture, see my "Uncommon Democracy in Mexico."

[92] Falling into this grouping was ex-president Calles, who did not hide his antagonism to Cárdenas despite their shared status as members of the "revolutionary family."

[93] In *Rural Mexico*, Whetten (p. 176) notes that as of 1940 (and this is after the significant increase in land titles to small owners generated by Cárdenas), 89.7 percent of all agricultural landowners in Mexico were either *ejidatarios* or small owners of privately held plots with under five hectares.

Mexico departed so radically from the East Asian path. This was an important historical juncture in twentieth-century economic development. When the 1929 world depression threw Mexico's agricultural exports into a tailspin, rural conditions started to deteriorate rapidly, bringing more rural migrants to the city who then drove down industrial wages by driving up the size of the labor force. Because Cárdenas's main concern during the 1930s was stemming rural-urban migration for the purposes of protecting the existent urban labor force from undue competition for scarce jobs, as much as for fueling rural prosperity per se, he prioritized agrarian programs intended to keep poor peasants in the countryside, with land redistribution obviously being a central element. One way he did so, in addition to implementing new agrarian legislations and carrying through old ones, was to found a new organization in the party – called the Confederación Nacional Campesina (CNC) – to help organize peasants for the purpose of land distribution. Through his reinvigoration of agrarian reform programs, and the political inclusion of campesinos, Cárdenas also was responding in kind to a radical activism among previously repressed labor unions, many of them communist-led, some of whom were as active in the countryside as in the city.[94] Yet all this meant that as he started Mexico down what he believed was a path toward recovery and eventual prosperity, Cárdenas paid almost no attention to the political – let alone economic – requisites of more prosperous family farmers. Indeed, the organization and development of the CNC had a particular purpose: to appease if not incorporate the poorest of the rural poor, not just Indians in traditional ejido villages, but also the landless and those with properties of less than five hectares, all of whom were among the most likely to support rural-based communist organizations or other leftist insurgent groups. Strategically speaking, it was for precisely this reason that this new sector of the party was labeled a "confederation of campesinos," since it was this language of the peasantry that was used most often by avowedly leftist organizations in their appeals to the rural constituency, and that most worried PNR leaders.

Whether or not the CNC grew in size and institutional stature because it asserted a campesino identity and employed an attendant peasant-like discourse that truly appealed to rural folk, or because it served as the primary institutional mechanism for redistributing land and linking these disenfranchised populations to the state, does not matter so much as the larger implications of its existence. One key consequence was that rural farmers who already owned their lands and who did not consider themselves peasants were pretty much excluded from the CNC and thus from the institutional structures of the state

---

[94] Article 123 of the Constitution, after all, had granted farm laborers the right to organize and strike too; it was not a privilege confined only to urban or industrial workers. And with rural conditions rapidly deteriorating in the early 1930s, many of these rural populations were becoming just as active as their urban counterparts.

(often because they were not contesting titles). Among these groups were a preponderance of the country's rural middle classes, or those more prosperous producers who had larger plot sizes (recall that most ejidatarios were granted land plots only under twenty hectares) and whose ownership rights to their lands were not in question. Further contributing to the exclusion felt by these rural middle classes was the fact that as the primary institutional mechanism for linking rural populations to the state, the CNC continually reinforced a peasant – and sometimes even a working-class – identity among its constituents, even as time wore on and ownership conditions changed. Indeed, despite Cárdenas's obvious orientation toward sustaining the development of a new class of landed small producers, and some successes in these regards, the CNC he created was infused with the rhetorics of peasantries (or campesinos) as well as a structure and a rights program that more closely paralleled those of a labor organization than those of a middle-class association. Lucio Mendieta y Nuñez's classic account of agrarian politics makes this point by underscoring the ways in which languages of the labor movement seeped into the CNC, in ways that strongly paralleled Perón's appeal to equivalent Argentine small agrarian producers. At its founding, among its stated aims were to:

1) maintain constant and direct relations between peasant organizations and their fraternal members;[95] 2) politically orient *rural workers* (*trabajadores de campo*); 3) put at its reach a public organ which could efficiently express their complaints and just petitions; 4) bring to the peasants in a comprehensible manner knowledge about education, agriculture, hygiene, industry, and law; 5) create a *class consciousness* and interest in national life among the rural masses.[96] [Emphases mine]

Moreover, while the CNC counted on a special section geared toward rural small industry along with sections on political orientation, law, and training, issues of small-farmer productivity played second fiddle to those of organizational unity, the development of a unified class consciousness, and political expression. The upshot was that the CNC's constituents failed to embrace a rural middle-class orientation or petit bourgeois producer mentality and skill set, in no small part because the Cárdenas government did not actively try to inculcate one, as had previous administrations (or as had the governments in Taiwan and South Korea). Rather, land distributed through the CNC was communally organized and cooperatively worked, even as it was "owned" by the government and not the people, factors which further impeded the development of middle-class, property-owning consciousness among the CNC's

---

[95] Members of the campesino organizations are called *agremiados*, a notion of fraternal membership or association that has frequently been translated as "union members," since a *gremio* is a form of a trade union.

[96] *Política agraria*, pp. 50–51.

rural constituency.[97] One result was that by the end of the 1930s, the voices of both urban and rural middle classes had become institutionally marginalized within the party, on the urban and national political scene, and with respect to the governing coalition of the state. Cárdenas may have been able to count on political support from constituents of the CTM and CNC, but the increasingly excluded middle classes – especially rural middle classes but also urban ones – soon became a source of growing political opposition, threatening to unite with landowning or capitalist enemies against the populist President Cárdenas. The ruling party thus found itself in an unstable political position and faced with a new surge of conflicts both within and outside the party that both sealed Cárdenas's fate and further set the developmental future of the nation.

Conflicting Languages and Competing Structures of Middle-Classness

In the last chapter's comparisons of class discourses in Taiwan and Argentina, we saw that discourses of middle "classness" were very much tied to political strategies formulated by national leaders as well as the ethnic, economic, and territorial experiences of rural and urban producers. The same was true in Mexico. But other determinants also left their mark: Ranging from institutional reforms in party structures to legal debates over categories of folk who were eligible to strike, together with already complicated racial, ethnic, and regional discourses, these factors produced conflicting languages and competing structures of middle-classness. The long-term result was a further muffling of voices that could represent middle classes in the party and state, both urban and rural. To the extent that these conflicting languages and competing structures of middle-classness were most evident and most divisive during the administration of Lázaro Cárdenas (1934–1940), they were in large part responsible for sidetracking his administration's efforts to chart an East Asian developmental path in the decades of the immediate postwar period.[98]

The difficulties in distinguishing middle-class from working-class identities were brought to the surface by the restructuring of the labor sector in 1935. Under Cárdenas, the CTM was organized to include state workers and other educated professionals alongside other occupational constituencies of the labor movement. With this shift, a divisive debate over the rights and

---

[97] For more on the impact of the state's ownership of ejidal lands as well as its direct intervention in the production and marketing process, see Nugent, *Spent Cartridges*, esp. pp. 110–119.

[98] The CNC, for its part, grouped small-scale rural producers in a so-called peasant or campesino sector infused with laborist rhetoric, while the CTM also incorporated state workers and other educated professionals as just another organized arm of the labor movement. But the ambiguities and tensions mounted over what constituted middle-classness, not just for farmers but also for urban populations.

organizational representation of state workers roared onto the political scene. Owing to its long-standing ties to the Confederación Regional de Obreros Mexicanos (CROM), the name of the labor organization that first linked the labor movement to the revolutionary state,[99] Mexico's state workers' federation (Federación Nacional de Trabajadores del Estado [FNTE]) defined itself as an organization of *trabajadores* or *obreros* (workers) rather than *empleados* (employees).[100] This tradition, which sharply distinguishes Mexico from the East Asian case, where we see much less elective affinity between public sector employees and the organized labor movement at early stages of state formation, gave Mexico's postrevolutionary leaders considerable pause. While Cárdenas seemed nonplussed, many of the country's political leaders were concerned enough about the connections between state employees and the industrial working class that they modified the Constitution to deny state workers (including the military) the right to strike. When Cárdenas later introduced new reforms in 1936 to expand the power and rights of the organized labor movement, this and other existent legal constraints on state workers were among the first to generate vocal opposition from the country's middle classes.

In the first round of struggles to extend industrial labor's rights to state workers, the FNTE leadership argued strongly for the right to strike, basing much of its claim on the fact that state workers were organized within the CTM and thus their juridical status should be the same as their fellow sectoral members. Yet because the FNTE included *all* state personnel, white-collar administrators and technical staff (empleados) as well as blue-collar government workers (trabajadores or obreros), this position was greeted with considerable controversy among the organization's membership, as well as from middle classes and in Mexican society at large. Granted, some state workers (most notably teachers) remained staunchly leftist in orientation and thus were strongly sympathetic to working-class rhetorics and causes as advocated by the CTM, including the right to strike. Others, however, had never been particularly radical. If anything, many had only accepted the working-class language of the FNTE, closer ties to the CTM, and the extension of political and civil rights in

---

[99] The Confederación Regional de Obreros Mexicanos (CROM), founded in 1918, was an offshoot of the Casa del Obrero Mundial. It dominated the Mexican labor movement during the 1920s, and many of its leaders took over as high-level officials in the government in the late 1920s, in the PNR in 1929 and after, and in the CTM after its founding in 1936. For more on these transformations, and the role of state workers within them, see my *Urban Leviathan*, Chap. 3.

[100] When state personnel explicitly identified themselves as workers, or *obreros*, they used a strict labor-capital analogy and saw the state as similar to other patrons; although sometimes state workers identified themselves as "obreros profesionales," who nonetheless had "proletarian aspirations and objectives." Letter by the Unión General de Trabajadores de los Establecimientos Fabriles, 20 August 1935. AGNM, Galería de Presidentes (Cárdenas), expediente 437/104.

order to defend themselves against political infighting within the bureaucracy or to improve working conditions within government agencies,[101] not because they automatically saw themselves as working class. Still, radicalized elements and the CTM leadership joined together to push a strongly laborist position, and many of the more traditional, and conservative, state workers began to express reservations about their avowed proletarian status and to tone down their demands for workplace rights. Rather than supporting strike legislation, they called for a Ley de Servicio Civil (Civil Service Law) that would merely regulate hours, wages, pensions, and promotions.[102]

The state was caught in a bind. One of Cárdenas's political aims was to strengthen labor legislation for the working class as a whole; yet he also was aware that growing opposition to his pro-labor stances from among public employees themselves could jeopardize his hold on power and the fate of the new party and the postrevolutionary state project in its entirety, especially given government employees' salience and location at the front lines between state and society. During this same time Cárdenas also was facing growing opposition from other urban middle classes in Mexico City, some of whom had recently organized in the Confederación de la Clase Media and who vociferously decried their exclusion from the party's deliberations and institutional structures. In a nod to both sides in the conflict, several years into his term President Cárdenas introduced in Congress a new statute intended to constitutionally protect state workers. This 1937 statute granted separate rights to so-called working-class employees of the state (called *trabajadores de base*, or "base workers," defined in terms of their location at the lower end of a payment, autonomy, and decision-making hierarchy) and middle-class employees of the state (called *trabajadores de confianza*, or "workers of confidence," who were higher paid and made decisions on the job requiring greater skills and discretion).[103]

---

[101] One 1936 document, arguing for state workers' right to strike, claimed that in many offices state workers were treated without respect – no better than "household help" – and asked to perform personal services at the whim of their supervisors. Ibid., expediente 545.2/1.

[102] Conservative bureaucrats who most opposed granting public employees juridical status as workers or their right to strike were especially reluctant to affiliate with the CTM or wave its ideological banner. Many higher-level state administrators and employees, some of whom traced their public service careers and initial political loyalties to the Porfiriato, worried about losing their capacity to uphold more moderate political positions if they were further linked with this radical labor confederation, which had signed a pact with the Communist Party. For a detailed account of conflicts among state workers within one government agency, see Instituto Nacional de Estudios Históricos de la Revolución Mexicana, *Historia del sindicato nacional de trabajadores de la Secretaría de Gobernación*.

[103] Lower-level state workers classified as *trabajadores de base* (manual laborers) were to be fully covered by the new statute, which bestowed on them the right to organize and strike. Higher-level workers with greater workplace autonomy were classified as *trabajadores de*

Still, this compromise was not enough to end the simmering conflict about class allegiance or the class identities of state workers, in part because there was little coherence between juridical status, institutional location, and the political salience of those who nonetheless preferred to identify themselves as middle-class employees (empleados) rather than workers (trabajadores). Many of those employed in government offices could be considered employees and identified themselves as such. Yet, there were those who were not necessarily high enough in the bureaucratic hierarchy to be considered trabajadores de confianza but who thought they should be recognized as more on the middle- than the working-class end of the trabajador lexicon. This in turn meant that many were institutionally lumped together with the more politically radical and worker self-identified trabajadores de base, who were now granted the right to organize and strike, as well as to join the CTM if they so desired. This was not just a problem for state employees who shunned leftist or union affiliations. Those state workers who eagerly sought closer linkages with the country's CTM-led union movement, especially teachers but also significant portions of the military rank and file who had served under Cárdenas during the Revolution – another category of state worker now denied the right to strike – were especially upset, particularly given their long history of radical activism. For one thing, the statute mandated that state workers organize agency by agency rather than by job classification, a requirement which limited working-class solidarity. For another, these agency-based organizations could shun the CTM, if members so desired, and affiliate with whichever federation they pleased.

With controversy continuing, the juridical statute proposed by Cárdenas in 1937 remained stalled in Congress for almost a year, where ongoing debate over its implementation deepened the class fault lines among state workers and within Mexican society at large. The government's March 1938 oil nationalization further raised the stakes, as conservative voices both within and outside the state workers' organization denounced the government's steady march to the left and decried the chaos that would ensue if state employees could mobilize, like industrial workers, and paralyze the nation through strikes.[104]

---

confianza (supervisory or "responsible" workers), thereby exempting them from the rights to organize and strike detailed in the statute (AGNM, Galería de Presidentes [Avila Camacho], statement of the Situación Jurídica de los Secretarios de Estudio y Cuenta de la Suprema Corte de Justicia de la Nación, expediente 542.2/10). The full text of the statute that was eventually approved with some modifications is entitled the Estatuto de los Trabajadores al Servicio de los Poderes de la Union, published in Mexico's *Diario oficial*, 5 December 1938.

[104] With right-wing spokesmen out in force drumming up public support, left-oriented forces also began to question the proposed statute mainly because they feared that granting organization and strike prerogatives to state workers without also requiring them to affiliate

Political problems hit a peak in May 1938 when right-wing military forces, led by provincial strongman General Saturnino Cedillo, attempted a coup d'état against Cárdenas. Much of the opposition stemmed from the clear leftward turn of the administration, especially after the oil nationalization. Yet many of the rebels were also disturbed by the growing "class" solidarity between the military rank and file and the labor movement, as well as the involvement of military personnel in the party's labor and peasant sectors.[105] The proposed statute, which categorized military employees as state workers, heightened their concerns because military personnel were juridically treated in class terms.[106] Most high-ranking military officers interpreted the categorization of military personnel as state workers – as well as the growing links between the armed forces and the union movement – as a threat to the military's independence and to their own personal power. Complicating matters, the move to treat military personnel as a category of state workers also exacerbated class tensions within the military rank and file itself, in much the same way it had among government employees. To be sure, some in the armed forces were eager to ally themselves institutionally and ideologically with the union movement or peasant federations,[107] thereby flagging their own working-class or campesino identities.[108] Yet other military personnel saw themselves more in professional terms, and felt their classification as trabajadores de confianza would juridically and ideologically link them to higher-level bureaucrats and state employees with middle-class sentiments. In short, it was ambiguity and conflict over who constituted the middle versus working classes and whether

with the CTM might actually allow the triumph of conservative forces both in the union movement and the state itself.

[105] Nava Nava, *Ideología del partido de la revolución Mexicana*, Vol. 1, pp. 286–287, argues in fact that General Saturnino Cedillo's May 1938 military rebellion was motivated in large part by a concern that Cárdenas's efforts "to create solidarity within the military for popular [read labor] causes were bearing fruit."

[106] Although most members of the army were to be classified as trabajadores de confianza in the new statute, and thus were exempted from the rights to organize and strike, the proposed reform did categorize thousands of military men employed in the manufacture of armaments and other military goods as trabajadores de base, which meant that some members of the armed forces had the right to organize and strike. See Mendieta y Nuñez, *La administración pública en México*, p. 181. Among workers categorized as trabajadores de base were those employed in the Dirección General de Materiales de Guerra, which reported directly to the Secretary of Defense.

[107] The categorization of some military men as trabajadores de base sustained this perspective.

[108] A 31 January 1938 document from the Frente Revolucionario de Intelectuales, signed by representatives from several organizations of state workers, health professionals, and artists, applauded Cárdenas for moves that appeared "to integrate a PARTY OF WORKERS AND SOLDIERS." AGNM, Galería de Presidentes (Cárdenas), expediente 544.61/103.

military personnel should be treated in such terms, either juridically or institutionally, that created a new round of problems for Cárdenas.

Growing opposition from senior military officers and high-level bureaucrats, coupled with continued pressure for political recognition of middle classes as distinct from working classes, drove the beleaguered president to a new compromise. Unwilling to drop the juridical statute and the rights it guaranteed, Cárdenas instead institutionally separated state workers from the CTM and reconstituted the party to provide two new distinct sectors for state employees and the military. In the new party, renamed the Partido de la Revolución Mexicana (PRM), the so-called military sector did not have the federation structure of the original labor and peasant sectors; rather, it was created to allow soldiers, sailors, and airmen to participate in party politics as individuals rather than as corporativist groupings.[109] State workers, however, were directly incorporated into the Federación de Sindicatos del Trabajadores al Servicio del Estado (FSTSE), which now included other middle-class employees who had not been active or organized in the FNTE, and which did operate as a corporatist sector within the PRM. Owing to its large and well-organized membership, the FSTSE formed the backbone of what was known as the party's "bureaucratic sector" and what Cárdenas occasionally called the "popular sector," or Sector Popular, foreshadowing its future role as the basis of the Confederación Nacional de Organizaciones Populares (CNOP).

Loyal to the Revolution, committed to populist principles, and eager to balance the nation's rural and urban development, with the 1938 reform of the party into these four distinct sectors Cárdenas did what he could to stem the tide of social and political opposition. But even the foundation of a new bureaucratic/popular sector for state workers did not end conflict over the structures and rhetorics of middle-classness. For one thing, although the establishment of a specialized institutional locale in the newly founded PRM helped Cárdenas deal with the problems of a potentially rebellious military and the earlier brouhaha over state workers' integration in the industrial labor sector, it did very little to stem opposition from powerful military leaders inside the party itself, especially the more conservative leaders who traced their roots to the provinces, of which General Juan Andreu Almazán was a leading

---

[109] According to González Casanova, Cárdenas proclaimed that the military would enjoy constitutionally guaranteed "political rights and should exercise them." In return, the military as an institution (and military personnel on active duty) could not participate in politics. With both the military and state workers organizationally distinct from labor, moreover, neither would be subordinated to the CTM. For more on this, see González Casanova, *El estado y los partidos políticos en México*, p. 120; Nava Nava, *Ideología del partido*, Vol. 1, p. 67; and Lozoya, *El ejército mexicano*, p. 66.

spokesman.[110] For another, with much of the upper ranks of the military peopled by the sons of the provincial middle classes, their diminishing political power vis-à-vis laborers, peasants, and state workers, combined with growing ideological conflicts with the radical rank and file, easily fed into existent regional and rural class tensions, adding more fuel to Cárdenas's conservative opposition. Both factors undermined ideological and institutional unity within the ranks of the military, further spurring some to identify with peasant comrades,[111] others with industrial laborers, and still others with state employees, while at the same time they eroded allegiance to the upper echelon of officers.[112]

But what about the traditional middle classes? Why did they, like the military, continue to form a strong core of opposition to Cárdenas even after his 1938 reforms widened the party's scope to include state workers, a key element of the urban middle class? The answer is relatively straightforward: Cárdenas failed to preempt middle-class opposition because his new "popular" sector did not adequately accommodate a broad enough spectrum of middle-class occupations, concerns, and demands, either rhetorically or substantively.

---

[110] Indeed, although this move may have accomplished the objective of institutionally distancing military personnel from the labor movement and state workers, it did not rid the military of radical elements. Many of the newly empowered enlisted men tended to be more progressive and supportive of Cárdenas's social policies than the conservative military leadership, something which kept many officers unhappy. So too family farmers and agricultural producers in the provinces, who tended to ally with regional military elites in opposition to Cárdenas's agrarian reforms, tended to be unhappy with the military reforms. These agriculturalists saw as threatening any reforms intended to educate and empower the military rank and file, since it was comprised mainly of poor peasants from rural areas who might challenge regional elites' social and political power if not kept under tight rein.

[111] McAlister, *The Military in Latin American Sociopolitical Evolution*, p. 203. Part of this owed to the fact that Cárdenas found it necessary to create agrarian militias because regional military elites and provincial agriculturalists were carrying out an armed campaign of terror and violence against rural campesinos during the late 1930s.

[112] Military disunity resulted from the classification of some military personnel, especially those in arms-related manufacturing, as trabajadores de base; and party leaders frequently insisted that soldiers "were no more than workers in arms." See September 1939 letter from General Heriberto Jara, president of the Central Committee of the PRM, AGNM, Galería de Presidentes (Cárdenas), 708.1/19. It was further limited by the dispersion of a small but notable proportion of the military rank and file across the party's sectors. And remember, the creation of a military "sector" that did not necessarily function as such in practice exacerbated this problem. To the extent that the new military sector lacked the same political power and corporate rights as the other sectors, its leadership now had relatively little formal say in party politics, especially in relation to other class forces with well-functioning sectoral structures: peasants, labor, and bureaucrats. See Garrido, *El partido de la revolución institucionalizada*, p. 305.

Even though Cárdenas often referred to this new institutional arm of the party interchangeably as both a bureaucratic and popular sector, in a clear attempt to appeal to both state workers and a broad variety of urban middle and lower middle classes, it was evident from early on that his principal concern in founding the sector was to politically accommodate state employees primarily – especially those now classified as trabajadores de confianza, who still lacked labor protections and other legal rights of organization and protest – rather than the middle class as a whole. The phrase "popular middle classes," later used to identify this sector's constituency, actually did not come into common usage until after 1940.[113] Accordingly, most citizens interpreted the PRM's new "popular" sector as institutionally and rhetorically embodying the same working-class and peasant objectives advanced by the party before 1938, only now they were presented in the language of populism rather than class.[114]

This does not necessarily mean that Cárdenas fully opposed middle-class embeddedness in the institutions and governing vision of the state. But his clear orientation toward the industrial working class and the country's landless peasants did make middle classes a lower priority, on their own, such that their inclusion was important in terms of working- and middle-class alliance building, at best, but not as an independent or institutionally autonomous force. More important, even if Cárdenas had wanted to include middle classes more systematically into his governing coalition, the PRM had no such groups readily at its side, and it lacked established institutional relationships to accommodate their potential participation.[115] The upshot was that without a

---

[113] Córdova, *La política de masas*, p. 84. Cárdenas began to use the term "popular" in 1936, when he and party allies promoted a Frente Popular Mexicano within the PNR to bring peasants and laborers together with other social and class forces to strengthen the party against internal and external opposition. See Léon and Marván, *La clase obrera en la historia de México*, pp. 238–301.

[114] Nor did the PRM leadership take Cárdenas's "popular" sector very seriously, at least as a format for a wide range of dissatisfied middle-class groups to participate. A June 1938 document of the PRM, for example, in which a new "Cultural and Popular Sector" is discussed, states that the party secretary "has not yet communicated... the names of the organizations pertaining to this sector that are capable of contributing to the development of the politico-social program of the Partido de la Revolución Mexicana." Moreover, in this fourteen-page document, the popular sector is the only one which has no organizations listed under its heading. AGNM, Galería de Presidentes (Cárdenas), report from Elias Campos V. to Comité Nacional del PRM, expediente 544.61/103, n.d. As such, Cárdenas's use of the term "popular" was thus intended not to institutionally accommodate the middle class as a whole so much as to legitimate a rhetorical politics of unity aimed at linking politically strategic constituents from all different class and social backgrounds together in support of the party leadership.

[115] It is only in late 1939, in fact, that one finds any clear evidence of organized middle-class groups outside the bureaucracy proclaiming allegiance to the popular sector of the

unified urban front of support, especially in the capital city, Cárdenas had a difficult time generating stable political support for his administration.[116] And, thus it was Cárdenas's failure to bring *urban* middle classes into his political coalition that led to some of the most serious political problems of his administration and, by so doing, inadvertently brought a further displacement of the Revolution's rural middle-class origins as well.

There were two specific concerns that captured the imagination of urban middle classes enough to mobilize against Cárdenas and the Mexican state in the 1940s and 1950s, both of which revolved around the tensions and ambiguities inherent in the class rhetorics and organizations that he advanced in the late 1930s, although they manifested themselves in different arenas. One had to do with urban servicing, an issue that could not be ignored in a highly urbanized country like Mexico, especially, when both political stability and economic progress rested so directly on conditions in the capital city. The other was education. Both issues were controversial enough to spur protest among Mexico City's middle classes, although their larger significance derived from the new political alliances that activism around these issues generated. Controversies over education joined rural and urban middle classes in the city and countryside together, in opposition to Cárdenas, while urban policy deficiencies brought both the urban poor and middle classes to question the Cárdenas regime at the territorial seat of government.

Problems of urban service delivery were no stranger to Mexico City's populations, given the size of the capital city and the magnitude of the resources necessary to administer to residents who spanned the class spectrum and participated in activities as diverse as commerce, industry, and agriculture. But during the Cárdenas administration conditions had worsened considerably, or at least that was the popular perception. This owed not only to problems of unemployment and impoverishment among urban residents in the aftermath of the Great Depression and in the wake of steady rural-urban migration, which even Cárdenas's land redistributions could not immediately turn around, but also to bureaucratic infighting and strikes in government agencies, which produced interruptions in critical public services in Mexico City.[117] Equally

---

PRM. Many of these groups appear to have been organized by the party leaders themselves in response to growing social unrest and clear public support for Almazán's candidacy.

[116] Although it helped, the U.S. decision to side with the PRM was not enough to quell Almazán's revolt or to eliminate internal political opposition to one-party rule. Throughout 1941, even after Almazán had formally laid down arms, violent conflict continued between pro- and anti-Almazanistas, especially in the provinces. AGNM, Galería de Presidentes (Cárdenas), expediente 556.6/28; and Galería de Presidentes (Avila Camacho) 703.2/7.

[117] The inverse occasionally occurred as well, with conservative employees undertaking disruptive actions against leftist agency administrators. This was evidenced in a letter requesting presidential action against "several employees of *Gobernación* in the *Bosque de Chapultepec*

important, Cárdenas's support for industry in order to generate working-class employment, coupled with his prioritization of agrarian reform, also led him to neglect critical urban services and the city's commercial sector. Under his administration, "the portion [of expenditures] destined for urban public works was reduced" and new social programs were introduced that mainly benefited organized labor, including extensive investments in health, education, and new housing for CTM and FSTSE constituents only.[118] Fewer resources went to water, drainage, street paving, public lighting, and markets, which had been the principal demands of nonunionized popular and middle-class residents, especially shopkeepers and small industries which relied on these services for their livelihoods.[119]

Cárdenas's neglect of urban services was an issue that united many of the city's residents against his administration. Insufficient access to water, drainage, electricity, and affordable housing generated anger among middle classes and urban poor alike, especially the self-employed urban poor who, unlike industrial laborers, were outside the CTM and thus lacked specialized workplace benefits or government-provided housing.[120] Urban middle classes

who launched attacks on said government and the P.R.M." AGNM, Galería de Presidentes (Cárdenas), 12 January 1939 letter to President Lázaro Cárdenas from the Congregación Ortíz, Municipio de Rosales, expediente 544.61/103. With lower-rung state workers now allowed to strike, tensions between the more working-class-identified state trabajadores de base, and the more middle-class trabajadores de confianza reached a new height. State administrators often found themselves directly challenged by the employees they supervised, especially when the latter went on strike. Further aggravating matters was the fact that strikes were often called for political purposes; that is, to express displeasure with the conservative actions or political orientations of higher-level bureaucrats.

[118] Perló Cohen, *El cardenismo y la ciudad de México*, p. 7.

[119] See Cárdenas's Plan Sexenal in ibid., p. 5. The pattern of national social expenditures further confirms the privileging of rural as opposed to urban populations. For example, Cárdenas dictated that all "increases in the quantity [of resources] assigned to the Department of Health be destined completely for services in the interior of the Republic, since Mexico City has received constant attention in health matters and the sanitary needs in the States are much more urgent." This not only alienated Mexico City residents but also exacerbated tensions within the Department of Public Health between *base* workers and *confianza* workers, the latter of whom relied on a high volume of activities to sustain power or personal gain (bribes).

[120] AGNM, Galería de la Dirección General de Gobierno, Series 2, 331.9 (29) expediente 14. So too did growing transport problems, which accelerated as Cárdenas took few actions against striking trolley workers. When floods paralyzed Mexico City in 1939, the government's neglect of the city's drainage system became a principal organizing issue around which a broad spectrum of the urban population rallied to express opposition. One such grassroots organization, notably called the Unificación Popular del Distrito Federal, identified scarcities in public services as one of the four vital problems facing Mexico in the late 1930s, along with the economy, the administration of justice, and national defense.

and the poor were also affected by the inflation and rising costs caused by the oil nationalization of 1938. Self-employed street vendors, artisans, and shopkeepers were not covered by minimum-wage legislation, unlike the industrial and state workers in the PRM, and suffered accordingly. And while Cárdenas proved willing to distribute urban and rural lands to workers and peasants, as well as to construct housing for bureaucrats and industrial workers, he refused to respond to demands by well-organized and highly mobilized renters (*inquilinarios*) and small shopkeepers for legislation on rent control.[121]

Contributing to the groundswell of urban and rural middle-class opposition to Cárdenas were growing concerns about his education programs, many of which were built around socialist rhetorics, which in the countryside usually entailed a clear privileging of exploited Indian peoples and landless peasants.[122] The content of public education in Mexico had long been under dispute, to be sure, owing to the postrevolutionary anticlericalism and attendant prohibitions on private religious schooling imposed by the ruling party. Yet when state workers were granted the rights to organize as unions and to strike, many in the public worried about the impact on education, since almost all school teachers were state workers classified as trabajadores de base, who were institutionally and juridically connected to the more radical labor movement. More important, the teachers' union was known to be among the nation's most radical, infused with communist elements, and its pedagogy was further radicalized by Cárdenas's open support for teacher training using socialist models of education.[123] Public concern about communism among teachers was particularly strong in Mexico City, where the teachers' union was linked to left-oriented intellectuals and where most of the nation's urban middle classes resided. Adding fuel to the fire, Cárdenas's use of campesino teachers to spread political education about class inequality and immiserization in the countryside alienated rural middle-class populations too, especially those tied to Cedillo and other potentially rebellious regional elites. Among the most contentious issues were debates over the proper place for discipline in the pedagogy of primary and secondary education. During the 1920s and 1930s most school textbooks were peppered with admonitions like "The good and

---

[121] Perló Cohen, *El cardenismo y la ciudad de México*, p. 38. Perhaps more than any other issue, the renters' movement brought together urban poor and urban middle-class businessmen in an anti-Cárdenas alliance, with marches and rent strikes common occurrences in Mexico City in 1938 and 1939.

[122] For more on this see Vaughan, *Cultural Politics*, esp. pp. 29–36.

[123] A 1938 editorial in the leading Mexico City daily reflected the growing concern about public education when it argued that the government should promote nationalism over class consciousness. Most Mexicans "aren't reds," the author protested, and teachers should end their ongoing "fetishism over the right to strike" and stop filling kids' minds with "Bolshevik propaganda." *El universal* (4 January 1938), p. 3.

obedient child will be rewarded" or "Work hard and you shall triumph!"[124] Under Cárdenas, however, "disciplinary prescriptions eased ... as the principle of class struggle privileged collective action over moralizing."[125] Not surprisingly, middle classes who had long held elective affinity with these moralizing claims were among the most upset by the pedagogic transformations that eliminated these disciplinary discourses.

By 1939 it was clear that Cárdenas had failed to stem citizen dissatisfaction, especially among rural and urban middle classes. These disenfranchised and dissatisfied forces became the political constituency for opposition candidate General Juan Andreu Almazán, who joined the presidential race in 1939. With a military foothold in the northern city of Monterrey, Almazán rallied support from provincial opponents of the PRM, including conservative factions in the military elite, the northern bourgeoisie, and small farmers threatened by Cárdenas's land distribution and agrarian reform. Yet he also relied on support from dissatisfied urban groups who felt excluded by Cárdenas's working class, pro-labor vision, namely, middle-class professionals, small shopkeepers, alienated state workers, and the self-employed urban poor. In this verbal war over city, class identities, and political rights, Almazán's appeals struck a powerful chord among both urban and rural middle classes, in no small part because he took advantage of the public's own recognition of the ambiguities and tensions over working- and middle-class identities as well their growing concerns about the privileges accorded certain class organizations at the expense of others, mainly in the capital city.[126] As it became clear that, armed with this political strategy, Almazán might triumph in the upcoming 1940 presidential election, the PRM united behind a recognition that it must change its direction and accommodate these concerns or risk losing power.

---

[124] Vaughan, *Cultural Politics*, p. 41.

[125] Ibid., p. 42.

[126] In order to tap this constituency, Almazán inaugurated his national campaign in the nation's capital and largest city, Mexico City, where he generated a crowd estimated at between two hundred and two hundred fifty thousand. During the campaign, he appealed directly to white-collar state workers by arguing against the recently implemented juridical statute. The PRM's candidate, Manuel Avila Camacho, responded by claiming that state workers have "class consciousness and won't swallow such clumsy bait or abandon their rights just for an attractive promise" (*El universal* [5 Sept. 1939]). Yet many of the non-Indian rural middle classes also responded to Almazán's call for an end to land reform and the restoration of protections on private property. Almazán's support for public housing delighted the urban lower middle class involved in the *inquilinario* movement; and his pro-Catholic stance and support for nonsecular education appealed to those who worried about leftist pedagogy in Mexico's schools. He even won support from some sectors of organized labor, not because of his policy orientation but because they feared the antidemocratic consequences of the PRM's monopoly on political power. For more on the 1940 election, see Contreras, *México: 1940*, pp. 140–143.

Uniting City and Country in the Politics of the Middle Class

With the aim of holding the reins of power, PRM operatives frantically sought to manipulate voting results in the 1940 election and did so successfully in many areas. Yet in Mexico City, home to the largest concentration of state workers and middle classes, the PRM was forced to acknowledge that it lost overwhelmingly to General Almazán.[127] Faced with an obvious expression of urban discontent that could not be hidden under the cover of electoral fraud, Mexico's political leaders immediately undertook a series of reforms aimed primarily at bringing a wider array of urban and rural middle classes into the governing coalition. These efforts began in April 1941, just four months after Avila Camacho took office as president, at which time party leaders established a new organization, the Confederación de Organizaciones Populares (COP), to serve as a coordinating body for a wide variety of groups in the capital city, including renters, shopkeepers, artisans, and other primarily middle-class professionals who were excluded from the CTM and the FSTSE. Shortly thereafter, the party-controlled Congress modified the Estatuto Jurídico by expanding the category of workers defined as trabajadores de confianza (thus further limiting state workers' right to strike), implemented a new Ley de Servicio Civil that regulated wages, hours, and promotions of confianza workers, and reformed an existent Ley de Pensiones Civiles de Retiro in order to guarantee housing for state employees and members of the military. The new government also introduced a strict rent control law for Mexico City, which addressed the housing concerns of those not covered by the new laws or previous labor legislation, which were mainly the city's middle classes.[128] The PRM, in short, compensated for its earlier failure to recognize urban middle classes as juridically, politically, and socially relevant.

The PRM's next task was to fundamentally reform the party's national sectoral structure so as to incorporate the urban poor and middle classes, both rural and urban, together with state workers in the governing coalition. Because the Mexico City–based COP had served so well as a format for distinct occupational sectors of the urban middle class to participate in local politics, party leaders decided to use the same type of organization on a national scale, a decision that ultimately reinforced the urban bias of this sector of the party – an issue to which I will return shortly. At its founding in 1943, the Confederación Nacional de Organizaciones Populares (CNOP), which was to represent the country's "popular middle classes," became the third principal sector of the party, which also was renamed the Partido Revolucionario Institucional (PRI) in order to formalize the significance of this break with Cárdenas's party

---

[127] For detailed analysis of the election fraud, see Medina Peña, *Del cardenismo al avilacamachismo*.
[128] In this period and until 1997, in fact, Mexico City's mayor was appointed by the president.

(PRM) and its sectoral structure. The newly established CNOP replaced the military and bureaucratic sectors (that had existed separately in the PRM) and included within it numerous predominantly middle-class groups, such as shopkeepers, street vendors, small industrialists, women's organizations, and family farmers or other small producers organized in federations of pequeños propietarios.

The CNOP's inclusion of pequeños propietarios, or small property holders, is especially significant for our understanding of the potential but ultimately unfulfilled promise of disciplinary development in postwar Mexico. Both in practice and in the lexicon of the times, this category of folk included those small and even medium-sized agricultural producers with lands greater than 50 hectares and whose holdings "usually ranged in size from 100 to 150 hectares of irrigable land or its equivalent."[129] According to Nathan Whetten, in both formal and informal usage the pequeño propiedad (small holding) was in fact understood as "that part of the hacienda which was exempt from expropriation when agrarian laws were applied. The pequeño propiedad, therefore, may be thought of as the nucleus of a former hacienda."[130] As such, this category is significant not just because it refers to small holders of a particular "middling" size (neither too small nor too large) or even because it underscores the genuinely rural middle-class character of the new CNOP. It is also significant, discursively and in terms of the CNOP's insitutional rationale, because it clearly shows that the state sought to appeal to those rural farmers whose rights or access to the lands preceded or somehow "stood outside" agrarian reform legislation. This, in turn, meant that the CNOP was targeting smaller producers, or rural middle classes, not already organized within the CNC.

Given the CNOP's constituency and the timing of its establishment on the heels of the PRM's near defeat at the ballot box, it is no surprise that among its founding principles were several moderate if not conservative tenets that appealed to traditional middle classes, both urban and rural, as well as to many of the heretofore disenfranchised segments of the urban poor. Nor is it a surprise that this organization was used to challenge the leftist orientation and hearty embrace of a radical agrarian reform program so evident in Cárdenas's initial class-oriented restructuring of the party in 1938. In the document announcing its creation, the party promised to use the CNOP to: 1) combat "prejudice and fanaticism" in education, 2) establish a full range of legal rights for professionals, 3) protect private property, 4) support small industry, 5) guarantee credit to small firms and farms, 6) promote the formation of

---

[129] Whetten, *Rural Mexico*, pp. 173–174. He further notes that in 1940 the average ejidatario held 18.1 hectares of land (p. 240).

[130] Ibid., p. 174.

cooperatives, and 7) solve the urban housing problem and defend the rights of renters.[131] In stark contrast to the language used by Cárdenas a few years earlier, moreover, President Avila Camacho and party leaders were careful to claim for the first time that this new organization represented the popular *middle* classes, not just the popular classes, hoping to cast their net broadly enough to tap the sentiments of those disenfranchised citizens bypassed by Cárdenas's policies and politics.

In addition to incorporating a broad range of urban and rural middle classes alongside state workers, the CNOP also functioned as the party organization through which the military participated in national politics.[132] After formal dissolution of the military sector and its delegate block in Congress, in fact, "the majority [of military delegates] *passed on to form part of the popular sector* [emphasis mine]."[133] Equally important, the military was now identified as a key beneficiary of land reform with land distribution mediated through the CNOP.[134] This shift not only helped undermine the peasant orientation of

---

[131] Confederación Nacional de Organizaciones Populares, *Primer consejo nacional*, pp. 2–4.

[132] It is commonly assumed by scholars that the military disappeared from party politics starting in 1941, once the military sector was eliminated as an autonomous institutional force in the PRM. See Knight, "The Rise and Fall of Cardenismo"; and Garrido, *El partido de la revolución institucionalizada*. Yet this was true in only a limited sense. Even without their own independent sector in the party, military personnel continued to participate after 1941, primarily through the newly formed CNOP; and they did so despite legislation that prevented those on active duty from running for office or participating in politics. Frequently, military personnel simply took leave from active military service for the duration of their involvement in Congress or party politics, only to return once their term ended. For discussion of this and other ways in which military personnel bypassed constitutional regulations and actively participated in politics during the 1940s, see Coronado Barajas, *De las limitaciones impuestas a los militares para actuar en la política*, pp. 60–64.

[133] Partido Revolucionario Institucional (PRI), *Historial documental de la CNOP*, Vol. 1, p. 44. With such a large number of military delegates formally adhering to the CNOP, moreover, they soon "acquired a numerical force that, in any given moment, could shift the balance of voting" in Congress (ibid., p. 45). Accordingly, even though the military – as an autonomous institution – was formally eliminated from the party in late 1940, military personnel nonetheless remained an essential social and political force within the party, by virtue of their affiliation with the CNOP. The CNOP's first secretary-general was a military officer, Lieutenant Colonel Antonio Nava Castillo, who openly identified himself as such on party documents; commissioned military officers held two of the most critical posts on the CNOP's National Executive Committee (secretary of finance and secretary of political affairs); and a Secretariat of Pre-Military and Sports Activities was created to formalize the military's institutional presence and represent its programmatic concerns within this new popular middle-class sector. For more on this, see Confederación Nacional de Organizaciones Populares, *Primer consejo nacional*, a mimeo, n.p.

[134] According to Whetten, "In 1941 a law was enacted permitting retired personnel from the armed forces of the nation to settle in colonies on the three types of land previously

Cárdenas's land reforms and challenged the privileges initially equated with membership in the CNC, it also revived a more rural middle-class view of agrarian development by shifting the emphasis away from ejidal distribution and more toward the development of agrarian "colonies" (*colonias agrarias*). Indeed, while recipients of ejido lands only had usufruct rights to specific plots (because the land was not theirs technically), the military and other privileged residents of these agrarian communities were able to purchase and own their lots, as well as use them for collateral.[135] With these measures in place, the CNOP's role as a key institutional location for the country's rural middle classes, and as an organization through which the military and the rural middle class both mingled and reinforced each other's disciplinary identity and ethos, was firmly established.

But if the foundation of the CNOP reinforced links between the military and rural middle classes, and if it effectively brought urban and rural middle classes into the governing coalition of the state, we again ask the question why Mexico still failed to follow the more successful East Asian path of disciplinary development – built on rural middle-class embeddedness in the state and a two-pronged approach toward agrarian and industrial development. After all, as of 1945 there were institutional mechanisms for inclusion of labor, rural middle classes, and state workers, three key forces that were well represented in the institutional and programmatic structures of the KMT and that led Taiwan, in particular, to such incredible developmental gains starting just a few years later. Additionally, as occurred in Taiwan, the CNOP effectively linked rural and urban middle classes on one hand, and the military and rural middle classes on the other, two key sets of alliances that in our East Asian cases helped insure that the rural development concerns of small and medium-sized producers would compete with – if not outweigh – urban industrial ones? So why did Mexico instead embrace ISI immediately after this key historical juncture and follow it for several decades, letting the small-farmer path of development almost completely fall by the wayside?

described: (a) properties which are being adequately farmed; b) properties which constitute an agricultural-industrial unit planned and carried out in accordance with modern technology; and c) properties in which direct administration is employed in more than 50 percent of the lands used for each type of enterprise). In such cases, the lands are an outright gift by the government. They are placed in workable condition. Houses and roads are constructed at government expense and at no cost to the colonists. The size of the plot which each receives is based upon his rank in the armed services. For an ordinary private the allotment is 6 hectares of irrigated or 12 hectares of seasonal land. The allotment for a division general is 100 hectares of irrigated land or 200 hectares of seasonal land or 5,000 hectares of pasture land. During the periods 1941–1944 three such colonies were established involving 124 colonists and 7,811 hectares of land. This would make an average of 63 hectares per person." See *Rural Mexico*, p. 170.

[135] Nugent, *Spent Cartridges*, p. 104.

To a certain degree, the answer is that it did not. In the initial years after the 1943 foundation of the CNOP, Mexico entered a short but noteworthy period of relative economic prosperity, at least as compared to previous periods. These gains were considered by most scholars to be the result of combined urban and rural development programs and government expenditures to sustain balanced rural and urban growth, in a hybrid developmental model that echoed that implemented in Taiwan. According to economic historian Enrique Cárdenas, Mexico saw clear industrial gains during the late 1940s and throughout the 1950s, because "previous infrastructural investments began to pay off in a large way, and the conditions of the 'Mexican miracle' were laid as ninety-five percent or more of domestic demand was met internally rather than through manufactured imports."[136] By the end of the 1940s and continuing into the early 1950s, moreover, the earlier commitment to land distribution and ejidal development also was paying off to a great extent, at least in terms of offering employment and a source of family support for many rural farmers. With newly distributed lands and existent small-farm operations buttressed by significant government support in the form of infrastructural investment, credit, and pricing policies for small rural producers, the material conditions for growth in the rural sector had become adequately established. Disciplinary development, or a pretty accurate reproduction of this model, was indeed starting to materialize. And this is not merely a general picture based on aggregate macroeconomic figures. Most of these successes were replicated in many – although surely not all – rural locales across the country, including those where plot sizes were quite small and where ejidos predominated.

In Daniel Nugent's highly nuanced study of agrarian reform in the village of Namiquipa, for example, the rural population's relatively critical stance on the political drawbacks of the ejido program comes across loud and clear, as do its longer-term failures to sustain the rural economy. But so too does the positive economic impact of Mexico's agrarian programs on the development of a small class of independent farmers. During the period from 1935 to 1965, Nugent argues convincingly, Namiquipa's small producers "were cultivating more lands [and] there was an up-and-down but on the whole steady increase in agricultural production."[137] He even goes so far as to highlight the ways in which agrarian programs actively buttressed the rural middle-class status of these folk, where the majority of the village's residents, despite the constraints of the ejido program, soon "owned or controlled all of their labor-power and all or almost all the means of production necessary to engage in agriculture," such that they subsequently could be regarded "as simple – or

---

[136] Quoted from Van Young, "Making Leviathan Sneeze," p. 151. Note again that this quote is drawn from Van Young's review of Enrique Cárdenas's *La hacienda pública y la política económica, 1929–1959.*

[137] *Spent Cartridges*, p. 132.

petty – commodity producers, which is to say the individuals labor upon their fields and organize their own productive activities, wage-labor plays an insignificant role in their process, and that portion of the final product of labor not consumed is sold to another party."[138] These gains were similarly matched in the non-ejido rural sector as well, in part owing to a massive agricultural colonization program initiated through the CNOP which poured money into agricultural "colonies."[139] It was only in the mid- to late-1960s, in fact, that Mexico's agricultural sector began to show insoluble problems and that manufacturing imports outweighed exports in such a way as to create serious current account imbalances, leading eventually to a severe debt crisis a decade later.

As implied above, the agricultural "good times" of the 1950s can be partially explained by the successes of the ejido program reestablished by Cárdenas, which in its early stages reinvigorated small-scale farm production. As one scholar put it, "As the *ejido* program gathered momentum and as large numbers of *haciendas* were expropriated, the work opportunities away from the farm began to diminish [from reduced demand for rural wage labor], and many of the *ejidos* tended to become virtually self-sufficient units of production."[140] However, some of it also can be explained by the heightened awareness of the plight of small producers in general, a sensitivity that was put on the agenda and later buttressed by the state's willingness to accommodate pequeña propiedad in the CNOP, as well as in larger political discourse, and to encourage their contributions to agricultural development. A 1948 newspaper account makes clear the growing political salience and increased social legitimacy of the small-farmer class in the period immediately after the CNOP was established. While "demogogues" may consider "small property to be of bourgeois character," the article states, especially if they take into account primarily the maximum allowable plot size afforded by the country's Agrarian Code, "in reality in our country there are thousands and thousands of small landowners with plots whose expanse is identical, sometimes smaller and other times slightly larger, than collective (*ejidal*) or small landlord (*minifundistas*) parcels, and whose social and economic condition does not differ that much from *ejidatarios*." And pequeña propriedad, the article goes on to suggest, "should be respected because its existence and development . . . is of national utility."[141]

[138] Ibid.

[139] For more on this program, see Whetten, *Rural Mexico*, pp. 152–182; and Mendieta y Nuñez, *Política agraria*, pp. 290–293.

[140] Whetten, *Rural Mexico*, p. 241.

[141] Mendieta y Nuñez, *Política agraria*, p. 212. This fascinating book presents a compilation of public opinion and statements on the country's agrarian policy from the postrevolutionary period until the late 1950s.

The significance of these claims rests not just in the fact that they underscore the importance of small rural producers, especially non-ejidatarios, but also in the fact that they were advanced by a group called the Confederación de Pequeños Propietarios (CPP), an organization of small rural producers both incorporated and politically empowered by the foundation of the CNOP in 1943. The CPP put these issues on the public agenda in the course of arguing for a major reform of the Agrarian Code, in the hopes that they would be successful in advocating for changes in the existent bureaucratic and legal structures, would help make small-property ownership more "efficient," and would do so without harming the "legitimate interests" of campesinos who had taken the ejidal route to petition for lands.[142] Indeed, in many ways the CPP played a role as the major advocate for institutionalizing the small-farmer path, by promoting policies of rural development that were in many ways equivalent to those advanced by the Taiwanese and South Korean states in conjunction with their small rural producers organizations, and that embodied a certain degree of disciplining. This is further evidenced in a 1947 article on the state's rural colonization programs, in which the CPP lauded the government's new efforts to develop agricultural colonies in rural areas (*fraccionamientos rurales*), arguing their superiority over *fraccionamientos urbanos* because they avoided middlemen whose gains came merely from speculation ("*no da al comprador los medios de pago*"). Moreover, in discussing this program, CPP spokesmen were quick to note that these agricultural colonies would only be successful "if they did not remain exclusively in the hands of private enterprises, but also [came] under the control of the government," a view of the importance of the state to the disciplinary project that paralleled those implemented in both our East Asian cases.[143]

Yet even with government support and strong optimism for these and other rural development programs among a newly empowered rural middle class, there were other serious obstacles that the CPP and other smaller-scale rural producers faced over the late 1950s and 1960s, which ultimately limited the utility and efficacy of the small-farmer path of rural development and disciplinary development in Mexico more generally. For example, despite the growing visibility of small farmers as a political and social force in this key historical juncture, eventually smaller-scale rural producers met the same fate as their counterparts in South Korea: an inability to keep production levels high, downward pressure on plot sizes, and growing rural unemployment, all of which materialized with a vengeance in the mid- to late-1960s. By the 1970s, Mexico was importing corn and other essential foodstuffs that earlier had been produced domestically. Underlying this trend was the fact that small and medium-sized rural producers had been almost completely

---

[142] Ibid., pp. 213–214.
[143] Ibid., p. 293.

crushed by competition from large agro-businesses choosing to produce goods for export rather than domestic markets, two interrelated processes that helped make the small-farmer vision of rural development a thing of the past. For another, economic obstacles directly associated with the ejido system and with the legal underpinnings of Mexico's agrarian reform and property ownership regulations contributed to the decline. Over time the subdivisivion of already precariously small ejidal lands among generations of recipients drove down average plot sizes, with demographic growth responsible for further pressures on land holdings. This was especially true among rural residents who felt some cultural or social allegiance to their community or village. In the words of one scholar, in order to remain in the countryside and work the land "children born into *ejidos* . . . must either purchase land, form new *ejidos*, or become agricultural laborers – landless peasants."[144] With ejidal land insufficient to sustain agricultural populations, rural-urban migration increased; and after two decades or so of self-sufficiency, many ejidos became merely a source of part-time employment.[145]

Yet even more significant from our vantage point were the larger politico-institutional constraints on the institutionalization of disciplinary development practices, which not only would entail thriving small-farmer production but also strong forward-backward linkages between rural and urban sectors as well as a strong disciplining of industrial capitalists and laborers. Indeed, although the CNOP allowed the plight of rural middle classes to be put on the political agenda, and although it gave new life to a vocal organization of pequeño propietarios organized as members of the CPP, the fact that this federation was itself institutionally embedded within the CNOP meant that small producers had very little power within the state to push the small-farmer path when the leadership in the CNOP and other key sectoral institutions of the party and state remained strongly committed to urban-based industrialization. As such, it was independent farmers' failures to cement themselves as a prosperous rural middle class, and their inability to hold political sway within the CNOP – and thus in the party-dominated state in its entirety – that explains why Mexico finally and decisively turned away from the small-farmer, East Asian–type development path. This outcome owed to more than just the

---

[144] Nugent, *Spent Cartridges*, p. 131.

[145] Whetten, *Rural Mexico*, p. 242. He also notes (p. 242) that problems of agrarian decline may have been facilitated by ejidatarios' failures to reinvest or expand production in a way that would help them increase market shares. "Gradually, the *ejidatarios* found that they could subsist, though very meagerly, on the *ejidos* without the necessity of working elsewhere, and, in the absence of wants that would stimulate them to look for outside work, they drifted into the custom of permitting the work on the *ejido* to represent the totality of their efforts." This view is very much in keeping with Mexican stereotypes about ejidatarios' "peasant ethos" and their incapacity to become small capitalists.

purely economic conditions that limited the development of an urban and rural middle class. As was the case at each other critical juncture in Mexico, in which the rural middle class started out auspiciously, poised to wield influence in the state and on subsequent developmental trajectories, it was the existence of unbridgeable divisions among rural producers and strong class alliances among urban producers and consumers that eventually limited the rural middle classes' capacity to sustain these goals, even after their organization in the CPP and their inclusion in party structures (i.e., the CNOP) in 1943. And as in past periods, the issues of race and regionalism again played a role in irreparably dividing the middle classes. After 1943, institutional dynamics associated with previous ventures in state formation also factored in, as did a new set of influences: geopolitics and nationalism. Moreover, in contrast to South Korea and Taiwan where geopolitical considerations and nationalism helped unify middle classes and link them to the state, in Mexico these same factors split rural and urban middle classes even as they increased the salience of the latter over the former within the state, ultimately pushing Mexico down the urban-dominated ISI path also pursued in Argentina.

Race, Nation, and the Geopolitics of Mexican Development

One of the biggest obstacles to uniting Mexico's rural middle class and preventing it from emerging as a salient economic and political force capable of pushing forward rural development as a national priority was the existence of two distinct institutional sectors of the party for representing rural producers (i.e., the CNC and CNOP), a state of affairs that resulted from the cumulative historical legacy of state formation and party building. Although in theory the newly founded CNOP held the promise of catapulting the previously excluded rural and urban middle classes into the limelight along with the already included ejidatorios, in practice the fact that the CNC already existed as a party sector with a very well defined aim (to facilitate land distribution claims), and that the CNOP was established apart from the CNC, meant that rural middle classes as a whole had neither a common institutional mechanism nor a common purpose to advance. Making matters worse, the existence of these two separate institutions further exacerbated already nascent divisions within the rural middle class that had long existed on the basis of size of landholding and race/ethnicity.

The CNC grouped the smallest of the small producers, who received their lands primarily through ejido legislation and as such tended to be of Indian descent, characteristics that reinforced the CNC's identity as a sector for so-called peasants, despite their membership status as small producers with usufruct rights to land, and despite the predominance of cultivation for exchange rather than use value. The fact that land was granted in the form of ejidos also meant that these small producers never were considered owners of the land. The CNOP, in contrast, grouped those more prosperous and long-standing small and medium-sized producers referred to as *pequeña propiedad* in the lexicon, who not only had direct ownership rights to the lands (and thus more incentive to produce and reinvest) but also were more likely to be mestizo. In short, the establishment of separate party sectors for ejidatorios on one hand and pequeños propietarios on the other reinforced social and political distinctions based on size, ownership, and race/ethnicity, thereby further legitimizing and reinforcing the differences between poor rural producers, who shared more in common with a so-called peasantry, and those we might call small rural capitalists. This division irreparably divided rural small producers in terms of interests, ideology, institutional unity, and thus organizational strength.

Daniel Nugent gives telling evidence not only of the arbitrariness of the distinction made between so-called peasants and rural small capitalists by government officials, but also of the insidious, racialized ways these distinctions were politically reinforced. The issue at hand involved Namiquipans' struggles to have agrarian reform legislation recognize the establishment of pequeñas propiedades within their ejidos. Even though Indians petitioned the state to allow them to hold their individual plots as small private properties, they were denied by government officials at the Comisión Nacional Agraria (CNA) because, in the words of CNA head Luis Cabrera, the owners of *"pequeña propiedad* ... were not to be peasants who lacked the proper entrepreneurial spirit ... ([and who would only] set themselves up in their ranchos and not develop the land due to their ideology), but capitalist farmers."[146] Thus, despite the fact that private property ownership among the nation's small farmers was heralded by government spokesmen as the hope for Mexico's future development, it was only *non*-Indians who would be allowed to become small capitalists, if you will, an economic marginalization that Nugent attributes to the government's desire to politically control native peoples (achieved by linking them to the state through the CNC's administration, management, and monitoring of their ejido activities). Whatever the origins, the situation did not bode well for the economic prospects of ejidatarios. As one article published in the Mexico City daily *El universal* in December 1953 noted, "It was not enough to put the land at the disposition of the rural proletariate [*sic*] if there was no restructuring of an adequate legal order to guarantee possession and utilization."[147]

That race and ethnicity divided the rural middle class to the point of producing distinct class discourses (i.e., campesinos, or peasants, versus pequeños

---

[146] *Spent Cartridges*, p. 102. Nugent goes on to say that "neither of the two *pequeñas propiedades* legally recognized within the Namiquipan *ejido* in 1926 belonged to peasants – they were both owned by *foráneos*" (outsiders, and ostensibly non-Indian).

[147] Mendieta y Núñez, *Política agraria*, p. 266.

propietarios, or small owners) among various small producers not only distinguishes the Mexican from the South Korean and Taiwanese experiences; it
also parallels in many ways the Argentine experience, where the foreign or
immigrant status of small rural producers served as a basis for distinguishing them from the long-standing (and near-fascist) rural middle-class families
outside of Perón's discourse. Yet the overall consequences were different in
Mexico than in Argentina, especially in terms of building coherence in the
government's large political coalition of support. In Argentina, even though
race and ethnicity split the rural middle class, it was precisely small farmers'
ethnically and racially cast "outsider" status that made it possible for Perón to
discursively draw them into a political coalition with their immigrant urban
working-class counterparts. In Mexico this did not occur, not just because
the industrial working class itself was divided by race, but also because the
institutionally bounded discourses used to refer to small producers (peasants
versus small capitalists) did not offer any clear basis for unification with industrial workers. In Mexico, then, the state built its legitimacy around three
distinct sectors with divergent class and social discourses, the ultimate effect
of which was to divide these forces as much as unite them into a single political
coalition.

This is not to suggest that the three-legged class-based structure of Mexico's
ruling party did not serve some function, nor even to suggest that it was not
a clever political strategy, albeit Machiavellian in conception. Indeed, much
of Mexico's political stability over the decades owed to the broadly cast class-
inclusiveness of its party structures, at least formally, a feat that was not
fully achieved until the establishment of the CNOP. This move gave the PRI
great legitimacy, a lease on political power lasting close to fifty years, and,
most important perhaps, the illusion of governing over what I have elsewhere
called an "uncommon democracy."[148] Still, although the foundation of the
CNOP may have been a brilliant preemptive political move because it helped
generate widespread political support among the previously disenfranchised,
the longer-term macroeconomic consequences were much more problematic.
The basic source of the problem lay not just in the fact that establishment
of separate sectors for peasants and small rural capitalists divided the rural
middle class in ways that prevented them from promoting the small-farmer
path of disciplinary development that brought measurable successes in the
East Asian context. Equally important was the fact that the logic of sectoral
composition and organization in the PRI effectively privileged urban over
rural populations, further restricting rural middle classes' capacities to wield
minimal political influence in the state either through the CNC or even from
within the CNOP, and catapulting urban-based workers, industrialists, and

---

[148] See my "Uncommon Democracy in Mexico."

middle classes into a loosely cast pro-ISI alliance where capitalists and laborers were accommodated and not disciplined.

The latter state of affairs was perhaps most damaging to Mexico's long-term economic prospects. Despite the fact that the CNOP was institutionally endowed with the structural capacity to link together rural and urban middle classes into one unified force, as occurred in Taiwan where strong ethnically bounded links between rural and urban middle classes helped sustain the state's overall disciplinary capacity, any cross-territorial middle-class cooperation in these regards was ultimately undermined by the urban orientation of the party's remaining constituencies. This occurred not just because two of the party's three sectors, the CTM and the CNOP, held within them so many urban-based populations (industrial laborers and state workers, the majority of whom resided in the Mexico City area), or because the only identifiably rural sector, the CNC, was the least powerful and the most controlled-from-above (representative socially marginalized Indians, to boot). It also resulted because within the CNOP itself, urban-based state employees and local residents of *colonias* soon dominated activities in such a way that rural middle classes eventually fell by the wayside, even within their formal representative body, paving the way for CNOP and CTM leaders to work together to promote the urbanization-led path of rapid industrial development built around domestic manufacturing for the internal (mainly urban) market, at the expense of small-farmer production in rural areas.

As at previous historical junctures, much of this owed to the unparalleled dominance of Mexico City and the PRI's decision that appeasing residents at its territorial base of power was a number one priority. This "urban overdetermination" of political and developmental outcomes was by the late 1940s and early 1950s even more overpowering than it had been in 1915 and again in 1939, since by this time the PRI also had established nearly indissoluble connections with industrialists in Mexico City. This occurred because in the mid-1930s the Mexico City–oriented national government introduced new statutes mandating changes in the private sector's formal organization in order to diminish the power and independence of regional businessmen's associations that had been challenging Cárdenas. Still, this is a response that raises more questions than it answers and thus deserves a bit more scrutiny. If we recognize that urban social, political, and even economic priorities had a history of commanding the activities of the party in general and the CNOP in particular, we must wonder why rural middle classes, be they in the CNC or the CNOP, still lent their sympathies and political support to the PRI by participating in these sectoral structures. This, after all, is more than a rhetorical question, at least with respect to rural middle classes and the CNOP. The allegiance of the CNC's "peasant" constituents can be explained partly by their heartfelt loyalty to Zapata, Villa, and the Revolution, their unabashed sympathies and personal enthusiasm for Cárdenas – the sector's founder and acknowledged champion of agrarian reform – and the patronage system, as well as the continued promise of fulfilling their claims for land. But understanding the allegiance of the CNOP's pequeños propietarios is much more difficult. Why did they not bolt the party and challenge it from without? This, after all, was not that farfetched an option. It was more or less in the same period that the CNOP was founded that Mexico's main opposition party, the Partido Acción Nacional (PAN), appeared on the scene. Founded in 1938, by the mid-1940s the PAN had presented itself as a forceful and potentially threatening political alternative to the official party, making its greatest inroads into the ruling party's constituency by aiming its message primarily toward Mexico's middle classes, many of whom at the time felt disenfranchised by the labor and peasant orientation of President Lázaro Cárdenas. And why did large numbers of military personnel, who also had become actively incorporated in the CNOP, not follow suit? This, after all, would have produced in Mexico a situation similar to that which developed in Argentina a few decades later: the middle-class military coup, in which middle classes and the military joined together to oppose the labor if not peasant orientation of the Peronists.

The answers to these questions, which hold the key to understanding Mexico's developmental trajectory, lie in a closer examination of the geopolitics of the time as well as of an attendant nationalism that combined with geopolitical conditions to link middle classes, the military, and industrialists to each other even as they produced a significant degree of rural middle-class participation in the CNOP.[149] The biggest single explanation for this was the advent of World War II. The war had a direct impact on the organizational successes of the CNOP and the longevity of one-party rule by uniting disparate class and ideological forces within this sector – and the party as a whole – around industrialization and against an external enemy (in ways that may have paralleled the nationalist project of industrialization in Taiwan and South Korea). The war also limited the possibility of U.S. support for armed military revolt (i.e., the middle-class military coup), provided the ideological grounding for a centrist path between communism and fascism, and spurred the economy sufficiently in order to generate medium-term prosperity, thus sustaining the truce among labor, peasants, and middle classes long enough for Mexico's new party structures to become truly institutionalized.

As in East Asia but to very different macroeconomic effect, global geopolitics and the long arm of the U.S. government were key players in these events

---

[149] To be sure, some of the country's rural middle classes, especially those pequeños propietarios with long-standing support for regional autonomy and strong (often pro-Catholic) links to urban middle classes in the provinces, did join the PAN, which became known as the semireligious party of the rural middle classes. But many others – in sufficient numbers to legitimize the PRI's hold on power for several more decades at least – lent full support to the party.

both in terms of what they did and what they did not do for the PRI. In 1940, the party was up against the wall in terms of growing opposition from military and middle-class groups, having fraudulently claimed victory and having expelled the real winner, Almazán. Refusing to accept the results of the election, Almazán and several of his military allies retreated north of the Mexican border and regrouped in San Antonio, Texas, where they declared a provisional government and vowed to struggle for democracy in Mexico. From there they shipped arms to guerrilla forces in northern Mexico in hopes of defeating the new president, Manuel Avila Camacho. Almazán's uprising, however, was dependent on at least tacit support from the U.S. government, and that support was not forthcoming, a stance that laid the first stone for the PRI's subsequent institutional reincarnation.[150] The outbreak of the war in September 1939 provided further incentives for the United States to strengthen its relations with Mexico's ruling party and reject Almazán's pleas for support.[151] The last thing the United States wanted was a burgeoning civil war on its southern border, which would form both a source of instability in the region and an opportunity for, in one analyst's words, "Nazis, Fascists, and Japanese to establish political, economic, and military beachheads in the New World."[152] However, it was not just the U.S.'s actions that turned the tide for Mexico.[153] Much as we have argued in the cases of South Korea and Taiwan, where U.S. political and financial support was similarly forthcoming for larger geopolitical and even ideological reasons, ultimately it was internal conditions that sustained military and middle-class support for the PRI, albeit internal conditions as inspired if not mediated by external developments.

[150] Lieuwen, *Mexican Militarism*, p. 138. Reluctance to support armed rebellion against the Mexican government also was partly the result of Franklin Roosevelt's Good Neighbor policy, which had forsworn U.S. intervention in Latin America's internal affairs. Even when Cárdenas expropriated U.S. oil companies in 1938, Roosevelt had resisted domestic pressure to invade Mexico, asking only that the U.S. firms involved be treated fairly.

[151] Almazán's appeal to Mexico's extreme right wing may also have been a concern to U.S. policy makers. Despite Cárdenas's left-leaning rhetoric and his criticisms of bourgeois democracy, both he and Avila Camacho consistently took a strong public stance against totalitarianism and the imperialistic objectives of the Axis powers. Almazán, in contrast, was known to count on political support from the neo-fascist Gold Shirts, a stance which hardly endeared him to a government intent on defeating world fascism. Thus the Roosevelt administration was eager to establish positive relations with both outgoing President Cárdenas – who now became secretary of defense – and incoming President Avila Camacho.

[152] Porter and Alexander, *The Struggle for Democracy*, p. 184.

[153] Although it helped, the U.S. decision to side with the PRM was not enough to quell Almazán's revolt or to eliminate internal political opposition to one-party rule. Throughout 1941, even after Almazán had formally laid down arms, violent conflict continued between pro- and anti-Almazanistas, especially in the provinces. AGNM, Galería de Presidentes (Cárdenas), expediente 556.6/28; and Galería de Presidentes (Avila Camacho) 703.2/7.

First and foremost, the outbreak of the war distracted much of the officer corps from party politics, and the PRM leadership actively played this card to its advantage.[154] Second, the government promoted a discourse of anti-imperialism and developed a massive campaign to "militarize" key sectors of civil society, mainly workers in factories, rural producers of all varieties, state employees, and local community organizations of *colonos* and *comerciantes*.[155] To militarize meant to teach skills of self-defense and to arm certain key populations; but it also served as a call to national unity, helping to reduce political differences and create solidarity among antagonistic class and social forces. The KMT had employed this strategy to great effect, as discussed earlier. In Mexico, this was accomplished through the creation of a five-thousand-man Civic Guard of the Mexican Revolution within the CNOP, which possessed a "semi-military character" and served as a mechanism to ideologically link the sector's middle-class constituents to the nation's armed forces under the banner of national unity.[156] Mexico stayed neutral for the first fifteen months of Avila Camacho's presidency, but when German submarines attacked Mexican ships in the Gulf in May 1942, the loss of Mexican life opened a floodgate of national support for the Allied cause. Thousands of citizens offered to join the Mexican army, and the public began debating the evils of Nazi imperialism and the importance of national struggles for world democracy. This further united disparate social and class groups in Mexico at a time when continued internal conflict might have irreparably weakened the ruling party's hold on power. It also reduced both the motive and opportunity for military rebellion by fully engaging the armed forces in the privileged mission of national defense. This in turn allowed the PRM leadership to justify the military's organizational existence within the party to progressives and conservatives alike, a stance that for the time being displaced the dilemma of which class identity (or sector) was most consistent with the military's identity and aim.[157]

One way the military's overall presence was legitimized and class-divisive issues were sidelined so as to keep middle-class opponents from leaving the party was through the project of "militarization," noted above, which broadened the social bases of military activity and erased the boundaries between military and civilian groups, no matter their class composition. Yet party leaders

---

[154] Lieuwen, *Mexican Militarism*, p. 143.

[155] AGNM, Galería de Presidentes (Avila Camacho), expedientes 545.2/14–1 and 545.2/80.

[156] Confederación Nacional de Organizaciones Populares, *Delegados de la Federación de Organizaciones Populares del D.F. en el primer consejo nacional de la CNOP*, p. 36.

[157] By late 1941, even the right-wing Gold Shirts, who had strongly supported Almazán, now "frankly and loyally" pledged their cooperation with the governing PRM "for the patriotic good," although this did not stop them in their search for "communist elements" inside the country's borders. AGNM, Galería de Presidentes (Avila Camacho), expediente 550/24.

also worked hard to present the armed forces as a democratic and equalizing force in society, introducing a program of military professionalization to help promote this new image. While in the past the army was comprised of relatively undisciplined renegades representing the "warrior soul of the race," it was now touted as much more: an "institutional body with authentically legitimate and democratic roots . . . formed of free and voluntary soldiers conscious of their responsibility" who deserved the "patriotic and enthusiastic" support of all the Mexican people.[158] In its new form, claimed General Felix Ireta, governor of Michoacan, the army "is the most alive, most pure, most perfect image of the Mexican Revolution. In it our workers, our peasants, our citizens of the middle class mix in a spirit of solidarity and fraternity."[159] The discourse of national unity inspired a common language, somewhere between the rhetorics of communism and fascism, that at least temporarily served to reconcile different ideological tendencies and bring seemingly disparate class-based forces and institutions together within the ruling party, in much the same way nationalist discourses helped unite potentially disparate class forces in South Korea under Park Chung Hee. Note, moreover, this all materialized in the 1940s when Mexico did begin to pursue the disciplinary developmental path.

As such, not only did the war effort bring much-needed internal political peace and stability to Mexico, because it was ideologically centrist, and palatable to so many different class and social forces, it also brought material results that benefited a wide variety of groups, beginning with the military. Massive amounts of government resources were poured into special services for the armed forces, from housing to medical care to their own community schools. These benefits pleased almost all groups within the military, giving incentive to both its conservative leaders and the rank and file to remain loyal and work with the party leadership. They also helped establish an organizational logic to unite disparate social and class forces within the CNOP. For example, the military now joined state employees as the recipients of special housing services. This policy helped unite the two social groups into a common middle-class constituency and explains why provision of housing was a founding principle of the CNOP in 1943. Furthermore, much of the wartime arms and machinery production was undertaken by military cooperatives, formed with government financial support under the guise of programs advanced by the CNOP. These policies reinforced the military's commitment to cooperatives, a form of small-producer organization identified at the CNOP's 1943 founding as a policy issue particularly dear to artisans, small shopkeepers, and small producers in both rural and urban locations. Finally, much of the government money spent on *colonias militares* supported the establishment of small-scale

---

[158] Ibid., expediente 135.2/206.
[159] Ibid., expediente 135.21/29.

service and commercial activities run by and for the military. These enterprises further linked the policy and political concerns of the military to those of other key middle-class constituents of the CNOP, not only shopkeepers and self-employed artisans but also other provincially based rural producers active in the associations of pequeños propietarios, while at the same time eliminating long-standing tensions between the military and industrial workers over the latter's special claims to social services under the earlier administration of Cárdenas.

In addition to the effects of war-related social spending on the CNOP's internal cohesiveness, the war had a powerfully stimulating effect on the national economy as a whole. The United States renegotiated Mexico's foreign debt with highly favorable terms, requiring it to pay only 10 percent of the principal plus interest over a twenty-year period. The United States also agreed to an annual purchase of Mexican silver, a \$40 million credit to stabilize the peso, a \$30 million line of credit at the Export-Import Bank, and a new commercial treaty that granted Mexico most-favored-nation status, thus reducing trade barriers on manufactured and agricultural products.[160] New sources of public and private investment flowed from north to south to support infrastructural development (most notably new highway and port construction) as well as industrial production. Most of Mexico's exports during this period consisted of agricultural produce and textiles. However, some of the most impressive growth took place in heavy industries directly involved in the war effort: iron and steel, motor vehicles, armaments, chemicals, and cement.[161] The long-term effects of these investments would be felt in the ISI path of the 1950s and the continuing expansion of the national economy, led in large part by industries that were first developed through the war effort during the early 1940s. It was in territorial terms, moreover, that the economic growth stimulated by the war had its greatest payoff, since most of the investments were located in Mexico City, where the government had greatest control over industry and the labor movement, and where U.S.-owned war production firms (among them GM, Chrysler, and Ford, which produced tanks and other war equipment and vehicles) were prone to locate.

With new life breathed into the nation's manufacturing sector, industrialists of all sizes, and especially those based primarily in Mexico City, found a reason to ally with the ruling party and its labor sector, a stance which gave the PRI renewed political legitimacy but which also reinforced the government's nascent commitment to ISI over the aims of rural development, especially of the small-farmer variety. The CTM was willing to go along because of increased job prospects, and as a consequence the labor movement took a more conciliatory stance toward capitalists and their ideological allies in the middle class, all

[160] Torres, *Historia de la revolución mexicana*, pp. 37, 58, 160.
[161] Porter and Alexander, *The Struggle for Democracy*, p. 184.

of which laid even stronger foundations for an urban-based capital-state-labor pact. This political alliance gave the party leadership significant legitimacy but it also limited its willingness to discipline either capitalists or laborers. More important perhaps, wartime industrial growth, and the promise of more to come, kept the three-tiered party structure politically legitimate and intact long enough to institutionalize solid political relations within and between each sector and the party leadership. In the 1946 presidential election, most of Mexico's citizens (77 percent) gave their approval to the party's new profile by supporting the ruling party's candidate, Miguel Alemán, who promised to maintain good relations with the United States as he led Mexico down the path of rapid, urbanization-led industrialization. The first civilian president in Mexico since 1911, Alemán came to office with particularly strong support from middle classes and the military. Labor split over his candidacy, with some of the most left-leaning sectors leaving the party to form the Partido Popular Socialista (PPS). Still, because of the geopolitical environment, much of the labor movement stayed loyal, as did the peasant sector. This broadly cast base of political support kept Alemán and subsequent party leaders loyal not just to centrist politics but also to the industrialization programs so successfully implemented during the war.

Accordingly, although the PRI ended up with a widely cast corporatist political structure that on the surface looked very similar to the KMT's in the breadth of its sectoral logic, and although this sustained important developmental gains in both agriculture and industry during the 1940s and 1950s, in the long run it differed significantly with respect to the political sway afforded rural middle classes and with respect to the overwhelming dominance of urban populations in the governing coalition. To be sure, just as in the East Asian cases, the form and character of the party was very much a product of the geopolitics of the time, which was similarly infused with struggles about ideology and political systems. The outcomes nonetheless were very different. External "geopolitical" factors helped establish strong linkages between rural middle classes and the state in South Korea (in a united front against North Korean communism) and rural and urban middle classes in Taiwan (in the face of both communist Chinese threats and KMT domination). In Mexico, however, geopolitics could neither unify rural and middle classes nor link the rural middle class to the state in any enduring fashion. For a short time, the advent of World War II and the U.S.-led struggle against fascism did help politically unite most social and class forces behind the party, under the guise of nationalism and national unity, in a fashion that temporarily supported a form of disciplinary development. But the economic and industrial impacts of World War II were more important in the long term, and they ultimately established an urban-industrial bias to the party's sectoral logic and structures. It was this urban bias, evident in larger party deliberations and in developmental objectives, that further disenfranchised CNC constituents even as it irreparably split the CNOP membership by relegating the claims of its rural middle class to the bottom of the agenda. By the late 1950s, a scant decade or so after the nationalist-infused geopolitical pacts had been forged, and some small-farmer agricultural development gains had been made, rural middle classes had practically dropped out of the CNOP's formal discourse, explaining why some of the region's most powerful opposition parties (PAN) and movements (ranging from Navismo in San Luis Potosi in the 1950s to El Barzón across northern states in the 1990s) have since then counted on independent rural middle classes to bolster their ranks.

Entrenching the Urban Leviathan

Once the capital-labor-state pact was forged and entrenched through the privileging of Mexico City–based industries and laborers during the extended period of production for World War II, it became increasingly unlikely that the state would recommit its developmental aims toward rural growth or a more equally balanced program of rural-urban development would actually materialize. Throughout the 1960s and 1970s, the party's labor and popular sectors reigned supreme in internal policy deliberations; and within the latter, it was state workers who effectively controlled the CNOP, at best taking into account the demands of mainly urban social movements – mostly in the capital city, again – in the later years of the 1970s and into the 1980s. Rural middle classes and their concerns shifted to the margins of policy making and political discourse, almost completely disappearing from view by the early 1960s (after a 1958 crisis over school textbooks temporarily put rural and urban middle-class ideological concerns in the spotlight and drove many to the PAN).[162] The steady eradication of rural middle classes from within the party's leading ranks reinforced the power of what I have elsewhere called Mexico's "urban leviathan," a party-led state whose political and economic aims revolved around the political and economic privileging of Mexico City residents to the exclusion of the country's majority rural populations.[163] And the continued privileging of Mexico City and its urban middle- and industrial working-class residents further reinforced the vicious cycle of rural middle-class exclusion.

With much of the party's institutional power resting in the hands of the party's labor sector, which developed its strongest ties with Mexico City–based industrialists, the Mexican government poured huge amounts of monies into programs and policies to sustain urbanization-led ISI, shunning any serious efforts at EOI. Over the 1960s and 1970s, Mexico City prospered as the site of what some would call the "Mexican miracle," the rapid development of

---

[162] For more on this, see Loaeza, *Clases medias y política en México*.

[163] See my *Urban Leviathan*.

a relatively productive manufacturing sector (for years sustaining an average economic growth rate of 6 percent), whose main aim was to "substitute" for foreign imports of industrial goods. This sector grew first by producing consumer goods and durables to be bought by Mexico's own residents, mainly urban consumers, many of them in the capital city and thus close to the producers. Later, Mexican industry moved to a second phase of development and began processing industrial inputs as opposed to merely finished consumer products. Most of these factories, again, were situated in Mexico City. This locational aspect of the government's macroeconomic development strategy was further sustained by the logic of the party, whose other main sector, the CNOP, had effectively become an institutional structure for urban residents, most but not all of whom lived in the capital city: state workers, street vendors, squatter communities, and myriad other neighborhood-based organizations.[164] Supporting ISI insured a modicum of employment for local residents at a relatively decent wage rate, since there was no need to keep wages down in order to compete with other countries' manufactured exports. It also provided industrial capitalists the opportunity to produce consumer durables that all urban residents could consume. Thus it was a policy that served multiple political purposes, the most important of which was keeping the labor and industrial capitalist constituencies happy. State workers also were content with the deal, because their employment was insured as long as the PRI remained in power and as long as the government continued with a commitment to strong state interventionism in social and economic policy making, which it did. And urban middle classes bought the consumer durables produced under the effective functioning of this political pact.

But the relatively smooth functioning of this setup also meant that making changes would be politically difficult. In economic terms, in particular, there was very little resolve on the part of the state or big industrialists to start manufacturing for export, especially in the late 1960s and early 1970s when South Korea and Taiwan were so successfully embarking on this same path. The same could be said for middle-class consumers and working-class producers of their products. Making the decision to pursue EOI then would have required more conscientious efforts to limit urban consumption and cap – if not reduce – wages to a greater extent than the party wanted, especially given the importance of the CTM to the PRI's electoral successes. It also would have entailed eliminating many of the medium-sized, consumer durables–producing industries that were located primarily in Mexico City and on whom party leaders had long counted for political support. The Mexico City–based CANACINTRA, or Cámara Nacional de Industrias de Transformación (National Chamber of Manufacturing Industries), had since the 1930s and 1940s informally been considered a "fourth" sector of the PRI, and its loyalty and

---

[164] For more on this, see my *Urban Leviathan*, especially Chap. 4.

support had long allowed the Mexican government to avoid being saddled with the potentially damaging "socialist" designation from private firms or governments abroad. Yet the long-term developmental costs of this "devil's bargain" were not cheap: The Mexican government accommodated the protectionist demands of the country's ISI industrialists, both large and small, and their labor force, going to bat for this broadly cast constituency as late as the mid-1980s by opposing Mexico's entry into the GATT. In order to counterbalance the market and pricing distortions produced by this high degree of protectionism, the government tried to keep a strong hold on labor in order to facilitate productivity and profit making in the manufacturing sector. But it was hard to deny labor their demands when owners themselves were coddled at every turn, and when labor was a main constituency in the PRI. This failure to equally discipline both capitalists and laborers was a vicious yet interconnected circle, sustained by the informal political pact that linked capital, urban labor, and the state together in a common project, with the government unable to make labor bear the brunt of austerity or cost cutting if the capitalists would not as well, and vice versa.

We should remember that in Taiwan considerable economic gains came from the self-discipline of key protagonists, not only of KMT-affiliated state workers, but also of small and medium-sized industrial producers involved in manufacturing or assembly for export, and even some large industrialists. In Mexico, however, the closest functional equivalent to the small urban-based industrial firms were the small and medium-sized firms organized into the Mexico City–based CANACINTRA; but they were even more highly protected and linked to the state and labor sectors than many large industrialists. This owed to the fact that a considerable number of the country's large industries, especially those with the capacity to export processed industrial goods, were located in northern regions of the country (many in Monterrey), away from the direct reach of the state. These same industrialists were also much more politically connected to the PAN, which further meant that the PRI-dominated government showed little inclination to encourage their industrial export aims. Small and medium-sized industries, in contrast, traced their economic and organizational history to their location in Mexico City and to the bargains they made with the postrevolutionary state; thus they were also more strongly linked to the PRI and its constituent sectors.[165]

Unlike in Taiwan, then, Mexico's small and medium-sized manufacturers did not discipline themselves, nor did state bureaucrats pursue policies that entailed imposition of strict performance standards on them. If anything, these smaller-scale industrial firms were handed a relatively free ride (at least until NAFTA snuffed out their advantages in these regards), given their

---

[165] For more on the history of the CANACINTRA and the role of its Mexico City location in the PRI's political history, see my *Urban Leviathan*, especially Chap. 3.

long-standing political relationships to the party and the state. They used these connections to the party and state to push the government to keep larger industrialists in different activities – like banking and finance – so that they, as smaller, less competitive, and less efficient firms could grow and prosper in ISI manufacturing without undue competition from these larger firms, many of which also established strong partnerships with foreign firms. This scenario was almost the exact opposite of what occurred in Taiwan, where big industries were protected (albeit in exchange for self-discipline) and smaller ones were disciplined or self-disciplined, often in order to facilitate their links to foreign firms upstream in lucrative international commodity chains. The upshot was that internal divisions among industrialists and the political links between smaller industrial firms and the state created numerous economic and political problems, such that in Mexico, it was difficult for the government to discipline or protect one set of industrial forces at the expense of the other.

If we return to the case of South Korea for a moment, we remember that much of the disciplining of capitalists and laborers grew inadvertently out of disciplinary programs that were initially intended to foster rural development. But by 1960, the urban biases in Mexican politics insured that few in the state or party – with the exception of the CNC's rank and file – had much sympathy for rural development per se, and thus they were not going to advance developmental changes in these regards. This was true even among military personnel. In South Korea, the military had been among the keenest supporters of small-farmer-oriented rural development programs; and as in those countries, in Mexico many military personnel also traced their personal origins or general sentiments to the small-farming experience, something discussed earlier in the chapter. Yet unlike in South Korea and even Taiwan, after World War II the greatest strategic challenge for the Mexican government and its military was not among rural areas but in the capital city, given the long-standing problems of the revolutionary leadership in sustaining hold on the physical seat of state in Mexico City.[166] To be sure, the military did become strategically concerned with rural areas and the emergence of agrarian-based opposition movements (communist and otherwise) starting in the late 1960s and early 1970s, when Mexico experienced a rise in rural-based guerrilla activities and other strong campesino-led social movements. But repression, not development aid, was the technique of choice to deal with these populations. By then, the urban

---

[166] This helps explain why the nation's largest, best, most elaborate military colony was established right in the capital city, a locational decision that further estranged much of the military from its rural roots. Indeed, there is an entire area of the city, bordering the president's private residence and within striking distance of the official presidential palace and most key state buildings and offices (in the Zocalo) that is called the *colonia militar*. In this development, as well, we see the territorial importance of Mexico City as the physical seat of state.

orientation of industrialization and the national economy was relatively well established in the state and society and the party-led government generally responded with violence toward rural folk rather than with an accommodation of their demands.[167]

Of course, if state bureaucrats had wanted to push the rural development route they might have been able to; but in the absence of a visible or salient force motivating them to do so, they would have had to rely on their own proclivities for inspiration. And as noted earlier, Mexico's bureaucrats may have been among the *least* likely to introduce a plan for sustaining agricultural development and using industrial exports to generate revenues to foster the rural sector and increase the ranks of small and medium-sized rural farmers. Recall that the state workers' federation, or FSTSE, had long been tied to the working class – institutionally, juridically, and even socially – and the majority of state workers resided in the capital city (as opposed to the South Korean and Taiwanese cases, where a majority of state workers still identified strongly with rural small farmers). Rural development was not high on most public sector workers' agenda, then, in no small part because years of living in Mexico City had made their connections to rural folk rather tenuous. Also remember that state workers had cultivated their greatest elective affinities with the urban-based organized labor movement (CTM), which also had little enthusiasm for rural development, especially if it meant reduced investment in industrial employment or major wage sacrifices on their part.[168]

---

[167] One other reason that Mexico's military personnel did not push the government to sustain small-farmer production or foster rural development in the same ways as their counterparts in South Korea and Taiwan, however, was the fact that many of their social links to rural populations were effectively severed by the party reforms that created the CNOP in 1943. Because the military became a key constituency in the CNOP, which thereafter steadily dedicated itself to the primarily urban concerns of its urban constituents, the military's concerns also became somewhat "urbanized," so to speak. Equally important, in this early "buyout" of the military, the state had invested massive monies in military programs, benefits, and services, in both city and countryside. Most rural-based *colonias militares* were so well funded and serviced by the government that few thought to complain about problems of rural development; and anyway, the fact that their connections to government policy makers were mediated through their involvement in the urban-based CNOP meant that even if the military still had held a strong position on rural development – as in South Korea and Taiwan – its capacity to translate these concerns into government policy would have been less direct.

[168] The limited commitment to rural development was further reinforced by the fact that those elected representatives in the Congress who ostensibly came from rural areas and were constitutionally required to carry forward their constituencies' concerns in the legislative arena, rarely resided (or even came from) the districts or states they were intended to represent. Most were selected to run for office based on their allegiance to the party and the

Owing to these historical developments, Mexico hobbled along with an "accommodating" rather than a "disciplinary" regime, in which a coalition of capitalists, laborers, and the state continued to call the developmental shots, in which rural development fell by the wayside, in which ISI reigned supreme long beyond its evident utility, and in which almost no single class force was disciplined, except perhaps for industrial labor at key crisis moments – and only then within limits. Yet the inherent weaknesses and limitations to this strategy weighed most heavily on the economy starting in the late 1970s and continuing throughout the 1980s. Much of this owed not just to the problems inherent in a developing economy and the fact that not enough attention was paid to exports to sustain the growing volume of imports. The urban biases of this model also weighed heavily on the economy and the state, mainly because they further weakened the country's macroeconomic health even as they reinforced rural middle-class political exclusion. With the continued growth of Mexico City, the capital became the source of massive government investments and subsidies for CNOP and CTM constituents. In turn, the countryside languished, except for a few prosperous regions where agro-exporting firms managed to create a niche for their products abroad even as they frequently destroyed smaller-farmers' capacities to sustain themselves. One immediate consequence was a steady acceleration of rural-urban migration, which in the years preceding the so-called 1960s miracle sent millions of unemployed agricultural laborers to Mexico's big cities.[169]

Sustained migration not only further limited the agricultural sector and its capacity to generate sufficient foodstuffs for urban consumption, forcing the government to import costly grains at the risk of growing current account imbalances; it also helped burst the capital city beyond its seams, since rural-urban migration most entrenched the demographic ranks of Mexico City, a locale that Octavio Paz has called a "monstrous inflated head, crushing the frail body that holds it up."[170] Both situations further weakened the national economic situation: the former by contributing to an overvalued peso, greater current account deficits, and a looming foreign exchange crisis; the latter by forcing the government to increase its subsidies to Mexico City. These developments, in turn, put considerable pressure on the federal budget and laid the foundation for a catastrophic foreign exchange crisis in the early 1980s,

---

government. As such, there was relatively little commitment to or understanding of the plight of small farmers from other forces either within the party or the state, especially as time wore on.

[169] For more on the disproportionate internal migration to large cities – as opposed to others – see my "Migration, Rank-Size Distribution, and Economic Development." Note however, that by the 1970s, most domestic destinations were eclipsed by international migration to the United States.

[170] Paz, *The Labyrinth of Solitude*, p. 343.

when revenues from oil exports dropped precipitously against a backdrop of rising imports. With a burgeoning debt crisis swelling throughout the late 1970s and reaching a peak in the 1980s, Mexico ended up looking very similar to South Korea, or shall we say vice versa, since earlier we saw that it was South Korea that abandoned the East Asian path to follow a more prototypically "Latin American" route, and since South Korea's debt crisis followed Mexico's by a few years.

Granted, the debt crisis that hit South Korea was neither as severe nor as long-lasting as the one crippling Mexico. Even now, at the cusp of a new millennium and several decades later, real wages in Mexico have not returned to the pre-crisis levels of the 1970s, despite some significant economic recovery in the industrial exporting sector, while South Korea has made some progress. Some of this owes to the fact that Mexico is an oil-exporting country and thus its debt problems revolved around oil prices in ways that South Korea's did not, which also makes it hard to compare the two on this score (although being an oil exporter can bring gains as well as losses). Additionally, in South Korea the fact that big businesses sustained most of their growth through industrial exports made that country's economy somewhat more stable even in the midst of growing debt burden; whereas in Mexico, because the capital-labor-state pact revolved around support for ISI industries, the country was practically brought to its knees by the currency devaluations that accompanied the crisis. This fundamental difference in the industrial and class foundations of the two economies further explains why debt crisis alone was not enough to relegate South Korea to the ranks of late-industrializing basket cases. Rather, it was a major banking crisis more than a decade later – showing the whole financial infrastructure of the country in the 1990s to be not much more than a paper game – that earned the country that status.

Still, the common thread that unites South Korea and Mexico in more recent periods is the absence of a rural middle class capable of sustaining a state seriously committed to disciplining capitalists, be they banking and/or industrial, even in the face of problematic economic conditions and immanent financial instability. As such, the apparent convergence of Mexico's and South Korea's economic paths owes to the fact that in both countries current account balances are highly dependent on the fate of the country's industrial sector and especially the extent to which manufacturing exports outweigh imports of both industry and agriculture. In these conditions, the failure to discipline capital and labor in ways that could turn around the crisis by contributing to the expansion of exports, as well as the failure to develop a strong agricultural sector so that food imports also could be capped, meant that after the 1980s both South Korea and Mexico were continually courting economic disaster. So what explains the similarities between Mexico and South Korea with regard to recent obstacles to economic development? The same factors that explain these states' inabilities to discipline industrial protagonists in the service of balanced national development.

First, both countries are now characterized by colossally strong linkages between big business groups and the state, linkages that have led to a similarly high degree of corruption and rent seeking in both private and public sectors. Second, both countries now hold a similarly active and well-mobilized labor movement, which has a clear political profile, even if it cannot achieve all its aims. Third, both countries have been characterized by a slow but steady pressure for democratization, fueled in no small part by mobilization on the part of labor and urban middle classes, many of whom reside in both countries' capital cities, Seoul and Mexico City.[171] This latter factor is significant because it has shifted many of the states' political concerns to the demands of urban classes, thereby snuffing out most efforts to accommodate rural middle classes, even in South Korea. It has also meant that over time the South Korean government has poured more monies into its capital, Seoul, a city pushed beyond its infrastructural bounds through steady streams of rural-urban migrants. As in Mexico, then, South Korea's economic livelihood and the government's political profile have become ever more tied to the capital city, a situation that stands in contrast to the early period of South Korean growth, when rural investments were as significant – if not more significant – than urban ones. In short, despite the fact that they looked so different from each other only three decades ago on all of these counts, today South Korea and Mexico are beginning to share similar patterns of dominant class influence in the state and similar cross-class relations between urban working and middle classes, while similar patterns of overurbanization and urban infrastructural scarcities in their capital cities have come to politically and economically dwarf the rest of the nation.

A Common Future?

But does this mean that both face similarly dim developmental prospects for the future? Probably not. There are some signs that historical legacies and political conditions still favor South Korea's exit from crisis and its more likely pursuit of a relatively solvent economic path. This is clear from a closer examination of the mid-1990s financial crisis, and the ways in which the South Korean government's response then differed from its response during debt crisis in the 1980s. In the early period, South Korea's government followed a macroeconomic stabilization strategy very similar to one frequently pursued among late developers with current account problems, including Mexico and Argentina: the all-too-familiar tack of disciplining labor (and thus bolstering

---

[171] For more on this, see Koo's "The Social and Political Character of the Korean Middle Classes," esp. pp. 62–65.

capitalists' short-term profit-making capacities) while also, to a certain extent, recalibrating the industrial sector to increase manufacturing exports. In the late 1990s financial crisis, however, South Korea rapidly revived its commitment to a strong disciplinary ethos, strongly clamping down on the country's offending capitalists, mainly banks. The government's renewed efforts to discipline and regulate capitalists may have been partly inspired by heavy pressure from international financial institutions and leaders worldwide who feared the longer-term impact of a domino-like East Asian financial crisis. Yet the government's disciplinary response reverberated in a resounding echo of its past practices.

The fact that most citizens were reported in the local presses as also willing to bite the bullet, by reducing their own consumption and increasing output with the aim of getting the economy back on track, further suggests that South Korea's political culture of discipline has deep roots, especially with respect to capitalists and especially when the national economy is at stake. The widespread support for the disciplinary ethos, or what might be considered a strong-arm route to modernity, may be further evidenced by one striking survey result generated from a public opinion poll conducted in South Korea in May 1997 in the midst of the financial crisis. When asked "Who would you most want to clone?" the overwhelming answer was Park Chung Hee, the military ruler who governed the country from 1961 to 1979.[172] This answer, which many interpreted as a popular response to the growing corruption of government-business relations that was on everyone's mind in 1997 (still a year before the "crisis"), was all the more startling considering that it came in the midst of South Korea's tortured transition to democracy, still in progress, thereby suggesting that the economic path Park forged and the austere manner in which he did so was still quite well appreciated by the country's citizenry, his nondemocratic credentials notwithstanding. Even more telling is the fact that one of the main stories still circulating about Park, during this revival in enthusiasm for his economically disciplinary hand, was that on the day he was assassinated by a member of his own junta, he was known to be wearing the cheapest underwear in Korea.

Mexico's historical legacies do not bode nearly so well for its exit from economic purgatory; and this is not merely because, unlike Park, past presidents have palaces and foreign bank accounts and stunning real estate properties (rather than cheap underwear) to prove it. Despite the recent reform of Article 27 to create the foundations for more small-scale ownership of agricultural lands, Mexico's government still has failed to match this property-owning reform with enough rural development assistance to truly transform the country's poor peasants into a vibrant rural middle class. As a result, agricultural market dynamics set in place by the late 1990s reform are creating more income

---

[172] "Mai" [Monthly discourse], 8 October 1977, p. 45.

polarization in the countryside, especially as bigger agricultural producers cultivating for external markets become successful enough to raise land prices and buy out fledgling small producers producing for the domestic market. The results are the same old story: rural poverty, rural exodus, and accelerating income, class, and spatial inequality in rural areas and between city and countryside, although much of the new migration is now headed northward to the United States. It is worth remembering that East Asia's developmental successes generally, and its rural gains in particular, stemmed from much more than merely giving lands to small producers and letting the market take its course. East Asian gains derived from conscious efforts to foster widespread rural development alongside industrial development, and to discipline capitalists in both city and countryside in the service of this vision. And it is on the latter count that Mexico's promise remains most unfulfilled.

Under the administration of Carlos Salinas in the early 1990s, and after a decade of debt crisis, the country may have initiated a fundamental transformation in the industrial sector and an about-face on the question of free trade, two interrelated shifts that Mexico bargained would increase domestic economic growth and that scholars, whose understanding of discipline is always grounded in the concept of market discipline, might highlight as the beginning of a new historical era. It also made considerable democratic headway by surpassing the power of the PRI's political dinosaurs and catapulting to power a new cadre of neoliberal technocrats.[173] But in retrospect, the latter changes appear to have been no more than skin-deep. Not only did the Salinas administration turn out to be one of Mexico's most corrupt; this occurred in no small part because he and his family members, among others in the one-party state, so obviously privileged rapacious capitalists and accepted kickbacks as part of the deal. To be sure, the approval of the NAFTA and the move to free trade in the 1990s did entail some undermining of the old capital-labor-state pact with ISI industrialists, something that could be understood as eliminating the shackles of "indiscipline" that had linked industrialists to the state and labor for so long, sustaining Mexico's inefficient and overprotected industrial sector. Yet under Salinas, and even his successor, Ernest Zedillo, the PRI-led state merely cultivated new relations with a nascent class of EOI industrialists; and rather than disciplining them, it pretty much let them do whatever they wanted. This, again, is evidenced by numerous reports of enormous state losses in the privatization of industries, government collusion in money laundering, and exchanges of monetary gifts and influences that transpired under the Salinas administration (and that paralleled the problems identified as causing the South Korean crisis in late 1998). And even now, the PAN's Vicente Fox is known to be just as well connected to the corporate classes in Mexico and is currently weathering a mini-scandal about campaign finance and money

---

[173] For one of the best accounts of this transformation, see Centeno's *Democracy Within Reason*.

laundering that links him to the nation's economic elite in ways that do not bode well for moral purity.

So what is the source of this endemic "moral weakness," if you choose to call it that, in the Mexican political economy? Tradition, of course, must account for some of it. The fact that a disciplinary strategy has hardly been part of the post–World War II Mexican policy repertoire could explain why there was not the same enthusiasm for it we saw in South Korea. This state of affairs may be directly traceable to the early disappearance of the small-farmer vision of development and to the rural petit bourgeois discourse that seem to have reached their peak between the 1920s and 1940s, but that declined steadily thereafter. Whatever the source, this state of affairs stands in contrast to the situation in South Korea, where the disciplinary ethos drew from and was reinforced by Park's strong relations to rural small producers less than a generation ago, a time period still present in the minds and lived experience of many South Koreans. In Mexico, however, languages and practices of discipline, especially with respect to capitalists, have not been a principal element in the political culture for decades, except for perhaps the brief period from 1940 to 1950 when rural and urban middle classes united in the CNOP.[174] In the absence of this political and cultural repertoire of action, Mexico's failure to discipline its capitalists and to pursue a less problem-ridden path of development is not all that surprising.

To suggest this is surely not to argue that economic success will permanently elude the nation. Changes can always be made. In its recent efforts to model itself after the successful late industrializers of East Asia, whose prosperity has been understood to result from their pursuit of an EOI path, Mexico will surely make some gains. In fact, a newfound commitment to EOI has already been formalized in trade treaties, government policies, and investment practices that have benefited certain portions of Mexican society, although clearly not all. But

---

[174] To the extent that languages or notions of discipline are at all related to the existence and self-understandings of middle classes, especially rural ones, it may be worth noting that since the 1950s, languages of middle-classness have almost disappeared, eclipsed in a peasant discourse or eschewed altogether. This may be best evidenced by the fact that despite its historical origins as a sector for the "popular middle classes," for years no party leader would dare mention publicly the middle classes as a serious political constituency or as a constituency worthy of government support. Except for a brief period in the 1960s, in fact, the CNOP has almost always been referred to as the popular sector; and even when those languages were dropped in the late 1980s when the CNOP's sectoral logic and organization were reformed in order to accommodate growing political opposition from social movements and other disenfranchised sectors of society, it was generally languages of citizenship or movements that the party adopted. For more on the changing discourses of the CNOP, and the shift from languages of (middle) class to citizenship, see my "New Social Movements, Old Party Structures."

the evidence presented here suggests that merely pursuing EOI – as opposed to ISI – will not necessarily guarantee economic success, even in this highly glob-alized world. For one thing, the global economy is constantly changing, such that the same development policies – be they EOI or ISI – may not always pro-duce the same economic results. For another, we seem to be reaching a stage at which all late industrializers cannot grow by exporting. This may have worked in earlier periods when so many late industrializers were importing; but if ev-eryone exports goods produced with disciplined capitalists and laborers, coun-tries may reach internal limits – often set by citizens themselves, who will balk at the disciplinary and consumption sacrifices that have to be made to pursue this path. Still, evidence from the past suggests that what has done countries well has not been solely their export-led orientation per se, but some sort of disciplinary infrastructure or self-disciplinary ethos that insured that the goals of producing competitively and efficiently will always take precedence over the gains of the banking and industrial elite, whether or not they are forging ahead with EOI or any other new strategy for growth. History has shown that states, especially those embedded with capitalists alone or with labor, often lack the capacity to impose this sort of discipline. There must be another class and political reference point for those state actors, then; and historically speak-ing, when an alliance of rural and urban middle classes serves in this capacity, we have been most likely to see states achieve and sustain their greatest disci-plinary potential. And once we recognize this, we must also wonder whether Mexico may still harbor some potential.

The glimmer of hope rests in a deeper understanding of several recent trends that may suggest that a partial change is under way, at least to the extent that for the first time in decades, we are beginning to see rural and urban middle classes emerge as independent, visible, and salient on both the political and economic scene. Some of these changes owe to the economic transformations that the country has experienced recently; others owe to the larger political transformations associated with the slow demise of the PRI and one-party rule and the new ascendance of the rural middle-class-based PAN. Here we mean not merely the steady democratization of Mexico's political system, but also the political and economic resurgence of Mexico's regions. Together, these changes have brought middle classes into the limelight for the first time in decades. Indeed, in just the past three years Mexico has seen a new and increasingly powerful organization of debtors called El Barzón, which counts on its greatest support in Mexico's northern agricultural states and which holds within its ranks a large number of small rural producers who were especially hard hit by the 1994 devaluation. They became a formidable voice of opposition to the now defeated PRI, with their anger fueled by the government's bailout of large banking and industrial firms, a sentiment that in many ways echoes the common view of bankers and big industrialists during the early years of Park Chung Hee's rise to power.

The larger significance of these rural farmers' self-organization becomes clear when we put the Barzón movement in the context of the rising support for the PAN in many of the heavily agricultural regions of the country. Middle classes in Mexico's far regions have long supported the PAN, but in the absence of true democratization their voices were not heard in the PRI. Now, with a political opening of the party system, and opposition governments in power in several key states, provincially based middle classes have the opportunity to throw their support to the PAN or other parties, and even to embed themselves in the state and its policy making in ways that make a difference for development policy. The PAN has made incredible gains in many states of the nation, in fact, and now holds the presidency. In theory, Mexico under Fox has the potential to bring the demands of rural middle classes front stage center and to introduce a form of disciplinary development. But Fox must considerably revise his current embeddedness with the nation's industrial and financial elite. The likelihood that he may be able to shift gears in this regard has been increased by the fact that in the past several years the basis for rural property owning has been fundamentally transformed in Mexico. As noted earlier, the reform of Article 27 has strengthened rural producers' property rights to agricultural lands and eliminated the ambiguities in ownership that plagued the original ejido legislation. One of the results of this reform is the increasing commercialization and marketization of rural production. At present, these changes seem to have brought more polarization in the countryside. But if the longer-term consequences of these property-owning transformations can be redirected to sustain the development of a more economically vibrant class of small and medium-sized rural producers, then we might also begin to see a shift in the political coalitions that sustain party politics or national economic policy making and the emergence of a more disciplinary ethos. At minimum, we would expect to see Mexico move away from the preoccupation with Mexico City and with urban-based ISI, two shifts that could leave considerable political space for rural middle classes to become important political and social forces.

Last are the cumulative effects of immigration, which in combination with transformations produced by the NAFTA could strengthen Mexico's regional economies and thus eliminate some of the stark differences between rural and urban areas that have characterized Mexico over the past five decades. Much of this owes to the fact that it is unemployed rural farmers or agricultural wage laborers who comprise the bulk of migrants. Most tend to relocate in the United States, and they generally send large remittances back to the rural areas to sustain small-farmer development. In a study of Namiquipan men working in the United States, Daniel Nugent found considerable evidence that "what they receive in wages they . . . [would] save and later deploy as capital to reproduce and sustain their units of production on the land."[175] Many of

---

[175] *Spent Cartridges*, p. 134.

these immigrants, or their families at least, also have gained increased social and political prominence in their communities, a state of affairs that helps push the democratization process by bringing folk without major loyalties to the PRI into the political arena. The result may be a major transformation in both the regional and economic sources of political influence.

All three of these factors have shifted the political and economic power away from Mexico City, reduced the role of industrial laborers and some industrial capitalists, and placed the middle classes, both rural and urban, in the forefront of civil society and opposition party politics for the first time in decades. The democratization of Mexico City has been especially helpful in achieving these gains in the urban sphere, in particular, bringing middle classes to the political arena who do not necessarily support the capital-labor-state pacts of the past. To the extent that along with these shifts regional imbalances are overcome, and Mexico is no longer dominated by an urban "leviathan" in which capitalists and laborers – alongside an urban middle class – predominate as the main source of political support or influence in the national state, Mexico might even start looking more like Taiwan. If what I have argued in this book is to be taken seriously, then, we could be somewhat optimistic about Mexico and its economic prospects (although politics are an entirely different matter).

Still, if we give time and place their due, as we also have done here, we must be prepared to accept the fact that these are different times now. As the new millennium begins, we live in a more globalized, higher technology world, one in which the global economy is very different than it was when Taiwan and South Korea catapulted to the head of the pack of late industrializers, and one in which space or location seem to matter less and less. Even if Mexican politics or state development policy were to reconnect to their rural middle-class roots, can we really be sure that national economic successes would be so easily forthcoming, especially now that both industrialization and agriculture have taken a back seat to other high-profile forces of economic organization and productivity, such as information technology? Further, is it possible that these new economic strategies presuppose such a high degree of "placelessness," and the disappearance of rural activities and rural farm lifestyles in particular, that the disciplinary culture of rural middle classes will itself disappear? And if so, will macroeconomic disciplining of key class actors also be a thing of the past; or, will other class or social forces draw on a disciplinary ethos enough to openly challenge rapacious capitalists, at least enough to lead their nations on a economically successful course, no matter what the developmental options pursued? I turn to these questions in my conclusion.

6

DISCIPLINARY DEVELOPMENT
IN A NEW MILLENNIUM

The Global Context of Past Gains and Future Prospects

Where to Now?

In this book I have tried to resurrect the analytic centrality of middle classes
in development theory while also rescuing a focus on history and domestic
politics in the study of late industrialization. With evidence drawn from four
late-developing countries, combined with analysis of several "early" developers, I have offered an argument that travels in time and across regions. My claim
is that successful economic development depends on a confluence of state and
societal capacities to discipline capitalists in a spatial context where such
actions can reinforce strong forward and backward linkages between industrial and agricultural sectors of the economy. Rural middle classes have been
key actors in achieving these aims, particularly when they are embedded in the
state or other equivalent institutions with coercive or policy-making power.
In seeking to account for the conditions that made this likely, I identified a
variety of historical factors – including legacies of urbanization and militarization, patterns of middle-class formation, processes of state formation, and
ethnicity as well as the cultural practices and national politics sustaining the
sway of these actors, identities, processes, and institutions – that together determined the likelihood that disciplining of capitalists occurred and sustained
economic development resulted. In this sense, historical contingency and path
dependency are considered as central to developmental successes as any rational bureaucratic commitment to finding the "proper" macroeconomic policy
techniques and prescriptions. Just the same, some of the key elements that
engendered disciplinary development in the countries studied here – namely,
the flowering of a vibrant rural middle class – were indeed generated through a
series of macroeconomic measures, normative aims, and policy commitments.
Strong state and/or societal support for smaller-scale, owner-occupied agricultural production, as embodied in land reform policies, is a case in point.

To recognize that a vibrant rural middle class can help guarantee the disciplining of capitalists, and in turn lay the foundations for macroeconomic

success, requires new ways of thinking about who or what sustains developmental progress among late industrializers. For one thing, it entails a shift in attention away from the two principal class protagonists of development that have dominated the literature for the last several decades – big manufacturing capitalists and waged industrial laborers – and an examination of the class force that has been missing in development studies for the last three decades: the middle class. For another, it requires that rural conditions be taken seriously in the study of industrialization. This not only presupposes much greater attention to social, political, and economic dynamics in both countryside and cities, and how they inform each other, it also involves a willingness to acknowledge the macroeconomic benefits of policy measures that sustain an entire class of smaller-scale agrarian producers and consumers, while also networking them across space and economic sectors in ways that bring large and small industrial producers into their orbit, and not merely vice versa. Only with this rural middle-class-based interactive dynamic at play, will countries be able to achieve self-generative developmental gains that spread relatively equally across city and countryside, thereby eliminating the market and political obstacles to national development identified with rural impoverishment and attendant patterns of overurbanization. Last and most important, much more attention must be paid to the state and societal conditions that make disciplining capitalists a serious normative possibility. To acknowledge this scholarly aim in itself requires a willingness to question the still popular assumption that whatever big investors or large industrialists think is good for their businesses is also good for market economies and for countries as a whole, a posture that in several of our cases produced the recipe for disaster.

In analyzing a variety of developmental experiences to arrive at this general argument, I found some significant similarities between early and late industrializers, and as such have concluded that my rural middle-class-based "model" of disciplinary development is comparatively and historically resilient. Its basic elements have been visible in cases as distinct as the United States and Britain in their formative years of economic development, centuries ago, and East Asia in just the past several decades. This is not to say that the timing of industrialization or the character of the global economy are entirely insignificant to my account. As the world economy becomes more complex and interconnected, the conditions necessary for the formation of a vibrant rural middle class, and for translating their disciplining of capitalists into national developmental gains, do not stay the same. Indeed, the rise of a vibrant small-producer agricultural class, the disciplining of capital, and the establishment of strong forward and backward linkages between rural and urban sectors may have been more easily achieved in early industrializers because the basic contours of national development in the eighteenth and nineteenth centuries rested primarily on market and production dynamics that unfolded in relatively circumscribed rural localities, like townships and regions. In this context local gains led ultimately to national gains, and not necessarily vice versa, while the stultifying weight of foreign investment and a globalizing economy on the state's capacity to discipline capitalists was much less apparent. The nineteenth-century experience also suggests that the more locally generated the dynamics of economic growth, the more likely the establishment of enduring community-based political institutions and social contracts for disciplining capitalists or for forging production and consumption networks among various local economic actors and activities.

Twentieth-century industrializers have not had the same luxury, and this inevitably makes disciplinary development even harder to achieve for those coming late to the development table. As the twentieth century unfolded, economic development had become primarily a national if not international affair, unfolding within the regulatory and macroeconomic policy confines of the nation-state – even if unevenly applied within a national territorial space. The presence of a well-entrenched global market for industrial goods and ever more powerful international actors whose global policy priorities, investment targets, manufacturing production strategies, and geopolitical aims also factored into national development dynamics further complicated the situation. Owing to these changes, countries that came late to the development game, including those in Latin America and East Asia, faced a much harder time establishing the will or political capacity to discipline capitalists within their national borders, especially because the latter frequently were empowered enough by foreign partners and external markets to sustain their hegemony and privilege vis-à-vis the national state. Likewise, the aim of establishing forward and backward linkages between rural and urban areas was a much more daunting challenge for late than for early industrializers, not only because the former frequently came to the development table with patterns of uneven development and extreme rural-urban polarization produced through years of segmented (frequently colonial) articulation in the global economy, but also because the ready existence and lure of a more globally networked economy changed many of the significant reference points for development, making almost any national effort to develop sectorally integrated, domestic-oriented internal markets seemed practically foolhardy if not quaintly premodern. Why hitch the national development wagon to local markets and domestic conditions – agricultural ones no less – at a time when integration into global markets and/or the drive to support bigger industry seemed to be offering so many more obvious financial gains?

Despite these structural obstacles, a good number of the twentieth-century's late developers *did* focus inward and achieve what we are calling disciplinary development; and those that were most successful, such as Taiwan and South Korea, did so with practices and an ethos that could be seen as a latter-day functional equivalent of the experience of early developers. It is these parallel successes that lead to the proposition that similarities or differences in developmental gains cannot be explained solely in terms of the distorting (or facilitating) dynamics of new global markets for manufacturing exports, or even the pre– and post–World War II timing of national industrialization, but rather in terms of similarities and differences in domestic political, class, cultural, and spatial conditions that pushed countries to industrial exporting in the first place. To be sure, South Korea and Taiwan, grouped together as similarly "late" late-developers, did seem to outdistance Mexico and Argentina in terms of their capacities to turn to industrial exporting early, through the auspices of disciplinary development, in part because of the advantages of "even more" backwardness (with apologies to Gerschenkron). The late-nineteenth- and early-twentieth-century advent of industrialization in Argentina and Mexico shifted political and economic balances of power from countryside to city early on, reducing the vibrancy of rural middle-class formation, the state's political will or capacity to discipline capital, and the likelihood of establishing strong domestic linkages between agriculture and industry in the postwar period of global expansion, although political factors also contributed to these outcomes. East Asia, in contrast, came to the game with limited industrialization and an agriculturally dominated economy that, in combination with geopolitical conditions and the pressures from rural-oriented populations holding sway in the state, made industrial exporting in order to generate foreign exchange for rural development much more desirable and possible.

Still, if we take into account the fact that in the long run Taiwan and Mexico outperformed their regional neighbors, South Korea and Argentina respectively, particularly in terms of achieving or committing to disciplinary development (even if only temporarily, as in the Mexican case), and if we consider that several of these countries vacillated back and forth in their disciplinary developmental potential (as occurred in Mexico and even South Korea to an extent), even this "early" versus "late" late-developing divide as a key to understanding prospects for success has its limits. Accordingly, we must consider that rather than global context or the timing of industrialization per se, it is internal social, political, and class conditions and how they vary that have been among the most critical determinants of developmental successes and relative failures, by prefiguring or setting limits on the likelihood that global integration through manufacturing exports will be an enduring or sustainable national policy of choice.

Discipline, Democracy, and Development

The four cases studied here also raise important questions about what role democracy – or its absence – might play in the dynamics of disciplinary development, and whether this could or should have been factored into our model. The idea that development somehow correlates with democracy is one of those claims that seems to circulate and recirculate in development circles. In our rapidly liberalizing world, this idea has produced a new generation of advocates, not just among U.S. State Department spokespeople but also within the halls of academe, so much so that it almost seems to have reached the status of a truism. How does this claim square with the narrative presented here? Of course, Mexico, Argentina, South Korea, and Taiwan are all countries where democracy has remained elusive for most of the past century, but some are much more economically sound than others. So whither causality? Still, the fact that at certain historical moments individual countries (such as Mexico) came closer to pursuing disciplinary development, and that in the case of Mexico at least, these were the periods of greatest democratic "potential" within a larger trajectory of one-party rule (during the 1950s, for example, when the PRI was perhaps its most inclusive and deliberative),[1] does suggest that the issue is more complicated than it may first appear. The possibility that there may be an implicit democratic logic in accounting for Mexico's near developmental gains, at least, combined with the fact that this book's argument rests on a deeper understanding of those middle-class forces that so many scholars have identified as the lifeblood of democracy, force a rethinking of the relationship between democracy and disciplinary development, if only briefly.

The proposition that democracy is essential to economic progress is actually quite dated, having been popularized in this country in the 1950s by Seymour Martin Lipset in his seminal book *Political Man*, in which middle classes also were considered to be key, and then resuscitated throughout subsequent decades in both quantitative study and political deliberation. Still, most of the scholars who have taken this position preferred to focus primarily on the more economically advanced countries of the world, if not the United States singularly, and if they offered comparative or historical study, as in much of the work by Edward Muller,[2] it was usually in the form of quantitative analysis where operational definitions of democracy generally left much to be desired.

Partly in response to the poverty of these works, several years ago Dietrich Rueschemeyer, John Stephens, and Evelyn Huber Stephens revisited the democracy-development debate with a quantitatively and qualitatively comprehensive comparative-historical study, perhaps the first of its kind in comparative breadth and historical scope. In this seminal book, titled *Capitalist Development and Democracy*, the authors also identified middle classes as key protagonists, at least in the achievement of democracy, an outcome whose origins they traced to trajectories of capitalist development in developed and developing countries alike. Their study suggested a path-dependent causal

---

[1] For more on an understanding of the "periodizaton" of Mexican democracy, see Davis and Brachet-Marquez, "Rethinking Democracy."

[2] One of his most comprehensive studies is "Democracy, Economic Development, and Income Inequality."

relationship between capitalist development and democracy, and not vice versa, as did Lipset and his followers. These differences may have owed to the fact that Rueschemeyer, Stephens, and Stephens were most interested in explaining the social origins of democracy and authoritarianism, not the prospects for development. But it also is noteworthy that the one developing region of the world they failed to examine in their study was East Asia, whose experience differs greatly from Latin America's, the developing region they focused upon with greatest care. Yet it is the East Asian experience that has motivated many scholars to embrace the premise that democracy is an unaffordable luxury for late industrializers. These competing claims, in short, may have a lot to do with which countries are studied.

Scholars who laud the economic successes of East Asia are among the most ardent proponents of the democracy-as-constraint proposition, precisely because their reading of East Asian successes (not just Taiwan and South Korea, but also Singapore, among others) entails recognition of the strong role of the state in restricting popular opposition and in supporting industry's efforts to develop and compete. Even those few who have recognized that the state may be imposing its heavy hand on capitalists as much as laborers also see such actions as inherently undemocratic. The general sense, then, has been that in any environment where a strong state is necessary to jump-start or guide economic development, democracy will remain elusive. The normative and ethical implications of this claim are troubling, of course, and that is why development theorists such as Amartya Sen have called for a redefinition of development that includes a commitment to democracy. However, our findings suggest that it may not be necessary to invoke normative concerns – or even to craft new definitions of development that embody these normative concerns – so much as to offer a more "deconstructed" view of democracy.

Generally speaking, the democracy-as-constraint view builds on much too simplistic a view of what constitutes democracy. Its main limitations owe to the fact that most scholars who invoke the notion of democracy focus primarily on competitive party politics and fail to take into account variations in state forms and in the wide range of territorial bases for bottom-up political participation and deliberation that exist even among countries all classified as sharing democratic or authoritarian regime type. In this book, we found otherwise. All four countries were nondemocracies to be sure, but some had structures and practices of participation that were more class inclusive than others, while also being built solidly on local-level participation and political incorporation. Those countries most likely to pursue disciplinary development were also those most likely to see the widest range of social inclusion and/or the most locally grounded structures for political participation. Moreover, in these instances rural middle-class embeddedness in the state – an important precondition for strong national commitment to disciplinary development – correlated with certain territorially decentralized political structures and practices built on the inclusion of some of these countries' most economically and politically powerless constituencies. Development trajectories, in short, are better explained by patterns of state formation than democracy (or authoritarianism) per se.

In those countries with a general commitment to disciplinary development, namely, South Korea in its pre-1975 period, Mexico in the 1950s, and Taiwan more generally, non-elite residents of rural areas participated in locally constituted farmers organizations and a variety of government-guided self-help programs that offered institutional mechanisms for posing demands and connecting populations to the national state, formally centralized as it was. That in Taiwan the state also counted on a very class-inclusive political party to complement and incorporate these farmers associations may explain why the commitment and durability of disciplinary development was stronger there than in South Korea, where political parties were top-down affairs with little connection to the state and where more ephemeral social movements and programs (i.e., Saemaul Undong) served as the glue linking rulers and ruled. In Argentina, in contrast, there were very few organizations, institutions, or mechanisms in rural areas that provided for deliberation or state participation in questions of governance or demand making, either with local or national objectives in mind. As a consequence, most of the rural poor and almost all of the rural middle class remained outside the nation's most important politically deliberative structures. The Peronist party, especially, has long been considered more a movement than a party, and unlike in South Korea, in Argentina this movement did not really develop strong institutional mechanisms to reach out to the rural poor, but concentrated instead on honing its urban working- or urban middle-class bases. Mexico, for its part, vacillated between the Argentine and Taiwanese political "models," with shifts correlating with development trajectories. That is, Mexico came closest to following a disciplinary development model when the ruling party crafted its most inclusive and vibrant organizations at the local level, including those that allowed farmers to connect to the PRI and the state alongside workers and peasants. When small farmers and poorer rural folk (i.e., campesinos) were marginalized in party politics – meaning that their capacities to deliberate and participate were constrained – disciplinary development remained elusive.

In all four of our countries, then, full democracy was far from flowering, at least if defined in a liberal democratic sense of competitive party politics built on individual voting rights. Collective identities and state-linked (if not -dominated) organizations served as the basis for most political participation and claim making. But even so, when rural-based organizations were included in these populist, clientelist, or corporatist practices and institutions, in real and not merely symbolic ways, they served as some sort of functional equivalent for a more inclusive and widely cast democratic participation, and this in turn correlated with greater developmental success. This may also owe to the fact that a more extensive inclusion of rural middle classes usually came hand in hand with incorporation of working classes (through the PRI in 1950s Mexico, through the KMT's wide-cast party structures in Taiwan, and through Park's populist regime); and this was a cross-class alliance that was not only relatively effective in guaranteeing state discipline of capitalists, but was also built around a quasi-democratic commitment to a broadly cast grass roots that included rural and urban working folk of modest means. Alternatively, when structures for participation excluded rural small producers, as in Argentina (or Mexico in the post-1960s period), not only was there less capacity for such widespread political participation among both rural and urban sectors, capitalists for their part had more power to overdetermine policy and political outcomes, thereby further undermining democratic commitments. All this suggests that there may exist some sort of loose relationship between disciplinary development – and especially the state's capacity to discipline capitalists – and a more territorially and class-inclusive participatory political system, even when competitive party politics and full democracy remain elusive.[3]

If we also return to Chapter 1's discussion of the United States and rethink this case in terms of the existence of local structures for inclusive political participation and deliberation, we find further evidence of the positive role played by rural middle-class participation and the politico-institutional foundations of developmental gains. Specifically, what many scholars of the United States have come to identify as a democracy-development dynamic also can be understood in light of the decentralization of political and economic life and, in particular, the opportunities this afforded for local participation and self-governance as well as economic growth. Political and economic decentralization sustained the creation of an economy and polity of small producers and by so doing helped augment citizens' social, economic, and political status on the local level. This situation further reinforced a locally grounded deliberative democracy in which town residents participated as relative equals. U.S. decentralized urban and political systems, in short, offered "spaces" for the dynamic interplay between rural middle-class formation and political participation on the local level. Hence we see that in the United States the relationship between democracy and development was based on local political participation, one in

---

[3] This claim, in many regards, turns upside down – or sideways – the arguments presented by Rueschemeyer, Stephens, and Stephens in *Capitalist Development and Democracy*. In their account of the relationship between development and democracy, the emergence of middle classes is central, especially to the extent that middle-class alliances and formation affect the entire balance of class power. As such, to the extent that capitalist development affects middle-class formation, certain forms of democracy are more or less likely. My proposition, conversely, is that to the extent that democracy or some version of it is associated with certain patterns of middle-class formation, patterns of successful economic development are more or less likely.

which local economic growth and local political participation mutually reinforced each other and in which rural middle classes were key actors. This, again, was as much an issue of state formation as democracy.

To be sure, the United States bears its own uniqueness, and the political and economic system generated in this country cannot readily be replicated elsewhere. But much of its uniqueness owes to the decentralized patterns of urbanization and the smaller-scale town-based structures of political participation. And a version of this has materialized in several of our late developers, despite their highly centralized political systems and the absence of formal democracy. Taiwan is a case in point, especially when examined in comparison to other relatively successful late developers, even South Korea. As one scholar of East Asia put it: "Local government on Taiwan gave the people there, to however limited a degree, some practical experience of competitive politics. . . . To win elections the party had to have an electoral organization linking it to the grassroots." This stood in stark contrast to "the almost total concentration of power in South Korea in the central government in Seoul."[4] And in Taiwan, for historical reasons, the most vibrant among these local electoral organizations linking the grass roots to the state were those organized on the town level and representing small-farmer producers. The result: hierarchically structured political capacities for farmers to send locally generated demands for rural development back up to the state, which ostensibly used this information for more efficient and targeted rural development programs – including a call for the disciplining of industrial capitalists in the service of these aims. Despite the KMT's clearly authoritarian character, then, not only was it much more embedded with rural middle classes than was the South Korean state or the Latin American states we examined, it offered quasi-democratic political structures for local deliberation and participation that paralleled political structures in the United States to a surprising degree, both politically and in terms of insuring discipline of capitalists.

All this suggests that we must be prepared to think in a more nuanced fashion about the analytic interconnections between democracy and development and to do so through the lens of institutions for rural middle-class political participation and divergent patterns of state formation. Sometimes formal democracy engenders rural middle-class participation and the promise of disciplinary development, and sometimes formal democracy (or democratic reform) reduces rural middle-class participation and/or shifts the political weight from countryside to city in ways that undermine the disciplinary developmental orientations we have analyzed here. It may actually be the case that, under certain conditions at least, formal democracy can make it harder to discipline capitalists and labor, depending on the territorial and institutional setup that buttresses electoral contests either locally or nationally. But whether this occurs will

---

[4] Moody, Jr., *Political Change on Taiwan*, p. 6.

depend on the character, location, nature, and empowerment of local participatory institutions. The point here is that considering the presence or absence of democracy is not enough. We also must factor into our theorizing an understanding of patterns of state formation, as well as of the class coalitions that materialize and are empowered by the particular structures and institutions of these states, paying special attention to the role that local structures of political participation play, independent of a regime's formal democratic status.

Globalization and Disciplinary Development: Good-bye to All That?

But is a focus on local participatory mechanisms, urbanization patterns, state forms, rural class formation, and social class coalitions enough to understand future prospects for disciplinary development, democratically based or not? As this book is brought to a close, it is hard to ignore the reality of increased and intensified globalization all over the world. The question thus arises as to how this phenomenon will affect prospects for development, not just among those still struggling to get a foothold in the competitive development game but also among those already embarked on some form of sustained macroeconomic growth with greater or lesser success, including the four late industrializers studied here. Do recent trends toward greater globalization suggest that our disciplinary development model's shelf life is about to expire, despite my claims about its historical resiliency drawn from these countries' experiences to date? This could be interpreted as a strange question to pose in the closing of a book that has firmly resisted globally oriented explanations by claiming similarities between early and late industrializers and by arguing that the character of the global economy when a country initiates its industrialization alone cannot fully explain its developmental trajectories. But asking this question is necessary, not just because as the new millennium unfolds both global and domestic conditions in late-industrializing countries do appear to be changing rather dramatically, but also because several leading theoretical paradigms point to this possibility.

One of the key premises shared by scholars of the increasingly popular world-systems theory is recognition of the importance played by historical changes in the timing, spread, and nature of capitalism and how these affect relations between "core" and "peripheral" countries and thus development trajectories. The implication often drawn from this body of theory, and from the work of globalization theorists more generally, is that structural obstacles posed by an increasingly globalized world economy make it difficult for late developers to pursue the same path to success as did early developers. One frequent explanation given for this is the fact that development possibilities are assumed to be determined and constrained by the global whole as well as by the relation of "parts" (i.e., individual countries) to that of the whole. In Andre Gunder Frank's words,

> What emerges from [a] review of early modern world economic history is that many of the specific "differences" are themselves generated by structured interaction in a common world economy/system. Far from being appropriate or necessary to understanding this or that specificity here or there, differentiation then becomes an obstacle to accounting for and comprehending it. Only a holistic perspective on and from the global whole that is more than the sum of its parts can offer any adequate comprehension of any one part and how and why it differs from any other."[5]

Frank argues, in short, that commonalities across countries in one global system "are both more common and more important even than the real differences [between countries], not to mention the many alleged differences that are not even real."[6]

Clearly this has not been the position advanced in this book, which loudly trumpets significant commonalities over time and key differences among late-developing countries today. But that does not mean we cannot find a place for understanding the impact of global conditions on the likelihood of disciplinary development, especially now as a new millennium takes hold, and, by so doing, still uphold the explanatory value of the model presented here. In searching for a guide, we turn to the work of those leading globalization theorists, such as Leslie Sklair, who are not constrained by assumptions about the parts-whole telos of world-system theory.[7] With Sklair's and others' focus on transnational practices, primarily economic ones, and how they span the border of national states, we can start to theorize the ways that a greater and more intensive globalization of the world economy has brought more developing countries and firms into world markets, turning ever more late industrializers into key exporters – and not just importers or consumers – of industrial and other manufactured goods.[8] Building on the market and production actions of corporations who at the prodding of their governments participate in new transnational networks and practices, new norms and expectations for domestic and global economic behavior get established. Slowly but surely these transformations, especially as they have unfolded over the last twenty years, have changed the global rules of the game, foreclosing past developmental options

[5] *ReOrient*, p. 342.
[6] Ibid., p. 341.
[7] See, in particular, *Globalization*; and his *Sociology of the Global System*.
[8] For more on the content of these transnational practices, see Sklair, *The Transnational Capitalist Class*; and Smith, *Transnational Urbanism*.

and presupposing future ones. One result is that developing countries face new global conditions and new domestic challenges.

The conceptual point I want to make here is borrowed from Max Weber and derives from his discussion of "switchmen of history." Under certain historical conditions and at certain historical moments, decisions made and paths followed will fundamentally recalibrate an entire system. Tracks may be jumped or directions reversed. This is what happened, I believe, when the East Asian tigers of South Korea and Taiwan successfully pursued export-led industrialization in the 1970s. Owing to unique domestic conditions in these countries – both class and political – these two East Asian tigers, along with several others, followed a globally oriented path of development that privileged export-led industrialization. Again, I have argued that these decisions were made not merely because the global economy existed out there to be "plugged into," or merely because South Korean and Taiwanese technocrats thought the global economy (the "whole") was such that these policy trajectories would work or be the most efficient option available for national development (the "parts"), but rather because the domestic class, political, and rural developmental aims of those nations and their citizens privileged the selection of this path so as to gain resources for agriculture. Remember, with similar global conditions as a backdrop, most Latin American countries did not pursue the same EOI strategy until much later, if at all, for reasons discussed in great detail in the pages of this book that also have to do with their neglect of rural populations. But even when Latin American governments finally turned to export-led industrialization several decades later, often under international pressure, their fate was irretrievably cast and generative developmental outcomes were not assured.

This happened in the following sequence of events. When the East Asian tigers broke new ground by pursuing EOI, the fact that they were among the first to do so helped insure that they prospered and benefited from global integration in stunning ways. This not only helped individual East Asian countries reverse directions and jump tracks, so to speak, it also catapulted them into the international limelight in ways that insured that they would be held up as models for the rest of the world. The "demonstration effect" was enormous, as was the economic and ideological weight of their successes. Year after year, decade after decade, country after country, other late industrializers were admonished to get with the program, so to speak, especially in "lagging" Latin America. Over time many did so, not just because they thought it might be a good idea to try a similar path, or even because a free market–obsessed IMF or World Bank prodded them to do so, although these not-so-gentle pressures surely factored into the reification of these dynamics, but also because over time they had less and less choice. Indeed, owing to the changing dynamics of the global economy, and the ways it increasingly harmed those who based domestic growth on ISI instead of EOI, the internal class structures of these late-industrializing countries themselves started to change. This meant that ISI became more costly to pursue; and as this happened wages fell, employment dropped, and in many countries, agriculture languished even further, except in those few exceptional places where national policies still linked rural and urban sectors or where governments offered alternative safety nets for rural populations. As a result, agricultural classes weakened, meaning that rural and urban political balances of power also shifted. (This, in essence, is what happened to South Korea in the 1980s as it temporarily became a victim to its own successes.) One result was that those pursuing ISI were under more pressure to pursue EOI, even as they were less likely to host the rural-based social and class forces that had initially made this a popular or politically feasible alternative elsewhere.

Even when Latin American countries were able to shift to EOI without much internal political upheaval, then, because capitalists were desperate for gains from somewhere, it was not with the same emphasis on linking rural and urban sectors, a failure that limited the generative potential of this strategy in terms of its contribution to the domestic economy. Moreover, by this time the externally derived benefits – at least as understood in terms of foreign exchange – were not all that great either. Much of this owed to the fact that the domestically determined path of export-led industrialization first advanced with great success in East Asia itself soon became a global modus operandi, building on a logic that drove ever more countries to hop on the industrial exporting bandwagon, which resulted in downward pressures on domestic wages fueling the cycle further by making it unlikely that industrialization for domestic consumption could remain the industrial policy of choice even in countries long committed to this path, let alone for newcomers.[9] And once this downward spiral kicked into place, those who came late to the game would and could not necessarily benefit and prosper in the same way as those who started and took advantage of the dynamic in the first place. The point here is that certain parts can affect and even "make" the whole, just as certain

---

[9] One of Frank's major aims was to break the myth of East versus West and to challenge conventional ways of treating them as conceptually unrelated locations. Along the way, he reintroduced the centrality of the economic history of the East to studies of the economic history of the so-called West, claiming that the latter generally, and incorrectly, has been understood as singularly relevant to the history of global capitalist development. Hence the stunningly apt title of his book, *ReOrient*. Well, I too have sought to reorient, and in that sense I owe a debt to Frank as I find myself sharing his overall conceptualization. It is just that as I bring closer examination of the East back into development theory, highlighting East Asia's unique paths and developmental successes in comparison to Latin America, I want to reorient our attention to the specific country histories that underlay that region of the world's developmental salience and as such reoriented global economic dynamics in the contemporary period. Unlike Frank, then, my eyes are not so much on the overly distant past but on the near past, how it made the present, and what this might mean for the immediate future.

countries can play a watershed or "switchman" role in the construction of an entire system of practices and expectations, by generating new models and practices – understood both ideologically and in terms of changing trade, labor, production, and exporting patterns – that subsequently fuel and embody the larger logic of that system.

But from the vantage point of our model of disciplinary development there is yet another more troubling way that increasing globalization of the economy, combined with the new transnational norms, practices, and markets that it is generating, will foreclose options that in the near and distant past brought significant national developmental gains to a privileged few late industrializers. I am speaking here of the ways that the increased acceleration and intensification of global trade have contributed to a greater disarticulation of city and countryside. Owing to the extensive global economic integration in production and consumption practices as well as commodity chains and other new innovations that flowered in the wake of the East Asian tigers' participation in the world economy, and owing to the recent advances in technology and communication that comprise what scholars such as Manuel Castells now call the rise of the information economy, cities all over the world are starting to tie their fate to each other more than to the countryside surrounding them.[10] As I have noted throughout the pages of this book, the forward and backward linkages between city and countryside have long been tenuous in the developing world, as has been the likelihood of uniting rural and urban social forces in a common political or development project. Such obstacles were precisely what prevented Latin American countries from early on taking the same developmental route followed in much of East Asia during the 1970s. But when they are bridged, the gains are enormous as we have seen in Taiwan. Now, globalization may be all but snuffing out the few rural-urban articulations that still remain within the developing country context, even as it limits the political likelihood that in the future, populations in the city and countryside will join together on a national scale in support of a disciplinary developmental project similar to that seen in Taiwan.

The implications of this observation for development theory and practice are not trivial. If we take seriously the fact that what we are calling disciplinary development was most likely to emerge in countries with a national government commitment to rural populations and conditions, something that itself was less likely in countries where national political systems and economic practices were dominated by a few large cities, then the prospects that developing countries in today's increasingly globalized world will be in a position to pursue a disciplinary development path truly are quite dim. We can see how and why by briefly summarizing some of the current research findings

---

[10] Castells's three-volume work on *The Rise of the Network Society* was one of the first and best treatments of this topic.

regarding globalization's impact on cities. In her seminal book *The Global City*, published more than a decade ago, Saskia Sassen introduced the idea that an intensified globalization of capital flows was creating new forms of urban activity concentrated in a few burgeoning cities, which themselves were characterized by an even greater concentration of social, economic, political, and even cultural resources.[11] As home to the world's largest multinational corporations, these so-called global cities are now drawing ever more resources and investments from around the world. The downside of these changes is less investment and growth in locales that remain outside this urban-based circuit of capital.

In her original work on the subject, Sassen made this point by highlighting the extent to which, with the globalization of leading cities like New York, developmental losses accrued to more industrially vulnerable cities such as Detroit and their surrounding regions, which lost out with the new restructuring of the national economy. Despite this note of caution, in much of the literature that followed the assumption was that global cities served as a source of unmitigated economic gain, primarily owing to their function as key nodes in the development of a new information- or service-linked international economy. Yet any optimism about the generative economic effects generated by the rise of global cities must be understood in light of the fact that those locales most likely to be recognized as hosting these gains were cities centered in the most affluent nations or economically promising regions of the world. New York, London, Paris, Tokyo, Hong Kong, and Singapore are some of the most frequently cited nominees. When one turns to most of the rest of the developing country context, then, especially to Latin America, or even to cities in developed countries whose economies are tied to industries now made obsolete by information technologies and global restructuring, both the local and national context of prosperity is missing, and so too the promise of national gains generated by these global cities. The source of the problem not only lies in the fact that most developing countries have been suffering over the last decades, and thus they still lack the strong national markets to take advantage of these new globally linked activities. It also lies in the fact that even when the urban economies of the principal cities in the developing world do flourish and bloom through global networks built on links with other prosperous cities or nations, these transformations frequently produce further social, political, and economic schisms within and between these cities and the rest of the nation. Indeed, domestic and international investment and support for agriculture, especially in the form of small-scale agrarian production, are more often than not a casualty of globalization. If there are gains, multinational agro-businesses tend to flourish in an environment of increased liberalization

---

[11] For some of the best writing on this topic, see Sassen's *The Global City*; and her *Globalization and Its Discontents*.

and globalization, usually to the detriment of small-farmer production, while the free flow of capital across borders creates instability in currency valuations in ways that can further harm these undercapitalized small producers most directly.

Accordingly, even in the prosperous East Asian tigers studied here, such as Taiwan, which were relatively successful in overcoming rural-urban disarticulation and sustaining a strong urban and rural middle class, the prospects of continuing along the same trajectory are diminishing as globalization brings more polarization both within cities and between cities and countryside, unless counteractive policy measures are put in place.[12] To the extent that globalization exacerbates social and economic polarization both within cities and nations, this situation can further undermine middle-class formation and past political coalitions that brought middle-class discipline to the nation-state and gave it the capacity to impose a disciplinary development strategy. Middle classes, remember, also serve as a key source of demand in countries trying to generate a national market for their goods (not to mention a key labor resource for service-related firms that sprout in global cities). But even more significantly, with globalization leading to ever more fragmentation of the long-standing social, economic, and political connections between cities and their hinterlands, with the balance of national political power shifting to a network of globally connected cities that transcends national bounds, it will be even harder to create a broad cross-territorial national political coalition of support for a development project that, like disciplinary development, is built on a vision of rural-urban synergy. Even if a national political project were to materialize in such conditions, disciplining of capital would be almost impossible, largely because political power balances will more likely shift to the cities, where most of the gains associated with global integration will be reflected in the increasing presence of multinational corporations, institutions, and the service sector (both high end and low end) that supports them.

The impact of all these shifts, in institutional terms at least, may be that existent state forms – understood in terms of the institutional reach and character of the nation-state and the territorially dispersed institutions of which it is comprised – also will become ever more distanced from these globally connected structures and agents of economic power, who will increasingly turn to like-minded allies and institutions outside their borders as a reference

---

[12] For more on the ways that globalization produces more polarization between city and countryside in the late-industrializing world, see McGee's "Globalization and Rural-Urban Linkages in the Developing World"; and Kane's "Feeding the World's Cities." For a general discussion of the negative impacts of globalization, both rural-urban disarticulation and social and economic polarization within cities themselves, see Lo and Yeung (eds.), *Globalization and the World of Large Cities*; United Nations Center for Human Settlements (Habitat), *Cities in a Globalizing World*; and Short and Kim, *Globalization and the City*.

point while bypassing the nation-state almost entirely.[13] It is worth noting that over the past decade or two, often through the encouragement of international agencies and lending institutions keen on creating macroeconomic efficiency through downsizing overcentralized national state apparatuses, most developing countries introduced massive decentralization programs. Yet now, the economic and political gains of globalization are themselves increasingly concentrated and centralized in one or two globally linked cities. To the extent that political institutions and practices are dispersed and decentralized across national territory, while resources and economic decision-making power are concentrated, we see the potential for a further weakening of the national state system as a whole as well as for political party systems whose constituencies will be national and not just local.

A worst-case scenario would be so much disjuncture between national-level political and economic structures of decision making so as to threaten the viability and legitimacy of the nation-state in its entirety, leading to more internal instability and even rebellion among those territorially and economically excluded from globalization's gains and the few cities it nurtures. If in response national states feel politically compelled to respond to the claims of *all* those within their national territory, as democracy so dictates, rather than accommodating only the privileged few living in a few globally linked urban locales, cities may balk at the attempts by the nation-state to rein them in. If they don't, then the state will ultimately become hostage to the city (in a paradoxical reversal of conventional understandings of their relationship). Either way, we may even see cities starting to act like nation-states, an alternative form of "rebellion" already under way in some European locations.[14] Yet by taking this route, globally networked cities will further fuel the cycle of state weakening as well as the state's incapacity to respond to the developmental or political demands of its rural populations. Perhaps the biggest casualty of this turn of events will be a government's capacity to discipline capitalists in the service of national gains, who now more than ever will be concentrated in the world's global cities or empowered vis-à-vis the national state. This scenario, to a great degree, could replicate around the world the experiences that in the past were so specific to Argentina, Mexico, and numerous late industrializers where the unparalleled power of classes and institutions in the capital city determined state decisions to accommodate capitalists and laborers and to ignore rural development, to disastrous macroeconomic effects.

---

[13] For further discussion of this, see Sassen's essay on the state and the global city in her *Globalization and Its Discontents*, pp. 195–215; and Brenner's "Global Cities, Global States."

[14] For more on the ways in which cities themselves become key actors negotiating with other global cities and external nation-states as much as their own, see Borja and Castells, *Local and Global*.

The Age of Indiscipline

It may be fitting to close this book with a concern about the state's diminishing capacity to discipline capitalists because recent evidence suggests that this may actually be a universal phenomenon linked to globalization, rather than a problem plaguing only late industrializers. The recent corruption scandals in the United States involving some of the largest and most powerful global firms (Enron, WorldCom, etc.) do indeed suggest that capitalist indiscipline – at least as reflected in big firms calling their own shots in the service of private profit with no heed for the law or aggregate national economic gain – is no longer a Third World problem. One reason for this may be the fact that the state's regulatory institutions (and if not the institutions, then the willingness of elected officials to enforce regulatory laws) have been weakening in the United States and other advanced countries, and not just in the late-industrializing world, as ever more empowered and globally networked capitalists seem to be building or managing corporations with greater impudence. The growing "indiscipline" of capitalists also might owe to the fact that, with globalization, social contracts that historically have been bounded in an allegiance or commitment to a circumscribed territory – be it a small rural community, as in the United States during early postcolonial periods of great economic gain, or in a larger "imagined" national community such as Taiwan and South Korea where a commitment to national progress underlay much of the state's disciplining of capital – no longer carry the same social, political, or even moral weight.

Before modern states and their regulatory laws played the role of disciplinarian for the "common good," churches and local communities did so by virtue of the social contracts they established with citizens. Over time, national states took over the role, with support from sufficient numbers of national citizens to legitimize them into law. In many developing countries, the willingness or capacity of the state to discipline corporate actors never reached the potential it did in the advanced capitalist world, with a few exceptions, for reasons discussed in the pages of this book. But as the world becomes more globalized and nation-states become more fragmented and splintered by virtue of the growing polarization in and between city and countryside, such discipline is becoming ever more elusive even in the so-called advanced world. For one thing, corporations today have much more political sway than they did even a few decades ago, because they also are territorially wrenched out of the social and political communities that would make them responsible to citizens. Instead, they are ever more embedded in transnational social networks and institutions that link them to each other and to the alternative "value" systems that sustain the undisciplined practices and ruthless financial aims of international firms that no doubt led to some of the excesses and corporate failures associated with Enron-like scandals. To the extent that globalization is creating a class of capitalists who themselves have less and less allegiance to a national community or its citizens, and who at best see their fate as linked to a transnational network of producers and consumers that are not necessarily tied to space or territory (including the cities that host their headquarters), the likelihood for state discipline is even less.

This prognosis all too eerily echoes the European experience in the centuries before the emergence of capitalism and modern state formation, when violence, political instability, fights over the reach of national states, and a global network of interlinked mercantile cities and powerful "corporate" actors unwilling to subordinate their interests to those of putative national states and imperial powers brought decades of war, bloodshed, and, ultimately, a recalibration of the global distribution of wealth and power. Oddly, then, this book ends as it started: by accentuating parallels as much as differences in the analysis of developmental prospects for both early and late developers. It may be that globalization is responsible for bringing us full circle to this originating methodological point. But even so, we stand behind the main substantive findings presented here. Prosperity and sustained economic success depend on the disciplining of capitalists and the creation of networks and forward-backward linkages among a variety of interconnected classes and economic sectors united in a well-circumscribed and manageable territorial space. Achieving this state of affairs will be the main normative and policy-making challenge of our times, not just because it has eluded so many late industrializers up until now, but because current globalization trends suggest that guaranteeing such conditions may become both more important and more problematic in years to come. The billion-dollar question is whether urban, rural, national, and international actors and institutions can be mobilized to produce these results in more than a few exceptional cases, and what this would take in an age of globalization. As with all billion-dollar questions, the answer clearly remains to be seen.

APPENDIX A

CASES, COMPARISONS, AND A NOTE ON
METHODOLOGY AND SOURCES

This book employs a comparative-historical methodology and does so for the standard reasons: to build and test hypotheses. By explicitly comparing Taiwan and South Korea with Argentina and Mexico, differences between East Asia and Latin America are considered. Yet with these four cases, there also is material to theorize developmental differences *within* the same regional contexts (i.e., between Mexico and Argentina, on one hand, and between South Korea and Taiwan on the other). After all, although both South Korea and Taiwan are considered great successes, the latter has not suffered the debt and banking crises that have plagued the former. In Latin America, similarly, there are significant differences: Mexico is uniformly considered to have forged a more stable macroeconomic path than Argentina, despite the recent gains (and setbacks) experienced by both. Argentina's current economic situation proves this view.

The selection of these particular four countries owes partly to the desire to hold constant the factors generally used to account for development trajectories. In all four cases equally interventionist, strong, and bureaucratized states with considerable power and institutional capacity guided national development during the initial periods of rapid and sustained industrialization. In each country the state held considerable political power to act with unrivaled authority, leading most scholars to conclude that these were "strong" states with considerable autonomous capacity. Moreover, each of their governments repressed or restricted democratic participation and civil liberties during critical junctures of industrial development, such that all four possessed semi-authoritarian political systems routinely identified as buttressing the state's institutional capacity to call the shots (military government in South Korea and Argentina, corporatist one-party rule in Taiwan and Mexico). And all four nations suffered under the weight of colonial and/or mercantilist core-periphery relations that distorted industrial development and favored the export of agricultural or other primary products before the period of political independence. Furthermore, in the first several decades after World War II all four shunned a full commitment to free-market strategies, choosing instead active state intervention in the market and direct regulation and involvement in industrial production. Those actions – which laid the foundations for later economic developments – included strong control of labor and aid to capitalists through such measures as protectionism, licensing, direct subsidies, and financing. Yet only the East Asian countries have achieved what can be understood as relative success, even though they doubted the magic of the market as much as did their Latin American counterparts. These differences are best evidenced by the fact that even as South Korea and Taiwan achieved sustained and considerable economic growth since the 1970s, with rising per capita incomes and relatively solid current account balances that helped militate against drastic cycles of devaluation, inflation, capital flight, and debt crisis, Mexico and Argentina did not.

Of course, the East Asian countries were blessed with massive doses of foreign aid, advanced for political as much as economic purposes. But not all countries on the receiving end of such aid, or even those that counted on increased direct foreign investment and substantial external development resources during the initial periods of industrialization, fared so well. Mexico also benefited from considerable U.S. financial aid, investment, and trade support in the period of postwar industrial development, and this contributed to the development of steel, petrochemicals, and the automobile industry;[1] and as in South Korea, most of this foreign aid and credit came in exchange for Mexico's support for U.S. geopolitical aims.[2] Yet rather than seeing the same general prosperity that flowered in South Korea and Taiwan, even with this financial assistance, Mexico's economy remained weak and vulnerable. Perhaps the main difference between these two sets of countries was that the East Asian nations initiated industrialization at a time in the development of the global economy when other advanced economies were seeking to cultivate low-wage imports from (not to) these countries. This surely gave the East Asians an "economic opportunity structure" – to appropriate Charles Tilly's notion – that the Latin Americans lacked.

Still, the timing of industrialization or even the more readily available markets for East Asian exports can account for only part of the story. What they cannot tell us, for one thing, is why East Asian government officials decided to partake of the new economic opportunities in the 1960s and early 1970s when it meant struggling against the domestic class and political interests of ISI industrialists, even when Latin American governments did not – despite their comparable eagerness to expand their economies during the same period of global capital expansion. Nor can the mere existence of global economic opportunity structures account for developmental differences within our regionally grouped pairs of countries, as well as similarities that span the Latin American–East Asian divide, either then or now, including the growing foreign debt burden and the banking crisis that hit South Korea in the 1980s and again in the late 1990s. The latter problems showed in fact that despite taking advantage of global opportunities for export, South Korea was not immune to the problems identified with the Latin American "model," even as Taiwan was spared.

Even between the Latin American countries under study here, there have been significant developmental differences, despite the similar global conditions in which they

---

[1] In the aftermath of World War II, Mexico received $90 million dollars in credits from 1940 to 1946 alone, for infrastructure and industrial development; it also received considerable direct foreign investment in industry, not only during its most intensive period of industrial takeoff, between 1940 and 1955, but also in subsequent decades.

[2] Much of this can be traced to joint efforts by the two countries to collaborate in the industrial production of materials for World War II. Torres, *México en la segunda guerra mundial*, pp. 205–211.

industrialized. Argentina's economy performed in a lackluster manner despite the fact that, in contrast to Mexico, it received *no direct* development aid or political accommodation from the United States during its initial industrialization because Argentina had backed the Axis powers. Unlike Mexico, and closer to the case of South Korea, however, Argentina severely limited direct foreign investment in manufacturing in the critical stage of industrial development. One result was that during the last several decades, Mexico and Argentina suffered through foreign exchange crises, recurrent bouts of spiraling inflation, debt problems that failed to disappear, general investor unease, and, most recently, a net drop in wages, growing income inequality, and a deterioration in the general standard of living, despite efforts to embrace neoliberal policy prescriptions and free trade economics.

Accordingly, developmental differences within and between these two regions of the world owe not only to variations in the timing, extent, and character of support for EOI over ISI, but to other factors relating to the ways that the East Asian countries developed leading sectors, diversified their economies, and established strong forward and backward sectoral linkages to achieve balanced rural and urban growth, enviable per capita income goals, and high educational and health standards.[3] In ascertaining why these developments have been more likely to materialize in East Asia than Latin America, my focus in this book is the rural middle class and its embeddedness with the state.

Two caveats having to do with methodology and the broadly cast comparative-historical framework employed in this study: While on the theoretical level much can be gained from a four-country study spanning decades for each case, such gains are not without cost. As the author of a closely documented historical study of a single country, Mexico, I know only too well the perils of grand treatments and the pleasures of detailed studies. Much will have to be sacrificed to paint the bigger picture. The hope is that a sufficiently plausible and compelling argument emerges that links middle-class formation to the rise of disciplinary states and thus the likelihood of successful economic development trajectories. Additionally, in a comparative-historical study of this scope, I have been forced to rely on secondary materials more than I would have had I undertaken a study of a single country. This has been especially true for the three countries that I did not know as well as Mexico upon beginning this project; and it is true even for Argentina, a Spanish-speaking country for which my own research on primary documents serves as the principal source of information. That in turn raises an additional problem of which I am fully aware: that the quality and character of the argument rests on the quality and character of the available sources.

---

[3] Among these countries, as economist Jagdish Bhagwati has argued, economic successes owe in no small part to whether EOI or ISI policies have been implemented early on, rather than to the state's autonomy or strength per se. And on these counts, South Korea and Taiwan turned relatively rapidly to highly successful EOI, itself built on a commitment to sectoral integration, the establishment of strong forward and backward linkages, and sustained per capita income spread much more equally across the population. Argentina and Mexico held to a highly problematic version of ISI characterized by a highly polarized and disarticulated economy and deep income inequalities. "Democracy and Development," p. 42.

Appendix A

As is clear in the chapters themselves, for Mexico and Argentina the availability of primary sources is less of a constraint than for South Korea and Taiwan because of the sheer volume of work on classes, class politics, and development, especially during each country's first several decades of industrial development. If there has been one part of the world where class and political economy have reigned supreme, Latin America wins top honors. For South Korea and Taiwan, however, such studies were not nearly as pervasive or accessible. The dearth of sources owes in part to the shorter duration of time since the development miracle hit; yet the real world of geopolitics and the subtle and not-so-subtle political constraints on left thinking also permeated both these societies and their academic institutions with direct implications for source materials. Additionally, East Asia's incredible successes inspired scholars over the last several decades to focus more on the state and the economy than on politics and classes, leave aside the middle classes. The rural middle classes, for their part, have hardly been studied at all (especially under that nomenclature, as noted in Chapter 2). In studies of South Korea and Taiwan, moreover, most research focused on the 1970s and 1980s, when the blossoming of East Asia's "miracle" first began to capture global attention. Few have studied the critical decades before, when the seeds of success were sown. Hence there is surprisingly little in any language that delves deeply into the 1950s and 1960s, especially at the level of detail necessary for a comprehensive study of rural and urban middle classes, their work, culture, and politics, and their relationships to other classes and the state in Taiwan and South Korea.

In the face of these obstacles, the best one can hope for is enough good primary material to serve as a starting point for understanding more complex historical conditions in each of the countries. Equally important are a relatively comprehensive body of major secondary works on each country, enough confidence in one's theoretical framework to move forward even if faced with gaps in the empirical material, sufficient intellectual integrity to know what points cannot be sustained, and, of course, a strong dose of humility to counter the relentless tendency for heady or baseless abstractions.

APPENDIX B

DEFINING THE MIDDLE CLASS: NOTES
ON BOUNDARIES AND EPISTEMOLOGY

Who are these middle classes that are hypothesized as so central to national development in this book, and what is the best way to study them as well as the state and class alliances they forge? These have been among the most difficult questions of this inquiry. Definitional quandaries about who constitutes the middle class and why have been among the most contentious and controversial themes in the study of society. Drawing boundaries around any class category is fraught with difficulties, as is theorizing their bases for action in the context of this boundary drawing. To be concerned with a class whose so-called objective foundations are considered fluid and unstable and which is characterized by extensive occupational diversity is to invite further controversy. Moreover, as Anthony Giddens and others have pointed out, one of the most interesting attributes of middle-classness is the *absence* of class identity or consciousness.[1] The turn to poststructuralist analysis has added to the confusion over definitions and the debates over boundary drawing by raising valid and serious questions about the relative worth of objective versus subjective definitions of class.[2] And if we also throw in the peculiarities of the developing world, where the middle class is in many ways a constantly moving target whose size, composition, and character change dramatically as the economy changes equally rapidly, the task is truly daunting. This is especially the case because most scholars of the newly industrializing world avoid using the notion of middle class, almost at all costs, for fear of the political and theoretical baggage it has frequently implied (for more on this, see Chapter 2). Accordingly, there is bound to be some scholarly conflict about the subject, no matter where the line is drawn.

Further complicating matters is the fact that in any study that attempts to differentiate rural from urban middle classes, like mine, yet another impediment comes

---

[1] As Giddens puts it: "Middle-class individuals normally lack a clear conception of class identity and, even when unionized, characteristically do not embrace any form of conflict consciousness." See Giddens, "The Growth of the New Middle Class," p. 121.

[2] Some have argued that precisely because the middle classes are so elusive, both theoretically and empirically speaking, the only way to study them is through a focus on their subjective struggles or the self-construction of middle-class identity. See Wacquant, "Making Class," especially his treatment of the writings of Kocka and Boltanski.

363

in the form of assumptions about the urban underpinnings of class differentiation or class formation. Even as some scholars have made headway in studying urban middle classes, especially the new middle class, rural forces are rarely analyzed in class terms, let alone middle-class terms. This, again, is especially the case in the study of developing countries, where it is assumed that cities, not the countryside, host if not engender the process of class differentiation and formation, and where many rural small producers are conceptualized as peasants, a term that obscures their class identity. Accordingly, to the extent that one chooses to question these assumptions and use class as a relevant category for understanding rural forces, middle class or otherwise, questions about how to analytically distinguish the urban from the rural also loom large. All this means that any argument built on a study of the actions and orientations of both rural and urban middle classes has to face the formidable problem of defining its central protagonists in a way that both acknowledges and makes sense of the ambiguity and imprecision inherent in the concept of middle class, in the assumed distinctions between urban and rural locales, in the epistemological differences in ways of knowing about class, and in the distinctively "classless" character of middle-classness. I rise to the challenge, but armed with several important qualifications.

First, I began the research by employing an operational definition of the middle class that was more starting than ending point. My substantive aim was to move beyond the preoccupation with big capitalists and wage laborers, two class forces already overstudied among developmentalists, and to initiate detailed study of those more "middling" sectors who work under different conditions and on many counts fall in an intermediate position on a social class continuum in which the two extremes are defined in terms of income, ownership, buying versus selling labor power, and autonomy on the job. As such, from the beginning I was aware that there was no guarantee that the forces I initially chose to examine as middle class would always be seen or see themselves as being in the middle of this continuum, either in one country or equally across different countries. Ascertaining why or why not has in fact been one of this book's primary concerns. In order to arrive at some final conclusions about middle classes and their political embeddedness in the state, even though I started out by using more "objective" criteria to initially target my central protagonists, I eventually examined both subjective and objective determinants of middle-class identity and alliances. My concern has always been understanding, or *verstehen* as Weber calls it, which means an appreciation of historical specificity and, in our case, a respect for the cultural, social, political, and economic dimensions of class identity, as well as questions of self-interpretation, not merely an allegiance to strictly cast, readily quantifiable, or easily operational categorizations.

Second, even as I proceeded under the assumption that middle-class identity is subjectively as well as objectively constructed in a multiplicity of ways, I still had to begin analysis from some initial vantage point, and I did so by starting with the assumption that the best definitional point of departure for targeting the relevant middle rungs of a more extreme social class continuum is also the most theoretically consensual and inclusive. And among scholars of different theoretical perspectives, ranging from those using income to those using labor process as criteria, there tends to be agreement that there are three basic occupational categories that comprise the middle class. They are: 1) *salaried employees* in commerce, services, industry, and the professions, as well as those employed by the state;[3] 2) *self-employed* artisans, craftsmen, and other independent rural or urban-based producers who in developing countries are frequently called petty commodity producers and would include among them small farmers; and 3) owners and operators of *small enterprises*, including family firms, in both industry and agriculture.[4]

As this last category indicates, for all scholars regardless of theoretical allegiance, size serves as an important yardstick for distinguishing middle classes (or petite bourgeoisie) from capitalists (i.e., the bourgeoisie) when it comes to enterprises. Owners of small firms tend to rely on nonwage labor, especially family labor, as well as themselves, a mix of work conditions that places small firms closer to the self-employed category than to capitalists.[5] Indeed, there is frequently a fine line between the activities of the individually self-employed, on one hand, and small businesses, on the other, at least in terms of labor process and in terms of articulation with larger firms in the economy. Moreover, small firms tend to differ considerably from larger firms in employment practices, stability and surety of income, access to credit and other productive inputs, as well as social and political power. It is for precisely these reasons, in fact, that the term "petite bourgeoisie" is so frequently used to refer to both the self-employed and small businesses and to differentiate them discursively from so-called capitalists.[6]

This broadly cast operational definition of the middle classes is not without problems. Many theorists would be wary of identifying the middle class in terms that specify only the outer boundaries separating them from capital and labor, but that do not give many clues as to differences within.[7] Most Weberian class analysts, for

---

[3] In Marxist terminology, salaried employees would include both semiautonomous wage earners and managers, two different categories of middle classes defined by their contradictory class location between capital and labor. See Wright, *Class, Crisis, and the State.*

[4] For a general theoretical understanding of the middle classes, both new and old, I draw upon the important work of the following authors, among others: Abercrombie and Urry, *Capital, Labour, and the Middle Classes*; Wright, *Class, Crisis, and the State*; Carchedi, "On the Economic Identification of the New Middle Class"; Goldthorpe, "On the Service Class"; Ross, "Marxism and the New Middle Classes"; Burris, "The Discovery of the New Middle Classes"; Hindess, *Politics and Class Analysis*; and Wacquant, "Making Class."

[5] See Berger, "The Uses of the Traditional Sector in Italy," for an interesting discussion of the economic rationale for focusing on the variable of firm size in understanding independent small property owners.

[6] All scholars, of course, do not collapse both the self-employed and small enterprises into a singular petit bourgeois category. Wright, for example, sees only the self-employed as purely petit bourgeois, while small firms are another category of middle classes with a contradictory class location straddled between the bourgeoisie and the petite bourgeoisie.

[7] Both Marxists and Weberians would agree that in modern societies capitalists and workers occupy entirely distinct class positions, and that the main source of capitalist profit is the labor of the working class. Both would also agree that the middle class is extraordinarily heterogeneous, holding within its bounds numerous occupations and persons with a wide variety of qualifications, earnings, skills, mobility, and work situations. In short, there is

example, hold that even within the intermediate strata there are important class distinctions (i.e., upper, middle, and lower middle class or "new" versus "old" middle classes), based on status criteria and differential access to property and the market, which prevent middle classes from acting as a singular force. Those writing within the Marxist tradition, on the other hand, tend to shun the claims of class hierarchies within the middle class, even though they too see internal distinctions, especially based on differences between new and old middle classes.[8] In contrast to Weberian analysts, for Marxists the most significant cleavages within the middle class owe to the extent to which work situation is closer to that of labor's or capital's, a problematic that is most pronounced with respect to the "new" middle classes. Such factors as level of exploitation, involvement in productive or unproductive labor, and control or autonomy in decision making all could lead to differences within these newer sectors of the middle class, with these differences reproducing or reinforcing the antagonistic class relations in society at large.[9] In Erik Olin Wright's terminology, the middle classes are best understood in terms of their contradictory class location, meaning that they hold elective affinities with both capital and labor.[10]

While many take a totalitarian position in this debate about the nature of divisions within the middle class and either define a priori or further delineate the middle strata in terms of a "structured affinity" with capital or labor, or even more precisely, in

---

agreement that there are fundamental differences in income, labor process, life chances, and ownership between the extremes of the class structure. Additionally, there is agreement on the diverse character of the occupations straddling the center regions of this polarized class structure. For a good overview of the different schools of thought, and where they converge or diverge, see Hindess, *Politics and Class Analysis*, p. 38.

[8] Mills's use and justification of this distinction is prototypical. He identifies old middle classes (farmers, businessmen, free professionals) as those associated with periods before extensive and deepening capitalist development; while new middle classes (managers, salaried professionals, salespeople, office workers) emerge with advanced capitalist development, partly due to the tendency for concentration in size and ownership. See *White Collar*, especially Mills's chapter on the new middle classes (pp. 63–76). See also the provocative work on middle classes by Urry, who in "Towards a Structural Theory of the Middle Class" analyzes the ways in which middle classes emerge in the interstices of two dichotomies (ownership/non-ownership of the means of production and production/nonproduction of value).

[9] See, for example, Poulantzas, *Classes in Contemporary Capitalism*; Abercrombie and Urry, *Capital, Labour, and the Middle Classes*; Cottrell, *Social Classes in Marxist Theory*; Carchedi, *On the Economic Identification of Social Classes*; and Clegg, Boreham, and Dow, *Class Politics and the Economy*.

[10] See *Class, Crisis, and the State*; and *Classes*. Note that in Wright's formulation, there are three basic class forces in society: the proletariat, the bourgeoisie, and the petty bourgeoisie; and middle classes are those workers (managers, small employers, and semiautonomous wage earners) who exist in a contradictory class location vis-à-vis these three classes. In our schema, we draw boundaries around the middle class in such a way as to consider the petty bourgeoisie as similarly situated with managers, small employers, and semiautonomous wage earners in a broadly defined middle class.

terms of market, income, status, and property differences, I do not. From my vantage point this would have been to put the cart before the horse. I fully expected that in the countries under study here income, market, status, and property differences vary considerably for intelligible historical reasons, and given these empirical variations, I naturally expected differences in objective and subjective definitions of the middle class. That is, differences in conditions across time and place affected whether people in similar occupations actually saw themselves in similar class terms or used these class languages in a self-referential sense. To a great extent, that turned out to be true (as is made most clear in the discussion of farmer-workers versus rural proletarians in the comparison of small rural producers in Taiwan and Argentina, respectively). What made an occupational category "middle class" in ethos and occupation, then, both from our vantage point and from the view of the subjects themselves, varied by country and even by time period within individual countries.

That there are significant differences within and between our Latin American and East Asian countries in terms of class structure in general and middle-class configurations, moreover, is precisely one of the central points of this book. In South Korea, for example, small farmers – even those on the margins of poverty – have held considerably greater status and cultural importance than their incomes would suggest. For this reason, in fact, state policy makers fashioned industrial development policies which accommodated their concerns and, in the process, helped initiate a more balanced and equitable development trajectory. In Mexico, in contrast, small farmers were more likely to remain out of the political and social picture, and for a variety of historical reasons, a large number have tended to identify more with the country's economically marginal classes, thereby considering themselves peasants (*campesinos*) rather than small farm owners (*pequeños propietarios*). It is also worth noting that in Mexico, in stark contrast to South Korea, the cultural weight of radical class discourses and the privileged political position of organized labor in the ruling party also meant that the incomes and status of industrial laborers frequently matched – if not surpassed – that of many salaried employees, despite their reduced autonomy on the job. This has not only had implications for working- and middle-class identities, and the relations between these two groups, but also for national development policy.

The point here is that income gains and status are frequently allocated within and between the middle class and other classes in a very different manner across time and place, such that there is not always the same direct correspondence between greater income or greater status and a middle- as opposed to working-class location, at least with the same regularity as in the advanced capitalist context. And it was precisely to avoid too narrowly defined or highly structured definitions that might prevent us from assessing variations and contingencies like those noted above that I shunned the use of income or status criterion as an entry point for identifying class; instead I stuck to the three most general and least debatable occupational categories of the middle class mentioned earlier (the self-employed, owners or operators of small enterprises, and employees). By examining the same sets of occupations in all the countries under study, and whether and why workers in them see themselves as middle class, I have been able to say something more exacting in terms of definitions, perhaps even modifying our understanding of how to identify middle classes in the developing country context. But again, that will be the ending – not starting – point of my research.

Finally, when early on in this study a fellow sociologist queried as to whether the South Korean farmers that I was treating as middle class also saw or talked about themselves as such, I was cued to the importance of being absolutely clear about whose voice is doing the defining, so to speak, and how this factors into my treatment and understanding of middle classes. As a consequence, I made considerable effort to insure that my substantive claims were derived not from privileging any particular subject's voice, but from a focus on the general life world – or everyday experience – of middle classes in each of these countries. That is, it has not been my intent to study only the self-conscious appropriation of languages of middle-classness by the protagonists themselves, or to use this as the sole or even preferred entry into the subject, although it does factor in. Rather, to the best of my ability I also have identified and thought about middle classes through analysis of how they live, how they work, what they aspire to economically and politically, and what they expect of fellow citizens, political parties, and their respective governments, as well as the myriad social, political, and economic organizations they have or have not joined. As Norbert Lechner reminds us, these everyday experiences teach people the practical skills and knowledge that inform their social and political behavior as well as the social meaning of their situation.[11] If we can grasp middle-class life worlds in our different countries, we can know more about who they are and why they do what they do.

Again, this is not to say that I have completely ignored language or that language is epistemologically unimportant in this study. In all of the cases under study, languages of class or classlessness play an important role in helping us understand how middle classes see themselves and why they act as they do.[12] Indeed, in several instances – especially in early periods of industrialization – groups that objectively speaking could be considered middle class shunned languages of class altogether, middle-class or otherwise. Yet as shall be clear, their efforts in this regard often reflected an effort to culturally and politically distinguish themselves from capital and labor. This state of affairs gives testament to one of the principal postures that defined middle classes in all the countries under study: the refusal to recognize the salience of class and the desire to repudiate class categories or class languages, a point noted earlier in reference to Giddens. For my purposes, this was methodologically and substantively relevant because it meant that even when the languages of middle-classness were missing, there often was other evidence of a self-conscious understanding of falling into a middling position between capital and labor. My aim in this book has been to find these linguistic silences and gauge the extent to which they, as well as middle-class voices, tell us something about development trajectories.

[11] "Some People Die of Fear," p. 33.

[12] For one of the best historical and ethnographic accounts of shifting languages of middle-classness, see Blumin's wonderful study, *The Emergence of the Middle Class*. Blumin examines how and why boundaries separating working and middle classes were drawn where they were, using an examination of languages of class and locating these transformations in the economic, social, and urban experience of colonial America.

APPENDIX C

TABLES

Table A. Urban Agglomeration in Capital Cities as Percentage of Total Population, 1950–2000 (in Thousands)

	1950	%	1960	%	1970	%	1980	%	1990	%	2000	%
Buenos Aires	4,722[a]	29.7	6,739	33.7	8,353	35.8	9,766	34.9	10,918[b]	33.5	11,454[c]	31.6
Mexico City	2,982	10.4	5,155	14.8	8,657	17.9	13,735	20.5	15,048	18.5	17,787	18.2
Seoul	1,446	7.2	2,445	9.8	5,443	17.1	8,364	21.9	10,627	24.8	9,895	21.4
Taipei	503	6.2	799	7.4	1,770	12.1	2,220	12.5	2,760	13.6	2,624	11.8

[a] The figure is for 1947.
[b] The figure is for 1991.
[c] The figure is for 2001.

Sources: International Historical Statistics, The Americas, 1750–1993, Third Edition, 1998, pp. 33, 38. International Historical Statistics, Africa, Asia, and Oceania, 1750–1993, Third Edition, 1998, pp. 42–43. Instituto Nacional de Estadística Geográfica e Informática, INEGI, Social and Demographic Statistics, www.inegi.gob.mx/. Instituto Nacional de Estadística y Censo, INDEC, Buenos Aires, Argentina. Economic Planning Board, Korea Statistical Yearbook, 2002, Korea, 2002, pp. 21, 77–78. Directorate-General of Budget Accounting and Statistics, National Statistics, www.dgbasey.gov.tw/, Republic of China, 2002.

Table B. *Urban and Rural Population, 1950–2000 (in Thousands)*

	Argentina			Mexico			Korea			Taiwan		
	Total	% Urban	% Rural	Total	% Urban	% Rural	Total	% Urban	% Rural	Total	% Urban	% Rural
1950	17,189	64.2	35.8	25,791	42.6	57.4	20,189[a]	17.2	82.8	8,128[b]	N.D.	N.D.
1960	20,956	67.6	32.4	34,923	50.7	49.3	25,003	27.7	72.3	10,792	N.D.	N.D.
1970	23,692	78.4	21.6	50,596	59.4	40.6	31,923	40.7	59.3	14,676	N.D.	N.D.
1980	28,094	82.9	17.1	67,570	66.3	33.7	38,124	56.9	43.1	17,805	69.7	30.3
1990	32,527	86.5	13.5	83,226	72.5	27.5	42,869	73.8	26.2	20,353	78.9	21.1
2000	37,032	89.4	10.6	97,966	74.4	25.6	46,136	82	18	22,216	83.5	16.5

[a] The figure is for 1949.
[b] The figure is for 1952.

Sources: Economic Commission for Latin America, *Statistical Bulletin for Latin America*, Vol. 2, no. 2, New York, 1965, pp. 9–10. Secretaría de Industria y Comercio, Dirección General de Estadística, *Anuario Estadístico de los Estados Unidos Mexicanos, 1960–1961*, Cap. 2, Mexico, 1963, p. 25. Economic Planning Board, *Korea Statistical Yearbook, 1962*, Korea, 1962, p. 21. International Bank for Reconstruction and Development/The World Bank, Development Data Group, The 2002 World Bank Development Indicators CD-ROM, Washington, D.C., 2002. Council for Planning and Development, *Taiwan Statistical Data Book, 2002*, Republic of China, 2002, p. 22.

Table C. Land Distribution Patterns in Latin America: Farm Households by Size of Cultivated Land in Argentina and Mexico (in Hectares)

ARGENTINA

	<5	5–25	25–100	100–200	200–1,000	1,000–5,000	>5,000
1952							
Number of farms	59,616	101,836	128,285	63,025	62,976	20,151	5,542
%	13.5	23.1	29.1	14.3	14.3	4.6	1.3
1960							
Number of farms	71,814	109,590	127,463	58,795	63,153	20,697	5,661
%	15.7	24	27.9	12.9	13.8	4.5	1.3
1969							
Number of farms	100,379	125,686	139,067	63,438	77,047	25,829	6,984
%	18.6	23.3	25.8	11.8	14.3	4.8	1.3

MEXICO

	<1	1.1–5	5.1–10	10.1–25	25.1–50
1950					
Number of farms	498,399	506,436	90,213	101,112	59,523
%	39.7	40.3	7.2	8.1	4.7
1960					
Number of farms	N.D.	N.D.	94,319	132,335	70,250
%	N.D.	N.D.	N.A.	N.A.	N.A.
1970					
Number of farms	255,020	266,756	101,918	101,702	60,335
%	32.5	34	13	12.9	7.7

Sources: For Argentina, Ministerio de Economía, Hacienda y Finanzas, Instituto Nacional de Estadística y Censos, Anuario Estadístico de la República Argentina, 1979–1980, Argentina, 1980, pp. 312–314. For Mexico, Instituto Nacional de Estadística Geográfica e Informática, INEGI, Estadísticas Históricas de México, Tomo 1, Second Edition, 1990, p. 375.

Table D. Land Distribution Patterns in East Asia: Farm Households by Size of Cultivated Land in Korea and Taiwan (in Hectares)

KOREA

	<0.3[a]	0.3–0.5	0.5–1	1–2	2–3	>3
1955						
Number of farms	420,402	543,414	689,745	445,632	122,441	5,551
%	18.9	24.4	31	20	5.5	0.2
1960						
Number of farms	463,415	545,209	706,689	485,933	141,371	6,389
%	19.7	23.2	30.1	20.7	6	0.3
1970						
Number of farms	390,893	395,902	824,347	639,369	123,391	37,299
%	16.2	16.4	34.2	26.5	5.1	1.5

TAIWAN

	<0.3	0.3–0.5	0.5–1	1–2	2–3	>3
1952						
Number of farms	288,955[b]		142,659	103,416	34,762	41,401
%	47.3		23.3	16.9	5.7	6.8
1960						
Number of farms	160,437	129,831	225,549	183,751	50,556	25,878
%	20.7	16.7	29.1	23.7	6.5	3.3
1970						
Number of farms	220,329	165,986	242,748	176,216	46,778	27,341
%	25.1	18.9	27.6	20	5.3	3.1

[a] The numbers in the column headings are in chia (1 chia = 0.9699 hectares).
[b] All farm holdings under 0.5 hectares.

Sources: For Korea, Economic Planning Board, Korea Statistical Yearbook, 1962, Republic of Korea, p. 88; 1974, p. 76; 2002, p. 180. For Taiwan, Ho, Economic Development of Taiwan, p. 352. Chinese-American Joint Commission on Rural Reconstruction, Taiwan Agricultural Statistics: 1901–1965, p. 192; 1961–1975, p. 112.

Table E. *GDP by Sector, 1950–2000*

	Argentina			Mexico			Korea			Taiwan		
	% Agriculture	% Industry	% Service	% Agriculture	% Industry	% Service	% Agriculture	% Industry	% Service	% Agriculture	% Industry	% Service
1950	21.5	28.6	49.9	23.8	32.5	43.7	44.3	12.6	42.6	32.2[a]	19.7[a]	48.1[a]
1960	17.7	35.1	47.2	23	36.1	40.9	36.3	20.3	43.4	28.5	26.9	44.6
1970	9.6	42.3	48.1	12.7	32.1	55.1	27.1	29.5	43.4	15.5	36.8	47.7
1980	6.4	41.2	52.4	9	33.6	57.4	14.8	39.9	45.3	7.7	45.7	46.6
1990	8.1	36	55.8	7.8	28.4	63.7	8.5	43.1	48.4	4.2	41.2	54.6
2000	4.8	27.6	67.7	4.4	28.4	67.3	4.6	42.7	52.7	2.1	32.4	65.5

[a] The figures are for 1952.

Sources: Carmen Llores de Azar, *Argentina: Evolución Económica, 1915–1976*, Argentina, 1980, pp. 101, 145. Presidencia de la República, Nacional Financiera, S.A., *Estadísticas Económicas de México*, Mexico, D.F., 1962, pp. 28. International Bank for Reconstruction and Development/The World Bank, Development Data Group, The 2002 World Bank Development Indicators CD-ROM, Washington, D.C., 2002. Economic Planning Board, *Korea Statistical Yearbook, 1962*, Korea, 1962, p. 81. Council for Planning and Development, *Taiwan Statistical Data Book, 2002*, Republic of China, 2002, p. 22.

BIBLIOGRAPHY

Author's Note: I use the Wade System to romanize Chinese in the text and in all references. But there are exceptions. If authors have written their titles in English, I use their spelling even if it is not the Wade System. All in-text Spanish translations from the original are my own; all Chinese translations have been provided by Yu-wen Fan.

Archives Consulted

Archivo del Ayuntamiento de México (AAM)
Archivo General de la Nación Mexicana (AGNM)

Works Consulted

Abercrombie, Nicholas, and John Urry. 1983. *Capital, Labour, and the Middle Classes.* London: George Allen and Unwin.

Abrams, Philip. 1982. *Historical Sociology.* Ithaca, N.Y.: Cornell University Press.

Adams, Richard N. 1967. "Political Power and Social Structures." Pp. 15–43 in Claudio Veliz (ed.), *The Politics of Conformity in Latin America.* London: Oxford University Press.

Adelman, Jeremy. 1999. *Colonial Legacies: The Problem of Persistence in Latin American History.* New York: Routledge.

Adelman, Jeremy. 1999. *Republic of Capital: Buenos Aires and the Legal Transformation of the Atlantic World.* Palo Alto, Calif.: Stanford University Press.

Ahn, Hae-kyun. 1972. *Administrative Changes and Elite Dynamics: The Changes of the Patterns of Elite Mobilization and Integration in Korea.* Pittsburgh, Pa.: University Center for International Studies, University of Pittsburgh.

Alam, Shahid M. 1989. *Government and Markets in Economic Development Strategies: Lessons from Korea, Taiwan, and Japan.* New York: Praeger.

Alavi, Hamza. 1973. "Peasant Classes and Primordial Loyalties." *Journal of Peasant Studies* 1/1.

Alavi, Hamza. 1965. *Peasants and Revolution.* Ann Arbor, Mich.: Radical Education Project.

375

Bibliography

Albert, Bill, and Adrian Graves (eds.). 1988. *The World Sugar Economy in War and Depression: 1914–1940*. London and New York: Routledge.

Amsden, Alice. 2000. *The Rise of the Rest: Challenges to the West from Late-Industrializing Economies*. New York and London: Oxford University Press.

Amsden, Alice. 1991. "Diffusion of Development: The Late Industrialization Model and Greater East Asia." *AEA Papers and Proceedings*, May 1991.

Amsden, Alice. 1989. *Asia's Next Giant: South Korea and Late Industrialization*. New York and London: Oxford University Press.

Amsden, Alice. 1985. "The State and Taiwan's Economic Development." In Peter B. Evans, Dietrich Rueschemeyer, and Theda Skocpol (eds.), *Bringing the State Back In*. Cambridge: Cambridge University Press.

Anderson, Perry. 1974. *Lineages of the Absolutist State*. London: New Left Books.

Anglade, Christian, and Carlos Fortin (eds.). 1985. *The State and Capital Accumulation in Latin America*. Pittsburgh, Pa.: University of Pittsburgh Press.

Appelbaum, Richard P., and Jeffrey Henderson (eds.). 1992. *States and Development in the Asian Pacific Rim*. London and Newbury Park: Sage Publications.

Aqua, Ronald. 1981. "The Role of Government in the Saemaul Movement." Pp. 409–426 in Man-Gap Lee (ed.), *Toward a New Community*. Seoul: Seoul National University.

Araiza, Luis. 1964. *Historia del movimiento obrero mexicano*. Four volumes. Mexico City: n.p.

Aristotle. 1952. *Politics* [trans. Ernest Barker]. Oxford: Clarendon Press.

Aston, T. H., and C. H. E. Philpin (eds.). 1985 (1976). *The Brenner Debate: Agrarian Class Structure and Economic Development in Pre-Industrial Europe*. Cambridge: Cambridge University Press.

Ayuntamiento de México. 1912. *Memoria del H. Ayuntamiento de México en 1911*. México, DF: Talleres Gráficos de la Nación.

Ban, Sung Hwan, Pal Yong Moon, and Dwight H. Perkins (eds.). 1980. *Rural Development*. Cambridge, Mass.: Harvard University Press.

Ban, Sung Hwan. 1977. "The New Community Movement." Pp. 206–235 in Chuk Kyo Kim (ed.), *Industrial and Social Development Issues*. Seoul: Korea Development Institute.

Bark, Dong Suh, and Chae-jin Lee. 1976. "Bureaucratic Elite and Development Orientations." In Dae Sook Suih and Chae-jin Lee (eds.), *Political Leadership in Korea*. Seattle, Wash.: University of Seattle Press.

Barkin, Kenneth D. 1970. *The Controversy Over German Industrialization, 1890–1902*. Chicago, Ill.: University of Chicago Press.

Barraclough, Solon (ed.). 1973. *Agrarian Structure in Latin America*. Lexington, Mass.: Lexington Books.

Bartra, Roger. 1993. *Agrarian Structure and Political Power in Mexico*. Baltimore, Md.: Johns Hopkins University Press.

Bechhofer, Frank, and Brian Elliot (eds.). 1981. *The Petite Bourgeoisie: Comparative Studies of the Uneasy Stratum*. New York: St. Martin's Press.

Bell, Daniel. 1960. *The End of Ideology*. Glencoe, Ill.: Free Press.

Bello, Waldon, and Stephanie Rosenfeld. 1990. *Dragons in Distress: Asia's Miracle Economies in Crisis*. San Francisco, Calif.: Institute for Food and Development Policy.

Bendix, Reinhard. 1964. *Nation-Building and Citizenship*. New York: John Wiley & Sons.

Berger, Peter. 1988. "An East Asian Development Model?" Pp. 3–12 in P. Berger and H. M. Hsiao (eds.). *In Search of an East Asian Development Model*. New Brunswick, N.J.: Transaction Books.

Berger, Peter, and Hsin-huang Michael Hsiao (eds.). 1988. *In Search of An East Asian Development Model*. New Brunswick, N.J.: Transaction Books.

Berger, Suzanne. 1981. "The Uses of the Traditional Sector in Italy: Why Declining Classes Survive." Pp. 71–90 in Frank Bechofer and Brian Elliot (eds.), *The Petite Bourgeoisie*. New York: St. Martin's Press.

Bergquist, Charles. 1986. *Labor in Latin America: Comparative Essays on Chile, Argentina, Venezuela, and Colombia*. Palo Alto, Calif.: Stanford University Press.

Bernstein, Henry. 1981. "Concepts for the Analysis of Contemporary Peasantries." Pp. 3–18 in Rosemary E. Galli (ed.), *The Political Economy of Rural Development: Peasants, International Capital, and the State*. Albany, N.Y.: SUNY Press.

Bethell, Leslie, and Ian Roxborough. 1993. *Latin America Between the Second World War and the Cold War, 1944–1948*. Cambridge: Cambridge University Press.

Bhagwati, Jagdish. 1992. "Democracy and Development." *The Journal of Democracy* 3/3: 35–37.

Biggert, Nicole Woolsey, and Mauro F. Guillén. 1999. "Developing Difference: Social Organization and the Rise of the Auto Industries of South Korea, Taiwan, Spain, and Argentina." *American Sociological Review* 64/5: 722–747.

Birdsall, Nancy, and Stephan Haggard. 2000. *After the Crisis: The Social Contract and the Middle Class in East Asia*. Washington, D.C.: Carnegie Endowment for International Peace.

Blumin, Stuart M. 1989. *The Emergence of the Middle Class: Social Experience in the American City, 1760–1900*. Cambridge: Cambridge University Press.

Boltanski, Luc. 1987. *The Making of a New Class*. Cambridge: Cambridge University Press.

Borja, Jordi, and Manuel Castells. 1997. *Local and Global: Management of Cities in the Information Age*. Sterling, Va.: Earthscan Publications.

Brandt, Vincent S. R. 1971. *A Korean Village Between Farm and Sea*. Cambridge, Mass.: Harvard University Press.

Brenner, Neil. 1988. "Global Cities, Global States: Global City Formation and State Territorial Restructuring in Contemporary Europe." *Review of International Political Economy* 5/1: 1–37.

Brenner, Robert. 1989. "Economic Backwardness in Eastern Europe in Light of Developments in the West." Pp. 15–52 in Daniel Chirot (ed.), *The Origins of Backwardness in Eastern Europe: Economics and Politics From the Middle Ages Until the Early Twentieth Century*. Berkeley: University of California Press.

Brenner, Robert. 1985. "Agrarian Class Structure and Economic Development in Pre-Industrial Europe." In T. H. Aston and C. H. E. Philpin (eds.), *The Brenner Debate: Agrarian Class Structure and Economic Development in Pre-Industrial Europe*. Cambridge: Cambridge University Press, 1985.

Brittan, Samuel. 1975. "The Economic Contradictions of Democracy." *British Journal of Sociology* 5.

Bibliography

Bullard, Monte R. 1997. *The Soldier and the Citizen: The Role of the Military in Taiwan's Development*. Armonk, N.Y., and London: M. E. Sharpe.

Burmeister, Larry L. 1988. *Research, Realpolitik, and Development in Korea: The State and the Green Revolution*. Boulder, Colo.: Westview Press.

Burris, Val. 1995. "The Discovery of the New Middle Classes." Pp. 15–55 in Arthur J. Vidich (ed.), *The New Middle Classes: Lifestyles, Status Claims, and Political Orientations*. New York: New York University Press.

Burris, Val. 1992. "Late Industrialization and Class Formation in East Asia." *Research in Political Economy* 13: 245–283.

Buve, Raymond Th. J. 1988. "Neither Carranza nor Zapata!: The Rise and Fall of a Peasant Movement That Tried to Challenge Both, Tlaxcala, 1910–1919." Pp. 338–375 in Friedrich Katz (ed.), *Riot, Rebellion, and Revolution*. Princeton, N.J.: Princeton University Press.

Calhoun, Craig. 1982. *The Question of Class Struggle: Social Foundations of Popular Radicalism During the Industrial Revolution*. Chicago, Ill.: University of Chicago Press.

Calvert, Susan, and Peter Calvert. 1989. *Argentina: Political Culture and Instability*. Pittsburgh, Pa.: University of Pittsburgh Press.

Canton, Dario. 1971. *La política de los militares argentinos: 1900–1971*. Mexico, DF: Siglo Veintiuno Editores.

Carchedi, Guglielmo. 1977. *On the Economic Identification of Social Classes*. London: Routledge and Kegan Paul.

Carchedi, Guglielmo. 1975. "On the Economic Identification of the New Middle Class." *Economy and Society* 4: 1–86.

Cardoso, Fernando Henrique, and Enzo Faletto. 1979. *Dependency and Development in Latin America*. Berkeley and Los Angeles: University of California Press (originally published in 1971).

Castells, Manuel. 1998. *The Rise of the Network Society*. Volume I: *The Information Age*. Oxford: Blackwell.

Castells, Manuel. 1992. "Four Asian Tigers with a Dragon Head: A Comparative Analysis of the State, Economy, and Society in the Asian Pacific Rim." Pp. 33–70 in Richard P. Appelbaum and Jeffrey Henderson (eds.), *States and Development in the Asian Pacific Rim*. London and Newbury Park, Ca: Sage Publications.

Centeno, Miguel. 1994. *Democracy Within Reason: Technocratic Revolution in Mexico*. University Park, Pa.: Penn State University Press.

Chang, Chi-yün. 1954. *The Kuomintang on the March*. Taipei: China Cultural Service.

Chang, Chi-yün. 1953. *The Rebirth of the Kuomintang: The Seventh National Congress*. Taipei: China Cultural Service.

Chang, Dal Joong. 1985. *Economic Control and Political Authoritarianism: The Role of Japanese Corporations in Korean Politics*. Seoul: Sogang University Press.

Chao, Tein-chen. 1985. *Industrial Organization in the Process of Economic Development: The Case of Taiwan, 1950–1980*. Louvain-la-Neurve: CIACO.

Chatterjee, Partha. 1982. "More on Modes of Power and the Peasantry." Occasional Paper no. 47. Calcutta: Centre for Studies in Social Science.

Cheng, Lu-lin, and Gary Gereffi. 1994. "The Informal Economy in East Asian Development." *International Journal of Urban and Regional Research* 18/2: 194–220.

Cheng, Tun-jen, and Stephan Haggard. 1992. "Regime Transformation in Taiwan: Theoretical and Comparative Perspectives." Pp. 1–32 in Tun-jen Cheng and

Stephan Haggard (eds.), *Political Change in Taiwan*. Boulder, Colo.: Lynne Rienner Publishers.

Cheng, Tun-jen. 1990. "Political Regimes and Development Strategies: South Korea and Taiwan." Pp. 139–178 in Gary Gereffi and Donald Wyman (eds.), *Manufacturing Miracles: Paths of Industrialization in Latin America and East Asia*. Princeton, N.J.: Princeton University Press.

Chevalier, Francois. 1967. "The *Ejido* and Political Stability in Mexico." Pp. 158–192 in Claudio Veliz (ed.), *The Politics of Conformity in Latin America*. London: Oxford University Press.

Chilcote, Ronald H., and Joel C. Edelstein (eds.). 1986. *Latin America: Capitalist and Socialist Perspectives of Development and Underdevelopment*. Boulder, Colo.: Westview Press.

Chirot, Daniel. 1989. "Causes and Consequences of Backwardness." Pp. 1–14 in Daniel Chirot (ed.), *The Origins of Backwardness in Eastern Europe: Economics and Politics From the Middle Ages Until the Early Twentieth Century*. Berkeley: University of California Press.

Chiu, Stephen W. K. 1996. "Unravelling the Hong Kong Exceptionalism: The Politics of Laissez-Faire in Industrial Takeoff." In Diane E. Davis (ed.), *Political Power and Social Theory*. Volume 10. Greenich, Conn., and London: JAI Press.

Chiu, Stephen W. K. 1992. *The State and the Financing of Industrialization in East Asia: Political Origins of Comparative Divergences*. Ph.D. diss., Princeton University.

Cho, Lee-jay, and Yoon Hyung Kim. 1991. "Major Economic Policies of the Park Administration." Pp. 15–40 in Lee-jay Cho and Yoon Hyung Kim (eds.), *Economic Development in the Republic of Korea: A Policy Perspective*. Honolulu: University of Hawaii Press.

Choi, Hochin. 1971. *The Economic History of Korea: From the Earliest Times to 1945*. Seoul: The Freedom Library.

Choi, Jang Jip. 1993. "Political Cleavages in South Korea." Pp. 13–51 in Hagen Koo (ed.), *State and Society in Contemporary Korea*. Ithaca, N.Y.: Cornell University Press.

Choi, Jang Jip. 1989. *Labor and the Authoritarian State: Labor Unions in South Korean Manufacturing Industries, 1961–1980*. Seoul: Korea University Press.

Choi, Sung-il, and Chae-jin Lee. n.d. "Environment, Policy, and Electoral Participation: A Comparison of Urban and Rural Areas." Pp. 165–180 in Chon Lim Kim (ed.), *Political Participation in Korea: Democracy, Mobilization, and Stability*. Santa Barbara and Oxford: CLIO Books.

Choue, Young Seek. 1965. *The Way to Korea's Prosperity*. Seoul: Korean Institute of Developing Area Studies, Kyung Hee University.

Ciria, Alberto. 1983. *Política y cultura popular: La argentina peronista*. Buenos Aires: Ediciones de la Flor.

Ciria, Alberto. 1964. *Partidos políticos y poder en la argentina moderna (1930–1946)*. Buenos Aires: Jorge Alvarez Editor.

Clegg, Stewart R., and S. Gordon Redding (eds.). 1990. *Capitalism in Contrasting Cultures*. New York: Walter de Gruyter.

Clegg, Stewart R., Winton Higgins, and Tony Spybey. 1990. "'Post-Confucianism,' Social Democracy, and Economic Culture." Pp. 31–78 in Stewart R. Clegg and

S. Gordon Redding (eds.), *Capitalism in Contrasting Cultures*. New York: Walter de Gruyter.

Clegg, Stewart, Paul Boreham, and Geoff Dow. 1986. *Class, Politics, and the Economy*. London: Routledge and Kegan Paul.

Coatsworth, John H. 1988. "Patterns of Rural Rebellion in Latin America: Mexico in Comparative Perspective." Pp. 21–65 in Friedrich Katz (ed.), *Riot, Rebellion, and Revolution*. Princeton, N.J.: Princeton University Press.

Cockcroft, James. 1980. *Mexico: Class Formation, Capital Accumulation, and the State*. New York: Monthly Review Press.

Coffin, Judith G. 1999. "A 'Standard' of Living? European Perspectives on Class and Consumption in the Early Twentieth Century." *International Journal of Labor and Working Class History* 55 (Spring): 6–26.

Collier, David, and Ruth Berins Collier. 1991. *Shaping the Political Arena*. Princeton, N.J.: Princeton University Press.

Collier, David, and Ruth Berins Collier. 1977. "Who Does What, to Whom, and How: Towards a Comparative Analysis of Latin American Corporatism." In James M. Malloy (ed.), *Authoritarianism and Corporatism in Latin America*. Pittsburgh, Pa.: University of Pittsburgh Press.

Collier, Ruth Berins. 1992. *The Contradictory Alliance: State-Labor Relations and Regime Change in Mexico*. Berkeley: Institute for International Affairs, University of California at Berkeley.

Confederación Nacional de Organizaciones Populares. n.d. *Primer conseijo nacional. Mexico*, DF: mimeo.

Confederación Nacional de Organizaciones Populares. 1944. *Delegados de la Federación de Organizaciones Populares del D. F. en el primer consejo nacional de la CNOP*. Mexico, DF: Talleres Gráficos de la Nación.

Contreras, Ariel José. 1977. *México 1940: Industrialización y crisis política*. Mexico City: Siglo Veintiuno Editores.

Conway, J. F. 1981. "Agrarian Petit-Bourgeois Responses to Capitalist Industrialization: The Case of Canada." In Franck Bechofer and Brian Elliott (eds.), *The Petite Bourgeoisie*. New York: St. Martin's Press.

Córdova, Arnaldo. 1974. *La política de masas del cardenismo*. Mexico City: Serie Popular Era.

Córdova, Arnaldo. 1973. *La ideología de la revolución mexicana: La formación del nuevo regimen*. Mexico, DF: Ediciones Era.

Cornblit, Oscar. 1967. "European Immigrants in Argentine History and Politics." Pp. 221–249 in Claudio Veliz (ed.), *The Politics of Conformity in Latin America*. London: Oxford University Press.

Coronado Barajas, Rafael. 1949. *De las limitaciones impuestas a los militares para actuar en la política*. Mexico: Tesis – Universidad Nacional Autónoma de México.

Corradi, Juan. 1985. *The Fitful Republic: Economy, Society, and Politics in Argentina*. Boulder, Colo.: Westview Press.

Costa, Bolivar. 1973. *O drama de classe media*. Rio de Janeiro: Paz e Terra.

Cottrell, Allin. 1984. *Social Classes in Marxist Theory*. London: Routledge and Kegan Paul.

Crozier, Michael, Samuel Huntington, and Jaji Watanuki. 1975. *The Crisis of Democracy: Report on the Governability of Democracies to the Trilateral Comission*. New York: New York University Press.

Cumberland, Charles C. 1967. *The Making of the Mexican Revolution*. Boston: D. C. Heath and Company.

Cumings, Bruce. 1990. *The Origins of the Korean War: The Roaring of the Cataract, 1947–1950*. Volume 2. Princeton, N.J.: Princeton University Press.

Cumings, Bruce. 1989. "The Abortive Abertura: South Korea in the Light of Latin American Experience." *New Left Review* 173 (January/February): 5–32.

Cumings, Bruce. 1987. "The Origins and Development of the Northeast Asian Political Economy: Industrial Sectors, Product Cycles, and Political Consequences." In Frederic Deyo (ed.), *The Political Economy of the New Asian Industrialism*. Ithaca, N.Y.: Cornell University Press.

Cumings, Bruce. 1981. *The Origins of the Korean War: Liberation and the Emergence of Separate Regimes, 1945–1947*. Princeton, N.J.: Princeton University Press.

Cúneo, Dardo. 1967. *Comportamiento y crisis de la clase empresaria*. Buenos Aires: Editorial Pleamar.

Cúneo, Dardo. 1965. *El desencuentro argentino 1930–1955*. Buenos Aires: n.p.

Dahrendorf, Ralph. 1959. *Class and Class Conflict in Industrial Society*. London: Routledge.

Davis, Diane E. 1997. "Confederación Nacional de Organizaciones Populares." In Michael Werner (ed.), *Encyclopedia of Mexico: History, Society, and Culture*. Chicago, Ill.: Fitzroy and Dearborn Publishers.

Davis, Diane. E. 1997. "New Social Movements, Old Party Structures: Discursive and Organizational Transformations in Mexican and Brazilian Party Politics." In William C. Smith and Roberto Patricio Korzeniewicz (eds.), *Politics, Social Change, and Economic Restructuring in Latin America*. Coral Gables, Fla.: North-South Center Press; Boulder, Colo.: distributed by Lynne Rienner Publishers.

Davis, Diane E., and Viviane Brachet-Marquez. 1997. "Rethinking Democracy: Mexico in Historical Perspective." *Comparative Studies in Society and History* 31: 86–119.

Davis, Diane E. 1995. "Uncommon Democracy in Mexico: Middle Classes and the Military in the Consolidation of One-Party Rule, 1936–1947." In Herrick Chapman and George Reid Andrews (eds.), *The Social Construction of Democracy, 1890–1990*. London: Macmillan Press.

Davis, Diane E. 1994. *Urban Leviathan: Mexico City in the Twentieth Century*. Philadelphia, Pa.: Temple University Press.

Davis, Diane E. 1993. "The Dialectic of Autonomy: State, Class, and Economic Crisis in Mexico, 1958–1982." *Latin American Perspectives* 20/3: 46–75.

Davis, Diane E. 1992. "Mexico's New Politics: Changing Positions on Free Trade." *World Policy Journal* 9/4: 655–672.

Davis, Diane E. 1989. "Divided Over Democracy: The Embeddedness of State and Class Conflicts in Contemporary Mexico." *Politics and Society* 17/3: 247–280.

Davis, Diane E. 1981. "Migration, Rank-Size Distribution, and Economic Development: The Case of Mexico." *Studies in Comparative International Development* 16/6: 84–107.

Bibliography

de Janvry, Alain. 1981. *The Agrarian Question and Reformism in Latin America*. Baltimore, Md.: Johns Hopkins University Press.

de Lasson, Aksel. 1976. *The Farmers' Association Approach to Rural Development: The Taiwan Case*. Saarbrucken, Germany: Verlad der SSIP.

de Palomino, Mirta L. 1988. *Tradición y poder: La sociedad rural argentina (1955–1983)*. Buenos Aires: CISEA, Grupo Editor Latinoamericano.

de Paoli, Pedro. 1960. *La reforma agraria*. Buenos Aires: Editorial A. Peña Lillo.

de Schweinitz, Karl. 1964. *Industrialization and Democracy: Economic Necessities and Political Possibilities*. New York: Free Press.

Democratic Republican Party. 1972. *DRP: Today and Tomorrow*. Seoul: Republic of Korea.

Deyo, Frederick. K. 1989. *Beneath the Miracle: Labor Subordination in the New Asian Industrialization*. Berkeley and Los Angeles: University of California Press.

di Tella, Guido, and Manuel Zymelman. 1967. *Las estapas del desarrollo económico Argentino*. Buenos Aires: Editorial Universitaria de Buenos Aires.

di Tella, Torcuato. 1990. *Latin American Politics: A Theoretical Framework*. Austin: University of Texas Press.

Dobb, Maurice. 1958. *Capitalism Yesterday and Today*. London: Lawrence and Wishart.

Dobb, Maurice. 1946. *Studies in the Development of Capitalism*. London: Routledge and Kegan Paul.

Dollar, David, and Kenneth L. Sokoloff. 1994. "Industrial Policy, Productivity, Growth, and Structural Change in the Manufacturing Industries: A Comparison of Taiwan and South Korea." Pp. 5–25 in Joel D. Aberbach, David Dollar, and Kenneth L. Sokoloff (eds.), *The Role of the State in Taiwan's Development*. Armonk, N.Y., and London: M. E. Sharpe.

Domínguez, Zeferino. 1913. *El servicio militar agrario y la pequeña propiedad*. Mexico, DF: Imprenta y Papelería "La Helveta."

Draper, Hal. 1977. *Karl Marx's Theory of Revolution*. New York: Monthly Review Press.

Duran, Marco Antonio. 1967. *El agrarismo mexicano*. Mexico, DF: Siglo Veintiuno Editores.

Eckert, Carter J. 1993. "The South Korean Bourgeoisie: A Class in Search of Hegemony." Pp. 95–131 in Hagen Koo (ed.), *State and Society in Contemporary Korea*. Ithaca, N.Y.: Cornell University Press.

Eckert, Carter J. 1991. *Offspring of Empire: The Kochanag Kims and the Colonial Origins of Korean Capitalism, 1876–1945*. Seattle and London: University of Washington Press.

Ehrenreich, John, and Barbara Ehrenreich. 1977. "The Professional-Managerial Class." *Radical America* 11: 7–31.

Eley, Geoff. 1990. "Edward Thompson, Social History, and Political Culture: The Making of a Working-Class Public Sphere." In Harvey J. Kaye and Keith McClelland (eds.), *E. P. Thompson: Critical Perspectives*. Philadelphia, Pa.: Temple University Press.

Emigh, Rebecca Jean. 1997. "The Spread of Sharecropping in Tuscany: The Political Economy of Transaction Costs." *American Sociological Review* 62/3: 423–443.

Engels, Friedrich. 1962. "Socialism: Utopian and Scientific." Pp. ii, 116–165 in Marx and Engels, *Selected Works*. Moscow: Foreign Languages Publishing House.

Escala, Alberto. 198? *Argentina: Estructura social y sectores intermedios*. Buenos Aires: Edicines Estudio.

Escárcega López, Everardo, and Saúl Escobar Toledo. 1990. *Historia de la cuestión agraria*. Volume 5: *El cardenismo: un parteaguas histórico en el proceso agrario nacional, 1934–1940* (primera parte). Mexico, DF: Siglo Veintiuno Editores.

Eckstein, Susan. 1977. *The Poverty of Revolution: The State and the Urban Poor in Mexico*. Princeton, N.J.: Princeton University Press.

Evans, Peter, and James Rauch. 1999. "Bureaucracy and Growth: A Cross-National Analysis of the Effects of 'Weberian' State Structures on Economic Growth." *American Sociological Review* 64/5: 748–765.

Evans, Peter. 1995. *Embedded Autonomy: States and Industrial Transformation*. Princeton, N.J.: Princeton University Press.

Evans, Peter, Dietrich Rueschemeyer, and Theda Skocpol (eds.). 1985. *Bringing the State Back In*. Cambridge: Cambridge University Press.

Evans, Peter. 1978. *Dependent Development: The Alliance of Multinational, State, and Local Capital in Brazil*. Princeton, N.J.: Princeton University Press.

Falcón, Romana. 1988. "Charisma, Tradition, and *Caciquismo*: Revolution in San Luis Potosi." Pp. 417–447 in Friedrich Katz (ed.), *Riot, Rebellion, and Revolution: Rural Social Conflict in Mexico*. Princeton, N.J.: Princeton University Press.

Fals-Borda, Orlando. 1955. *Peasant Society in the Colombian Andes: A Sociological Study of Saucío*. Jacksonsville: University of Florida Press.

Fitzgerald, E. V. K. "The Financial Constraint on Relative Autonomy." Pp. 211–235 in Christian Anglade and Carlos Fortin (eds.), *The State and Capital Accumulation in Latin America*. Pittsburgh, Pa.: University of Pittsburgh Press.

Fligstein, Neil. 1996. "Politics As Markets: A Political-Cultural Approach to Market Institutions." *American Sociological Review* 61/4: 656–673.

Forni, Floreal H., and María I. Tort. 1992. "Las transformaciones de la explotación familiar en la producción de cereales de la región pampeana." Pp. 142–158 in Jorge Raul Jorrat and Ruth Santu (eds.), *Después de Germani: Exploraciones sobre estructura social de Argentina*. Buenos Aires: Editorial PAIDA.

Foucault, Michael. 1977. *Discipline and Punish: The Birth of the Prison*. New York: Pantheon Books.

Frank, Andre Gunder. 1998. *ReOrient: Global Economy in the Asian Age*. Berkeley and Los Angeles: University of California Press.

Franklin, S. H. 1969. *The European Peasantry: The Final Phase*. London: Methuen & Co.

Gallin, Bernard. 1966. *Hsin Hsing, Taiwan: A Chinese Village in Change*. Berkeley and Los Angeles: University of California Press.

Garrido, Luis Javier. 1982. *El partido de la revolución institucionalizada: La formación del nuevo estado en México*. Mexico City: Siglo Veintiuno Editores.

Geddes, Barbara. 1994. *Politician's Dilemma: Building State Capacity in Latin America*. Berkeley and Los Angeles: University of California Press.

Geerligs, H. C. Prinsen. 1912. *The World's Cane Sugar Industry: Past and Present*. Manchester: Norman Rodger.

Geiger, Theodor. 1994 (1932). "The Old and New Middle Classes." Pp. 191–194 in Anton Kaes, Martin Jay, and Edward Dimendberg, *The Weimar Republic Sourcebook*. Berkeley and Los Angeles: University of California Press.

Bibliography

Gereffi, Gary. 1994. "Industrial Restructuring and National Development Strategies: A Comparison of Taiwan, South Korea, Brazil, and Mexico." Pp. 581–616 in Hsin-huang Michael Hsiao, Wei-yuan Cheng, and Hou-sheng Chan (eds.), *Taiwan: A Newly Industrialized State*. Taipei: National Taiwan University.

Gereffi, Gary. 1990. "Big Business and the State." In Gary Gereffi and Donald Wyman (eds.), *Manufacturing Miracles: Paths of Industrialization in Latin America and East Asia*. Princeton, N.J.: Princeton University Press.

Gereffi, Gary, and Donald Wyman (eds.). 1990. *Manufacturing Miracles: Paths of Industrialization in Latin America and East Asia*. Princeton, N.J.: Princeton University Press.

Gereffi, Gary. 1983. *The Pharmaceutical Industry and Dependency in the Third World*. Princeton, N.J.: Princeton University Press.

Germani, Gino. 1955. *La estructura social de la Argentina*. Buenos Aires: Raigal.

Gerry, Chris, and Chris Birkbeck. 1981. "The Petty Commodity Producer in Third World Cities: Petit Bourgeois or 'Disguised' Proletarian?" Pp. 121–154 in Frank Bechofer and Brian Elliott (eds.), *The Petite Bourgeoisie: Comparative Studies of the Uneasy Stratum*. New York: St. Martin's Press.

Gerschenkron, Alexander. 1962. *Economic Backwardness in Historical Perspective*. Cambridge, Mass.: Harvard University Press.

Giddens, Anthony. 1995. "The Growth of the New Middle Class." Pp. 103–133 in Arthur J. Vidich (ed.), *The New Middle Classes: Lifestyles, Status Claims, and Political Orientations*. New York: New York University Press.

Gilbert, Alan, and Joseph Gugler. 1992. *Cities, Poverty, and Development: Urbanization in the Third World*. Oxford: Oxford University Press.

Gilbert, Jess, and Carolyn Howe. 1991. "Beyond 'State vs. Society': Theories of the State and New Deal Agricultural Policies." *American Sociological Review* 56: 204–220.

Gillespie, Richard. 1989. *Soldiers of Perón: Argentina's Montoneros*. Oxford: Oxford University Press.

Gilly, Adolfo. 1983. *The Mexican Revolution*. London: Verso (translated by Patrick Camiller).

Girbal de Blacha, Noemí. 1988. *Estado, chacareros y terratenientes (1919–1930)*. Buenos Aires: Centro Editor de América Latína.

Glasberg, Davita Silsen. 1987. "International Finance Capital and the Relative Autonomy of the State: Mexico's Foreign Debt Crisis." *Research in Political Economy* 10: 83–108.

Gold, Thomas B. 1986. *State and Society in the Taiwan Miracle*. Armonk, N.Y.: M. E. Sharpe.

Goldthorpe, John. 1982. "On the Service Class, Its Formation and Future." Pp.162–185 in Anothony Giddens and Gavin Mackenzie (eds.), *Social Class and the Division of Labour: Essays in Honour of Ilya Nuestadt*. Cambridge: Cambridge University Press.

González Casanova, Pablo. 1981. *El estado y los partidos políticos en México: Ensayos*. México, D.F.: Ediciones Era.

Gorski, Philip S. 1993. "The Protestant Ethic Revisited: Disciplinary Revolution and State Formation in Holland and Prussia." *American Journal of Sociology* 99/2 (September): 265–316.

Bibliography

Graham, W. Fred. 1971. *The Constructive Revolutionary: Johan Calvin and His Socio-Economic Impact*. Richmond, Va.: John Knox Press

Gramsci, Antonio. 1957. "The Southern Question." Pp. 28–55 in *The Modern Prince and Other Writings*. New York: International Publishers.

Granovetter, Mark. 1985. "Economic Action and Social Structure: The Problem of Embeddedness." *American Journal of Sociology* 91/3: 481–510.

Guardino, Peter. 1996. *Peasants, Politics, and the Formation of Mexico's National State: Guerrero, 1800–1857*. Stanford, Calif.: Stanford University Press.

Gugler, Joseph (ed.). 1988. *The Urbanization of the Third World*. Oxford: Oxford University Press.

Guillén, Mauro F. 2001. *The Limits of Convergence: Globalization and Organizational Change in Argentina, South Korea, and Taiwan*. Princeton, N.J.: Princeton University Press.

Gulalp, Haldun. 1987. "Capital Accumulation, Classes, and the Relative Autonomy of the State." *Science and Society* 51: 287–313.

Gwynne, R. N. 1985. *Industrialization and Urbanization in Latin America*. London: Croom Helm.

Haggard, Stephan, and Chien-kuo Pang. 1994. "The Transition to Export-Led Growth in Taiwan." Pp. 47–90 in Joel Aberbach, David Dollar, and Kenneth L. Sokoloff (eds.), *The Role of the State in Taiwan's Development*. Armonk, N.Y., and London: M. E. Sharpe.

Haggard, Stephan, and Chung-in Moon. 1993. "The State, Politics, and Economic Development in Postwar South Korea." Pp. 51–94 in Hagen Koo (ed.), *State and Society in Contemporary Korea*. Ithaca, N.Y.: Cornell University Press.

Haggard, Stephan. 1990. *Pathways From the Periphery: The Politics of Growth in the Newly Industrializing Countries*. Ithaca, N.Y.: Cornell University Press.

Hahn, Bae-ho, and Kyu-taik, Kim. 1963. "Korean Political Leaders (1952–1962): Their Social Origins and Skills." *Asian Survey* 3 (July): 305–323.

Hahn, Sung Joe K. S. 1981. "The Political Philosophy of the Saemaul Movement." Pp. 99–131 in Man-gap Lee (ed.), *Toward a New Community*. Seoul: Seoul National University.

Hall, Peter. 1986. *Governing the Economy*. Oxford: Oxford University Press.

Halperin-Donghi, Tulio. 1975. *Politics, Economics, and Society in Argentina in the Revolutionary Period*. Cambridge: Cambridge University Press.

Hamilton, Clive. 1986. *Capitalist Industrialization in Korea*. Boulder, Colo.: Westview Press.

Hamilton, Gary. 1998. "Culture and Organization in Taiwan's Market Economy." Pp. 41–78 in Robert W. Hefner (ed.), *Market Cultures: Society and Morality in the New Asian Capitalisms*. Boulder, Colo.: Westview Press.

Hamilton, Nora, and Timothy Harding (eds.). 1986. *Modern Mexico: State, Economy, and Social Conflict*. Beverly Hills, Calif.: Sage Publications.

Hamilton, Nora. 1982. *The Limits of State Autonomy: Post-revolutionary Mexico*. Princeton, N.J.: Princeton University Press.

Hart, John M. 1987. *Anarchism and the Mexican Working Class, 1860–1931*. Austin: University of Texas Press, 2nd edition.

Hart, John Mason. 1987. *Revolutionary Mexico: The Coming and Process of the Mexican Revolution*. Berkeley: University of California Press.

Hartland-Thunberg, Penelope. 1990. *China, Hong Kong, Taiwan, and the World Trading System.* New York: St. Martin's Press.

Harvey, David. 1989. *The Condition of Postmodernity: An Enquiry Into the Origins of Cultural Change.* Oxford: Basil Blackwell.

Hazell, Peter, and Steven Haggblade. 1993. "Farm-Nonfarm Growth Linkages and the Welfare of the Poor." Pp. 190–204 in Michael Lipton and Jacques van der Gaag (eds.), *Including the Poor.* Washington, D.C.: The World Bank.

Hill, Christopher. 1966. "Protestantism and the Rise of Capitalism." In David Landes (ed.), *The Rise of Capitalism.* New York: Macmillan.

Hillerbrand, Hans J. (ed.). 1968. *The Protestant Reformation.* New York: Harper & Row.

Hindess, Barry. 1987. *Politics and Class Analysis.* London: Basil Blackwell.

Hirschman, Albert O. 1977. *The Passions and the Interests: Political Arguments for Capitalism Before Its Triumph.* Princeton, N.J.: Princeton University Press.

Ho, Samuel. 1978. *Economic Development of Taiwan, 1860–1970.* New Haven, Conn.: Yale University Press.

Ho, Yu In, and Kim Byung Hee. 1981. "The Economic Plight of Korean Farmers." *Korean Scope* 2/4 (September): 6–30.

Hobsbawm, Eric. 1990. *Nations and Nationalism Since 1780: Program, Myth, Reality.* Cambridge: Cambridge University Press.

Hobsbawm, Eric. 1987. *The Age of Empire: 1875–1914.* New York: Pantheon Books.

Hobsbawm, Eric, Witold Kula, Ashok Mitra, K. N. Raj, and Ignacy Sachs (eds.). 1980. *Peasants in History: Essays in Honour of Daniel Thorner.* Delhi: Oxford University Press.

Hobsbawm, Eric. 1967. "Peasants and Rural Migrants in Politics." Pp. 43–66 in Claudio Veliz (ed.), *The Politics of Conformity in Latin America.* London: Oxford University Press.

Hodges, Donald C. 1995. *Mexican Anarchism After the Revolution.* Austin: University of Texas Press.

Horowitz, Joel. 1990. *Argentine Unions, the State, and the Rise of Perón.* Berkeley: Institution of International Studies, University of California at Berkeley.

Hsiao, Hsin-huang Michael. 1993. "Discovering East Asian Middle Classes: Formation, Differentiation, and Politics." Pp. 1–23 in Hsin-huang Michael Hsiao (ed.), *Discovery of the New Middle Classes in East Asia.* Taipei: Institute of Ethnology, Academia Sinica.

Hsiao, Hsin-huang Michael. 1992. "The Labor Movement in Taiwan: A Retrospective and Prospective Look." Pp. 151–167 in Denis F. Simon and Michael Y. M. Kau (eds.), *Taiwan: Beyond the Economic Miracle.* Armonk, N.Y., and London: M. E. Sharpe.

Hsiao, Hsin-huang Michael. 1991. "The Changing State-Society Relation in the ROC: Economic Change, the Transformation of the Class Structure, and the Rise of Social Movements." Pp. 127–140 in Ramon H. Myers (ed.), *Two Societies in Opposition.* Palo Alto, Calif.: Hoover Institution Press.

Hsiao, Hsin-huang Michael. 1989. "The Middle Classes in Taiwan: Origins, Formation, and Significance." Pp. 151–165 in Hsin-huang Michael Hsiao, Wi-Yuan

Cheng, and Hou-Sheng Chan (eds.), *Taiwan: A Newly Industrialized State*. Taipei: Department of Sociology, National Taiwan University.

Hsiao, Hsin-huang Michael. 1981. *Government Agricultural Strategies in Taiwan and South Korea: A Macro-Sociological Assessment*. Taipei: Academia Sinica.

Hsu, Cheng-kuang. 1976. "Ecological Change and Economic Activities in Yen Village," *Bulletin of the Institute of Ethnology, Academia Sinica* 42: 1–39.

Huang, Chun-chieh. 1991. *Nung-fu-huei yu T'ai-wan chi-yen: 1949–1979 (Joint Commission on Rural Reconstruction and Taiwan's Experience: 1949–1979)*. Taipei: San-min shu-chiu.

Huer, Jon. 1989. *Marching Orders: The Role of the Military in South Korea's Economic Miracle, 1961–1971*. New York: Greenwood Press.

Huntingon, Samuel H. 1968. *Political Order in Changing Societies*. New Haven, Conn.: Yale University Press.

Im, Hyug Baeg. 1987. "The Rise of Bureaucratic-Authoritarianism." *World Politics* 39:2, 231–257.

Instituto Nacional de Estudios Históricos de la Revolución Mexicana (INEHRM). 1986. *Historia del Sindicato Nacional de Trabajadores de Secretaria de Gobernación*. Mexico, DF: Secretaria de Gobernación, INEHRM.

Ionescu, Ghita, and Ernest Gellner (eds.). 1969. *Populism: Its Meaning and National Characteristics*. New York: Macmillan.

Iturrieta, Anibal. n.d. *El pensamiento peronista*. Buenos Aires: n.p.

Jacobs, Norman. 1975. *The Korean Road to Modernization*. Champaign-Urbana: University of Illinois Press.

Jacoby, Erich H. 1980. "Has Land Reform Become Obsolete?" Pp. 296–307 in Eric Hobsbawm et al. (eds.), *Peasants in History*. Delhi: Oxford University Press.

Janelli, Roger L. 1993. *Making Capitalism: The Social and Cultural Construction of a South Korean Conglomerate*. Stanford, Calif.: Stanford University Press.

Jiang, Ping-lung, and Wen-cheng Wu. 1992. "The Changing Role of the KMT in Taiwan's Political System." Pp. 75–94 in Tun-jen Cheng and Stephan Haggard (eds.), *Political Change in Taiwan*. Boulder, Colo.: Lynne Rienner Publishers.

Johnson, Dale (ed.). 1985. *Middle Classes in Dependent Countries*. Beverly Hills, Calif.: Sage Publications.

Johnson, John J. 1958. *Political Change in Latin America: The Emergence of the Middle Sectors*. Palo Alto, Calif.: Stanford University Press.

Jones, Gareth Stedman. 1971. *Outcast London: A Study in the Relationship Between Classes in Victorian Society*. Oxford: Clarendon Press.

The Journal of Democracy 3/3 (July 1992).

Ka, Chih-ming. 1995. *Japanese Colonialism in Taiwan: Land Tenure, Development, and Dependency, 1895–1945*. Boulder, Colo.: Westview Press.

Ka, Chih-Ming. 1992. "Farmers, the State, and the Relationship Between the Agricultural and Industrial Sector in Taiwan: The Continuation and Transformation of Family Farms During Agricultural Development." Paper presented at the Conference on the State and Society Under Democratization. Yueh-han-Tang, National Tsing Hua University, Taipei, Taiwan, March 7–8.

Kane, Hal. 1998. "Feeding the World's Cities." Pp. 497–518 in Fu-chen Lo and Yue-man Yeung (eds.), *Globalization and the World of Large Cities*. New York: United Nations University Press.

Bibliography

Katznelson, Ira, and Aristide Zolberg (eds.). 1986. *Working-Class Formation*. Princeton, N.J.: Princeton University Press.

Kay, Cristóbal. 2001. *Asia's and Latin America's Development in Comparative Perspective: Landlords, Peasants, and Industrialization*. The Hague: Institute for Social Studies, Working Paper Series No. 336 (May).

Keon, Michael. 1977. *Korean Phoenix: A Nation From the Ashes*. Englewood Cliffs, N.J.: Prentice-Hall.

Kim, Eun Mee. 1997. *Big Business, Strong State: Collusion and Conflict in South Korean Development, 1960–1990*. Albany: State University of New York Press.

Kim, Hae-kyun. 1972. *Administrative Changes and Elite Dynamics: The Changes of the Patterns of Elite Mobilization and Integration in Korea*. Pittsburgh, Pa.: University Center for International Studies, University of Pittsburgh.

Kim, Jungsae. 1975. "Recent Trends in the Government's Management of the Economy." Pp. 255–279 in Edward Reynolds Wright (ed.), *Korean Politics in Transition*. Seattle and London: University of Washington Press.

Kim, Kwang Suk, and Michael Roemer (eds.). 1979. *Growth and Structural Transformation*. Cambridge, Mass.: Council on East Asian Studies, Harvard University.

Kim, Kyong-dong. 1987. "The Distinctive Features of South Korean Development." Pp. 197–219 in Peter Berger and Hsin-huang Michael Hsiao (eds.), *In Search of an East Asian Development Model*. New Brunswick, N.J.: Transaction Books.

Kim, Kyong-dong. 1979. *Man and Society in Korea's Economic Growth: Sociological Studies*. Seoul: National University Press.

Kim, Quee-young. 1983. *The Fall of Syngman Rhee*. Korea Research Monograph 7. Berkeley: Institute of East Asian Studies, University of California at Berkeley.

Kim, Se-jin. 1971. *The Politics of Military Revolution in Korea*. Chapel Hill: University of North Carolina Press.

King, Roger, and John Raynor. 1969. *The Middle Class*. Essex: Longman.

Knight, Alan. 1991. "The Rise and Fall of Cardenismo, c.1930–c.1946." In Leslie Bethell (ed.), *Mexico Since Independence*. Cambridge: Cambridge University Press.

Knight, Alan. 1986. *The Mexican Revolution*. Volumes 1 and 2. Lincoln: University of Nebraska Press.

Knight, Alan. 1980. "Peasant and Caudillo in Revolutionary Mexico, 1910–1917." Pp. 17–59 in D. A. Brading, *Peasant and Caudillo in the Mexican Revolution*. London: Cambridge University Press.

Kocka, Jürgen. 1989. *Les employes en Allemagne, 1850–1980*. Paris: Editions de la Maison des Sciences de l'Homme.

Kocka, Jürgen. 1982. "Class Formation, Interest Articulation, and Public Policy: The Origins of the German White-Collar Class in the Late Nineteenth and Early Twentieth Century." In Suzanne Berger (ed.), *Organizing Interests in Western Europe*. Cambridge: Cambridge University Press.

Kohli, Atul. 1998. "Japan's Contribution to Korea's Economic Success." JOSPOD Session #6, Massachusetts Institute of Technology Faculty Club, April 15, 1998.

Kohli, Atul. 1990. "Democracy and Development." In John P. Lewis and Valeriana Kallab (eds.), *Development Strategies Reconsidered*. New Brunswick, N.J.: Transaction Publishers.

Koo, Hagen. 1993. "The Social and Political Character of the Korean Middle Classes." Pp. 54 75 in Hsin-huang Michael Hsiao (ed.), *Discovery of the New Middle Classes in East Asia*. Taipei: Institute of Ethnology, Academia Sinica.

Koo, Hagen. 1993. "The State, *Minjung*, and the Working Class in South Korea." Pp. 131–163 in Hagen Koo (ed.), *State and Society in Contemporary Korea*. Ithaca, N.Y.: Cornell University Press.

Koo, Hagen. 1993. "Work, Culture, and Consciousness of the Korean Working Class." Paper presented at a conference on East Asian Labor in Comparative Perspective, October 1–3, 1993, Tahoe City, California.

Koo, Hagen. 1991. "Middle Classes, Democratization, and Class Formation: The Case of South Korea." *Theory and Society* 20/4: 485–509.

Koo, Hagen. 1990. "From Farm to Factory: Proletarianization in Korea." *American Sociological Review* 55 (October): 669–681.

Koo, Hagen. 1989. "The State, Industrial Structure, and Labor Politics: Comparisons of South Korea and Taiwan." Pp. 21–37 in *Industrial East Asia: Tasks and Challenges*. Seoul: The Korean Sociological Association.

Koo, Hagen. 1987. "The Interplay of State, Social Class, and World System in East Asian Development: The Cases of South Korea and Taiwan." Pp. 165–181 in Frederick Deyo (ed.), *The Political Economy of the New Asian Industrialism*. Ithaca, N.Y.: Cornell University Press.

Kristof, Nicholas D. 1977. "Seoul Plans to Ask the IMF for a Minimum of $20 Billion." *New York Times*, 22 November 1977, P. A1.

Krueger, Ann O. 1993. *The Political Economy of Policy Reform in Developing Countries*. Cambridge, Mass.: MIT Press.

Kuo, Shirley W. Y., Gustav Ranis, and John C. H. Fei. 1981. *The Taiwan Success Story: Rapid Growth With Improved Distribution in the Republic of China, 1952–1979*. Boulder, Colo.: Westview Press.

Kwon, Tai Hwan, Hae Young Lee, Yunshik Chang, and Eui-young Yu. 1975. *The Population of Korea*. Seoul: Seoul National University (The Population Studies and Development Center).

Kyung, Cho Chung. 1962. *New Korea: New Land of the Morning Calm*. New York: Macmillan.

Landes, David. 1998. *The Wealth and Poverty of Nations: Why Some Are So Rich and Some So Poor*. New York: W. W. Norton & Company.

Landes, David. 1969. *The Unbound Prometheus: Technological Change and Industrial Development in Western Europe From 1750 to the Present*. New York: Cambridge University Press, 1969.

Landes, David (ed.) 1966. *The Rise of Capitalism*. New York: Macmillan.

Lattuada, Mario J. 1988. *Política agraria y partidos políticos (1946–1983)*. Buenos Aires: Centro Editor de América Latína.

Lattuada, Mario J. 1986. *La política agraria peronista (1943–1983)*. Buenos Aires: Centro Editor de América Latína.

Lattuada, Mario J. 1987. *Política agraria del liberalismo-conservador (1946–1985)*. Buenos Aires: Centro Editor de América Latína.

Lechner, Norbert. 1992. "Some People Die of Fear." In Juan Corradi, Patricia Weiss Fagen, and Manuel Antonio Garreton (eds.), *Fear at the Edge: State Terror and Resistance in Latin America*. Berkeley: University of California Press.

Bibliography

Lederer, Emil, and Jacob Marshak. 1995. "The New Middle Class." Pp. 55–87 in Arthur J. Vidich (ed.), *The New Middle Classes: Lifestyles, Status Claims, and Political Orientations*. New York: New York University Press.

Lee, Hahn-been. 1967. "Political Change and Administrative Development in Korea Since 1945." *Korean Journal of Administration* 10: 1–23.

Lee, Hyo-jae. 1971. *Life in Urban Korea*. Seoul: Taewan Publishing Company.

Lee, Man-gap (ed.). 1981. *Toward a New Community: Reports of the International Research-Seminar on the Saemaul Movement*. Seoul: Seoul National University.

Lee, Man-gap. 1969. "Rural People and Their Modernization." Pp. 70–91 in C. I. Eugene Kim and Ch'angboh Chee (eds.), *Aspects of Social Change in Korea*. Kalamazoo, Mich.: Korea Research and Publications, Inc.

Lee, T. H. 1971. *Inter-Sectoral Capital Flows in the Development of Taiwan: 1895–1960*. Ithaca, N.Y.: Cornell University Press.

Lee, Wen-jer. 1970. "Taiwan's New Land Reform." *Free China Review* 20/7: 13–18.

Lee, Yeon-ho. 1997. *The State, Society, and Big Business in South Korea*. London and New York: Routledge.

Lee, Young-ho. 1975. "The Politics of Democratic Experiment." Pp. 13–44 in Edward Reynolds Wright (ed.), *Korean Politics in Transition*. Seattle and London: University of Washington Press.

Leeds, Anthony. 1994 [1977]. "Mythos and Pathos: Some Unpleasantries on Pleasantries." Pp. 109–144 in Roger Sanjek (ed.), *Cities, Classes, and the Social Order*. Ithaca, N.Y.: Cornell University Press.

Lenin, Vladimir. 1956. *The Development of Capitalism in Russia*. Moscow: Foreign Languages Publishing House.

León, Samuel, and Ignacio Marván. 1985. *La clase obrera en la história de México: En el Cardenismo (1934–1940)*. Mexico City: Siglo Veintiuno Editores.

Lerman, Arthur J. 1978. *Taiwan's Politics: The Provincial Assemblyman's World*. Washington, D.C.: University Press of America.

Lewis, Roy, and Angus Maude. 1950. *The English Middle Classes*. New York: Alfred A. Knopf.

Li, K. T. 1988. *The Evolution of Policy Behind Taiwan's Development Success*. New Haven, Conn.: Yale University Press.

Lie, John. 1991. "Review: Rethinking the 'Miracle' – Economic Growth and Political Struggles in South Korea." *Bulletin of Concerned Asian Scholars* 23/4: 66–71.

Lieuwen, Edwin. 1981. *Mexican Militarism: The Rise and Fall of the Revolutionary Army, 1910–1940*. Westport, Conn.: Greenwood Press.

Lim, Timothy C. 1994. "Explaining Development in South Korea and East Asia: A Review of the Last Dozen Years of Research." *Korean Studies* 18: 171–203.

Lim, Timothy C. 1993. "The Developmental State, Political Leadership, and Late Industrialization in South Korea." Unpublished Manuscript, Department of Political Science, University of Hawaii at Manoa.

Lipset, Seymour Martin, and Aldo Solari (eds.). 1967. *Elites in Latin America*. New York: Oxford University Press.

Lipset, Seymour Martin. 1960. *Political Man*. Garden City, N.Y.: Doubleday.

Lipton, Michael. 1977 (1976). *Why Poor People Stay Poor: Urban Bias in World Development*. Cambridge: Cambridge University Press.

Bibliography

Lipton, Michael. 1974. "Towards a Theory of Land Reform." Pp. 269–316 in David Lehmann (ed.), *Peasants, Landlords and Governments: Agrarian Reform in the Third World*. New York: Holmes and Meier.

Lloyd, Jane-Dale. 1998. "Rancheros and Rebellion: The Case of Northwestern Chihuahua, 1905–1909." Pp. 107–133 in Daniel Nugent (ed.), *Rural Revolt in Mexico: U.S. Intervention and the Domain of Subaltern Politics*. Durham, N.C.: Duke University Press.

Lo, Fu-chen, and Yue-man Yeung (eds.). 1998. *Globalization and the World of Large Cities*. New York: United Nations University Press.

Loaeza, Soledad. 1988. *Clases medias y política en México*. Mexico City: Siglo Veintiuno Editores.

Lovell, John P. 1975. "The Military and Politics in Postwar Korea." Pp. 153–199 in Edwin Reynolds Wright (ed.), *Korean Politics in Transition*. Seattle and London: University of Washington Press.

Lovell, John P. 1969. "The Military As an Instrument for Political Development in South Korea." Pp. 13–29 in Andrew C. Nahm (ed.), *Studies in the Developmental Aspects of Korea*. School of Graduate Studies and Institute of International and Area Studies, Western Michigan University.

Lozoya, Jorge Alberto. 1970. *El ejército mexicano, 1911–1965*. México: Colegio de México.

Lu, Ya-li. 1991. "Political Modernization in the ROC: The Kuomintang and the Inhibited Political Center." Pp. 111–126 in Ramon Myers (ed.), *Two Societies in Opposition*. Stanford, Calif.: Hoover Institution Press.

Mafud, Julio. 1985. *Sociología de la clase media argentina*. Buenos Aires: El Juglar.

Mallon, Florencia E. 1983. *The Defense of Community in Peru's Central Highlands*. Princeton, N.J.: Princeton University Press.

Markiewicz, Dana. 1993. *The Mexican Revolution and the Limits of Agrarian Reform, 1915–1946*. Boulder, Colo.: Lynne Rienner.

Martínez Estrada, Ezequiel. 1948. *Muerte y transfiguración de Martín Fierro: Ensayo de interpretación de la vida argentina*. 2 Volumes. Mexico City: Fondo de Cultura Económica.

Marx, Karl. 1972 [1852]. *The Eighteenth Brumaire of Louis Bonaparte*. Pp. 426–535 in Robert C. Tucker (ed.), *The Marx-Engels Reader*. New York.: W. W. Norton & Company.

Marx, Karl. 1965. *The German Ideology*. London: Lawrence & Wishart.

Marx, Karl. 1861–1863. *Marx's Economic Manuscripts of 1861–1863, Part Three: Relative Surplus; Productivity of Capital, Productive and Unproductive Labour* (Notebook XXI: 1329). http://www.marxists.org/archive/marx/works/1861/economic/ch38.htm

Mason, Edward S., Mahn Je Kim, Dwight Perkins, Kwang Suk Kim, and David C. Cole. 1980. *The Economic and Social Modernization of the Republic of Korea*. Cambridge, Mass.: Harvard University Press.

Mattson, Kevin. 1998. *Creating a Democratic Public: The Struggle for Urban Participatory Democracy During the Independence Era*. University Park, Pa.: Pennsylvania State University Press.

Bibliography

McAlister, Lyle, Anthony P. Maingot, and Robert A. Potash. 1970. *The Military in Latin American Sociopolitical Evolution: Four Case Studies*. Washington, D.C.: Center for Research in Social Systems.

McBride, G. M. 1971 [c. 1923]. *The Land Systems of Mexico*. New York: Octagon Books.

McClelland, David. 1963. "The Achievement Motive in Economic Growth." In Bert F. Hoselitz and Wilbert E. Moore (eds.), *Industrialization and Society*. Paris: UNESCO.

McCormack, Gavan. 1978. "The South Korean Economy: GNP Versus the People." Pp. 91–111 in Gavan McCormack and Mark Selden (eds.), *Korea; North and South: The Deepening Crisis*. New York: Monthly Review Press.

McGee, Terence G. 1998. "Globalization and Rural-Urban Linkages in the Developing World." Pp. 471–496 in Fu-chen Lo and Yue-man Yeung (eds.), *Globalization and the World of Large Cities*. New York: United Nations University Press.

McGee, Terence G. 1971. *The Urbanization Process in the Third World: Explorations in Search of a Theory*. London: Bell Press.

McMichael, Philip. 1995. *Food and Agrarian Orders in the World-Economy*. Westport, Conn.: Praeger.

McNeill, John T. 1954. *The History and Character of Calvinism*. New York: Oxford University Press.

Medina Peña, Luis. 1976. *Del cardenismo al avilacamachismo: Historia de la revolución mexicana*. Mexico City: El Colegio de México.

Mellor, John W., and Bruce F. Johnston. 1984. "The World Food Equation: Interrelation Among Development, Employment, and Food Consumption." *Journal of Economic Literature* 22/2 (June): 531–574.

Mendieta y Nuñez, Lucio. 1957. *Política agraria*. Mexico, DF: Instituto de Investigaciones Sociales, UNAM.

Mendieta y Nuñez, Lucio. 1943. *La administración pública en México*. México: Imprenta Universitaria.

Merkel, Ina. 1999. "Working People and Consumption Under Really-Existing Socialism: Perspectives from the German Democratic Republic." *International Journal of Labor and Working-Class History* 55 (Spring): 92–111.

Metraux, Daniel. 1991. *Taiwan's Political and Economic Growth in the Late Twentieth Century*. Queenstown, Ontario: Edwin Mellen Press.

Metzger, Thomas H. 1991. "The Chinese Reconciliation of Moral-Sacred Values With Modern Pluralism: Political Discourse in the ROC, 1949–1989." Pp. 3–56 in Ramon H. Myers (ed.), *Two Societies in Opposition: The Republic of China and the People's Republic of China After Forty Years*. Stanford, Calif.: Hoover Institution.

Migdal, Joel, Atul Kohli, and Vivienne Shue (eds.). 1994. *State Power and Social Forces*. Cambridge: Cambridge University Press.

Migdal, Joel. 1974. *Peasants, Politics, and Revolution*. Princeton, N.J.: Princeton University Press.

Mills, C. Wright. 1951. *White Collar: The American Middle Classes*. London: Oxford University Press.

Ministry of Public Education. 1966. *Profile of President Park Chung Hee*. Seoul: Ministry of Public Education (January).

Misra, Joya. 1996. Review of *In Search of National Economic Success: Balancing Competition and Cooperation* by Lane Kenworthy, Sage Publications, 1995, and *National Competitiveness in a Global Economy* by David P. Rapkin and William P. Avery (eds.), Lynne Rienner Publishers, 1995. *Contemporary Sociology* 25/5: 605–608.

Misztal, Bronislaw. 1981. "The Petite Bourgeoisie in Socialist Society." Pp. 90–105 in Frank Bechhofer and Brian Elliott (eds.), *The Petite Bourgeoisie: Comparative Studies of the Uneasy Stratum*. New York: St. Martin's Press.

Mitchell, Clyde C. 1949. "Land Reform in South Korea." *Pacific Affairs* 22/2: 144–154.

Molina Enríquez, Andrés. 1986 (1932 first edition). *La revolución agraria de México, 1910–1920.* Volume 5. Mexico, DF: Miguel Angel Porrua, S.A.

Moody, Peter R., Jr. 1992. *Political Change on Taiwan: A Study of Ruling Party Adaptability.* New York: Praeger.

Moore, Barrington, Jr. 1966. *Social Origins of Dictatorship and Democracy: Lord and Peasant in the Making of the Modern World.* Boston: Beacon Press.

Muller, Edward M. 1988. "Democracy, Economic Development, and Income Inequality." *American Sociological Review* 53 (February): 50–68.

Murmis, Miguel, and Juan Carlos Portantiero. 1971. *Estudios sobre los orígenes del peronismo.* Volume 1. Buenos Aires: Siglo Veintiuno Argentina Ediciones.

Myers, Ramon H., and Yamada Saburo. 1984. "Agricultural Development in the Empire." Pp. 421–435 in Ramon H. Myers and Mark R. Peattie (eds.), *The Japanese Colonial Empire: 1895–1945.* Princeton, N.J.: Princeton University Press.

Myers, Ramon H., and Mark Peattie (eds.). 1984. *The Japanese Colonial Empire: 1895–1945.* Princeton, N.J.: Princeton University Press.

Nava Nava, Carmen. 1984. *Ideología del Partido de la Revolución Mexicana.* México: Centro de Estudios de la Revolución Mexicana.

Neumann, W. Lawrence. 1985. "The Political Ideology of the American Petite Bourgeoisie: Potential Allies of Workers or Capitalists?" *Journal of Political and Military Sociology* 13 (Fall): 239–264.

Niehoff, Justin D. "The Villager As Industrialist: Ideologies of Household Manufacturing in Rural Taiwan." *Modern China* 13/3: 278–309.

Norden, Deborah. 1996. *Military Rebellion in Argentina: Between Coups and Consolidation.* Lincoln: University of Nebraska Press.

Nugent, Daniel. 1993. *Spent Cartridges of Revolution: An Anthropological History of Namiquipa, Chihuahua.* Chicago, Ill.: University of Chicago Press.

Nun, José. 1976. "The Middle-Class Military Coup Revisited." Pp. 49–86 in Abraham Lowenthal (ed.), *Armies and Politics in Latin America.* New York: Holmes and Meier Publishers.

Nun, José. 1967. "The Middle-Class Military Coup." Pp. 66–119 in Claudio Veliz (ed.), *The Politics of Conformity in Latin America.* London: Oxford University Press.

O'Donnell, Guillermo. 1986. "Toward an Alternative Conceptualization of South American Politics." Pp. 239–275 in Peter F. Klaren and Thomas J. Bossert (eds.), *Promise of Development: Theories of Change in Latin America.* Boulder, Colo.: Westview Press.

O'Donnell, Guillermo, Phillipe Schmitter, and Laurence Whitehead (eds.). 1986. *Transitions From Authoritarian Rule: Prospects for Democracy.* Baltimore, Md.: Johns Hopkins University Press.

O'Donnell, Guillermo. 1973. *Modernization and Bureaucratic-Authoritarianism: Studies in South American Politics.* Berkeley, Calif.: Institute of International Studies.

OECD. 1993. *Small and Medium-sized Enterprises: Technology and Competitiveness.* Paris: OECD.

Office of Planning and Coordination. 1968. *Evaluation of the First Year Program (1967), The Second Five-Year Economic Development Plan.* Seoul: Republic of Korea, Office of the Prime Minister.

Ogle, George E. 1990. *South Korea: Dissent Within the Economic Miracle.* London: Zed Books.

Oh, Young-kyun. 1967. "Agrarian Reform and Economic Development: A Case Study of Korean Agriculture." *Korean Quarterly* 9/2:91–137.

Paige, Jeffery M. 1975. *Agrarian Revolution: Social Movements and Export Agriculture in the Underdeveloped World.* New York: Macmillan.

Paik, Wan Ki. 1991. "The Formation of the Governing Elites in Korean Society," Pp. 42–57 in Gerald E. Cohen and Bun Woong Kim (eds.), *A Dragon's Progress: Development Administration in Korea.* Hartford, Conn.: Kumarian Press.

Pak, Ki Hyuk, and Sidney W. Gamble. 1975. *The Changing Korean Village.* Seoul: Shin-Hung Press.

Pak, Ki Hyuk. 1968. "Economic Effects of Land Reform in the Republic of Korea." *Land Reform, Land Settlement, and Cooperatives* 1: 13–27. Rome: FAO.

Pak, Ki Hyuk. 1962. "The Outlook of Korean Agriculture in the Five-Year Plan." *Korean Affairs* 1/1 (March–April) : 1–26.

Papanek, Gustav. 1988. "The New Asian Capitalism: An Economic Portrait." Pp. 27–79 in Peter Berger and Hsin-huang Michael Hsiao (eds.), *In Search of an East Asian Development Model.* New Brunswick, N.J.: Transaction Books.

Pappi, Franz Urban. 1981. "The Petite Bourgeoisie and the New Middle Class: Differentiation or Homogenisation of the Middle Strata in Germany." In Frank Bechofer and Brian Elliot (eds.), *The Petite Bourgeoisie.* New York: St. Martin's Press.

Park, Chung Hee. 1979. *Korea Reborn: A Model for Development.* Englewood Cliffs, N.J.: Prentice-Hall.

Park, Chung Hee. 1971. *Rebuilding a Nation.* Seoul: n.p.

Park, Chung Hee. 1967. *The Road Toward Economic Self-Sufficiency and Prosperity.* Seoul: Ministry of Public Information.

Park, Chung Hee. 1962. *The Country, the Revolution, and I.* Seoul: Hollym Corporation Publishers.

Park, Chung Hee. 1962. *Our Nation's Path: Ideology of Social Reconstruction*, mimeo. Seoul: American Embassy, February 1962.

Park, Ki Hyuk. 1981. "Contribution of the Saemaul Movement to National Economic Development." Pp. 163–195 in Man-gap Lee (ed.), *Toward a New Community.* Seoul: Seoul National University.

Park, Sung-jo. 1980. *Economic Development and Social Change in Korea.* Frankfurt and New York: Campus-Verlag.

Parker, David S. 1998. *The Idea of the Middle Class: White-Collar Workers and Peruvian Society, 1900–1950.* University Park, Pa.: Pennsylvania State University Press.

Partido Revolucionario Institucional (PRI). 1984. *Historial Documental de la CNOP.* Vol. I, II, III. Mexico, DF: Edicap, Instituto de Capacitación Politica.

Bibliography

Pavón Pereyra, Enrique. 1973. *Perón tal como es*. Buenos Aires: Editorial Machacha Guemes.

Paz, Octavio. 1985. *The Labyrinth of Solitude*. New York: Grove Press.

Perló Cohen, Manuel. 1988. "El cardenismo y la ciudad de México: Historia de un conflicto." Paper presented at the seminar "Mexico: 1931–1980." Coordinacion de Humanidades, Universidad Nacional Autónoma de México, March 1988.

Ph, Young-kyun. 1967. "Agrarian Reform and Economic Development: A Case Study of Korean Agriculture." *Korean Quarterly* 9/2: 91–137.

Pirenne, Henri. 1936. *The Economic and Social History of Medieval Europe*. London: Routledge and Kegan Paul.

Porter, Charles D., and Robert J. Alexander. 1961. *The Struggle for Democracy in Latin America*. New York: Macmillan.

Portes, Alejandro, Manuel Castells, and Lauren Benton (eds.). 1989. *The Informal Economy: Studies in Advanced and Less Developed Countries*. Baltimore, Md.: Johns Hopkins University Press.

Portes, Alejandro, and A. Douglas Kincaid. 1989. "Sociology and Development in the 1990s: Critical Challenges and Empirical Trends." *Sociological Forum* 4/4: 479–503.

Portes, Alejandro, and John Walton. 1981. *Labor, Class, and the International System*. New York: Academic Press.

Pouchepadass, Jacques. 1980. "Peasant Classes in Twentieth Century Agrarian Movements in India." Pp. 136–156 in Eric Hobsbawm et al. (eds.), *Peasants in History*. Delhi: Oxford University Press.

Poulantzas, Nicos. 1978. *Classes in Contemporary Capitalism*. London: Verso.

Pozas, Ricardo, and Isabel H. de Pozas. 1971. *Los indios en las clases sociales de México*. Mexico: Siglo XXI Editores.

Przeworski, Adam. 1991. *Democracy and the Market*. Cambridge: Cambridge University Press.

Przeworski, Adam. 1977. "The Process of Class Formation from Kautsky's 'The Class Struggle' to Recent Controversies." *Politics and Society* 7: 354–401.

Ranis, Gustav, and Frances Stewart. 1987. "Rural Linkages in the Philippines and Taiwan." Pp. 140–191 in Frances Stewart (ed.), *Macro-Policies for Appropriate Technology in Developing Countries*. Boulder and London: Westview Press.

Ratinoff, Luis. 1967. "The New Urban Groups: The Middle Classes," Pp. 61–94 in Seymour Martin Lipset and Aldo Solari (eds.), *Elites in Latin America*. New York: Oxford University Press.

Redfield, Robert. 1969. *Peasant Society and Culture*. Chicago, Ill.: University of Chicago Press.

Reed, Edward P. 1981. "Village Cooperation and the Saemaul Movement." Pp. 273–298 in Man-gap Lee (ed.), *Toward a New Community*. Seoul: Seoul National University.

Rhee, Jong-chan. 1994. *The State and Industry in South Korea: The Limits of the Authoritarian State*. London and New York: Routledge.

Rho, Chung-hyun. 1993. *Public Administration and the Korean Transformation: Concepts, Policies, and Value Conflicts*. Hartford, Conn.: Kumarian Press.

Roberts, Bryan. 1992. "Transitional Cities." Pp. 50–65 in Richard M. Morse and Jorge E. Hardoy (eds.), *Rethinking the Latin American City*. Washington, D.C.: Woodrow Wilson Center Press.

Roberts, Bryan. 1978. *Cities of Peasants: The Political Economy of Urbanization in the Third World*. London: Edward Arnold.

Rock, David (ed.). 1994. *Latin America in the 1940s*. Berkeley: University of California Press.

Rock, David. 1993. *Authoritarian Argentina: The Nationalist Movement, Its History, and Its Impact*. Berkeley: University of California Press.

Rock, David. 1987. *Argentina, 1516–1987: From Spanish Colonization to Alfonsín*. Berkeley: University of California Press.

Rock, David. 1975. "Radical Populism and the Conservative Elite, 1912–1930." Pp. 66–88 in David Rock (ed.), *Argentina in the Twentieth Century*. Pittsburgh, Pa.: University of Pittsburgh Press.

Romero, José Luis. 1963. *A History of Argentine Political Thought*. Stanford, Calif.: Stanford University Press.

Roseberry, William, Lowell Gudmundson, and Mario Samper Kutsbach (eds.). 1995. *Coffee, Society, and Power in Latin America*. Baltimore, Md.: Johns Hopkins University Press.

Roseberry, William. 1993. "Beyond the Agrarian Question in Latin America." Pp. 318–371 in Frederick Cooper, Allen F. Isaacman, Florencia E. Mallon, William Roseberry, and Steve J. Stern, *Confronting Historical Paradigms: Peasants, Labor, and the Capitalist World System in Africa and Latin America*. Madison: University of Wisconsin Press.

Ross, George. 1978. "Marxism and the New Middle Classes: French Critiques." *Theory and Society* 5/2: 163–190.

Rostow, Walter W. 1960. *The Stages of Economic Growth*. Cambridge: Cambridge University Press.

Rourke, Francis E. 1982. "Urbanism and American Democracy," Pp. 344–357 in Alexander B. Callow, Jr. (ed.), *American Urban History*. Oxford: Oxford University Press.

Rueschemeyer, Dietrich, Evelyn Huber Stephens, and John D. Stephens. 1992. *Capitalist Development and Democracy*. Chicago, Ill.: University of Chicago Press.

Rueschemeyer, Dietrich, and Peter Evans. 1985. "The State and Economic Transformation: Toward an Analysis of the Conditions Underlying Effective Intervention." Pp. 44–78 in Peter B. Evans, Dietrich Rueschemeyer, and Theda Skocpol (eds.), *Bringing the State Back In*. Cambridge: Cambridge University Press.

Ruiz, Ramón Eduardo. 1976. *La revolución mexicana y el movimiento obrero, 1911–1913*. Mexico, DF: Ediciones Era.

Sachs, Jeffrey. 1985. "External Debt and Macroeconomic Performance in Latin America and East Asia." *Brookings Papers on Economic Activity* 2: 523–573.

Salem, Ellen. 1981. "Korean Rural Development: A Historical Perspective." Pp. 27–45 in Man-gap Lee (ed.), *Toward a New Community*. Seoul: Seoul National University.

Sanderson, Susan R. Walsh. 1984. *Land Reform in Mexico: 1910–1980*. Orlando, Fla.: Academic Press.

Bibliography

Sassen, Saskia. 1998. *Globalization and Its Discontents: Essays on the New Mobility of People and Money*. New York: The New Press

Sassen, Saskia. 1991. *The Global City: New York, London, Tokyo*. Princeton, N.J.: Princeton University Press.

Sawers, Larry. 1996. *The Other Argentina: The Interior and National Development*. Boulder, Colo.: Westview Press.

Sayer, Derek. 1991. *Capitalism and Modernity: An Excursus on Marx and Weber*. London: Routledge.

Scase, Robert. 1982. "The Petty Bourgeoisie and Modern Capitalism: A Consideration of Recent Theories." Pp. 148–161 in Anthony Giddens and Gavin Mackenzie (eds.), *Social Class and the Divison of Labour*. Cambridge: Cambridge University Press.

Schryer, Frans J. 1980. *The Rancheros of Pisaflores: The History of a Peasant Bourgeoisie in Twentieth Century Mexico*. Toronto: University of Toronto Press.

Scott, James. 1976. *The Moral Economy of the Peasant*. New Haven, Conn.: Yale University Press.

Scott, Robert E. 1967. "Political Elites and Political Modernization: The Crisis of Transition." Pp. 117–146 in Seymour Martin Lipset and Aldo Solari (eds.), *Elites in Latin America*. New York: Oxford University Press.

Sewell, William H., Jr. 1980. *Work and Revolution in France: The Language of Labor from the Old Regime to 1848*. Cambridge: Cambridge University Press.

Shadlen, Kenneth C. 2000. "Neoliberalism, Corporatism, and Small Business Political Activism in Contemporary Mexico." *Latin American Research Review* 35: 73–106.

Shadlen, Kenneth C. 1997. *Corporatism and the Organization of Business Interests: Small Industry and the State in Post-revolutionary Mexico*. Ph.D. diss., University of California at Berkeley.

Shanin, Teodor. 1966. "The Peasantry As Political Factor." *Sociological Review* 14/1: 5–27.

Shieh, G. S. 1992. *"Boss" Island: The Subcontracting Network and Micro-Enterpreneurship in Taiwan's Development*. New York: Peter Lang.

Shieh, Milton J. T. 1970. *The Kuomintang: Selected Historical Documents, 1894–1969*. n.p.: St. John's University.

Shik, Shin Bum (ed.). 1970. *Major Speeches by Korea's Park Chung Hee*. Seoul: Hollym Corporation Publishers.

Shin, Gi-wook. 1995. "Marxism, Anti-Americanism, and Democracy in South Korea: An Examination of Nationalist Intellectual Discourse." *Positions* 3/2: 203–229.

Short, John Rennie, and Yeong-Hyun Kim. 1999. *Globalization and the City*. London: Longman.

Shulgovski, Anatoli. 1968. *México en la encrucijada de su historia*. Mexico, DF: Ediciones de Cultura Popular.

Shumway, Nicolas. 1991. *The Invention of Argentina*. Berkeley and Los Angeles: University of California Press.

Silin, Robert H. 1976. *Leadership and Values: The Organization of Large-Scale Taiwanese Enterprises*. Cambridge, Mass.: Harvard University Press.

Silva, Eduardo. 1993. "Capitalist Coalitions, the State, and Neoliberal Economic Restructuring: Chile, 1973–1988." *World Politics* 45: 526–59.

Silva Hérzog, Jesús. 1946. *Un ensayo sobre la revolución mexicana*. Mexico, DF.: Cuadernos Americanos.

Simon, Denis Fred. 1988. "External Incorporation and Internal Reform." Pp. 138–151 in Edwin A. Winckler and Susan Greenhalgh (eds.), *Contending Approaches to the Political Economy of Taiwan*. Armonk, N.Y.: M. E. Sharpe.

Sjoberg, Gideon. 1960. *The Pre-Industrial City*. New York: Free Press.

Sklair, Leslie. 2002. *Globalization: Capitalism and Its Alternatives*. New York: Oxford University Press.

Sklair, Leslie. 2001. *The Transnational Capitalist Class*. New York: Basil Blackwell.

Sklair, Leslie. 1991. *Sociology of the Global System*. Baltimore, Md.: Johns Hopkins University Press.

Skocpol, Theda. 1992. *Protecting Soldiers and Mothers*. Cambridge, Mass.: Belknap/Harvard University Press.

Skocpol, Theda. 1979. *States and Social Revolutions: A Comparative Analysis of France, Russia, and China*. Cambridge: Cambridge University Press.

Slatta, Richard W. 1992. *Gauchos and the Vanishing Frontier*. Lincoln: University of Nebraska Press, 2nd edition.

Smith, Michael P. 2001. *Transnational Urbanism: Locating Globalization*. Malden: Blackwell Publishers.

Smith, Michael Peter. 1999. "Transnationalism and the City." Pp. 119–140 in Robert Beauregard and Sophie Body-Gendrot (eds.), *The Urban Moment: Cosmopolitan Essays on the Late Twentieth Century*. Thousand Oaks, Calif: Sage Publications.

Smith, Peter. 1969. *Politics and Beef in Argentina*. New York: Columbia University Press.

Song, Byung-Nap. 1990. *The Rise of the Korean Economy*. London: Oxford University Press.

Sorenson, Clark W. 1988. *Over the Mountains Are Mountains: Korean Peasant Households and Their Adaptations to Rapid Industrialization*. Seattle and London: University of Washington Press.

Speier, Hans. 1995. "Bureaucracy and Masked Class Membership." Pp. 151–161 in Arthur J. Vidich (ed.), *The New Middle Classes: Lifestyles, Status Claims, and Political Orientations*. New York: New York University Press.

Speier, Hans. 1985. *German White Collar Workers and the Rise of Hitler*. New Haven, Conn.: Yale University Press.

Stallings, Barbara. 1985. "International Lending and the Relative Autonomy of the State: A Case Study of Twentieth-Century Peru." *Politics and Society* 14: 257–287.

Stavenhagen, Rodolfo. 1971. *Las clases sociales en las sociedades agrarias*. Mexico: Siglo Veintiuno.

Stavenhagen, Rodolfo. 1968. "Aspectos sociales de la estructura agraria en México." In *Neolatifundismo y explotación*. Mexico: Editorial Nuestro Tiempo.

Stedman Jones, Gareth. 1971. *Outcast London: A Study in the Relationship Between Classes in Victorian Society*. Oxford: Clarendon Press.

Steinberg, Marc. 1991. "Talkin' Class: Discourse, Ideology, and Their Roles in Class Conflict." In Scott G. McNall, Rhonda F. Levine, and Rick Fantasia (eds.), *Bringing Class Back In*. Boulder, Colo.: Westview Press.

Steinmo, Sven, Kathleen Thelen, and Frank Longstreth (eds.). 1992. *Structuring Politics: Historical Institutionalism in Comparative Analysis*. Cambridge: Cambridge University Press.

Stephens, Evelyne Huber, and John D. Stephens. 1986. *Democratic Socialism in Jamaica: The Political Movement and Social Transformation in Dependent Capitalism*. Princeton, N.J.: Princeton University Press.

Sung, Byung-nak. 1990. *The Rise of the Korean Economy*. London: Oxford University Press.

Supreme Council for National Reconstruction. 1961. *Military Revolution in Korea*. Seoul: The Secretariat, Supreme Council for National Reconstruction, November 5, 1961.

Supreme Council for National Reconstruction. 1961. *Revolution's First Two Months' Achievements*. Seoul: Office of Public Information, Supreme Council for National Reconstruction, August 15, 1961.

Tan, Chester C. 1971. *Chinese Political Thought in the Twentieth Century*. Garden City, N.Y.: Doubleday.

Tannenbaum, Frank. 1968. *Peace by Revolution: Mexico After 1910*. New York: Columbia University Press.

Tawney, R. H. 1936. *Religion and the Rise of Capitalism: A Historical Study*. London: John Murray.

Taylor, Carl C. 1948. *Rural Life in Argentina*. Baton Rouge: Louisiana State University Press.

Tejada, Luis. 1985. *La cuestion del pan: el anarcosindicalismo en el Peru, 1880–1919*. Lima: Instituto Nacional de Cultura, Banco Industrial de Peru.

Teng, Hsueh-ping. 1954. *T'ai-wan nung-ts'un fang-wen chi (Visiting Rural Areas in China)*. N.p.

Thompson, Edward P. 1966. *The Making of the English Working Class*. New York: Vintage.

Tien, Hung-mao. 1989. *The Great Transition: Political and Social Change in the Republic of China*. Stanford, Calif.: Hoover Institution Press.

Tilly, Charles. 1992. *Coercion, Capital, and European States*. London and New York: Basil Blackwell.

Tobler, Hans Werner. 1988. "Peasants and the Shaping of the Revolutionary State." Pp. 487–520 in Friedrich Katz (ed.), *Riot, Rebellion, and Revolution*. Princeton, N.J.: Princeton University Press.

Torres, Blanca. 1979. *Historia de la revolución mexicana (1940–1952): México en la regunda guerra mundial*. Mexico City: El Colegio de Mèxico.

Tsiang, S. C. 1985. "Foreign Trade and Investment As Boosters for Take-off: The Experience of Taiwan." Pp. 27–56 in Vittorio Corbo, Anne O. Krueger, and Fernando Ossa (eds.), *Export-Oriented Development Strategies: The Success of Five Newly Industrializing Countries*. Boulder, Colo.: Westview Press.

Tucker, Robert C. (ed.). 1972. *The Marx-Engels Reader*. New York: W. W. Norton & Company.

Turner, John E., Vicki L. Hesli, Dong Suh Bark, and Hoon Yu. 1993. *Villages Astir: Community Development, Tradition, and Change in Korea*. Westport, Conn., and London: Praeger.

Bibliography

United Nations Center for Human Settlements (Habitat). 2001. *Cities in a Globalizing World*. London: Earthscan.

Urry, John. 1971. "Towards a Structural Theory of the Middle Class." *Acta Sociologica* 16/3: 175–188.

Van Young, Eric. 1999. "Making Leviathan Sneeze: Recent Works on Mexico and the Mexican Revolution." *Latin American Research Review* 34/3: 143–165.

Vaughan, Mary Kay. 1997. *Cultural Politics in Revolution: Teachers, Peasants, and Schools in Mexico, 1930–1940*. Tucson: University of Arizona Press.

Veliz, Claudio (ed.). 1967. *The Politics of Conformity in Latin America*. London: Oxford University Press.

Vidich, Arthur J. (ed.). 1995. *The New Middle Classes: Lifestyles, Status Claims, and Political Orientations*. New York: New York University Press.

Vogel, Ezra F. 1991. *The Four Little Dragons: The Spread of Industrialization in East Asia*. Cambridge, Mass.: Harvard University Press.

Wacquant, Loic J. D. 1991. "Making Class: The Middle Class(es) in Social Theory and Social Structure." Pp. 39–64 in Scott G. McNall, Rhonda F. Levine, and Rick Fantasia (eds.), *Bringing Class Back In: Contemporary and Historical Perspectives*. Boulder, Colo.: Westview Press.

Wade, Robert. 1990. *Governing the Market: Economic Theory and the Role of Government in East Asian Industrialization*. Princeton, N.J.: Princeton University Press.

Wade, Robert. 1982. *Irrigation and Agricultural Policies in South Korea*. Boulder, Colo.: Westview Press.

Waisman, Carlos. 1987. *The Reversal of Development in Argentina: Postwar Counterrevolutionary Policies and Their Structural Consequences*. Princeton, N.J.: Princeton University Press.

Walsh, Casey. 2001. "Eugenic Acculturation: Manuel Gamio, Migration Studies, and the Anthropology of Development in Mexico, 1910–1940." Unpublished mimeo.

Walton, John. 1977. *Elites and Economic Development: Comparative Studies in the Political Economy of Latin American Cities*. Austin: University of Texas Press.

Warman, Arturo. 1988. "The Political Project of Zapatismo." Pp. 321–337 in Friedrich Katz (ed.), *Riot, Rebellion, and Revolution*. Princeton, N.J.: Princeton University Press.

Warman, Arturo. 1980. *We Come to Object: The Peasants of Morelos and the National State*. Baltimore, Md.: Johns Hopkins University Press.

Weber, Eugen. 1976. *Peasants Into Frenchmen: The Modernization of Rural France, 1870–1914*. Stanford, Calif.: Stanford University Press.

Weber, Max. 1961. *General Economic History*. Translated by Frank H. Knight. New York: Collier Books.

Weber, Max. 1964 (1958). "Capitalism and Rural Society in Germany." Pp. 363–395 in Hans H. Gerth and C. Wright Mills (eds. and trans.), *From Max Weber: Essays in Sociology*. New York: Oxford University Press.

Weber, Max. 1930. *The Protestant Ethic and the Spirit of Capitalism* (translated by Talcott Parsons). London: George Allen & Unwin.

Whetten, Nathan L. 1948. *Rural Mexico*. Chicago, Ill.: University of Chicago Press.

Whittaker, Arthur P. 1964. *Argentina*. Englewood Cliffs, N.J.: Prentice-Hall.

Williamson, Edwin. 1992. *The Penguin History of Latin America*. London: Penguin Books.

Winckler, Edwin A., and Susan Greenhalgh. 1988. *Contending Approaches to the Political Economy of Taiwan*. Armonk, N.Y., and London: M. E. Sharpe.

Wolf, Eric R. 1968. *Peasant Wars of the Twentieth Century*. New York: Harper and Row, 1968.

Wolf, Eric R. 1966. *Peasants*. Englewood Cliffs, N.J.: Prentice-Hall.

Wolf, Eric R. 1955. "Types of Latin American Peasantry: A Preliminary Discussion." *American Anthropologist* 57/3 (part I): 452–471.

Womack, John, Jr. 1969. *Zapata and the Mexican Revolution*. New York: Alfred A. Knopf.

Woo, Jung-en. 1991. *Race to the Swift: State and Finance in South Korean Industrialization*. New York: Columbia University Press.

Woo Cumings, Meredith. 1996. "The Ties That Bind? Autonomy, Embeddedness, and Industrial Development." Pp. 307–321 in Diane E. Davis (ed.), *Political Power and Social Theory*. Volume 10. Greenwich, Conn., and London: JAI Press.

Wood, Gord S. 1994. "Inventing American Capitalism." *New York Review of Books* (June 9, 1994): 44–49.

Wright, Erik Olin. 1985. *Classes*. London: New Left Books.

Wright, Erik Olin. 1978. *Class, Crisis, and the State*. London: New Left Books.

Wu, Mai-teh. 1996. "Class Identity Without Class Consciousness? Working-Class Orientations in Taiwan." Pp. 77–102 in Elisabeth Perry (ed.), *Workers' Identities in East Asia*. Berkeley: Center for East Asian Studies, University of California.

Yager, Joseph A. 1988. *Transforming Agriculture in Taiwan: The Experience of the Joint Commission on Rural Reconstruction*. Ithaca, N.Y., and London: Cornell University Press.

Ya-li, Lu. 1991. "Political Modernization in the ROC: The Kuomintang and the Inhibited Political Center." Pp. 111–126 in Ramon H. Myers (ed.), *Two Societies in Opposition: The Republic of China and the People's Republic of China After Forty Years*. Stanford, Calif.: Hoover Institution.

Yu, Tal-young. 1962. "The National Reconstruction Movement in Retrospect and Prospect." *Korean Affairs* 1/3: 291–300.

Zeitlin, Maurice. 1984. *The Civil Wars in Chile: Or, the Bourgeois Revolutions That Never Were*. Princeton, N.J.: Princeton University Press.

Zeitlin, Maurice, and James Petras (ed.). 1968. *Latin America: Reform or Revolution?* Greenwich, Conn.: Fawcett.

INDEX

Index

Index

Index

Index